SUPER LCCS™

Gale's
Library of Congress
Classification Schedules

Combined
with Additions
and Changes
through 2004

ISSN 1088-1921

Class E-F

History: America

SUPER LCCS™

Gale's
Library of Congress
Classification Schedules

Combined
with Additions
and Changes
through 2004

Compiled from sources enumerated on verso

THOMSON
GALE

Detroit • New York • San Francisco • San Diego • New Haven, Conn. • Waterville, Maine • London • Munich

THOMSON
GALE

SUPERLCCS

Gale's Library of Congress Classification Schedules Combined with Additions and Changes Through 2004

Classes E-F, History: America, Washington, 2000, issued by Library of Congress, Cataloging Policy and Support Office, Library Services, and combined with revisions published in *L.C. Classification—Additions and Changes,* List 281 (Jan.-Mar., 2001) through List 284 (Oct.-Dec., 2001) and *Library of Congress Classification Weekly Lists,* 2002-2004.

Project Editor
Michael Reade

Editorial
Kathleen Droste

Manufacturing
Keith Helmling

For more information, contact
Thomson Gale
27500 Drake Rd.
Farmington Hills, MI 48334-3535
Or you can visit our Internet site at
http://www.gale.com

LIBRARY OF CONGRESS CATALOG CARD NUMBER 2001027702

ISBN 0-7876-8437-6 (This cumulation)
ISBN 0-7876-8429-5 (Complete Set)
ISBN 0-7876-8522-4 (Microfiche cumulation)
ISBN 0-7876-8514-3 (Microfiche complete set)

Printed in the United States of America
10 9 8 7 6 5 4 3 2 1

CONTENTS

PREFACE

This publication integrates each of the latest editions of the Library of Congress classification schedules with all pertinent changes found in the Library's quarterly publication *LC Classification—Additions and Changes.* The material included in each volume covers the period from the publication date of each schedule through December, 2001 (List 284) and *Library of Congress Classification Weekly Lists,* 2002-2004. This series of cumulations has been prepared by a staff of professional librarians at Gale Group.

A Valuable Tool

The use of this publication eases the painstaking task of classification immeasurably. No longer is it necessary to determine where and how the additions and changes relate to the schedule. All classification information from the lists through 2004 has been interfiled into one sequence.

Validation Procedures

The full text of each schedule and its index have been meticulously combined with the changes from the quarterly *LC Classification—Additions and Changes* and *Library of Congress Classification Weekly Lists.* Although there is no official connection between Gale and the Library of Congress (LC) in the preparation of this publication, LC generously provided the editors with information when questions of form or problems of interpretation arose during the integration process.

Frequency of publication

Completely updated volumes of *Library of Congress Classification Schedules Combined with Additions and Changes and Weekly Lists* are published annually.

A Standardized Gale Style

In 1994 a new Gale classification database was constructed that allowed for a more efficient, accurate, and flexible interaction with the data. Data elements were normalized and the varying styles of the printed schedules were standardized into one Gale style. Much of this style originated with the announced Library of Congress changes in which footnotes would be eliminated; "Divide like" notes would be replaced with developments; "General works" captions would be reinstated; and many internal tables changed into external tables.

A Noteworthy Gale Feature

In the schedules Gale is adding editorial notes in textual situations where such notes would be beneficial to users. These notes direct the user to another location or define, clarify, or elaborate abbreviated or ambiguous instruction or description. These notes are easily identified by the label "GALE NOTE."

For example, many times in the Library of Congress text, the word "modified" appears after a table reference when subtopics are listed below such a caption that contains a table reference. In these cases, the cataloger would adjust the table by integrating the subtopics into the table development. Whenever a table modification is implied or when the word "modified" appears following a table reference in the Library of Congress text, the following GALE NOTE will appear:

> GALE NOTE To develop this number range, integrate the subtopics
> into the table structure.

Some Gale notes reiterate Library of Congress instruction in places lacking such direction. For example, the Library of Congress occasionally adds the definition of ".x" in cutter number tables. Gale will add this following definition to all tables that contain this symbolic cutter number:

> GALE NOTE ".x" represents the cutter number for ...

Each year Gale will systematically add new notes to make *SUPERLCCS* easier to use and to make its content more accessible to its users.

The GALE NOTE is just one of the many suggestions adopted from recommendations made by an Advisory Board.

Notes Relating to Specific Volumes

The Library of Congress recently published seven new editions: *Class H: Social Sciences; Subclass KB: Religious Law; Subclass KF: Law of the United States; Subclass P-PZ: Language and Literature Tables; Subclass PN: Literature (General); Subclass PQ: French, Italian, Spanish, and Portuguese Literature; and Class Q: Science.* The new, expanded *Subclass KB: Religious Law* includes and supercedes the old edition: *Subclasses KBR, KBU: History of Canon Law. Law of the Roman Catholic Church. The Holy See.* These new editions are incorporated into Gale's current 2005 publication cycle.

In 1999 Library of Congress issued a new schedule, *K Tables, Form Division Tables for Law.* Since some of the law schedules already include tables at the end of the text, Gale, as a convenience to its customers, will include these new K Tables at the end of those schedules to which they apply. Tables of subdivisions referred to in the text of the Class P schedules are found in a separate schedule, *Language and Literature Tables,* reissued by the Library of Congress in 1998.

Suggestions Are Welcome

The editors welcome your comments and suggestions for enhancing or improving this work. Please write to: The Editors, SUPERLCCS, Gale Group, 27500 Drake Rd., Farmington Hills, MI 48331-4253. Phone no.: 1-800-877-4253; Fax no. 248-699-8062. E-mail address: SuperLCCS@thomson.com.

SYNOPSIS

E	AMERICA
E	UNITED STATES
F	UNITED STATES LOCAL HISTORY
F	BRITISH AMERICA
F	FRENCH AMERICA
F	LATIN AMERICA. SPANISH AMERICA

OUTLINE

E	11-143	America
	11-29	General
	29	Elements in the population
	31-49.2	North America
	51-73	Pre-Columbian America. The Indians
	75-99	Indians of North America
	81-83	Indian wars
	99	Indian tribes and cultures
	101-135	Discovery of America and early explorations
	103-110	Pre-Columbian period
	111-120	Columbus
	121-135	Post-Columbian period. El Dorado
	141-143	Descriptive accounts of America. Earliest to 1810
E	151-887	United States
	151-169.12	General
	171-183.9	History
	171-180	General
	173	Sources and documents
	175-175.7	Historiography
	176-176.8	Biography
	179.5	Historical geography
	181	Military history
	182	Naval history
	183-183.3	Political history
	183.7-183.9	Diplomatic history. Foreign and general relations
	183.8	Relations with individual countries, A-Z
	184-185.98	Elements in the population
	184.5-185.98	Afro-Americans
	185.2-185.89	Status and development since emancipation
	185.96-185.98	Biography. Genealogy
	186-199	Colonial history, 1607-1775
	186-189	General
	191-199	By period
	191	1607-1689
	195-199	1689-1775
	196	King William's War, 1689-1697
	197	Queen Anne's War, 1702-1713
	198	King George's War, 1744-1748
	199	French and Indian War, 1755-1763
	201-298	The Revolution, 1775-1783

E

	United States - Continued
300-453	Revolution to the Civil War, 1775/83-1861
300-302.6	General
302	Collected works of American statesmen
302.1	Political history
302.5-302.6	Biography (Late eighteenth century)
303-440.5	By period
303-309	1775-1789. The Confederation, 1783-1789
310-337	1789-1809. Constitutional period
310.7	Diplomatic history. Foreign and general relations
311-320	Washington's administrations, 1789-1797
321-330	John Adams' administration, 1797-1801
323	Troubles with France, 1796-1800
331-337	Jefferson's administrations, 1801-1809
333	Purchase of Louisiana, 1803
335	War with Tripoli, 1801-1805
336-336.5	Neutral trade and its restrictions, 1800-1810
337.5	Nineteenth century (General)
337.8-400	Early nineteenth century, 1801/1809-1845
337.8-340	General
337.8	Collected works of American statesmen
339-340	Biography
341-370	Madison's administrations, 1809-1817
351-364.9	War of 1812
365	War with Algeria, 1815
371-375	Monroe's administrations, 1817-1825
373	Missouri Compromise, 1820
374	Diplomatic history. Foreign relations
376-380	John Quincy Adams' administration, 1825-1829
381-385	Jackson's administrations, 1829-1837
384.3	Nullification
386-390	Van Buren's administration, 1837-1841
391-392	William H. Harrison's administration, March 4-April 4, 1841
396-400	Tyler's administration, April 4, 1841-1845
398	Northeastern boundary disputes, 1783-1845
401-415.2	Mexican War, 1846-1848
408	Mexican cession of 1848
415.6-440.5	Middle nineteenth century, 1845/1848-1861
415.6-415.9	General
415.6	Collected works of American statesmen
415.8-415.9	Biography
416-420	Polk's administration, 1845-1849
421-423	Taylor's administration, 1849-July 9, 1850
423	Slavery question, 1849-1853
426-430	Fillmore's administration, July 9, 1850-1853
431-435	Pierce's administration, 1853-1857
433	Slavery question, 1853-1857
436-440.5	Buchanan's administration, 1857-1861
438	Slavery question, 1857-1861
440.5	State of the country, November 1860-March 4, 1861
441-453	Slavery in the United States. Antislavery movements
456-655	Civil War period, 1861-1865
456-459	Lincoln's administrations, 1861-April 15, 1865
461-655	The Civil War, 1861-1865
482-489	Confederate States of America
491-586	Armies. Troops
591-600	Naval histroy
660-738	Late nineteenth century, 1865-1900
660-664	General
660	Collected works of American statesmen
661.7	Diplomatic history. Foreign and general relations
663-664	Biography

E		United States
		Late nineteenth century, 1865-1900 - Continued
	666-670	Johnson's administration, April 15, 1865-1869
	668	Reconstruction, 1865-1877
	669	Purchase of Alaska, 1867
	671-680	Grant's administrations, 1869-1877
	681-685	Hayes' administration, 1877-1881
	686-687.9	Garfield's administration, March 4-September 19, 1881
	691-695	Arthur's administration, September 19, 1881-1885
	696-700	Cleveland's first administration, 1885-1889
	701-705	Benjamin Harrison's administration, 1889-1893
	706-710	Cleveland's second administration, 1893-1897
	711-738	McKinley's first administration, 1897-1901
	713	Annexation in 1898 of the Hawaii, the Philippines, and Puerto Rico
	714-735	War of 1898 (Spanish-American War)
	740-837.7	Twentieth century
	740-749	General
	740.5	Sources and documents
	742.5	Collected works of American statesmen
	743-743.5	Political history
	743.5	Un-American activities
	744-744.5	Diplomatic history. Foreign and general relations
	745	Military history
	746	Naval history
	747-748	Biography
	751	McKinley's second administration, March 4- September 14, 1901
	756-760	Theodore Roosevelt's administrations, September 14, 1901-1909
	761-765	Taft's administration, 1909-1913
	766-783	Wilson's administrations, 1913-1921
	768	Purchase of Danish West Indies (Virgin Islands), 1917
	780	Internal history during World War I
	784-805	1919-1933. Harding-Coolidge-Hoover era. "The twenties"
	785-786	Harding's administration, 1921-August 2, 1923
	791-796	Coolidge's administration, August 2, 1923- 1929
	801-805	Hoover's administration, 1929-1933
	806-812	Franklin Delano Roosevelt's administrations, 1933-April 12, 1945
	813-816	Truman's administrations, April 12, 1945-1953
	835-837.7	Eisenhower's administrations, 1953-1961
	838-887	Later twentieth century, 1961-
	838-840.8	General
	838.3	Sources and documents
	839.5-839.8	Political history
	839.8	Un-American activities
	840-840.2	Diplomatic history. Foreign and general relations
	840.6-840.8	Biography (General)
	841-843	Kennedy's administration, 1961-November 22, 1963
	842.9	Assassination, funeral, memorial services, etc.
	846-851	Johnson's administrations, November 22, 1963-1969
	855-861	Nixon's administrations, 1969-August 9, 1974
	860-861	Watergate Affair. Resignation
	865-868	Ford's administration, August 9, 1974-1977
	872-875	Carter's administration, 1977-1981
	876-880	Reagan's administrations, 1981-1989
	877.3	Assassination attempt
	881-884	Bush administration, 1989-1993
	885-887	Clinton administrations, 1993-

F	1-975	United States local history
	1-15	New England
	16-30	Maine
	31-45	New Hampshire
	46-60	Vermont
	61-75	Massachusetts
	76-90	Rhode Island
	91-105	Connecticut
	106	Atlantic coast. Middle Atlantic States
	116-130	New York
	131-145	New Jersey
	146-160	Pennsylvania
	161-175	Delaware
	176-190	Maryland
	191-205	District of Columbia. Washington
	206-220	The South. South Atlantic States
	221-235	Virginia
	236-250	West Virginia
	251-265	North Carolina
	266-280	South Carolina
	281-295	Georgia
	296-301	Gulf States. West Florida
	306-320	Florida
	321-335	Alabama
	336-350	Mississippi
	350.5-355	Mississippi River and Valley. Middle West
	366-380	Louisiana
	381-395	Texas
	396	Old Southwest. Lower Mississippi Valley
	406-420	Arkansas
	431-445	Tennessee
	446-460	Kentucky
	461-475	Missouri
	476-485	Old Northwest. Northwest Territory
	486-500	Ohio
	516-520	Ohio River and Valley
	521-535	Indiana
	536-550	Illinois
	550.5-553.2	The Lake region. Great Lakes
	561-575	Michigan
	576-590	Wisconsin
	590.3-596.3	The West. Trans-Mississippi Region. Great Plains
	597	The Northwest
	598	Missouri River and Valley
	601-615	Minnesota
	616-630	Iowa
	631-645	North Dakota
	646-660	South Dakota
	661-675	Nebraska
	676-690	Kansas
	691-705	Oklahoma
	721-722	Rocky Mountains. Yellowstone National Park
	726-740	Montana
	741-755	Idaho
	756-770	Wyoming
	771-785	Colorado
	786-790	New Southwest. Colorado River, Canyon, and Valley
	791-805	New Mexico
	806-820	Arizona
	821-835	Utah
	836-850	Nevada

F		United States local history - Continued
	850.5-851.5	Pacific States
	851.7	Cascade Range
	852-854	Pacific Northwest. Columbia River and Valley. Northwest boundary since 1846
	856-870	California
	871-885	Oregon
	886-900	Washington
	901-951	Alaska
	951	Bering Sea and Aleutian Islands
	965	The territories of the United States (General)
	970	Insular possessions of the United States (General)
	975	Central American, West Indian, and other countries protected by and having close political affiliations with the United States (General)
F	1001-1140	British America
	1001-1140	Canada
	1001-1035	General
	1035.8	Maritime provinces. Atlantic coast of Canada
	1036-1040	Nova Scotia. Acadia
	1041-1045	New Brunswick
	1046-1049.7	Prince Edward Island
	1050	St. Lawrence Gulf, River, and Valley (General)
	1051-1055	Quebec
	1056-1059.7	Ontario
	1060-1060.97	Canadian Northwest. Northwest Territories
	1061-1065	Manitoba
	1067	Assiniboia
	1070-1074.7	Saskatchewan
	1075-1080	Alberta
	1086-1089.7	British Columbia
	1090	Rocky Mountains of Canada
	1090.5	Arctic regions
	1091-1095.5	Yukon
	1096-1100.5	Mackenzie
	1101-1105.7	Franklin
	1106-1110.5	Keewatin
	1121-1139	Newfoundland
	1135-1139	Labrador
	1140	The Labrador Peninsula
		Other than Canada
		Bahamas, *see* F1650+
		Bermudas, *see* F1630+
		British East and West Florida, 1763-1783, *see* F301, F314
		British Guiana, *see* F2361+
		British Honduras (Belize), *see* F1441+
		British West Indies, *see* F2131+
		Falkland Islands, *see* F3031+
		Thirteen North American Colonies before 1776, *see* E186+
F		Dutch America
		Colony in Brazil, 1625-1661, *see* F2532
		Dutch Guiana, *see* F2401+
		Dutch West Indies, *see* F2141
		New Netherlands to 1664, *see* F122.1
		New Sweden (Dutch possession, 1655-1664), *see* F167
F	1170	French America
	1170	Saint Pierre and Miquelon
		Other French America
		Colony in Brazil, 1555-1567, *see* F2529
		Colony in Florida, 1562-1565, *see* F314

F		French America
		Other French America - Continued
		French Guiana, *see* F2441+
		French West Indies, *see* F2151
		Louisiana, 1698-1803, *see* F372
		New France and Acadia, 1600-1763, *see* F1030, F1038
F	1201-3799	Latin America. Spanish America
	1201-1392	Mexico
	1218.5-1221	Antiquities. Indians
	1401-1419	Latin America (General)
	1421-1440	Central America
	1435-1435.3	Mayas
	1441-1457	Belize
	1461-1477	Guatemala
	1481-1497	Salvador (El Salvador)
	1501-1517	Honduras
	1521-1537	Nicaragua
	1541-1557	Costa Rica
	1561-1577	Panama
	1569.C2	Canal Zone. Panama Canal
	1601-1629	West Indies
	1630-1640	Bermudas
	1650-1660	Bahamas
	1741-1991	Greater Antilles
	1751-1854.9	Cuba
	1788-1788.22	Communist regime
	1861-1896	Jamaica
	1900-1941	Haiti (Island). Hispaniola
	1912-1930	Haiti (Republic)
	1931-1941	Dominican Republic
	1951-1983	Puerto Rico
	1991	Navassa
	2001-2151	Lesser Antilles
		Groups of islands, by geographical distribution
	2006	Leeward Islands
	2011	Windward Islands
	2016	Islands along Venezuela coast
	2033-2129	Individual islands
		Groups of islands, by political allegiance
	2131-2133	British West Indies
	2136	Virgin Islands of the United States
	2141	Netherlands West Indies. Dutch West Indies
	2151	French West Indies
	2155-2191	Caribbean area. Caribbean Sea
	2201-3799	South America
	2201-2239	General
	2251-2299	Colombia
	2301-2349	Venezuela
	2351	Guiana
	2361-2391	Guyana. British Guiana
	2401-2431	Surinam
	2441-2471	French Guiana
	2501-2659	Brazil
	2661-2699	Paraguay
	2701-2799	Uruguay
	2801-3021	Argentina
	3031-3031.5	Falkland Islands
	3051-3285	Chile
	3301-3359	Bolivia
	3401-3619	Peru
	3701-3799	Ecuador

General

E11-E29 are reserved for works which are actually comprehensive in scope. A book on travel would only occasionally be classified here; the numbers for the United States, Spanish America, etc., would usually accomodate all works, the choice being determined by the main country or region covered

11 **Periodicals. Societies. Collections (serial)**

For international American Conferences, see F1404+

Collections (Nonserial). Collected works

12 Several authors

13 Individual authors

14 **Dictionaries. Gazetteers. Geographic names**

General works, see E18

History

16 Historiography

16.5 Study and teaching

Biography

17 Collective

Individual, *see* country, period, etc.

18 General works

Including comprehensive works on America

18.5 Chronology, chronological tables, etc.

18.7 Juvenile works

18.75 General special

By period

Pre-Columbian period, *see* E51+, E103+

18.82 1492-1810

Cf. E101+, Discovery and exploration of America

Cf. E141+, Earliest accounts of America to 1810

18.83 1810-1900

18.85 1901-

19 **Pamphlets, addresses, essays, etc.**

Including radio programs, pageants, etc.

20 **Social life and customs. Civilization. Intellectual life**

21 **Historic monuments (General)**

21.5 **Antiquities (Non-Indian)**

21.7 **Historical geography**

Description and travel. Views

Cf. F851, Pacific Coast

Cf. G419+, Travels around the world and in several parts of the world including America and other countries

Cf. G575+, Polar discoveries

Earliest to 1606, *see* E141+

1607-1810, *see* E143

27 1811-1950

27.2 1951-1980

27.5 1981-

Elements in the population

29.A1 General works

29.A2-.Z Individual elements, A-Z

29.A75 Asians

29.B35 Basques

Blacks, *see* E29.N3

29.B75 British

29.C35 Canary Islanders

29.C37 Catalans

29.C5 Chinese

29.C73 Creoles

29.C75 Croats

29.C94 Czechs

29.D25 Danube Swabians

General

Elements in the population

29.A2-.Z Individual elements, A-Z — Continued

29.E37 East Indians

29.E87 Europeans

29.F8 French

29.G26 Galicians (Spain)

29.G3 Germans

29.H9 Huguenots

29.I74 Irish

29.I8 Italians

29.J3 Japanese

29.J5 Jews

29.N3 Negroes. Blacks

(29.O6) Orientals, *see* E29.A75

29.P6 Poles

29.R83 Russian Germans

29.R84 Russians

29.S65 Spaniards

29.S83 Swedes

29.Y67 Yoruba

North America

The numbers "E31-46" like "E11-29" are to be assigned to works actually comprehensive in scope; for example, a book dealing principally with British America with a few pages at the end on the United States would be classed in F1001-1035, regardless of title. Most works having United States in the title relate so largely to this country that they are classed in E151-839

31 **Periodicals. Societies. Collections**

35 **Dictionaries. Gazetteers. Geographic names**

Biography

36 Collective

Individual, *see* country, period, etc.

38 **General works**

38.5 **Juvenile works**

39 **Pamphlets, addresses, essays, etc.**

39.5 **Pictorial works**

40 **Social life and customs. Civilization. Intellectual life**

40.5 **Geography**

41 **Description and travel**

43 **Antiquities (non-Indian)**

43.5 **National and state parks and reservations (Collective descriptive works)**

History

Cf. E101+, Discovery and exploration of America

Cf. F1411+, History of Latin America

45 General works

46 General special

46.5 Military history

Elements in the population

49 General works

49.2.A-.2.Z Individual elements, A-Z

For a list of racial, ethnic, and religious elements (with cutter numbers), see E184.A+

South America, see F2201+

Pre-Columbian America. The Indians

For language, see Subclass PM

51 **Periodicals. Societies. Collections (Serial)**

Including anthropological records, Archaeological Institute of America

For American Antiquarian Society, see E172

51.5 **Congresses**

Collections (nonserial). Collected works

53 Several authors

54 Individual authors

Pre-Columbian America. The Indians — Continued

54.5 **Dictionaries. Directories. Guides to tribes**

Study and teaching. Research

55.5 General works

55.6 Audiovisual aids

55.6.Z9A-.Z9Z Catalogs of materials

56 **Museums. Exhibitions**

Including collections of antiquities

Subarrange by author

57 **Theory. Methods of investigation**

Including biography (Arranged by biographee), e.g. William Jones

58 **General works**

58.4 **Juvenile works**

59.A-.Z **Topics, A-Z**

59.A32 Aesthetics

59.A35 Agriculture

59.A5 Anthropometry

Antiquities, *see* E61

59.A67 Architecture

59.A68 Arms and armor. Weapons

59.A7 Art

59.A73 Arts

59.A8 Astronomy

59.B3 Baskets

59.B43 Beadwork

Boats, *see* E59.C2

59.C18 Cannibalism

59.C2 Canoes. Boats

59.C22 Captivities

59.C25 Cartography

59.C46 Children

59.C5 Chronology

59.C55 City planning

59.C59 Commerce

59.C6 Costume. Adornment

59.C73 Craniology

59.C9 Cremation

Culture, *see* E58

59.D35 Dance

59.D45 Dentistry

59.D58 Diseases

59.D66 Dolls

59.D69 Domestic animals

59.D9 Dwellings

59.E3 Economic conditions

Including employment

59.E4 Education

59.E75 Ethnic identity

59.F53 First contact with Europeans

59.F6 Folklore. Legends

59.F63 Food

59.G3 Games. Recreation. Sports

59.G55 Goldwork

Government, Tribal, *see* E59.T75

Government and politics, *see* E59.P73

59.G6 Government relations

59.H54 Hindu influences

59.I4 Implements

59.I5 Industries

59.I53 Influence on other civilizations

Pre-Columbian America. The Indians

59.A-.Z **Topics, A-Z — Continued**

59.L3 Land tenure
59.L4 Leatherwork. Tanning
Legends, *see* E59.F6
Literature, *see* PM151+
59.M3 Masks
59.M33 Material culture
59.M34 Mathematics
59.M4 Medicine
59.M47 Metalwork
59.M58 Migrations
59.M65 Missions
59.M66 Mixed descent
59.M7 Money
59.M8 Mortuary customs
59.N5 Narcotics
59.N8 Numeration
59.P42 Petroglyphs. Rock painting
59.P45 Philosophy
Picture writing, *see* E59.W9
Popular attitudes toward Indians, *see* E59.P89
59.P73 Politics and government
59.P75 Population
59.P8 Pottery
59.P87 Psychology
59.P89 Public opinion. Popular attitudes toward Indians
59.P92 Public welfare
Recreation, *see* E59.G3
59.R38 Religion. Mythology
59.R56 Rites and ceremonies
59.R6 Roads. Trails
Rock paintings, *see* E59.P42
59.S35 Science
59.S37 Sculpture
59.S45 Sexual behavior
59.S54 Shell engraving
59.S64 Social conditions
59.S65 Social life and customs
Sports, *see* E59.G3
59.S7 Statistics
59.T35 Textile fabrics
59.T6 Tobacco pipes
Trails, *see* E59.R6
59.T73 Transpacific influences
59.T75 Tribal government
59.W3 Warfare
Weapons, *see* E59.A68
59.W8 Women
59.W9 Writing. Picture writing

61 **Archaeology of the Americans. Origin of the Indians in general**

65 **Latin America (General)**

For Spanish treatment of the Indians, see F1411

For special, class in local history, usually under the country; in certain cases with state or province; e.g., F1219, Mexico; F1529.M9, Mosquito Reservation

North America (north of Mexico)

71 General works

For works on Indians only, see E77+

Mound builders. Mounds

Class here general works only

Pre-Columbian America. The Indians
North America (north of Mexico)
Mound builders. Mounds — Continued
For mounds in a particular state, province, or region, see E78.A+
(74.A-.Z) By state, province, or region, A-Z
Indians of North America
75 **Periodicals. Societies. Collections**
76 **Congresses**
76.2 **Dictionaries. Directories. Guides to tribes**
Biographies of Indianists
76.4 Collective
76.45.A-.45.Z Individual, A-Z
Subarrange by Table E1 at the end of the text
76.6 **Study and teaching**
76.7 Research
76.8 **Historiography**
Museums. Exhibitions
76.85 General works
76.86.A-.86.Z Special institutions. By place, A-Z
General works
77 Comprehensive works
77.2 Addresses, essays, lectures
77.4 Juvenile works
77.5 Pictorial works
77.6 Minor works
Archaeology
77.8 Periodicals. Societies. Collections. Congresses
77.9 General treatises
77.92 Juvenile works
77.94 Minor works
78.A-.Z **By state, province, or region ,A-Z**
Including Indian antiquities
Class all mounds and archaeological sites within a county or toher division of a state, with the state, subarranging by author, e.g., mounds in Franklin County, Ohio, are classed in E78.O3
Class Indian reservations here under state unless held by a single tribe, when they are classes in E99
For Canada (General), see E78.C2
For works limited to specific tribes, see E99.A+
78.A28 Alabama
78.A3 Alaska
78.A34 Alberta
78.A66 Appalachian Region
Including Blue Ridge Mountains
78.A7 Arizona
78.A8 Arkansas
78.A88 Atlantic States
Blue Ridge Mountains, *see* E78.A66
78.B9 British Columbia
78.C15 California
78.C2 Canada (General)
Including the Canadian Northwest
Cf. E92, Government relations
Cf. E78.B9, British Columbia; E78.N9, Nova Scotia; etc.
78.C45 Chattahoochee River Valley
78.C5 Churchill River Watershed (Sask. and Man.)
78.C6 Colorado
78.C617 Colorado Plateau
78.C62 Colorado River Valley
78.C63 Columbia Plateau
78.C64 Columbia River Valley

Indians of North America

78.A-.Z **By state, province, or region ,A-Z — Continued**

78.C7 Connecticut

78.D2 Dakota Territory

For North Dakota, see E78.N75

For South Dakota, see E78.S63

78.D3 Delaware

78.D5 Delaware Valley

78.D54 Delmarva Peninsula

78.D6 District of Columbia

78.E2 Eastern North America. Woodlands

78.F6 Florida

78.F73 Franklin (District)

78.G3 Georgia

78.G67 Great Basin

78.G7 Great Lakes

78.G73 Great Plains

78.H83 Hudson Valley

78.I18 Idaho

78.I3 Illinois

78.I5 Indian Territory

Including the five civilized tribes before 1907

For the five civilized tribes after 1907, see E78.O45

78.I53 Indiana

78.I6 Iowa

78.K15 Kankakee Valley

78.K16 Kansas

78.K25 Keewatin (District)

78.K3 Kentucky

78.L3 Labrador

78.L58 Little Colorado River Valley (New Mexico and Arizona)

78.L8 Louisiana

78.M16 Mackenzie

78.M2 Maine

78.M25 Manitoba

78.M28 Maritime Provinces

78.M3 Maryland

78.M4 Massachusetts

78.M6 Michigan

78.M65 Middle Atlantic States

78.M67 Middle West

78.M7 Minnesota

78.M73 Mississippi

78.M75 Mississippi Valley

78.M8 Missouri

78.M82 Missouri Valley

78.M9 Montana

78.N3 Nebraska

78.N4 Nevada

78.N46 New Brunswick

78.N5 New England

78.N54 New Hampshire

78.N6 New Jersey

78.N65 New Mexico

78.N7 New York

78.N72 Newfoundland

78.N74 North Carolina

78.N75 North Dakota

Northeastern States, *see* E78.E2

78.N76 Northwest (Old)

Indians of North America

78.A-.Z **By state, province, or region ,A-Z — Continued**

78.N77 Northwest (Pacific)
78.N78 Northwest coast of North America
78.N79 Northwest Territories
78.N8 Northwestern States
78.N9 Nova Scotia. Acadia
78.O3 Ohio
78.O4 Ohio Valley
78.O45 Oklahoma

Including the five civilized tribes after 1907

For the five civilized tribes before 1907, see E78.I5

78.O5 Ontario
78.O6 Oregon
78.O9 Ozark Mountains
78.P2 Pacific Coast
78.P24 Pacific Crest Trail
78.P4 Pennsylvania
Plains Indians, *see* E78.G73
Plateau Indians, *see* E78.G67
78.P7 Prairie Provinces
78.P8 Puget Sound
78.Q3 Quebec
78.R37 Republican River Valley (Nebraska and Kansas)
78.R4 Rhode Island
78.R56 Rio Grande Valley
78.R63 Rocky Mountains
78.S2 Saskatchewan
78.S6 South Carolina
78.S63 South Dakota
78.S65 Southern States
78.S7 Southwest, New

Including Four Corners Region

Cf. F802.B25, Cliff Dwellings in Frijoles Canyon

Cf. F817.C3, Cliff Dwellings in Canyon de Chelly National Monument

78.S8 Southwest, Old
78.S87 Superior, Lake
78.S9 Susquehanna Valley
78.T3 Tennessee
78.T33 Tennessee River Region
78.T4 Texas
Ungava, *see* E78.Q3
78.U55 Utah
78.V5 Vermont
78.V7 Virginia
78.W3 Washington (State)
78.W5 The West
78.W6 West Virginia
78.W8 Wisconsin
Woodlands, *see* E78.E2
78.W95 Wyoming
78.Y44 Yellowstone National Park. Yellowstone River Valley
78.Y8 Yukon Territory

Indian wars

81 General works
82 Wars of the colonial period (General)
83 Individual wars

For biographies, assign first cutter for biographee

Arrnaged chronologically

For wars and uprisings in Virginia, 1609-1676 (Massacres of 1622 and 1641, etc.), see F229

	Indians of North America
	Indian wars
83	Individual wars — Continued
83.63	Pequot War, 1636-1638
83.65	Dutch-Indian War, 1643-1645. Kieft's War
83.655	New York Uprising, 1655
83.663	Esopus Wars, 1659-1676
83.67	King Philip's War, 1675-1676
83.69	Frontenac's Expedition, 1696
	King William's War, 1689-1697, *see* E196
	Queen Anne's War, 1702-1713, *see* E197
83.71	Tuscarora War, 1711-1713
83.713	Yamassee War, 1715-1716
83.72	Eastern Indian Wars (New England), 1722-1726
	Including Pigwacket Fight, 1725; Sébastien Rasles (Râle, Rasle); etc.
83.73	Natchez Massacre, 1729
83.739	Chickasaw War, 1739-1740
	King George's War, 1744-1748, *see* E198
	French and Indian War, 1755-1763, *see* E199
83.759	Cherokee War, 1759-1761
83.7595	Wyoming Massacre, 1763
83.76	Pontiac's Conspiracy, 1763-1765
	Biography: Henry Bouquet, etc.
83.77	Dunmore's War, 1774. Battle of Point Pleasant
83.775	Indian Wars, 1775-1783
	Campaigns of the Revolution, see E230+
	Wyoming Massacre, 1778, see E241.W9
	Cherry Valley Massacre, 1778, see E241.C5
	Sullivan's Campaign, 1779, see E235
	Crawford's Campaign, 1782, see E238
83.79	Northwestern Indian Wars (Ohio Valley), 1790-1795
	Including Harmar's Expedition, 1790; Scott's Expedition, May 1791; Wilkinson's Expedition, August 1791; St. Clair's Campaign, November 1791
83.794	Wayne's Campaign, 1793-1795
83.81	Battle of Tippecanoe, 1811
83.812	Indian Wars, 1812-1815
	Campaigns of the War of 1812, *see* E355.2
83.813	First Creek War, 1813-1814
	Including Jackson's execution of the Tennessee militiamen
83.817	First Seminole War, 1817-1818
	Including the execution of Ambrister and Arbuthnot
83.818	Arikara War, 1823
83.83	Black Hawk War, 1832
	Biography: Black Hawk, the Sauk chief, etc.
83.835	Second Seminole War, 1835-1842
83.836	Second Creek War, 1836
	Thomas Sidney Jesup, etc.
83.837	Comanche War, 1840
83.838	Temecula Massacre, 1847
83.84	Pacific Northwest Indian wars, 1847-1865
	Including Cayuse War, 1847-1850; Rogue River War, 1850; Yakima War, 1855-1858; Spokane Expedition, 1858
83.854	Dakota Indian or Sioux War, 1855-1856
	Including Harney's Expedition
83.855	Third Seminole War, 1855-1858
83.8565	Battle of Maricopa Wells, 1857
	Mountain Meadow Massacre, 1857, *see* F826
83.857	Spirit Lake Massacre, 1857
83.8575	Battle of Solomon's Fork, 1857
83.8577	Battle of Crooked Creek, 1859

Indians of North America

Indian wars

83 Individual wars — Continued

83.858 Mill Creek War, 1857-1865

83.859 Navaho (Navajo) War, 1858-1868

83.86 Dakota Indian or Sioux War, 1862-1865

Including uprising in Minnesota (Battles of Birch Coulee, Fort Ridgely, New Ulm, Wood Lake), 1862; Battle of Whitestone Hill, 1863; Battle of Killdeer Mountain, July 1864; Platt Bridge Fight, July 1865; Powder River Campaign, July-October 1865

83.863 Indian wars, 1862-1865

Including Shoshoni War, 1863-1865; Cheyenne War, 1864; Sand Creek Massacre, 1864; Battle of Adobe Walls, 1864

Cf. E83.858, Mill Creek War

Cf. E83.859, Navaho War

Cf. E83.86, Sioux War

83.866 Indian wars, 1866-1898

Including Fort Phil Kearney Massacre, 1866; Warren Wagon Train Massacre, 1871; Red Cloud War, 1866-1867

Biography: George Crook, Nelson Appleton Miles, etc.

83.867 Black Hawk War (Utah), 1865-1872

83.8675 Battle of Camp Cady, 1866

83.868 Battle of Beecher Island, 1868

83.869 Washita Campaign, 1868-1869

83.8695 Battle of Summit Springs, 1869

83.8697 Battle of Belly River, 1870

83.87 Modoc War, 1872-1873

83.875 Red River War, 1874-1875

Including Cheyenne Outbreak

83.876 Dakota Indian or Sioux War, 1876

Including Battle of the Little Big Horn

83.8765 Battle of the Butte, 1877

83.877 Nez Percé War, 1877

Including Battle of the Big Hole

83.879 Ute War, 1879

Including White River Massacre

Riel Rebellion, *see* F1060.9

83.88 Apache War, 1882-1886

83.89 Dakota Indian or Sioux War, 1890-1891. Messiah War

Including Death of Chief Sitting Bull; Wounded Knee Massacre, 1890

83.895 Chippewa War, 1898

Captivities

Including adventures and experiences of those taken captive by the Indians

85 General works. Collected narratives

87.A-.Z Individual captivities, A-Z

Prefer classification in E83 or E99 if captivity relates to a particular war or tribe

88 **Individual memoirs of early explorers, traders, trappers, etc., giving accounts of their experiences among the Indians**

For memoirs relating to a specific tribe, see E99.A+

Biography

89 Collective

Including portraits

90.A-.Z Individual, A-Z

Class individuals identified with specific tribes in E99 unless better known in connection with specific wars in which case class with the war in E83.63-.895

Subarrange by Table E1 at the end of the text

GALE NOTE *The cutter number(s) listed below have been given only as examples by the Library of Congress*

Black Hawk, Sauk chief, *see* E83.83

Pocahontas, *see* E99.P85

Sitting Bull, Dakota chief, *see* E99.D1

Indians of North America

Biography

90.A-.Z Individual, A-Z — Continued

90.T2 Tegakouita, Catharine

Government relations

Including government agencies dealing with Indians, Indian rights associations, biography, treatment of Indians, reservations (General), and government services for Indians (General)

For works limited to specific regions or states, see E78.A+

For works limited to specific tribes, see E99.A+

91 General works

92 Canada

Cf. E78.C2, Indians in Canada

93 United States

(94) Law, *see* Class K

(95) Treaties, *see* Class K

Social life and customs, see E98.S7

Education

For works limited to specific tribes, see E99.A+

96 General works

Canada

96.2 General works

Indian schools

96.5 General works

96.6.A-.6.Z Individual schools. By name, A-Z

GALE NOTE *The cutter number(s) listed below have been given only as examples by the Library of Congress*

96.6.S17 St. Pauls's Indian Residential School, Cardston, Alta.

96.65.A-.65.Z By region or province, A-Z

United States

97 General works

97.3 Finance

Indian schools

97.5 General works

97.55 Tribal colleges. Indian community colleges

97.6.A-.6.Z Individual schools. By name, A-Z

GALE NOTE *The cutter number(s) listed below have been given only as examples by the Library of Congress*

97.6.B87 Bureau of Indian Affairs School, Bethel, Alaska

97.6.C35 Cherokee National Female Seminary, Tahlequah, Okla.

97.6.F66 Fort Shaw Indian School (Great Falls, Mont.)

97.6.H3 Hampton Institute, Hampton, Va.

Cf. LC2851.H27+, African-American education at Hampton Institute

97.6.J69 Johnson's Indian School, White Sulphur, Ky.

97.6.M5 Moor's Indian Charity School, Lebanon, Conn.

Cf. LD1420+, Dartmouth College, Hanover, N.H.

97.6.R35 Rapid City Indian School

97.6.S2 Santee Normal Training School, Santee, Nebr.

97.6.T4 Thomas Indian School, Iroquois, N.Y.

97.6.U54 University of California. Tecumseh Center

97.65.A-.65.Z By region or state, A-Z

97.8 **Indian libraries. Library service to Indians**

97.9 **Indian archives**

98.A-.Z **Other topics, A-Z**

For works limited to specific geographic areas, if specific tribes are not indicated, see E78.A+

For works limited to specific tribes, see E99.A+

98.A15 Adoption

98.A2 Aesthetics

Afro-American relations, *see* E98.R28

98.A27 Aged

	Indians of North America
98.A-.Z	**Other topics, A-Z — Continued**
98.A3	Agriculture
	Alcohol use, *see* E98.L7
98.A55	Anthropometry
	Antiquities, *see* E77.8+, E78.A+
	Appropriations, *see* E91+
98.A63	Architecture
98.A65	Arms and armor. Weapons
98.A7	Art
	For modern art by Indian artists, see Class N
98.A73	Arts
98.A84	Asian influences
98.A88	Astronomy
98.B3	Baskets
98.B46	Beadwork
98.B54	Biology. Ethnobiology
98.B6	Boats. Canoes
98.B7	Botany (Economic). Ethnobotany
98.B8	Buffalo
	Burial customs, *see* E98.M8
98.B87	Business enterprises
98.C14	Calendar
	Captivities, *see* E85+
98.C17	Cartography
	Including works about maps of Indian lands
98.C3	Census
98.C47	Charitable contributions. Philanthropy
98.C5	Children
	Citizenship, *see* E91+
98.C55	Chronology
	Claims
98.C6	By Indians
98.C62	Against Indians
98.C7	Commerce
98.C73	Communication
98.C76	Copperwork
98.C79	Cosmology
98.C8	Costume. Adornment
	Crafts, *see* E98.I5
98.C85	Craniology
98.C87	Crime. Police
	Including Indian reservation police
	Criminal justice system, *see* Class K
98.C89	Cultural assimilation
	Cf. E91+, Government relations and treatment of Indians
	Culture, *see* E77
98.D2	Dance
98.D6	Diseases
98.D65	Dolls
98.D67	Domestic animals
98.D8	Drama
98.D9	Dwellings. Furniture
98.E2	Economic conditions
	Education, *see* E97+
98.E5	Embroidery
98.E6	Employment
98.E83	Ethics
98.E85	Ethnic identity
	Ethnobiology, *see* E98.B54

	Indians of North America
98.A-.Z	**Other topics, A-Z — Continued**
	Ethnobotany, *see* E98.B7
98.F3	Financial affairs
	Including trust estates, revolving credit fund, relief
	Cf. E98.P3, Pensions
98.F38	Fire use
98.F39	First contact with Europeans
98.F4	Fishing
98.F58	Folk literature
	For legends and tales, see E98.F6
98.F6	Folklore. Legends
	For individual tribes, see E99.A+
98.F7	Food
98.F73	Footwear
98.G18	Gambling
	Including gambling on Indian reservations
98.G2	Games. Recreation. Sports
98.G44	Genealogy
	Government relations, *see* E91+
	Handicraft, *see* E98.I5
98.H35	Handicapped
	History, *see* E77+
	Homosexuality, *see* E98.S48
98.H55	Horses
	Hospitals, *see* RA981.A35
98.H58	Housing
98.H77	Humor
98.H8	Hunting
98.I4	Implements. Utensils
98.I5	Industries
	Including handicraft, mining, etc.
	For basketry, see E98.B3
	For silversmithing, see E98.S55
	For textile industry, see E98.T35
98.I54	Interviews
98.I75	Irrigation
98.J48	Jewelry
98.K48	Kinship
98.K54	Knives
98.L3	Land tenure
	Land transfers, *see* E91+
	Language, *see* PM1+
98.L4	Leatherwork. Tanning
	Legends, *see* E98.F6
98.L7	Liquor use. Alcohol use
98.M2	Magic
98.M27	Marriage customs and rites
98.M3	Masks
	Mass media, *see* P94.5.I53
98.M34	Material culture
98.M35	Medals
98.M4	Medicine. Medicine men
	Cf. E98.D6, Diseases
	Mental health, *see* RC451.5.I5
98.M45	Metalwork
98.M5	Military capacity and organization. Indians as soldiers
98.M6	Missions (General)
	Including biography of missionaries
	Prefer tribe or local

	Indians of North America
98.A-.Z	**Other topics, A-Z**
98.M6	Missions (General) — Continued
	For Jesuit missions in New France, see F1030.7+
98.M63	Mixed descent
98.M7	Money. Wampum
98.M8	Mortuary customs
	Music (Music scores), *see* M1669, ML3557
98.N2	Names
98.N5	Narcotics. Drugs
	Newspapers, *see* PN4883
	Origin, *see* E61
98.O7	Oratory. Speeches, addresses, etc.
	Ornaments, *see* E98.C8
98.O76	Orphanages
98.P23	Painting
98.P3	Pensions
98.P34	Petroglyphs. Rock paintings
	Philanthropy, *see* E98.C47
98.P5	Philosophy
98.P53	Physical anthropology
	Including physical characteristics, beauty, etc.
	Cf. E98.A55, Anthropometry
(98.P74)	Poetry
	For poetry in Indian languages, see PM151+
	For poetry by Indians in non-Indian languages, see Subclasses PR, PS, etc.
	Police, *see* E98.C87
	Politics and government, *see* E98.T77
98.P76	Population
	Portraits (Collected), *see* E89+
98.P8	Pottery
98.P86	Powwows
98.P9	Property
	Including appraisal, removal of restrictions, timber contracts, wills, etc.
98.P95	Psychology
	Cf. BF432.I5, Intelligence of Indians
98.P99	Public opinion about Indians. Popular attitudes toward Indians
	Recreation, *see* E98.G2
98.R28	Relations with Afro-Americans
98.R3	Religion. Mythology
	Including creation, future life, katcinas, occultism, revivalism, rites and ceremonies, shamanism, etc.
98.R4	Removal
	Reservations, *see* E78.A+, E91+, E99.A+
98.R5	Riding gear
98.R53	Rites and ceremonies
	Rock paintings, *see* E98.P34
98.S26	Salt
98.S3	Sandpaintings
	Scalping, *see* E98.W2
98.S43	Science
98.S46	Services for
98.S48	Sexual behavior
	Including homosexuality
98.S5	Sign language
98.S55	Silversmithing
98.S6	Slavery
	Smoking, *see* E98.T6
98.S67	Social conditions
98.S7	Social life and customs

	Indians of North America
98.A-.Z	**Other topics, A-Z — Continued**
98.S75	Societies
	Speeches, addresses, etc., *see* E98.O7
	Sports, *see* E98.G2
	Suffrage, *see* E91+
98.S9	Suicide
98.S94	Sweatbaths
98.T2	Tattooing
98.T24	Taxation
98.T35	Textile fabrics. Weaving
	Including blankets, rugs, etc.
98.T6	Tobacco pipes. Smoking
98.T65	Totems
	Including totem poles
98.T7	Trails
98.T73	Transatlantic influences
98.T75	Trapping
	Treaties, *see* Class K
98.T77	Tribal government. Politics and government
98.U72	Urban residence
	Utensils, *see* E98.I4
98.W2	Warfare. Scalping
	Wars, *see* E81+
	Weapons, *see* E98.A65
	Weaving, *see* E98.T35
98.W49	Wife abuse
	Wills, *see* E98.P9
98.W8	Women
98.W86	Writing
98.Y68	Youth
	Tribes and cultures, A-Z
	Including those Mexican tribes which are also found in the United States
	For biographies, assign second cutter for biographees
99.A12	Abitibi
99.A13	Abnaki. Abenaki
99.A15	Achomawi
99.A16	Acoma
99.A18	Adena culture
99.A28	Ahtena
99.A34	Aleuts
99.A349	Algonkin
99.A35	Algonquian
99.A4	Alibamu
99.A45	Alsea
	Anasazi culture, *see* E99.P9
99.A6	Apache
99.A62	Apalachee
99.A63	Apalachicola
99.A7	Arapaho
99.A8	Arikara
99.A82	Arosaguntacook
99.A83	Assateague
99.A84	Assiniboin
99.A86	Athapascan
	Atikamekw, *see* E99.T33
99.A87	Atsina
99.A875	Atsugewi
99.A88	Attacapa
99.B33	Bannock

Indians of North America

Tribes and cultures, A-Z — Continued

99.B37	Basket-Maker
99.B376	Bearlake
(99.B38)	Bellabella, *see* E99.H45
99.B39	Bellacoola
99.B4	Beothuk
99.B5	Biloxi
99.B6	Bocootawwonauke
99.B7	Brotherton
99.B8	Brulé
99.C12	Caddo
99.C13	Caddoan
99.C15	Cahokia
99.C155	Cahuilla
99.C18	Calusa
99.C19	Campo
99.C2	Capote
	Carrier, *see* E99.T17
99.C23	Casas Grandes culture
99.C24	Catawba
99.C26	Cathlamet
(99.C27)	Caughnawaga, *see* E99.M8
99.C3	Cayuga
99.C32	Cayuse
99.C37	Chaco culture
99.C4	Chakchiuma
99.C48	Chasta
99.C483	Chastacosta
99.C49	Chehalis
99.C4925	Chelan
99.C493	Chemehuevi
99.C495	Cheraw
99.C5	Cherokee
99.C526	Chetco
99.C53	Cheyenne
99.C55	Chickasaw
	Chilcotin, *see* E99.T78
99.C552	Chilkat
99.C5523	Chilliwack
99.C553	Chilula
99.C56	Chimariko
99.C565	Chimmesyan
99.C57	Chinook
99.C58	Chinookan
99.C59	Chipewyan
99.C6	Chippewa
99.C68	Chiricahua
99.C7	Chitimacha
99.C8	Choctaw
99.C815	Chumash. Chumashan
99.C82	Clallam
99.C83	Clayoquot
99.C832	Clovis culture
99.C834	Coahuiltecan
99.C835	Cochimi
99.C84	Cochiti
99.C842	Cocopa
99.C844	Colville
99.C85	Comanche

Indians of North America

Tribes and cultures, A-Z — Continued

99.C86	Comox
99.C87	Conestoga
99.C873	Conoy
	Including Piscataway
99.C874	Coos
99.C87414	Coosa
99.C8742	Coquille
99.C8743	Coree
(99.C8744)	Costanoan, *see* E99.O32
99.C875	Cowichan
99.C877	Cowlitz
99.C88	Cree
99.C9	Creek
99.C91	Croatan. Lumbee
99.C92	Crow
99.C94	Cupeño
99.D1	Dakota. Sioux
	Including Chief Sitting Bull
	For death of Chief Sitting Bull, see E83.89
99.D2	Delaware
	Dena'ina, *see* E99.T185
99.D25	Dene Thá
99.D4	Dhegiha
99.D5	Diegueño
99.D8	Dudley
99.D9	Duwamish
99.E42	Entiat
99.E5	Erie
99.E7	Eskimos
	Including Inuit
99.E8	Esopus
99.E85	Esselen
99.E9	Eyak
	Five civilized tribes, *see* E78.I5, E99.C5, E99.C55, E99.C8, E99.C9, E99.S28
99.F65	Folsom culture
99.F67	Fort Ancient culture
99.F7	Fox
99.F75	Fremont culture
99.G15	Gabrieleño
	Gitksan, *see* E99.K55
99.G67	Gosiute
99.G82	Guale
99.H15	Hackensack
99.H2	Haida
99.H23	Haisla
99.H26	Han
99.H28	Hasinai
99.H3	Havasupai
99.H45	Heiltsuk
99.H6	Hidatsa
99.H65	Hitchiti
99.H68	Hohokam culture
99.H69	Hopewell culture
99.H7	Hopi
99.H72	Houma
99.H75	Hualapai
99.H795	Hunkpapa
99.H8	Hupa

Indians of North America

Tribes and cultures, A-Z — Continued

99.H9	Huron
	Including Wyandot Indians
99.I2	Illinois
99.I5	Ingalik
	Inuit, *see* E99.E7
99.I6	Iowa
99.I69	Iroquoian
99.I7	Iroquois
99.I8	Isleta
99.J4	Jemez
99.J5	Jicarilla
99.J8	Juaneño
99.J9	Jumano
99.K15	Kainah
99.K16	Kalapuyan
99.K17	Kalispel
99.K18	Kamia
99.K2	Kansa
99.K23	Karankawa
99.K25	Karok
99.K258	Kashaya
99.K26	Kaska
99.K264	Kaskaskia
99.K267	Kato
99.K269	Kawaiisu
99.K28	Kawchottine
99.K3	Keeche
99.K39	Keresan
99.K396	Kichai
99.K4	Kickapoo
99.K5	Kiowa
99.K52	Kiowa Apache
99.K55	Kitksan. Gitksan
99.K59	Kiyuksa
99.K7	Klamath
99.K76	Klikitat
99.K77	Koasati
	Kootenai, *see* E99.K85
99.K79	Koyukon
99.K82	Kuitsh
99.K83	Kusso
99.K84	Kutchin
99.K85	Kutenai
99.K9	Kwakiutl
99.L2	Laguna
	Lakes, *see* E99.S546
99.L25	Lamar culture
99.L3	Lassik
99.L35	Lekwungen. Songhees
99.L4	Lillooet
99.L5	Lipan
99.L9	Luiseño
	Lumbee, *see* E99.C91
99.L95	Lummi
99.L98	Lutuamian
99.M115	Madehsi
99.M12	Mahican
99.M18	Maidu

Indians of North America
Tribes and cultures, A-Z — Continued

99.M19	Makah
99.M195	Malecite
99.M198	Manahoac
99.M2	Mandan
99.M22	Manhattan
99.M23	Manso
99.M25	Maricopa
99.M27	Martis culture
99.M3	Mascouten
99.M4	Mashpee
99.M42	Massachuset
99.M424	Massawomeck
99.M43	Mattole
99.M433	Mayas *Cf. F1435+, Central America* *Cf. F1445+, British Honduras* *Cf. F1465+, Guatemala*
99.M435	Mdewakanton
99.M44	Menominee
99.M45	Mescalero
99.M46	Methow
99.M47	Métis
99.M48	Miami
99.M6	Micmac
99.M615	Mikasuki
99.M62	Mikinakwadshiwininiwak
99.M625	Mill Creek
99.M63	Mimbreño
99.M64	Mingo
99.M642	Miniconjou
99.M65	Minisink
99.M68	Missisauga
99.M6815	Mississippian culture
99.M682	Missouri
99.M683	Mistassin
99.M69	Miwok
99.M693	Mixed descent *For Métis, see E99.M47*
99.M697	Moache
99.M698	Mobile
99.M7	Modoc
99.M75	Mogollon Apache
99.M76	Mogollon culture *Including Mimbres culture*
99.M77	Mohave
99.M8	Mohawk
99.M83	Mohegan
99.M84	Molala
99.M85	Monacan
99.M86	Mono
99.M87	Montagnais
99.M88	Montauk
99.M89	Moquelumnan
99.M9	Moravian
99.M917	Muckleshoot
99.M92	Multnomah
99.M93	Munsee
99.M95	Muskhogean

	Indians of North America
	Tribes and cultures, A-Z — Continued
99.N125	Nahane
99.N14	Nanticoke
99.N16	Narranganset
99.N18	Naskapi
99.N19	Natchesan
99.N2	Natchez
99.N22	Natsitkutchin
99.N23	Naugatuck
99.N25	Nauset
99.N3	Navajo
99.N45	Nehalem
99.N46	Nespelim
99.48	Neutral Nation
99.N5	NezPercé
99.N6	Niantic
99.N65	Nipissing
99.N7	Nipmuc
99.N73	Nisenan
99.N734	Niska
99.N74	Nisqually
99.N815	Nomlaki
99.N84	Nooksack
99.N85	Nootka
99.N9	Norridgewock
99.N93	Nottoway
99.N96	Ntlakyapamuk
99.N97	Numic
99.O22	Occaneechi
99.O3	Oglala
99.O32	Ohlone
	Ojibwa, *see* E99.C6
(99.O33)	Oka, *see* E99.M8
99.O35	Okinagan
99.O4	Omaha
99.O45	Oneida
99.O5	Oneota (Great Plains)
99.O58	Onondaga
99.O63	Oohenonpa
99.O68	Oowekeeno
99.O8	Osage
99.O87	Oto
99.O9	Ottawa
99.P2	Paiute
99.P215	Palaihnihan
99.P22	Paloos
99.P225	Pamlico
99.P23	Pamunkey
99.P24	Panamint
99.P244	Panhandle culture
99.P25	Papago. Tohono O'Odham
99.P26	Pascagoula
99.P27	Passamaquoddy
99.P29	Patwin
99.P292	Paugusset
99.P3	Pawnee
99.P32	Payaya
99.P34	Pecos
99.P35	Pee Dee

Indians of North America

Tribes and cultures, A-Z — Continued

99.P4	Pennacook
99.P5	Penobscot
99.P515	Peoria
99.P52	Pequawket
99.P53	Pequot
99.P57	Piankashaw
99.P575	Picuris
99.P58	Piegan
99.P6	Pima
99.P62	Piman
99.P63	Piro Pueblo
	Piscataway, *see* E99.C873
	Plains Indians, *see* E78.G73
99.P64	Pocasset
99.P65	Pomo
99.P7	Ponca
99.P8	Potawatomi
99.P83	Potomac
99.P84	Poverty Point culture
99.P85	Powhatan
	Including Pocahontas
99.P9	Pueblo
	Including Anasazi culture and cliff dwellings
99.P98	Puyallup
99.Q2	Quapaw
99.Q5	Quileute
99.Q6	Quinaielt
99.Q7	Quinnipiac
99.R18	Rappahannock
99.S14	Saclan
(99.S15)	Saint Regis, *see* E99.M8
99.S16	Sakonnet
	Salado culture, *see* E99.S547
99.S17	Salinan
99.S2	Salish
99.S21	Salishan
	Including Coast Salish and Puget Sound Salish
99.S2115	Samish
99.S212	San Felipe
99.S213	San Ildefonso
99.S214	Sandia
99.S215	Sanpoil
99.S217	Sans Arc
99.S22	Santee
99.S223	Santo Domingo
99.S225	Saone
99.S226	Saponi
99.S227	Sarsi
99.S23	Sauk
99.S25	Scaticook (Connecticut)
99.S252	Scaticook (New York)
99.S258	Sechelt
99.S26	Sekani
99.S28	Seminole
99.S3	Seneca
	Senijextee, *see* E99.S546
99.S31	Serrano
99.S32	Sewee

Indians of North America

Tribes and cultures, A-Z — Continued

99.S325	Shahaptian
99.S33	Shasta
99.S332	Shastan
99.S35	Shawnee
99.S38	Shinnecock
99.S39	Shoshonean
99.S4	Shoshoni
99.S45	Shuswap
(99.S5)	Sia, *see* E99.Z52
99.S53	Sihasapa
99.S54	Siksika
99.S544	Siletz
99.S546	Sin Aikst. Senijextee. Lakes Indians
99.S547	Sinagua culture *Including Salado culture*
99.S55	Sinkiuse-Columbia
99.S56	Sinkyone
99.S6	Siouan
	Sioux, *see* E99.D1
99.S62	Sisseton
99.S622	Siuslaw
99.S623	Siwanoy
99.S627	Skagit
99.S63	Skitswish
99.S64	Skokomish
99.S65	Slave
99.S66	Snoqualmie
99.S665	Sokoki
	Songhees, *see* E99.L35
99.S68	Spokan
99.S7	Squawmish
99.S72	Stalo
99.S75	Stillaquamish
99.S8	Stockbridge
99.S85	Suquamish
99.S95	Susquehanna
99.T114	Tabeguache
99.T115	Taensa
99.T12	Tahltan
99.T15	Takelma
99.T17	Takulli
99.T18	Tamaroa
99.T185	Tanai. Dena'ina
99.T187	Tanana
99.T2	Taos
99.T315	Tawakoni
99.T32	Tenino
99.T325	Tequesta
99.T33	Têtes de Boule. Atikamekw
99.T34	Teton
99.T35	Tewa
99.T4	Thlingchadinne
99.T52	Tigua. Tiwa
99.T53	Tillamook
99.T54	Timiskaming
99.T55	Timucua
99.T56	Tinne
99.T57	Tionontati

Indians of North America

Tribes and cultures, A-Z — Continued

	Tiwa, *see* E99.T52
99.T58	Tlakluit
99.T6	Tlingit
	Tohono O'Odham, *see* E99.P25
99.T7	Tolowa
99.T73	Tonikan
99.T75	Tonkawa
99.T77	Tsattine
99.T772	Tsetsaut
99.T78	Tsilkotin
99.T8	Tsimshian
99.T83	Tubatulabal
99.T845	Tukkuthkutchin
99.T85	Tukuarika
99.T87	Tulalip
99.T875	Tunica
99.T88	Tunxis
99.T9	Tuscarora
99.T92	Tutchone
99.T96	Tutelo
99.T97	Tututni
99.T98	Twana
99.T986	Tzotzil
	Cf. F1221.T9, Mexico
99.U35	Uinta
99.U4	Umatilla
99.U45	Umpqua
99.U8	Ute
99.U85	Uto-Aztecan
99.V8	Vuntakutchin
99.W114	Waccamaw
99.W12	Wachuset
99.W125	Waco
99.W13	Wahpekute
99.W135	Wahpeton
99.W15	Wailaki
99.W16	Wakashan
99.W18	Walla Walla
99.W185	Walpapi
99.W19	Wamesit
99.W2	Wampanoag
99.W3	Wanapum
99.W34	Wappinger
99.W35	Wappo
99.W36	Warm Spring Apache
99.W37	Wasco
99.W38	Washo
99.W4	Wawenock
99.W45	Wea
99.W48	Weeden Island culture
99.W5	Welsh
	Including the tradition and theories about this mythic tribe
99.W53	Wenatchi
99.W54	Wenrohronon
99.W56	Wet'suwet'en
99.W6	Wichita
99.W63	Wiechquaeskeck
99.W65	Wiminuche

Indians of North America

Tribes and cultures, A-Z — Continued

99.W7 Winnebago
99.W78 Wintu
99.W79 Wintun
99.W8 Wiyat
99.W84 Woodland culture
99.W9 Wyam
99.Y18 Yahuskin
99.Y2 Yakama. Yakima
99.Y212 Yakonan
99.Y22 Yamassee
99.Y225 Yampa
99.Y23 Yana
99.Y25 Yankton
99.Y26 Yanktonai
Yaqui, *see* F1221.Y3
99.Y5 Yavapai
99.Y7 Yokayo
99.Y75 Yokuts
99.Y77 Yoncalla
99.Y9 Yuchi
99.Y92 Yukian
99.Y94 Yuma
99.Y95 Yuman
99.Y97 Yurok
99.Z52 Zia. Sia
99.Z9 Zuñi

Discovery of America and early explorations

Including early to about 1607

101 **General works**

Pre-Columbian period

103 General works

Special

105 Norse. Vinland

Including biography of Liev Eiriksson, Kensington rune stone

For Greenland, see G725+

109.A-.Z Other, A-Z
109.A35 African
109.B3 Basque
109.C37 Catalan
109.C44 Celtic
109.C5 Chinese
109.D2 Danish
109.D9 Dutch
109.E2 East Indian
109.E3 Egyptian
109.G7 Greek
109.I57 Indonesian
109.I6 Irish
109.I8 Italian

Including voyages of the brothers Niccolò and Antonio Zeno

109.M34 Malian
109.P5 Phoenician
109.P8 Portuguese
109.S7 Spanish
109.T74 Trojan
109.W4 Welsh

For the tradition of the Welsh Indians, see E99.W5

Discovery of America and early explorations — Continued

Background factors of the discovery, and resulting conditions

Including the influence of Paolo del Pozzo Toscanelli, Martin Behaim

Columbus (Cristoforo Colombo)

111 General works

Including biography

112 Special

Including autographs, birthplace, canonization, celebrations, coat of arms, education, friends, iconography, landfall, language, marriage, monuments, name. relics, ships, tomb

For bibliography of Columbus, see Z8187

113 Family

Including the Colombo, Colón, Moniz, and Perestrello families

Writings of Columbus

114 Collected works

Including collected letters and collectiond of documents concerning him

Arranged alphabetically by editor

Individual works

First letter (Santangel)

115 Spanish text. By date

Including facsimiles and reprints without translation

115.2 Translations. By language, A-Z, and date of imprint

With or without facsimiles or reprints of Spanish text

115.3 Pharaphrases and works about the letter. By author

Second letter (Sánchez)

116 Spanish text. By date

Including facsimiles and reprints without translation

Translations

116.1 Latin. By date

Including the earliest translation as well as others made from it; facsimiles and texts

116.2 Other. By initial letter of language and date

With or without facsimiles or reprints of Spanish text

116.3 Pharaphrases and works about the letter. By author

117 Other writings

For his journal, see E118

118 Voyages. Journal of Columbus

119 Coluimbus celebrations, 1892-1893

Arranged alphabetically by place

Cf. T400+, National and international exhibitions

119.2 Columbus quincentennial, 1192-1993

120 Pamphlets, addresses, essays, etc.

Including poetry, drama, Columbus Day celebrations and programs

Cf. Subclasses PN-PZ, Literature

Post-Columbian period. El Dorado

Including successors of Columbus to about 1607

121 General works

Cf. G199.2+, History of geographical discoveries, explorations, and travels

Cf. G575+, Polar discoveries

Cf. G640+, Search for the Northwest Passage

Spanish and Portuguese

123 General works

Including Line of Demarcation drawn by Pope Alexander VI in 1493 and modified by Treaty of Tordesillas, 1494

Cf. E141+, Descriptive accounts of America before 1607

Cf. F314, Spanish settlement in Florida before 1821

Cf. F1230, Spanish settlement in Mexico before 1810

Cf. F1411, History of Spanish America before 1600

Cf. F3442, Spanish settlement in Peru before 1820

Cf. G278+, History of geographical discoveries by the Spanish and the Portuguese

Discovery of America and early explorations

Post-Columbian period. El Dorado

Spanish and Portuguese — Continued

Individual explorers, A-Z

GALE NOTE *The cutter number(s) listed below have been given only as examples by the Library of Congress*

125.A3 Aguilar, Jerónimo de

Subarrange by Table E1 at the end of the text

125.A35 Aguirre, Lope de

Subarrange by Table E1 at the end of the text

125.B2 Balboa, Vasco Núñez de

Subarrange by Table E1 at the end of the text

125.B7 Boyl, Bernardo

Subarrange by Table E1 at the end of the text

125.C11 Cabral, Pedro Alvares

Subarrange by Table E1 at the end of the text

125.C12 Cabrillo, Juan Rodríquez

Subarrange by Table E1 at the end of the text

125.C2 Caminha, Pedro Vaz de

Subarrange by Table E1 at the end of the text

125.C4 Casas, Bartolomé de las

Subarrange by Table E1 at the end of the text

For the tracts of Las Casas, see F1411

125.C8 Cosa, Juan de la

Subarrange by Table E1 at the end of the text

125.F3 Federmann, Nikolaus

Subarrange by Table E1 at the end of the text

125.F35 Fernández, Juan

Subarrange by Table E1 at the end of the text

125.F9 Fuca, Juan de

Subarrange by Table E1 at the end of the text

125.G2 García, Diego de Moguer

Subarrange by Table E1 at the end of the text

125.G6 Gómez, Esteban

Subarrange by Table E1 at the end of the text

125.G8 Grijalva, Juan de

Subarrange by Table E1 at the end of the text

125.M3 Marco da Nizza, Father

Subarrange by Table E1 at the end of the text

125.N3 Narváez, Pánfilo de

Subarrange by Table E1 at the end of the text

125.N9 Núñez Cabeza de Vaca, Alvar

Subarrange by Table E1 at the end of the text

125.O58 Ordás, Diego de

Subarrange by Table E1 at the end of the text

125.O6 Orellano, Francisco de

Subarrange by Table E1 at the end of the text

125.P2 Pancaldo, León

Subarrange by Table E1 at the end of the text

125.P5 Pinzón, Martín Alonso

Subarrange by Table E1 at the end of the text

125.P52 Pinzón, Vincente Yáñez

Subarrange by Table E1 at the end of the text

125.P7 Ponce de León, Juan

Subarrange by Table E1 at the end of the text

125.S23 Sarmiento de Gamboa, Pedro

Subarrange by Table E1 at the end of the text

125.S3 Schmidel, Ulrich

Subarrange by Table E1 at the end of the text

Discovery of America and early explorations
Post-Columbian period. El Dorado
Spanish and Portuguese
Individual explorers, A-Z — Continued
125.S7 Soto, Hernando de
Subarrange by Table E1 at the end of the text
125.U8 Ursúa, Pedro de
Subarrange by Table E1 at the end of the text
125.V3 Vásquez de Coronado, Francisco
Subarrange by Table E1 at the end of the text
125.V5 Vespucci, Amerigo
Subarrange by Table E1 at the end of the text
125.V6 The name "America"
English
127 General works
129.A-.Z Individual explorers, A-Z
129.C1 Cabot, John an d Sebastian
Subarrange by Table E1 at the end of the text
129.D7 Drake, Sir Francis
Subarrange by Table E1 at the end of the text
Cf. G420.D7, Voyage of circumnavigation
129.G4 Gilbert, Sir Humphrey
Subarrange by Table E1 at the end of the text
129.H4 Hawkins, Sir Richard
Subarrange by Table E1 at the end of the text
129.H8 Hudson, Henry
Subarrange by Table E1 at the end of the text
Cf. F127.H8, Hudson: Fulton celebration, 1909
129.R2 Raleigh, Sir Walter
Subarrange by Table E1 at the end of the text
Cf. DA86.22.R2, Biography
Cf. F229, Raleigh's Roanoke colonies, 1584-1590
French
Cf. F314, French colony in Florida
Cf. 1030, New France
131 General works
133.A-.Z Individual explorers, A-Z
133.C3 Cartier, Jacques
Subarrange by Table E1 at the end of the text
133.P3 Paulmier de Gonneville, Binot
Subarrange by Table E1 at the end of the text
133.T47 Thevet, André
Subarrange by Table E1 at the end of the text
133.V5 Verrazzano, Giovanni da
Subarrange by Table E1 at the end of the text
135.A-.Z Other, A-Z
GALE NOTE *The cutter number(s) listed below have been given only as examples by the Library of Congress*
135.D9 Dutch
135.G3 German. Welsers
135.I8 Italian
Allusions
Including works on subjetcs other than America, containing illusions to the discovery and to the New World
For the books being classified with the subjects of which they treat or the literature to which they belong, e.g., the polyglot Psalter edited by Agostino Giustiniani, see BS1419, and the Sentencias catholocias del divi, poeta Dant, compiled by Jaume Ferrer de Blanes, seePS3937.F4
Descriptive accounts of America. Earliest to 1810
141 **Earliest to 1606**
cluding 16th century travels

Descriptive accounts of America. Earliest to 1810

141 **Earliest to 1606 — Continued**

Cf. E101+, Discoveries

Cf. F1411, History of Latin America to 1600

143 **1607-1810. Latin America**

For English colonies, see E162

For Latin America since 1810, see F1409

For New France, 1603-1763, see F1030

For other local, see corresponding country and period divisions in Class F

General
151 **Periodicals. Societies. Collections**
Including general societies for the preservation of places of historic or other national interest, e.g. American Scenic and Historic Preservation Society
For geographic societies, see G3
For historical periodicals and societies, see E171-172 , E186 , etc.
For patriotic societies, see E172.7, E181, E182, E186, E202, etc.
154 **Gazetteers**
Directories
154.5 General
154.7 Social directories. Social registers
(154.9) Business and trade directories, *see* HF5035-5068
Recreational directories, *see* E158
155 **Geographic names**
Cf. E98.N2, Indian names
Cf. G104+, Geographic names and terms (General)
156 **General works**
Electronic information resource catalogs, see E175.88
158 **Guidebooks. Handbooks**
Including directories of summer and winter resorts, excursions, etc.
159 **Historic monuments (General)**
Including mansions, mission buildings, public buildings
For individual mansions, mission buildings, public buildings, etc., see local divisions
For roads, see HE356.A+
For historical and descriptive works on regions traversed by a road, see Class F
For general questions of the location and removal of the national capital, see F195
Cf. E179.5, Boundaries
Cf. G109, Distances
Cf. GB494+, Altitudes
159.5 **Antiquities (Non-Indian)**
160 **National and state parks and reservations (Collective descriptive works)**
Including national forests as parks
Cf. SD426+, Forest reserves
For works on individual parks, including theory, management and description, see the subject or local division, e.g. E475.81, Chickamauga and Chattanooga National Military Park; F868.Y6, Yosemite National Park
For works on theory, management and history, etc., of U.S. parks and public reservations in general, see SB482.A1+
161 **Social life and customs (General)**
Including antiquities, museums, etc., illustrative of American life, e.g. Henry Ford Museum and Greenfield Village, Dearborn, Mich.
Cf. E169.1+, Civilization, Intellectual life
By period, *see* E162+
161.3 **Geography**
Description and travel
For travel before era of settlement, see E141+
For regions, see Class F, Local history, e.g. F106, Atlantic coast; F206-220, Southern States; F351-354, Mississippi Valley; F476-485, Old Northwest; F591-595, The West
161.5 History of travels. Travel anthologies
By period
Including works on civilization, social life
Class general works of travel through the country in 1785 in E164, not in F106, Atlantic States
162 1607-1764
Including general descriptive works on the British colonies in America including Thanksgiving Day and customs
Cf. F7, Thanksgiving Day in New England
Cf. GT4975, Festivals
163 1765-1783
164 1784-1811

General

Description and travel

By period — Continued

165 1812-1844

166 1845-1860

167 1861-1865

For travels in the Confederate States, see F214

168 1866-1913

169 1914-1944

169.02 1945-1980

169.04 1981-

Civilization. Intellectual life

Including national characteristics, ideals, Americanization

Cf. E161, Social life and customs (General)

Cf. JK1758, Manuals for foreign-born citizens

169.1 General works

By period

Early to 1865, *see* E162+

1866-1945, *see* E169.1

169.12 1945-

Biography (Americanization literature), *see* E184+

History

171 **Periodicals. Yearbooks**

172 **Societies**

Including historical departments of other organizations, e.g. Museums, libraries

Cf. E175.4, Historiography

Geographic societies, *see* G3

Patriotic hereditary societies

172.7 General works

Individual societies, *see* E181-182, E186, E202, etc.

Political and patriotic societies primarily interested in social objectives, *see* HS2321+

172.9 **Congresses, seminars, etc.**

173 **Sources and documents. Collections. Collected works**

Including exhibitions of source materials

174 **Dictionaries and encyclopedias**

174.5 **Chronology. Chronological tables, etc.**

Historiography

For general works on state and local historiography, see E180.5

175 General works. History

175.1 Pamphlets, etc.

175.4 Institutions

Including programs, reports, methods of organization and work

Including the work of government commissions, historical societies, etc.

175.4.C3 Carnegie Institution of Washington. Division of Historical Research

Biography of historians

Including general criticism of their works

Class criticism of a particular work with the work

175.45 Collective

175.5.A-.5.Z Individual, A-Z

Subarrange by Table E1 at the end of the text

GALE NOTE *The cutter number(s) listed below have been given only as examples by the Library of Congress*

175.5.B38 Beard, Charles Austin

175.7 Methodology

Including theory, comparison and criticism, etc. Research

Study and teaching

Class here study and teaching in colleges, universities, and secondary schools

175.8 General works

175.85 Criticism of textbooks (General)

Cf. E468.5, Criticism of textbooks on the Civil War

History — Continued

175.87 **Film catalogs**

175.88 **Electronic information resource catalogs**

175.9 **Philosophy of American history**

Biography (Collective)

176 General

For general United States biography not limited to political life, see CT210+

For biography of individual periods, see the period, e.g. E302.5, 1775-1829

Presidents

For the biography of each president, see his administration, e.g. E312, Washington; E322, Jefferson

Presidential inaugurations are classed in local history, e.g. F128.44, New York City, for Washington's first inauguration in 1789; but F158.44, Philadelphia, for his second in 1793; F197-200, Washington, D.C., for the inaugurations of Jefferson and succeeding presidents

For the White House, see F204.W5

176.1 General works

176.2 Wives of Presidents

176.25 Fathers of Presidents

176.3 Mothers of Presidents

176.4 Relations with women

176.45 Children and grandchildren of Presidents

176.47 Staff

176.472.A-.472.Z Relations with specific ethnic groups, A-Z

176.472.A34 African Americans

176.472.J47 Jews

176.48 Pets

176.49 Vice-Presidents

176.5 Portraits

Class here works emphasizing historical aspects

For works emphasizing the artistic aspects or the artist, see N7593+

176.6 Hall of Fame, New York University

176.8 Juvenile works

Biography (Individual), see under periods in national or state history, e.g. E195, United States, 1689-1775; E207, Revolution; F122, New York State before 1775; and under topics, e.g E181-182, Military and naval leaders; E185.97, Afro-Americans

For the life of a representative in Congress and governor of a state, see state history unless his national career has been decidedly more prominent

General works

178 Comprehensive works

178.1 Textbooks

178.2 Outlines, syllabi, etc.

For chronology, see E174.5

178.25 Examinations, questions, etc.

178.3 Juvenile works

Including collections of stories from American history for children

Cf. PE1127.H5+, English readers on United States history

178.4 Comic and satirical works

Including humor of American history

178.5 Pictorial works

178.6 Addresses, essays, lectures, etc.

178.9 Poetical works. Rhyming histories

For general collections of American historical poems, see PS595.H5

Collections or single poems on a particular event are classed with the subject, e.g. E233 , Ballads and poems relating to the Burgoyne campaign

179 General special

Including topics such as disasters, floods, pageants, vigilance committees, etc. in general not otherwise provided for

For local, see Class F

History — Continued

179.5 **Historical geography**

Including Boundaries (General), the frontier, history of territorial expansion, public domain, regionalism, etc.

For boundaries (Special), see F912.B7, Alaska; F550.5+, F597, North; E398, F27.B7, F42.B7, F57.B7, F127.B7, Northeast; F854, F880, Northwest; F317.B7, Southeast before 1819; F392.B7, F786, Southwest

For anthropogeography, see GF503+

Cf. E713, Expansion controversy, imperialism, etc.

Cf. JK2551+, Territorial government and administration

History of states and counties, collectively

Class counties limited to one state with that state

180 General works

180.5 State and local historiography

General special

181 Military history

Including battles of more than two wars

For battles of more than two wars in the twentieth century, see E745

Including military societies, veterans' organizations, etc., covering more than one war: Medal of Honor Legion of the United States, Military Order of Foreign Wars of the United States, Military Order of the Purple Heart, Society of American Wars of the United States, Veterans of Foreign Wars of the United States, etc.

For Grand Army of the Republic (Civil War), see E462.1

Including military biography not limited to one war: William Selby Harney, John Joseph Pershing, Hugh Lenox Scott, Leonard Wood, etc.

Cf. U52-53, Biography (Military science)

For military history of the twentieth century, see E745

For military history of individual wars, see the war, e.g. E230-239, Revolution; E470-478, Civil War

182 Naval history (United States Navy and Marine Corps)

Including naval battles of more than two wars

Including naval societies, veterans' organizations, etc., covering more than one war: Naval Order of the United States, United States Navy Veteran Association, etc.

For National Association of Naval Veterans (Civil War), see E462.5

Naval biography not limited to one war: Smedley Darlington Butler; Stephen Decatur, 1752-1808; Robley Dunglison Evans; Ernest Joseph King; Edward Yorke Macauley; Alfred Thayer Mahan; Richard Worsam Meade; Hiram Paulding; Matthew Calbraith Perry; John Woodward Philip; George Henry Preble; Francis Asbury Roe; Stephen Clegg Rowan; Benjamin Franklin Sands; Charles Steedman; Thomas Truxtun; etc.

Cf. V62+, Biography (Naval science)

For naval history of the twentieth century, see E746

For naval history of individual wars, see the war, e.g. E271, Revolution; E591-600, Civil War

Political history

Political history of a period or administration is classed with the period or administration, e.g. E188, Colonial history; E801, Hoover's administration

183 General works

183.3 Political collectibles. Political Americana

Diplomatic history. Foreign and general relations

General works on the diplomatic history of a period or administration are classed with the period or administration, e.g. E313, Washington's administration; E661.7, Period since Civil War; E744, Twentieth century

All the works on relations with a specific country are classed in E183.8, regardless of administration or period

Cf. JZ1482, Monroe Doctrine

183.7 General works

(183.75) Relations with special groups of countries

For Africa, see DT38

For Barbary States (1801-1809), see E335

History

General special

Diplomatic history. Foreign and general relations

(183.75) Relations with special groups of countries — Continued

For Central American, West Indian, and other countries protected by and having close political affiliations with the United States, see F975

For Europe (1945-), see D1065.U5

For The Far East (Far Eastern question), see DS518.8

For Latin America, see F1418

For Islamic countries, see DS35.74.U6

For International American Conference, see F1405

For Near East, see DS63.2.U5

For Oceania, see DU30

For West Indies, see F1622

183.8.A-.8.Z Relations with individual countries, A-Z

183.9 Other (not A-Z)

Elements in the population

184.A-.Z **Elements, A-Z**

The cutter numbers are intended to be used as a guide for the best distribution of numbers and not to be used as a fixed standard or to affect numbers already assigned

Including racial and ethnic groups and religious bodies which have significance in the history of the United States

Elements in individual regions, states, cities, etc., are classed with the region, state, city, etc., e.g. F128.9.G3, Germans in New York (City)

For voyages of discovery by various nationalities, see E101+; G220+

184.A1 General works

Including foreign elements (General), minorities, race conflicts, and problems, etc.

184.A2 Acadians. Cajuns

184.A23 Afghans

184.A24 Africans

For works on Afro-Americans in the United States in general or in individual regions or states, see E185.5+ or E441+

For works on Afro-Americans in individual counties, cities, or towns, see Class F. If the pertinent number in Class F provides for an A-Z arrangement for elements in the population, assign ".N4"

184.A26 Afrikaners

184.A3 Albanians

184.A4 Alsatians

Amish, *see* E184.M45

184.A65 Arabs

184.A67 Argentines

184.A7 Armenians

184.A75 Asians

184.A8 Assyrians

184.A9 Austrians

184.A95 Azoreans

184.B13 Bangladeshis

184.B15 Basques

184.B2 Belgians

184.B26 Bengalis

184.B67 Bohemians. Czechs

184.B674 Bolivians

184.B675 Bosnians

184.B676 Brass Ankles

184.B68 Brazilians

184.B7 British

Including the English

For other nationalities, see the nationality, e.g. E184.S3, Scotch

184.B8 Bulgarians

Byelorussians, *see* E184.W6

Elements in the population

184.A-.Z Elements, A-Z — Continued

Cajuns, *see* E184.A2

Cambodians, *see* E184.K45

184.C2 Canadians

184.C22 Canary Islanders

184.C24 Cape Verdeans

184.C27 Caribbeans

184.C29 Catalans

184.C3 Catholics

Cf. E184.C36, Chaldean Catholics

184.C34 Central Americans

184.C36 Chaldean Catholics

184.C4 Chileans

184.C5 Chinese

184.C58 Colombians

184.C6 Cornish

184.C8 Covenanters

184.C87 Creoles

184.C9 Cretans

184.C93 Croats. Croatians

184.C97 Cubans

Czechs, *see* E184.B67

Danes, *see* E184.S19

184.D6 Dominicans (Dominican Republic)

184.D78 Druzes

184.D9 Dutch

184.E17 East Europeans

184.E2 East Indians

Cf. E184.G84, Gujaratis

Cf. E184.K35, Kanarese

Cf. E184.M37, Marathas

Cf. E184.P28, Pakistanis

Cf. E184.P36, Panjabis

184.E28 Ecuadorians

184.E38 Egyptians

(184.E5) English, *see* E184.B7

184.E7 Estonians

184.E74 Ethiopians

184.E95 Europeans

Cf. E184.E17, East Europeans

184.F4 Filipinos

184.F5 Finns

184.F57 Flemings

184.F8 French

Cf. E184.A2, Acadians

Cf. E184.F85, French Canadians

Cf. E184.H9, Huguenots

184.F85 French Canadians

Cf. E184.A2, Acadians

184.F89 Friends. Society of Friends. Quakers

184.F894 Frisians

184.G24 Gambians

184.G27 Georgians (Transcaucasians)

184.G3 Germans

Cf. E184.M7, Moravians

Cf. E184.R85, Russian Germans

Cf. E184.S78, Swabians

For Palatines, see E184.P3

184.G44 Ghanaians

	Elements in the population
184.A-.Z	**Elements, A-Z — Continued**
184.G7	Greeks
184.G75	Grenadians
184.G82	Guatemalans
184.G84	Gujaratis
184.G86	Guyanese
184.H27	Haitians
184.H3	Hawaiians
	Hispanic Americans, *see* E184.S75
184.H55	Hmong (Asian people)
184.H9	Huguenots
184.H95	Hungarians
184.H97	Hutterite Brethren
184.I3	Icelanders
	Indians, *see* E75+
184.I43	Indochinese
184.I45	Indonesians
184.I5	Iranians
184.I55	Iraquis
184.I6	Irish *Cf. E184.S4, Scotch-Irish*
184.I7	Israelis *Cf. E184.J5, Jews*
184.I8	Italians
	Jackson Whites, *see* E184.R3
184.J27	Jamaicans
184.J3	Japanese *For Japanese-American war relocation centers, see D769.8.A6*
(184.J5)	Jews, *see* E184.3+ *This number is not valid for works about Jews in the United States as a whole. The Cutter number .J5 may be used under those numbers in United States local history that are subarranged by this list of Cutter numbers, e.g. F73.9.J5, Jews in Massachusetts*
	Jugoslavs, *see* E184.Y7
184.K3	Kalmyks
184.K35	Kanarese
184.K45	Khmers. Cambodians
184.K6	Koreans
184.L27	Laos
184.L34	Lebanese
184.L4	Letts. Latvians
184.L53	Liberians
184.L55	Liechtensteiners
184.L7	Lithuanians
184.L88	Luxemburgers
184.M3	Macedonians
184.M33	Malians
184.M34	Maltese
184.M37	Marathas
184.M44	Melungeons
184.M45	Mennonites. Amish
184.M47	Mestizos
184.M5	Mexicans
184.M53	Minorcans
184.M7	Moravians
184.M8	Mormons
184.M83	Mountain people *Cf. F210, Southern States*
184.M88	Muslims

Elements in the population

184.A-.Z **Elements, A-Z — Continued**

(184.N4) Negroes, *see* E184.5+, E441+, or Class F

Assign the cutter .N4 only for numbers in Class F that provide for an A-Z arrangement for elements in the population

184.N53 Nicaraguans

184.N55 Nigerians

Norwegians, *see* E184.S2

(184.O6) Orientals, *see* E184.A75

184.P25 Pacific Islanders

184.P28 Pakistanis

184.P3 Palatines

184.P33 Palestinians

184.P35 Panamanians

184.P36 Panjabis

Persians, *see* E184.I5

184.P47 Peruvians

184.P7 Poles

184.P8 Portuguese

184.P85 Puerto Ricans

184.R3 Ramapo Mountain people

184.R8 Romanians

184.R85 Russian Germans

184.R9 Russians

Ruthenians, *see* E184.U5

184.R93 Rwandans

184.S15 Salvadorans

184.S16 Sami Americans

184.S17 Samoans

Scandinavians

184.S18 General

184.S19 Danes

184.S2 Norwegians

184.S23 Swedes

184.S3 Scotch. Scots

184.S4 Scotch-Irish

184.S5 Serbs

184.S53 Shakers

184.S54 Sierra Leoneans

184.S55 Sikhs

184.S6 Slavs

Cf. E184.B67, Bohemians. Czechs

Cf. E184.B8, Bulgarians

Cf. E184.C93, Croats

Cf. E184.P7, Poles

Cf. E184.R9, Russians

Cf. E184.S5, Serbs

Cf. E184.S64, Slovaks

Cf. E184.S65, Slovenes

Cf. E184.U5, Ukrainians

Cf. E184.Y7, Yugoslavs

184.S64 Slovaks

184.S65 Slovenes

184.S67 Somalis

184.S68 Sorbs

184.S69 South Asians

184.S695 Southeast Asians

184.S7 Spaniards

184.S75 Spanish Americans

Cf. E184.C34, Central Americans

	Elements in the population
184.A-.Z	**Elements, A-Z**
184.S75	Spanish Americans — Continued
	Cf. E184.M5, Mexicans
184.S77	Sudanese
184.S78	Swabians
	Swedes, *see* E184.S23
184.S9	Swiss
184.S98	Syrians
184.T35	Taiwanese
184.T4	Thais
184.T53	Tibetans
184.T88	Turks
184.U5	Ukrainians
	Including Ruthenians
184.V53	Vietnamese
184.W35	Walloons
184.W4	Welsh
184.W5	Wesorts
184.W54	West Indians
184.W6	White Russians
184.Y36	Yao (Southeast Asian people)
184.Y44	Yemenites
184.Y66	Yoruba
184.Y7	Yugoslavs
184.2	**Americans in foreign countries**
	Americans in a particular country are classified with that country
	Jews
	Including Italian Jews, Russian Jews, etc.
184.3	Periodicals
184.312	Congresses
184.32	Collections. Sources
184.33	Historiography
184.34	Study and teaching
184.35	History (General). General works
	For history of Judaism in the United States, including synagogues and congregations, see BM203+
	By period
184.3512	Colonial period to 1776
184.352	1776-1880
184.353	1880-1925
184.354	1925-1945
184.355	1945-
184.36.A-.36.Z	Special topics, A-Z
184.36.A34	Afro-American-Jewish relations
	Antisemitism, *see* DS146.U6
184.36.E25	Economic conditions
	For special aspects of economic conditions, see Class H
184.36.E84	Ethnic identity
	For relations between American Jews and Israel, see DS132
184.36.E86	Ethnic relations
184.36.I58	Intellectual life
184.36.P64	Politics and government
184.36.S65	Social conditions. Social life and customs
	Including family, youth, children, etc.
	For special aspects of social conditions, including specific activities, services, etc., see Class H
	For religious life, see BM723+
184.36.W64	Women
	Including collective biography

Elements in the population
Jews — Continued
By region, state, etc., *see* Class F
Biography and memoirs
184.37.A1-.37.A19 Collective
184.37.A2-.37.Z Individual, A-Z
For collective biography of women, see E184.36.W64
Afro-Americans
Including works on free Afro-Americans in the United States before 1863
Periodicals, societies, etc., *see* E185.5
184.5 Congresses
184.6 Collections. Sources
184.65 Historiography
184.7 Study and teaching. Afro-American studies
184.7.Z9 Catalogs of audiovisual materials
185 General works. History (General)
Cf. E440.92+, Slavery in the United States
Cf. E448, Colonization
Cf. E453, Emancipation
Cf. GN645, Black race (Anthropology)
Cf. HT973.2+, Slave trade (General)
Cf. HV3181+, Protection, assistance, and relief for Afro-Americans
Cf. JX4447, Slave trade (International law)
Cf. LC2701+, Education of Afro-Americans
History (By period)
185.18 To 1863
Including free Afro-Americans
For free Afro-Americans in an individual state, see E185.93.A+
185.2 1863-1877
Including from emancipation to the end of the reconstruction period, the Afro- American as a ward of the nation, ex-slaves, slave pensions, Freedmen's Bureau (Bureau of Refugees, Freedmen, and Abandoned Lands)
For Reconstruction in the United States, 1865-1877, see E668
For Reconstruction in individual southern states, see the state, e.g. F231, Virginia; F259, North Carolina
For Freedmen, by state, see E185.93.A+
1877-1964. Reconstruction to Civil Rights Act of 1964
185.5 Periodicals. Societies. Collections
Including periodicals and societies before emancipation, and post 1964
Cf. HS2259+, Fraternal and social societies
Museums. Exhibitions, etc.
185.53.A1 General works
185.53.A3-.53.Z By city and museum, A-Z
185.6 General works
185.61 Race relations
Including attitudes, discriminations, loyalties, prejudices; civil rights; interracial cooperation, movements, and practices; segregation
Cf. BP221+, Black Muslims
Cf. JK1923+, Afro-American suffrage
Cf. LC212.5+, Racial segregation in schools
For relations with indians, see E98.R28
For relations with Jewish Americans, see E184.36.A34
185.615 1964-
For periodicals, societies, etc., see E185.5
Special topics
185.62 Intermarriage of races. Miscegnation. Mulattoes
185.625 Psychosocial factors. Race identity
185.63 Afro-Americans in the Armed Forces
Cf. D639.N4, Afro-Americans in World War I, 1914-1918
Cf. D810.N4, Afro-Americans in World War II, 1939-1945

Elements in the population
Afro-Americans
Special topics
185.63 Afro-Americans in the Armed Forces — Continued
Cf. E269.N3, Afro-Americans in the Revolution, 1775-1783
Cf. E540.N3, Afro-Americans in the Civil War, 1861-1865 (Union Army)
Cf. E585.A35, Afro-Americans in the Civil War, 1861-1865 (Confederate Army)
Cf. E725.5.N3, Afro-Americans in the Spanish-American War, 1898
Crime. Delinquency, *see* HV6197.A+
(185.7) Religion. Afro-American churches
For Black Muslims, see BP221+
For Afro-American churches (General), Afro-American clergy, etc., see BR563.N4
For Afro-American religions not limited to Christianity, see BL1+
185.8 Economic conditions
For special aspects of economic conditions, see Class H
The professions, *see* the individual profession
185.86 Social conditions. Social life and customs
Including family, women, youth, children, etc.
Health. Physical condition, *see* Class R
185.89.A-.89.Z Other topics, A-Z
185.89.E8 Ethnobotany
Gay African Americans, *see* HQ76.27.A37
Housing, *see* HD7293.A1+
Iconography, *see* Class N
185.89.N3 Names
Relations with Jewish Americans, *see* E184.36.A34
Relations with Indians, *see* E98.R28
185.89.R45 Reparations
Transportation, *see* HE1+
By region, state, etc.
185.9 African Americans in the North
185.912 African Americans in the Appalachian Region
185.915 African Americans in the Middle West and Old Northwest
185.917 African Americans in New England
185.92 African Americans in the South
For pre-1964 material, see E185 or E185.6
185.923 African Americans in the Southwest
185.925 African Americans in the West
185.93.A-.93.W By state, A-W
For Afro-Americans in an individual county, city, or town, see Class F, e.g. F128.9.N3, Afro-Americans in New York
For slavery in an individual state, see E445.A+
185.93.A3 Alabama
185.93.A4 Alaska
185.93.A7 Arizona
185.93.A8 Arkansas
185.93.C2 California
185.93.C6 Colorado
185.93.C7 Connecticut
185.93.D4 Delaware
185.93.D6 District of Columbia
185.93.F5 Florida
185.93.G4 Georgia
185.93.H3 Hawaii
185.93.I15 Idaho
185.93.I2 Illinois
185.93.I4 Indiana
185.93.I64 Iowa
185.93.K16 Kansas
185.93.K3 Kentucky

Elements in the population

Afro-Americans

By region, state, etc.

185.93.A-.93.W By state, A-W — Continued

185.93.L6 Louisiana

185.93.M15 Maine

185.93.M2 Maryland

185.93.M3 Massachusetts

185.93.M5 Michigan

185.93.M55 Minnesota

185.93.M6 Mississippi

185.93.M7 Missouri

185.93.M8 Montana

185.93.N5 Nebraska

185.93.N52 Nevada

185.93.N53 New Hampshire

185.93.N54 New Jersey

185.93.N55 New Mexico

185.93.N56 New York

185.93.N6 North Carolina

185.93.N7 North Dakota

185.93.O2 Ohio

185.93.O4 Oklahoma

185.93.O7 Oregon

185.93.P41 Pennsylvania

185.93.R4 Rhode Island

185.93.S7 South Carolina

Including the Sea Islands

185.93.S8 South Dakota

185.93.T3 Tennessee

185.93.T4 Texas

185.93.U8 Utah

185.93.V4 Vermont

185.93.V8 Virginia

185.93.W3 Washington

185.93.W5 West Virginia

185.93.W58 Wisconsin

185.93.W9 Wyoming

185.94 Afro-Americans living in foreign countries (Collectively)

For Afro-Americans in a particular country, see the country

Biography. Genealogy

185.96 Collective

Including biographical dictionaries and directories

Class here general collected biography, including collected biography of Afro- Americans in public life covering several or all periods of United States history

For biography of Afro-Americans in public life covering a single period of United States history, see the period

For Afro-Americans associated with a special field, see the field

For Afro-Americans of special regions or states, see E185.9+

For Afro-Americans of an individual county, city, or town, see Class F

185.97.A-.97.Z Individual, A-Z

For biography of slaves, see E444, E449+

For Afro-Americans associated with a special field (including politics), see the field or period of activity

For Afro-Americans of special regions or states, see E185.9+

For Afro-Americans in an individual county, city, or town, see Class F, e.g. F128.9.N3, New York (City)

GALE NOTE *The cutter number(s) listed below have been given only as examples by the Library of Congress*

Carver, George Washington, *see* S417.A+

Elements in the population

Afro-Americans

Biography. Genealogy

185.97.A-.97.Z Individual, A-Z — Continued

185.97.R63 Robeson, Paul

Subarrange by Table E1 at the end of the text

For Robeson as a singer, see ML420.R73

185.97.T8 Truth, Sojourner

Subarrange by Table E1 at the end of the text

185.97.W4 Washington, Booker Taliaferro

Subarrange by Table E1 at the end of the text

185.97.Z9 Anonymous

185.98 Biography of persons other than Afro-Americans identified primarily with Afro-Americans

185.98.A1 Collective

185.98.A3-.98.Z Individual, A-Z

Subarrange by Table E1 at the end of the text

Colonial history, 1607-1775

Including earliest permanent English settlements on the Atlantic Coast to the American Revolution

Including the thirteen colonies

186 **Periodicals. Societies**

e.g. The Prince Society and its publications

186.3-.99 **Patriotic societies**

Under each (unless otherwise indicated):

	Official publications
.A1-.A4	Serial publications
.A5-.A69	Monographs
.A7	Nonofficial publications
.A8-.W	State branches. By state, A-W

Under each:

	Official publications
A1-A4	Serial publications
A5-A7	Monographs
A8-Z	Nonofficial publications

186.3 Society of Colonial Wars

Subarrange by table below E186.3-.99

186.4 National Society of the Colonial Dames of America

Subarrange by table below E186.3-.99

186.5 Colonial Dames of America

Subarrange by table below E186.3-.99

186.6 Order of the Founders and Patriots of America

Subarrange by table below E186.3-.99

186.7 Colonial Daughters of the Seventeenth Century

Subarrange by table below E186.3-.99

186.8 Daughters of Founders and Patriots of America

Subarrange by table below E186.3-.99

186.99.A-.99.Z Other, A-Z

Under each:

GALE NOTE *".x" represents the cutter number for the patriotic society*

	Official publications
.xA1-.xA4	Serial publications
.xA5-.xA7	Monographs
.xA8-.xZ	Nonofficial publications

186.99.C55 Colonial Dames of the XVII Century

Subarrange by table below E186.99.A-.99.Z

186.99.D3 Daughters of the American Colonists

Subarrange by table below E186.99.A-.99.Z

186.99.H55 Hereditary Order of Descendants of Colonial Governors

Subarrange by table below E186.99.A-.99.Z

Colonial history, 1607-1775

186.3-.99 **Patriotic societies**

186.99.A-.99.Z Other, A-Z — Continued

186.99.N33 National Society of the Colonial Daughters of America

Subarrange by table below E186.99.A-.99.Z

186.99.O6 Order of Colonial Lords of Manors in America

Subarrange by table below E186.99.A-.99.Z

Order of Washington, *see* E202.7

186.99.P6 The Pilgrims

Subarrange by table below E186.99.A-.99.Z

186.99.S5 Sons and Daughters of the Pilgrims

Subarrange by table below E186.99.A-.99.Z

187 **Collections. Collected works**

Including monographs, essays, documents, sources, etc.

187.A5 American colonial tracts monthly

187.A53 American political tracts

187.C72 Colonial pamphlets

187.F69 Force, Peter. Tracts and other papers

187.H42 Hazard, Ebenezer. Historical collections

187.O7 Original narratives of early American history

187.2 **Historiography**

Biography

187.5 Collective. Genealogy

Including comprehensive lists of English immigrants

For lists of immigrants of non-English nationalities, see E184.A+

For biography of later colonial period, beginning with French and Indian War, see E302.5; genealogy of New England in F3; etc.

Individual, *see* E191-199, E302.6, and individual wars

188 **General works**

Cf. E82-83, Indian wars

Cf. E101+, Discovery and exploration of America to 1607

Cf. E141+, General accounts of America to 1810

Cf. E162, Travel and description

Cf. F7, New England to 1775

Cf. F229, Raleigh's Roanoke colonies, 1584-1590

Cf. F314, French Huguenot colonies

Cf. F1030, British North America

Cf. F2131, British West Indies

Cf. F2361+, British Guiana

Cf. JV1000+, Administration of British colonies

188.5 **Addresses, essays, lectures, sermons, etc.**

189 **Minor works**

Including pamphlets, pageants, etc., and otherwise unprovided-for topics

For discussions on European origin of American institutions, see Class D, unless largely American history

By period

191 1607-1689

Cf. E83.63, Pequot War, 1636-1638

Cf. E83.663, War with Esopus Indians, 1658-1664

Cf. E83.67, King Philip's War, 1675-1676

Cf. F7, Council for New England, 1620; Plymouth Company, 1606; United Colonies of New England, 1643-1684; etc.

Cf. F7.5, Governor Andros and his government, 1688

Cf. F22, Popham Colony, Maine

Cf. F229, Virginia Company of London

1689-1775

Including attempts at union; Albany Congress of 1754; last years of colonial government, 1763- 1775; etc.

Including biography: Sir William Johnson, William Shirley, etc.

Cf. E83.71, Tuscarora War, 1711-1713

Colonial history, 1607-1775

By period

1689-1775 — Continued

Cf. E83.72, Wars with the eastern Indians (New England), 1722-1726

Cf. E83.739, Wars with the Chickasaw Indians, 1739-1740

Cf. E83.76, Pontiac's Conspiracy, 1763-1765

Cf. E210+, Political history, disputes with Great Britain

Cf. E215.2, Stamp Act Congress, 1765

Cf. F517, Ohio Company

Cf. F1032, Quebec Act, 1774

Cf. F2272.5, Cartagena Expedition, 1741

195 General works

196 King William's War, 1689-1697

Including the destruction of Schenectady, 1690; capture of Port Royal (Nova Scotia), 1690; Quebec Expedition, 1690; Massacre at Haverhill, 1697; etc.

197 Queen Anne's War, 1702-1713

Including Massacres at Deerfield (1704), Haverhill (1708), etc.; Church's expedition to the eastward; capture of Port Royal (Nova Scotia), 1710; Walker's expedition to Quebec, 1711; etc.

Cf. D281+, War of Spanish Succession, 1710-1714

Cf. E83.71, Tuscarora War, 1711-1713

198 King George's War, 1744-1748

Including the siege and capture of Louisburg (Cape Breton Island), 1745

Including biography: Sir William Pepperell, etc.

Cf. D291+, War of the Austrian Succession, 1740-1748

Cf. F1036+, Nova Scotia, Acadia, Cape Breton Island

199 French and Indian War, 1755-1763

Including Washington at Fort Necessity, 1754; Braddock's defeat, 1755; Battle of Lake George, 1755; siege of Fort William Henry, 1757; expeditions against Ticonderoga and Crown Point, 1755-1759; second siege and capture of Louisburg, 1758; capture of Fort Frontenac, 1758; Niagara and Quebec campaigns, 1759

Including biography: John Bradstreet; François Gaston, duc de Lévis; Louis Joseph de Montcalm-Gozon, marquis de Saint-Veran; Robert Rogers; etc.

Cf. E83.759, Cherokee War, 1759-1761

Cf. E195+, Albany Congress, 1754

Cf. F1038, Winslow's expedition for expulsion of the Acadians, 1755

Cf. F1781, Siege of Havana, 1762-1763

Elements in the population, *see* E184.A+

The Revolution, 1775-1783

201 **Periodicals. Societies (Research)**

202 **Societies (Patriotic and hereditary)**

Including reports, registers, etc.

For collections of documents, memoirs, etc., see E203, e.g. E203.S49, Publications of the Seventy-Six Society

202.1 Society of the Cincinnati

Subarrange by table below E186.3-.99

202.2 Daughters of the Cincinnati

Subarrange by table below E186.3-.99

202.3 Sons of the American Revolution

Subarrange by table below E186.3-.99

202.4 Sons of the Revolution

Subarrange by table below E186.3-.99

Including proposals for the union of Sons of the Revolution and Sons of the American Revolution

202.5 Daughters of the American Revolution

Subarrange by table below E186.3-.99

202.6 Daughters of the Revolution

Subarrange by table below E186.3-.99

202.7 Order of Washington

Subarrange by table below E186.3-.99

The Revolution, 1775-1783

202 **Societies (Patriotic and hereditary) — Continued**

202.8 Washington Society of Maryland

Subarrange by table below E186.3-.99

202.9 Children of the American Revolution

Subarrange by table below E186.3-.99

202.99.A-.99.Z Other, A-Z

Subarrange by table below E186.99.A-.99.Z

GALE NOTE *The cutter number(s) listed below have been given only as examples by the Library of Congress*

202.99.M64 Military Order of Pulaski

Subarrange by table below E186.99.A-.99.Z

202.99.O63 Order of LaFayette

Subarrange by table below E186.99.A-.99.Z

202.99.O65 Order of the Descendants of the Signers of the Secret Pact or Prior Declaration of Independence

Subarrange by table below E186.99.A-.99.Z

Museums, exhibitions, see E289

203 **Collections. Collected works**

Including documents, essays, letters, journals, memoirs, etc.

For collections of anecdotes, see E296

204 **Congresses, seminars, etc.**

Biography

Including portraits

206 Collective

Especially military and naval leaders

For signers of the Declaration of Independence, see E221

For statesmen of the Revolutionary period, see E302.5

207.A-.Z Individual, A-Z

Including lives of military and naval commanders and staff officers

For regimental officers and privates, see regimental histories in E263.A+, or personal narratives in E275.A2+

For Scouts and spies, see E279+

Cf. E302.6.A+, Lives of individual statesmen

GALE NOTE *The cutter number(s) listed below have been given only as examples by the Library of Congress*

207.A3 Alexander, William

Subarrange by Table E1 at the end of the text

Called Lord Stirling

207.A4 Allen, Ethan

Subarrange by Table E1 at the end of the text

207.B2 Barry, John

Subarrange by Table E1 at the end of the text

207.B48 Biddle, Nicholas

Subarrange by Table E1 at the end of the text

207.B5 Biddle, Owen

Subarrange by Table E1 at the end of the text

207.B58 Bigelow, Timothy

Subarrange by Table E1 at the end of the text

207.B8 Brown, John, 1744-1780

Subarrange by Table E1 at the end of the text

207.C5 Clark, George Rogers

Subarrange by Table E1 at the end of the text

207.C62 Clinton, James

Subarrange by Table E1 at the end of the text

207.D3 Davidson, William Lee

Subarrange by Table E1 at the end of the text

207.D9 Duportail, Louis Lebègue de Presle

Subarrange by Table E1 at the end of the text

The Revolution, 1775-1783

Biography

207.A-.Z Individual, A-Z — Continued

207.E3 Elbert, Samuel

Subarrange by Table E1 at the end of the text

207.G2 Gadsden, Christopher

Subarrange by Table E1 at the end of the text

207.G3 Gates, Horatio

Subarrange by Table E1 at the end of the text

207.G56 Glover, John

Subarrange by Table E1 at the end of the text

207.G9 Greene, Nathanael

Subarrange by Table E1 at the end of the text

207.H7 Hopkins, Ezek

Subarrange by Table E1 at the end of the text

207.H85 Howe, Robert

Subarrange by Table E1 at the end of the text

207.J7 Jones, John Paul

Subarrange by Table E1 at the end of the text

207.K14 Kalb, Jean, baron de

Subarrange by Table E1 at the end of the text

207.K74 Knox, Henry

Subarrange by Table E1 at the end of the text

207.K8 Kósciusko, Tadeusz Andrzej

Subarrange by Table E1 at the end of the text

Cf. DK4348.K67, Polish patriot

207.L2 Lafayette, Marquis de

Subarrange by Table E1 at the end of the text

Including Lafayette in America

Cf. DC146.L2, Lafayette in France

207.L22 Lamb, John

Subarrange by Table E1 at the end of the text

207.L47 Lee, Charles

Subarrange by Table E1 at the end of the text

207.L5 Lee, Henry

Subarrange by Table E1 at the end of the text

207.M3 Marion, Francis

Subarrange by Table E1 at the end of the text

207.M5 Mercer, Hugh

Subarrange by Table E1 at the end of the text

207.M6 Mifflin, Thomas

Subarrange by Table E1 at the end of the text

207.M7 Montgomery, Richard

Subarrange by Table E1 at the end of the text

207.M8 Morgan, Daniel

Subarrange by Table E1 at the end of the text

207.M85 Moultrie, William

Subarrange by Table E1 at the end of the text

207.M9 Moylan, Stephen

Subarrange by Table E1 at the end of the text

207.M95 Muhlenberg, John Peter Gabriel

Subarrange by Table E1 at the end of the text

207.N2 Nash, Francis

Subarrange by Table E1 at the end of the text

207.O13 O'Brien, Jeremiah

Subarrange by Table E1 at the end of the text

207.P2 Parsons, Samuel Holden

Subarrange by Table E1 at the end of the text

207.P3 Paterson, John

Subarrange by Table E1 at the end of the text

The Revolution, 1775-1783

Biography

207.A-.Z Individual, A-Z — Continued

207.P63 Pickens, Andrew

Subarrange by Table E1 at the end of the text

207.P68 Pitcairn, John

Subarrange by Table E1 at the end of the text

207.P7 Pomeroy, Seth

Subarrange by Table E1 at the end of the text

207.P75 Prescott, William

Subarrange by Table E1 at the end of the text

207.P8 Pułaski, Kazimierz

Subarrange by Table E1 at the end of the text

Cf. DK4348.P8, Polish patriot

207.P9 Putnam, Israel

Subarrange by Table E1 at the end of the text

207.R32 Reed, James

Subarrange by Table E1 at the end of the text

207.S3 Schuyler, Philip John

Subarrange by Table E1 at the end of the text

207.S79 Stark, John

Subarrange by Table E1 at the end of the text

207.S8 Steuben, Friedrich Wilhelm, Baron von

Subarrange by Table E1 at the end of the text

207.S9 Sullivan, John

Subarrange by Table E1 at the end of the text

207.S95 Sumter, Thomas

Subarrange by Table E1 at the end of the text

207.T13 Talbot, Silas

Subarrange by Table E1 at the end of the text

207.T45 Thomas, John

Subarrange by Table E1 at the end of the text

207.T57 Tilghman, Tench

Subarrange by Table E1 at the end of the text

207.T8 Tucker, Samuel

Subarrange by Table E1 at the end of the text

207.W2 Ward, Artemas

Subarrange by Table E1 at the end of the text

207.W26 Ward, Samuel

Subarrange by Table E1 at the end of the text

207.W27 Warner, Seth

Subarrange by Table E1 at the end of the text

207.W35 Wayne, Anthony

Subarrange by Table E1 at the end of the text

207.W63 Wickes, Lambert

Subarrange by Table E1 at the end of the text

207.W65 Willett, Marinus

Subarrange by Table E1 at the end of the text

207.W7 Williams, Otho Holland

Subarrange by Table E1 at the end of the text

207.W78 Wood, James

Subarrange by Table E1 at the end of the text

207.W8 Woodhull, Nathaniel

Subarrange by Table E1 at the end of the text

207.W9 Wooster, David

Subarrange by Table E1 at the end of the text

208 **General works. History (General)**

For travel, manners, and customs of the period, see E163

The Revolution, 1775-1783 — Continued

209 **General special**

Including pamphlets, pictorial works, chronological tables, etc., and otherwise unprovided-for topics, such as historiography, the Revolution as a social movement, religious aspects, legends

Political history

Including the causes and origins of the Revolution and the controversies which preceded it, 1763-1775; the influence of the American clergy, legal aspects, trade, western lands, etc.

For controversies in individual colonies before 1763, see E263.A+, e.g. E263.M4, Massachusetts

210 General works (Other than contemporary)

211 Contemporary works

For sermons and addresses of a general character, see E297

Special questions and events

215 General works

215.1 Commercial restrictions (General). Enforcement of trade and navigation laws. Writs of assistance

215.2 Stamp Act, 1765. Stamp Act Congress, New York, 1765

215.3 Townshend Acts, 1767. Nonimportation agreements of 1768-1769

Including Townshend Acts repealed in April 1770, except for a tax on tea

215.4 Mutiny Act, 1765. Boston Massacre, March 5, 1770

Including the quartering of troops in Boston

215.5 Taxation and representation

215.6 Gaspee affair, June 1772

215.7 Resistance to the tea tax. Boston Tea Party, December 1773

215.8 Boston Port Bill, 1774

215.9 Mecklenburg Resolves, 1775

Including the so-called Mecklenburg Declaration of Independence

215.95 The "Olive branch" petition to George III, 1775

216 Other special topics (not A-Z)

Including Committees of correspondence and safety; efforts to enlist aid of other British possessions, as Canada and Ireland; Paul Revere's ride; Sons of Liberty; the Duché letters; etc.

For Loyalists in the colonies, see E277+

For The parsons' cause, Va., see F229

For War of the Regulators, N.C., see F257

221 **Declaration of Independence**

Including collective biography of the signers

Military operations

Cf. E271+, Naval history

230 General works

Including campaigns and battles (General) and lists of battles

For individual battles, see E241.A+

Class orderly books with campaigns in E231-239 or in E255-268 with the military organization to which they belong

For Indian wars, 1775-1783, see E83.775

230.5.A-.5.Z By region, A-Z

Class regions within a state under the name of the state

GALE NOTE *The cutter number(s) listed below have been given only as examples by the Library of Congress*

230.5.M6 Middle States

230.5.N4 New York (State). Hudson Valley

230.5.O3 Ohio Valley

230.5.V3 Vermont. Mount Independence

Campaigns. By year

231 1775

Including Beginnings, Canadian invasion, siege of Boston (1775-1776), Patriots' Day (April 19), etc.

232 1776

Including British occupation of New York, Washington's retreat up the Hudson and through New Jersey, etc.

The Revolution, 1775-1783
Military operations
Campaigns. By year — Continued
233 1777
Including Burgoyne's invasion, St. Leger's invasion, Howe's occupation of Philadelphia, Jane McCrea, etc.
For Saratoga Campaign, see E241.S2
234 1778
Including Clark's Expedition, Butler's Indian Campaign, Valley Forge, etc.
235 1779
Including Penobscot Expedition, Sullivan's Indian Campaign, etc.
236 1780
Including Benedict Arnold's treason, campaigns in the South, etc.
Cf. E278.A7, Arnold as a loyalist
237 1781
Including Campaigns in the Carolinas and Virginia, Clark's Expedition against Detroit, etc.
For Mutiny of the Pennsylvania line, see E255
238 1782
Including Crawford's Indian Campaign, etc.
239 1783
Including British evacuation of New York, Evacuation Day, etc.
For Newburgh addresses, see E255
241.A-.Z Individual battles, A-Z
Including attacks, capture and burning of cities, massacres, sieges, etc.
Class battles, sieges, etc., in E231+, if preferred
241.B33 Bedford, N.Y. (Westchester Co.), 1779
241.B4 Bennington, Vt., 1777
241.B65 Blue Licks, Ky., 1782
Boston siege, 1775-1776, *see* E231
241.B76 Bound Brook, N.J., 1777
241.B8 Brandywine, Pa., 1777
Brooklyn, N.Y., 1776, *see* E241.L8
241.B87 Bull's Ferry, N.J., 1780
241.B9 Bunker Hill, Mass., 1775
241.C17 Camden, S.C., 1780
241.C2 Carleton's Raid, 1778
241.C4 Charleston, S.C., 1780
241.C48 Chelsea, Mass., 1775
241.C5 Cherry Valley, N.Y., 1778
241.C52 Chestnut Hill, Pa., 1777
241.C56 Clapps Mill, N.C., 1781
241.C7 Concord, Mass., 1775
241.C73 Cooch's Bridge, Del., 1777
241.C8 Cowan's Ford, Tenn., 1781
241.C9 Cowpens, S.C., 1781
241.C94 Crooked Billet, Pa., 1778
241.C96 Cumberland, Fort, N.B., 1776
241.D2 Danbury, Conn., 1777
241.E39 Elizabeth, N.J., 1780
241.E4 Elizabethtown, N.C., 1781
241.F16 Fairfield, Conn., 1779
Falmouth, Me., *see* E241.P8
241.F55 Flamborough Head, England, 1779
241.F74 Freeland, Fort, Warrior Run, Pa., 1779
241.G3 Germantown, Pa., 1777
241.G6 Great Bridge, Va., 1775
241.G8 Groton Heights, Conn., 1781
241.G9 Guilford Court House, N.C., 1781
241.H2 Harlem Heights, N.Y., 1776

The Revolution, 1775-1783

Military operations

241.A-.Z Individual battles, A-Z — Continued

241.H8 Hubbardton, Vt., 1777

241.K48 Kettle Creek, Ga., 1779

241.K5 King's Mountain, S.C., 1780

241.K6 Kingston, N.Y., 1777

241.L6 Lexington, Mass., 1775

241.L65 Lindley's Mill, N.C., 1781

241.L7 Little Egg Harbor, N.J., 1778

241.L8 Long Island, N.Y., 1776

241.M5 Mercer, Fort, N.J., 1777

241.M6 Minisink, N.Y., 1779

241.M7 Monmouth, N.J., 1778

241.M8 Moore's Creek Bridge, N.C., 1776

241.M9 Moultrie, Fort, S.C., 1776

241.N5 New Haven, Conn., 1779

241.N56 Newtown, N.Y., 1779

241.O6 Oriskany, N.Y., 1777

241.P2 Paoli, Pa., 1777

241.P24 Paulus Hook, N.J., 1779

241.P3 Pell's Point, N.Y., 1776

241.P55 Piqua, Ohio, 1780

241.P8 Portland, Me., 1775

241.P9 Princeton, N.J., 1777

241.Q3 Quebec (City), 1775-1776

241.R3 Red Bank, N.J., 1777

241.R4 Rhode Island, 1778

241.R53 Ridgefield, Conn., 1777

241.S2 Saratoga, N.Y., 1777

241.S26 Savannah, Ga., 1779

241.S53 Short Hills, N.J., 1777

241.S6 Springfield, N.J., 1780

241.S7 Stanwix, Fort, N.Y., 1777

241.S8 Stony Point, N.Y., 1779

241.T5 Ticonderoga, N.Y., 1775

241.T7 Trenton, N.J., 1776

241.V14 Valcour Island, Lake Champlain, 1776

241.W3 Washington, Fort, N.Y., 1776

241.W5 White Plains, N.Y., 1776

241.W9 Wyoming, Pa., 1778

241.Y6 Yorktown, Va., 1781

249 **Diplomatic history. Treaty of Paris, 1783**

Including alliances, claims of foreigners against the United States, diplomatic relations with individual countries, missions to foreign powers, propaganda, Treaty of 1778

Cf. E265, French participation in the war, French auxiliaries

Cf. E313+, Final withdrawal of British troops from western posts

249.3 **Foreign public opinion**

Armies. Troops

251 General works

The American Army

255 General works

Including bounties; the Conway Cabal; Mutiny of the Pennsylvania Line, 1781; Newburgh addresses; pensioners; registers and lists not confined to single states; war claims; etc.

For orderly books, see E231+

Cf. E281, Lists of prisoners

Cf. UB373+, Military pensions (General)

Continental army

259 General works

The Revolution, 1775-1783

Armies. Troops

The American Army

Continental army — Continued

260 Military organizations raised by Congress directly

Including Commander in Chief's Guard, Lee's Legion, etc.

263.A-.W By state, A-W

Including the British American colonies; each state's part in the war and previous controversy

Including collections; histories (General, and regimental); rolls and orderly books; registers; addresses honoring patriots; diaries, journals, letters, and memoirs of officers, etc.; state continental line; state troops and militia, including minutemen

For histories of counties and towns in the war, see local history, e.g. F74.W9, Worcester, Mass.

Cf. E230+, Military operations in a state

Cf. E277+, American loyalists in individual states

263.C2 Canada (Province of Quebec)

Including biography: Antoine Paulint, etc.

Cf. E216, Efforts to enlaid of Canada

Cf. E263.N9, Nova Scotia and dependencies

Cf. E269.C27, Canadians in the American army

263.C5 Connecticut

Including biography: Jonathan Trumbull, etc.

263.D3 Delaware. Delmarva Peninsula

Including biography: Thomas Rodney, etc.

263.F6 Florida (East and West)

263.G3 Georgia

Including biography: Lyman Hall, etc.

263.I5 Indiana

263.K4 Kentucky

263.L68 Louisiana

Maine, *see* E263.M4

263.M3 Maryland

Including biography: John Gunby, John Eager Howard, etc.

Cf. E263.D3, Delmarva Peninsula

263.M4 Massachusetts (and Maine)

Including biography: Joseph Hawley, Josiah Quincy (1744-1775), Joseph Warren, etc.

263.N4 New Hampshire

Including biography: Joseph Cilley, etc.

263.N5 New Jersey

Including biography: Moore Furman, Margaret (Hill) Morris, etc.

263.N6 New York

Including biography: Simon Boerum, Henry Ludington, etc.

263.N8 North Carolina (and Tennessee)

Including biography: Joseph Graham, etc.

For Tennessee alone, see E263.T4

Cf. E215.9, Mecklenburg Resolutions, 1775

Cf. F257, War of the Regulators, 1766-1771

263.N84 Old Northwest

263.N9 Nova Scotia (and dependencies)

Cf. E263.C2, Canada (Province of Quebec)

263.O3 Ohio

263.P4 Pennsylvania and Delaware Valley (General)

Including biography: John Bayard, John Rosbrugh, etc.

Quebec, *see* E263.C2

263.R4 Rhode Island

Including biography: Israel Angell, etc.

Cf. E215.6, Gaspee Affair, June 1772

263.S7 South Carolina

Including biography: John Drayton, Eliza (Yonge) Wilkinson, etc.

The Revolution, 1775-1783

Armies. Troops

The American Army

263.A-.W By state, A-W — Continued

263.T4 Tennessee

For Tennessee with North Carolina, see E263.N8

263.T45 Texas

263.V5 Vermont

263.V8 Virginia

Including biography: Theodorick Bland, John Champe, Filippo Mazzei, Leven Powell, etc.

Cf. E83.77, Dunmore's War, 1774

Cf. E263.D3, Delmarva Peninsula

263.W5 West Indies. Bermudas

265 Auxiliaries

Including French participation; histories; lists; personal letters, journals, and narratives of soldiers and sailors; etc.

Including biography: Comte de Rochambeau, etc.

For Marquis de Lafayette, see E207.L2

The British Army

Including histories; lists; personal diaries; journals, letters, and narratives; etc.

For Tory regiments, see E277.6.A+

267 General works

268 German mercenaries. Hessians

For Germans in the American Army, see E269.G3

269.A-.Z **Participation by race, ethnic group, religious group, etc., A-Z**

Afro-Americans, *see* E269.N3

269.B2 Baptists

269.C27 Canadians

269.C3 Catholics

269.C5 Church of England (Anglicans)

269.D88 Dutch

269.F67 Foreigners (General)

French auxiliaries, *see* E265

269.F8 Friends. Quakers

German mercenaries, *see* E268

269.G3 Germans

269.H3 Haitians

269.I5 Indians

269.I6 Irish

269.J5 Jews

Loyalists, *see* E277+

269.M6 Moravians

269.N3 Negroes. Afro-Americans

269.P6 Poles

269.P9 Presbyterians

269.S36 Scots-Irish

269.S63 Spaniards

269.S8 Swedes

269.W4 Welsh

Colleges and their participation

270.A1 General works

270.A2-.Z Individual colleges, A-Z

GALE NOTE *The cutter number(s) listed below have been given only as examples by the Library of Congress*

270.P9 Princeton University

270.Y2 Yale University

Naval history. Naval operations

Including British and French fleets in the West Indies; narratives of sailors, privateers, etc.

The Revolution, 1775-1783

Naval history. Naval operations — Continued

For the lives of naval leaders, see E206+

For naval operations forming part of military movements, see E231+

271 General works

273.A-.Z Individual ships, A-Z

273.P75 Providence

Personal narratives and other accounts (General)

Including diaries, journals, letters, memoirs, reminiscences, etc.

For narratives relating to special campaigns, battles, or regiments, see E231+ or E263.A+

For narratives of British soldiers, see E267+

For narratives of French auxiliaries, see E265

For narratives of German mercenaries, see E268

For narratives of loyalists, see E278.A+

For narratives of prisoners, see E281

For narratives of naval service, see E271

Cf. E203, Collections of source material

Cf. E296, Anecdotes

275.A2 Collections

275.A3-.Z Individual narratives

276 **Women and the war**

Loyalists. Traitors

Including biography and narratives of loyalists; loyalists in exile (General) and in England; treatment of Tories, e.g. sequestration, confiscation, and sale of estates; etc.

For Loyalists in individual provinces of Canada, see F1036+, F1041+, F1056+

277 General works

277.6.A-.6.Z Loyalist regiments, etc.

GALE NOTE *The cutter number(s) listed below have been given only as examples by the Library of Congress*

277.6.B9 Butler's Rangers

277.6.D3 De Lancey's Brigade (Loyalist)

277.6.M2 Maryland Loyalists Regiment

277.6.N5 New Jersey Volunteers

277.6.Q6 Queen's Rangers

278.A-.Z Individual loyalists, A-Z

GALE NOTE *The cutter number(s) listed below have been given only as examples by the Library of Congress*

278.A3 Alexander, Robert

Subarrange by Table E1 at the end of the text

278.A4 Allen, Jolley

Subarrange by Table E1 at the end of the text

278.A7 Arnold, Benedict

Subarrange by Table E1 at the end of the text

Cf. E236, Arnold's treason

278.A72 Arnold, Margaret (Shippen)

Subarrange by Table E1 at the end of the text

278.B9 Butler, Walter

Subarrange by Table E1 at the end of the text

278.C4 Chandler, John

Subarrange by Table E1 at the end of the text

278.C5 Christie, James

Subarrange by Table E1 at the end of the text

278.C7 Connolly, John

Subarrange by Table E1 at the end of the text

278.C8 Cornell, Samuel

Subarrange by Table E1 at the end of the text

278.C9 Curwen, Samuel

Subarrange by Table E1 at the end of the text

278.D94 Dulany, Daniel

Subarrange by Table E1 at the end of the text

The Revolution, 1775-1783

Loyalists. Traitors

278.A-.Z Individual loyalists, A-Z — Continued

278.F2 Fanning, David

Subarrange by Table E1 at the end of the text

278.G14 Galloway, Joseph

Subarrange by Table E1 at the end of the text

278.G4 Gilbert, Thomas

Subarrange by Table E1 at the end of the text

278.L5 Leonard, Daniel

Subarrange by Table E1 at the end of the text

278.M13 McAlpine, John

Subarrange by Table E1 at the end of the text

278.M8 Moody, James

Subarrange by Table E1 at the end of the text

278.M98 Murray, James

Subarrange by Table E1 at the end of the text

278.S6 Smyth, John Ferdinand Dalziel

Subarrange by Table E1 at the end of the text

278.T9 Tuttle, Stephen

Subarrange by Table E1 at the end of the text

278.V27 Van Schaack, Henry Cruger

Subarrange by Table E1 at the end of the text

278.V54 Vernon, Thomas

Subarrange by Table E1 at the end of the text

278.W6 Wilkins, Isaac

Subarrange by Table E1 at the end of the text

Secret service. Spies

279 General works

280.A-.Z Individual spies, A-Z

GALE NOTE *The cutter number(s) listed below have been given only as examples by the Library of Congress*

280.A5 André, John

Subarrange by Table E1 at the end of the text

Including his captors: John Paulding, Isaac Van Wart, David Williams

280.C95 Crosby, Enoch

Subarrange by Table E1 at the end of the text

280.H2 Hale, Nathan

Subarrange by Table E1 at the end of the text

280.H8 Howe, John

Subarrange by Table E1 at the end of the text

280.T7 Townsend, Robert

Subarrange by Table E1 at the end of the text

281 **Prisoners and prisons**

Including exchanges, prison life, prison ships, prisoners' narratives, etc.

283 **Medical and hospital services. Hospitals, etc.**

Including biography: Jonathan Potts, etc.

Celebrations. Anniversaries

For special celebrations in the form of expositions, see T400+

For monuments and memorials, see by place in Class F

285 General works

Special centennials

1876

For works limited to the 1876 exposition, see T825

285.2 General works

The Revolution, 1775-1783
Celebrations. Anniversaries
Special centennials
1876 — Continued
285.25.A-.25.W By state, A-W
Under each:
GALE NOTE *".x" represents the cutter number for the state*
.x General works
.x2A-.x2Z By city, A-Z
1926 exposition, *see* T826.3
1976
285.3 General works
285.4.A-.4.W By state, A-W
Subarrange by table below E285.25.A-.25.W
Special days
Evacuation Day, November 25, *see* E239
Fourth of July
Class here general works on the observance of the day, including specific celebrations and addresses
For works of distinct local interest, see Class F
286.A1-.A19 General works
286.A2-.Z Individual celebrations and addresses. By place and date
GALE NOTE *The cutter number(s) listed below have been given only as examples by the Library of Congress*
286.B74 1774 Boston, 1774
286.B74 1933 Boston, 1933
Patriots' Day, April 19, *see* E231
289 **Museums. Exhibitions**
Including bells, flags, relics, trophies, etc.
Cf. NK806, Collectibles
(295) **Poetry, ballads, songs. Drama, pageants, see Class P**
296 **Anecdotes**
Cf. E203, Collections of source material
Cf. E275.A2+, Personal narratives
297 **Sermons. Prayers**
For sermons on a specific subject, see the subject
298 **Comic and satirical histories. Humor, caricatures, etc.**
Revolution to the Civil War, 1775/1783-1861
For history of the Revolutionary War, see E201+
For history of the Civil War, see E461+
300 **Historiography**
301 **General works**
Including works covering the preliminaries of the Revolution to the close of the Civil War, 1765-1865
For political history of slavery, see E338-459
Cf. E183.7+, Diplomatic history, 1783-1865
Cf. E398, Northeast boundary question
Cf. E440.92+, Slavery and the antislavery movement
Cf. F550.5+; F597, Northern boundary
Cf. F854; F880, Northwest boundary
302.A-.Z **Collected works of American statesmen (Revolutionary group), A-Z**
For works of statesmen of the early nineteenth century, see E337.8.A+
For works of statesmen of the middle nineteenth century, see E415.6.A+
GALE NOTE *The cutter number(s) listed below have been given only as examples by the Library of Congress*
302.A26 Adams, John
Subarrange by Table E3 at the end of the text
302.F8 Franklin, Benjamin
Subarrange by Table E3 at the end of the text
For his literary works and biography, see PS745+

Revolution to the Civil War, 1775/1783-1861

302.A-.Z **Collected works of American statesmen (Revolutionary group), A-Z — Continued**

302.J44 Jefferson, Thomas

Subarrange by Table E3 at the end of the text

302.M19 Madison, James

Subarrange by Table E3 at the end of the text

Washington, George, *see* E312.7

302.1 **Political history**

Including the supremacy of the fathers of the republic

Cf. E210+, Political history of the Revolution

Cf. E357+, Political history of the War of 1812

Cf. E407, Political history of the War with Mexico

Biography (Late eighteenth century)

For Revolutionary leaders, especially military commanders, see E206+

302.5 Collective

For signers of the Declaration of Independence, collectively, see E221

302.6.A-.6.Z Individual, A-Z

GALE NOTE *The cutter number(s) listed below have been given only as examples by the Library of Congress*

302.6.A2 Adams, Samuel

Subarrange by Table E2A at the end of the text

302.6.A5 Ames, Fisher

Subarrange by Table E2A at the end of the text

302.6.A7 Armstrong, John

Subarrange by Table E2A at the end of the text

302.6.B14 Bache, Benjamin Franklin

Subarrange by Table E2A at the end of the text

302.6.B17 Baldwin, Abraham

Subarrange by Table E2A at the end of the text

302.6.B19 Baldwin, Simeon

Subarrange by Table E2A at the end of the text

302.6.B2 Bartlett, Josiah

Subarrange by Table E2A at the end of the text

302.6.B3 Bayard, James Asheton

Subarrange by Table E2A at the end of the text

302.6.B6 Blount, William

Subarrange by Table E2A at the end of the text

302.6.B7 Boudinot, Elias

Subarrange by Table E2A at the end of the text

302.6.B8 Bradley, Stephen Row

Subarrange by Table E2A at the end of the text

302.6.B84 Breckinridge, John

Subarrange by Table E2A at the end of the text

302.6.B9 Burr, Aaron

Subarrange by Table E2A at the end of the text

For Burr's conspiracy, see E334

302.6.B91 Jumel, Eliza (Bowen)

Subarrange by Table E2A at the end of the text

302.6.B93 Burr, Esther (Edwards)

Subarrange by Table E2A at the end of the text

302.6.B954 Alston, Theodosia Burr

Subarrange by Table E2A at the end of the text

302.6.C11 Cabot, George

Subarrange by Table E2A at the end of the text

302.6.C2 Campbell, George Washington

Subarrange by Table E2A at the end of the text

302.6.C3 Carroll, Charles (Charles Carroll of Carrollton)

Subarrange by Table E2A at the end of the text

302.6.C33 Carroll, Daniel

Subarrange by Table E2A at the end of the text

Revolution to the Civil War, 1775/1783-1861
Biography (Late eighteenth century)

302.6.A-.6.Z	Individual, A-Z — Continued
302.6.C4	Chase, Samuel *Subarrange by Table E2A at the end of the text*
302.6.C55	Clark, Abraham *Subarrange by Table E2A at the end of the text*
302.6.C6	Clinton, George *Subarrange by Table E2A at the end of the text*
302.6.C7	Cooper, Thomas *Subarrange by Table E2A at the end of the text*
302.6.D14	Dallas, Alexander James *Subarrange by Table E2A at the end of the text*
302.6.D16	Dana, Francis *Subarrange by Table E2A at the end of the text*
302.6.D2	Davie, William Richardson *Subarrange by Table E2A at the end of the text*
302.6.D25	Deane, Silas *Subarrange by Table E2A at the end of the text*
302.6.D3	Dearborn, Henry *Subarrange by Table E2A at the end of the text*
302.6.D45	Dexter, Samuel *Subarrange by Table E2A at the end of the text*
302.6.D5	Dickinson, John *Subarrange by Table E2A at the end of the text*
302.6.D8	Duane, James *Subarrange by Table E2A at the end of the text*
302.6.D82	Duane, William *Subarrange by Table E2A at the end of the text*
302.6.E15	Eaton, William *Subarrange by Table E2A at the end of the text*
302.6.E3	Ellery, William *Subarrange by Table E2A at the end of the text*
302.6.E4	Ellsworth, Oliver *Subarrange by Table E2A at the end of the text*
302.6.F24	Farragut, George *Subarrange by Table E2A at the end of the text*
302.6.F56	FitzSimons, Thomas *Subarrange by Table E2A at the end of the text*
302.6.F6	Fowler, John *Subarrange by Table E2A at the end of the text*
302.6.F7-.6.F8	Franklin, Benjamin *For his collected works, see E302.F8*
	Autobiography
302.6.F7A2	English. By date
302.6.F7A3-.6.F7Z3	Translations. By language and date
302.6.F7Z4-.6.F7Z99	Commentaries
302.6.F75	Letters
302.6.F75A1-.6.F75A6	Collections. By title
302.6.F75A7	Single letters. By date
302.6.F8	Biography
302.6.G16	Gallatin, Albert *Subarrange by Table E2A at the end of the text*
302.6.G37	Gerry, Elbridge *Subarrange by Table E2A at the end of the text*
302.6.G47	Giles, William Branch *Subarrange by Table E2A at the end of the text*
302.6.G66	Gorham, Nathaniel *Subarrange by Table E2A at the end of the text*

Revolution to the Civil War, 1775/1783-1861
Biography (Late eighteenth century)

302.6.A-.6.Z Individual, A-Z — Continued

302.6.G95 Gwinnett, Button
Subarrange by Table E2A at the end of the text

302.6.H2 Hamilton, Alexander
Subarrange by Table E2A at the end of the text
For his collected works, see E302.H2

302.6.H22 Hamilton, Elizabeth (Schuyler)
Subarrange by Table E2A at the end of the text

Hancock, John

302.6.H23 General works
Subarrange by Table E2A at the end of the text

302.6.H24 Hancock, Dorothy (Quincy)
Subarrange by Table E2A at the end of the text

302.6.H27 Hanson, John
Subarrange by Table E2A at the end of the text

302.6.H29 Harper, Robert Goodloe
Subarrange by Table E2A at the end of the text

302.6.H4 Henry, John
Subarrange by Table E2A at the end of the text

302.6.H5 Henry, Patrick
Subarrange by Table E2A at the end of the text

302.6.H6 Hillegas, Michael
Subarrange by Table E2A at the end of the text

302.6.H63 Hillhouse, James
Subarrange by Table E2A at the end of the text

302.6.H65 Hindman, William
Subarrange by Table E2A at the end of the text

302.6.H7 Hooper, William
Subarrange by Table E2A at the end of the text

302.6.H78 Hopkins, Stephen
Subarrange by Table E2A at the end of the text

302.6.H8 Hosmer, Titus
Subarrange by Table E2A at the end of the text

302.6.H89 Humphreys, David
Subarrange by Table E2A at the end of the text

302.6.H9 Huntington, Benjamin
Subarrange by Table E2A at the end of the text

302.6.H93 Husbands, Herman
Subarrange by Table E2A at the end of the text

302.6.I6 Ingersoll, Jared
Subarrange by Table E2A at the end of the text

302.6.I7 Iredell, James
Subarrange by Table E2A at the end of the text

302.6.J4 Jay, John
Subarrange by Table E2A at the end of the text
For Jay's Treaty, see E314

302.6.J65 Johnson, Thomas
Subarrange by Table E2A at the end of the text

302.6.J7 Johnson, William Samuel
Subarrange by Table E2A at the end of the text

302.6.K3 Kavanagh, Edward
Subarrange by Table E2A at the end of the text

302.6.K5 King, Rufus
Subarrange by Table E2A at the end of the text

302.6.L26 Langdon, John
Subarrange by Table E2A at the end of the text

302.6.L3 Laurens, Henry
Subarrange by Table E2A at the end of the text

Revolution to the Civil War, 1775/1783-1861
Biography (Late eighteenth century)

302.6.A-.6.Z Individual, A-Z — Continued
302.6.L4 Lee, Richard Henry
Subarrange by Table E2A at the end of the text
302.6.L6 Lewis, Francis
Subarrange by Table E2A at the end of the text
302.6.L66 Livermore, Edward St. Loe
Subarrange by Table E2A at the end of the text
302.6.L67 Livingston, Anne Home (Shippen)
Subarrange by Table E2A at the end of the text
Livingston, Edward
302.6.L68 General works
Subarrange by Table E2A at the end of the text
302.6.L684 Livingston, Louise (Davezac) Moreau
Subarrange by Table E2A at the end of the text
302.6.L7 Livingston, Philip
Subarrange by Table E2A at the end of the text
302.6.L72 Livingston, Robert R.
Subarrange by Table E2A at the end of the text
302.6.L75 Livingston, William
Subarrange by Table E2A at the end of the text
302.6.L8 Logan, George
Subarrange by Table E2A at the end of the text
302.6.L9 Lyon, Matthew
Subarrange by Table E2A at the end of the text
302.6.M12 McHenry, James
Subarrange by Table E2A at the end of the text
302.6.M13 McKean, Thomas
Subarrange by Table E2A at the end of the text
302.6.M14 Maclay, William
Subarrange by Table E2A at the end of the text
302.6.M17 Macon, Nathaniel
Subarrange by Table E2A at the end of the text
302.6.M35 Marshall, Humphrey
Subarrange by Table E2A at the end of the text
302.6.M4 Marshall, John
Subarrange by Table E2A at the end of the text
Including John Marshall Day
302.6.M432 Mason, Armistead Thomson
Subarrange by Table E2A at the end of the text
302.6.M45 Mason, George
Subarrange by Table E2A at the end of the text
302.6.M7 Morris, Gouverneur
Subarrange by Table E2A at the end of the text
Morris, Robert
302.6.M8 General works
Subarrange by Table E2A at the end of the text
302.6.M81 Morris, Mary (White)
Subarrange by Table E2A at the end of the text
302.6.M88 Mulligan, Hercules
Subarrange by Table E2A at the end of the text
302.6.O8 Otis, James
Subarrange by Table E2A at the end of the text
302.6.P14 Paine, Robert Treat
Subarrange by Table E2A at the end of the text
Paine, Thomas, *see* JC178.V2
302.6.P3 Paterson, William
Subarrange by Table E2A at the end of the text

Revolution to the Civil War, 1775/1783-1861
Biography (Late eighteenth century)

302.6.A-.6.Z Individual, A-Z — Continued
302.6.P5 Pickering, Timothy
Subarrange by Table E2A at the end of the text
302.6.P54 Pinckney, Charles
Subarrange by Table E2A at the end of the text
302.6.P55 Pinckney, Charles Cotesworth
Subarrange by Table E2A at the end of the text
32.6.P57 Pinckney, Thomas
Subarrange by Table E2A at the end of the text
302.6.P6 Pinkney, William
Subarrange by Table E2A at the end of the text
302.6.P73 Plumer, William
Subarrange by Table E2A at the end of the text
302.6.P84 Pollock, Oliver
Subarrange by Table E2A at the end of the text
302.6.P86 Pope, John
Subarrange by Table E2A at the end of the text
302.6.P93 Preston, Francis
Subarrange by Table E2A at the end of the text
302.6.Q7 Quincy, Josiah, 1772-1864
Subarrange by Table E2A at the end of the text
302.6.R18 Randolph, Edmund
Subarrange by Table E2A at the end of the text
302.6.R2 Randolph, John
Subarrange by Table E2A at the end of the text
302.6.R27 Read, George
Subarrange by Table E2A at the end of the text
302.6.R3 Reed, Joseph
Subarrange by Table E2A at the end of the text
302.6.R6 Rodney, Caesar
Subarrange by Table E2A at the end of the text
302.6.R61 Rodney, Caesar Augustus
Subarrange by Table E2A at the end of the text
302.6.R77 Ross, Betsy (Griscom)
Subarrange by Table E2A at the end of the text
302.6.R79 Ross, George, 1730-1779
Subarrange by Table E2A at the end of the text
302.6.R8 Ross, James
Subarrange by Table E2A at the end of the text
302.6.R85 Rush, Benjamin
Subarrange by Table E2A at the end of the text
302.6.R89 Rutledge, John, 1739-1800
Subarrange by Table E2A at the end of the text
302.6.R9 Rutledge, John, 1766-1819
Subarrange by Table E2A at the end of the text
302.6.S13 Sailly, Peter
Subarrange by Table E2A at the end of the text
302.6.S17 Salomon, Haym
Subarrange by Table E2A at the end of the text
302.6.S3 Sawyer, Lemuel
Subarrange by Table E2A at the end of the text
302.6.S45 Sevier, John
Subarrange by Table E2A at the end of the text
302.6.S5 Sherman, Roger
Subarrange by Table E2A at the end of the text
302.6.S57 Smith, Jeremiah
Subarrange by Table E2A at the end of the text

Revolution to the Civil War, 1775/1783-1861
Biography (Late eighteenth century)
302.6.A-.6.Z Individual, A-Z — Continued
302.6.S59 Smith, William Stephens
Subarrange by Table E2A at the end of the text
302.6.S7 Spaight, Richard Dobbs
Subarrange by Table E2A at the end of the text
302.6.S85 Stockton, Richard
Subarrange by Table E2A at the end of the text
302.6.S98 Symmes, John Cleves
Subarrange by Table E2A at the end of the text
302.6.T18 Tait, Charles
Subarrange by Table E2A at the end of the text
302.6.T2 Tallmadge, Benjamin
Subarrange by Table E2A at the end of the text
302.6.T23 Taylor, John
Subarrange by Table E2A at the end of the text
302.6.T4 Thomas, Ebenezer Smith
Subarrange by Table E2A at the end of the text
302.6.T48 Thomson, Charles
Subarrange by Table E2A at the end of the text
302.6.T8 Tompkins, Daniel D.
Subarrange by Table E2A at the end of the text
302.6.T93 Tyler, Mary Hunt (Palmer)
Subarrange by Table E2A at the end of the text
302.6.V33 Varnum, James Mitchell
Subarrange by Table E2A at the end of the text
302.6.V4 Varnum, Joseph Bradley
Subarrange by Table E2A at the end of the text
302.6.W15 Washington, Bushrod
Subarrange by Table E2A at the end of the text
302.6.W2 Webster, Pelatiah
Subarrange by Table E2A at the end of the text
302.6.W4 Weems, Mason Locke
Subarrange by Table E2A at the end of the text
302.6.W5 Whipple, William
Subarrange by Table E2A at the end of the text
302.6.W55 Williams, William
Subarrange by Table E2A at the end of the text
302.6.W6 Williamson, Hugh
Subarrange by Table E2A at the end of the text
302.6.W62 Willing, Thomas
Subarrange by Table E2A at the end of the text
302.6.W64 Wilson, James
Subarrange by Table E2A at the end of the text
302.6.W67 Wingate, Paine
Subarrange by Table E2A at the end of the text
302.6.W68 Wisner, Henry
Subarrange by Table E2A at the end of the text
302.6.W7 Witherspoon, John
Subarrange by Table E2A at the end of the text
302.6.W85 Wolcott, Oliver
Subarrange by Table E2A at the end of the text
By period
1775-1789. The Confederation, 1783-1789
303 General works
Including Continental Congress, 1774-1788. Articles of Confederation. The Constitution. Foreign relations, 1783-1789
For Constitutional history, see JK111+
For Revolution, see E201+

Revolution to the Civil War, 1775/1783-1861

By period

1775-1789. The Confederation, 1783-1789

303 General works — Continued

For Shay's Rebellion, see F69

303.2 Bicentennial celebrations for the Constitution

309 Territorial questions

Including cession of western land claims to the general government by Connecticut, Massachusetts, New York, North Carolina, and Virginia, 1781-1786. Northwest Ordinance, 1787

For Georgia land cessions of 1802, see F290

For South Carolina cession of 1787, see F292.B7

1789-1809. Constitutional period

310 General works

310.7 Diplomatic history. Foreign and general relations

For diplomatic history of special periods, see E313-314,E323,E333-336,E357, etc.

Washington's administrations, 1789-1797

For wars with the northwestern Indians, 1790-1795, see E83.79

Cf. HG2525+, United States banks (First and second)

311 General works

Biography of George Washington, 1732-1799

For bibliography, see Z8950

312 General works. Washington as president

312.1 Societies

312.15 Reminiscences of contemporaries, anecdotes, calendars, etc.

312.17 Special

Including personality, character, religion, etc.; relations with special classes or individuals; etc.

312.19 Ancestry. Family. Servants

Including biography, e.g. Martha Washington

For genealogy of the Washingtons and genealogical tables, see CS71.A+

312.195 Sulgrave Manor

Including the home of the Washington family in England

Including publications of Sulgrave Institution

By period

312.2 Early life to 1775

312.23 Expeditions to the Ohio, 1753-1754. Participation in French and Indian War

For general accounts of Braddock's campaign, see E199

Military career as commander-in-chief, 1775-1783

312.25 General works

Cf. E201+ , The American Revolution

312.27 Itineraries, etc.

Class individual headquarters with locality in Class F

312.29 Period after the Revolution, 1783-1799

For period of the Presidency, 1789-1797, see E311+

312.3 Death. Funeral. Memorial services

Including memorial publications

For funeral addresses and sermons, see E312.62+

For tomb, see E312.5

Iconography

312.4 General works

312.43 Portraits, etc.

For medals, see CJ5801+

Monuments, statues, etc.

312.45 General works

Local monuments, statues, etc., *see* Class F, e.g. F203.4.W3 , Washington monument in Washington, D.C.

312.5 Homes and haunts

Including birthplace, Wakefield, Va.; Mount Vernon; Washington estate; Washington's tomb and relics

Revolution to the Civil War, 1775/1783-1861
By period
1789-1809. Constitutional period
Washington's administrations, 1789-1797
Biography of George Washington, 1732-1799 — Continued
312.6 Anniversaries. Celebrations. Memorials (since 1800 only)
Including Washington's birthday, centennial celebrations, etc.
For funeral and memorial services, 1799-1800, see E312.3
Addresses, essays, lectures. Sermons
312.62 Collections
312.63 Individual
(312.65) Poetry. Drama. Fiction, *see* Subclasses P-PZ
312.66 Juvenile works
Music, *see* Class M
312.67 Other works
Including questions and answers on his life
Writings of Washington
312.7 Collected works. By date
312.72 Partial collections. Selected works. By date
Letters
Collections
312.74 General. By date
312.75.A-.75.Z By subject, A-Z
GALE NOTE *The cutter number(s) listed below have been given only as examples by the Library of Congress*
312.75.A2-.75.A3 Agriculture
312.75.M4-.75.M5 Freemasons
312.75.R3-.75.R4 Religion
Revolution, *see* E203
312.75.S6-.75.S7 Society of the Cincinnati
312.76 Individual letters. By date
312.77 Spurious letters. Editions. By date
312.78 Rules of civility. By date
312.79 Selections. Extracts
Including maxims, prayers, sayings, etc.
312.8 Diaries. Journals. By date
For selected Revolutionary orders, see E230
312.81 Accounts. Editions. By date
Addresses and messages
312.83 Addresses to officers of the army, March 15, 1783
312.85 Circular letter, June 18, 1783
Another edition has title "Last official address ... to the legislatures of the United States"
Addressed to the governors of the several states
Editions arranged by place of publication
312.87 Farewell address to the army, November 2, 1783
312.9 Speeches and messages as President. By date
312.95 Farewell address, 1796. By date
Subarrange by place of publication
312.952 History and criticism
312.99 Will. Editions, by date
Diplomatic history. Foreign relations
Including Neutrality proclamation of 1793; withdrawal of British garrisons from western posts; embargo of 1794; Treaty with Spain, 1795; etc.
Including activities of foreign ministers Adet, Genet, and Casa Yrujo
313 General works
314 Jay's Treaty
Signed November 1794, ratified August 1795
For British right of search, see E357.2
315 Whisky insurrection of Pennsylvania, 1794

Revolution to the Civil War, 1775/1783-1861
By period
1789-1809. Constitutional period
Washington's administrations, 1789-1797 — Continued
320 Presidential campaign of 1796
John Adams' administration, 1797-1801
For Washington, D.C., selected as capital, see F195
321 General works
Biography of John Adams, 1735-1826
For his collected works, see E302.A26
For his speeches and messages as President, see J82.A2+
322 General works
Subarrange by Table E2 at the end of the text
322.1 Adams family (not genealogy)
323 Troubles with France, 1796-1800
Including "XYZ" letters, naval conflicts, etc.
For French spoilation claims before 1800, see JX238.F72+
326 Fries Rebellion, 1798-1799
Alien and sedition laws, 1798
327 General works
328 Kentucky and Virginia Resolutions
330 Presidential campaign of 1800
Jefferson's administrations, 1801-1809
For the Chesapeake affair, see E357.2
For impressment of American seamen, see E357.2
For Lewis and Clark Expedition, 1804-1806, see F592.3+
331 General works
Biography of Thomas Jefferson, 1743-1826
For bibliography, see Z8452
332 General works. Jefferson as president and statesman
For autobiography, see E332.9.A8
332.15 Reminiscences of contemporaries. Anecdotes
332.2 Special
Including Jefferson's personality, character, religion, catholicity, etc.; his attitude toward civil and religious liberty, state rights, freedom of the press, etc.; his knowledge of government, language, science, the fine and useful arts, etc.
Including Jefferson as scholar, humanist, author, architect, musician, educator, social reformer, farmer, inventor, etc.
For Jefferson as president and statesman, see E332
For Jefferson as legislator, see E332.3+
For Jefferson as diplomat, see E332.45
For Jefferson as traveler, see E332.745
For Jefferson as philosopher, see B885
Including Jefferson's relations with special classes, e.g. Jews; Slaves; Relations with contemporaries, e.g. Alexander Hamilton; James Madison
332.25 Ancestry. Family. Family life
Including biography, e.g. Martha (Jefferson) Randolph, his daughter
By period
332.27 Early life
Including frontier life in western Virginia; education; admission to the bar, 1764; professional career, 1767-1774; marriage
Public life
332.3 General works
332.4 State politics
Including service in Virginia House of Burgesses, 1770; Virginia legislature, 1776-1778; governor, 1779-1781
332.45 International diplomacy
Including Jefferson as treaty negotiator with European powers, 1784; Minister to France, 1785-1789

Revolution to the Civil War, 1775/1783-1861
By period
1789-1809. Constitutional period
Jefferson's administrations, 1801-1809
Biography of Thomas Jefferson, 1743-1826
By period
Public life — Continued
332.5 National politics
Including Jefferson as delegate to the Continental Congress, 1775-1776, 1781, 1783-1784; Secretary of State, 1790-1793; Vice-president, 1796-1800
Cf. E221, Declaration of Independence
Cf. E320, Presidential campaign of 1796
Cf. E330, Presidential campaign of 1800
Cf. E337, Presidential campaigns of 1808
Cf. HG521, History of United States money, 1783-1860
Cf. JK2311+, Democratic (Democratic-Republican) Party
For Presidency, 1801-1809, see E331+
332.6 Later life
Including his financial difficulties; sale of library to Congress, 1815; death and burial; funeral and memorial services, 1826-1827; Memorial publications
For the founding of the University of Virginia, 1819, see LD5660+
For funeral addresses and sermons, see E332.76+
For his tomb, see E332.74
Iconography
332.7 General works
332.72 Portraits, etc.
Cf. Subclass NE, Engraved portraits
For medals, see CJ5801+
332.73 Monuments, statues, etc.
Including foreign monuments and statues, e.g. the Jefferson statue at Angers, France
For local monuments and statues, see Class F, e.g. the Thomas Jefferson Memorial in Washington, F203.4.J4
332.74 Homes and haunts
Including his birthplace, Shadwell, Va.; Monticello with tomb and relics; Graff House, Philadelphia; Hôtel de Langear, Paris; etc.
332.745 Journeys
Including those in America and Europe
332.75 Anniversaries. Celebrations. Memorials
Including memorials since 1827; Jefferson's birthday; centennial celebrations, etc.
For funeral and memorial services, 1826-1827, see E332.6
Addresses, essays, lectures. Sermons
332.76 Collections
332.77 Individual
(332.78) Poetry. Drama. Fiction, *see* Subclasses P-PZ
Music, *see* Class M
332.79 Juvenile works
332.795 Other works
Including the Thomas Jefferson quiz book
332.799 Uncataloged pamphlets, clippings, etc.
Writings of Jefferson
For speeches and messages as President, see J82.A3+
(332.8) Collected works, *see* E302.J44
(332.82) Selected works, *see* E302.J44
Correspondence
332.84 Calendar of correspondence
332.85 Collections of letters (General). By date
332.86 Selected letters (General). By date

Revolution to the Civil War, 1775/1783-1861
By period
1789-1809. Constitutional period
Jefferson's administrations, 1801-1809
Writings of Jefferson
Correspondence — Continued
Special
332.87 Letters. By subject, A-Z
In general, prefer classification in Classes A-Z, e.g. PA70.U6, Letters concerning philology and the classics
332.88.A-.88.Z Letters. By correspondent, A-Z
GALE NOTE *The cutter number(s) listed below have been given only as examples by the Library of Congress*
332.88.D8 Dupont de Nemours, Pierre Samuel
332.88.J4 Jefferson, Randolph
332.9.A-.9.Z Individual works, A-Z
In general, prefer classification by subject in Classes A-Z
GALE NOTE *The cutter number(s) listed below have been given only as examples by the Library of Congress*
332.9.A8 Autobiography (1743-1790)
332.9.C6 Commonplace books. Literary Bible
Declaration of Independence, *see* E221
Jefferson Bible, *see* BS2549.J3+
Literary Bible, *see* E332.9.C6
Notes on the state of Virginia, *see* F230
Summary view of the rights of British America, *see* E211
(332.95) Addresses, essays, lectures, *see* E302.J44
(332.98) Doubtful or spurious works, *see* classification by subject
(332.99) Criticism and evaluation of Jefferson's writings, *see* E332.2
333 Purchase of Louisiana, 1803
Including Treaty of Paris, 1803; diplomatic and political aspects; etc.
For the region purchased, see F351+, F366+
333.7 Presidential campaign of 1804
334 Burr's conspiracy, 1805-1807. Wilkinson's participation
For Burr, Aaron (Biography), see E302.6.B9
For Mississippi Valley, see F353
For Wilkinson, James (Biography), see E353.1.W6
335 War with Tripoli, 1801-1805
Called also Tripolitan War or Tripoline War
Including general relations with Barbary States; Treaty of Peace and Amity; the capture and destruction of the frigate Philadelphia; etc.
Including biography: James Barron, Richard Valentine Morris, Mordecai Manuel Noah, Edward Preble, Richard Somers, etc.
For war with Algeria, see E365
Neutral trade and its restriction, 1800-1810
Including French spoliations after 1800
For controversies with England, see E357+
For orders in Council, see HF3505.9
336 General works
336.5 Embargo, December 1807-March 1809
For Embargo acts: Text, and effects on commerce, see HF3027.1
337 Presidential campaign of 1808
337.5 Nineteenth century (General)
Early nineteenth century, 1801/1809-1845
Including Slavery controversy in politics, general works on "manifest destiny," territorial expansion, etc.
For Antimasonic controversy, 1827-1845, see HS525-527
Cf. E440.92, Moral and economic aspects of slavery in the United States
337.8.A-.8.Z Collected works of American statesmen, A-Z
For works of statesmen of the middle nineteenth century, see E415.6.A+

Revolution to the Civil War, 1775/1783-1861

By period

Early nineteenth century, 1801/1809-1845

337.8.A-.8.Z Collected works of American statesmen, A-Z — Continued

GALE NOTE *The cutter number(s) listed below have been given only as examples by the Library of Congress*

337.8.A2 Adams, John Quincy

337.8.C13 Calhoun, John Caldwell

337.8.C55 Clay, Henry

337.8.E9 Everett, Edward

337.8.J3 Jackson, Andrew

337.8.W24 Webster, Daniel

338 General works

Biography

For the middle nineteenth century, see E415.8+

339 Collective

340.A-.Z Individual, A-Z

GALE NOTE *The cutter number(s) listed below have been given only as examples by the Library of Congress*

340.A4 Allen, Charles

Subarrange by Table E2A at the end of the text

340.B2 Bancroft, George

Subarrange by Table E2A at the end of the text

340.B4 Benton, Thomas Hart

Subarrange by Table E2A at the end of the text

340.B57 Binney, Horace, 1780-1875

Subarrange by Table E2A at the end of the text

340.B6 Birney, James Gillespie

Subarrange by Table E2A at the end of the text

340.B67 Branch, John

Subarrange by Table E2A at the end of the text

340.B8 Brockenbrough, William Henry

Subarrange by Table E2A at the end of the text

340.B88 Brown, James

Subarrange by Table E2A at the end of the text

340.B9 Burges, Tristam

Subarrange by Table E2A at the end of the text

340.B98 Butler, Benjamin Franklin, 1795-1858

Subarrange by Table E2A at the end of the text

340.C15 Calhoun, John Caldwell

Subarrange by Table E2A at the end of the text

340.C3 Cass, Lewis

Subarrange by Table E2A at the end of the text

340.C4 Choate, Rufus

Subarrange by Table E2A at the end of the text

340.C5 Cilley, Jonathan

Subarrange by Table E2A at the end of the text

Including the Graves-Cilley duel

340.C6 Clay, Henry

Subarrange by Table E2A at the end of the text

340.C62 Clayton, Augustin Smith

Subarrange by Table E2A at the end of the text

340.C65 Clinton, De Witt

Subarrange by Table E2A at the end of the text

340.C7 Cook, Daniel Pope

Subarrange by Table E2A at the end of the text

340.C76 Corwin, Thomas

Subarrange by Table E2A at the end of the text

340.C89 Crawford, William Harris

Subarrange by Table E2A at the end of the text

Revolution to the Civil War, 1775/1783-1861
By period
Early nineteenth century, 1801/1809-1845
Biography

340.A-.Z Individual, A-Z — Continued

340.C9 Crittenden, John Jordan
Subarrange by Table E2A at the end of the text

340.D14 Dallas, George Mifflin
Subarrange by Table E2A at the end of the text

340.D4 DeForest, David Curtis
Subarrange by Table E2A at the end of the text

340.D7 Dodge, Henry
Subarrange by Table E2A at the end of the text

340.E8 Everett, Edward
Subarrange by Table E2A at the end of the text

340.E9 Ewing, Thomas
Subarrange by Table E2A at the end of the text

340.F16 Fairfield, John
Subarrange by Table E2A at the end of the text

340.F86 Frelinghuysen, Theodore
Subarrange by Table E2A at the end of the text

340.G2 Gaston, William
Subarrange by Table E2A at the end of the text

340.G48 Gilpin, Henry Dilworth
Subarrange by Table E2A at the end of the text

340.G8 Grundy, Felix
Subarrange by Table E2A at the end of the text

340.H2 Hammond, Charles
Subarrange by Table E2A at the end of the text

340.H26 Hardin, Benjamin
Subarrange by Table E2A at the end of the text

340.H4 Hayne, Robert Young
Subarrange by Table E2A at the end of the text

340.H9 Huntington, Jabez Williams
Subarrange by Table E2A at the end of the text

340.I5 Ingersoll, Charles Jared
Subarrange by Table E2A at the end of the text

340.I53 Ingersoll, Joseph Reed
Subarrange by Table E2A at the end of the text

340.J3 Jarvis, Leonard
Subarrange by Table E2A at the end of the text

340.J69 Johnson, Richard Mentor
Subarrange by Table E2A at the end of the text

340.K2 Kaufman, David Spangler
Subarrange by Table E2A at the end of the text

340.K33 Kendall, Amos
Subarrange by Table E2A at the end of the text

340.K54 King, William Rufus
Subarrange by Table E2A at the end of the text

340.L4 Lawrence, Abbott
Subarrange by Table E2A at the end of the text

340.L5 Legaré, Hugh Swinton
Subarrange by Table E2A at the end of the text

340.L7 Linn, Lewis Fields
Subarrange by Table E2A at the end of the text

340.M17 McDuffie, George
Subarrange by Table E2A at the end of the text

340.M2 McLean, John
Subarrange by Table E2A at the end of the text

Revolution to the Civil War, 1775/1783-1861

By period

Early nineteenth century, 1801/1809-1845

Biography

340.A-.Z Individual, A-Z — Continued

340.M3 Mangum, Willie Person

Subarrange by Table E2A at the end of the text

340.M34 Mason, Jeremiah

Subarrange by Table E2A at the end of the text

340.M4 Menefee, Richard Hickman

Subarrange by Table E2A at the end of the text

340.M5 Mercer, Charles Fenton

Subarrange by Table E2A at the end of the text

340.M7 Monroe, James, 1799-1870

Subarrange by Table E2A at the end of the text

340.M8 Morris, Thomas

Subarrange by Table E2A at the end of the text

340.M83 Morrow, Jeremiah

Subarrange by Table E2A at the end of the text

340.O8 Otis, Harrison Gray

Subarrange by Table E2A at the end of the text

340.P3 Pearce, James Alfred

Subarrange by Table E2A at the end of the text

340.P54 Phelps, Samuel Shethar

Subarrange by Table E2A at the end of the text

340.P75 Poindexter, George

Subarrange by Table E2A at the end of the text

340.P77 Poinsett, Joel Roberts

Subarrange by Table E2A at the end of the text

340.P88 Prentiss, Samuel

Subarrange by Table E2A at the end of the text

340.P9 Prentiss, Seargent Smith

Subarrange by Table E2A at the end of the text

Including the Prentiss-Tucker duel

340.R6 Ritchie, Thomas

Subarrange by Table E2A at the end of the text

340.R7 Robertson, George

Subarrange by Table E2A at the end of the text

340.R88 Royall, Anne (Newport)

Subarrange by Table E2A at the end of the text

340.R9 Rush, Richard

Subarrange by Table E2A at the end of the text

340.S18 Saltonstall, Leverett

Subarrange by Table E2A at the end of the text

340.S75 Stevenson, Andrew

Subarrange by Table E2A at the end of the text

Story, Joseph, *see* KF8745.A+

Taney, Roger Brooke, *see* KF8745.A+

340.T47 Thompson, Richard Wigginton

Subarrange by Table E2A at the end of the text

340.V7 Vinton, Samuel Finley

Subarrange by Table E2A at the end of the text

340.W3 Wayne, James Moore

Subarrange by Table E2A at the end of the text

340.W4 Webster, Daniel

Subarrange by Table E2A at the end of the text

340.W53 White, Hugh Lawson

Subarrange by Table E2A at the end of the text

340.W65 Wilmot, David

Subarrange by Table E2A at the end of the text

Revolution to the Civil War, 1775/1783-1861
By period
Early nineteenth century, 1801/1809-1845
Biography
340.A-.Z Individual, A-Z — Continued
340.W73 Winthrop, Robert Charles
Subarrange by Table E2A at the end of the text
340.W79 Wirt, William
Subarrange by Table E2A at the end of the text
340.W8 Woodbury, Levi
Subarrange by Table E2A at the end of the text
340.W95 Wright, Silas
Subarrange by Table E2A at the end of the text
Jefferson's administrations, 1801-1809, *see* E331+
Madison's administrations, 1809-1817
For war with Algeria, 1815, see E365
For Presidential campaign of 1816, see E370
Cf. E83.81, Battle of Tippecanoe, 1811
Cf. E83.813, First Creek War, 1813-1814
Cf. E357+, Troubles with England since 1797
Cf. F314, Seizure of West Florida west of the Perdido
341 General works
Biography of James Madison, 1751-1836
For his collected works, see E302.M19
For his speeches and messages as President, see J82.A4+
342 General
Subarrange by Table E2 at the end of the text
342.1 Madison's family (not genealogy)
Including biography, e.g. Dorothy (Payne) Todd Madison (Dolly Madison)
349 Presidential campaign of 1812
War of 1812
Periodicals. Societies. Collections
351 General works
Societies of veterans
351.2 National Convention of the Soldiers of the War of 1812
351.23 Pennsylvania Association of the Defenders of the Country in the War of 1812
351.27 New England Association of Soldiers of the War of 1812
351.28 New York State Convention of the Soldiers of the War of 1812
351.3-353.6 Patriotic societies of descendants
Under each:

.A1-.A49	Official publications
.A5A-.A5Z	History of the society
.A6-.Z	By state

351.3 Society of the War of 1812
Subarrange by table below E351.3-353.6
351.32 Society of the Second War with Great Britain in the State of New York
Subarrange by table below E351.3-353.6
351.5 Military Society of the War of 1812
Subarrange by table below E351.3-353.6
351.6 National Society of United States Daughters of 1812
Subarrange by table below E351.3-353.6
Biography
353 Collective
Including chiefly military and naval leaders
For statesmen and politicians, see E302.5+, E339+
353.1.A-.1.Z Individual, A-Z
GALE NOTE *The cutter number(s) listed below have been given only as examples by the Library of Congress*
353.1.A19 Adair, John
Subarrange by Table E1 at the end of the text

Revolution to the Civil War, 1775/1783-1861
By period
Early nineteenth century, 1801/1809-1845
Madison's administrations, 1809-1817
War of 1812
Biography
353.1.A-.1.Z Individual, A-Z — Continued
353.1.B2 Bainbridge, William
Subarrange by Table E1 at the end of the text
353.1.B26 Barney, Joshua
Subarrange by Table E1 at the end of the text
353.1.B5 Biddle, James
Subarrange by Table E1 at the end of the text
353.1.B8 Brock, Sir Isaac
Subarrange by Table E1 at the end of the text
353.1.B9 Brown, Jacob
Subarrange by Table E1 at the end of the text
353.1.C75 Covington, Leonard
Subarrange by Table E1 at the end of the text
353.1.C8 Croghan, George
Subarrange by Table E1 at the end of the text
353.1.D29 Decatur, Stephen, 1779-1820
Subarrange by Table E1 at the end of the text
353.1.E4 Elliot, Jesse Duncan
Subarrange by Table E1 at the end of the text
353.1.G14 Gaines, Edmund Pendleton
Subarrange by Table E1 at the end of the text
353.1.H2 Hampton, Wade, 1754-1835
Subarrange by Table E1 at the end of the text
353.1.H8 Hull, Isaac
Subarrange by Table E1 at the end of the text
353.1.H9 Hull, William
Subarrange by Table E1 at the end of the text
353.1.J7 Jones, Jacob
Subarrange by Table E1 at the end of the text
353.1.L4 Lawrence, James
Subarrange by Table E1 at the end of the text
353.1.M15 McArthur, Duncan
Subarrange by Table E1 at the end of the text
353.1.M2 Macdonough, Thomas
Subarrange by Table E1 at the end of the text
353.1.M3 Macomb, Alexander
Subarrange by Table E1 at the end of the text
353.1.M8 Morris, Charles
Subarrange by Table E1 at the end of the text
353.1.P4 Perry, Oliver Hazard
Subarrange by Table E1 at the end of the text
353.1.P7 Porter, David
Subarrange by Table E1 at the end of the text
353.1.R5 Ripley, Eleazer Wheelock
Subarrange by Table E1 at the end of the text
353.1.R7 Rodgers, John
Subarrange by Table E1 at the end of the text
353.1.S8 Stewart, Charles
Subarrange by Table E1 at the end of the text
353.1.W6 Wilkinson, James
Subarrange by Table E1 at the end of the text
354 General works
Cf. E165, Manners and customs, and general travel, 1812-1845

Revolution to the Civil War, 1775/1783-1861
By period
Early nineteenth century, 1801/1809-1845
Madison's administrations, 1809-1817
War of 1812 — Continued
Military operations, 1812-1815
Cf. E83.812, Indian wars, 1812-1815

355 General works
Including campaigns and battles (General) and lists of battles
For individual battles, see E356.A+

355.1.A-.1.Z By region, A-Z
Including campaigns of the northwestern army, the war in the north, in the south, etc., in general

E355.1.N5 Campaigns upon the Niagara frontier

Campaigns. By year

355.2 1812
Including campaigns in the north and northwest covering Detroit, Lake Champlain, Niagara, etc.

355.4 1813
Including campaigns in the east, north, and northwest covering Chesapeake Bay, Lake Champlain, Lake Erie, Lake Ontario, St Lawrence River, etc.
Cf. E83.813, First Creek War, 1813-1814

355.6 1814-1815
Including campaigns in the east, north, and south covering Chesapeake Bay, Lake Champlain, New Orleans, Niagara, etc.
For the capture and burning of Washington, see E356.W3

356.A-.Z Individual battles, A-Z
Including attacks; capture and burning of cities; sieges
Battles, sieges, etc., may be classed in E355.2+

356.B2 Baltimore, 1814
Including the battle of North Point and the bombardment of Fort McHenry
Class here also the Fort McHenry National Monument and Historic Shrine

356.B3 Beaver Dams, Ont., 1813
356.B5 Bladensburg, Md., 1814
356.B6 Boquet River, N.Y., 1814
Bridgewater, Ont., *see* E356.L9
356.B8 Brownstown, Mich., 1812
356.C2 Campbell's Island, 1814
In Mississippi River east of Moline, Ill.
356.C3 Caulk's Field, Md., 1814
Champlain, Lake, *see* E356.P7
356.C4 Chateauguay, N.Y., 1813
356.C53 Chicago, 1812
356.C55 Chippewa, Ont., 1814
356.C74 Cook's Mills, Ont., 1814
356.C8 Craney Island, Va., 1813
Dearborn, Fort, *see* E356.C53
356.D4 Detroit, 1812
356.D8 Dudley's defeat
356.E5 Erie, Fort, Ont., 1814
356.E6 Erie, Lake, 1813
Including Perry Memorial, Put-in-Bay, Ohio
Frenchtown, Mich., *see* E356.R2
356.G4 George, Fort, Ont., 1812
356.H3 Harrison, Fort, Ind., 1812
356.L9 Lundy's Lane, Ont., 1814
356.M15 Mackinac, Mich., 1812
On Mackinac Island, Lake Huron
356.M19 Malcolm's Mills, Ont., 1814
McHenry, Fort, *see* E356.B2

Revolution to the Civil War, 1775/1783-1861
By period
Early nineteenth century, 1801/1809-1845
Madison's administrations, 1809-1817
War of 1812
Military operations, 1812-1815
356.A-.Z Individual battles, A-Z — Continued
356.M5 Meigs, Fort, Ohio, 1813
356.N5 New Orleans, 1815
Including Chalmette National Historical Park
Niagara, Ont., *see* E356.L9
North Point, *see* E356.B2
356.P6 Pigeon Roost, Ind., 1812
356.P7 Plattsburg, N.Y., 1814
356.Q3 Queenston (Queenston Heights), Ont., 1812
356.R2 Raisin River, Mich., 1813
356.S34 Sackets Harbor, N.Y., 1813
356.S7 Stephenson, Fort, Ohio, 1813
356.S8 Stonington, Conn., 1814
356.T3 Thames, Ont., 1813
356.T68 Toronto, 1813
356.W3 Washington, D.C., 1814
York, Ont., *see* E356.T68
Political history
Including controversy with England, 1797-1812
Cf. E314, Jay's Treaty
Cf. E336+, Neutral trade and its restrictions, 1800-1810
Cf. E336.5, Embargo, December 1807-March 1809
357 General works
Right of search and impressment
357.2 General works
357.3 The Chesapeake-Leopard Affair, 1807
Opposition to the war by the New England Federalists
357.6 General works
357.7 Hartford Convention, 1814
357.9 Effects of the war
358 Diplomatic history. Foreign relations
Treaty of Ghent, 1814; Treatment of Alien enemies; Fisheries; Boundaries; etc.
Armies. Troops
359 General works
The American Army
359.2 Regulars
359.24 Infantry
359.25 Cavalry
359.26 Artillery
359.3 Militia
359.4 Pensioners. Bounties. Claims
359.5.A-.5.W The states and their participation, A-W
359.5.C7 Connecticut
359.5.F6 Florida
359.5.G4 Georgia
359.5.I53 Indiana
359.5.K5 Kentucky
359.5.L8 Louisiana
359.5.M2 Maryland
359.5.M3 Massachusetts
359.5.N3 New Hampshire
359.5.N4 New Jersey
359.5.N6 New York
359.5.N7 North Carolina

Revolution to the Civil War, 1775/1783-1861
By period
Early nineteenth century, 1801/1809-1845
Madison's administrations, 1809-1817
War of 1812
Armies. Troops
The American Army
359.5.A-.5.W The states and their participation, A-W — Continued
359.5.O2 Ohio
359.5.P3 Pennsylvania
359.5.T47 Texas
359.5.V3 Vermont
359.5.V8 Virginia
The British Army
359.8 General works
359.85 Canadian participation
359.9.A-.9.Z Participation by race, ethnic group, etc., A-Z
359.9.A35 Afro-Americans
359.9.J5 Jews
Negroes, *see* E359.9.A35
360 Naval history
Including naval battles on the ocean; naval blockades; narratives of sailors, privateers; etc.
For biography of naval leaders, see E353+
For Chesapeake-Leopard Affair, see E357.3
For naval battles in connection with military operations, see E355+
Secret service. Spies
360.5 General works
360.6.A-.6.Z Individual spies, A-Z
360.6.H5 Henry, John (British)
Subarrange by Table E1 at the end of the text
361.A-.Z Personal narratives, A-Z
For prisoners' narratives, see E362
For sailors' narratives, see E360
362 Prisoners and prisons
Including lists of prisoners, prison life, prisoners' narratives, etc., as well as accounts of the Dartmoor Massacre, 1815 (Dartmoor Military Prison, England)
362.5 Medical and hospital services. Hospitals
363 Celebrations. Anniversaries. Museums
Including exhibitions
Illustrative material
(364) Poetry, ballads, songs. Drama, pageants, *see* Class P
364.3 Anecdotes
Cf. E360, Personal narratives of sailors and soldiers
Cf. E361.A+, Personal narratives of sailors and soldiers
Cf. Subclasses PN-PT, Literature
364.5 Addresses, essays, lectures. Sermons. Prayers
364.9 Other (not A-Z)
365 War with Algeria, 1815
Cf. E335, Relations with the Barbary States in general
370 Presidential campaign of 1816
Monroe's administrations, 1817-1825
For the First Seminole War, 1817-1818, see E83.817
371 General works
372 Biography of James Monroe, 1758-1831
Subarrange by Table E2 at the end of the text
For his collected works, see E302.M72+
For his speeches and messages as President, see J82.A5+
373 Missouri Compromise, 1820
Cf. E433, Repeal of the Missouri Compromise, 1854

Revolution to the Civil War, 1775/1783-1861
By period
Early nineteenth century, 1801/1809-1845
Monroe's administrations, 1817-1825
373 Missouri Compromise, 1820 — Continued
Cf. E446, Early American slavery and political agitation growing out of it
Cf. F466, Missouri history
374 Diplomatic history. Foreign relations
For the execution of Arbuthnot and Ambrister, 1818, see E83.817
For Monroe doctrine, see JZ1482
For the Spanish Treaty of 1819 and cession of Florida, see F314
375 Presidential campaign of 1824
Including charge of a corrupt bargain between Adams and Clay
John Quincy Adams' administration, 1825-1829
For Northeastern boundary dispute, see E398
For Panama Congress, 1826, see F1404
For Tariff of 1828, see HF1754
376 General works
Biography of John Quincy Adams, 1767-1845
For his collected works, see E337.8.A2
For his speeches and messages as President, see J82.A6+
377 General works
Subarrange by Table E2 at the end of the text
377.2 Adams' family (not genealogy)
Including biography of individual families
Diplomatic history, *see* E376+
380 Presidential campaign of 1828
Jackson's administrations, 1829-1837
For Bank of the United States, 1816-1836, see HG2525+
For Black Hawk War, see E83.83
For Northeastern boundary troubles, see E398
For Second Creek War, see E83.836
For Second Seminole War, see E83.835
For Tariff of 1833, see HF1754
381 General works
Biography of Andrew Jackson, 1767-1845
Cf. E83.813, Execution of Tennessee militiamen, First Creek War
For his collected works, see E337.8.J3
For his speeches and messages as President, see J82.A7+
382 General
Subarrange by Table E2 at the end of the text
Jackson's family
382.1.A1 General works
382.1.D6 Donelson, Emily Tennessee (Donelson)
382.1.J2 Jackson, Rachel (Donelson)
383 Presidential campaign of 1832
384.3 Nullification
For tariff controversy, see HF1754
Cf. F273, South Carolina politics, 1775-1865
384.7 Removal of deposits from the Bank of the United States. Vote of censure, 1834. Expunging resolutions, 1834-1837
Cf. HG2525+, Bank of the United States, 1816-1836
384.8 Diplomatic history. Foreign relations
For Mexican protest against advance of United States troops, see F390
For Texan War of Independence, and recognition by United States, see F390
385 Presidential campaign of 1836
Van Buren's administration, 1837-1841
For Alton riot, 1837, see F549.A4
For "Amistad" case, see E447
For Aroostook War, and Northeast boundary troubles, see E398

Revolution to the Civil War, 1775/1783-1861

By period

Early nineteenth century, 1801/1809-1845

Van Buren's administration, 1837-1841 — Continued

For Canadian Rebellion, 1837, and destruction of the "Caroline," see F1032

For independent treasury, see HG2535+

For movement for annexation of Texas, see F390

For Panic of 1837, see HB3717

For removal of the Creek Indians to the West, see E99.C9

For Second Seminole War, 1835-1842, see E83.835

386 General works

387 Biography of Martin Van Buren, 1782-1862

Subarrange by Table E2 at the end of the text

For his collected works, see E337.8.A2

For his speeches and messages as President, see J82.A8+

390 Presidential campaign of 1840

W.H. Harrison's administration, March 4-April 4, 1841

391 General works

392 Biography of William H. Harrison, 1773-1841

Subarrange by Table E2 at the end of the text

For his collected works, see E337.8.A+

For his speeches and messages as President, see J82.B1+

Tyler's administration, April 4, 1841-1845

For his attempt to reestablish Bank of the United States, see HG2525+

For Dorr's Rebellion, 1842, see F83.4

For question of the annexation of Texas, see F390

For tariff, see HF1754

396 General works

Including explosion of the frigate "Princeton," 1844

397 Biography of John Tyler, 1790-1862

Subarrange by Table E2 at the end of the text

For his collected works, see E337.8.A+

For his speeches and messages as President, see J82.B2+

398 Northeastern boundary dispute, 1783-1845

Including the Aroostook War, 1839; Webster-Ashburton Treaty (known also as Treaty of Washington, Ashburton Treaty), 1842

After 1845 reports on boundary disputes are classed with locality, e.g. F27.B7, Maine; F42.B7, New Hampshire; F127.B7, New York

400 Presidential campaign of 1844

Mexican War, 1846-1848

401 Periodicals. Collections (Serial)

Societies

401.1 Aztec Club of 1847

401.2 Guadalupe Club of 1848, Washington, D.C

401.3 National Association of Veterans of the Mexican War

401.34 Michigan Association of Veterans of the War with Mexico

401.36 Ohio State Association of Mexican War Veterans

401.7 Dames of 1846

Biography

Includes chiefly military and naval leaders

For statesmen and politicians, see E339+ and E415.8+

403 Collective

403.1.A-.1.Z Individual, A-Z

GALE NOTE *The cutter number(s) listed below have been given only as examples by the Library of Congress*

403.1.B9 Butler, William Orlando

Subarrange by Table E1 at the end of the text

403.1.C7 Connor, David

Subarrange by Table E1 at the end of the text

Cf. E410, Naval history

Revolution to the Civil War, 1775/1783-1861
By period
Mexican War, 1846-1848
Biography
403.1.A-.1.Z Individual, A-Z — Continued
403.1.D6 Doniphan, Alexander William
Subarrange by Table E1 at the end of the text
403.1.H2 Hamer, Thomas Lyon
Subarrange by Table E1 at the end of the text
403.1.H87 Hungerford, Daniel Elihu
Subarrange by Table E1 at the end of the text
403.1.K2 Kearny, Stephen Watts
Subarrange by Table E1 at the end of the text
403.1.P6 Pillow, Gideon Johnson
Subarrange by Table E1 at the end of the text
For Pillow's court-martial, see E405.6
403.1.Q8 Quitman, John Anthony
Subarrange by Table E1 at the end of the text
403.1.R2 Ransom, Truman Bishop
Subarrange by Table E1 at the end of the text
403.1.S4 Scott, Winfield
Subarrange by Table E1 at the end of the text
403.1.S5 Shields, James
Subarrange by Table E1 at the end of the text
403.1.S6 Sloat, John Drake
Subarrange by Table E1 at the end of the text
403.1.S8 Stockton, Robert Field
Subarrange by Table E1 at the end of the text
403.1.W8 Wool, John Ellis
Subarrange by Table E1 at the end of the text
Cf. E405.4, Wool's campaign in Mexico
Cf. E601+, Civil War reminiscences
403.1.W9 Worth, William Jenkins
Subarrange by Table E1 at the end of the text
404 General works
Military operations
Cf. E410, Naval history
For individual battles, see E406.A+
405 General works
Campaigns
For general works, see E405
405.1 Taylor's campaign, 1846-1847
Including campaign along the Rio Grande and in northern Mexico
405.2 Campaigns in and the occupation of New Mexico and California
Including expeditions made by Doniphan, Kearny, Stockton, etc.
405.4 Chihuahua Campaign, 1846-1848
Including Wool's march from San Antonio to Saltillo
405.6 Scott's Campaign, 1847
From Veracruz to Mexico City
406.A-.Z Individual battles, etc., A-Z
406.A48 Alvarado, Veracruz, Mexico, 1846
406.B9 Buena Vista, Mexico, 1847
406.C4 Cerro Gordo, Mexico, 1847
406.C47 Chapultepec, Mexico, 1847
406.C5 Churubusco, Mexico, 1847
406.C6 Contreras, Mexico, 1847
406.M3 Matamoros, Mexico, 1846
406.M6 Mexico City, 1847
406.M65 Molino del Rey, Mexico, 1847
406.M7 Monterrey, Mexico, 1846

Revolution to the Civil War, 1775/1783-1861
By period
Mexican War, 1846-1848
Military operations
406.A-.Z Individual battles, etc., A-Z — Continued
406.P3 Palo Alto, Mexico, 1846
406.R4 Resaca de la Palma, Mexico, 1846
406.S2 San Pasqual, Calif., 1846
406.S25 Santa Clara, Calif., 1847
406.V4 Veracruz, Mexico, 1847
407 Political history
Including causes of the war
Cf. F390, Revolt and annexation of Texas
408 Diplomatic history. Treaty of Guadalupe Hidalgo, 1848
Including the Mexican cessions of 1848
Cf. F786, Mexican boundary after 1848, and the Gadsden Purchase, 1853
Armies. Troops
409 General works
The American Army
409.2 Regulars
409.4 Pensioners. Bounties. Claims
For United States military pensions (General), see UB373+
409.5.A-.5.W The states and their participation, A-W
409.5.C6 Connecticut
409.5.D6 District of Columbia
409.5.I4 Illinois
409.5.I7 Indiana
409.5.I72 Iowa
409.5.K4 Kentucky
409.5.M2 Maryland
409.5.M56 Mississippi
409.5.N6 New York
409.5.O3 Ohio
409.5.P3 Pennsylvania
409.5.S7 South Carolina
409.5.T4 Tennessee
409.5.T45 Texas
409.7 Registers, lists of the dead and wounded, etc.
409.8 The Mexican Army
410 Naval history
Including narratives of sailors
For biography of naval leaders, see E403+
For operations in connection with military campaigns, see E405+
411 Personal narratives
For prisoners' narratives, see E412
For sailors' narratives, see E410
412 Prisoners and prisons
Including lists of prisoners, prison life, prisoners' narratives, etc.
412.5 Medical and hospital services. Hospitals
413 Celebrations. Anniversaries
Cf. E401.1+, Societies of veterans
War poetry, drama, etc., *see* Class P
415 Addresses, essays, lectures. Sermons
415.2.A-.2.Z Special topics, A-Z
415.2.A78 Art and the war
415.2.D48 Desertions
415.2.P82 Public opinion
415.2.S43 Secret service

Revolution to the Civil War, 1775/1783-1861

By period — Continued

Middle nineteenth century, 1845/1848-1861

415.6.A-.6.Z Collected works of American statesmen, A-Z

For works of statesmen of the early nineteenth century, see E337.8.A+

GALE NOTE *The cutter number(s) listed below have been given only as examples by the Library of Congress*

415.6.D16 Dana, Richard Henry

Subarrange by Table E3 at the end of the text

415.6.J65 Johnson, Andrew

Subarrange by Table E3 at the end of the text

415.6.J94 Julian, George Washington

Subarrange by Table E3 at the end of the text

Lincoln, Abraham, *see* E457.91+

415.6.P55 Phillips, Wendell

Subarrange by Table E3 at the end of the text

415.6.S51 Seward, William Henry

Subarrange by Table E3 at the end of the text

415.6.S93 Sumner, Charles

Subarrange by Table E3 at the end of the text

415.6.T57 Tilden, Samuel Jones

Subarrange by Table E3 at the end of the text

415.7 General works

From the outbreak of the Mexican War through the period of reconstruction after the Civil War, 1845-1877

Including political aspects of the slavery question, extension of slavery to the territories, squatter sovereignty, etc.

For wars with the Pacific coast Indians, 1847-1865, see E83.84

Cf. F1783, Cuban question, 1810-1899

Cf. JK2341, American Party (Know-Nothing Party)

Biography

For military leaders of the Civil War, see E467+

For military leaders of the Mexican War, see E403+

415.8 Collective

415.9.A-.9.Z Individual, A-Z

GALE NOTE *The cutter number(s) listed below have been given only as examples by the Library of Congress*

415.9.B4 Bell, John

Subarrange by Table E2A at the end of the text

415.9.B45 Belmont, August

Subarrange by Table E2A at the end of the text

415.9.B6 Black, Jeremiah Sullivan

Subarrange by Table E2A at the end of the text

415.9.B79 Breckinridge, John Cabell

Subarrange by Table E2A at the end of the text

415.9.B84 Broderick, David Colbreth

Subarrange by Table E2A at the end of the text

415.9.B88 Browning, Orville Hickman

Subarrange by Table E2A at the end of the text

415.9.B9 Brownlow, William Gannaway

Subarrange by Table E2A at the end of the text

415.9.C18 Cameron, Simon

Subarrange by Table E2A at the end of the text

415.9.C19 Campbell, John Archibald

Subarrange by Table E2A at the end of the text

415.9.C4 Chase, Salmon Portland

Subarrange by Table E2A at the end of the text

415.9.C55 Clay, Cassius Marcellus

Subarrange by Table E2A at the end of the text

Revolution to the Civil War, 1775/1783-1861
By period
Middle nineteenth century, 1845/1848-1861
Biography

415.9.A-.9.Z Individual, A-Z — Continued

415.9.C6 Clayton, John Middleton
Subarrange by Table E2A at the end of the text

415.9.C63 Clingman, Thomas Lanier
Subarrange by Table E2A at the end of the text

415.9.C68 Colfax, Schuyler
Subarrange by Table E2A at the end of the text

415.9.C96 Curtis, Benjamin Robbins
Subarrange by Table E2A at the end of the text

415.9.C98 Cushing, Caleb
Subarrange by Table E2A at the end of the text

415.9.D15 Dana, Richard Henry
Subarrange by Table E2A at the end of the text
For his collected works, see E415.6.D16

415.9.D26 Davis, Henry Winter
Subarrange by Table E2A at the end of the text
For his collected works, see E415.6.A+

415.9.D27 Dayton, William Lewis
Subarrange by Table E2A at the end of the text

415.9.D48 Dickinson, Anna Elizabeth
Subarrange by Table E2A at the end of the text

415.9.D5 Dickinson, Daniel Stevens
Subarrange by Table E2A at the end of the text

415.9.D6 Dix, John Adams
Subarrange by Table E2A at the end of the text

415.9.D73 Douglas, Stephen Arnold
Subarrange by Table E2A at the end of the text
For Lincoln-Douglas debates, see E457.4

415.9.D9 Dunn, William McKee
Subarrange by Table E2A at the end of the text

415.9.F4 Fessenden, William Pitt
Subarrange by Table E2A at the end of the text

415.9.F5 Field, David Dudley
Subarrange by Table E2A at the end of the text

415.9.F55 Field, Maunsell Bradhurst
Subarrange by Table E2A at the end of the text

415.9.F64 Floyd, John Buchanan
Subarrange by Table E2A at the end of the text

415.9.F7 Foote, Henry Stuart
Subarrange by Table E2A at the end of the text

415.9.F8 Frémont, John Charles
Subarrange by Table E2A at the end of the text

415.9.G4 Giddings, Joshua Reed
Subarrange by Table E2A at the end of the text

415.9.G7 Graham, William Alexander
Subarrange by Table E2A at the end of the text

415.9.G8 Greeley, Horace
Subarrange by Table E2A at the end of the text
For the presidential campaign of 1872, see E675

415.9.G85 Grimes, James Wilson
Subarrange by Table E2A at the end of the text

415.9.G86 Grinnell, Josiah Bushnell
Subarrange by Table E2A at the end of the text

415.9.G89 Grow, Galusha Aaron
Subarrange by Table E2A at the end of the text

Revolution to the Civil War, 1775/1783-1861

By period

Middle nineteenth century, 1845/1848-1861

Biography

415.9.A-.9.Z Individual, A-Z — Continued

415.9.H15 Hale, John Parker

Subarrange by Table E2A at the end of the text

415.9.H2 Hamlin, Hannibal

Subarrange by Table E2A at the end of the text

415.9.H28 Harris, Benjamin Gwinn

Subarrange by Table E2A at the end of the text

For the Harris court-martial, 1865, see E458.8

415.9.H35 Haskin, John Bussing

Subarrange by Table E2A at the end of the text

415.9.H6 Hicks, Thomas Holliday

Subarrange by Table E2A at the end of the text

415.9.H65 Hilliard, Henry Washington

Subarrange by Table E2A at the end of the text

415.9.H9 Hunter, Robert Mercer Taliaferro

Subarrange by Table E2A at the end of the text

415.9.J5 Jenckes, Thomas Allen

Subarrange by Table E2A at the end of the text

415.9.J6 Jones, George Wallace

Subarrange by Table E2A at the end of the text

415.9.J7 Jones, J. Glancy

Subarrange by Table E2A at the end of the text

415.9.J95 Julian, George Washington

Subarrange by Table E2A at the end of the text

For his collected works, see E415.6.J94

415.9.K35 Kennedy, John Pendleton

Subarrange by Table E2A at the end of the text

415.9.K52 King, Horatio

Subarrange by Table E2A at the end of the text

415.9.K7 Körner, Gustav Philipp

Subarrange by Table E2A at the end of the text

415.9.L2 Lane, Joseph

Subarrange by Table E2A at the end of the text

415.9.L38 Lawrence, Amos Adams

Subarrange by Table E2A at the end of the text

415.9.L4 Lawrence, William Beach

Subarrange by Table E2A at the end of the text

415.9.L7 Lieber, Francis

Subarrange by Table E2A at the end of the text

415.9.L89 Lovejoy, Owen

Subarrange by Table E2A at the end of the text

415.9.M16 Maclay, William Brown

Subarrange by Table E2A at the end of the text

415.9.M18 Marcy, William Learned

Subarrange by Table E2A at the end of the text

415.9.M19 Mason, Charles

Subarrange by Table E2A at the end of the text

415.9.M2 Mason, James Murray

Subarrange by Table E2A at the end of the text

415.9.M3 Maury, Dabney Herndon

Subarrange by Table E2A at the end of the text

415.9.M4 Memminger, Christopher Gustavus

Subarrange by Table E2A at the end of the text

415.9.M5 Meredith, William Morris

Subarrange by Table E2A at the end of the text

Revolution to the Civil War, 1775/1783-1861
By period
Middle nineteenth century, 1845/1848-1861
Biography

415.9.A-.9.Z Individual, A-Z — Continued
415.9.P4 Pendleton, George Hunt
Subarrange by Table E2A at the end of the text
415.9.P78 Pomeroy, Samuel Clarke
Subarrange by Table E2A at the end of the text
415.9.R75 Rollins, Edward Henry
Subarrange by Table E2A at the end of the text
415.9.R76 Rollins, James Sidney
Subarrange by Table E2A at the end of the text
415.9.S4 Seward, William Henry
Subarrange by Table E2A at the end of the text
For his collected works, see E415.6.S51
415.9.S5 Seymour, Horatio
Subarrange by Table E2A at the end of the text
415.9.S53 Sickles, Daniel Edgar
Subarrange by Table E2A at the end of the text
415.9.S58 Slidell, John
Subarrange by Table E2A at the end of the text
415.9.S64 Smith, Gerrit
Subarrange by Table E2A at the end of the text
415.9.S72 Soulé, Pierre
Subarrange by Table E2A at the end of the text
415.9.S74 Speed, James
Subarrange by Table E2A at the end of the text
415.9.S84 Stevens, Thaddeus
Subarrange by Table E2A at the end of the text
415.9.S88 Stuart, Alexander Hugh Holmes
Subarrange by Table E2A at the end of the text
415.9.S9 Sumner, Charles
Subarrange by Table E2A at the end of the text
For his collected works, see E415.6.S93
For works on Brooks' assault, see E434.8
415.9.T12 Taft, Alphonso
Subarrange by Table E2A at the end of the text
415.9.T45 Thompson, Jacob
Subarrange by Table E2A at the end of the text
415.9.T5 Tilden, Samuel Jones
Subarrange by Table E2A at the end of the text
For his collected works, see E415.6.T57
415.9.T6 Toombs, Robert Augustus
Subarrange by Table E2A at the end of the text
415.9.T86 Trumbull, Lyman
Subarrange by Table E2A at the end of the text
415.9.T88 Tuck, Amos
Subarrange by Table E2A at the end of the text
415.9.T93 Tyler, Robert
Subarrange by Table E2A at the end of the text
415.9.V2 Vallandigham, Clement Laird
Subarrange by Table E2A at the end of the text
415.9.W16 Wade, Benjamin Franklin
Subarrange by Table E2A at the end of the text
415.9.W2 Walker, Robert James
Subarrange by Table E2A at the end of the text
415.9.W39 Weed, Thurlow
Subarrange by Table E2A at the end of the text

Revolution to the Civil War, 1775/1783-1861
By period
Middle nineteenth century, 1845/1848-1861
Biography
415.9.A-.9.Z Individual, A-Z — Continued
415.9.W6 Wilson, Henry
Subarrange by Table E2A at the end of the text
415.9.W8 Wise, Henry Alexander
Subarrange by Table E2A at the end of the text
415.9.Y2 Yancey, William Lowndes
Subarrange by Table E2A at the end of the text
415.9.Y9 Yulee, David Levy
Subarrange by Table E2A at the end of the text
Polk's administration, 1845-1849
Including government of the newly acquired Spanish possessions in the Southwest; slavery in the territories; slavery question in politics; Wilmot Proviso, 1846; etc.
For annexation of Texas, 1845, see F390
For Oregon question and Northwestern boundary to 1846, see F880
416 General works
Biography of James K. Polk, 1795-1849
For his collected works, see E415.6.A+
For his speeches and messages as President, see J82.B3+
417 General works
Subarrange by Table E2 at the end of the text
417.1 Polk, Sarah (Childress)
420 Presidential campaign of 1848
Taylor's administration, 1849-July 9, 1850
For admission of California, see F864
For organization of New Mexico and Utah territories, see F801, F826
For payment to Texas for claim on part of New Mexico, see F801
421 General works
422 Biography of Zachary Taylor, 1784-1850
Subarrange by Table E2 at the end of the text
For his collected works, see E415.6.A+
For his speeches and messages as President, see J82.B4+
For his campaign, 1846-1847, see E405.1
423 Slavery question, 1849-1853
Including Clay's Omnibus Bill (Compromise of 1850); Southern Convention, Nashville, 1850
For fugitive slaves and the new law of 1850, see E450
Fillmore's administration, July 9, 1850-1853
426 General works
427 Biography of Millard Fillmore, 1800-1874
Subarrange by Table E2 at the end of the text
For his collected works, see E415.6.A+
For his speeches and messages as President, see J82.B5+
429 Diplomatic history, 1849-1853. Foreign relations
Including intervention; political refugees from abroad; etc.
For Clayton-Bulwer Treaty, 1850, see F1438
For Cuban question, see F1783
430 Presidential campaign of 1852
Pierce's administration, 1853-1857
For American Party (Know-Nothing Party), see JK2341
For bombardment of Greytown, Nicaragua, 1854, see F1536.S2
For the Cuban question, see F1783
For the Filibuster War in Nicaragua, 1855-1857, see F1526
For the Gadsden purchase, 1853, see F786
For the Third Seminole War, 1855-1858, see E83.855
For the Wars with Pacific coast Indians, see E83.84

Revolution to the Civil War, 1775/1783-1861
By period
Middle nineteenth century, 1845/1848-1861
Pierce's administration, 1853-1857 — Continued
431 General works
Including diplomatic history; the Ostend Manifesto, October 1854
Biography of Franklin Pierce, 1804-1869
For his collected works, see E415.6.A+
For his speeches and messages as President, see J82.B6+
432 General
Subarrange by Table E2 at the end of the text
432.2 Pierce family (not genealogy)
Including biography of individual members
433 Slavery question, 1853-1857
Including repeal of the Missouri Compromise, 1854; Kansas-Nebraska Bill, May 1854
For Kansas troubles, see F685
For moral and economic aspects of the slavery question, see E449+
For squatter sovereignty, see E415.7
434.5 Election of speaker of the House
434.8 Brooks' assault on Senator Sumner, 1856
435 Presidential campaign of 1856
Buchanan's administration, 1857-1861
For Cuban question, see F1783
For Mill Creek War, 1857-1865, see E83.858
For Mormon Rebellion, 1857-1859, see F826
For Paraguay Expedition, see F2686
For Spirit Lake Massacre, 1857, see E83.857
For Walker's Filibuster wars, 1855-1860, see F1526
436 General works
Biography of James Buchanan, 1791-1868
For his collected works, see E337.8.A+
For his speeches and messages as President, see J82.B7+
437 General works
Subarrange by Table E2 at the end of the text
437.1 Buchanan family (not genealogy)
Including biography, e.g. Harriet Lane, 1830-1903
438 Slavery question, 1857-1861
Including attempt to revive slave trade, 1858, Lincoln's Cooper Institute address
For Dred Scott decision, 1857, see E450
For Harpers Ferry raid, 1859, see E451
For Kansas and the Lecompton Constitution, see F685
For Lincoln-Douglas debates, 1858, see E457.4
For squatter sovereignty, see E415.7
440 Presidential campaign of 1860
440.5 State of the country, November 1860- March 4, 1861
Including attempts at compromise (Crittenden Compromise, December 18, 1860; Crittenden Resolution, July 22, 1861; etc.); Peace Conference at Washington (Border Slave State Convention), 1861; secession of certain states
Cf. E458.1, Political history, March 4-December 31, 1861
Cf. E471.1, Opening events of Civil War
Slavery in the United States. Antislavery movements
Including general works on slavery in the South
Cf. HT851+, Slavery and the slave trade (General)
For various political aspects of the slavery question of the Revolution to the Civil War period, see E301+, including especially E373, E407, E415.7, E416, E423, E433, E438, E440.5
For general works on Afro-Americans, including the period since the Civil War, see E185
Periodicals, *see* E446, E449
441 General works
Including history of slavery in general
For history by period, see E446+

Revolution to the Civil War, 1775/1783-1861

Slavery in the United States. Antislavery movements — Continued

442 The internal slave trade. Slave markets and auctions

443 Slave life

Including duties of slaves and masters, overseers

444 Biography. Personal narratives of slaves

For biography of fugitive slaves, see E450

Cf. E449, Life and writings of Frederick Douglass

445.A-.W By state, A-W

Including history of antislavery movements

For slavery in an individual county, see under the state

Cf. E185.93.A+, Afro-Americans in individual states

445.A3 Alabama

445.C7 Connecticut

445.D3 Delaware

445.D6 District of Columbia

445.F6 Florida

445.G3 Georgia

445.I2 Illinois

445.I3 Indiana

445.K16 Kansas

Cf. F685, Struggle between pro-slavery and antislavery parties

445.K5 Kentucky

445.L8 Louisiana

445.M3 Maryland

445.M4 Massachusetts

445.M6 Mississippi

445.M67 Missouri

445.N2 Nebraska

445.N5 New England

445.N54 New Jersey

445.N55 New Mexico

445.N56 New York

Cf. F128.4, Negro plot in New York City, 1741

445.N8 North Carolina

445.P3 Pennsylvania

445.R4 Rhode Island

445.S7 South Carolina

Cf. F273, Trouble with Massachusetts over its Afro-American citizens in South Carolina

Cf. F279.C4, Charleston Insurrection (Denmark Vesey's Rebellion), 1822

445.T3 Tennessee

445.T47 Texas

445.V8 Virginia

Cf. F232.S7, Southampton Insurrection (Nat Turner's Rebellion), 1831

Cf. F234.R5, Richmond Insurrection (Gabriel's Insurrection), 1800

445.W8 Wisconsin

History of slavery to 1830

Including controversial literature

446 General works

Including attempts to revive slave trade, early anti-slavery movements, etc.

Cf. E309, Northwest Ordinance of 1787

Cf. E373, Missouri Compromise, 1820

447 Slave insurrections (General)

Including mutiny on slave ships, e.g Amistad (Schooner); Creole (Brig)

For individual insurrections, see local history, e.g. F279.C4, Charleston Insurrection (Denmark Vesey's Rebellion), 1822; F128.4, New York Negro plot, 1741; F234.R5, Richmond Insurrection (Gabriel's Insurrection), 1800; F232.S7, Southampton Insurrection (Nat Turner's Rebellion), 1831

Revolution to the Civil War, 1775/1783-1861

Slavery in the United States. Antislavery movements — Continued

448 Colonization

Including the American Colonization Society and affiliated organizations: their origin, plans, history, etc.; also modern colonization societies

Cf. DT621+, Liberia

History of slavery, 1830-1863. Period of abolition agitation

Including controversial literature

Cf. E337.8+, Political aspects of slavery question

Cf. E416+, Wilmot Proviso, 1846

Cf. E423, Compromise of 1850

Cf. E434.8, Brooks' assault on Senator Sumner, 1856

Cf. F273, Dispute between Massachusetts and South Carolina over Afro-American citizens of Massachusetts, 1845

Cf. F549.A4, Alton Riot, 1837

Cf. F685, Struggle between proslavery and antislavery parties in Kansas

449 General works

Including biography: Frederick Douglass, William Lloyd Garrison, William Jay, Lucretia (Coffin) Mott, Wendell Phillips

450 Fugitive slaves

Including biographies and narratives of fugitive slaves, e.g. John Anderson, Eliza Harris, James Williams; fugitive slave law; personal liberty laws; slaves in free states; underground railroad; biographies and narratives of protectors of slaves, e.g. Levi Coffin, Jonathan Walker, Laura S. Haviland

Including such events and cases as the Garrison mob, Boston, 1835; case of the slave child, Med Slater, 1836; Isaac Brown case, 1847; Dred Scott case, 1848-1857; South Bend slave case, 1849; Randolph epistles, 1850; Christiana Riot, 1851, and trial of Castner Hanway and others for assault on Edward Gorsuch; Sherman M. Booth case, 1854; Anthony Burns case in Boston, 1854; Addison White rescue, 1857; Oberlin-Wellington rescue, 1858; Jonathan Lemmon slave case, 1860

Cf. KF4545.S5, Fugitive slave act

For court records of individual trials, see KF223+

451 John Brown's Raid at Harpers Ferry, W. Va., 1859

Including the capture, trial, execution, and biography of John Brown

Cf. F685, John Brown in Kansas

453 Slaves and the slavery question in the Civil War

Including "Contrabands"; slavery in the Confederate States of America; emancipation of the slaves in general; Emancipation Proclamation (Manifesto by Abraham Lincoln on September 22, 1862, that on January 1, 1863, he would declare free all slaves held in parts of the United States not in the possession of the Union armies)

For local material, see E445.A+ or E185.93.A+

Cf. E185.2, Freedmen, Freedmen's Bureau (Bureau of Refugees, Freedmen, and Abandoned Lands), etc.

Cf. E185.93.S7, Port Royal Mission, S.C.

Cf. E540.N3, Afro-American soldiers in the Union Army

Cf. E585.A35, Afro-American soldiers in the Confederate Army

Cf. JK169, Thirteenth, fourteenth, and fifteenth amendments to the Constitution

Civil War period, 1861-1865

Lincoln's administrations, 1861-April 15, 1865

For election and events preceding inauguration, see E440+

For presidential campaign of 1864, see E458.4

For wars with Dakota Indians, 1862-1863, see E83.86

For other Indian wars, 1862-1863, see E83.863

456 General works

Biography of Abraham Lincoln, 1809-1865

For his collected works, see E457.91+

For his speeches and messages as President, see E457.94

457 General works. Lincoln as president and statesman

Subarrange by Table E2 at the end of the text

Including campaign biographies of 1860, 1864

Civil War period, 1861-1865

Lincoln's administrations, 1861-April 15, 1865

Biography of Abraham Lincoln, 1809-1865

457 General works. Lincoln as president and statesman — Continued

Cf. E456,E458+, Political history of the country, 1861-1865

457.1 Societies

457.15 Anecdotes relating to Lincoln

Including personal reminiscences of contemporaries, but not formal biographies

457.2 Special

Including Lincoln's personality (Character, kindness, loyalty, etc.), religion, education, books and reading, etc. Attitude toward slavery, temperance and prohibition, etc.

Including Lincoln as lawyer, freemason, writer, speaker, etc.

For Lincoln as president and statesman, see E457

Including Lincoln's relations with special classes, e.g. Jews, private soldiers, etc.

457.25 Family life

Including biography, e.g. Mary (Todd) Lincoln; Thomas (Tad) Lincoln

By period

Early life to 1861

For campaign biographies, see E457

Cf. F532.S6, Lincoln Boyhood National Memorial

Cf. F549.S7, Lincoln's home in Springfield, Ill

457.3 General works

457.32 To 1830

Including lineage, family, and parents (Thomas Lincoln, Nancy (Hanks) Lincoln, Sarah (Bush) Johnston Lincoln), etc.

Including birthplace (Hodgenville, Ky.), boyhood and youth in Kentucky and Indiana

Cf. F532.S6, Nancy Hanks Lincoln Memorial

457.35 1830-1846

Including first years in Illinois; Black Hawk War, 1832; Illinois legislature, professional career; etc.

Including Ann Rutledge, marriage, etc.

Cf. E457.25, Family life

457.4 1846-1861

Including national politics; congressional service; Lincoln-Douglas debates, 1858; journey to Washington; etc.

Cf. E415.7, E449, The slavery question

Cf. E440, Presidential campaign of 1860

Cf. E440.5, State of the country, November 1860-March 1861

457.45 1861-1865

Cf. E458.4, Presidential campaign of 1864

Cf. E461+, The Civil War

Cf. E475.35, Gettysburg address

457.5 Assassination

Including the conspirators (Booth, Surratt, etc.)

For the trials of Booth, Surratt, etc., see KF223+

457.52 Death

Including funeral journey to Springfield, burial, memorial services throughout the country and abroad, guard of honor, tomb, etc.

Cf. E457.8, Funeral sermons

457.6 Monuments. Statues. Portraits

Including life and death masks, etc.; monuments, statues, etc. located in foreign countries

For local monuments, statues, etc., in the United States, see Class F, e.g. in Washington, D.C., F203.4.L72, Lincoln statue (Lincoln Park); F203.4.L73, Lincoln Memorial

Cf. E457.32, Birthplace, Hodgenville, Kentucky

Cf. E457.52, Lincoln Tomb, Springfield, Ill.

For medals, see CJ5801+

457.63 Caricatures and cartoons

Including satirical and comic works

Civil War period, 1861-1865

Lincoln's administrations, 1861-April 15, 1865

Biography of Abraham Lincoln, 1809-1865 — Continued

457.64 Homes and haunts of Lincoln (General)

For early years, see E457.32 or E457.35

For Springfield home, see F549.S7

457.65 Museums. Exhibitions. Lincoln relics

Including Lincoln Museum (Ford Theatre), Washington, D.C.; Oldroyd collection of Lincoln relics

For medals, see CJ5801+

457.7 Anniversaries. Celebrations. Memorials since 1865

Including centennials, Lincoln Day

For funeral and memorial services, see E457.52

457.8 Addresses, essays, lectures. Sermons (Funeral, etc.)

Class here addresses which have been delivered since the assassination

For addresses delivered before April 1865, see E440, E457, or E458.1-.5

Cf. E457.15, Personal reminiscences

Cf. E457.52, Funeral services

(457.9) Poetry. Drama. Fiction, *see* Class P

Music, *see* Class M

457.905 Juvenile works

457.909 Lincolniana

Including miscellaneous printed matter, minor pamphlets

Reserved for material not separately cataloged

Writings of Lincoln

Classification by subject is preferred

457.91 Collected works. By date

457.92 Partial collections. Selected works. Selections. By date

Including collections of speeches (Three or more)

457.94 State papers, messages, inaugural addresses. By date

Under each:

.A2-.A29 Text

.A3-.Z History and criticism

457.94 1861 First inaugural address

457.94 1865 Second inaugural address

457.95 Addresses, essays, lectures. By date

For collections of speeches, see E457.92

For Lincoln-Douglas debates, 1858, see E457.4

Letters

457.96 Individual. By date

457.962 Collections. By date

457.98 Minor works

Including history of the Fisher murder mystery; a facsimile of an indenture drawn up, October 25, 1841, by Lincoln and signed by his father

457.99 Stories, anecdotes, poems, axioms, brief extracts, etc., attributed to Lincoln

Arrange alphabetically by editor or title

Political history (Contemporary works)

Including questions at issue between North and South, the internal policies of the United States, etc.

For treaties published after the close of the war, see E459

For sermons and addresses, see E649+

For foreign public opinion, see E469.8

458 General works

Including collections and works covering more than a single year

458.1 March 4-December 31, 1861

Cf. E440.5, State of the nation, November 1860-March 4, 1861

458.2 1862

458.3 1863

Cf. E453, Emancipation of the slaves

Civil War period, 1861-1865

Lincoln's administrations, 1861-April 15, 1865

Political history (Contemporary works) — Continued

458.4 1864

Including presidential campaign of 1864; campaign literature; etc.

458.5 January-May 1865

458.7 Union men in the South. Refugees

458.8 Confederate sympathizers in the North. "Copperheads," "Butternuts," etc.

Including conspiracies, e.g. Northwestern Conspiracy, 1864; disloyal organizations: Knights of the Golden Circle, Order of American Knights or Sons of Liberty, Order of the Lone Star, etc.; suspension of the writ of habeas corpus; prisoners of state; Harris court-martial, 1865; etc.

Cf. E615+, Union prisons

Cf. JK343, Military rule, martial law, etc., within states or districts during the Civil War

459 Political history (Non-contemporary works)

Including publications since May 1865

For treatises only

For addresses, sermons, etc., see E649+

For contemporary publications, see E458+

The Civil War, 1861-1865

461 **Periodicals**

For Confederate periodicals, see E482

Societies of veterans, etc.

For Confederate societies, see E483

For regimental associations of veterans, see regiment in E492

462 General works

462.Z7 Minor publications not separately cataloged

Individual societies, etc.

Under each (unless otherwise indicated):

	Official publications
.A1-.A4	Serial publications
.A5-.A69	Monographs
.A7A-.A7Z	Nonofficial publications
.A8-.W	State branches. By state, A-W

Under each:

	Official publications
A1-A4	Serial publications
A5-A7	Monographs
A8-Z	Nonofficial publications

462.1 Grand Army of the Republic

Subarrange by table above E462.1

462.15 Women's Relief Corps

Subarrange by table above E462.1

462.17 Ladies of the Grand Army of the Republic

Subarrange by table above E462.1

462.18 Legion of Loyal Women, Washington, D.C.

Subarrange by table above E462.1

462.2 Military Order of the Loyal Legion of the United States

Subarrange by table above E462.1

462.25 Dames of the Loyal Legion

Subarrange by table above E462.1

462.3 Military Order of the Medal of Honor

Subarrange by table above E462.1

462.4 Union Veteran Legion of the United States

Subarrange by table above E462.1

462.5 National Association of Naval Veterans

Subarrange by table above E462.1

462.6 Veteran Brotherhood of the State of Kansas

Subarrange by table above E462.1

The Civil War, 1861-1865

Societies of veterans, etc.

Individual societies, etc. — Continued

462.7 Union League of America

Subarrange by table above E462.1

462.84 Union clubs

Subarrange by table above E462.1

For local Union clubs, see HS2721+

462.9 Sons of Union Veterans of the Civil War

Subarrange by table above E462.1

462.92 Soldiers' and Sailors' National Union League of Washington, D.C.

Subarrange by table above E462.1

462.93 Washington, D.C. Old Guard

Subarrange by table above E462.1

462.94 Order of American Freemen

Subarrange by table above E462.1

462.96 Union White Boys in Blue

Subarrange by table above E462.1

462.97 Philadelphia. War Veterans' Club

Subarrange by table above E462.1

462.98 National Soldiers Historical Association

Subarrange by table above E462.1

462.99.A.99.Z Other societies, etc., A-Z

GALE NOTE *The cutter number(s) listed below have been given only as examples by the Library of Congress*

462.99.D2 Daughters of Union Veterans of the Civil War

Subarrange by table below E186.99.A-.99.Z

First Defenders, *see* E493.9

National Association of Civil War Army Nurses, *see* E621

462.99.N27 National Veteran Club of the United States

Subarrange by table below E186.99.A-.99.Z

462.99.O65 Order of Stars and Stripes

Subarrange by table below E186.99.A-.99.Z

462.99.S6 Society for Correct Civil War Information

Subarrange by table below E186.99.A-.99.Z

462.99.S62 Society of the Army and Navy of the Gulf

Subarrange by table below E186.99.A-.99.Z

462.99.U53 Union Society of the Civil War

Subarrange by table below E186.99.A-.99.Z

462.99.U57 Union Soldiers' Alliance, Washington, D.C.

Subarrange by table below E186.99.A-.99.Z

462.99.U63 Union Veterans' Union

Subarrange by table below E186.99.A-.99.Z

United States Veteran Signal Corps Association, *see* E608

463 Patriotic societies during the war

Including Loyal League of Union Citizens, Loyal National League of the State of New York, Loyal Publication Society, etc.

For Loyal Union League clubs, see HS2721+

464 Collections. Collected works

Including papers read before Loyal Legion, Grand Army of the Republic

Cf. E458+, Collections of political pamphlets

Cf. E484, Confederate collections

Cf. E655, Anecdotes of the Civil War

Biography

467 Collective (Union and Confederate)

For nurses, see E621+

For prisoners of war, see E611+

For rolls of college men in the war, see E541.A+ and E586.A+

467.1.A-.1.Z Individual, A-Z

Including chiefly lives of commanders and other officers

The Civil War, 1861-1865

Biography

467.1.A-.1.Z Individual, A-Z — Continued

Cf. E415.9.A+, Biography of political leaders except a few like Davis, Stanton, and Benjamin whose careers culminated in the war

Cf. E495+, E545+, Regimental officers and privates

Cf. E601+, Personal narratives of war service

GALE NOTE *The cutter number(s) listed below have been given only as examples by the Library of Congress*

467.1.A2 Adams, Charles Francis, 1807-1886

Subarrange by Table E1 at the end of the text

467.1.A3 Alexander, Andrew Jonathan

Subarrange by Table E1 at the end of the text

467.1.A4 Allen, Henry Watkins

Subarrange by Table E1 at the end of the text

467.1.A54 Anderson, Richard Heron

Subarrange by Table E1 at the end of the text

467.1.A78 Arrowsmith, George

Subarrange by Table E1 at the end of the text

467.1.A8 Ashby, Turner

Subarrange by Table E1 at the end of the text

467.1.B14 Bailey, Theodorus

Subarrange by Table E1 at the end of the text

467.1.B16 Baker, Edward Dickenson

Subarrange by Table E1 at the end of the text

467.1.B23 Banks, Nathaniel Prentice

Subarrange by Table E1 at the end of the text

467.1.B25 Barlow, Francis Channing

Subarrange by Table E1 at the end of the text

467.1.B26 Barnes, James

Subarrange by Table E1 at the end of the text

467.1.B29 Bartlett, William Francis

Subarrange by Table E1 at the end of the text

467.1.B3 Bayard, George Dashiell

Subarrange by Table E1 at the end of the text

467.1.B38 Beauregard, Pierre Gustave

Subarrange by Table E1 at the end of the text

467.1.B39 Beaver, James Addams

Subarrange by Table E1 at the end of the text

467.1.B397 Benedict, Lewis

Subarrange by Table E1 at the end of the text

467.1.B4 Benjamin, Judah Philip

Subarrange by Table E1 at the end of the text

467.1.B5 Berry, Hiram Gregory

Subarrange by Table E1 at the end of the text

467.1.B6 Birney, David Bell

Subarrange by Table E1 at the end of the text

467.1.B7 Boomer, George Boardman

Subarrange by Table E1 at the end of the text

467.1.B73 Bowen, John Steven

Subarrange by Table E1 at the end of the text

467.1.B75 Bragg, Braxton

Subarrange by Table E1 at the end of the text

467.1.B77 Brown, Joseph Newton

Subarrange by Table E1 at the end of the text

467.1.B8 Burnside, Ambrose Everett

Subarrange by Table E1 at the end of the text

467.1.B87 Butler, Benjamin Franklin (1818-1893)

Subarrange by Table E1 at the end of the text

The Civil War, 1861-1865

Biography

467.1.A-.1.Z Individual, A-Z — Continued

467.1.B9 Butterfield, Daniel

Subarrange by Table E1 at the end of the text

467.1.C52 Chetlain, Augustus Louis

Subarrange by Table E1 at the end of the text

467.1.C97 Curtis, Samuel Ryan

Subarrange by Table E1 at the end of the text

467.1.C98 Cushing, William Barker

Subarrange by Table E1 at the end of the text

467.1.C99 Custer, George Armstrong

Subarrange by Table E1 at the end of the text

467.1.D13 Dahlgren, John Adolphus

Subarrange by Table E1 at the end of the text

467.1.D24 Davis, Charles Henry

Subarrange by Table E1 at the end of the text

467.1.D26 Davis, Jefferson

Subarrange by Table E1 at the end of the text

467.1.D27 Davis, Varina (Howell). "Mrs. Jefferson Davis"

Subarrange by Table E1 at the end of the text

467.1.D28 Davis, Varina Anne Jefferson

Subarrange by Table E1 at the end of the text

467.1.D6 Dodge, Grenville Mellen

Subarrange by Table E1 at the end of the text

467.1.D9 Du Pont, Samuel Francis

Subarrange by Table E1 at the end of the text

467.1.E13 Early, Jubal Anderson

Subarrange by Table E1 at the end of the text

467.1.E4 Elliott, Stephen

Subarrange by Table E1 at the end of the text

467.1.E47 Ellsworth, Ephraim Elmer

Subarrange by Table E1 at the end of the text

467.1.E86 Ewell, Richard Stoddert

Subarrange by Table E1 at the end of the text

467.1.E9 Ewing, Charles

Subarrange by Table E1 at the end of the text

467.1.F23 Farragut, David Glasgow

Subarrange by Table E1 at the end of the text

467.1.F64 Flusser, Charles Williamson

Subarrange by Table E1 at the end of the text

467.1.F68 Foote, Andrew Hull

Subarrange by Table E1 at the end of the text

467.1.F72 Forrest, Nathan Bedford

Subarrange by Table E1 at the end of the text

467.1.F83 Franklin, William Buel

Subarrange by Table E1 at the end of the text

467.1.F87 French, Samuel Gibbs

Subarrange by Table E1 at the end of the text

467.1.F9 Fritchie, Barbara (Hauer)

Subarrange by Table E1 at the end of the text

467.1.G29 Geary, John White

Subarrange by Table E1 at the end of the text

467.1.G6 Gooding, Oliver Paul

Subarrange by Table E1 at the end of the text

467.1.G66 Gordon, John Brown

Subarrange by Table E1 at the end of the text

467.1.G68 Gorgas, Josiah

Subarrange by Table E1 at the end of the text

The Civil War, 1861-1865

Biography

467.1.A-.1.Z Individual, A-Z — Continued

467.1.G79 Greene, George Sears
Subarrange by Table E1 at the end of the text

467.1.G88 Grout, William Wallace
Subarrange by Table E1 at the end of the text

467.1.H18 Halleck, Henry Wager
Subarrange by Table E1 at the end of the text

467.1.H19 Hampton, Wade, 1818-1902
Subarrange by Table E1 at the end of the text

467.1.H2 Hancock, Winfield Scott
Subarrange by Table E1 at the end of the text

467.1.H4 Hartranft, John Frederick
Subarrange by Table E1 at the end of the text

467.1.H44 Hatton, Robert
Subarrange by Table E1 at the end of the text

467.1.H58 Hood, John Bell
Subarrange by Table E1 at the end of the text

467.1.H6 Hooker, Joseph
Subarrange by Table E1 at the end of the text

467.1.H7 Hovey, Alvin Peterson
Subarrange by Table E1 at the end of the text

467.1.H8 Howard, Oliver Otis
Subarrange by Table E1 at the end of the text

467.1.H885 Humphreys, Andrew
Subarrange by Table E1 at the end of the text

467.1.H89 Hunt, Henry Jackson
Subarrange by Table E1 at the end of the text

467.1.H9 Hunter, David
Subarrange by Table E1 at the end of the text

467.1.J15 Jackson, Thomas Jonathan
Subarrange by Table E1 at the end of the text

467.1.J73 Johnston, Albert Sidney
Subarrange by Table E1 at the end of the text

467.1.J74 Johnston, Joseph Eggleston
Subarrange by Table E1 at the end of the text

467.1.K24 Kearny, Philip
Subarrange by Table E1 at the end of the text

467.1.L4 Lee, Robert Edward
Subarrange by Table E1 at the end of the text

467.1.L5 Logan, Thomas Muldrup
Subarrange by Table E1 at the end of the text

467.1.L55 Longstreet, James
Subarrange by Table E1 at the end of the text

467.1.L6 Lowell, Charles Russell
Subarrange by Table E1 at the end of the text

467.1.L9 Lyon, Nathaniel
Subarrange by Table E1 at the end of the text

467.1.M2 McClellan, George Brinton
Subarrange by Table E1 at the end of the text
Cf. E458.4, Presidential campaign of 1864

467.1.M24 McCulloch, Ben
Subarrange by Table E1 at the end of the text

467.1.M35 Maffitt, John Newland
Subarrange by Table E1 at the end of the text

467.1.M38 Meade, George Gordon
Subarrange by Table E1 at the end of the text

467.1.M4 Meagher, Thomas Francis
Subarrange by Table E1 at the end of the text

The Civil War, 1861-1865

Biography

467.1.A-.1.Z Individual, A-Z — Continued

467.1.M6 Mitchel, Ormsby Macknight

Subarrange by Table E1 at the end of the text

467.1.M86 Morgan, John Hunt

Subarrange by Table E1 at the end of the text

467.1.M87 Mosby, John Singleton

Subarrange by Table E1 at the end of the text

467.1.O7 Ord, Edward Otho Cresap

Subarrange by Table E1 at the end of the text

467.1.P26 Parsons, Lewis Baldwin

Subarrange by Table E1 at the end of the text

467.1.P365 Pemberton, John Clifford

Subarrange by Table E1 at the end of the text

467.1.P37 Pendleton, William Nelson

Subarrange by Table E1 at the end of the text

467.1.P4 Perkins, George Hamilton

Subarrange by Table E1 at the end of the text

467.1.P51 Pettigrew, James Johnston

Subarrange by Table E1 at the end of the text

467.1.P57 Pickett, George Edward

Subarrange by Table E1 at the end of the text

467.1.P7 Polk, Leonidas

Subarrange by Table E1 at the end of the text

467.1.P78 Porter, David Dixon

Subarrange by Table E1 at the end of the text

467.1.P8 Porter, Fitz-John

Subarrange by Table E1 at the end of the text

For conduct at 2d battle of Bull Run and court-martial, see E473.772

467.1.P82 Porter, Horace

Subarrange by Table E1 at the end of the text

467.1.R2 Ramseur, Stephen Dodson

Subarrange by Table E1 at the end of the text

467.1.R25 Rawlins, John Aaron

Subarrange by Table E1 at the end of the text

467.1.R4 Reynolds, John Fulton

Subarrange by Table E1 at the end of the text

467.1.R7 Rosecrans, William Starke

Subarrange by Table E1 at the end of the text

467.1.S32 Schenck, Robert Cumming

Subarrange by Table E1 at the end of the text

467.1.S35 Schofield, John McAllister

Subarrange by Table E1 at the end of the text

467.1.S4 Sedgwick, John

Subarrange by Table E1 at the end of the text

467.1.S47 Semmes, Raphael

Subarrange by Table E1 at the end of the text

467.1.S54 Sheridan, Philip Henry

Subarrange by Table E1 at the end of the text

467.1.S55 Sherman, William Tecumseh

Subarrange by Table E1 at the end of the text

467.1.S552 Sherman, Ellen (Ewing)

Subarrange by Table E1 at the end of the text

467.1.S58 Sigel, Franz

Subarrange by Table E1 at the end of the text

467.1.S63 Slocum, Henry Warner

Subarrange by Table E1 at the end of the text

467.1.S75 Smith, William Farrar

Subarrange by Table E1 at the end of the text

The Civil War, 1861-1865

Biography

467.1.A-.1.Z Individual, A-Z — Continued

467.1.S8 Stanton, Edwin McMasters

Subarrange by Table E1 at the end of the text

467.1.S84 Steedman, James Barrett

Subarrange by Table E1 at the end of the text

467.1.S85 Stephens, Alexander Hamilton

Subarrange by Table E1 at the end of the text

467.1.S87 Stone, Charles Pomeroy

Subarrange by Table E1 at the end of the text

467.1.S9 Stuart, James Ewell Brown

Subarrange by Table E1 at the end of the text

467.1.T4 Thomas, George Henry

Subarrange by Table E1 at the end of the text

467.1.T8 Tucker, John Randolph

Subarrange by Table E1 at the end of the text

467.1.T9 Tyler, Daniel

Subarrange by Table E1 at the end of the text

467.1.T98 Tyndale, Hector

Subarrange by Table E1 at the end of the text

467.1.W13 Wadsworth, James Samuel

Subarrange by Table E1 at the end of the text

467.1.W2 Wallace, Lewis

Subarrange by Table E1 at the end of the text

Cf. PS3130+, Wallace as an author, his works, and criticism of those works

467.1.W3 Wallace, William Henry Lamme

Subarrange by Table E1 at the end of the text

467.1.W4 Warren, Gouverneur Kemble

Subarrange by Table E1 at the end of the text

Cf. E477.675, Warren court-martial

467.1.W46 Welles, Gideon

Subarrange by Table E1 at the end of the text

467.1.W5 Wheeler, Joseph

Subarrange by Table E1 at the end of the text

467.1.W61 Whiting, William Henry Chase

Subarrange by Table E1 at the end of the text

467.1.W69 Wilder, John Thomas

Subarrange by Table E1 at the end of the text

467.1.W72 Williams, Alpheus Starkey

Subarrange by Table E1 at the end of the text

467.1.W74 Wilson, James Harrison

Subarrange by Table E1 at the end of the text

467.1.W77 Winslow, John Ancrum

Subarrange by Table E1 at the end of the text

467.1.W81 Wistar, Isaac Jones

Subarrange by Table E1 at the end of the text

467.1.W94 Wright, Marcus Joseph

Subarrange by Table E1 at the end of the text

Comprehensive works. General histories

Cf. E167, Description and travel, 1861-1865

Cf. E458+, Causes, aims, etc., of the war

Cf. E470+, Military operations

Cf. E482+, F214, The Confederate States of America

468 General works

468.3 Chronology

Cf. E470.1, Chronological lists of battles

468.5 Historiography

Including criticism of histories and textbooks, accuracy and bias of writers, etc.

Cf. E175.85, Criticisms of textbooks, (General)

The Civil War, 1861-1865

Comprehensive works. General histories — Continued

468.7 Pictorial works

Including works important solely or chiefly for the illustrations

468.8 Soldiers' almanacs

468.9 General special

Including otherwise unprovided for topics such as propaganda, name of the war, influence, etc.

Cf. E488.5, Confederate propaganda in foreign countries

Diplomatic history

Including Trent Affair, 1861; Gilmore and Jacquess' conference with Jefferson Davis, 1864; Hampton Roads Conference, 1865; construction of Confederate war vessels in England; etc.

Cf. E440.5, Washington Peace Conference, 1860

Cf. E470.95, Confederates in Canada, and St. Albans Raid

Cf. E488, Confederate diplomatic history

Cf. E596+, Confederate navy

Cf. F1233, French intervention in Mexico

Cf. JX238.A4+, Alabama claims

469 General works

469.8 Foreign public opinion

Cf. E458+, Contemporary addresses on the war

Military operations

470 General works

Including campaigns and battles (General); military histories of the war; narratives of commanders; etc.

For works restricted to a special region, campaign, or battle, see E470+

For lists of battles, see E470.1

Cf. E468+, General history of the war

Cf. E601+, Personal narratives of minor officers and privates

470.1 Battles (Alphabetical or chronological lists)

For individual battles, see E471+

By region

Including military operations of individual armies

Eastern border states

Including Virginia, Maryland, District of Columbia, and Pennsylvania, Army of the James, Army of the Potomac, Army of Virginia, Army of Northern Virginia (C.S.A.)

Personal narratives of service in the Army of the Potomac, if not classed under campaign or regiment, should be classed in E601 rather than E470.2

470.2 General works

470.3 Shenandoah Valley

Western border states

Including Ohio Valley and central Mississippi Valley (West Virginia, Kentucky, Tennessee, Ohio, Indiana, Illinois, Missouri, Arkansas), Army of West Virginia

470.4 General works

470.45 Border warfare. Guerrillas

470.5 Cumberland and Tennessee Valleys. Chattanooga region

Including armies of the Cumberland and the Tennessee, Army of Tennessee (C.S.A.)

470.6 Lower South

Including North Carolina, South Carolina, Georgia, and region west

For Sherman's march, see E476.69

470.65 South Atlantic coast line

Including Siege of Charleston, 1863-1865; supplies for Savannah

Cf. E475.6+, Engagements in Charleston Harbor, 1863

Cf. E476.4+, Engagements in Charleston Harbor, 1864

For Naval operations and blockade running, see E591+

470.7 Gulf States

Including Florida, Alabama, Mississippi, Louisiana, Texas

For Society of the Army and Navy of the Gulf, see E462.99.S62

For naval operations and blockade running, see E591+

470.8 Mississippi Valley

The Civil War, 1861-1865
Military operations
By region — Continued
470.9 Trans-Mississippi region
Including Texas, Indian Territory, Kansas, New Mexico, Missouri, Arkansas, etc., Army of the Pacific
470.95 Northern frontier of the United States
Including Confederates in Canada; St. Albans (Vt.) Raid, 1864
By campaign and battle
Cf. E467.1.A+, Biography of leaders
Cf. E468+, Comprehensive histories of the war
Cf. E470, General military histories, and memoirs of commanders
Cf. E470.2+, Military operations by region, and history of armies
Cf. E493.1, History of corps and divisions
Cf. E493.5, History of brigades
Cf. E495+, E551+, History of regiments
Cf. E547, History of corps, divisions, amd brigades
A history of a regiment in a particular campaign or battle is classed in E471-478, rather than E495-582
The literature of the national military parks at Chickamauga and Chattanooga, Gettysburg, Vicksburg, etc., and descriptive works dealing with the battlefield are classed with the battle
For local guidebooks, see Class F, e.g. F444.C4, Chattanooga
For naval operations in connection with military movements, see E471-478 rather than E591
Opening events
471 General works
471.1 South Carolina, December 20, 1860- April 14, 1861
Including Charleston Harbor (Fort Sumter)
Other southern states
Cf. E440.5, E458.1, E551+, General political history
471.5 General works
471.51 Georgia, January 3-26, 1861
471.52 Alabama and Mississippi, January 4-20, 1861
471.53 Florida, January 6-August 31, 1861
Including Fort Jefferson, Dry Tortugas
471.54 North Carolina, January 9-May 20, 1861
471.55 Louisiana, January 10-February 19, 1861
471.56 Texas and New Mexico, February 1-June 11, 1861
471.57 Arkansas, Indian Territory, and Missouri, February 7-May 9, 1861
Maryland, Pennsylvania, Virginia, and West Virginia, April 16-July 31, 1861
472.1 General works
472.13 Conflict between United States troops and mob in Baltimore, April 19
472.14 Engagement at Big Bethel, June 10
472.16 Operations in Shenandoah Valley, July 2-25
472.17 Campaign in West Virginia, July 6-17
Including Battle of Rich Mountain, July 11
Bull Run Campaign, July 16-22
Including First battle of Bull Run (Manassas), July 21
472.18 General works
472.182 Manassas Battlefield Confederate Park
472.183 Manassas National Battlefield Park
Missouri, Arkansas, Kansas and Indian Territory, May 10-November 19, 1861
472.2 General works
472.23 Battle of Wilson's Creek, August 10
472.25 Siege of Lexington, Mo., September 13-20
472.28 Engagement at Belmont, Mo., and demonstration from Paducah upon Columbus, Ky., November 7
Texas, New Mexico, and Arizona, June 11-February 1, 1862
472.3 General works
472.32 Skirmish at Mesilla, evacuation of Fort Fillmore, and surrender of Union forces at San Augustine, July 25-27

The Civil War, 1861-1865

Military operations

By campaign and battle — Continued

472.4 Kentucky and Tennessee, July 1-November 19, 1861

472.5 North Carolina and southeastern Virginia, August 1, 1861-January 11, 1862

Maryland, northern Virginia, and West Virginia, August 1, 1861-March 17, 1862

472.6 General works

472.63 Operations on the Potomac near Leesburg, Va.

Including engagement at Ball's Bluff and action near Edward's Ferry, October 21-24

Coasts of South Carolina, Georgia, and middle and east Florida, August 21, 1861-April 11, 1862

Including Port Royal Expedition, November, 1861

472.7 General works

472.79 Bombardment and capture of Fort Pulaski, Ga., April 10-11

West Florida, southern Alabama, southern Mississippi, and Louisiana, September 1, 1861-May 12, 1862

472.8 General works

472.88 Bombardment and capture of Forts Jackson and Saint Philip and occupation of New Orleans, by Union forces, April 18-May 1

Cf. E510, General Butler's government of Louisiana

Kentucky, Tennessee, north Alabama, and southwest Virginia, November 19, 1861- March 4, 1862

Including Anna E. Carroll's claim

472.9 General works

472.96 Capture of Fort Henry, Tenn., February 6

472.97 Siege and capture of Fort Donelson, Tenn., February 12-16

Missouri, Arkansas, Kansas, and Indian Territory, November 19, 1861-April 10, 1862

473.1 General works

473.15 Operations at New Madrid, Mo., and Island No. 10, and descent upon Union City, Tenn., February 28-April 8

473.17 Battle of Pea Ridge, March 6-8

473.2 Southeastern Virginia, January 11-March 17, 1862

Including naval engagement in Hampton Roads, Merrimac and Monitor

North Carolina, January 11-August 20, 1862

Including Burnside's Expedition, capture of Elizabeth City, N.C., September 10

473.3 General works

473.31 Battle of Roanoke Island, February 8

473.34 Battle of New Bern, March 14

Texas, New Mexico, and Arizona, February 1- September 20, 1862

Including Battle of Nueces River, August 10

473.4 General works

473.46 Expedition from southern California through Arizona to northwestern Texas and New Mexico, April 13-September 20

Including California column

Kentucky, Tennessee, northern Mississippi, northern Alabama, and southwest Virginia, March 4-June 10, 1862

473.5 General works

473.52 Cumberland Gap campaign, March 28-June 18

473.54 Battle of Shiloh, April 6-7

Including Shiloh National Military Park

473.55 Raid on Confederate line of communication between Chattanooga, Tenn., and Marietta, Ga., April 7-12

Including Andrews' railroad raid

473.56 Advance upon and siege of Corinth, Miss., and pursuit of the Confederate forces, April 29-June 10

473.59 Attack on Chattanooga, Tenn., June 7-8

Peninsular campaign, Va., March 17-September 2, 1862

473.6 General works

473.61 Siege of Yorktown, April 5-May 4

473.63 Battle of Williamsburg, May 5

473.64 Occupation of Norfolk and Portsmouth, May 10

473.65 Battle of Fair Oaks, May 31-June 1

The Civil War, 1861-1865

Military operations

By campaign and battle

Peninsular campaign, Va., March 17-September 2, 1862 — Continued

473.66 Stuart's raid, June 13-15

473.68 Seven days' battles, June 25-July 1

Including Battles of Mechanicsville (Beaver Dam Creek), June 26; Gaines' Mill, June 27; Savage Station, June 29; Glendale (Frayser's Farm), June 30; Malvern Hill, July 1

Northern Virginia, West Virginia, and Maryland, March 17-September 2, 1862

Including General Pope's Virginia campaign

473.7 General works

473.72 Battle of Kernstown, Va., March 23

473.74 Operations in the Shenandoah Valley, May 15-June 17

473.76 Battle of Cedar Mountain, August 9

Campaign in northern Virginia, August 16-September 2

Including Battles of Groveton, August 28-29; Bull Run (Second battle), August 30; Chantilly, September 1

473.77 General works

473.772 Fitz-John Porter case

473.8 Missouri, Arkansas, Kansas, Indian Territory, and the Department of the Northwest, April 10-November 20, 1862

Cf. E83.86, Sioux Indian War, 1862-1865

Coasts of South Carolina, Georgia, and middle and east Florida, April 12, 1862-June 11, 1863

473.9 General works

473.92 Engagement at Secessionville (James Island), S.C., June 16, 1862

473.96 Engagement in Charleston Harbor, April 7, 1863

West Florida, southern Alabama, southern Mississippi, and Louisiana, May 12, 1862- May 14, 1863. Texas, New Mexico, and Arizona, September 20, 1862-May 14, 1863

Including Battle of Galveston, January 1, 1863

For Grierson's raid, April 17-May 2, 1863, see E475.23

474.1 General works

474.11 Operations against Vicksburg, Miss., and Baton Rouge, La., May 18-August 6, 1862

Including The Essex (U.S. ironclad) and Arkansas (Confederate ironclad)

474.17 Operations against and about Port Hudson, La., March 7-27, 1863

474.18 Operations in west Louisiana, April 9-May 14, 1863

Kentucky, middle and east Tennessee, north Alabama, and southwest Virginia, June 10-October 31, 1862

474.3 General works

474.32 Morgan's first Kentucky raid, July 4-28

474.34 Action at and surrender of Murfreesboro, Tenn., July 13

474.37 Battle of Richmond, Ky., August 30

474.38 Evacuation of Cumberland Gap, Tenn., September 17-October 3

474.39 Battle of Perryville, Ky., October 8

West Tennessee and northern Mississippi, June 10, 1862-January 20, 1863

474.4 General works

474.42 Engagement at Iuka, Miss., September 19

474.44 Battle of Corinth, Miss., and pursuit of the Confederate forces, October 3-12

474.46 Forrest's expedition into west Tennessee, December 15-January 2

474.47 Operations against Vicksburg, December 20-January 3

474.48 Expedition against Arkansas Post or Fort Hindman, Ark., and operations in that vicinity, January 4-17

North Carolina and southeastern Virginia, August 20, 1862-June 3, 1863

474.5 General works

474.52 Expedition from New Bern, to Goldsboro, N.C., December 11-20, 1862

474.55 Siege of Washington, N.C. and pursuit of the Confederate forces, March 30-April 20, 1863

Northern Virginia, West Virginia, Maryland, and Pennsylvania, September 3-November 14, 1862

474.6 General works

The Maryland campaign, September 3-20

Including siege of Harper's Ferry, September 14-15

474.61 General works

The Civil War, 1861-1865
Military operations
By campaign and battle
Northern Virginia, West Virginia, Maryland, and Pennsylvania, September 3-November 14, 1862
The Maryland campaign, September 3-20 — Continued
474.65 Battle of Antietam, September 17
Including Antietam National Cemetery
474.67 Stuart's expedition into Maryland and Pennsylvania, October 9-12
Kentucky, middle and east Tennessee, north Alabama, and southwest Virginia, November 1, 1862-January 20, 1863
474.7 General works
474.75 Morgan's second Kentucky raid, December 22-January 2
474.77 The Stone's River or Murfreesboro, Tenn. campaign, December 26-January 5
Including Stones River National Military Park
Northern Virginia, West Virginia, Maryland, and Pennsylvania, November 15, 1862-January 25, 1863
474.8 General works
474.85 Battle of Fredericksburg, Va., December 11-15
Including Fredericksburg and Spotsylvania County National Military Park
Missouri, Arkansas, Kansas, Indian Territory, and the Department of the Northwest, November 20, 1862-December 31, 1863
Including Battles of Helena, Ark., July 4; and Baxter Springs, Kans., October 6
Cf. E83.86, Sioux Indian War, 1862-1865
474.9 General works
474.92 Battle of Prairie Grove, Ark., December 7, 1862
474.94 Battle of Fayetteville, Ark., April 18, 1863
474.96 Advance of Union forces upon Little Rock, Ark., August 1-September 14, 1863
474.97 Quantrill's raid into Kansas and pursuit by Union forces, August 20-28
Including the Lawrence massacre and burning, August 21
474.98 Shelby's raid in Arkansas and Missouri, September 22-October 26
Kentucky, middle and east Tennessee, north Alabama, and southwest Virginia, January 21-August 10, 1863
Including Streight's raid toward Rome, Ga., April-May 1863
475.1 General works
475.16 The middle Tennessee or Tullahoma campaign, June 23-July 7
475.18 Morgan's raid in Kentucky, Indiana, and Ohio, July 2-26
Mississippi and West Tennessee
Including operations in Arkansas and Louisiana connected with the siege of Vicksburg, January 20-August 10, 1863
475.2 General works
475.22 Yazoo Pass expedition, February 24-April 8
475.23 Grierson's raid from La Grange, Tenn., to Baton Rouge, La., April 17-May 2
475.24 Battle of Port Gibson, Miss., May 1
475.26 Battle of Champion's Hill, May 16
475.27 Siege of Vicksburg, Miss., May 19-July 4
Including Vicksburg National Military Park
475.29 The Jackson, Miss., campaign, July 5-25
Northern Virginia, West Virginia, Maryland, and Pennsylvania, January 26-June 3, 1863
Including Battle of Kelly's Ford, March 17
475.3 General works
475.35 The Chancellorsville campaign, April 27- May 6
475.38 The Stoneman raid, April 29-May 7
West Florida, southern Alabama, southern Mississippi, Louisiana, Texas, and New Mexico, May 14-December 31, 1863
Including engagements at Milliken's Bend, June 7, and Sabine Pass, September 8
For siege of Vicksburg, see E475.27
475.4 General works
475.42 Siege of Port Hudson, La., May 22-July 8

The Civil War, 1861-1865

Military operations

By campaign and battle — Continued

475.5 North Carolina, Virginia, West Virginia, Maryland, Pennsylvania, and Department of the East, June 3-August 3, 1863

Including Battle of Middleburg, Va., June 17-18

Cf. F128.44, Draft riots in New York City, June 13-16

The Gettysburg campaign, June 3-August 1

Including Battle of Hanover, Pa., June 30

475.51 General works

475.53 Battle of Gettysburg

475.55 Gettysburg National Cemetery

Including dedication, national monument, and Lincoln's Gettysburg address

475.56 Gettysburg National Military Park

Including state, regimental, and other monuments

For acccounts of the battle, see E475.53

475.57 Fiftieth anniversary celebration, 1913

475.58 Seventy-fifth anniversary celebration, 1938

475.582 One-hundredth anniversary celebration, 1963

Coasts of South Carolina and Georgia. Middle and east Florida, June 12- December 31, 1863

475.6 General works

475.62 Charleston Harbor, April-December, 1863

475.63 Operations on Morris Island, S.C., July 10-September 7

Including attack and fall of Battery Wagner

475.65 Bombardment of Fort Sumter, August 17- December 31

475.68 Engagement in Charleston Harbor, September 7-8

North Carolina, Virginia, West Virginia, Maryland, and Pennsylvania, August 4-December 31, 1863

475.7 General works

475.75 The Bristoe, Va., campaign, October 9-22

475.76 Expeditions from Beverly and Charleston against Lewisburg, W. Va., November 1-7

Including Battle of Droop Mountain, W. Va., November 6

475.78 Mine Run, Va., campaign, November 26- December 2

Kentucky, southwest Virginia, Tennessee, Mississippi, north Alabama, and north Georgia, August 11-October 19, 1863

475.8 General works

475.81 Chickamauga, Ga., campaign, August 16- September 22

Including Chickamauga and Chattanooga National Park

475.85 East Tennessee campaign, August 16-October 19

475.87 Wheeler and Roddey's raid, September 30- October 17

475.88 Chalmer's raid in west Tennessee and northern Mississippi, October 4-17

Kentucky, southwest Virginia, Tennessee, Mississippi, north Alabama, and north Georgia, October 20-December 31, 1863

475.9 General works

475.92 Reopening of the Tennessee River, October 26-29

Including skirmish at Brown's Ferry and engagement at Wauhatchie, Tenn., October 29

475.94 Knoxville, Tenn., campaign, November 4- December 23

Including Attack upon Fort Sanders, November 29

475.97 Chattanooga-Ringgold campaign, November 23-27

Including Battles of Lookout Mountain and Missionary Ridge

Kentucky, southwest Virginia, Tennessee, Mississippi, Alabama, and north Georgia, January 1-April 30, 1864

476.1 General works

476.14 The Meridian, Miss., expedition, February 3-March 6

Including cooperating expeditions from Memphis and up the Yazoo River

476.17 Forrest's expedition into west Tennessee and Kentucky, March 16-April 14

Including Massacre at Fort Pillow, April 12

North Carolina, Virginia, West Virginia, Maryland, and Pennsylvania, January 1-April 30, 1864

476.2 General works

476.23 Expedition against New Bern, N.C., January 28-February 10

The Civil War, 1861-1865
Military operations
By campaign and battle
North Carolina, Virginia, West Virginia, Maryland, and Pennsylvania, January 1-April 30, 1864 — Continued
476.27 Kilpatrick's expedition against Richmond, February 28-March 4
Including Dahlgren's raid
Louisiana and the trans-Mississippi states and territories, January 1-June 30, 1864
476.3 General works
476.33 Red River, La., campaign, March 10-May 22
Including Battle of Pleasant Hill, La., April 9
476.35 Camden, Ark., expedition, March 23-May 3
Including Battle of Fitzhugh's Woods, April 1
South Carolina, Florida, and coast of Georgia, January 1-November 13, 1864
476.4 General works
476.41 Operations in Charleston Harbor and vicinity, January 1-November 13
476.43 Florida expedition, February 5-22
Including Battle of Olustee, February 20
Southeastern Virginia and North Carolina, May 1-June 12, 1864
476.5 General works
476.52 Campaign from the Rapidan to the James, May 4-June 12
Including Battle of the Wilderness, May 5-7; Spottsylvania, May 8-21; Cold Harbor, June 3
476.57 Operations on the south side of the James, May 4-June 2
Including Bermuda Hundred, Va., May 16-30
476.59 Engagement at Petersburg, Va., June 9
Northern Virginia, West Virginia, Maryland, and Pennsylvania, May 1-August 3, 1864
476.6 General works
476.62 Expedition against the Virginia and Tennessee Railroad, May 2-19
476.64 Engagement at New Market, Va., May 15
476.65 Lynchburg campaign, May 26-June 29
476.66 Operations in the Shenandoah Valley, Maryland, and Pennsylvania, June 23-August 3
Including Maryland campaign: Battle of Monocacy River, July 9; attack on Fort Stevens, Washington, D.C., July 11-12
For burning of Chambersburg, Pa., July 30, see F159.C4
476.69 Sherman's march, May 1864-April 1865
Cf. E476.7, Atlanta, Ga., campaign, May 1-September 8, 1864
Cf. E476.87, Operations in north Georgia and north Alabama, September 29-November 13, 1864
Cf. E477.41, Savannah campaign, November 15-December 21
Cf. E477.7, North Carolina (from February 1), South Carolina, southern Georgia, and east Florida, January 1-June 30, 1865
476.7 Atlanta, Ga., campaign, May 1-September 8, 1864
Including Battles of New Hope Church, May 24-28; Kennesaw Mountain, June 27; Peachtree Creek, July 20; Jonesboro (Jonesborough), August 31-September 1; capture of Atlanta, September 1
Including Kennesaw Mountain National Battlefield Park
Kentucky, southwest Virginia, Tennessee, Mississippi, Alabama, and north Georgia, May 1-November 13, 1864
For Atlanta campaign, see E476.7
476.8 General works
476.82 Morgan's raid into Kentucky, May 31-June 20
476.83 Expedition from Memphis, Tenn., into Mississippi, June 1-13
476.84 Expedition from La Grange, Tenn., to Tupelo, Miss., July 5-21
476.85 Operations in Mobile Bay, August 2-23
476.87 Operations in north Georgia and north Alabama, September 29-November 13
Including Battle of Allatoona, October 5
Southeastern Virginia and North Carolina, June 13-July 31, 1864
476.9 General works
Richmond campaign, June 13-July 31
476.91 General works

The Civil War, 1861-1865
Military operations
By campaign and battle
Southeastern Virginia and North Carolina, June 13-July 31, 1864
Richmond campaign, June 13-July 31 — Continued
476.93 Siege of Petersburg. Battle of Petersburg Crater
Including Petersburg National Military Park
Louisiana and the trans-Mississippi states and territories, July 1-December 31, 1864
Cf. E83.863, Indian campaigns in Dakota
477.1 General works
477.16 Price's Missouri expedition, August 29- December 2
Including Battles of Pilot Knob, September 27; Westport, October 21-23; Big Blue, October 22
Southeastern Virginia and North Carolina, August 1-December 31, 1864
477.2 General works
477.21 Richmond campaign, August 1-December 31
Including Weldon Railroad; battle and capture of Fort Harrison, September 29-30
477.28 Expedition to and operations against Fort Fisher, N.C., December 7-27
Northern Virginia, West Virginia, Maryland, and Pennsylvania, August 4-December 31, 1864
477.3 General works
477.33 Shenandoah Valley campaign, August 7- November 28
Including Battles of Winchester, September 19; Fisher's Hill, September 22; Cedar Creek, October 19
South Carolina, Georgia, and Florida, November 14-December 31, 1864
477.4 General works
477.41 Savannah campaign, November 15-December 21
477.44 Engagement at Honey Hill, S.C., November 30
Kentucky, southwest Virginia, Tennessee, Mississippi, Alabama, and north Georgia, November 14, 1864-January 23, 1865
477.5 General works
477.52 Campaign in north Alabama and middle Tennessee, November 14, 1864-January 23, 1865
Including Battles of Spring Hill, Tenn., November 29; Franklin, Tenn., November 30; Nashville, December 15-16
Northern and southeastern Virginia, North Carolina (January 1-31), West Virginia, Maryland, and Pennsylvania, January 1-June 30, 1865
477.6 General works
477.61 Richmond campaign, January 1-April 3
Including attack on Fort Stedman, March 25; evacuation of Petersburg, April 2
477.63 Expedition to and capture of Fort Fisher, N.C., January 3-17
477.65 Expedition from Winchester to the front of Petersburg, February 27-March 28
Appomattox campaign, March 29-April 9
Including Battles of Gravelly Run, Dinwiddie Courthouse, Five Forks
477.67 General works
477.675 Warren court-martial
North Carolina (from February 1), South Carolina, southern Georgia, and east Florida, January 1-June 30, 1865
Including Campaign of the Carolinas
477.7 General works
477.75 Capture and burning of Columbia, S.C., February 17-18
477.8 Louisiana and the trans-Mississippi states and territories, January 1-June 30, 1865
Cf. E83.863, Indian campaigns
Kentucky, southwestern Virginia, Tennessee, northern and central Georgia, Mississippi, Alabama, and west Florida, January 1-June 30, 1865
Including Stoneman's raid, March 24-April 15; Gillem's raid, April 15-25
477.9 General works
477.94 Mobile campaign, March 17-May 4
477.96 Wilson's raid from Chickasaw to Selma, Ala., and Macon, Ga., March 22-April 24
Including Capture of Columbus, Ga., April 16
477.98 Pursuit and capture of Jefferson Davis, May 1-10

The Civil War, 1861-1865
Military operations
By campaign and battle — Continued
478.1 Pacific coast, January 1, 1861-June 30, 1865
For expedition from southern California through Arizona to northwestern Texas and New Mexico, April 13-September 20, 1862, see E473.46
Cf. E83.86, Indian campaigns
Cf. E83.863, Indian wars
Finance. Commerce. Confiscations, etc.
Including abandoned and confiscable property, blockade, government contracts, purchase of products from insurgents, war claims
Cf. HF3027.6, History of United States commerce during Civil War
Cf. HJ251+, Public finance of Civil War
Cf. HJ2371+, Revenue and taxation during Civil War
Cf. JK347, Military rule, martial law, etc., during Civil War
480 General works
480.5 Confederate States of America
Confederate States of America
482 Periodicals
483 Societies
483.1 United Confederate Veterans
483.2 Confederate Veteran Association of Kentucky
483.25 Society of the Army and Navy of the Confederate States, Maryland
483.28 Grand Camp Confederate Veterans, Department of Virginia
483.4 Sons of Confederate Veterans
Formerly United Sons of Confederate Veterans
483.5 United Daughters of the Confederacy
483.55 Children of the Confederacy
483.7 Southern Historical Society
483.72 Confederate Southern Memorial Association
483.75 Confederate Memorial Literary Society
483.99.A-.99.Z Other societies, A-Z
483.99.C78 Confederate Veterans' Association of Fulton County, Georgia
484 Collections. Collected works
Biography (Collective and individual), *see* E467+
Description and travel, social conditions, etc., *see* F214
487 History (General). Political history
Including administration of Jefferson Davis and memoirs and reminiscences of civil officials and noncombatants
Cf. E458+, Political history and causes of the war
Cf. E468, General histories of the war
Cf. E470+, Military operations
Cf. JK9663+, C.S.A. documents
488 Diplomatic history
Cf. E469+, Diplomatic history of the United States
Cf. E596+, Foreign-built Confederate cruisers
Military history, *see* E470.2+, E545+
Naval history, *see* E591+
Economic history, *see* HC105.65
Addresses, sermons, etc., *see* E650
Commemorations, Memorial Day, *see* E645
Battle Abbey, Richmond, *see* F234.R5
Flags, *see* E646
Hospitals, *see* E625
Military prisons, *see* E611
488.5 Propaganda in foreign countries
Secret Service, Signal Corps., *see* E608
Union men in the South, *see* E458.7
489 Other (not A-Z)

The Civil War, 1861-1865 — Continued
Armies. Troops
The Union Army
491 General works
Including administration, organization, volunteering, conscription, Southern federals, statistics, numbers and losses, Civil War medals of honor, transportation, supplies, etc.
Arms of the service
492 General works
United States regular troops
For general histories of regular army organizations, see UA24+
492.3 General works
492.4 Infantry
Subarrange by number or name of regiment, A-Z. By author, A-Z
492.5 Cavalry
Subarrange by number or name of regiment, A-Z. By author, A-Z
492.6 Artillery
Subarrange by number or name of regiment, A-Z. By author, A-Z
492.7 Other (not A-Z)
Including Balloon Service, Corps of Engineers, Sharpshooters, etc.
For Secret Service, Signal Corps, see E608
Afro-American regiments
For general subject of Afro-Americans in the war, see E540.N3
For various state regiments of Afro-Americans, see E495+
492.9 General works
492.94 Infantry
Subarrange by number or name of regiment, A-Z. By author, A-Z
492.95 Cavalry
Subarrange by number or name of regiment, A-Z. By author, A-Z
493.1 Corps. Divisions
Including associations, societies, unions, etc., of individual corps
Subarrange by number or name of corps, A-Z. By author, A-Z
493.5 Brigades
Subarrange by number or name of brigade, A-Z. By author, A-Z
Including associations, reunions, etc., of individual brigades
For a brigade consisting entirely of troops from a single state whether infantry or cavalry, see E495-537, subdivision .4 under state number, e.g. E507.4.C9, Crocker's Iowa Brigade
493.9 First defenders or Minute Men of 1861
Including works on the troops who responded to President Lincoln's first call of April 15, 1861
494 Registers, lists of the dead and wounded, etc.
Including lists of soldiers and officers from more than one state and veterans residing in particular states
For veterans residing in a county or town, see local biography in Class F
For lists of prisoners, see E611
495-537 By state
Including state political history, 1861-1865; quotas in war; war governors
For a comprehensive history of a state militia regiment, see UA50+
For military operations in a state, see E470.2+
For relief associations, see E629
Alabama
For campaigns and battles, see E471+
For Civil War, campaigns and battles, see E470.6, E470.7
For Confederate history, see E471.52, E551.1+
495 General works
495.1 Official publications on the raising, equipment, and service of the troops in the war
495.2 Adjutant Generals' reports for 1861-1865
495.3 Lists of soldiers. Lists of the state's dead
For the seceded states, this subdivision is used for Union troops

The Civil War, 1861-1865
Armies. Troops
The Union Army
495-537 By state
Alabama — Continued
495.4 Histories of the states' troops
Including collected biographies or lists of officers, general associations of survivors, the draft, state brigades, state memorials and monuments, the state's battle flags, lists of citizens serving in organizations of other states
For the seceded states, this subdivision is used for Union troops
Military organizations
For the seceded states, this subdivision is used for Union troops
495.5 Infantry
For the seceded states, this subdivision is used for Union troops
Subarrange by number or name of regiment, A-Z. By author, A-Z, e.g. E527.5.L6, Logan Guards
495.6 Cavalry
For the seceded states, this subdivision is used for Union troops
Subarrange by number or name of regiment, A-Z. By author, A-Z
495.7 Artillery, Heavy
For the seceded states, this subdivision is used for Union troops
Subarrange by number or name of regiment, A-Z. By author, A-Z
495.8 Artillery, Light
For the seceded states, this subdivision is used for Union troops
Subarrange by number or name of regiment, A-Z. By author, A-Z
495.9 Other (not A-Z)
For the seceded states, this subdivision is used for Union troops
History of a town or county's participation in the Civil War, and local lists of soldiers, are classed in local history (F1-900). If, however, the town was the seat of military operations, as Chambersburg, Pa., the literature is found in E471-478, or where several sieges or battles are covered, in E470.2-.9 (e.g., a history of all military operations around Richmond)
495.95 Arizona
Not to be further subdivided
Arkansas
For Confederate history, see E471.57, E553.1+
For campaigns and battles, see E470.4+, E470.8-.9, E471+
496 General works
496.1 Official publications on the raising, equipment, and service of the troops in the war
496.2 Adjutant Generals' reports for 1861-1865
496.3 Lists of soldiers. Lists of the state's dead
For the seceded states, this subdivision is used for Union troops
496.4 Histories of the states' troops
Including collected biographies or lists of officers, general associations of survivors, the draft, state brigades, state memorials and monuments, the state's battle flags, lists of citizens serving in organizations of other states
For the seceded states, this subdivision is used for Union troops
Military organizations
For the seceded states, this subdivision is used for Union troops
496.5 Infantry
For the seceded states, this subdivision is used for Union troops
Subarrange by number or name of regiment, A-Z. By author, A-Z, e.g. E527.5.L6, Logan Guards
496.6 Cavalry
For the seceded states, this subdivision is used for Union troops
Subarrange by number or name of regiment, A-Z. By author, A-Z
496.7 Artillery, Heavy
For the seceded states, this subdivision is used for Union troops
Subarrange by number or name of regiment, A-Z. By author, A-Z

The Civil War, 1861-1865

Armies. Troops

The Union Army

495-537 By state

Arkansas

Military organizations — Continued

496.8 Artillery, Light

For the seceded states, this subdivision is used for Union troops

Subarrange by number or name of regiment, A-Z. By author, A-Z

496.9 Other (not A-Z)

For the seceded states, this subdivision is used for Union troops

History of a town or county's participation in the Civil War, and local lists of soldiers, are classed in local history (F1-900). If, however, the town was the seat of military operations, as Chambersburg, Pa., the literature is found in E471-478, or where several sieges or battles are covered, in E470.2-.9 (e.g., a history of all military operations around Richmond)

California

Cf. E473.46, The California column, 1862

497 General works

497.1 Official publications on the raising, equipment, and service of the troops in the war

497.2 Adjutant Generals' reports for 1861-1865

497.3 Lists of soldiers. Lists of the state's dead

For the seceded states, this subdivision is used for Union troops

497.4 Histories of the states' troops

Including collected biographies or lists of officers, general associations of survivors, the draft, state brigades, state memorials and monuments, the state's battle flags, lists of citizens serving in organizations of other states

For the seceded states, this subdivision is used for Union troops

Military organizations

For the seceded states, this subdivision is used for Union troops

497.5 Infantry

For the seceded states, this subdivision is used for Union troops

Subarrange by number or name of regiment, A-Z. By author, A-Z, e.g. E527.5.L6, Logan Guards

497.6 Cavalry

For the seceded states, this subdivision is used for Union troops

Subarrange by number or name of regiment, A-Z. By author, A-Z

497.7 Artillery, Heavy

For the seceded states, this subdivision is used for Union troops

Subarrange by number or name of regiment, A-Z. By author, A-Z

497.8 Artillery, Light

For the seceded states, this subdivision is used for Union troops

Subarrange by number or name of regiment, A-Z. By author, A-Z

497.9 Other (not A-Z)

For the seceded states, this subdivision is used for Union troops

History of a town or county's participation in the Civil War, and local lists of soldiers, are classed in local history (F1-900). If, however, the town was the seat of military operations, as Chambersburg, Pa., the literature is found in E471-478, or where several sieges or battles are covered, in E470.2-.9 (e.g., a history of all military operations around Richmond)

Colorado

498 General works

498.1 Official publications on the raising, equipment, and service of the troops in the war

498.2 Adjutant Generals' reports for 1861-1865

498.3 Lists of soldiers. Lists of the state's dead

For the seceded states, this subdivision is used for Union troops

498.4 Histories of the states' troops

Including collected biographies or lists of officers, general associations of survivors, the draft, state brigades, state memorials and monuments, the state's battle flags, lists of citizens serving in organizations of other states

The Civil War, 1861-1865
Armies. Troops
The Union Army
495-537 By state
Colorado
498.4 Histories of the states' troops — Continued
For the seceded states, this subdivision is used for Union troops
Military organizations
For the seceded states, this subdivision is used for Union troops
498.5 Infantry
For the seceded states, this subdivision is used for Union troops
Subarrange by number or name of regiment, A-Z. By author, A-Z, e.g. E527.5.L6, Logan Guards
498.6 Cavalry
For the seceded states, this subdivision is used for Union troops
Subarrange by number or name of regiment, A-Z. By author, A-Z
498.7 Artillery, Heavy
For the seceded states, this subdivision is used for Union troops
Subarrange by number or name of regiment, A-Z. By author, A-Z
498.8 Artillery, Light
For the seceded states, this subdivision is used for Union troops
Subarrange by number or name of regiment, A-Z. By author, A-Z
498.9 Other (not A-Z)
For the seceded states, this subdivision is used for Union troops
History of a town or county's participation in the Civil War, and local lists of soldiers, are classed in local history (F1-900). If, however, the town was the seat of military operations, as Chambersburg, Pa., the literature is found in E471-478, or where several sieges or battles are covered, in E470.2-.9 (e.g., a history of all military operations around Richmond)
Connecticut
Including biography: William Alfred Buckingham, etc.
499 General works
499.1 Official publications on the raising, equipment, and service of the troops in the war
499.2 Adjutant Generals' reports for 1861-1865
499.3 Lists of soldiers. Lists of the state's dead
For the seceded states, this subdivision is used for Union troops
499.4 Histories of the states' troops
Including collected biographies or lists of officers, general associations of survivors, the draft, state brigades, state memorials and monuments, the state's battle flags, lists of citizens serving in organizations of other states
For the seceded states, this subdivision is used for Union troops
Military organizations
For the seceded states, this subdivision is used for Union troops
499.5 Infantry
For the seceded states, this subdivision is used for Union troops
Subarrange by number or name of regiment, A-Z. By author, A-Z, e.g. E527.5.L6, Logan Guards
499.6 Cavalry
For the seceded states, this subdivision is used for Union troops
Subarrange by number or name of regiment, A-Z. By author, A-Z
499.7 Artillery, Heavy
For the seceded states, this subdivision is used for Union troops
Subarrange by number or name of regiment, A-Z. By author, A-Z
499.8 Artillery, Light
For the seceded states, this subdivision is used for Union troops
Subarrange by number or name of regiment, A-Z. By author, A-Z
499.9 Other (not A-Z)
For the seceded states, this subdivision is used for Union troops

The Civil War, 1861-1865
Armies. Troops
The Union Army
495-537 By state
Connecticut
Military organizations
499.9 Other (not A-Z) — Continued
History of a town or county's participation in the Civil War, and local lists of soldiers, are classed in local history (F1-900). If, however, the town was the seat of military operations, as Chambersburg, Pa., the literature is found in E471-478, or where several sieges or battles are covered, in E470.2-.9 (e.g., a history of all military operations around Richmond)
Dakota Territory, *see* E530.1+
Delaware
500 General works
500.1 Official publications on the raising, equipment, and service of the troops in the war
500.2 Adjutant Generals' reports for 1861-1865
500.3 Lists of soldiers. Lists of the state's dead
For the seceded states, this subdivision is used for Union troops
500.4 Histories of the states' troops
Including collected biographies or lists of officers, general associations of survivors, the draft, state brigades, state memorials and monuments, the state's battle flags, lists of citizens serving in organizations of other states
For the seceded states, this subdivision is used for Union troops
Military organizations
For the seceded states, this subdivision is used for Union troops
500.5 Infantry
For the seceded states, this subdivision is used for Union troops
Subarrange by number or name of regiment, A-Z. By author, A-Z, e.g. E527.5.L6, Logan Guards
500.6 Cavalry
For the seceded states, this subdivision is used for Union troops
Subarrange by number or name of regiment, A-Z. By author, A-Z
500.7 Artillery, Heavy
For the seceded states, this subdivision is used for Union troops
Subarrange by number or name of regiment, A-Z. By author, A-Z
500.8 Artillery, Light
For the seceded states, this subdivision is used for Union troops
Subarrange by number or name of regiment, A-Z. By author, A-Z
500.9 Other (not A-Z)
For the seceded states, this subdivision is used for Union troops
History of a town or county's participation in the Civil War, and local lists of soldiers, are classed in local history (F1-900). If, however, the town was the seat of military operations, as Chambersburg, Pa., the literature is found in E471-478, or where several sieges or battles are covered, in E470.2-.9 (e.g., a history of all military operations around Richmond)
District of Columbia
For campaigns and battles, see E470.2+, E471+
501 General works
501.1 Official publications on the raising, equipment, and service of the troops in the war
501.2 Adjutant Generals' reports for 1861-1865
501.3 Lists of soldiers. Lists of the state's dead
For the seceded states, this subdivision is used for Union troops
501.4 Histories of the states' troops
Including collected biographies or lists of officers, general associations of survivors, the draft, state brigades, state memorials and monuments, the state's battle flags, lists of citizens serving in organizations of other states
For the seceded states, this subdivision is used for Union troops
Military organizations
For the seceded states, this subdivision is used for Union troops

The Civil War, 1861-1865
Armies. Troops
The Union Army
495-537 By state
District of Columbia
Military organizations — Continued
501.5 Infantry
For the seceded states, this subdivision is used for Union troops
Subarrange by number or name of regiment, A-Z. By author, A-Z, e.g. E527.5.L6, Logan Guards
501.6 Cavalry
For the seceded states, this subdivision is used for Union troops
Subarrange by number or name of regiment, A-Z. By author, A-Z
501.7 Artillery, Heavy
For the seceded states, this subdivision is used for Union troops
Subarrange by number or name of regiment, A-Z. By author, A-Z
501.8 Artillery, Light
For the seceded states, this subdivision is used for Union troops
Subarrange by number or name of regiment, A-Z. By author, A-Z
501.9 Other (not A-Z)
For the seceded states, this subdivision is used for Union troops
History of a town or county's participation in the Civil War, and local lists of soldiers, are classed in local history (F1-900). If, however, the town was the seat of military operations, as Chambersburg, Pa., the literature is found in E471-478, or where several sieges or battles are covered, in E470.2-.9 (e.g., a history of all military operations around Richmond)
Florida
For Confederate history, see E471.53, E558.1+
For campaigns and battles, see E470.6-.7, E471+
502 General works
502.1 Official publications on the raising, equipment, and service of the troops in the war
502.2 Adjutant Generals' reports for 1861-1865
502.3 Lists of soldiers. Lists of the state's dead
For the seceded states, this subdivision is used for Union troops
502.4 Histories of the states' troops
Including collected biographies or lists of officers, general associations of survivors, the draft, state brigades, state memorials and monuments, the state's battle flags, lists of citizens serving in organizations of other states
For the seceded states, this subdivision is used for Union troops
Military organizations
For the seceded states, this subdivision is used for Union troops
502.5 Infantry
For the seceded states, this subdivision is used for Union troops
Subarrange by number or name of regiment, A-Z. By author, A-Z, e.g. E527.5.L6, Logan Guards
502.6 Cavalry
For the seceded states, this subdivision is used for Union troops
Subarrange by number or name of regiment, A-Z. By author, A-Z
502.7 Artillery, Heavy
For the seceded states, this subdivision is used for Union troops
Subarrange by number or name of regiment, A-Z. By author, A-Z
502.8 Artillery, Light
For the seceded states, this subdivision is used for Union troops
Subarrange by number or name of regiment, A-Z. By author, A-Z
502.9 Other (not A-Z)
For the seceded states, this subdivision is used for Union troops

The Civil War, 1861-1865

Armies. Troops

The Union Army

495-537 By state

Florida

Military organizations

502.9 Other (not A-Z) — Continued

History of a town or county's participation in the Civil War, and local lists of soldiers, are classed in local history (F1-900). If, however, the town was the seat of military operations, as Chambersburg, Pa., the literature is found in E471-478, or where several sieges or battles are covered, in E470.2-.9 (e.g., a history of all military operations around Richmond)

Georgia

For Confederate history, see E471.51, E559.1+

For campaigns and battles, see E470.6, E471+

503 General works

503.1 Official publications on the raising, equipment, and service of the troops in the war

503.2 Adjutant Generals' reports for 1861-1865

503.3 Lists of soldiers. Lists of the state's dead

For the seceded states, this subdivision is used for Union troops

503.4 Histories of the states' troops

Including collected biographies or lists of officers, general associations of survivors, the draft, state brigades, state memorials and monuments, the state's battle flags, lists of citizens serving in organizations of other states

For the seceded states, this subdivision is used for Union troops

Military organizations

For the seceded states, this subdivision is used for Union troops

503.5 Infantry

For the seceded states, this subdivision is used for Union troops

Subarrange by number or name of regiment, A-Z. By author, A-Z, e.g. E527.5.L6, Logan Guards

503.6 Cavalry

For the seceded states, this subdivision is used for Union troops

Subarrange by number or name of regiment, A-Z. By author, A-Z

503.7 Artillery, Heavy

For the seceded states, this subdivision is used for Union troops

Subarrange by number or name of regiment, A-Z. By author, A-Z

503.8 Artillery, Light

For the seceded states, this subdivision is used for Union troops

Subarrange by number or name of regiment, A-Z. By author, A-Z

503.9 Other (not A-Z)

For the seceded states, this subdivision is used for Union troops

History of a town or county's participation in the Civil War, and local lists of soldiers, are classed in local history (F1-900). If, however, the town was the seat of military operations, as Chambersburg, Pa., the literature is found in E471-478, or where several sieges or battles are covered, in E470.2-.9 (e.g., a history of all military operations around Richmond)

Illinois

For campaigns and battles, see E470.4+, E471+

505 General works

505.1 Official publications on the raising, equipment, and service of the troops in the war

505.2 Adjutant Generals' reports for 1861-1865

505.3 Lists of soldiers. Lists of the state's dead

For the seceded states, this subdivision is used for Union troops

505.4 Histories of the states' troops

Including collected biographies or lists of officers, general associations of survivors, the draft, state brigades, state memorials and monuments, the state's battle flags, lists of citizens serving in organizations of other states

For the seceded states, this subdivision is used for Union troops

The Civil War, 1861-1865

Armies. Troops

The Union Army

495-537 By state

Illinois — Continued

Military organizations

For the seceded states, this subdivision is used for Union troops

505.5 Infantry

For the seceded states, this subdivision is used for Union troops

Subarrange by number or name of regiment, A-Z. By author, A-Z, e.g. E527.5.L6, Logan Guards

505.6 Cavalry

For the seceded states, this subdivision is used for Union troops

Subarrange by number or name of regiment, A-Z. By author, A-Z

505.7 Artillery, Heavy

For the seceded states, this subdivision is used for Union troops

Subarrange by number or name of regiment, A-Z. By author, A-Z

505.8 Artillery, Light

For the seceded states, this subdivision is used for Union troops

Subarrange by number or name of regiment, A-Z. By author, A-Z

505.9 Other (not A-Z)

For the seceded states, this subdivision is used for Union troops

History of a town or county's participation in the Civil War, and local lists of soldiers, are classed in local history (F1-900). If, however, the town was the seat of military operations, as Chambersburg, Pa., the literature is found in E471-478, or where several sieges or battles are covered, in E470.2-.9 (e.g., a history of all military operations around Richmond)

505.95 Indian Territory

Not to be further subdivided

For Confederate history, see E471.57, E561

For campaigns and battles, see E470.9, E471+

For preliminaries of the war, see E471.57

For Indian tribes, see E99.A+

Indiana

Including biography: Oliver Perry Morton, etc.

For campaigns and battles, see E470.4+, E471+

506 General works

506.1 Official publications on the raising, equipment, and service of the troops in the war

506.2 Adjutant Generals' reports for 1861-1865

506.3 Lists of soldiers. Lists of the state's dead

For the seceded states, this subdivision is used for Union troops

506.4 Histories of the states' troops

Including collected biographies or lists of officers, general associations of survivors, the draft, state brigades, state memorials and monuments, the state's battle flags, lists of citizens serving in organizations of other states

For the seceded states, this subdivision is used for Union troops

Military organizations

For the seceded states, this subdivision is used for Union troops

506.5 Infantry

For the seceded states, this subdivision is used for Union troops

Subarrange by number or name of regiment, A-Z. By author, A-Z, e.g. E527.5.L6, Logan Guards

506.6 Cavalry

For the seceded states, this subdivision is used for Union troops

Subarrange by number or name of regiment, A-Z. By author, A-Z

506.7 Artillery, Heavy

For the seceded states, this subdivision is used for Union troops

Subarrange by number or name of regiment, A-Z. By author, A-Z

506.8 Artillery, Light

For the seceded states, this subdivision is used for Union troops

The Civil War, 1861-1865
Armies. Troops
The Union Army
495-537 By state
Indiana
Military organizations
506.8 Artillery, Light — Continued
Subarrange by number or name of regiment, A-Z. By author, A-Z
506.9 Other (not A-Z)
For the seceded states, this subdivision is used for Union troops
History of a town or county's participation in the Civil War, and local lists of soldiers, are classed in local history (F1-900). If, however, the town was the seat of military operations, as Chambersburg, Pa., the literature is found in E471-478, or where several sieges or battles are covered, in E470.2-.9 (e.g., a history of all military operations around Richmond)
Iowa
Including biography: Samuel Jordan Kirkwood
507 General works
507.1 Official publications on the raising, equipment, and service of the troops in the war
507.2 Adjutant Generals' reports for 1861-1865
507.3 Lists of soldiers. Lists of the state's dead
For the seceded states, this subdivision is used for Union troops
507.4 Histories of the states' troops
Including collected biographies or lists of officers, general associations of survivors, the draft, state brigades, state memorials and monuments, the state's battle flags, lists of citizens serving in organizations of other states
For the seceded states, this subdivision is used for Union troops
Military organizations
For the seceded states, this subdivision is used for Union troops
507.5 Infantry
For the seceded states, this subdivision is used for Union troops
Subarrange by number or name of regiment, A-Z. By author, A-Z, e.g. E527.5.L6, Logan Guards
507.6 Cavalry
For the seceded states, this subdivision is used for Union troops
Subarrange by number or name of regiment, A-Z. By author, A-Z
507.7 Artillery, Heavy
For the seceded states, this subdivision is used for Union troops
Subarrange by number or name of regiment, A-Z. By author, A-Z
507.8 Artillery, Light
For the seceded states, this subdivision is used for Union troops
Subarrange by number or name of regiment, A-Z. By author, A-Z
507.9 Other (not A-Z)
For the seceded states, this subdivision is used for Union troops
History of a town or county's participation in the Civil War, and local lists of soldiers, are classed in local history (F1-900). If, however, the town was the seat of military operations, as Chambersburg, Pa., the literature is found in E471-478, or where several sieges or battles are covered, in E470.2-.9 (e.g., a history of all military operations around Richmond)
Kansas
For campaigns and battles, see E470.9, E471+
508 General works
508.1 Official publications on the raising, equipment, and service of the troops in the war
508.2 Adjutant Generals' reports for 1861-1865
508.3 Lists of soldiers. Lists of the state's dead
For the seceded states, this subdivision is used for Union troops
508.4 Histories of the states' troops
Including collected biographies or lists of officers, general associations of survivors, the draft, state brigades, state memorials and monuments, the state's battle flags, lists of citizens serving in organizations of other states

The Civil War, 1861-1865
Armies. Troops
The Union Army
495-537 By state
Kansas
508.4 Histories of the states' troops — Continued
For the seceded states, this subdivision is used for Union troops
Military organizations
For the seceded states, this subdivision is used for Union troops
508.5 Infantry
For the seceded states, this subdivision is used for Union troops
Subarrange by number or name of regiment, A-Z. By author, A-Z, e.g. E527.5.L6, Logan Guards
508.6 Cavalry
For the seceded states, this subdivision is used for Union troops
Subarrange by number or name of regiment, A-Z. By author, A-Z
508.7 Artillery, Heavy
For the seceded states, this subdivision is used for Union troops
Subarrange by number or name of regiment, A-Z. By author, A-Z
508.8 Artillery, Light
For the seceded states, this subdivision is used for Union troops
Subarrange by number or name of regiment, A-Z. By author, A-Z
508.9 Other (not A-Z)
For the seceded states, this subdivision is used for Union troops
History of a town or county's participation in the Civil War, and local lists of soldiers, are classed in local history (F1-900). If, however, the town was the seat of military operations, as Chambersburg, Pa., the literature is found in E471-478, or where several sieges or battles are covered, in E470.2-.9 (e.g., a history of all military operations around Richmond)
Kentucky
For Confederate history, see E564.1+
For campaigns and battles, see E470.4+, E470.5, E470.8, E471+
509 General works
509.1 Official publications on the raising, equipment, and service of the troops in the war
509.2 Adjutant Generals' reports for 1861-1865
509.3 Lists of soldiers. Lists of the state's dead
For the seceded states, this subdivision is used for Union troops
509.4 Histories of the states' troops
Including collected biographies or lists of officers, general associations of survivors, the draft, state brigades, state memorials and monuments, the state's battle flags, lists of citizens serving in organizations of other states
For the seceded states, this subdivision is used for Union troops
Military organizations
For the seceded states, this subdivision is used for Union troops
509.5 Infantry
For the seceded states, this subdivision is used for Union troops
Subarrange by number or name of regiment, A-Z. By author, A-Z, e.g. E527.5.L6, Logan Guards
509.6 Cavalry
For the seceded states, this subdivision is used for Union troops
Subarrange by number or name of regiment, A-Z. By author, A-Z
509.7 Artillery, Heavy
For the seceded states, this subdivision is used for Union troops
Subarrange by number or name of regiment, A-Z. By author, A-Z
509.8 Artillery, Light
For the seceded states, this subdivision is used for Union troops
Subarrange by number or name of regiment, A-Z. By author, A-Z
509.9 Other (not A-Z)
For the seceded states, this subdivision is used for Union troops

The Civil War, 1861-1865

Armies. Troops

The Union Army

495-537 By state

Kentucky

Military organizations

509.9 Other (not A-Z) — Continued

History of a town or county's participation in the Civil War, and local lists of soldiers, are classed in local history (F1-900). If, however, the town was the seat of military operations, as Chambersburg, Pa., the literature is found in E471-478, or where several sieges or battles are covered, in E470.2-.9 (e.g., a history of all military operations around Richmond)

Louisiana

Including the administration of the Department of the Gulf by General Benjamin Franklin Butler in 1862

For Confederate history, see E471.55, E565.1+

For campaigns and battles, see E470.7, E471+

510 General works

510.1 Official publications on the raising, equipment, and service of the troops in the war

510.2 Adjutant Generals' reports for 1861-1865

510.3 Lists of soldiers. Lists of the state's dead

For the seceded states, this subdivision is used for Union troops

510.4 Histories of the states' troops

Including collected biographies or lists of officers, general associations of survivors, the draft, state brigades, state memorials and monuments, the state's battle flags, lists of citizens serving in organizations of other states

For the seceded states, this subdivision is used for Union troops

Military organizations

For the seceded states, this subdivision is used for Union troops

510.5 Infantry

For the seceded states, this subdivision is used for Union troops

Subarrange by number or name of regiment, A-Z. By author, A-Z, e.g. E527.5.L6, Logan Guards

510.6 Cavalry

For the seceded states, this subdivision is used for Union troops

Subarrange by number or name of regiment, A-Z. By author, A-Z

510.7 Artillery, Heavy

For the seceded states, this subdivision is used for Union troops

Subarrange by number or name of regiment, A-Z. By author, A-Z

510.8 Artillery, Light

For the seceded states, this subdivision is used for Union troops

Subarrange by number or name of regiment, A-Z. By author, A-Z

510.9 Other (not A-Z)

For the seceded states, this subdivision is used for Union troops

History of a town or county's participation in the Civil War, and local lists of soldiers, are classed in local history (F1-900). If, however, the town was the seat of military operations, as Chambersburg, Pa., the literature is found in E471-478, or where several sieges or battles are covered, in E470.2-.9 (e.g., a history of all military operations around Richmond)

Maine

Including biography: Abner Coburn, Israel Washburn, etc.

511 General works

511.1 Official publications on the raising, equipment, and service of the troops in the war

511.2 Adjutant Generals' reports for 1861-1865

511.3 Lists of soldiers. Lists of the state's dead

For the seceded states, this subdivision is used for Union troops

511.4 Histories of the states' troops

Including collected biographies or lists of officers, general associations of survivors, the draft, state brigades, state memorials and monuments, the state's battle flags, lists of citizens serving in organizations of other states

The Civil War, 1861-1865
Armies. Troops
The Union Army
495-537 By state
Maine
511.4 Histories of the states' troops — Continued
For the seceded states, this subdivision is used for Union troops
Military organizations
For the seceded states, this subdivision is used for Union troops
511.5 Infantry
For the seceded states, this subdivision is used for Union troops
Subarrange by number or name of regiment, A-Z. By author, A-Z, e.g. E527.5.L6, Logan Guards
511.6 Cavalry
For the seceded states, this subdivision is used for Union troops
Subarrange by number or name of regiment, A-Z. By author, A-Z
511.7 Artillery, Heavy
For the seceded states, this subdivision is used for Union troops
Subarrange by number or name of regiment, A-Z. By author, A-Z
511.8 Artillery, Light
For the seceded states, this subdivision is used for Union troops
Subarrange by number or name of regiment, A-Z. By author, A-Z
511.9 Other (not A-Z)
For the seceded states, this subdivision is used for Union troops
History of a town or county's participation in the Civil War, and local lists of soldiers, are classed in local history (F1-900). If, however, the town was the seat of military operations, as Chambersburg, Pa., the literature is found in E471-478, or where several sieges or battles are covered, in E470.2-.9 (e.g., a history of all military operations around Richmond)
Maryland
For Confederate history, see E566.1+
For campaigns and battles, see E470.2+, E471+
For prisoners of state, see E458.8
512 General works
512.1 Official publications on the raising, equipment, and service of the troops in the war
512.2 Adjutant Generals' reports for 1861-1865
512.3 Lists of soldiers. Lists of the state's dead
For the seceded states, this subdivision is used for Union troops
512.4 Histories of the states' troops
Including collected biographies or lists of officers, general associations of survivors, the draft, state brigades, state memorials and monuments, the state's battle flags, lists of citizens serving in organizations of other states
For the seceded states, this subdivision is used for Union troops
Military organizations
For the seceded states, this subdivision is used for Union troops
512.5 Infantry
For the seceded states, this subdivision is used for Union troops
Subarrange by number or name of regiment, A-Z. By author, A-Z, e.g. E527.5.L6, Logan Guards
512.6 Cavalry
For the seceded states, this subdivision is used for Union troops
Subarrange by number or name of regiment, A-Z. By author, A-Z
512.7 Artillery, Heavy
For the seceded states, this subdivision is used for Union troops
Subarrange by number or name of regiment, A-Z. By author, A-Z
512.8 Artillery, Light
For the seceded states, this subdivision is used for Union troops
Subarrange by number or name of regiment, A-Z. By author, A-Z
512.9 Other (not A-Z)
For the seceded states, this subdivision is used for Union troops

The Civil War, 1861-1865

Armies. Troops

The Union Army

495-537 By state

Maryland

Military organizations

512.9 Other (not A-Z) — Continued

History of a town or county's participation in the Civil War, and local lists of soldiers, are classed in local history (F1-900). If, however, the town was the seat of military operations, as Chambersburg, Pa., the literature is found in E471-478, or where several sieges or battles are covered, in E470.2-.9 (e.g., a history of all military operations around Richmond)

Massachusetts

Including biography: John Albion Andrew

513 General works

513.1 Official publications on the raising, equipment, and service of the troops in the war

513.2 Adjutant Generals' reports for 1861-1865

513.3 Lists of soldiers. Lists of the state's dead

For the seceded states, this subdivision is used for Union troops

513.4 Histories of the states' troops

Including collected biographies or lists of officers, general associations of survivors, the draft, state brigades, state memorials and monuments, the state's battle flags, lists of citizens serving in organizations of other states

For the seceded states, this subdivision is used for Union troops

Military organizations

For the seceded states, this subdivision is used for Union troops

513.5 Infantry

For the seceded states, this subdivision is used for Union troops

Subarrange by number or name of regiment, A-Z. By author, A-Z, e.g. E527.5.L6, Logan Guards

513.6 Cavalry

For the seceded states, this subdivision is used for Union troops

Subarrange by number or name of regiment, A-Z. By author, A-Z

513.7 Artillery, Heavy

For the seceded states, this subdivision is used for Union troops

Subarrange by number or name of regiment, A-Z. By author, A-Z

513.8 Artillery, Light

For the seceded states, this subdivision is used for Union troops

Subarrange by number or name of regiment, A-Z. By author, A-Z

513.9 Other (not A-Z)

For the seceded states, this subdivision is used for Union troops

History of a town or county's participation in the Civil War, and local lists of soldiers, are classed in local history (F1-900). If, however, the town was the seat of military operations, as Chambersburg, Pa., the literature is found in E471-478, or where several sieges or battles are covered, in E470.2-.9 (e.g., a history of all military operations around Richmond)

Michigan

514 General works

514.1 Official publications on the raising, equipment, and service of the troops in the war

514.2 Adjutant Generals' reports for 1861-1865

514.3 Lists of soldiers. Lists of the state's dead

For the seceded states, this subdivision is used for Union troops

514.4 Histories of the states' troops

Including collected biographies or lists of officers, general associations of survivors, the draft, state brigades, state memorials and monuments, the state's battle flags, lists of citizens serving in organizations of other states

For the seceded states, this subdivision is used for Union troops

Military organizations

For the seceded states, this subdivision is used for Union troops

The Civil War, 1861-1865

Armies. Troops

The Union Army

495-537 By state

Michigan

Military organizations — Continued

514.5 Infantry

For the seceded states, this subdivision is used for Union troops

Subarrange by number or name of regiment, A-Z. By author, A-Z, e.g. E527.5.L6, Logan Guards

514.6 Cavalry

For the seceded states, this subdivision is used for Union troops

Subarrange by number or name of regiment, A-Z. By author, A-Z

514.7 Artillery, Heavy

For the seceded states, this subdivision is used for Union troops

Subarrange by number or name of regiment, A-Z. By author, A-Z

514.8 Artillery, Light

For the seceded states, this subdivision is used for Union troops

Subarrange by number or name of regiment, A-Z. By author, A-Z

514.9 Other (not A-Z)

For the seceded states, this subdivision is used for Union troops

History of a town or county's participation in the Civil War, and local lists of soldiers, are classed in local history (F1-900). If, however, the town was the seat of military operations, as Chambersburg, Pa., the literature is found in E471-478, or where several sieges or battles are covered, in E470.2-.9 (e.g., a history of all military operations around Richmond)

Minnesota

For Indian wars, see E83.86, E83.863

515 General works

515.1 Official publications on the raising, equipment, and service of the troops in the war

515.2 Adjutant Generals' reports for 1861-1865

515.3 Lists of soldiers. Lists of the state's dead

For the seceded states, this subdivision is used for Union troops

515.4 Histories of the states' troops

Including collected biographies or lists of officers, general associations of survivors, the draft, state brigades, state memorials and monuments, the state's battle flags, lists of citizens serving in organizations of other states

For the seceded states, this subdivision is used for Union troops

Military organizations

For the seceded states, this subdivision is used for Union troops

515.5 Infantry

For the seceded states, this subdivision is used for Union troops

Subarrange by number or name of regiment, A-Z. By author, A-Z, e.g. E527.5.L6, Logan Guards

515.6 Cavalry

For the seceded states, this subdivision is used for Union troops

Subarrange by number or name of regiment, A-Z. By author, A-Z

515.7 Artillery, Heavy

For the seceded states, this subdivision is used for Union troops

Subarrange by number or name of regiment, A-Z. By author, A-Z

515.8 Artillery, Light

For the seceded states, this subdivision is used for Union troops

Subarrange by number or name of regiment, A-Z. By author, A-Z

515.9 Other (not A-Z)

For the seceded states, this subdivision is used for Union troops

History of a town or county's participation in the Civil War, and local lists of soldiers, are classed in local history (F1-900). If, however, the town was the seat of military operations, as Chambersburg, Pa., the literature is found in E471-478, or where several sieges or battles are covered, in E470.2-.9 (e.g., a history of all military operations around Richmond)

The Civil War, 1861-1865

Armies. Troops

The Union Army

495-537 By state — Continued

Mississippi

For Confederate history, see E471.52, E568.1+

For campaigns and battles, see E470.6-.7, E471+

516 General works

516.1 Official publications on the raising, equipment, and service of the troops in the war

516.2 Adjutant Generals' reports for 1861-1865

516.3 Lists of soldiers. Lists of the state's dead

For the seceded states, this subdivision is used for Union troops

516.4 Histories of the states' troops

Including collected biographies or lists of officers, general associations of survivors, the draft, state brigades, state memorials and monuments, the state's battle flags, lists of citizens serving in organizations of other states

For the seceded states, this subdivision is used for Union troops

Military organizations

For the seceded states, this subdivision is used for Union troops

516.5 Infantry

For the seceded states, this subdivision is used for Union troops

Subarrange by number or name of regiment, A-Z. By author, A-Z, e.g. E527.5.L6, Logan Guards

516.6 Cavalry

For the seceded states, this subdivision is used for Union troops

Subarrange by number or name of regiment, A-Z. By author, A-Z

516.7 Artillery, Heavy

For the seceded states, this subdivision is used for Union troops

Subarrange by number or name of regiment, A-Z. By author, A-Z

516.8 Artillery, Light

For the seceded states, this subdivision is used for Union troops

Subarrange by number or name of regiment, A-Z. By author, A-Z

516.9 Other (not A-Z)

For the seceded states, this subdivision is used for Union troops

History of a town or county's participation in the Civil War, and local lists of soldiers, are classed in local history (F1-900). If, however, the town was the seat of military operations, as Chambersburg, Pa., the literature is found in E471-478, or where several sieges or battles are covered, in E470.2-.9 (e.g., a history of all military operations around Richmond)

Missouri

For Confederate history, see E471.57, E569.1+

For campaigns and battles, see E470.4+, E470.9, E471+

517 General works

517.1 Official publications on the raising, equipment, and service of the troops in the war

517.2 Adjutant Generals' reports for 1861-1865

517.3 Lists of soldiers. Lists of the state's dead

For the seceded states, this subdivision is used for Union troops

517.4 Histories of the states' troops

Including collected biographies or lists of officers, general associations of survivors, the draft, state brigades, state memorials and monuments, the state's battle flags, lists of citizens serving in organizations of other states

For the seceded states, this subdivision is used for Union troops

Military organizations

For the seceded states, this subdivision is used for Union troops

517.5 Infantry

For the seceded states, this subdivision is used for Union troops

Subarrange by number or name of regiment, A-Z. By author, A-Z, e.g. E527.5.L6, Logan Guards

517.6 Cavalry

For the seceded states, this subdivision is used for Union troops

The Civil War, 1861-1865
Armies. Troops
The Union Army
495-537 By state
Missouri
Military organizations
517.6 Cavalry — Continued
Subarrange by number or name of regiment, A-Z. By author, A-Z
517.7 Artillery, Heavy
For the seceded states, this subdivision is used for Union troops
Subarrange by number or name of regiment, A-Z. By author, A-Z
517.8 Artillery, Light
For the seceded states, this subdivision is used for Union troops
Subarrange by number or name of regiment, A-Z. By author, A-Z
517.9 Other (not A-Z)
For the seceded states, this subdivision is used for Union troops
History of a town or county's participation in the Civil War, and local lists of soldiers, are classed in local history (F1-900). If, however, the town was the seat of military operations, as Chambersburg, Pa., the literature is found in E471-478, or where several sieges or battles are covered, in E470.2-.9 (e.g., a history of all military operations around Richmond)
Nebraska
518 General works
518.1 Official publications on the raising, equipment, and service of the troops in the war
518.2 Adjutant Generals' reports for 1861-1865
518.3 Lists of soldiers. Lists of the state's dead
For the seceded states, this subdivision is used for Union troops
518.4 Histories of the states' troops
Including collected biographies or lists of officers, general associations of survivors, the draft, state brigades, state memorials and monuments, the state's battle flags, lists of citizens serving in organizations of other states
For the seceded states, this subdivision is used for Union troops
Military organizations
For the seceded states, this subdivision is used for Union troops
518.5 Infantry
For the seceded states, this subdivision is used for Union troops
Subarrange by number or name of regiment, A-Z. By author, A-Z, e.g. E527.5.L6, Logan Guards
518.6 Cavalry
For the seceded states, this subdivision is used for Union troops
Subarrange by number or name of regiment, A-Z. By author, A-Z
518.7 Artillery, Heavy
For the seceded states, this subdivision is used for Union troops
Subarrange by number or name of regiment, A-Z. By author, A-Z
518.8 Artillery, Light
For the seceded states, this subdivision is used for Union troops
Subarrange by number or name of regiment, A-Z. By author, A-Z
518.9 Other (not A-Z)
For the seceded states, this subdivision is used for Union troops
History of a town or county's participation in the Civil War, and local lists of soldiers, are classed in local history (F1-900). If, however, the town was the seat of military operations, as Chambersburg, Pa., the literature is found in E471-478, or where several sieges or battles are covered, in E470.2-.9 (e.g., a history of all military operations around Richmond)
Nevada
519 General works
519.1 Official publications on the raising, equipment, and service of the troops in the war
519.2 Adjutant Generals' reports for 1861-1865
519.3 Lists of soldiers. Lists of the state's dead
For the seceded states, this subdivision is used for Union troops

The Civil War, 1861-1865

Armies. Troops

The Union Army

495-537 By state

Nevada — Continued

519.4 Histories of the states' troops

Including collected biographies or lists of officers, general associations of survivors, the draft, state brigades, state memorials and monuments, the state's battle flags, lists of citizens serving in organizations of other states

For the seceded states, this subdivision is used for Union troops

Military organizations

For the seceded states, this subdivision is used for Union troops

519.5 Infantry

For the seceded states, this subdivision is used for Union troops

Subarrange by number or name of regiment, A-Z. By author, A-Z, e.g. E527.5.L6, Logan Guards

519.6 Cavalry

For the seceded states, this subdivision is used for Union troops

Subarrange by number or name of regiment, A-Z. By author, A-Z

519.7 Artillery, Heavy

For the seceded states, this subdivision is used for Union troops

Subarrange by number or name of regiment, A-Z. By author, A-Z

519.8 Artillery, Light

For the seceded states, this subdivision is used for Union troops

Subarrange by number or name of regiment, A-Z. By author, A-Z

519.9 Other (not A-Z)

For the seceded states, this subdivision is used for Union troops

History of a town or county's participation in the Civil War, and local lists of soldiers, are classed in local history (F1-900). If, however, the town was the seat of military operations, as Chambersburg, Pa., the literature is found in E471-478, or where several sieges or battles are covered, in E470.2-.9 (e.g., a history of all military operations around Richmond)

New Hampshire

520 General works

520.1 Official publications on the raising, equipment, and service of the troops in the war

520.2 Adjutant Generals' reports for 1861-1865

520.3 Lists of soldiers. Lists of the state's dead

For the seceded states, this subdivision is used for Union troops

520.4 Histories of the states' troops

Including collected biographies or lists of officers, general associations of survivors, the draft, state brigades, state memorials and monuments, the state's battle flags, lists of citizens serving in organizations of other states

For the seceded states, this subdivision is used for Union troops

Military organizations

For the seceded states, this subdivision is used for Union troops

520.5 Infantry

For the seceded states, this subdivision is used for Union troops

Subarrange by number or name of regiment, A-Z. By author, A-Z, e.g. E527.5.L6, Logan Guards

520.6 Cavalry

For the seceded states, this subdivision is used for Union troops

Subarrange by number or name of regiment, A-Z. By author, A-Z

520.7 Artillery, Heavy

For the seceded states, this subdivision is used for Union troops

Subarrange by number or name of regiment, A-Z. By author, A-Z

520.8 Artillery, Light

For the seceded states, this subdivision is used for Union troops

Subarrange by number or name of regiment, A-Z. By author, A-Z

520.9 Other (not A-Z)

For the seceded states, this subdivision is used for Union troops

The Civil War, 1861-1865
Armies. Troops
The Union Army
495-537 By state
New Hampshire
Military organizations
520.9 Other (not A-Z) — Continued
History of a town or county's participation in the Civil War, and local lists of soldiers, are classed in local history (F1-900). If, however, the town was the seat of military operations, as Chambersburg, Pa., the literature is found in E471-478, or where several sieges or battles are covered, in E470.2-.9 (e.g., a history of all military operations around Richmond)
New Jersey
Including biography: Joel Parker, etc.
521 General works
521.1 Official publications on the raising, equipment, and service of the troops in the war
521.2 Adjutant Generals' reports for 1861-1865
521.3 Lists of soldiers. Lists of the state's dead
For the seceded states, this subdivision is used for Union troops
521.4 Histories of the states' troops
Including collected biographies or lists of officers, general associations of survivors, the draft, state brigades, state memorials and monuments, the state's battle flags, lists of citizens serving in organizations of other states
For the seceded states, this subdivision is used for Union troops
Military organizations
For the seceded states, this subdivision is used for Union troops
521.5 Infantry
For the seceded states, this subdivision is used for Union troops
Subarrange by number or name of regiment, A-Z. By author, A-Z, e.g. E527.5.L6, Logan Guards
521.6 Cavalry
For the seceded states, this subdivision is used for Union troops
Subarrange by number or name of regiment, A-Z. By author, A-Z
521.7 Artillery, Heavy
For the seceded states, this subdivision is used for Union troops
Subarrange by number or name of regiment, A-Z. By author, A-Z
521.8 Artillery, Light
For the seceded states, this subdivision is used for Union troops
Subarrange by number or name of regiment, A-Z. By author, A-Z
521.9 Other (not A-Z)
For the seceded states, this subdivision is used for Union troops
History of a town or county's participation in the Civil War, and local lists of soldiers, are classed in local history (F1-900). If, however, the town was the seat of military operations, as Chambersburg, Pa., the literature is found in E471-478, or where several sieges or battles are covered, in E470.2-.9 (e.g., a history of all military operations around Richmond)
New Mexico
For Confederate history, see E471.56, E571.1+
For campaigns and battles, see E470.9, E471+
522 General works
522.1 Official publications on the raising, equipment, and service of the troops in the war
522.2 Adjutant Generals' reports for 1861-1865
522.3 Lists of soldiers. Lists of the state's dead
For the seceded states, this subdivision is used for Union troops
522.4 Histories of the states' troops
Including collected biographies or lists of officers, general associations of survivors, the draft, state brigades, state memorials and monuments, the state's battle flags, lists of citizens serving in organizations of other states
For the seceded states, this subdivision is used for Union troops

The Civil War, 1861-1865
Armies. Troops
The Union Army
495-537 By state
New Mexico — Continued
Military organizations
For the seceded states, this subdivision is used for Union troops
522.5 Infantry
For the seceded states, this subdivision is used for Union troops
Subarrange by number or name of regiment, A-Z. By author, A-Z, e.g. E527.5.L6, Logan Guards
522.6 Cavalry
For the seceded states, this subdivision is used for Union troops
Subarrange by number or name of regiment, A-Z. By author, A-Z
522.7 Artillery, Heavy
For the seceded states, this subdivision is used for Union troops
Subarrange by number or name of regiment, A-Z. By author, A-Z
522.8 Artillery, Light
For the seceded states, this subdivision is used for Union troops
Subarrange by number or name of regiment, A-Z. By author, A-Z
522.9 Other (not A-Z)
For the seceded states, this subdivision is used for Union troops
History of a town or county's participation in the Civil War, and local lists of soldiers, are classed in local history (F1-900). If, however, the town was the seat of military operations, as Chambersburg, Pa., the literature is found in E471-478, or where several sieges or battles are covered, in E470.2-.9 (e.g., a history of all military operations around Richmond)
New York
Cf. F128.44, Draft riots, New York City
523 General works
523.1 Official publications on the raising, equipment, and service of the troops in the war
523.2 Adjutant Generals' reports for 1861-1865
523.3 Lists of soldiers. Lists of the state's dead
For the seceded states, this subdivision is used for Union troops
523.4 Histories of the states' troops
Including collected biographies or lists of officers, general associations of survivors, the draft, state brigades, state memorials and monuments, the state's battle flags, lists of citizens serving in organizations of other states
For the seceded states, this subdivision is used for Union troops
Military organizations
For the seceded states, this subdivision is used for Union troops
523.5 Infantry
For the seceded states, this subdivision is used for Union troops
Subarrange by number or name of regiment, A-Z. By author, A-Z, e.g. E527.5.L6, Logan Guards
523.6 Cavalry
For the seceded states, this subdivision is used for Union troops
Subarrange by number or name of regiment, A-Z. By author, A-Z
523.7 Artillery, Heavy
For the seceded states, this subdivision is used for Union troops
Subarrange by number or name of regiment, A-Z. By author, A-Z
523.8 Artillery, Light
For the seceded states, this subdivision is used for Union troops
Subarrange by number or name of regiment, A-Z. By author, A-Z
523.9 Other (not A-Z)
For the seceded states, this subdivision is used for Union troops

The Civil War, 1861-1865
Armies. Troops
The Union Army
495-537 By state
New York
Military organizations
523.9 Other (not A-Z) — Continued
History of a town or county's participation in the Civil War, and local lists of soldiers, are classed in local history (F1-900). If, however, the town was the seat of military operations, as Chambersburg, Pa., the literature is found in E471-478, or where several sieges or battles are covered, in E470.2-.9 (e.g., a history of all military operations around Richmond)
North Carolina
For Confederate history, see E471.54, E573.1+
For campaigns and battles, see E470.6, E471+
524 General works
524.1 Official publications on the raising, equipment, and service of the troops in the war
524.2 Adjutant Generals' reports for 1861-1865
524.3 Lists of soldiers. Lists of the state's dead
For the seceded states, this subdivision is used for Union troops
524.4 Histories of the states' troops
Including collected biographies or lists of officers, general associations of survivors, the draft, state brigades, state memorials and monuments, the state's battle flags, lists of citizens serving in organizations of other states
For the seceded states, this subdivision is used for Union troops
Military organizations
For the seceded states, this subdivision is used for Union troops
524.5 Infantry
For the seceded states, this subdivision is used for Union troops
Subarrange by number or name of regiment, A-Z. By author, A-Z, e.g. E527.5.L6, Logan Guards
524.6 Cavalry
For the seceded states, this subdivision is used for Union troops
Subarrange by number or name of regiment, A-Z. By author, A-Z
524.7 Artillery, Heavy
For the seceded states, this subdivision is used for Union troops
Subarrange by number or name of regiment, A-Z. By author, A-Z
524.8 Artillery, Light
For the seceded states, this subdivision is used for Union troops
Subarrange by number or name of regiment, A-Z. By author, A-Z
524.9 Other (not A-Z)
For the seceded states, this subdivision is used for Union troops
History of a town or county's participation in the Civil War, and local lists of soldiers, are classed in local history (F1-900). If, however, the town was the seat of military operations, as Chambersburg, Pa., the literature is found in E471-478, or where several sieges or battles are covered, in E470.2-.9 (e.g., a history of all military operations around Richmond)
North Dakota, *see* E530.1+
Ohio
For campaigns and battles, see E470.4+, E471+
525 General works
525.1 Official publications on the raising, equipment, and service of the troops in the war
525.2 Adjutant Generals' reports for 1861-1865
525.3 Lists of soldiers. Lists of the state's dead
For the seceded states, this subdivision is used for Union troops
525.4 Histories of the states' troops
Including collected biographies or lists of officers, general associations of survivors, the draft, state brigades, state memorials and monuments, the state's battle flags, lists of citizens serving in organizations of other states
For the seceded states, this subdivision is used for Union troops

The Civil War, 1861-1865

Armies. Troops

The Union Army

495-537 By state

Ohio — Continued

Military organizations

For the seceded states, this subdivision is used for Union troops

525.5 Infantry

For the seceded states, this subdivision is used for Union troops

Subarrange by number or name of regiment, A-Z. By author, A-Z, e.g. E527.5.L6, Logan Guards

525.6 Cavalry

For the seceded states, this subdivision is used for Union troops

Subarrange by number or name of regiment, A-Z. By author, A-Z

525.7 Artillery, Heavy

For the seceded states, this subdivision is used for Union troops

Subarrange by number or name of regiment, A-Z. By author, A-Z

525.8 Artillery, Light

For the seceded states, this subdivision is used for Union troops

Subarrange by number or name of regiment, A-Z. By author, A-Z

525.9 Other (not A-Z)

For the seceded states, this subdivision is used for Union troops

History of a town or county's participation in the Civil War, and local lists of soldiers, are classed in local history (F1-900). If, however, the town was the seat of military operations, as Chambersburg, Pa., the literature is found in E471-478, or where several sieges or battles are covered, in E470.2-.9 (e.g., a history of all military operations around Richmond)

Oklahoma, *see* E505.95

Oregon

526 General works

526.1 Official publications on the raising, equipment, and service of the troops in the war

526.2 Adjutant Generals' reports for 1861-1865

526.3 Lists of soldiers. Lists of the state's dead

For the seceded states, this subdivision is used for Union troops

526.4 Histories of the states' troops

Including collected biographies or lists of officers, general associations of survivors, the draft, state brigades, state memorials and monuments, the state's battle flags, lists of citizens serving in organizations of other states

For the seceded states, this subdivision is used for Union troops

Military organizations

For the seceded states, this subdivision is used for Union troops

526.5 Infantry

For the seceded states, this subdivision is used for Union troops

Subarrange by number or name of regiment, A-Z. By author, A-Z, e.g. E527.5.L6, Logan Guards

526.6 Cavalry

For the seceded states, this subdivision is used for Union troops

Subarrange by number or name of regiment, A-Z. By author, A-Z

526.7 Artillery, Heavy

For the seceded states, this subdivision is used for Union troops

Subarrange by number or name of regiment, A-Z. By author, A-Z

526.8 Artillery, Light

For the seceded states, this subdivision is used for Union troops

Subarrange by number or name of regiment, A-Z. By author, A-Z

526.9 Other (not A-Z)

For the seceded states, this subdivision is used for Union troops

The Civil War, 1861-1865
Armies. Troops
The Union Army
495-537 By state
Oregon
Military organizations
526.9 Other (not A-Z) — Continued
History of a town or county's participation in the Civil War, and local lists of soldiers, are classed in local history (F1-900). If, however, the town was the seat of military operations, as Chambersburg, Pa., the literature is found in E471-478, or where several sieges or battles are covered, in E470.2-.9 (e.g., a history of all military operations around Richmond)
Pennsylvania
For campaigns and battles, see E470.2+, E471+
527 General works
527.1 Official publications on the raising, equipment, and service of the troops in the war
527.2 Adjutant Generals' reports for 1861-1865
527.3 Lists of soldiers. Lists of the state's dead
For the seceded states, this subdivision is used for Union troops
527.4 Histories of the states' troops
Including collected biographies or lists of officers, general associations of survivors, the draft, state brigades, state memorials and monuments, the state's battle flags, lists of citizens serving in organizations of other states
For the seceded states, this subdivision is used for Union troops
Military organizations
For the seceded states, this subdivision is used for Union troops
527.5 Infantry
For the seceded states, this subdivision is used for Union troops
Subarrange by number or name of regiment, A-Z. By author, A-Z, e.g. E527.5.L6, Logan Guards
527.6 Cavalry
For the seceded states, this subdivision is used for Union troops
Subarrange by number or name of regiment, A-Z. By author, A-Z
527.7 Artillery, Heavy
For the seceded states, this subdivision is used for Union troops
Subarrange by number or name of regiment, A-Z. By author, A-Z
527.8 Artillery, Light
For the seceded states, this subdivision is used for Union troops
Subarrange by number or name of regiment, A-Z. By author, A-Z
527.9 Other (not A-Z)
For the seceded states, this subdivision is used for Union troops
History of a town or county's participation in the Civil War, and local lists of soldiers, are classed in local history (F1-900). If, however, the town was the seat of military operations, as Chambersburg, Pa., the literature is found in E471-478, or where several sieges or battles are covered, in E470.2-.9 (e.g., a history of all military operations around Richmond)
Rhode Island
528 General works
528.1 Official publications on the raising, equipment, and service of the troops in the war
528.2 Adjutant Generals' reports for 1861-1865
528.3 Lists of soldiers. Lists of the state's dead
For the seceded states, this subdivision is used for Union troops
528.4 Histories of the states' troops
Including collected biographies or lists of officers, general associations of survivors, the draft, state brigades, state memorials and monuments, the state's battle flags, lists of citizens serving in organizations of other states
For the seceded states, this subdivision is used for Union troops
Military organizations
For the seceded states, this subdivision is used for Union troops

The Civil War, 1861-1865
Armies. Troops
The Union Army
495-537 By state
Rhode Island
Military organizations — Continued
528.5 Infantry
For the seceded states, this subdivision is used for Union troops
Subarrange by number or name of regiment, A-Z. By author, A-Z, e.g. E527.5.L6, Logan Guards
528.6 Cavalry
For the seceded states, this subdivision is used for Union troops
Subarrange by number or name of regiment, A-Z. By author, A-Z
528.7 Artillery, Heavy
For the seceded states, this subdivision is used for Union troops
Subarrange by number or name of regiment, A-Z. By author, A-Z
528.8 Artillery, Light
For the seceded states, this subdivision is used for Union troops
Subarrange by number or name of regiment, A-Z. By author, A-Z
528.9 Other (not A-Z)
For the seceded states, this subdivision is used for Union troops
History of a town or county's participation in the Civil War, and local lists of soldiers, are classed in local history (F1-900). If, however, the town was the seat of military operations, as Chambersburg, Pa., the literature is found in E471-478, or where several sieges or battles are covered, in E470.2-.9 (e.g., a history of all military operations around Richmond)
South Carolina
For Confederate history, see E471.1, E577.1+
For campaigns and battles, see E470.6, E471+
Cf. E185.93.S7, Afro-Americans in the Sea Island District
529 General works
529.1 Official publications on the raising, equipment, and service of the troops in the war
529.2 Adjutant Generals' reports for 1861-1865
529.3 Lists of soldiers. Lists of the state's dead
For the seceded states, this subdivision is used for Union troops
529.4 Histories of the states' troops
Including collected biographies or lists of officers, general associations of survivors, the draft, state brigades, state memorials and monuments, the state's battle flags, lists of citizens serving in organizations of other states
For the seceded states, this subdivision is used for Union troops
Military organizations
For the seceded states, this subdivision is used for Union troops
529.5 Infantry
For the seceded states, this subdivision is used for Union troops
Subarrange by number or name of regiment, A-Z. By author, A-Z, e.g. E527.5.L6, Logan Guards
529.6 Cavalry
For the seceded states, this subdivision is used for Union troops
Subarrange by number or name of regiment, A-Z. By author, A-Z
529.7 Artillery, Heavy
For the seceded states, this subdivision is used for Union troops
Subarrange by number or name of regiment, A-Z. By author, A-Z
529.8 Artillery, Light
For the seceded states, this subdivision is used for Union troops
Subarrange by number or name of regiment, A-Z. By author, A-Z
529.9 Other (not A-Z)
For the seceded states, this subdivision is used for Union troops

The Civil War, 1861-1865

Armies. Troops

The Union Army

495-537 By state

South Carolina

Military organizations

529.9 Other (not A-Z) — Continued

History of a town or county's participation in the Civil War, and local lists of soldiers, are classed in local history (F1-900). If, however, the town was the seat of military operations, as Chambersburg, Pa., the literature is found in E471-478, or where several sieges or battles are covered, in E470.2-.9 (e.g., a history of all military operations around Richmond)

South Dakota. Dakota Territory

For Indian wars, see E83.86, E83.863

530 General works

530.1 Official publications on the raising, equipment, and service of the troops in the war

530.2 Adjutant Generals' reports for 1861-1865

530.3 Lists of soldiers. Lists of the state's dead

For the seceded states, this subdivision is used for Union troops

530.4 Histories of the states' troops

Including collected biographies or lists of officers, general associations of survivors, the draft, state brigades, state memorials and monuments, the state's battle flags, lists of citizens serving in organizations of other states

For the seceded states, this subdivision is used for Union troops

Military organizations

For the seceded states, this subdivision is used for Union troops

530.5 Infantry

For the seceded states, this subdivision is used for Union troops

Subarrange by number or name of regiment, A-Z. By author, A-Z, e.g. E527.5.L6, Logan Guards

530.6 Cavalry

For the seceded states, this subdivision is used for Union troops

Subarrange by number or name of regiment, A-Z. By author, A-Z

530.7 Artillery, Heavy

For the seceded states, this subdivision is used for Union troops

Subarrange by number or name of regiment, A-Z. By author, A-Z

530.8 Artillery, Light

For the seceded states, this subdivision is used for Union troops

Subarrange by number or name of regiment, A-Z. By author, A-Z

530.9 Other (not A-Z)

For the seceded states, this subdivision is used for Union troops

History of a town or county's participation in the Civil War, and local lists of soldiers, are classed in local history (F1-900). If, however, the town was the seat of military operations, as Chambersburg, Pa., the literature is found in E471-478, or where several sieges or battles are covered, in E470.2-.9 (e.g., a history of all military operations around Richmond)

Tennessee

For Confederate history, see E579.1+

For campaigns and battles, see E470.4+, E471+

531 General works

531.1 Official publications on the raising, equipment, and service of the troops in the war

531.2 Adjutant Generals' reports for 1861-1865

531.3 Lists of soldiers. Lists of the state's dead

For the seceded states, this subdivision is used for Union troops

531.4 Histories of the states' troops

Including collected biographies or lists of officers, general associations of survivors, the draft, state brigades, state memorials and monuments, the state's battle flags, lists of citizens serving in organizations of other states

For the seceded states, this subdivision is used for Union troops

The Civil War, 1861-1865

Armies. Troops

The Union Army

495-537 By state

Tennessee — Continued

Military organizations

For the seceded states, this subdivision is used for Union troops

531.5 Infantry

For the seceded states, this subdivision is used for Union troops

Subarrange by number or name of regiment, A-Z. By author, A-Z, e.g. E527.5.L6, Logan Guards

531.6 Cavalry

For the seceded states, this subdivision is used for Union troops

Subarrange by number or name of regiment, A-Z. By author, A-Z

531.7 Artillery, Heavy

For the seceded states, this subdivision is used for Union troops

Subarrange by number or name of regiment, A-Z. By author, A-Z

531.8 Artillery, Light

For the seceded states, this subdivision is used for Union troops

Subarrange by number or name of regiment, A-Z. By author, A-Z

531.9 Other (not A-Z)

For the seceded states, this subdivision is used for Union troops

History of a town or county's participation in the Civil War, and local lists of soldiers, are classed in local history (F1-900). If, however, the town was the seat of military operations, as Chambersburg, Pa., the literature is found in E471-478, or where several sieges or battles are covered, in E470.2-.9 (e.g., a history of all military operations around Richmond)

Texas

For Confederate history, see E471.56, E580.1+

For campaigns and battles, see E470.7, E470.9, E471+

532 General works

532.1 Official publications on the raising, equipment, and service of the troops in the war

532.2 Adjutant Generals' reports for 1861-1865

532.3 Lists of soldiers. Lists of the state's dead

For the seceded states, this subdivision is used for Union troops

532.4 Histories of the states' troops

Including collected biographies or lists of officers, general associations of survivors, the draft, state brigades, state memorials and monuments, the state's battle flags, lists of citizens serving in organizations of other states

For the seceded states, this subdivision is used for Union troops

Military organizations

For the seceded states, this subdivision is used for Union troops

532.5 Infantry

For the seceded states, this subdivision is used for Union troops

Subarrange by number or name of regiment, A-Z. By author, A-Z, e.g. E527.5.L6, Logan Guards

532.6 Cavalry

For the seceded states, this subdivision is used for Union troops

Subarrange by number or name of regiment, A-Z. By author, A-Z

532.7 Artillery, Heavy

For the seceded states, this subdivision is used for Union troops

Subarrange by number or name of regiment, A-Z. By author, A-Z

532.8 Artillery, Light

For the seceded states, this subdivision is used for Union troops

Subarrange by number or name of regiment, A-Z. By author, A-Z

532.9 Other (not A-Z)

For the seceded states, this subdivision is used for Union troops

The Civil War, 1861-1865
Armies. Troops
The Union Army
495-537 By state
Texas
Military organizations
532.9 Other (not A-Z) — Continued
History of a town or county's participation in the Civil War, and local lists of soldiers, are classed in local history (F1-900). If, however, the town was the seat of military operations, as Chambersburg, Pa., the literature is found in E471-478, or where several sieges or battles are covered, in E470.2-.9 (e.g., a history of all military operations around Richmond)
532.95 Utah
Not to be further subdivided
Vermont
Cf. E470.95, St. Albans Raid, 1864
533 General works
533.1 Official publications on the raising, equipment, and service of the troops in the war
533.2 Adjutant Generals' reports for 1861-1865
533.3 Lists of soldiers. Lists of the state's dead
For the seceded states, this subdivision is used for Union troops
533.4 Histories of the states' troops
Including collected biographies or lists of officers, general associations of survivors, the draft, state brigades, state memorials and monuments, the state's battle flags, lists of citizens serving in organizations of other states
For the seceded states, this subdivision is used for Union troops
Military organizations
For the seceded states, this subdivision is used for Union troops
533.5 Infantry
For the seceded states, this subdivision is used for Union troops
Subarrange by number or name of regiment, A-Z. By author, A-Z, e.g. E527.5.L6, Logan Guards
533.6 Cavalry
For the seceded states, this subdivision is used for Union troops
Subarrange by number or name of regiment, A-Z. By author, A-Z
533.7 Artillery, Heavy
For the seceded states, this subdivision is used for Union troops
Subarrange by number or name of regiment, A-Z. By author, A-Z
533.8 Artillery, Light
For the seceded states, this subdivision is used for Union troops
Subarrange by number or name of regiment, A-Z. By author, A-Z
533.9 Other (not A-Z)
For the seceded states, this subdivision is used for Union troops
History of a town or county's participation in the Civil War, and local lists of soldiers, are classed in local history (F1-900). If, however, the town was the seat of military operations, as Chambersburg, Pa., the literature is found in E471-478, or where several sieges or battles are covered, in E470.2-.9 (e.g., a history of all military operations around Richmond)
Virginia
Including biography of Governor Francis Harrison Pierpont
For Confederate history, see E581.1+
For campaigns and battles, see E470.2+, E471+
534 General works
534.1 Official publications on the raising, equipment, and service of the troops in the war
534.2 Adjutant Generals' reports for 1861-1865
534.3 Lists of soldiers. Lists of the state's dead
For the seceded states, this subdivision is used for Union troops

The Civil War, 1861-1865
Armies. Troops
The Union Army
495-537 By state
Virginia — Continued
534.4 Histories of the states' troops
Including collected biographies or lists of officers, general associations of survivors, the draft, state brigades, state memorials and monuments, the state's battle flags, lists of citizens serving in organizations of other states
For the seceded states, this subdivision is used for Union troops
Military organizations
For the seceded states, this subdivision is used for Union troops
534.5 Infantry
For the seceded states, this subdivision is used for Union troops
Subarrange by number or name of regiment, A-Z. By author, A-Z, e.g. E527.5.L6, Logan Guards
534.6 Cavalry
For the seceded states, this subdivision is used for Union troops
Subarrange by number or name of regiment, A-Z. By author, A-Z
534.7 Artillery, Heavy
For the seceded states, this subdivision is used for Union troops
Subarrange by number or name of regiment, A-Z. By author, A-Z
534.8 Artillery, Light
For the seceded states, this subdivision is used for Union troops
Subarrange by number or name of regiment, A-Z. By author, A-Z
534.9 Other (not A-Z)
For the seceded states, this subdivision is used for Union troops
History of a town or county's participation in the Civil War, and local lists of soldiers, are classed in local history (F1-900). If, however, the town was the seat of military operations, as Chambersburg, Pa., the literature is found in E471-478, or where several sieges or battles are covered, in E470.2-.9 (e.g., a history of all military operations around Richmond)
Washington (State)
535 General works
535.1 Official publications on the raising, equipment, and service of the troops in the war
535.2 Adjutant Generals' reports for 1861-1865
535.3 Lists of soldiers. Lists of the state's dead
For the seceded states, this subdivision is used for Union troops
535.4 Histories of the states' troops
Including collected biographies or lists of officers, general associations of survivors, the draft, state brigades, state memorials and monuments, the state's battle flags, lists of citizens serving in organizations of other states
For the seceded states, this subdivision is used for Union troops
Military organizations
For the seceded states, this subdivision is used for Union troops
535.5 Infantry
For the seceded states, this subdivision is used for Union troops
Subarrange by number or name of regiment, A-Z, and by author, A-Z
535.6 Cavalry
For the seceded states, this subdivision is used for Union troops
Subarrange by number or name of regiment, A-Z. By author, A-Z
535.7 Artillery, Heavy
For the seceded states, this subdivision is used for Union troops
Subarrange by number or name of regiment, A-Z. By author, A-Z
535.8 Artillery, Light
For the seceded states, this subdivision is used for Union troops
Subarrange by number or name of regiment, A-Z. By author, A-Z
535.9 Other (not A-Z)
For the seceded states, this subdivision is used for Union troops

The Civil War, 1861-1865
Armies. Troops
The Union Army
495-537 By state
Washington (State)
Military organizations
535.9 Other (not A-Z) — Continued
History of a town or county's participation in the Civil War, and local lists of soldiers, are classed in local history (F1-900). If, however, the town was the seat of military operations, as Chambersburg, Pa., the literature is found in E471-478, or where several sieges or battles are covered, in E470.2-.9 (e.g., a history of all military operations around Richmond)
West Virginia
For Confederate history, see E582.1+
For campaigns and battles, see E470.4+, E471+
536 General works
536.1 Official publications on the raising, equipment, and service of the troops in the war
536.2 Adjutant Generals' reports for 1861-1865
536.3 Lists of soldiers. Lists of the state's dead
For the seceded states, this subdivision is used for Union troops
536.4 Histories of the states' troops
Including collected biographies or lists of officers, general associations of survivors, the draft, state brigades, state memorials and monuments, the state's battle flags, lists of citizens serving in organizations of other states
For the seceded states, this subdivision is used for Union troops
Military organizations
For the seceded states, this subdivision is used for Union troops
536.5 Infantry
For the seceded states, this subdivision is used for Union troops
Subarrange by number or name of regiment, A-Z. By author, A-Z, e.g. E527.5.L6, Logan Guards
536.6 Cavalry
For the seceded states, this subdivision is used for Union troops
Subarrange by number or name of regiment, A-Z. By author, A-Z
536.7 Artillery, Heavy
For the seceded states, this subdivision is used for Union troops
Subarrange by number or name of regiment, A-Z. By author, A-Z
536.8 Artillery, Light
For the seceded states, this subdivision is used for Union troops
Subarrange by number or name of regiment, A-Z. By author, A-Z
536.9 Other (not A-Z)
For the seceded states, this subdivision is used for Union troops
History of a town or county's participation in the Civil War, and local lists of soldiers, are classed in local history (F1-900). If, however, the town was the seat of military operations, as Chambersburg, Pa., the literature is found in E471-478, or where several sieges or battles are covered, in E470.2-.9 (e.g., a history of all military operations around Richmond)
Wisconsin
537 General works
537.1 Official publications on the raising, equipment, and service of the troops in the war
537.2 Adjutant Generals' reports for 1861-1865
537.3 Lists of soldiers. Lists of the state's dead
For the seceded states, this subdivision is used for Union troops
537.4 Histories of the states' troops
Including collected biographies or lists of officers, general associations of survivors, the draft, state brigades, state memorials and monuments, the state's battle flags, lists of citizens serving in organizations of other states
For the seceded states, this subdivision is used for Union troops
Military organizations
For the seceded states, this subdivision is used for Union troops

The Civil War, 1861-1865
Armies. Troops
The Union Army
495-537 By state
Wisconsin
Military organizations — Continued
537.5 Infantry
For the seceded states, this subdivision is used for Union troops
Subarrange by number or name of regiment, A-Z, and by author, A-Z
537.6 Cavalry
For the seceded states, this subdivision is used for Union troops
Subarrange by number or name of regiment, A-Z. By author, A-Z
537.7 Artillery, Heavy
For the seceded states, this subdivision is used for Union troops
Subarrange by number or name of regiment, A-Z. By author, A-Z
537.8 Artillery, Light
For the seceded states, this subdivision is used for Union troops
Subarrange by number or name of regiment, A-Z. By author, A-Z
537.9 Other (not A-Z)
For the seceded states, this subdivision is used for Union troops
History of a town or county's participation in the Civil War, and local lists of soldiers, are classed in local history (F1-900). If, however, the town was the seat of military operations, as Chambersburg, Pa., the literature is found in E471-478, or where several sieges or battles are covered, in E470.2-.9 (e.g., a history of all military operations around Richmond)
540.A-.Z Participation by race, ethnic group, religious group, etc., A-Z
Afro-Americans, *see* E540.N3
540.B4 Belgians
540.C3 Catholics
540.C47 Children
540.C5 Christians. Clergy. Churches (General)
540.C94 Czechs
540.F6 Foreigners (General). Immigrants
Cf. E540.G3, Germans
Cf. E540.H6, Hungarians
Cf. E540.I6, Irish
540.F8 Friends
540.G3 Germans
540.H6 Hungarians
Immigrants, *see* E540.F6
540.I3 Indians
For Indian wars, 1861-1865, see E83.86, E83.863
540.I6 Irish
540.I8 Italians
540.J5 Jews
540.M5 Methodists
540.M54 Mexicans
540.N3 Negroes. Afro-Americans
For United States Afro-American regiments, see E492.9
For state Afro-American regiments, see E495+
Cf. E453, Slavery as affected by the war
540.P64 Poles
540.P9 Presbyterians
540.S8 Swedes
541.A-.Z Colleges, schools, etc., and their participation, A-Z
Cf. E586.A+, Confederate colleges, schools, etc.
GALE NOTE *The cutter number(s) listed below have been given only as examples by the Library of Congress*
541.A5 Amherst College
541.B7 Bowdoin College

The Civil War, 1861-1865

Armies. Troops

The Union Army

541.A-.Z Colleges, schools, etc., and their participation, A-Z — Continued

541.B8 Brown University

541.D22 Dartmouth College

541.E13 East Maine Conference Seminary, Bucksport

541.H2 Harvard University

541.I6 Iowa. University

541.M3 Marietta College

541.N2 Nazareth Hall, Nazareth, Pa

541.N5 New York. City College

541.O2 Oberlin College

541.P4 Pennsylvania. University

541.P9 Princeton University

541.U5 Union University, Schenectady, N.Y

541.W7 Williams College

541.Y2 Yale University

The Confederate States Army

545 General works

Including administration, organization, volunteering, conscription, statistics, transportation, supplies

For amnesty, see E668

For flags, see E646

For separate armies, see E470.2+

Arms of service

546 General works

For individual corps, divisions, etc., which are confined to a single state, see E551-582 with subdivision .4 under each

546.4 Infantry

546.5 Cavalry

546.6 Artillery

546.7 Other (not A-Z)

For Secret Service, Signal Corps, see E608

547 Corps. Divisions. Brigades

Including associations, etc.

For corps, divisions, and brigades confined to one state, see E551-582 with subdivision .4 under each

GALE NOTE *The cutter number(s) listed below have been given only as examples by the Library of Congress*

547.C6 Cleburne's Division

547.F6 Forrest's Cavalry Corps

547.H2 Hampton's Cavalry Division

547.M8 Morgan's Cavalry Division

547.P5 Pickett's Division

547.W5 Wheeler's Cavalry Corps

548 Registers, lists of the dead and wounded, etc.

In general, lists of soldiers and officers from more than one state and veterans residing in particular states are classed here

For veterans residing in a county or town, see local biography in Class F

For lists of prisoners, see E615+

By state

Including individual Confederate States and border states with troops in the Confederate States Army

Under the border states (Kentucky, Maryland, Missouri, and West Virginia, and territory of New Mexico), the subdivisions ".3-.9" are used for Confederate troops, all general and political history of the state being classed in E509, E512, E517, E522, and E536

For military operations in a state, see E470.2+

For southern relief agencies, see E634

The Civil War, 1861-1865
Armies. Troops
The Confederate States Army
By state — Continued
Alabama
For preliminaries of the war, see E471.52
For Union history, see E495.1+
For campaigns and battles, see E470.6, E471+
551 General works
551.1 Official publications on the raising, equipment, and service of the troops in the war
551.2 Adjutant Generals' reports for 1861-1865
551.3 Lists of soldiers. Lists of the state's dead
551.4 Histories of the states' troops
Including collected biographies or lists of officers, general associations of survivors, the draft, state brigades, state memorials and monuments, the state's battle flags, lists of citizens serving in organizations of other states
Military organizations
A comprehensive history of a state militia regiment is classed in UA50-549 even if Civil War service is given
For regimental associations of veterans, see the regiment
551.5 Infantry
Subarrange by number or name of regiment, A-Z. By author, A-Z, e.g. E527.5.L6, Logan Guards
551.6 Cavalry
Subarrange by number or name of regiment, A-Z. By author, A-Z
551.7 Artillery, Heavy
Subarrange by number or name of regiment, A-Z. By author, A-Z
551.8 Artillery, Light
Subarrange by number or name of regiment, A-Z. By author, A-Z
551.9 Other (not A-Z)
Arizona
552 General works
552.1 Official publications on the raising, equipment, and service of the troops in the war
552.2 Adjutant Generals' reports for 1861-1865
552.3 Lists of soldiers. Lists of the state's dead
552.4 Histories of the states' troops
Including collected biographies or lists of officers, general associations of survivors, the draft, state brigades, state memorials and monuments, the state's battle flags, lists of citizens serving in organizations of other states
Military organizations
552.5 Infantry
Subarrange by number or name of regiment, A-Z. By author, A-Z, e.g. E527.5.L6, Logan Guards
552.6 Cavalry
Subarrange by number or name of regiment, A-Z. By author, A-Z
552.7 Artillery, Heavy
Subarrange by number or name of regiment, A-Z. By author, A-Z
552.8 Artillery, Light
Subarrange by number or name of regiment, A-Z. By author, A-Z
552.9 Other (not A-Z)
Arkansas
For preliminaries of the war, see E471.57
For Union history, see E496.1+
For campaigns and battles, see E470.4+, E471+
553 General works
553.1 Official publications on the raising, equipment, and service of the troops in the war
553.2 Adjutant Generals' reports for 1861-1865
553.3 Lists of soldiers. Lists of the state's dead

The Civil War, 1861-1865

Armies. Troops

The Confederate States Army

By state

Arkansas — Continued

553.4 Histories of the states' troops

Including collected biographies or lists of officers, general associations of survivors, the draft, state brigades, state memorials and monuments, the state's battle flags, lists of citizens serving in organizations of other states

Military organizations

553.5 Infantry

Subarrange by number or name of regiment, A-Z. By author, A-Z, e.g. E527.5.L6, Logan Guards

553.6 Cavalry

Subarrange by number or name of regiment, A-Z. By author, A-Z

553.7 Artillery, Heavy

Subarrange by number or name of regiment, A-Z. By author, A-Z

553.8 Artillery, Light

Subarrange by number or name of regiment, A-Z. By author, A-Z

553.9 Other (not A-Z)

Florida

For preliminaries of the war, see E471.53

For Union history, see E502.1+

For campaigns and battles, see E471+

558 General works

558.1 Official publications on the raising, equipment, and service of the troops in the war

558.2 Adjutant Generals' reports for 1861-1865

558.3 Lists of soldiers. Lists of the state's dead

558.4 Histories of the states' troops

Including collected biographies or lists of officers, general associations of survivors, the draft, state brigades, state memorials and monuments, the state's battle flags, lists of citizens serving in organizations of other states

Military organizations

558.5 Infantry

Subarrange by number or name of regiment, A-Z. By author, A-Z, e.g. E527.5.L6, Logan Guards

558.6 Cavalry

Subarrange by number or name of regiment, A-Z. By author, A-Z

558.7 Artillery, Heavy

Subarrange by number or name of regiment, A-Z. By author, A-Z

558.8 Artillery, Light

Subarrange by number or name of regiment, A-Z. By author, A-Z

558.9 Other (not A-Z)

Georgia

For preliminaries of the war, see E471.51

For Union history, see E503.1+

For campaigns and battles, see E470.6, E471+

559 General works

559.1 Official publications on the raising, equipment, and service of the troops in the war

559.2 Adjutant Generals' reports for 1861-1865

559.3 Lists of soldiers. Lists of the state's dead

559.4 Histories of the states' troops

Including collected biographies or lists of officers, general associations of survivors, the draft, state brigades, state memorials and monuments, the state's battle flags, lists of citizens serving in organizations of other states

Military organizations

559.5 Infantry

Subarrange by number or name of regiment, A-Z. By author, A-Z, e.g. E527.5.L6, Logan Guards

The Civil War, 1861-1865
Armies. Troops
The Confederate States Army
By state
Georgia
Military organizations — Continued
559.6 Cavalry
Subarrange by number or name of regiment, A-Z. By author, A-Z
559.7 Artillery, Heavy
Subarrange by number or name of regiment, A-Z. By author, A-Z
559.8 Artillery, Light
Subarrange by number or name of regiment, A-Z. By author, A-Z
559.9 Other (not A-Z)
561 Indian Territory
Not to be further subdivided
For preliminaries of the war, see E471.57
For campaigns and battles, see E470.9, E471+
For individual Indian tribes, see E99.A+
Kentucky
For Union history, see E509.1+
For campaigns and battles, see E470.4-.5, E470.8, E471+
564 General works
564.1 Official publications on the raising, equipment, and service of the troops in the war
564.2 Adjutant Generals' reports for 1861-1865
564.3 Lists of soldiers. Lists of the state's dead
564.4 Histories of the states' troops
Including collected biographies or lists of officers, general associations of survivors, the draft, state brigades, state memorials and monuments, the state's battle flags, lists of citizens serving in organizations of other states
This subdivision is used for Confederate troops
Military organizations
564.5 Infantry
This subdivision is used for Confederate troops
Subarrange by number or name of regiment, A-Z. By author, A-Z, e.g. E527.5.L6, Logan Guards
564.6 Cavalry
This subdivision is used for Confederate troops
Subarrange by number or name of regiment, A-Z. By author, A-Z
564.7 Artillery, Heavy
This subdivision is used for Confederate troops
Subarrange by number or name of regiment, A-Z. By author, A-Z
564.8 Artillery, Light
This subdivision is used for Confederate troops
Subarrange by number or name of regiment, A-Z. By author, A-Z
564.9 Other (not A-Z)
This subdivision is used for Confederate troops
Louisiana
For preliminaries of the war, see E471.55
For campaigns and battles, see E471+
565 General works
565.1 Official publications on the raising, equipment, and service of the troops in the war
565.2 Adjutant Generals' reports for 1861-1865
565.3 Lists of soldiers. Lists of the state's dead
565.4 Histories of the states' troops
Including collected biographies or lists of officers, general associations of survivors, the draft, state brigades, state memorials and monuments, the state's battle flags, lists of citizens serving in organizations of other states

The Civil War, 1861-1865
Armies. Troops
The Confederate States Army
By state
Louisiana — Continued
Military organizations
565.5 Infantry
Subarrange by number or name of regiment, A-Z. By author, A-Z, e.g. E527.5.L6, Logan Guards
565.6 Cavalry
Subarrange by number or name of regiment, A-Z. By author, A-Z
565.7 Artillery, Heavy
Subarrange by number or name of regiment, A-Z. By author, A-Z
565.8 Artillery, Light
Subarrange by number or name of regiment, A-Z. By author, A-Z
565.9 Other (not A-Z)
Maryland
For Union history, see E512.1+
For campaigns and battles, see E470.2+, E471+
566 General works
566.1 Official publications on the raising, equipment, and service of the troops in the war
566.2 Adjutant Generals' reports for 1861-1865
566.3 Lists of soldiers. Lists of the state's dead
566.4 Histories of the states' troops
Including collected biographies or lists of officers, general associations of survivors, the draft, state brigades, state memorials and monuments, the state's battle flags, lists of citizens serving in organizations of other states
This subdivision is used for Confederate troops
Military organizations
566.5 Infantry
This subdivision is used for Confederate troops
Subarrange by number or name of regiment, A-Z. By author, A-Z, e.g. E527.5.L6, Logan Guards
566.6 Cavalry
This subdivision is used for Confederate troops
Subarrange by number or name of regiment, A-Z. By author, A-Z
566.7 Artillery, Heavy
This subdivision is used for Confederate troops
Subarrange by number or name of regiment, A-Z. By author, A-Z
566.8 Artillery, Light
This subdivision is used for Confederate troops
Subarrange by number or name of regiment, A-Z. By author, A-Z
566.9 Other (not A-Z)
This subdivision is used for Confederate troops
Mississippi
For preliminaries of the war, see E471.52
For Union history, see E516.1+
For campaigns and battles, see E470.6, E471+
568 General works
568.1 Official publications on the raising, equipment, and service of the troops in the war
568.2 Adjutant Generals' reports for 1861-1865
568.3 Lists of soldiers. Lists of the state's dead
568.4 Histories of the states' troops
Including collected biographies or lists of officers, general associations of survivors, the draft, state brigades, state memorials and monuments, the state's battle flags, lists of citizens serving in organizations of other states
Military organizations
568.5 Infantry
Subarrange by number or name of regiment, A-Z. By author, A-Z, e.g. E527.5.L6, Logan Guards

The Civil War, 1861-1865
Armies. Troops
The Confederate States Army
By state
Mississippi
Military organizations — Continued
568.6 Cavalry
Subarrange by number or name of regiment, A-Z. By author, A-Z
568.7 Artillery, Heavy
Subarrange by number or name of regiment, A-Z. By author, A-Z
568.8 Artillery, Light
Subarrange by number or name of regiment, A-Z. By author, A-Z
568.9 Other (not A-Z)
Missouri
For preliminaries of the war, see E471.57
For Union history, see E517.1+
For campaigns and battles, see E470.4+, E471+
569 General works
569.1 Official publications on the raising, equipment, and service of the troops in the war
569.2 Adjutant Generals' reports for 1861-1865
569.3 Lists of soldiers. Lists of the state's dead
569.4 Histories of the states' troops
Including collected biographies or lists of officers, general associations of survivors, the draft, state brigades, state memorials and monuments, the state's battle flags, lists of citizens serving in organizations of other states
This subdivision is used for Confederate troops
Military organizations
569.5 Infantry
This subdivision is used for Confederate troops
Subarrange by number or name of regiment, A-Z. By author, A-Z, e.g. E527.5.L6, Logan Guards
569.6 Cavalry
This subdivision is used for Confederate troops
Subarrange by number or name of regiment, A-Z. By author, A-Z
569.7 Artillery, Heavy
This subdivision is used for Confederate troops
Subarrange by number or name of regiment, A-Z. By author, A-Z
569.8 Artillery, Light
This subdivision is used for Confederate troops
Subarrange by number or name of regiment, A-Z. By author, A-Z
569.9 Other (not A-Z)
This subdivision is used for Confederate troops
New Mexico
For preliminaries of the war, see E471.56
For campaigns and battles, see E470.9, E471+
571 General works
571.1 Official publications on the raising, equipment, and service of the troops in the war
571.2 Adjutant Generals' reports for 1861-1865
571.3 Lists of soldiers. Lists of the state's dead
571.4 Histories of the states' troops
Including collected biographies or lists of officers, general associations of survivors, the draft, state brigades, state memorials and monuments, the state's battle flags, lists of citizens serving in organizations of other states
Military organizations
571.5 Infantry
Subarrange by number or name of regiment, A-Z. By author, A-Z, e.g. E527.5.L6, Logan Guards
571.6 Cavalry
Subarrange by number or name of regiment, A-Z. By author, A-Z

The Civil War, 1861-1865
Armies. Troops
The Confederate States Army
By state
New Mexico
Military organizations — Continued
571.7 Artillery, Heavy
Subarrange by number or name of regiment, A-Z. By author, A-Z
571.8 Artillery, Light
Subarrange by number or name of regiment, A-Z. By author, A-Z
571.9 Other (not A-Z)
North Carolina
For preliminaries of the war, see E471.54
For Union history, see E524.1+
For campaigns and battles, see E470.6, E471+
573 General works
573.1 Official publications on the raising, equipment, and service of the troops in the war
573.2 Adjutant Generals' reports for 1861-1865
573.3 Lists of soldiers. Lists of the state's dead
573.4 Histories of the states' troops
Including collected biographies or lists of officers, general associations of survivors, the draft, state brigades, state memorials and monuments, the state's battle flags, lists of citizens serving in organizations of other states
Military organizations
573.5 Infantry
Subarrange by number or name of regiment, A-Z. By author, A-Z, e.g. E527.5.L6, Logan Guards
573.6 Cavalry
Subarrange by number or name of regiment, A-Z. By author, A-Z
573.7 Artillery, Heavy
Subarrange by number or name of regiment, A-Z. By author, A-Z
573.8 Artillery, Light
Subarrange by number or name of regiment, A-Z. By author, A-Z
573.9 Other (not A-Z)
Oklahoma, *see* E561
South Carolina
For preliminaries of the war, see E471.1
For Union history, see E529.1+
For campaigns and battles, see E470.6, E471+
577 General works
577.1 Official publications on the raising, equipment, and service of the troops in the war
577.2 Adjutant Generals' reports for 1861-1865
577.3 Lists of soldiers. Lists of the state's dead
577.4 Histories of the states' troops
Including collected biographies or lists of officers, general associations of survivors, the draft, state brigades, state memorials and monuments, the state's battle flags, lists of citizens serving in organizations of other states
Military organizations
577.5 Infantry
Subarrange by number or name of regiment, A-Z. By author, A-Z, e.g. E527.5.L6, Logan Guards
577.6 Cavalry
Subarrange by number or name of regiment, A-Z. By author, A-Z
577.7 Artillery, Heavy
Subarrange by number or name of regiment, A-Z. By author, A-Z
577.8 Artillery, Light
Subarrange by number or name of regiment, A-Z. By author, A-Z
577.9 Other (not A-Z)
Tennessee
For campaigns and battles, see E470.4-.5, E471+

The Civil War, 1861-1865
Armies. Troops
The Confederate States Army
By state
Tennessee — Continued
579 General works
579.1 Official publications on the raising, equipment, and service of the troops in the war
579.2 Adjutant Generals' reports for 1861-1865
579.3 Lists of soldiers. Lists of the state's dead
579.4 Histories of the states' troops
Including collected biographies or lists of officers, general associations of survivors, the draft, state brigades, state memorials and monuments, the state's battle flags, lists of citizens serving in organizations of other states
Military organizations
579.5 Infantry
Subarrange by number or name of regiment, A-Z. By author, A-Z, e.g. E527.5.L6, Logan Guards
579.6 Cavalry
Subarrange by number or name of regiment, A-Z. By author, A-Z
579.7 Artillery, Heavy
Subarrange by number or name of regiment, A-Z. By author, A-Z
579.8 Artillery, Light
Subarrange by number or name of regiment, A-Z. By author, A-Z
579.9 Other (not A-Z)
Texas
For preliminaries of the war, see E471.56
For Union history, see E532.1+
For campaigns and battles, see E470.9
580 General works
580.1 Official publications on the raising, equipment, and service of the troops in the war
580.2 Adjutant Generals' reports for 1861-1865
580.3 Lists of soldiers. Lists of the state's dead
580.4 Histories of the states' troops
Including collected biographies or lists of officers, general associations of survivors, the draft, state brigades, state memorials and monuments, the state's battle flags, lists of citizens serving in organizations of other states
Military organizations
580.5 Infantry
Subarrange by number or name of regiment, A-Z. By author, A-Z, e.g. E527.5.L6, Logan Guards
580.6 Cavalry
Subarrange by number or name of regiment, A-Z. By author, A-Z
580.7 Artillery, Heavy
Subarrange by number or name of regiment, A-Z. By author, A-Z
580.8 Artillery, Light
Subarrange by number or name of regiment, A-Z. By author, A-Z
580.9 Other (not A-Z)
Virginia
For Union history, see E534.1+
581 General works
581.1 Official publications on the raising, equipment, and service of the troops in the war
581.2 Adjutant Generals' reports for 1861-1865
581.3 Lists of soldiers. Lists of the state's dead
581.4 Histories of the states' troops
Including collected biographies or lists of officers, general associations of survivors, the draft, state brigades, state memorials and monuments, the state's battle flags, lists of citizens serving in organizations of other states

The Civil War, 1861-1865
Armies. Troops
The Confederate States Army
By state
Virginia — Continued
Military organizations
581.5 Infantry
Subarrange by number or name of regiment, A-Z. By author, A-Z, e.g. E527.5.L6, Logan Guards
581.6 Cavalry
Subarrange by number or name of regiment, A-Z. By author, A-Z
581.7 Artillery, Heavy
Subarrange by number or name of regiment, A-Z. By author, A-Z
581.8 Artillery, Light
Subarrange by number or name of regiment, A-Z. By author, A-Z
581.9 Other (not A-Z)
West Virginia
For Union history, see E536.1+
For campaigns and battles, see E470.4+
582 General works
582.1 Official publications on the raising, equipment, and service of the troops in the war
582.2 Adjutant Generals' reports for 1861-1865
582.3 Lists of soldiers. Lists of the state's dead
582.4 Histories of the states' troops
Including collected biographies or lists of officers, general associations of survivors, the draft, state brigades, state memorials and monuments, the state's battle flags, lists of citizens serving in organizations of other states
This subdivision is used for Confederate troops
Military organizations
582.5 Infantry
This subdivision is used for Confederate troops
Subarrange by number or name of regiment, A-Z. By author, A-Z, e.g. E527.5.L6, Logan Guards
582.6 Cavalry
This subdivision is used for Confederate troops
Subarrange by number or name of regiment, A-Z. By author, A-Z
582.7 Artillery, Heavy
This subdivision is used for Confederate troops
Subarrange by number or name of regiment, A-Z. By author, A-Z
582.8 Artillery, Light
This subdivision is used for Confederate troops
Subarrange by number or name of regiment, A-Z. By author, A-Z
582.9 Other (not A-Z)
This subdivision is used for Confederate troops
585.A-.Z Participation by race, ethnic group, religious group, etc., A-Z
585.A35 Afro-Americans
585.C54 Children
585.I53 Indians
Negroes, *see* E585.A35
586.A-.Z Colleges, schools, etc., and their participation, A-Z
GALE NOTE *The cutter number(s) listed below have been given only as examples by the Library of Congress*
586.N8 North Carolina. University
586.S5 Shreveport, La. Centenary College of Louisiana
586.S7 South Carolina. University
586.U5 U.S. Military Academy, West Point
586.V5 Virginia Military Institute, Lexington, Va.
586.V6 Virginia. Univerity

The Civil War, 1861-1865 — Continued

Naval history

591 General works. The Union Navy

Including naval operations, registers, naval reminiscences, individual fleets or squadrons

Cf. E462.5, National Association of Naval Veterans

Cf. E467+, Lives of naval commanders

Cf. E470+, Naval operations in combination with military campaigns, e.g Monitor-Merrimac battle

Cf. E480, Naval contracts

595.A-.Z Individual ships, A-Z

GALE NOTE *The cutter number(s) listed below have been given only as examples by the Library of Congress*

595.C5 Cherokee (Steamer)

595.C9 Cumberland (Frigate)

595.H2 Hartford (Sloop)

595.K2 Kearsarge (Corvette)

595.L5 Lehigh (Monitor)

595.M7 Monitor (Ironclad)

595.R6 Roanoke (Steamer)

The Confederate States Navy

Including registers, naval reminiscences, privateers and cruisers

Cf. E469+, Construction of cruisers abroad

596 General works

599.A-.Z Individual ships, A-Z

GALE NOTE *The cutter number(s) listed below have been given only as examples by the Library of Congress*

599.A3 Alabama (Confederate cruiser)

599.A4 Albemarle (Ram)

599.A8 Atlanta (Ram)

599.F6 Florida (Privateer)

599.M5 Merrimac (Frigate)

599.S2 Savannah (Privateer)

599.S5 Shenandoah (Cruiser)

599.S8 Sumter (Cruiser)

600 Blockade and blockade running

Personal narratives and other accounts

The narratives of general or staff officers are usually classed in E470, unless relating to special armies or campaigns, in which case they are classed in E470.2-.9 or E471-478

For biography of commanding officers, see E467+

The narratives of regimental officers and privates are usually classed in E495-537 or E551-552 if they contain rolls or are otherwise valuable for regimental histories. If they are of value for military history of special campaigns, they are classed in E471+

The narratives of noncombatants are usually classed in E470-478, if relating to military operations; otherwise in E456, E468, E491, E545; F214; or under state in E495-582

Cf. E464, E484, Collections of narratives

Cf. E591+, Sailors' narratives

Cf. E611+, Prisoners' narratives

Cf. E628, Women's narratives

Cf. E621+, Nurses' narratives

Cf. E655, Collections of anecdotes

601 Union narratives

Including journals, diaries, letters, etc.

Cf. E458.7, Refugees from the South

605 Confederate narratives

Cf. E487, Memoirs and reminiscences of Confederate civil officials and noncombatants

Cf. F214, The South (Travel and description during the Civil War)

607 **Army life. The private soldier**

608 **Secret Service. Signal Corps**

Including United States Veteran Signal Corps Association, telegraph service, United States Military Telegraph Corps, spies, scouts, etc. (North and South)

The Civil War, 1861-1865

608 **Secret Service. Signal Corps — Continued**

Cf. E473.55, Andrews' Railroad Raid, 1862

609 **Press. Censorship**

Prisoners and prisons

Including prison life

Confederate prisons

611 General works

Including general lists of prisoners, exchanges

612.A-.Z Individual prisons. By name of prison or city, A-Z

GALE NOTE *The cutter number(s) listed below have been given only as examples by the Library of Congress*

612.A5 Andersonville, Ga. Military Prison

612.B3 Belle Isle Prison, Richmond

612.C2 Cahaba, Ala. Military Prison

612.D2 Danville, Va. Military Prison

612.L6 Libby Prison, Richmond

612.L7 Liggon's Tobacco Warehouse Prison, Richmond

612.M1 Macon, Ga. Military Prison

612.M2 Madison, Ga. Military Prison

612.R6 Richmond prisons (Collective)

612.S15 Salisbury, N.C. Military Prison

612.T9 Tyler, Tex. Camp Ford

Union prisons

Cf. E458.8, Treason and traitors in the North, prisoners of state, and suspension of habeas corpus

Cf. JK343+, Military rule, martial law, etc., within states during a civil war

615 General works

616.A-.Z Individual prisons. By name of prison or city, A-Z

GALE NOTE *The cutter number(s) listed below have been given only as examples by the Library of Congress*

616.A4 Alton, Ill. Military Prison

616.C4 Camp Chase, Columbus, Ohio

616.D3 Fort Delaware, Del.

616.D4 Camp Dennison, Ohio

616.D7 Camp Douglas, Chicago, Ill.

616.E4 Elmira, N.Y. Military Prison

616.J7 Johnson's Island, Lake Erie

616.L2 Fort Lafayette, N.Y.

616.L8 Point Lookout, Md.

616.M8 Camp Morton, Ind.

616.O4 Old Capitol Prison, Washington, D.C.

616.R6 Rock Island, Ill. Military Prison

Washington, D.C. Old Capitol, *see* E616.O4

Medical and hospital services. Sanitary services

Including ambulance service; hospitals; mortality and health statistics; nurses, physicians, surgeons; transportation of the wounded

621 General, and the North

Including National Association of Army Nurses of the Civil War

Including biography: Mary Ann Bickerdyke, John Hill Brinton

625 The South

Including biography

628 **Women's work**

Relief. Charities

629 General, and the North

Including southern relief agencies and associations

United States Sanitary Commission

631.A1-.A7 Official publications

631.A8-.Z4 Branch societies. By name

Including publications of and about these societies

The Civil War, 1861-1865

Relief. Charities

629 General, and the North

United States Sanitary Commission — Continued

631.Z5 General works

Western Sanitary Commission

631.5.A1-.5.A7 Official publications

631.5.A8-.5.Z General works

631.7.A-.7.Z Local sanitary commissions. By state, city, etc., A-Z

631.7.A1 General works

632 Sanitary fairs

634 The South

Including southern relief agencies

635 **Religion in the armed forces (North and South)**

Including religious life of the personnel; work of chaplains, church denominations, United States Christian Commission, Young Men's Christian Association, etc.

Including religious and other tracts

Celebrations. Memorials. Monuments

Cf. E495+, Civil War history of the states

For national cemeteries located on battlefields, see E471-478. Those located elsewhere are classed in local history, e.g. F234.A7, Arlington, Va.

For registers of the dead (General), see E494, E548

For registers of deceased prisoners of war, see E611+

For reunion of veterans of a single state or group of states, see E494, E548

641 General, and the North

642 Memorial Day services and addresses

645 The South. Confederate Memorial Day

Including services and addresses

646 War museums. Exhibitions. Flags. Trophies

Cf. E495+, subdivision ".4", Battle flags of individual states

646.5 **Antiquities**

Illustrative material

647 Cartoons

Addresses, essays, lectures. Sermons, prayers

649 The North

Including those delivered since the war

For those delivered during the war, see E458+

For Lincoln memorial address, see E457.8

For Memorial Day addresses, see E642

650 The South

Including southern addresses and sermons made during the war and after

For Confederate Memorial Day addresses, see E645

655 Anecdotes. Collections of short narratives

Cf. E464, General collections

Cf. E484, Confederate collections

For literature, see Subclasses PN-PT

656 Motion pictures about the war

Late nineteenth century, 1865-1900

660.A-.Z **Collected works of American statesmen, A-Z**

Including works of statesmen of the twentieth century to 1921

GALE NOTE *The cutter number(s) listed below have been given only as examples by the Library of Congress*

660.B6 Blaine, James Gillespie

Subarrange by Table E3 at the end of the text

660.B87 Bryan, William Jennings

Subarrange by Table E3 at the end of the text

660.D3 Depew, Chauncey Mitchell

Subarrange by Table E3 at the end of the text

660.G2 Garfield, James Abram

Subarrange by Table E3 at the end of the text

Late nineteenth century, 1865-1900

660.A-.Z **Collected works of American statesmen, A-Z — Continued**

660.G756 Grant, Ulysses Simpson

Subarrange by Table E3 at the end of the text

660.H29 Harrison, Benjamin

Subarrange by Table E3 at the end of the text

660.L75 Lodge, Henry Cabot

Subarrange by Table E3 at the end of the text

660.M14 McKinley, William

Subarrange by Table E3 at the end of the text

660.R7 Roosevelt, Theodore

Subarrange by Table E3 at the end of the text

660.S3 Schurz, Carl

Subarrange by Table E3 at the end of the text

660.T11 Taft, William Howard

Subarrange by Table E3 at the end of the text

660.W71 Wilson, Woodrow

Subarrange by Table E3 at the end of the text

661 **General works**

Cf. E83.866, Indian wars, 1866-1898

Cf. E185, Afro-Americans, the race question

Cf. E668, Reconstruction, 1865-1877

Cf. E741, Twentieth century

661.7 **Diplomatic history. Foreign and general relations**

For relations with individual countries, see E183.8.A+

For relations with Latin America, see F1418

Biography

Including biography of statesmen of the early twentieth century

663 Collective

664.A-.Z Individual, A-Z

GALE NOTE *The cutter number(s) listed below have been given only as examples by the Library of Congress*

664.A19 Adams, Charles Francis, 1835-1915

Subarrange by Table E2A at the end of the text

664.A55 Angell, James Burrill

Subarrange by Table E2A at the end of the text

664.A6 Anthony, Henry Bowen

Subarrange by Table E2A at the end of the text

664.B123 Bacon, Robert

Subarrange by Table E2A at the end of the text

664.B2 Bailey, Joseph Weldon

Subarrange by Table E2A at the end of the text

664.B3 Bayard, Thomas Francis

Subarrange by Table E2A at the end of the text

664.B5 Belmont, Perry

Subarrange by Table E2A at the end of the text

664.B55 Bigelow, John

Subarrange by Table E2A at the end of the text

664.B6 Blaine, James Gillespie

Subarrange by Table E2A at the end of the text

For his collected works, see E660.B6

664.B62 Blaine, Harriet Bailey

Subarrange by Table E2A at the end of the text

"Mrs. J.G. Blaine"

664.B64 Bland, Richard Parks

Subarrange by Table E2A at the end of the text

664.B69 Bonaparte, Charles Joseph

Subarrange by Table E2A at the end of the text

664.B819 Brandeis, Louis Dembitz

Subarrange by Table E2A at the end of the text

Late nineteenth century, 1865-1900

Biography

664.A-.Z Individual, A-Z — Continued

664.B87 Bryan, William Jennings

Subarrange by Table E2A at the end of the text

For his collected works, see E660.B87

664.C22 Cannon, Joseph Gurney

Subarrange by Table E2A at the end of the text

664.C29 Carpenter, Matthew Hale

Subarrange by Table E2A at the end of the text

664.C4 Chandler, Zachariah

Subarrange by Table E2A at the end of the text

664.C45 Choate, Joseph Hodges

Subarrange by Table E2A at the end of the text

664.C49 Clark, Champ

Subarrange by Table E2A at the end of the text

664.C543 Cockran, William Bourke

Subarrange by Table E2A at the end of the text

664.C75 Conkling, Roscoe

Subarrange by Table E2A at the end of the text

664.C78 Cox, Jacob Dolson

Subarrange by Table E2A at the end of the text

664.C8 Cox, Samuel Sullivan

Subarrange by Table E2A at the end of the text

664.D28 Davis, Jeff

Subarrange by Table E2A at the end of the text

664.D4 Depew, Chauncey Mitchell

Subarrange by Table E2A at the end of the text

For his collected works, see E660.D3

664.D58 Dingley, Nelson, Jr.

Subarrange by Table E2A at the end of the text

664.E88 Evarts, William Maxwell

Subarrange by Table E2A at the end of the text

664.F46 Field, Stephen Johnson

Subarrange by Table E2A at the end of the text

664.F52 Fish, Hamilton

Subarrange by Table E2A at the end of the text

664.F53 Fisk, Clinton Bowen

Subarrange by Table E2A at the end of the text

664.F69 Foraker, Joseph Benson

Subarrange by Table E2A at the end of the text

664.G2 Gardner, Augustus Peabody

Subarrange by Table E2A at the end of the text

664.G34 George, James Zachariah

Subarrange by Table E2A at the end of the text

664.G67 Gorman, Arthur Pue

Subarrange by Table E2A at the end of the text

664.G73 Grady, Henry Woodfin

Subarrange by Table E2A at the end of the text

664.H24 Hanna, Marcus Alonzo

Subarrange by Table E2A at the end of the text

664.H27 Harlan, James

Subarrange by Table E2A at the end of the text

664.H31 Harris, Isham Green

Subarrange by Table E2A at the end of the text

664.H41 Hay, John

Subarrange by Table E2A at the end of the text

664.H49 Hendricks, Thomas Andrews

Subarrange by Table E2A at the end of the text

Late nineteenth century, 1865-1900
Biography
664.A-.Z Individual, A-Z — Continued
664.H53 Hill, Benjamin Harvey
Subarrange by Table E2A at the end of the text
664.H65 Hoar, George Frisbie
Subarrange by Table E2A at the end of the text
664.H73 Hobart, Garret Augustus
Subarrange by Table E2A at the end of the text
664.H86 Hughes, Charles Evans
Subarrange by Table E2A at the end of the text
664.I4 Ingalls, John James
Subarrange by Table E2A at the end of the text
664.K4 Kerr, Michael Crawford
Subarrange by Table E2A at the end of the text
664.L16 LaFollette, Robert Marion
Subarrange by Table E2A at the end of the text
664.L2 Lamar, Lucius Quintus Cincinnatus
Subarrange by Table E2A at the end of the text
664.L7 Lodge, Henry Cabot
Subarrange by Table E2A at the end of the text
For his collected works, see E660.L75
664.L83 Logan, John Alexander
Subarrange by Table E2A at the end of the text
664.M8 Morrill, Justin Smith
Subarrange by Table E2A at the end of the text
664.M82 Morton, Julius Sterling
Subarrange by Table E2A at the end of the text
664.M85 Morton, Levi Parsons
Subarrange by Table E2A at the end of the text
664.N4 Nelson, Knute
Subarrange by Table E2A at the end of the text
664.P15 Page, Walter Hines
Subarrange by Table E2A at the end of the text
664.P2 Palmer, John McAuley
Subarrange by Table E2A at the end of the text
664.P41 Penrose, Boies
Subarrange by Table E2A at the end of the text
664.P53 Phelps, William Walter
Subarrange by Table E2A at the end of the text
664.P62 Pinchot, Gifford
Subarrange by Table E2A at the end of the text
664.P7 Platt, Orville Hitchcock
Subarrange by Table E2A at the end of the text
664.P72 Platt, Thomas Collier
Subarrange by Table E2A at the end of the text
664.P73 Plumb, Preston B.
Subarrange by Table E2A at the end of the text
664.Q2 Quay, Matthew Stanley
Subarrange by Table E2A at the end of the text
664.R3 Reed, Thomas Brackett
Subarrange by Table E2A at the end of the text
664.R35 Reid, Whitelaw
Subarrange by Table E2A at the end of the text
664.R7 Root, Elihu
Subarrange by Table E2A at the end of the text
664.R93 Rusk, Jeremiah McLain
Subarrange by Table E2A at the end of the text
664.S39 Schurz, Carl
Subarrange by Table E2A at the end of the text

Late nineteenth century, 1865-1900

Biography

664.A-.Z Individual, A-Z

664.S39 Schurz, Carl — Continued

For his collected works, see E660.S3

664.S57 Sherman, John

Subarrange by Table E2A at the end of the text

664.S68 Smoot, Reed

Subarrange by Table E2A at the end of the text

664.S78 Stanford, Leland

Subarrange by Table E2A at the end of the text

664.S896 Straus, Oscar Solomon

Subarrange by Table E2A at the end of the text

664.T2 Teller, Henry Moore

Subarrange by Table E2A at the end of the text

664.T57 Tillman, Benjamin Ryan

Subarrange by Table E2A at the end of the text

664.V2 Vance, Zebulon Baird

Subarrange by Table E2A at the end of the text

664.W24 Wanamaker, John

Subarrange by Table E2A at the end of the text

664.W337 Watson, Thomas Edward

Subarrange by Table E2A at the end of the text

664.W55 Wharton, Francis

Subarrange by Table E2A at the end of the text

664.W675 Williams, John Sharp

Subarrange by Table E2A at the end of the text

664.W76 Windom, William

Subarrange by Table E2A at the end of the text

664.W8 Wolcott, Edward Oliver

Subarrange by Table E2A at the end of the text

Johnson's administration, April 15, 1865-1869

666 General works

Including impeachment of the President

Cf. E83.868, Beecher Island Fight

Cf. F1032, Fenian invasion of Canada, 1866

Cf. KF5076.J6, Impeachment (Legal aspects)

Biography of Andrew Johnson, 1808-1875

For his collected works, see E415.6.J65

For his speeches and messages as President, see J82.B9+

667 General works

Subarrange by Table E2 at the end of the text

667.1 Johnson family (not genealogy)

Including biography of individual families

668 Reconstruction, 1865-1877

Including Amnesty; Ku-Klux Klan; relations of seceded states to the Union; removal of political disabilities

Cf. E185.2, Afro-Americans during reconstruction

Cf. F216, Travel in the South during reconstruction

For reconstruction in individual states, see the state in Class F

669 Diplomatic history. Foreign relations

Including proposed annexation of Danish West Indies, 1867-1869; purchase of Alaska, 1867

Cf. F901+, Alaska, Klondike region, Bering Sea, and Aleutian Islands

Cf. F1233, French in Mexico

670 Presidential campaign of 1868

Grant's administrations, 1869-1877

671 General works

Including Grant and Sumner controversy; Liberal Republicans; etc.

Cf. E83.87, Modoc War, 1872-1873

Cf. E83.876, Dakota Indian War, Custer Massacre, 1876

Late nineteenth century, 1865-1900

Grant's administrations, 1869-1877

671 General works — Continued

Cf. E668, Reconstruction

Cf. HB3717, Panic of 1873

Cf. HG527, Specie Resumption Act, January 1875

Cf. HJ5021, Whisky Ring, 1875

Cf. JK681+, Civil service reform

Cf. T825, Centennial Exposition, Philadelphia, 1876

Biography of Ulysses Simpson Grant, 1822-1885

For his collected works, see E660.G756

For his speeches and messages as President, see J82.C1+

672 General works

Subarrange by Table E2 at the end of the text

672.1 Grant family (not genealogy)

Including biography of individual members

673 Diplomatic history. Foreign relations

Including proposed annexation of Santo Domingo, 1869-1871; sale of arms to France

Cf. F854, Northwest San Juan border

Cf. F1033, Fenian invasions of Canada, 1870-1871

Cf. F1785, Cuban question; Virginius affair, October-December, 1873

Cf. F1938.2+, Dominican Republic foreign relations

675 Presidential campaign of 1872

680 Presidential campaign of 1876

Including Hayes-Tilden contest, Electoral Commission

Hayes' administration, 1877-1881

681 General works

Cf. E83.877, Nez Percé War, 1877

Cf. E83.879, Ute War, 1879

Cf. HG527, Resumption of gold payments, 1879

Biography of Rutherford Birchard Hayes, 1822-1893

For his collected works, see E660.A+

For his speeches and messages as President, see J82.C2+

682 General works

Subarrange by Table E2 at the end of the text

682.1 Hayes family (not genealogy)

Including biography of individual members

685 Presidential campaign of 1880

Garfield's administration, March 4-September 19, 1881

686 General works

Including Blaine's foreign policy

Cf. E691, Arthur's administration

Cf. E701, Harrison's administration

Biography of James Abram Garfield, 1831-1881

For his collected works, see E660.A+

For his speeches and messages as President, see J82.C3+

687 General works

Subarrange by Table E2 at the end of the text

687.2 Garfield's family (not genealogy)

Including biography of individual families

687.9 Assassination. Guiteau

Arthur's administration, September 19, 1881-1885

691 General works

Cf. E83.88, Apache War, 1883-1886

692 Biography of Chester Alan Arthur, 1830-1886

Subarrange by Table E2 at the end of the text

For his collected works, see E660.A+

For his speeches and messages as President, see J82.C4+

695 Presidential campaign of 1884

Late nineteenth century, 1865-1900 — Continued

Cleveland's first administration, 1885-1889

696 General works

For Cleveland's second administration, see E706+

Cf. E83.88, Apache War, 1883-1886

697 Biography of Grover Cleveland, 1837-1908

Subarrange by Table E2 at the end of the text

For his collected works, see E660.A+

For his speeches and messages as President, see J82.C5+

697.5 Cleveland family (not genealogy)

Including biography of individual members

700 Presidential campaign of 1888

Benjamin Harrison's administration, 1889-1893

701 General works

Cf. E83.89, Dakota Indian War, 1890-1891

Cf. F1405, International American Conference, 1889-1890

Cf. HF1755, McKinley Tariff Act, 1890

Cf. JX238.F8+, Bering Sea fur seal controversy

Biography of Benjamin Harrison, 1833-1901

For his collected works, see E660.H29

For his speeches and messages as President, see J82.C6+

702 General works

Subarrange by Table E2 at the end of the text

702.2 Harrison family (not genealogy)

Including biography of individual members

705 Presidential campaign of 1892

Cleveland's second administration, 1893-1897

706 General works

For Cleveland's first administration, see E696+

Cf. DU627.19+, Hawaiian Revolution, 1893-1898

Cf. F2331.B7, Venezuela-British Guiana boundary controversy

Cf. HF1755, Wilson-Gorman Tariff Act, 1894

Cf. HG529+, Currency question, 1890-1900

710 Presidential campaign of 1896

McKinley's first administration, 1897-1901

711 General works

For McKinley's second administration, see E751+

Cf. DS771, Boxer Insurrection in China, 1900

Cf. E713, Territorial expansion

Cf. HF1756+, Dingley tariff

Biography of William McKinley, 1843-1901

For his collected works, see E660.M14

For his speeches and messages as President, see J82.C8+

711.6 General works

Subarrange by Table E2 at the end of the text

711.9 Assassination. Czolgosz

711.95 McKinley, Ida (Saxton)

713 Diplomatic history. Foreign relations

Including imperialism; territorial expansion, e. g. Hawaiian Islands; Philippine Islands

Cf. DS679+, Annexation of Philippine Islands, 1898

Cf. DU627.3+, Annexation of Hawaiian Islands, 1898

Cf. E179.5, Historical geography of United States

Cf. F970, Insular possessions of the United States as a whole

Cf. F1786, Question of Cuban annexation

Cf. F1975, Annexation of Puerto Rico, 1898

War of 1898 (Spanish-American War)

714 Periodicals. Collections

714.3.A-.3.Z Societies

GALE NOTE *The cutter number(s) listed below have been given only as examples by the Library of Congress*

Late nineteenth century, 1865-1900
McKinley's first administration, 1897-1901
War of 1898 (Spanish-American War)

714.3.A-.3.Z	Societies — Continued
714.3.A12	Spanish War Veterans (1899-1904)
714.3.N2-.3.N8	Naval and Military Order of the Spanish-American War
714.3.S48-.3.S5	Service Men of the Spanish War (1899-1904)
714.3.S67-.3.S68	Society of the Army of Santiago de Cuba
714.3.U57-.3.U95	United Spanish War Veterans
	Biography
	For individual narratives, see E729
714.5	Collective
714.6.A-.6.Z	Individual, A-Z
	GALE NOTE *The cutter number(s) listed below have been given only as examples by the Library of Congress*
714.6.D51	Dewey, George
	Subarrange by Table E2A at the end of the text
714.6.D55	Dickinson, Walter Mason
	Subarrange by Table E2A at the end of the text
714.6.R8	Rowan, Andrew Summers
	Subarrange by Table E2A at the end of the text
714.6.S3	Schley, Winfield Scott
	Subarrange by Table E2A at the end of the text
	Cf. E727, Court-martial
715	Comprehensive works. General histories
	Military operations. Campaigns and battles
717	General works
717.1	Cuban Campaign
	Including Santiago Campaign; battles of El Caney, San Juan Hill, Santiago
	Cf. E727 , Naval battle off Santiago
	Cf. F1786 , Cuban Revolution, 1895-1898
717.3	Puerto Rican Campaign
717.7	Philippine Campaign. Battle of Manila Bay
	Cf. DS679+, Philippine Insurrection
	Battles, *see* E717+
	Political history
	Including question of intervention after destruction of the "Maine"; public opinion
721	General works
721.6	Destruction of the Maine (Battleship), February 15, 1898
723	Diplomatic history. Treaty of Paris, 1898
	For legal works, including texts of the treaty and related documents, see KZ1389+
	Armies. Troops
725	General works
	United States Army. Corps. Brigades
725.3	General works
725.4	Infantry
	Including regulars and volunteers
	Subarranged by regiment, e.g E725.4.9th for Ninth regiment (Volunteer)
725.45	Cavalry
	Including regulars and volunteers
	Subarranged by regiment, e.g E725.45.1st for First regiment (Volunteer), "The Rough Riders"
725.46	Artillery
725.47	Other (not A-Z)
	Including engineers, Signal Corps
725.5.A-.5.Z	Participation by race, ethnic group, etc., A-Z
	Afro-Americans, *see* E725.5.N3
725.5.C5	Churches
725.5.G3	Germans
725.5.J4	Jews

Late nineteenth century, 1865-1900
McKinley's first administration, 1897-1901
War of 1898 (Spanish-American War)
Armies. Troops
United States Army. Corps. Brigades
725.5.A-.5.Z Participation by race, ethnic group, etc., A-Z — Continued
725.5.N3 Negroes. Afro-Americans
725.6.A-.6.Z Colleges, schools, etc., and their participation, A-Z
GALE NOTE *The cutter number(s) listed below have been given only as examples by the Library of Congress*
725.6.H3 Harvard University
725.6.P7 Princeton University
725.8 Registers, lists of the dead and wounded, etc.
725.9 Spanish Army
726.A-.W By state, A-W. Regimental histories
726.A3 Alabama
726.C1 California
726.C7 Connecticut
726.F6 Florida
726.I2 Illinois
726.I3 Indiana
726.I4 Iowa
726.K2 Kansas
726.K37 Kentucky
726.L8 Louisiana
726.M4 Massachusetts
726.M6 Michigan
726.M7 Minnesota
726.M8 Missouri
726.N3 New Hampshire
726.N4 New Jersey
726.N5 New York
726.N8 North Carolina
726.O3 Ohio
726.P4 Pennsylvania
726.R4 Rhode Island
726.T4 Tennessee
726.V5 Vermont
726.W6 Wisconsin
Naval history
727 General works. United States Navy
Naval operations including battle of Santiago and destruction of Cervera's fleet but not battle of Manila Bay, which is classed in E717.7 ; court-martial of Schley; individual squadrons and ships
Cf. E721.6 , Destruction of the Maine (Battleship)
727.8 Spanish Navy
729 Personal narratives and other accounts
Including diaries, letters, reminiscences
Cf. E727 , Sailors' narratives
Cf. E730 , Prisoners' narratives
730 Prisoners and prisons
Including prison life
731 Medical and hospital services. War relief work
Including camps, Red Cross, sanitary services
733 Celebrations. Monuments
734 Museums. Exhibitions. Flags. Trophies
735 Addresses, essays, lectures
738 Presidential campaign of 1900
Twentieth century
740 **Periodicals. Societies. Collections (Serial)**

Twentieth century — Continued

740.5 **Sources and documents**

740.7 **Dictionaries and encyclopedias**

741 **General works**

742 **Addresses, essays, lectures, etc. (Collected). By several authors or an individual author**

742.5.A-.5.Z **Collected works of American statesmen, A-Z**

For works of statesmen of the early 20th century to 1921, see E660.A+

For works of statesmen prominent after 1960, see E838.5.A+

742.5.E37 Eisenhower, Dwight David

Subarrange by Table E3 at the end of the text

742.5.H66 Hoover, Herbert Clark

Subarrange by Table E3 at the end of the text

742.5.R6 Roosevelt, Franklin Delano

Subarrange by Table E3 at the end of the text

742.5.T6 Truman, Harry S.

Subarrange by Table E3 at the end of the text

Political history

743 General works

743.5 Un-American activities

Including propaganda, spies and espionage, subversive activities, fifth column

For Soviet propaganda in the United States, see DK272.U6

For Anti-Soviet propaganda in the United States, see DK272.7.U6

Diplomatic history. Foreign and general relations

For relations with individual countries, or groups of countries, see E183.8.A+; F1418

744 General works

744.5 Cultural relations (General)

e.g. The work and publications of the U.S Department of State's Office of Information and Educational Exchange; the U.S. Information Agency; Voice of America

For works treating only of American information libraries, see Z675.G7

Cultural relations with individual countries or groups of countries are classed with foreign relations, e.g. E183.6; F1418; etc.

745 **Military history**

For military societies established before 1951, see E181

Including military biography of World Wars I-II and the Korean War, e.g. Claire Lee Chennault; Douglas MacArthur; George Catlett Marshall; George Smith Patton; Jonathan Mayhew Wainright, etc.

For biographees whose careers extend into the Vietnamese Conflict, see E840.5.A+

For military history of individual wars, see the war, e.g. D509-680, World War I, 1914-1918; D731-838, World War II, 1939-1945; DS918-921.7, Korean War, 1950-1953

746 **Naval history**

Including naval battles of more than two wars

Including naval biography, not limited to one war (Collective and individual): William Frederick Halsey

For naval history of individual wars, see the war, e.g. DS920, Korean War

Biography

747 Collective

748.A-.Z Individual, A-Z

GALE NOTE *The cutter number(s) listed below have been given only as examples by the Library of Congress*

748.B32 Baruch, Bernard Mannes

Subarrange by Table E2A at the end of the text

748.B63 Bloom, Sol

Subarrange by Table E2A at the end of the text

748.B7 Borah, William Edgar

Subarrange by Table E2A at the end of the text

748.D22 Dawes, Charles Gates

Subarrange by Table E2A at the end of the text

748.D48 Dewey, Thomas Edmund

Subarrange by Table E2A at the end of the text

Twentieth century

Biography

748.A-.Z Individual, A-Z — Continued

748.D868 Dulles, John Foster

Subarrange by Table E2A at the end of the text

748.F24 Farley, James Aloysius

Subarrange by Table E2A at the end of the text

748.G23 Garner, John Nance

Subarrange by Table E2A at the end of the text

748.G53 Glass, Carter

Subarrange by Table E2A at the end of the text

748.H93 Hull, Cordell

Subarrange by Table E2A at the end of the text

748.I28 Ickes, Harold Le Claire

Subarrange by Table E2A at the end of the text

748.L23 La Guardia, Fiorello Henry

Subarrange by Table E2A at the end of the text

748.L7 Lilienthal, David Eli

Subarrange by Table E2A at the end of the text

748.L86 Long, Huey Pierce

Subarrange by Table E2A at the end of the text

748.L893 Lucas, Scott Wike

Subarrange by Table E2A at the end of the text

748.M52 Mellon, Andrew William

Subarrange by Table E2A at the end of the text

748.M75 Morrow, Dwight Whitney

Subarrange by Table E2A at the end of the text

748.N65 Norris, George William

Subarrange by Table E2A at the end of the text

748.S63 Smith, Alfred Emanuel

Subarrange by Table E2A at the end of the text

748.S88 Stimson, Frederic Jesup

Subarrange by Table E2A at the end of the text

748.T2 Taft, Robert Alphonso

Subarrange by Table E2A at the end of the text

748.W225 Walker, Frank C.

Subarrange by Table E2A at the end of the text

748.W23 Wallace, Henry Agard

Subarrange by Table E2A at the end of the text

748.W7 Wilke, Wendell Lewis

Subarrange by Table E2A at the end of the text

748.Y74 Young, Owen D.

Subarrange by Table E2A at the end of the text

749 **Pamphlets, addresses, etc.**

McKinley's second administration, March 4-September 14, 1901

For McKinley's first administration, see E711+

For presidential campaign of 1900, see E738

751 General works

Biography and assassination of McKinley, *see* E711.6+

Theodore Roosevelt's administrations, September 14, 1901-1909

756 General works

Including negotiations for purchase of Danish West Indies, policy in Russo-Japanese War

Cf. F912.B7 , Alaska boundary question, 1903

Cf. F1566.5 , Panama foreign relations, 1903

Cf. HD6250.A+ , Child labor legislation

Biography of Theodore Roosevelt, 1858-1919

For his collected works, see E660.R7

For his speeches and messages as President, see J82.C9+

757 General works

Subarrange by Table E2 at the end of the text

Twentieth century

Theodore Roosevelt's administrations, September 14, 1901-1909

Biography of Theodore Roosevelt, 1858-1919 — Continued

757.2 Roosevelt memorials

Including reports

Cf. F129.O98 , Sagamore Hill, Oyster Bay, N.Y.

Cf. F203.4.T5 , Theodore Roosevelt Island, D.C.

757.3 Roosevelt family (not genealogy)

758 Presidential campaign of 1904

760 Presidential campaign of 1908

Taft's administration, 1909-1913

761 General works

Cf. HD2771+ , Regulation of corporations

Cf. HF1732+ , Reciprocity with Canada

Cf. HF1756+ , Payne-Aldrich tariff, 1909

Biography of William Howard Taft, 1857-1930

For his collected works, see E660.T11

For his speeches and messages as President, see J82.D1+

762 General works

Subarrange by Table E2 at the end of the text

762.1 Taft family (not genealogy)

Including biography, e.g. Helen (Herron) Taft

765 Presidential campaign of 1912

Wilson's administrations, 1913-1921

766 General works

For period of World War I, see E780

Cf. HG2559+ , Establishment of Federal Reserve System

Cf. HV5089 , 18th amendment to Constitution, 1919 (Prohibition)

Cf. JK1888-1896 , 19th amendment to Constitution, 1920 (Woman suffrage)

Biography of Woodrow Wilson, 1856-1924

For his collected works, see E660.W71

For his speeches and messages as President, see J82.D2+

767 General works

Subarrange by Table E2 at the end of the text

767.1 Special (not A-Z)

767.3 Wilson family (not genealogy)

Including biography, e.g. Edith (Bolling) Galt Wilson

768 Diplomatic history. Foreign relations

Including purchase of Danish West Indies (Virgin Islands)

Cf. D570, Participation of the United States in World War I

Cf. D619, Relation of United States to World War I prior to its entry

For frontier troubles with Mexico, 1913, see F1234

For Occupation of Veracruz, 1914, see F1234

For Pershing Expedition, 1916, see F1234

769 Presidential campaign of 1916

772 Woodrow Wilson Foundation

780 Internal history during World War I

783 Presidential campaign of 1920

784 **1919-1933. Harding-Coolidge-Hoover era. "The twenties"**

Harding's administration, 1921-August 2, 1923

785 General works

Including history of Teapot Dome oil scandal

Cf. HD242.5 , Oil leases

Cf. HF1756+ , Fordney-McCumber Tariff Act, 1922

Cf. JX235+ , Conference on the Limitation of Armament, Washington, 1921-1922; Four-Power Treaty Relating to Pacific Possessions

786 Biography of Warren Gamaliel Harding, 1865-1923

Subarrange by Table E2 at the end of the text

For his collected works, see E742.5.A+

For his speeches and messages as President, see J82.D3+

Twentieth century

784 **1919-1933. Harding-Coolidge-Hoover era. "The twenties"**

Harding's administration, 1921-August 2, 1923

786 Biography of Warren Gamaliel Harding, 1865-1923 — Continued

786.2 Harding family (not genealogy)

Including biography, e.g. Florence Kling Harding

Coolidge's administrations, August 2, 1923-1929

791 General works

Cf. D649.G3A+ , Dawes and Young plans

Cf. JX1952, JX1987+, Kellogg-Briand Pact of 1928 (Pact of Paris renouncing war)

Biography of Calvin Coolidge, 1872-1933

For his collected works, see E742.5.A+

For his speeches and messages as President, see J82.D4+

792 General works

Subarrange by Table E2 at the end of the text

792.1 Coolidge family (not genealogy)

Including biography, e.g. Calvin Coolidge, Jr.

795 Presidential campaign of 1924

796 Presidential campaign of 1928

796.Z9 Campaign literature not separately cataloged

796.Z93 Democratic

796.Z95 Republican

Hoover's administration, 1929-1933

801 General works

Cf. HB3717 , Stock market crash, 1929

Cf. HF1756+ , Hawley-Smoot Tariff Act, 1930

Cf. HG3729.A+, Reconstruction Finance Corporation (created 1932)

Cf. JX1974+, London Naval Conference and Treaty, Three-Power Treaty (Limitation of naval armament)

Biography of Herbert Clark Hoover, 1874-1964

For his collected works, see E742.5.A+

For his speeches and messages as President, see J82.D5+

802 General works

Subarrange by Table E2 at the end of the text

802.1 Hoover family (not genealogy)

Including biography, e.g. Lou (Henry) Hoover

805 Presidential campaign of 1932

F.D. Roosevelt's administrations, 1933-April 12, 1945

806 General works

Period of the "New Deal"

Including works covering the Roosevelt and Truman administrations, 1933-1953

Cf. D731+, World War II, 1939-1945

Cf. DS686+, Commonwealth of the Philippines, 1935-1946

Cf. HD7121+, Social security

Cf. HF1732+, Reciprocal Trade Agreement Act, 1934, and trade agreements

Cf. TK1421+, Tennessee Valley Authority (created 1932)

Biography of Franklin Delano Roosevelt, 1882-1945

Cf. F129.H99, Hyde Park

For his collected works, see E742.5.R6

For his speeches and messages as President, see J82.D6+

807 General works

Subarrange by Table E2 at the end of the text

807.1 Roosevelt family (not genealogy)

Including biography, e.g. Eleanor Roosevelt

807.3 Assassination attempt

Including biography of Giuseppe Zangara

810 Presidential campaign of 1936

811 Presidential campaign of 1940

812 Presidential campaign of 1944

Twentieth century — Continued
Truman's administrations, April 12, 1945-1953
813 General works
Including Period of the "Fair Deal"
Cf. D845, North Atlantic Treaty, 1949
Cf. DS686.5, Republic of the Philippines, 1946-
Cf. HC60, Point four program, Technical assistance program
Cf. HC240, Marshall Plan (European Recovery Program), Foreign Assistance Act, 1948
Cf. JX1976+, United Nations
Cf. UA646.3+, North Atlantic Treaty Organization
Cf. UB343, Selective Service Act, 1948
Biography of Harry S. Truman, 1884-1972
For his collected works, see E742.5.T6
For his speeches and messages as President, see J82.D7+
814 General works
Subarrange by Table E2 at the end of the text
814.1 Truman family (not genealogy)
Including biography, e.g. Margaret (Truman) Daniels
815 Presidential campaign of 1948
816 Presidential campaign of 1952
Eisenhower's administrations, 1953-1961
835 General works
Cf. D839, Geneva Conference, 1955
Cf. DS921.7, Korean armistice, 1953
Cf. E743.5, Internal security, subversive activities, etc.
Cf. HD242.5, Tidelands oil controversy
Cf. HD9698+, Atoms for peace program
Cf. LC212.5+, Segregation in schools
Biography of Dwight David Eisenhower, 1890-1969
For his collected works, see E742.5.E37
For his speeches and messages as President, see J82.D8+
836 General works
Subarrange by Table E2 at the end of the text
837 Eisenhower family (not genealogy)
Including biography, e.g. Mamie (Doud) Eisenhower
837.5 Presidential campaign of 1956
837.7 Presidential campaign of 1960
Later twentieth century, 1961-2000
838 **Periodicals. Societies**
Collections
838.3 Sources and documents
838.5.A-.5.Z Collected works of American statesmen, A-Z
838.5.K4 Kennedy, John Fitzgerald
Subarrange by Table E3 at the end of the text
838.6 **Dictionaries and encyclopedias**
839 **General works**
839.3 **Minor works. Pamphlets**
839.4 **Addresses, essays, lectures, etc. (Collected). By several authors or an individual author**
Political history
839.5 General works
839.8 Un-American activities
Including propaganda, spies and espionage, subversive activities
Diplomatic history. Foreign and general relations
For relations with individual countries or groups of countries, see E183.8.A+
840 General works
840.2 Cultural relations (General)
e.g. The work and publications of the U.S. Department of State's Office of Information and Educational Exchange; the U.S. Information Agency; Voice of America; etc.
Cultural relations with individual countries or groups of countries are classed with foreign relations, e.g. E183.8; F1418; etc.

Later twentieth century, 1961-2000 — Continued

Military, naval, and air force history

840.4 General works

840.5.A-.5.Z Biography, A-Z

Subarrange by Table E1 at the end of the text

Biography (General)

840.6 Collective

840.8.A-.8.Z Individual, A-Z

GALE NOTE *The cutter number(s) listed below have been given only as examples by the Library of Congress*

840.8.K4 Kennedy, Robert F.

Subarrange by Table E2A at the end of the text

840.8.K58 Kissinger, Henry

Subarrange by Table E2A at the end of the text

Kennedy's administration, 1961-November 22, 1963

Including Cuban missile crisis

841 General works

Biography of John Fitzgerald Kennedy, 1917-1963

842.A-.Z8 General works. Kennedy as President and statesman

Subarrange by Table E2 at the end of the text

For his collected works, see E838.5.K4

For his speeches and messages issued as official documents, see KF70.A47+

For his speeches and messages as President, see J82.D9+

842.Z9 Juvenile works on all or portions of Kennedy's life

842.1 Special (not A-Z)

By period

842.3 Naval career, 1941-1945

842.47 Visit to Ireland, 1963

842.5 Monuments, portraits, statues, etc.

Class here also monuments, etc. located in foreign countries

For medals, see CJ5801+

842.9 Assassination, funeral, memorial services, etc.

843 Kennedy family (not genealogy)

Including biography, e.g. Jacqueline (Bouvier) Kennedy

For Jacqueline (Kennedy) Onassis, see CT275.A+

Johnson's administrations, November 22, 1963-1969

846 General works

Biography of Lyndon Baines Johnson, 1908-1973

For his collected works, see E838.5.A+

For his speeches and messages as President, see J82.E1+

847 General works

Subarrange by Table E2 at the end of the text

847.2 Special (not A-Z)

848 Johnson family (not genealogy)

Including biography, e.g. Claudia Alta (Taylor) Johnson

850 Presidential campaign of 1964

851 Presidential campaign of 1968

Nixon's administrations, 1969-August 9, 1974

855 General works

Biography of Richard Milhous Nixon, 1913-1994

For his collected works, see E838.5.A+

For his speeches and messages as President, see J82.E2+

856 General works

Subarrange by Table E2 at the end of the text

857 Nixon family (not genealogy)

Including biography, e.g. Thelma (Ryan) Nixon

859 Presidential campaign of 1972

860 Watergate Affair, 1972-1974

861 Impeachment question. Resignation

Later twentieth century, 1961-2000 — Continued

Ford's administration, August 9, 1974-1977

865 General works

Biography of Gerald R. Ford, 1913-

For his collected works, see E838.5.A+

For his speeches and messages as President, see J82.E3+

866 General works

Subarrange by Table E2 at the end of the text

866.3 Assassination attempts

Including biography of Lynette Fromme

867 Ford family (not genealogy)

Including biography of individual members

868 Presidential campaign of 1976

Carter's administration, 1977-1981

872 General works

Biography of Jimmy Carter, 1924-

For his collected works, see E838.5.A+

For his speeches and messages as President, see J82.E4+

873 General works

Subarrange by Table E2 at the end of the text

873.2 Special (not A-Z)

874 Carter family (not genealogy)

Including biography of individual members

Iran Hostage Crisis, 1979-1981, *see* E183.8.A+

875 Presidential campaign of 1980

Reagan's administration, 1981-1989

876 General works

Biography of Ronald Reagan, 1911-

For his collected works, see E838.5.A+

For his speeches and messages as President, see J82.E5+

For his acting career, see PN2287.R25

877 General works

Subarrange by Table E2 at the end of the text

877.2 Special (not A-Z)

877.3 Assassination attempt

Including biography of John Hinckley

878 Reagan family (not genealogy)

Including biography of individual members

879 Presidential campaign of 1984

880 Presidential campaign of 1988

881 **Bush administration, 1989-1993**

Biography of George Bush, 1924-

For his collected works, see E838.5.A+

For his speeches as President, see J82.E6

882 General works

Subarrange by Table E2 at the end of the text

882.2 Special (not A-Z)

883 Bush family (not genealogy)

Including biography of individual members

884 Presidential campaign of 1992

Clinton's administrations, 1993-2001

885 General works

Biography of Bill Clinton, 1946-

For his collected works, see E838.5.A+

For his speeches as President, see J82.E7

886 General works

Subarrange by Table E2 at the end of the text

886.2 Special (not A-Z)

887 Clinton family (not genealogy)

Including biography of individual members

Later twentieth century, 1961-2000

Clinton's administrations, 1993-2001 — Continued

888 Presidential campaign of 1996

889 Presidential campaign of 2000

Twenty-first century

895 **Diplomatic history. Foreign and general relations**

For relations with individual countries, see E183.8.A-.8.Z

For relations with Latin America, see F1418

George W. Bush's administration, 2001-

902 General works

Biography of G. W. Bush, 1946-

For his collected works, see E838.5

For speeches and messages as president, see J82.E8

903 General works

Subarrange by Table E2 at the end of the text

903.2 Special (not A-Z)

904 Bush family (not genealogy)

Including biography of individual members

905 Presidential campaign of 2004

New England
1 **Periodicals. Societies. Collections**
1.5 **Museums. Exhibitions, exhibits**
2 **Gazetteers. Dictionaries. Geographic names**
2.3 **Guidebooks**
3 **Biography (Collective). Genealogy (Collective)**
3.2 **Historiography**
Historians, *see* E175.5.A+
3.5 **Study and teaching**
4 **General works. Histories**
4.3 **Juvenile works**
Pamphlets, addresses, essays, etc.
4.5 General
4.6 Anecdotes, legends, pageants, etc.
5 **Historic monuments (General). Illustrative material**
6 **Antiquities (Non-Indian)**
By period
7 Early to 1775
Including the Plymouth Company, 1606; Council for New England, 1620; United Colonies of New England, 1643-1684; Puritans; Pilgrims; Thanksgiving Day in New England
Including individual voyagers after 1607, e.g. Bartholomew Gosnold, John Smith, George Waymouth
Cf. BF1575+, Witchcraft in New England
Cf. E83.63, Pequot War, 1636-1638
Cf. E83.67, King Philip's War, 1675-1676
Cf. E83.72, War with eastern Indians, 1722-1726
Cf. E105, Norsemen, Vinland
Cf. E121+, Early voyages before 1607
Cf. E162, Thanksgiving Day in the United States
Cf. E196, King William's War, 1689-1697
Cf. E197, Queen Anne's War, 1702-1713
Cf. E198, King George's War, 1744-1748
Cf. E199, French and Indian War, 1755-1763
Cf. F22, Popham Colony
Cf. F67, Puritans in Massachusetts
Cf. F68, Pilgrims in New Plymouth Colony
7.5 Dominion of New England, 1686-1689
Including consolidation of New England colonies and regions into one province; later (1688), enlarged by the addition of New York and New Jersey
Including relations with Governor Edmund Andros; Revolution of 1689
8 1775-1865
Cf. E357.6+, Opposition to War of 1812
9 1865-1950
Including New England hurricane, 1938
For effects of hurricane on an individual state or city, see the local classification number
10 1951-
12.A-.Z **Regions, A-Z**
For Berkshire Hills, see F72.B5
12.A74 Atlantic Coast
12.C7 Connecticut River and Valley
Cf. F42.C65, New Hampshire
Cf. F57.C7, Vermont
Cf. F72.C7, Massachusetts
Cf. F102.C7, Connecticut
Isle of Shoals, *see* F42.I8
Merrimac River and Valley, *see* F42.M4, F72.M6
White Mountains, *see* F41
Elements in the population
15.A1 General works

New England
Elements in the population — Continued
15.A2-.Z Individual elements
For list of racial, ethnic, and religious elements (with cutter numbers), see E184.A+
Maine
16 **Periodicals. Societies. Collections**
16.5 **Museums. Exhibitions, exhibits**
17 **Gazetteers. Dictionaries. Geographic names**
17.3 **Guidebooks**
18 **Biography (Collective). Genealogy (Collective)**
18.2 **Historiography**
Historians, *see* E175.5.A+
18.5 **Study and teaching**
19 **General works. Histories**
19.3 **Juvenile works**
Pamphlets, addresses, essays, etc.
19.5 General
19.6 Anecdotes, legends, pageants, etc.
20 **Historic monuments (General). Illustrative material**
21 **Antiquities (Non-Indian)**
By period
22 Early to 1620
Including attempts at colonization: Pemaquid, Me.; Popham Colony
23 1620-1775
Including Lygonia Colony (Plough Patent); Trelawney Plantation
Including biography: Edward Godfrey
Cf. E83.72, War with Eastern Indians, 1722-1726
Cf. F27.K3, Kennebec Patent
Cf. F27.M95, Muscongus or Waldo Patent
Cf. F29.B9, Pejepscot Purchase
Cf. F1036+, Acadia
Cf. F1039.B7, Boundary between French and English possessions in Acadia
24 1775-1865
Including separation from Massachusetts and admission as a state, March 15, 1820
Including biography: William King
Cf. E230+, Military operations and battles
Cf. E263.M4, Maine in the Revolution (General)
Cf. E398, International boundary troubles and the Aroostook War, 1839
Cf. E511.1+, Civil War, 1861-1865 (General)
25 1865-1950
Including biography: Harris Merrill Plaisted, etc.
Cf. D570.85.M2+ , World War I, 1914-1918
Cf. D769.85.M2+ , World War II, 1939-1945
1951-
26 General works
Biography
26.3 Collective
26.32.A-.32.Z Individual, A-Z
GALE NOTE *See note at the head of Table F5 at the end of the text for further instructions on how to subdivide this number*
27.A-.Z **Regions, counties, etc., A-Z**
27.A15 Counties
27.A16 Regions
27.A17 Rivers
27.A18 Lakes
27.A19 Islands
Acadia National Park, *see* F27.M9
27.A4 Allagash River and Valley
27.A5 Androscoggin Co.
Including Lake Androscoggin, Snow Falls

Maine

27.A-.Z **Regions, counties, etc., A-Z — Continued**

27.A53 Androscoggin River and Valley

27.A7 Aroostook Co.

Including Aroostook River and Valley (General, and Maine)

Cf. F1044.A7 , New Brunswick

27.A75 Atlantic Coast

Bartlett Island, *see* F27.M9

Baxter State Park, *see* F27.P5

27.B49 Blue Hill Bay

Bluff Island, *see* F27.Y6

27.B7 Boundaries

Cf. E398, Northeastern boundary disputes, 1783-1845

Cf. F42.B7, New Hampshire boundary

Cf. F1039.B7, Ancient boundary of Acadia

27.C3 Casco Bay and islands (Collectively)

For individual islands, see F27.C9

27.C9 Cumberland Co.

Including Orr's Island, Peak Island, Sebago Lake

For Saco Bay, see F27.Y6

For Saco River and Valley, see F27.S15

27.D2 Dead River and Valley

Dochet Island, *see* F27.W3

27.F8 Franklin Co.

Friendship Long Island, *see* F27.K7

Great Gott Island, *see* F27.H3

27.H3 Hancock Co.

Including Great Gott Island, Little Cranberry Island, Little Gott Island, Long Island, Swans Island, Union River and Valley, Union River Bay

For Mount Desert Island, see F27.M9

Isles of Shoals, *see* F42.I8

Islesboro Island, *see* F27.W16

Kennebago Lake, *see* F27.R2

27.K2 Kennebec Co.

Including Lake Cobbosseecontee

27.K3 Kennebec Patent. Plymouth Company (1749-1816)

27.K32 Kennebec River and Valley

27.K7 Knox Co.

Including Friendship Long Island

For Matinicus Island, see F27.M3

27.L7 Lincoln Co.

For Monhegan Island, see F27.M7

Little Cranberry Island, *see* F27.H3

Little Gott Island, *see* F27.H3

Long Island, *see* F27.H3

27.M18 Magalloway Island

27.M3 Matinicus Island

27.M7 Monhegan Island

27.M8 Moosehead Lake region

27.M9 Mount Desert Island

Including Acadia National Park, Bartlett Island

Cf. F1038, Jesuit station, 1609

Moxie Pond, *see* F27.S7

27.M95 Muscongus or Waldo Patent

Including greater part of Waldo and Knox and a portion of Lincoln counties

27.O9 Oxford Co.

Including Oxford Hills, Parmachenee Lake

Oxford Hills, *see* F27.O9

Parmachenee Lake, *see* F27.O9

	Maine
27.A-.Z	**Regions, counties, etc., A-Z — Continued**
27.P3	Passamaquoddy Bay, Maine
	Cf. F1044.P3 , New Brunswick
	Pejepscot Patent (Brunswick), *see* F29.B9
27.P37	Penobscot Bay region
27.P38	Penobscot Co.
27.P4	Penobscot River and Valley
27.P48	Piscataqua River and Valley, Maine
	Cf. F42.P4 , General, and New Hampshire
27.P5	Piscataquis Co.
	Including Baxter State Park, Debsconeag Lake region, Mount Katahdin, Chesuncook Lake, Sebec Lake
	Pond Island, *see* F27.W3
27.R2	Rangeley Lakes. Kennebago Lake
	Roque Island, *see* F27.W3
	Saco Bay, *see* F27.Y6
27.S15	Saco River and Valley
27.S18	Sagadahoc Co.
	St. Croix (Dochet) Island, *see* F27.W3
27.S2	St. Croix River and Valley (General, and Maine)
	Cf. F1044.S17 , New Brunswick
27.S25	St. George (George's) River
27.S3	St. John River and Valley, Maine
	Cf. F1044.S2, General, and New Brunswick
	Sebec Lake, *see* F27.P5
	Sheepscot River and Valley, *see* F27.W16
	Snow Falls, *see* F27.A5
27.S7	Somerset Co.
	Including Moxie Pond
	Stratton Island, *see* F27.Y6
	Swans Island, *see* F27.H3
27.T48	Thompson Lake and Region
	Union River and Valley. Union River Bay, *see* F27.H3
27.W16	Waldo Co.
	Including Islesboro Island, Sheepscot River and Valley
	For Waldo Patent, see F27.M95
27.W3	Washington Co.
	Including Narraguagus Valley, Pond Island, St. Croix (Dochet) Island, Roque Island
27.Y6	York Co.
	Including Bluff Island, Boon Island, Saco Bay, Stratton Island
	For Saco River and Valley, see F27.S15
29.A-.Z	**Cities, towns, etc., A-Z**
	GALE NOTE *The cutter number(s) listed below have been given only as examples by the Library of Congress*
29.A9	Augusta
29.B2	Bangor
29.B3	Bar Harbor
29.B9	Brunswick
	Including Pejepscot Purchase. Pejepscot Company (Brunswick Proprietors)
29.K3	Kennebunk
29.P9	Portland
29.Y6	York
	Elements in the population
30.A1	General works
30.A2-.Z	Individual elements
	For list of racial, ethnic, and religious elements (with cutter numbers), see E184.A+
	New Hampshire
31	**Periodicals. Societies. Collections**
31.5	**Museums. Exhibitions, exhibits**

New Hampshire — Continued

32 **Gazetteers. Dictionaries. Geographic names**
32.3 **Guidebooks**
33 **Biography (Collective). Genealogy (Collective)**
33.2 **Historiography**
Historians, *see* E175.5.A+
33.5 **Study and teaching**
34 **General works. Histories**
34.3 **Juvenile works**
Pamphlets, addresses, essays, etc.
34.5 General
34.6 Anecdotes, legends, pageants, etc.
35 **Historic monuments (General). Illustrative material**
36 **Antiquities (Non-Indian)**
By period
37 Early to 1775. Mason's Grant
Including biography: John Mason
Cf. E83.72 , Wars with eastern Indians, 1722-1726
Cf. E199 , French and Indian War, 1755-1763
Cf. F52 , New Hampshire Grants
38 1775-1865
Including biography: William Henry Young Hackett, Isaac Hill, etc.
Cf. E263.N4 , New Hampshire in the Revolution
Cf. E359.5.N3 , War of 1812
Cf. E520.1+ , Civil War, 1861-1865 (General)
39 1865-1950
Including biography: Harry Bingham, Charles Doe
Cf. D570.85.N25+ , World War I, 1914-1918
Cf. D769.85.N25+ , World War II, 1939-1945
Cf. E726.N3 , War of 1898 (Spanish-American War)
40 1951-
41 **White Mountains**
41.1 Periodicals. Societies. Collections
41.2 Gazetteers. Dictionaries. Geographic names
41.25 Guidebooks
41.3 General works
41.32 Pamphlets, addresses, essays, etc.
41.37 Historic monuments (General). Illustrative material
By period
41.44 Early to 1865
41.5 1865-1950
41.52 1951-
41.6.A-.6.Z Regions, places, etc., A-Z
For political divisions, see F42-44
GALE NOTE *The cutter number(s) listed below have been given only as examples by the Library of Congress*
41.6.F8 Franconia Notch
Old Man of the Mountain, *see* F41.6.P9
41.6.P9 The Profile
41.6.W3 Mount Washington
42.A-.Z **Regions, counties, etc., A-Z**
42.A15 Counties
42.A16 Mountains
42.A17 Rivers
42.A18 Lakes
42.A19 Islands
42.B4 Belknap Co.
42.B7 Boundaries
For New York-New Hampshire dispute over New Hampshire Grants, see F52

New Hampshire

42.A-.Z **Regions, counties, etc., A-Z — Continued**

42.C3 Carroll Co.

Including Mount Pequawkwet (Kearsarge), Ossipee Mountain Park

For Mount Kearsarge, Merrimack Co., see F42.M5

42.C5 Cheshire Co.

Including Mount Monadnock

42.C65 Connecticut River and Valley, N.H.

Cf. F12.C7 , New England

42.C7 Coos Co.

Including Indian Stream

42.G7 Grafton Co.

Including Newfound (Pasquaney) Lake, Mount Moosilaukee

42.H6 Hillsboro (Hillsborough) Co.

Including Uncanoonuc Mountains

42.I8 Isles of Shoals

Kearsarge, Mount, Carroll Co., *see* F42.C3

Kearsarge, Mount, Merrimack Co., *see* F42.M5

Magalloway Valley, *see* F27.M18

42.M4 Merrimac River and Valley, N.H.

Cf. F72.M6 , General, and Massachusetts

42.M5 Merrimack Co.

Including Mount Kearsarge

Odiorne Point Stat Park, *see* F42.R7

42.P4 Piscataqua River and Valley (General, and N.H.)

Cf. F27.P48 , Maine

42.R7 Rockingham Co.

Including Lake Massabesic, Odiorne Point State Park

For Isles of Shoals, see F42.I8

42.S8 Strafford Co.

42.S87 Sullivan Co.

42.S9 Sunapee Lake

Waterville Valley, *see* F44.W32

Welch Island, *see* F42.W7

White Mountains, *see* F41

42.W7 Lake Winnipesaukee

Including Welch Island

44.A-.Z **Cities, towns, etc., A-Z**

GALE NOTE *The cutter number(s) listed below have been given only as examples by the Library of Congress*

44.C7 Concord

44.D7 Dover

44.M2 Manchester

44.N2 Nashua

44.P8 Portsmouth

44.W32 Waterville

Including Waterville Valley

Elements in the population

45.A1 General works

45.A2-.Z Individual elements

For a list of racial, ethnic, and religious elements (with cutter numbers), see E184.A+

Vermont

46 **Periodicals. Societies. Collections**

46.5 **Museums. Exhibitions, exhibits**

47 **Gazetteers. Dictionaries. Geographic names**

47.3 **Guidebooks**

48 **Biography (Collective). Genealogy (Collective)**

48.2 **Historiography**

Historians, *see* E175.5.A+

48.5 **Study and teaching**

Vermont — Continued

49 **General works. Histories**

49.3 **Juvenile works**

Pamphlets, addresses, essays, etc.

49.5 General

49.6 Anecdotes, legends, pageants, etc.

50 **Historic monuments (General). Illustrative material**

51 **Antiquities (Non-Indian)**

By period

52 Early to 1791

Including New Hampshire Grants; Green Mountain boys

Including biography: Ira Allen, Thomas Chittenden

Cf. E263.V5 , Vermont in the Revolution (General)

Cf. E230+ , Military operations and battles

Cf. F37 , New Hampshire colonial history

Cf. F122 , New York colonial history

Cf. F127.A3 , Albany Co., N.Y.

Cf. F127.W3 , Charlotte (now Washington) County, N.Y.

53 1791-1865

Including admission as a state, March 4, 1791

Including biography: Jacob Collamer, etc.

Cf. E359.5.V3, War of 1812

Cf. E355, Military operations

Cf. E533.1+, Civil War, 1861-1865 (General)

Cf. E470.95, St. Alban's Raid

54 1865-1950

Cf. D570.85.V5+, World War I, 1914-1918

Cf. D769.85.V5+, World War II, 1939-1945

Cf. E726.V5, War of 1898 (Spanish-American War)

1951-

55 General works

Biography

55.2 Collective

55.22.A-.22.Z Individual, A-Z

GALE NOTE *See note at the head of Table F5 at the end of the text for further instructions on how to subdivide this number*

57.A-.Z **Regions, counties, etc., A-Z**

57.A15 Counties

57.A16 Mountains

57.A17 Rivers

57.A18 Lakes

57.A19 Islands

57.A2 Addison Co.

Including Lake Dunmore

57.B4 Bennington Co.

Including Hoosic River and Valley, Vt.

Cf. F72.B5, Massachusetts

Cf. F127.H73, General, and New York

57.B7 Boundaries

Cf. F42.B7, New Hampshire boundary

Cf. F72.B7, Massachusetts boundary

Cf. F127.B7, New York boundary

For New Hampshire-New York dispute over land in the present state of Vermont, see F52

57.C2 Caledonia Co.

57.C4 Lake Champlain region, Vt.

Cf. F57.G7 , Grand Isle Co.

Cf. F127.C6 , General, and New York

57.C5 Chittenden Co.

57.C7 Connecticut River and Valley, Vt.

Cf. F12.C7 , New England

	Vermont
57.A-.Z	**Regions, counties, etc., A-Z — Continued**
57.E7	Essex Co.
57.F8	Franklin Co.
	For Missisquoi River and Valley, see F57.M7
57.G7	Grand Isle Co.
57.G8	Green Mountains
	Hoosic River and Valley, Vt., *see* F57.B4
57.L2	Lamoille Co.
57.L22	Lamoille River and Valley
57.M3	Mount Mansfield
57.M5	Lake Memphremagog region, Vt.
	Cf. F1054.M5 , Quebec
57.M7	Missisquoi River and Valley, Vt.
	Cf. F1054.B8 , General, and Quebec
57.O56	Ompompanoosuc Parish
	Cf. F59.N9 , Norwich
	Cf. F59.T4 , Thetford
57.O6	Orange Co.
57.O7	Orleans Co.
	Including Willoughby Lake
	For Missisquoi River and Valley, see F57.M7
57.R9	Rutland Co.
	Including Lake Bomoseen
57.W3	Washington Co.
	Willoughby Lake, *see* F57.O7
57.W6	Windham Co.
57.W7	Windsor Co.
57.W73	Winooski River
59.A-.Z	**Cities, towns, etc., A-Z**
	GALE NOTE *The cutter number(s) listed below have been given only as examples by the Library of Congress*
59.B4	Bennington
59.B8	Brattleboro
59.B9	Burlington
59.M7	Montpelier
59.N9	Norwich
	Ompompanoosuc Parish, *see* F57.O56
59.T4	Thetford
	Elements in the population
60.A1	General works
60.A2-.Z	Individual elements
	For a list of racial, ethnic, and religious elements (with cutter numbers), see E184.A+
	Massachusetts
61	**Periodicals. Societies. Collections**
61.5	**Museums. Exhibitions, exhibits**
62	**Gazetteers. Dictionaries. Geographic names**
62.3	**Guidebooks**
63	**Biography (Collective). Genealogy (Collective)**
63.2	**Historiography**
	Historians, *see* E175.5.A+
63.5	**Study and teaching**
64	**General works. Histories**
64.3	**Juvenile works**
	Pamphlets, addresses, essays, etc.
64.5	General
64.6	Anecdotes, legends, pageants, etc.
65	**Historic monuments (General). Illustrative material**
66	**Antiquities (Non-Indian)**

Massachusetts — Continued
By period
Early to 1775
67 General
Including Dorchester Company; Massachusetts Bay Company; persecution of Quakers; Province of Massachusetts; Puritans; etc.
Including biography: Roger Conant, Thomas Dudley, John Endecott, Daniel Gookin, Anne (Marbury) Hutchinson, Thomas Hutchinson, Cotton Mather, Increase Mather, Peter Oliver, Thomas Pownall, John Read, Timothy Ruggles, Samuel Sewall, John Winthrop (1588-1649), etc.
Cf. BF1575, Witchcraft delusion
Cf. E83.67, King Philip's War, 1675-1676
Cf. E83.72, War with the eastern Indians, 1722-1726
Cf. E196, King William's War, 1689-1697
Cf. E197, Queen Anne's War, 1702-1713
Cf. E198, King George's War, 1744-1748
Cf. E199, French and Indian War, 1755-1763
Cf. F7.5, Andros and his province of New England, 1688-1689
68 New Plymouth Colony
Including pilgrims; annexation to Massachusetts, 1691 (forming the counties of Barnstable, Bristol, and Plymouth); etc.
Including Pilgrim Society, Plymouth; Society of Mayflower Descendants; etc.
For Old Colony Historical Society, Taunton, see F74.T2
Including biography: Isaac Allerton, William Bradford, William Brewster, Miles Standish, etc.
69 1775-1865
Including Shays' Rebellion, 1786-1787
Including biography: James Bowdoin, Christopher Gore, David Henshaw, Samuel Howe, Amos Lawrence, Theophilus Parsons, Samuel Phillips, William Phillips, Paul Revere, Caleb Strong
Cf. E263.M4 , Massachusetts and the Revolution
Cf. E210+, Preliminaries (Revolution)
Cf. E216, Paul Revere's ride
Cf. E230+, Military operations and battles
Cf. E309, F483, Cession of western lands
Cf. E359.5.M3, War of 1812
Cf. E513.1+, Civil War, 1861-1865 (General)
Cf. F127.G2, F127.H7, F127.T6, Lands in western New York
Cf. F273, Trouble with South Carolina over Afro-American citizens, 1845
70 1865-1950
Including biography: James Michael Curley, Frederic Thomas Greenhalge, Samuel Hoar, Roger Wolcott, etc.
Cf. D570.85.M4+, World War I, 1914-1918
Cf. D769.85.M4+, World War II, 1939-1945
Cf. E726.M4, War of 1898 (Spanish-American War)
1951-
71 General works
Biography
71.2 Collective
71.22.A-.22.Z Individual, A-Z
GALE NOTE *See note at the head of Table F5 at the end of the text for further instructions on how to subdivide this number*
72.A-.Z **Regions, counties, etc., A-Z**
72.A15 Counties
72.A16 Mountains
72.A17 Rivers
72.A18 Lakes
72.A19 Islands
Barnstable Co., *see* F72.C3
72.B5 Berkshire Co.
Including Berkshire Hills, Greylock Mountain, Hoosic River and Valley, Mass., Mohawk Trail, Mount Everett

Massachusetts

72.A-.Z **Regions, counties, etc., A-Z**

72.B5 Berkshire Co. — Continued

Cf. F57.B4, Vermont

Cf. F127.H73, General, and New York, Hoosic River and Valley

Cf. F127.M55, New York, Mohawk Trail

72.B57 Blackstone River and Valley

Cf. F87.B55 , General, and Rhode Island

Boon Lake, *see* F72.M7

"Boston Ten Townships," N.Y., *see* F127.T6

72.B7 Boundaries

Cf. F42.B7 , New Hampshire boundary

Cf. F1039.B7 , Ancient boundary of Acadia

For Massachusetts territorial claims to western New York, see F127.G2

72.B8 Bristol Co.

72.B9 Buzzards Bay region

72.C3 Cape Cod. Barnstable Co.

Including Cape Cod Bay, Sparrow-hawk (Ship) wreck (1626)

Chappaquiddick Island, *see* F72.M5

72.C46 Charles River

72.C7 Connecticut River and Valley, Mass.

Cf. F12.C7, New England

Dukes Co., *see* F72.M5

72.E5 Elizabeth Islands

Including Cuttyhunk, Nashawena, Naushon, Nonamesset, Pasque, and Penikese Islands

72.E7 Essex Co.

Including Cape Ann, Ipswich (Agawam) River, North Shore, Saugus River

72.F8 Franklin Co.

Including Deerfield River, Pocumtuck Valley

72.H2 Hampden Co.

72.H3 Hampshire Co.

Including Mill River, Mount Holyoke, Mount Tom

72.H7 Housatonic River and Valley, Mass.

Cf. F102.H7 , General, and Connecticut

72.M5 Martha's Vineyard. Dukes Co.

Including Chappaquiddick Island

"Massachusetts Ten Townships," N.Y., *see* F127.T6

72.M6 Merrimac River and Valley (General, and Mass.)

Cf. F42.M4, New Hampshire

72.M7 Middlesex Co.

Including Lake Boon, Concord River, Middlesex Fells Reservation, Minute Man National Historical Park, Walden Pond

Middlesex Fells Reservation, *see* F72.M7

72.M73 Millers River and Valley

Minute Man National Historical Park, *see* F72.M7

72.N2 Nantucket Co.

Including Nantucket, Muskeget, and Tuckernuck Islands

72.N6 No Mans Land (Island)

72.N8 Norfolk Co.

Peddocks Island, *see* F72.P7

Pioneer Valley, *see* F72.C7

72.P6 Plum Island

72.P7 Plymouth Co.

Including North River, South Shore, Peddocks Island

72.S86 Sudbury River and Valley

72.S9 Suffolk Co.

Cf. F73 , Boston

72.S94 Swift River Valley. Quabbin Reservoir. Ware River Valley

Walden Pond, *see* F72.M7

Massachusetts

72.A-.Z **Regions, counties, etc., A-Z — Continued**

72.W9 Worcester Co.

Including Wachusett Mountain, Lake Quinsigamond

73 **Boston**

73.1 Periodicals. Societies. Collections

73.15 Museums. Exhibitions, exhibits

For Foreign Exhibition, 1883, see T460

73.18 Guidebooks

73.25 Biography (Collective). Genealogy (Collective)

Including vital records, epitaphs

73.27 Historiography

73.29 Study and teaching

73.3 General works. Histories

73.33 Juvenile works

Pamphlets, addresses, essays, etc.

73.35 General

73.36 Anecdotes, legends, pageants, etc.

73.37 Historic monuments (General). Illustrative material

73.39 Antiquities (Non-Indian)

By period

73.4 Early to 1775

Including the fires of 1711, 1737, 1760, etc.

Including biography: William Blackstone, etc.

Cf. E215, Events just prior to the Revolution

73.44 1775-1865

Cf. E450, Fugitive slave riots

73.5 1865-1950

Including fire of 1872

1951-

73.52 General works

Biography

73.53 Collective

73.54.A-.54.Z Individual, A-Z

GALE NOTE *See note at the head of Table F5 at the end of the text for further instructions on how to subdivide this number*

Sections. Localities. Districts, etc.

73.6 General works

73.61 Cemeteries

Including Copp's Hill Burial Ground, Granary Burial Ground, King's Chapel Burial Ground, Mount Hope Cemetery

73.62 Churches

73.625 Hotels, taverns, etc.

73.627 Places of amusement

73.63 Harbor

73.64 Monuments. Statues

GALE NOTE *The cutter number(s) listed below have been given only as examples by the Library of Congress*

73.64.A1 General works

73.64.B4 Beacon Hill Monument

73.64.W4 Wendell Phillips Statue

73.65 Parks. Squares. Circles

Including Boston Common, Franklin Park

73.67 Streets. Bridges. Railroads, etc.

GALE NOTE *The cutter number(s) listed below have been given only as examples by the Library of Congress*

73.67.A1 General works

73.67.P3 Park Street

73.67.S7 State Street

73.67.T7 Tremont Street

	Massachusetts
73	**Boston**
	Sections. Localities. Districts, etc.
73.67	Streets. Bridges. Railroads, etc. — Continued
73.67.W3	Washington Street
73.68.A-.68.Z	Suburbs. Sections of the city. Rivers
73.68.B32	Back Bay
73.68.B4	Beacon Hill
	Brighton, *see* F74.B73
73.68.C3	Castle Island
	Charlestown, *see* F74.C4
	Dorchester, *see* F74.D5
73.68.E2	East Boston
73.68.L43	Leather District
73.68.N65	North End
73.68.R2	Rainsford Island
73.68.R67	Roslindale
	Roxbury, *see* F74.R9
73.68.S7	South Boston
73.68.T5	Thompson Island
73.68.W47	West End
	West Roxbury, *see* F74.W59
73.69	Wards
	Buildings
73.7	Collective
73.8.A-.8.Z	Individual, A-Z
	GALE NOTE *The cutter number(s) listed below have been given only as examples by the Library of Congress*
73.8.C9	Crown Coffee House
73.8.F2	Faneuil Hall Market
73.8.O4	Old State House
73.8.P3	Parker House
73.8.S8	State House
	Elements in the population
73.9.A1	General works
73.9.A2-.9.Z	Individual elements
	For a list of racial, ethnic, and religious elements (with cutter numbers), see E184.A+
74.A-.Z	**Other cities, towns, etc., A-Z**
	GALE NOTE *The cutter number(s) listed below have been given only as examples by the Library of Congress*
74.B73	Brighton
74.C1	Cambridge
74.C4	Charlestown
74.C8	Concord
74.D5	Dorchester
74.G9	Groton
74.L98	Lynn
74.P8	Plymouth
74.P96	Provincetown
74.R9	Roxbury
74.S1	Salem
74.S8	Springfield
	Subarrange by Table F2 at the end of the text
74.T2	Taunton
	Including Old Colony Historical Society
74.W59	West Roxbury
74.W9	Worcester
	Elements in the population
75.A1	Collective

Massachusetts
Elements in the population — Continued
75.A2-.Z Individual elements
For a list of racial, ethnic, and religious elements (with cutter numbers), see E184.A+
Rhode Island
76 **Periodicals. Societies. Collections**
76.5 **Museums. Exhibitions, exhibits**
77 **Gazetteers. Dictionaries. Geographic names**
77.3 **Guidebooks**
78 **Biography (Collective). Genealogy (Collective)**
78.2 **Historiography**
Historians, *see* E175.5.A+
78.5 **Study and teaching**
79 **General works. Histories**
79.3 **Juvenile works**
Pamphlets, addresses, essays, etc.
79.5 General
79.6 Anecdotes, legends, pageants, etc.
80 **Historic monuments (General). Illustrative material**
81 **Antiquities (Non-Indian)**
By period
82 Early to 1775
Including First Rhode Island Charter, 1663; the Narragansett country; union of plantations at Newport, Portsmouth, Providence, and Warwick, 1636-1643
Including biography: John Clarke, Samuel Gorton, Roger Williams, etc.
Cf. E83.67, King Philip's War, 1675-1676
1775-1865
83 General
Cf. E215.6, Gaspee affair
Cf. E263.R4, Rhode Island in the Revolution (General)
Cf. E230+, Military operations and battles
Cf. E528.1+, Civil War, 1861-1865 (General)
83.4 Dorr Rebellion, 1842
Including biography: Thomas Wilson Dorr, etc.
84 1865-1950
Cf. D570.85.R4+, World War I, 1914-1918
Cf. D769.85.R4+, World War II, 1939-1945
Cf. E726.R4, War of 1898 (Spanish-American War)
85 1951-
87.A-.Z **Regions, counties, etc., A-Z**
87.A15 Counties
87.A16 Mountains
87.A17 Rivers
87.A18 Lakes
87.A19 Islands
87.B55 Blackstone River and Valley (General, and Rhode Island)
Cf. F72.B57 , Massachusetts
87.B6 Block Island (Manisees)
87.B7 Boundaries
Cf. F72.B7, Massachusetts boundary
Cf. F82, Massachusetts claims to Narragansett country
Cf. F102.B7, Connecticut boundary
87.B86 Bristol Co.
87.K3 Kent Co.
87.N2 Narragansett Bay region
87.N5 Newport Co.
For Block Island, see F87.B6
For Rhode Island (Island), see F87.R4
87.P3 Pawtuxet River and Valley
87.P5 Pettaquamscutt Purchase

Rhode Island

87.A-.Z **Regions, counties, etc., A-Z — Continued**

87.P9 Providence Co.

87.R4 Rhode Island (Island) (Aquidneck)

87.S25 Sakonnet River and Region

87.W3 Washington Co.

89.A-.Z **Cities, towns, etc., A-Z**

GALE NOTE *The cutter number(s) listed below have been given only as examples by the Library of Congress*

89.N5 Newport

89.P9 Providence

Subarrange by Table F2 at the end of the text

Elements in the population

90.A1 General works

90.A2-.Z Individual elements

For a list of racial, ethnic, and religious elements (with cutter numbers), see E184.A+

Connecticut

91 **Periodicals. Societies. Collections**

91.5 **Museums. Exhibitions, exhibits**

92 **Gazetteers. Dictionaries. Geographic names**

92.3 **Guidebooks**

93 **Biography (Collective). Genealogy (Collective)**

93.2 **Historiography**

Historians, *see* E175.5.A+

93.5 **Study and teaching**

94 **General works. Histories**

94.3 **Juvenile works**

Pamphlets, addresses, essays, etc.

94.5 General

94.6 Anecdotes, legends, pageants, etc.

94.8 **Geography**

95 **Historic monuments (General). Illustrative material**

96 **Antiquities (Non-Indian)**

By period

Early to 1775

Including early grants by the Council for New England; Dutch posts; etc.

Including biography: John Winthrop, 1606-1676

Cf. E83.63, Pequot War, 1636-1638

Cf. E83.67, King Philip's War, 1675-1676

Cf. E199, French and Indian War, 1755-1763

Cf. F7.5, Government of Andros, 1688-1689

Cf. F157.W9, Claims to Wyoming Valley, Susquehanna Company

97 General works

98 New Haven Colony

Cf. F102.N5, New Haven County

Cf. F104.N6, New Haven

99 1775-1865

Cf. E263.C5, Connecticut in the Revolution (General)

Cf. E230+, Military operations and battles in the Revolution

Cf. E309, F483, F497.W5, Cession of western lands

Cf. E357.7, Hartford Convention, 1814

Cf. E359.5.C7, War of 1812

Cf. E409.5.C6, War with Mexico, 1845-1848

Cf. E499.1+, Civil War, 1861-1865 (General)

Cf. F157.W9, Susquehanna claims

100 1865-1950

Cf. D570.85.C8+, World War I, 1914-1918

Cf. D769.85.C8+, World War II, 1939-1945

Cf. E726.C7, War of 1898 (Spanish-American War)

101 1951-

Connecticut — Continued

102.A-.Z **Regions, counties, etc., A-Z**

102.A15 Counties

102.A16 Mountains

102.A17 Rivers

102.A18 Lakes

102.A19 Islands

102.B7 Boundaries

Cf. F72.B7, Massachusetts boundary

Cf. F127.B7, New York boundary

Cf. F157.W9, Pennsylvania-Connecticut boundary dispute ("Connecticut Gore," Susquehanna Company)

102.C2 Lake Candlewood

102.C7 Connecticut River and Valley, Conn.

Cf. F12.C7, New England

102.F2 Fairfield Co.

Including Norwalk Islands and Sheffield Island

Firelands, *see* F497.W5

Fishers Island, *see* F127.F5

102.H3 Hartford Co.

102.H7 Housatonic River and Valley (General, and Conn.)

Cf. F72.H7, Massachusetts

102.L6 Litchfield Co.

Including Highland Lake, Litchfield Hills

For Berkshire Hills, see F72.B5

Long Island, *see* F127.L8

102.M6 Middlesex Co.

102.N2 Naugatuck River and Valley

102.N5 New Haven Co.

Including Leetes Island

Cf. F98, New Haven Colony

102.N7 New London Co.

102.T4 The Thimbles

102.T6 Tolland Co.

Western Reserve, *see* F497.W5

Westmoreland (township, 1774; county, 1775), *see* F157.W9

102.W7 Windham Co.

104.A-.Z **Cities, towns, etc., A-Z**

GALE NOTE *The cutter number(s) listed below have been given only as examples by the Library of Congress*

104.H3 Hartford

104.L7 Litchfield

104.N6 New Haven

Subarrange by Table F2 at the end of the text

104.N7 New London

104.N93 Norwich

104.S8 Stamford

Elements in the population

105.A1 General works

105.A2-.Z Individual elements

For a list of racial, ethnic, and religious elements (with cutter numbers), see E184.A+

106 **Atlantic coast of North America. Middle Atlantic States**

Including the eastern United States as a whole; Atlantic States (Maine to Florida); Middle States; Appalachian Mountains (General)

Class here descriptive and historic works after 1825

For earlier works, see E162-165 , E186-375

Cf. F157.D4, Delaware River and Valley

Cf. F157.S8, Susquehanna River and Valley

Cf. F172.D3, Delaware Bay and region

Cf. F187.C5, Chesapeake Bay and region

106 **Atlantic coast of North America. Middle Atlantic States — Continued**
Cf. F187.P8, Potomac River and Valley
Cf. F217.A65, Appalachian Mountains, Southern
Cf. F1035.8, Atlantic coast of Canada

New York
116 **Periodicals. Societies. Collections**
New York Historical Society
Collections
116.N62 First and second series, 1811-1859
116.N63 John Watts de Peyster Publication Fund series
Formerly Publication Fund series
116.N638 Quarterly bulletin, 1917-
116.N64 Proceedings, 1843-1849
116.N65 Annual report of the Executive Committee
116.N66 Charter, constitution, etc. Editions by date
116.N67 Lists of members. Editions by date
116.N68 Anniversary address. By date
116.N69 Inaugural address of President. By date
116.N7-.N76 Other official publications. By title
116.N77A-.N77Z Publications about the society or its officers. By author or name of officer
116.5 **Museums. Exhibitions, exhibits**
117 **Gazetteers. Dictionaries. Geographic names**
117.3 **Guidebooks**
118 **Biography (Collective). Genealogy (Collective)**
118.2 **Historiography**
Historians, *see* E175.5.A+
118.5 **Study and teaching**
119 **General works. Histories**
119.3 **Juvenile works**
Pamphlets, addresses, essays, etc.
119.5 General
119.6 Anecdotes, legends, pageants, etc.
120 **Historic monuments (General). Illustrative material**
121 **Antiquities (Non-Indian)**
By period
Early to 1775
Including English province, 1664-1774; Dutch reconquest, 1673-1674; Leisler's Rebellion, 1689; Agrarian conflicts, 1711-1715
Including biography: Nicholas Bayard; William Burnet; Cadwallader Colden; Thomas Dongan, Earl of Limerick; Caleb Heathcote; Jacob Leisler; etc.
Cf. E101+, Early voyages to America
Cf. E196, King William's War, 1689-1697
Cf. E199, French and Indian War, 1755-1763
Cf. F7.5, Andros and his government, 1688-1689
Cf. F52, New Hampshire Grants
Cf. F1030, French explorations, invasions, and missionaries in western New York
Cf. HD196.A+, Agrarian conflicts, 1711-1715
122 General works
122.1 New Netherlands. Dutch Colony, 1610-1664
Including biography: Arent van Curler, Adriaen van der Donck, Jonas Michaelius, Peter Minuit, Peter Stuyvesant, etc.
Cf. E83.655, Indian uprising of 1655
Cf. E83.663, Esopus Indian War, 1663-1664
Cf. F127.R32, Rensselaerswyck
Cf. F167, Subjugation of the Swedes on the Delaware, 1655
123 1775-1865
Including biography: John Watts DePeyster, James Kent, John Alsop King, Elias Warner Leavenworth, Henry Cruse Murphy, Daniel D. Tompkins, Stephen Van Rensselaer, etc.
Cf. E263.N6, New York in the Revolution (General)
Cf. E230+, Military operations and battles in the Revolution

New York

By period

123 1775-1865 — Continued

Cf. E359.5.N6, War of 1812 (General)

Cf. E355+, Military operations and battles in the War of 1812

Cf. E409.5.N6, War with Mexico, 1845-1848 (General)

Cf. E523.1+, Civil War, 1861-1865 (General)

Cf. F1032, Burning of the "Caroline"; the McLeod case

Cf. HD199, Antirent movement, 1835-1846

Cf. HS525+, Antimasonic Controversy, 1827-1845

Cf. TC625.E6, Erie Canal

124 1865-1950

Including biography: John Alden Dix, Daniel Drew, Roswell Pettibone Flower, Herbert Henry Lehman, Patrick Henry McCarren, James Aloysius O'Gorman, John Boyd Thacher, etc.

Cf. D570.85.N4+, World War I, 1914-1918

Cf. D769.85.N4+, World War II, 1939-1945

Cf. E726.N5, War of 1898 (Spanish-American War)

1951-

125 General works

Biography

125.2 Collective

125.3.A-.3.Z Individual, A-Z

GALE NOTE *See note at the head of Table F5 at the end of the text for further instructions on how to subdivide this number*

127.A-.Z **Regions, counties, etc., A-Z**

127.A15 Counties

127.A16 Mountains

127.A17 Rivers

127.A18 Lakes

127.A19 Islands

127.A2 Adirondack Mountains

Including Esther Mountain, Mount Marcy, etc.

127.A3 Albany Co.

Including Helderberg Mountains

Cf. F52 , New Hampshire

Cf. F127.R32 , Rensselaerswyck

127.A4 Allegany Co.

127.A43 Allegany State Park

127.A45 Allegheny River and Valley, N.Y.

Cf. F157.A5, General, and Pennsylvania

Allens Creek and Valley, *see* F127.M6

Altona Flat Rock, *see* F127.C77

Au Sable River and Valley, *see* F127.E8

127.B4 Beaver Kill and Beaver Kill Valley

Big Moose Lake, *see* F127.H5

127.B48 Black River

"Boston Ten Townships," *see* F127.T6

127.B7 Boundaries

Cf. F72.B7, Massachusetts boundary

Cf. F142.B7, New Jersey boundary

For Massachusetts territorial claims to western New York, see F127.G2

For New Hampshire-New York dispute over New Hampshire Grants, see F52

Bronx Co., *see* F128.68.B8

127.B8 Broome Co.

Cf. F127.G2, Genesee region

Cf. F127.T6, "Massachusetts (or Boston) Ten Townships"

127.C28 Castleton Island State Park

127.C3 Catskill Mountains

Including Kaaterskill Park, Rip Van Winkle Trail

127.C4 Cattaraugus Co.

New York

127.A-.Z **Regions, counties, etc., A-Z — Continued**

127.C5 Cayuga Co.

127.C52 Cayuga Lake

127.C6 Lake Champlain region (General, and N.Y.)

Including Champlain Valley; Lake Champlain Tercentenary, 1909

Cf. F57.C4, Vermont

Cf. F57.G7, Grand Isle Co., Vt.

Charlotte Co. (1772), *see* F127.W3

127.C7 Chautauqua Co.

Including Chautauqua Creek and Valley, Lake Chautauqua, Portage Trail

127.C72 Chemung Co.

127.C73 Chemung River and Valley (General, and N.Y.)

Cf. F157.C37 , Pennsylvania

127.C76 Chenango Co.

127.C765 Chenango River and Valley. Chenango Canal

Clermont State Park, *see* F127.L73

127.C77 Clinton Co.

Including Altona Flat Rock

127.C8 Columbia Co.

127.C83 Constitution Island

Cornwall Co., *see* F23

127.C85 Cortland Co.

Cumberland Co. (1768), *see* F52

127.D3 Delaware Co.

127.D4 Delaware River and Valley, N.Y.

Cf. F142.D4, New Jersey

Cf. F157.D4, General, and Pennsylvania

Cf. F172.D4, Delaware

127.D8 Dutchess Co.

Including Little (or Upper) Nine Partners Patent, etc.

127.E5 Erie Canal

127.E6 Erie Co.

127.E65 Lake Erie region, N.Y.

Cf. F555, Lake Erie (General)

127.E8 Essex Co.

Including Au Sable River and Valley, Au Sable Chasm, etc.

Esther Mountain, *see* F127.A2

127.F4 Finger Lakes region

Cf. F127.C52, Cayuga Lake, etc.

Fire Island, *see* F127.S9

127.F5 Fishers Island

Cf. F129.S74 , Southold

127.F8 Franklin Co.

Including Mount Seward, Saranac Lakes

127.F88 Fulton Chain Lakes and Region

127.F9 Fulton Co.

Gardiner's Island, *see* F129.E13

127.G15 Gateway National Recreation Area (General, and New York)

Cf. F142.G37, New Jersey

127.G19 Genesee Co.

127.G2 Genesee region. Genesee River and Valley

Including Phelps-Gorham Purchase (1788), etc.

Cf. F127.H7, Holland Purchase

Cf. F127.T6, "Massachusetts (or Boston) Ten Townships"

127.G3 Lake George

Gloucester Co. (1770), *see* F52

Grand Island, *see* F129.G68

127.G7 Greene Co.

For Catskill Mountains, see F127.C3

New York

127.A-.Z **Regions, counties, etc., A-Z — Continued**

Grindstone Island, *see* F127.T5

127.H2 Hamilton Co.

Including Blue Mountain Lake, Long Lake, Raquette Lake

Hamptons, *see* F127.S9

Helderberg Mountains, *see* F127.A3

127.H5 Herkimer Co.

Including West Canada Creek, Big Moose Lake

Hiawatha Island, *see* F127.S96

127.H7 Holland Purchase. Treaty of Big Tree, 1797

127.H73 Hoosic River and Valley (General, and N.Y.)

Cf. F57.B4, Vermont

Cf. F72.B5, Massachusetts

127.H8 Hudson River and Valley (General, and N.Y.)

Including Highlands; Hudson-Fulton Celebration, 1909; Palisades

Cf. F142.B4, New Jersey Palisades

Cf. F142.H83, New Jersey

Irondequoit Creek and Valley, *see* F127.M6

127.J4 Jefferson Co.

127.K4 Keuka Lake

127.K5 Kings Co.

Cf. F129.B7 , Borough of Brooklyn

127.L6 Lewis Co.

127.L7 Livingston Co.

Including Hemlock Lake

127.L73 Livingston Manor. Clermont State Park

127.L8 Long Island

For Fishers Island, see F127.F5

For Shelter Island, see F127.S54

Cf. F127.K5, Kings Co.

Cf. F127.N2, Nassau Co.

Cf. F127.Q3, Queens Co.

Cf. F127.S9, Suffolk Co.

127.M2 Madison Co.

Manhasset Neck, *see* F127.N2

Marcy, Mount, *see* F127.A2

"Massachusetts (or Boston) Ten Townships," *see* F127.T6

127.M4 Military tract (set off from Tryon Co., 1782)

127.M5 Minisink region

For Minisink Patent (1704), see F142.B7

127.M55 Mohawk River and Valley

Including Mohawk Trail, N.Y.

For Mohawk Trail, Mass., see F72.B5

127.M6 Monroe Co.

Including Allens Creek and Valley, Irondequoit Creek and Valley

127.M7 Montgomery Co.

Including Tryon Co. (1772-1784)

127.N2 Nassau Co.

Including Manhasset Neck

New Hampshire Grants, *see* F52

New York Co., *see* F128+

127.N38 New York State Seaway Trail

127.N5 Niagara Co.

127.N6 Niagara River and region (General, and N.Y.)

Including Niagara frontier, Niagara River and Valley, etc.

Cf. F1059.N5, Niagara Peninsula, Ontario

127.N8 Niagara Falls

Including State Reservation, Goat Island

Cf. F1059.Q3 , Queen Victoria Niagara Falls Park, Ontario

New York

127.A-.Z **Regions, counties, etc., A-Z — Continued**

127.O5 Oneida Co.

127.O52 Oneida Lake

127.O6 Onondaga Co.

Including Onondaga Lake

127.O7 Ontario Co.

Cf. F127.G2, Genesee region

Cf. F127.H7, Holland Purchase

127.O72 Lake Ontario region, N.Y.

Cf. F556, Lake Ontario (General)

127.O8 Orange Co.

Including Newburgh Bay

For Highlands, see F127.H8

For Minisink region, see F127.M5

For Wawayanda Patent (1703), see F142.B7

127.O9 Orleans Co.

127.O91 Oswego Co.

127.O93 Otsego Co.

Ozonia Lake, *see* F127.S2

Palisades of the Hudson, *see* F127.H8

Phelps-Gorham Purchase (1788), *see* F127.G2

127.P9 Putnam Co.

127.Q3 Queens Co.

Cf. F128.68.Q4, Borough of Queens

Raquette Lake, *see* F127.H2

127.R3 Rensselaer Co.

Including Taconic Mountains

127.R32 Rensselaerswyck. The Van Rensselaer Manor

Cf. HD199, Antirent movement, 1835-1846

Richmond Co., *see* F127.S7

Robins Island, *see* F127.S9

127.R6 Rockland Co.

127.S2 St. Lawrence Co.

Including Black Lake, Ozonia Lake

127.S23 St. Lawrence River and Valley, N.Y.

Cf. F127.T5, Thousand Islands

Cf. F1050, General, and Canada

127.S235 Sampson State Park

Saranac Lakes, *see* F127.F8

127.S26 Saratoga Co.

Including Mount McGregor, etc.

127.S27 Schenectady Co.

127.S3 Schoharie Co.

Including Schoharie Creek and Valley, etc.

127.S33 Schroon River and Valley

127.S34 Schuyler Co.

Including Watkins Glen

Seaway Trail, *see* F127.N38

127.S4 Seneca Co.

127.S43 Seneca Lake

Shawangunk Mountains, *see* F127.U4

127.S54 Shelter Island

127.S7 Staten Island. Richmond Co. Borough of Richmond

127.S8 Steuben Co.

Including Canisteo River

127.S9 Suffolk Co.

Including Fire Island, Fire Island State Park, Hamptons, Robins Island

For Fishers Island, see F127.F5

New York

127.A-.Z **Regions, counties, etc., A-Z — Continued**

127.S91 Sullivan Co.

For Minisink region, see F127.M5

127.S96 Susquehanna River and Valley, N.Y.

Including Hiawatha Island

Cf. F157.S8, General, and Pennsylvania

Cf. F187.S8, Maryland

127.T5 Thousand Islands

Including Carleton Island, Grenell Island, Grindstone Island

127.T6 Tioga Co. "Massachusetts (or Boston) Ten Townships"

Cf. F127.G2, Genesee region

127.T7 Tompkins Co.

Tryon Co. (1772-1784), *see* F127.M7

127.T83 Tug Hill region

127.U4 Ulster Co.

Including Lake Minnewaska, Mohonk Lake, Mount Meenahga, Shawangunk Mountains

For Catskill Mountains, see F127.C3

For Minisink region, see F127.M5

127.U54 Unadilla River and Valley

127.W2 Warren Co.

Including Luzerne Lake

Cf. F127.G3 , Lake George

127.W3 Washington Co.

Including Charlotte County (1772)

Cf. F52, New Hampshire Grants

Cf. F127.G3, Lake George

Wawayanda Patent (1703), *see* F142.B7

127.W4 Wayne Co.

127.W5 Westchester Co.

Including Fordham Manor, Philipsburg Manor, Van Cortlandt Manor

Cf. F128.68.B8, Borough of the Bronx

127.W9 Wyoming Co.

127.Y3 Yates Co.

New York (City). New York (County)

128.1 Periodicals. Societies. Collections

128.15 Museums. Exhibitions, exhibits

For World's Fair, 1939-1940, see T785

128.18 Guidebooks

128.25 Biography (Collective). Genealogy (Collective)

128.27 Historiography

128.29 Study and teaching

128.3 General works. Histories

128.33 Juvenile works

Pamphlets, addresses, essays, etc.

128.35 General

128.36 Anecdotes, legends, pageants, etc.

128.37 Historic monuments. Illustrative material

128.39 Antiquities (Non-Indian)

By period

128.4 Early to 1775

Including New Amstersdam; Negro plot, 1741

Including biography: Annetje Jane Bogardus, etc.

Cf. F122+, New York (State)

128.44 1775-1865

Including fire, 1835; Draft riot, 1863

Including biography: Michael Floy, Philip Hone, Fernando Wood, etc.

Cf. E263.N6, New York in the Revolution

Cf. E230+, Military operations and battles in the Revolution

New York

New York (City). New York (County)

By period — Continued

128.47 1865-1900

Including Riot, 1871; Blizzard, 1888

Including biography: Richard Croker, Andrew Haswell Green, John Kelly, Abram Stevens Hewitt, William Marcy Tweed, etc.

128.5 1901-1950. Greater New York

Including "General Slocum" disaster, 1904

Including biography: Edward Joseph Flynn, William Jay Gaynor, Seth Low, James John Walker, etc.

Cf. F127.Q3, Queens County

Cf. F127.S7, Staten Island, Richmond County

Cf. F129.B7, Brooklyn

1951-1980

128.52 General works

Biography

128.53 Collective

128.54.A-.54.Z Individual, A-Z

GALE NOTE *See note at the head of Table F5 at the end of the text for further instructions on how to subdivide this number*

1981-

128.55 General works

Biography

128.56 Collective

128.57.A-.57.Z Individual, A-Z

Sections. Localities. Districts, etc.

128.6 General works

128.61.A-.61.Z Cemeteries

GALE NOTE *The cutter number(s) listed below have been given only as examples by the Library of Congress*

128.61.A1 General works

128.61.W8 Woodlawn Cemetery

128.62 Churches

For architecture, see Subclass NA

For religious aspects, see Subclass BX

128.625 Hotels, taverns, etc.

128.627 Places of amusement

128.63 Harbor

128.64.A-.64.Z Monuments. Statues

GALE NOTE *The cutter number(s) listed below have been given only as examples by the Library of Congress*

128.64.A1 General works

128.64.G7 Grant Monument (Grant's Tomb)

128.64.L6 Statue of Liberty

128.65.A-.65.Z Parks. Squares. Circles

GALE NOTE *The cutter number(s) listed below have been given only as examples by the Library of Congress*

128.65.A1 General works

128.65.B3 Battery

128.65.B8 Bronx Parkway

128.65.C3 Central Park

128.65.C5 City Hall Park

128.65.R5 Riverside Park

128.65.Z6 Zoological Park

128.67.A-.67.Z Streets. Bridges. Railroads, etc.

GALE NOTE *The cutter number(s) listed below have been given only as examples by the Library of Congress*

128.67.A1 General works

128.67.B6 Bowery

New York
New York (City). New York (County)
Sections. Localities. Districts, etc.
128.67.A-.67.Z Streets. Bridges. Railroads, etc. — Continued
128.67.B7 Broadway
128.67.F4 Fifth Avenue
128.67.F7 Forty-second Street
128.67.P3 Park Avenue
128.67.R6 Riverside Drive
128.67.W2 Wall Street
128.68.A-.68.Z Suburbs. Sections of the city. Rivers
GALE NOTE *The cutter number(s) listed below have been given only as examples by the Library of Congress*
128.68.A1 General works
128.68.B6 Bloomingdale
128.68.B8 Bronx (Borough)
Including Morrisania Manor, Pelham Manor, etc.
Cf. F127.W5, Westchester Co.
Brooklyn (Borough), *see* F129.B7
128.68.C47 Chinatown
128.68.C5 City Island
Coney Island, *see* F129.C75
128.68.G7 Governor's Island
128.68.G8 Greenwich Village
128.68.H3 Harlem
128.68.H4 Harlem River
128.68.L5 Little Italy
Long Island City, *see* F129.L78
128.68.Q4 Queens (Borough)
Cf. F127.Q3, Queens County
Richmond (Borough), *see* F127.S7
Rockaway Beach, *see* F129.R8
Staten Island, *see* F127.S7
128.68.S9 Stuyvesant Village
128.68.W2 Washington Heights
128.69 Wards
Buildings
128.7 General works. Collective
128.8.A-.8.Z Individual, A-Z
GALE NOTE *The cutter number(s) listed below have been given only as examples by the Library of Congress*
128.8.M8 Morris Mansion (Jumel Mansion)
128.8.P4 Pennsylvania Station
128.8.R7 Rockefeller Center
128.8.V2 Van Cortlandt Mansion
128.8.W82 Woolworth Building
Elements in the population
128.9.A1 General works
128.9.A2-.9.Z Individual elements
For a list of racial, ethnic, and religious elements (with cutter numbers), see E184.A+
129.A-.Z **Other cities, towns, etc., A-Z**
GALE NOTE *The cutter number(s) listed below have been given only as examples by the Library of Congress*
129.A1 General works
129.A3 Albany
Subarrange by Table F2 at the end of the text
129.B7 Brooklyn
A borough of New York (City)
129.B8 Buffalo
Subarrange by Table F2 at the end of the text

New York
129.A-.Z Other cities, towns, etc., A-Z — Continued
129.C75 Coney Island
129.E13 East Hampton
Including Gardiner's Island, Gardiner Manor
129.G68 Grand Island
129.H99 Hyde Park
129.L78 Long Island City
129.O98 Oyster Bay
Including Sagamore Hill
129.R7 Rochester
Subarrange by Table F2 at the end of the text
129.R8 Rockaway Beach
129.S3 Saratoga Springs
129.S74 Southold
Cf. F127.F5, Fishers Island
Elements in the population
130.A1 General works
130.A2-.Z Individual elements
For a list of racial, ethnic, and religious elements (with cutter numbers), see E184.A+
New Jersey
131 **Periodicals. Societies. Collections**
131.5 **Museums. Exhibitions, exhibits**
132 **Gazetteers. Dictionaries. Geographic names**
132.3 **Guidebooks**
133 **Biography (Collective). Genealogy (Collective)**
133.2 **Historiography**
Historians, *see* E175.5.A+
133.5 **Study and teaching**
134 **General works. Histories**
134.3 **Juvenile works**
Pamphlets, addresses, essays, etc.
134.5 General
134.6 Anecdotes, legends, pageants, etc.
135 **Historic monuments (General). Illustrative material**
136 **Antiquities (Non-Indian)**
By period
137 Early to 1775
Including Plowden's New Albion Grant; East and West Jersey, 1676-1702
Including biography: Sir George Carteret, John Fenwick, William Franklin, etc.
Cf. E198, King George's War, 1744-1748
Cf. F142.S2, Fenwick's Colony
Cf. F167, New Sweden
138 1775-1865
Including biography: Richard Stockton Field, William Churchill Houston, Andrew Kirkpatrick, etc.
Cf. E263.N5, New Jersey in the Revolution
Cf. E230+, Military operations and battles in the Revolution
Cf. E359.5.N4, War of 1812 (General)
Cf. E521.1+, Civil War, 1861-1865 (General)
139 1865-1950
Including biography: Harold Giles Hoffman, John Peter Jackson, Henry Cooper Pitney, etc.
Cf. D570.85.N3+, World War I, 1914-1918
Cf. D769.85.N3+, World War II, 1939-1945
Cf. E726.N4, War of 1898 (Spanish-American War)
1951-
140 General works
Biography
140.2 Collective

New Jersey
By period
1951-
Biography — Continued
140.22.A-.22.Z Individual, A-Z
GALE NOTE *See note at the head of Table F5 at the end of the text for further instructions on how to subdivide this number*
142.A-.Z **Regions, counties, etc., A-Z**
142.A15 Counties
142.A16 Mountains
142.A17 Rivers
142.A18 Lakes
142.A19 Islands
142.A79 Atlantic Coast
142.A8 Atlantic Co.
Barnegat Bay, *see* F142.O2
142.B4 Bergen Co.
Including Hackensack River and Valley; New Jersey Palisades
Cf. F127.H8, New York
142.B7 Boundaries
Including Minisink and Wawayanda Patents
Cf. F172.B7, Delaware boundary
142.B9 Burlington Co.
Including Rancocas Valley
142.C16 Camden Co.
142.C2 Cape May Co.
142.C9 Cumberland Co.
Deal Lake, *see* F142.M7
142.D3 Delaware Bay region, N.J.
Cf. F172.D3 , General, and Delaware
142.D4 Delaware River and Valley, N.J.
Cf. F127.D4, New York
Cf. F157.D4, General, and Pennsylvania
Cf. F172.D4, Delaware
Delaware Water Gap, *see* F157.D5
142.E8 Essex Co.
Including Nutley area
142.G37 Gateway National Recreation Area
Cf. F127.G15, General, and New York
142.G5 Gloucester Co.
142.H35 Hackensack Meadowlands
142.H7 Lake Hopatcong
142.H8 Hudson Co.
142.H83 Hudson River and Valley, N.J.
Cf. F127.H8, General, and New York
Cf. F142.B4, New Jersey Palisades
142.H9 Hunterdon Co.
142.J4 Jersey Shore
142.L65 Long Beach Island
142.M5 Mercer Co.
142.M6 Middlesex Co.
142.M64 Millstone River and Valley
142.M7 Monmouth Co.
Including Deal Lake, Monmouth Patent, Navesink River and Valley, Shark River
142.M8 Morris Co.
142.M85 Morristown National Historical Park
142.M9 Mullica River
Navesink River and Valley, *see* F142.M7
New Albion Grant, *see* F137
142.N48 New Jersey Coastal Heritage Trail

New Jersey

142.A-.Z **Regions, counties, etc., A-Z — Continued**

142.O2 Ocean Co.

Including Barnegat Bay, Long Beach, Sedge Islands

Palisades of New Jersey, *see* F142.B4

Palisades of the Hudson (Interstate park), *see* F127.H8

142.P2 Passaic Co.

Including Ringwood Manor

142.P3 Passaic River and Valley

142.P5 Pine Barrens. Pinelands National Reserve

Pinelands National Reserve, *see* F142.P5

142.R16 Ramapo River and Valley, N.J.

142.R2 Raritan River and Valley

142.S2 Salem Co.

Including John Fenwick's colony

Sedge Islands, *see* F142.O2

142.S6 Somerset Co.

Staten Island, *see* F127.S7

142.S9 Sussex Co.

For Minisink Patent, see F142.B7

For Minisink region, see F127.M5

142.U5 Union Co.

142.W2 Warren Co.

For Delaware Water Gap, see F157.D5

142.W47 Wharton State Forest

144.A-.Z **Cities, towns, etc., A-Z**

GALE NOTE *The cutter number(s) listed below have been given only as examples by the Library of Congress*

144.A1 General works

144.A8 Atlantic City

144.C2 Camden

East Orange, *see* F144.O6

144.E4 Elizabeth

144.J5 Jersey City

Subarrange by Table F2 at the end of the text

144.N6 Newark

Subarrange by Table F2 at the end of the text

144.O6 Orange (East, South, West)

144.P4 Paterson

South Orange, *see* F144.O6

144.T7 Trenton

Subarrange by Table F2 at the end of the text

West Orange, *see* F144.O6

Elements in the population

145.A1 General works

145.A2-.Z Individual elements

For a list of racial, ethnic, and religious elements (with cutter numbers), see E184.A+

Pennsylvania

146 **Periodicals. Societies. Collections**

146.5 **Museums. Exhibitions, exhibits**

147 **Gazetteers. Dictionaries. Geographic names**

147.3 **Guidebooks**

148 **Biography (Collective). Genealogy (Collective)**

148.2 **Historiography**

Historians, *see* E175.5.A+

148.5 **Study and teaching**

149 **General works. Histories**

149.3 **Juvenile works**

Pamphlets, addresses, essays, etc.

149.5 General

Pennsylvania

Pamphlets, addresses, essays, etc. — Continued

149.6 Anecdotes, legends, pageants, etc.

149.8 **Geography**

150 **Historic monuments (General). Illustrative material**

151 **Antiquities (Non-Indian)**

By period

Early to 1775

152 General

Including Grant to Penn, 1681; the Paxton boys

Including biography: Andrew Hamilton, Sir William Keith, James Logan, Francis Daniel Pastorius, Richard Peters, Michael Schlatter, Conrad Weiser, etc.

Cf. E83.76, Pontiac's Conspiracy, 1763-1765

Cf. E198, King George's War, 1744-1748

Cf. E199, French and Indian War, 1755-1763

Cf. F157.W5, Virginia claims in southwestern Pennsylvania

Cf. F157.W9, Connecticut claims in northeastern Pennsylvania

152.2 The proprietors: William Penn and family

153 1775-1865

Including Harrisburg Convention, 1788; Buckshot War, 1838

Including biography: Charles Biddle, Benjamin Chew, James Cooper, William John Duane, Thomas Earle, John Bannister Gibson, Joseph Hiester, Ellis Lewis, Joseph Ritner, William Rodman, George Washington Woodward, etc.

Cf. E263.P4, Pennsylvania in the Revolution

Cf. E230+, Military operations and battles in the Revolution

Cf. E315, Whisky Rebellion, 1794

Cf. E326, Fries' Rebellion, 1798-1799

Cf. E359.5.P3, War of 1812

Cf. E409.5.P3, War with Mexico, 1845-1848

Cf. E527+, Civil War, 1861-1865 (General)

Cf. E470.2, E471+, Campaigns and battles in the Civil War

Cf. F157.W9, Connecticut settlers in Wyoming Valley, Susquehanna claim

154 1865-1950

Including biography: John Wallace Crawford; John A. Lemon; Arthur George Olmsted; Samuel Whitaker Pennypacker; George Ross, 1841-1894; etc.

Cf. D570.85.P4+, World War I, 1914-1918

Cf. D769.85.P4+, World War II, 1939-1945

Cf. E726.P4, War of 1898 (Spanish-American War)

Cf. HV6452.A+, Molly Maguires

1951-

155 General works

Biography

155.2 Collective

155.3.A-.3.Z Individual, A-Z

GALE NOTE *See note at the head of Table F5 at the end of the text for further instructions on how to subdivide this number*

157.A-.Z **Regions, counties, etc., A-Z**

157.A15 Counties

157.A16 Mountains

157.A17 Rivers

157.A18 Lakes

157.A19 Islands

157.A2 Adams Co.

For Conewago Creek and Valley, see F157.C75

157.A4 Allegheny Co.

157.A5 Allegheny River and Valley (General, and Pa.)

Cf. F127.A45, New York

157.A7 Armstrong Co.

157.B16 Bald Eagle Mountain

Pennsylvania

157.A-.Z **Regions, counties, etc., A-Z — Continued**

157.B2 Beaver Co.

Including Ohio River and Valley, Pa.

Cf. F516+, General

157.B23 Beaver River and Valley

157.B25 Bedford Co.

157.B3 Berks Co.

Including Oley Valley

157.B5 Blair Co.

157.B65 Blue Mountains

157.B7 Boundaries. Mason and Dixon's Line

For Connecticut claims in northeastern Pennsylvania, see F157.W9

For Virginia claim to land south and east of the Ohio River, see F157.W5

Cf. F127.B7, New York boundary

Cf. F497.B7, Ohio boundary

157.B76 Bradford Co.

157.B77 Brandywine Creek and Valley (General, and Pennsylvania)

Cf. F172.B78, Delaware

157.B8 Bucks Co.

For Perkiomen River and Valley, see F157.M7

Buffalo Creek and Valley, *see* F157.U5

157.B87 Butler Co.

157.C16 Cambria Co.

157.C18 Cameron Co.

157.C2 Carbon Co.

157.C3 Centre Co.

Including Penn's Cave, etc.

157.C37 Chemung River and Valley, Pa.

Cf. F127.C73, General, and New York

157.C4 Chester Co.

157.C5 Clarion Co.

157.C52 Clarion River

157.C53 Clearfield Co.

157.C6 Clinton Co.

157.C67 Cocalico Creek and Valley

157.C7 Columbia Co.

157.C73 Conemaugh River and Valley

Conestoga Creek and Valley, *see* F157.L2

157.C75 Conewago Creek and Valley

157.C76 Cook Forest Park

157.C77 Crawford Co.

Including Conneaut Lake

157.C8 Cumberland Co.

Including Old Cumberland Co. (Formed 1750)

157.C85 Cumberland Road. National Road

Cf. HE356.C8, Traffic engineering

157.C9 Cumberland (Kittochtinny) Valley

Including Cumberland and Franklin Counties

For Franklin County only, see F157.F8

157.D2 Dauphin Co.

157.D28 Delaware and Lehigh National Heritage Corridor

157.D3 Delaware Co.

157.D4 Delaware River and Valley (General, and Pa.)

Cf. F127.D4, New York

Cf. F142.D4, New Jersey

Cf. F172.D4, Delaware

157.D5 Delaware Water Gap

157.E4 Elk Co.

157.E45 Endless Mountains

Pennsylvania

157.A-.Z **Regions, counties, etc., A-Z — Continued**

157.E6 Erie Co.

Including Lake Erie region, Pa.

Cf. F555, Lake Erie (General)

157.F2 Fayette Co. (Formed 1783)

Cf. F157.W5, Old Westmoreland Co.

157.F65 Forbes Road

157.F7 Forest Co.

157.F8 Franklin Co.

Including Cumberland Valley (the part in Franklin Co.), Conococheague Creek and Valley

Cf. F157.C9, Cumberland Valley (General, and Cumberland Co.)

Cf. F187.W3, Conococheague Creek, Md.

157.F9 Fulton Co.

157.G8 Greene Co. (Formed 1796)

Cf. F157.W5 , Old Westmoreland Co.

157.H9 Huntingdon Co.

Independence National Historical Park, *see* F158.65.I3

157.I3 Indiana Co.

157.J4 Jefferson Co.

157.J6 Juniata Co.

157.J7 Juniata River and Valley

157.L15 Lackawanna Co.

157.L17 Lackawanna River and Valley

157.L2 Lancaster Co.

Including Conestoga Creek, Mill Creek and Valley, Pequea Creek

157.L3 Lawrence Co.

League Island, *see* F158.68.L4

157.L4 Lebanon Co.

157.L5 Lehigh Co.

157.L6 Lehigh River and Valley

157.L8 Luzerne Co.

157.L9 Lycoming Co.

157.M2 McKean Co.

157.M3 Mahoning River and Valley, Pa.

Cf. F497.M2 , General, and Ohio

Mason and Dixon's line, *see* F157.B7

157.M5 Mercer Co.

157.M55 Mifflin Co.

Mill Creek and Valley, *see* F157.L2

157.M58 Monongahela River and Valley (General, and Pa.)

Cf. F247.M6, West Virginia

157.M6 Monroe Co.

Including Pocono Mountains, etc.

For Delaware Water Gap, see F157.D5

157.M7 Montgomery Co.

Including Perkiomen River and Valley, etc.

157.M8 Montour Co.

157.N7 Northampton Co.

157.N8 Northumberland Co.

157.O26 Octoraro Creek and Valley (General and Pennsylvania)

Cf. F187.O27, Maryland

Ohio River and Valley, *see* F157.B2

Oley Valley, *see* F157.B3

157.P44 Pennsylvania Dutch Country

Cf. F157.L2, Pennsylvania Dutch in Lancaster County

157.P5 Perry Co.

157.P56 Philadelphia Co.

Cf. F158.44 , Consolidation Act merging the county into the city in 1854

157.P6 Pike Co.

Pennsylvania

157.A-.Z **Regions, counties, etc., A-Z — Continued**

157.P63 Pine Creek (Potter County-Lycoming County)

157.P64 Pine Creek Gorge Natural Area

157.P8 Potter Co.

157.S3 Schuylkill Co.

157.S33 Schuylkill River and Valley

157.S47 Shenango River and Valley

157.S49 Sinnamahoning Creek

157.S5 Snyder Co.

157.S6 Somerset Co.

157.S67 Sullivan Co.

Including Eagle's Mere

157.S7 Susquehanna Co.

157.S8 Susquehanna River and Valley (General, and Pa.)

Cf. F127.S96, New York

Cf. F187.S8, Maryland

157.S9 West Branch of the Susquehanna

157.T5 Tioga Co.

157.U5 Union Co.

Including Buffalo Creek and Valley

157.V4 Venango Co.

157.W2 Warren Co.

157.W3 Washington Co. (Formed 1781)

Cf. F157.W5, Old Westmoreland Co.

157.W35 Wayne Co.

157.W5 Westmoreland Co.

Including Old Westmoreland County, formed 1773 (present-day Westmoreland, Washington, Fayette, and Greene Counties); boundary disputes with Virginia until 1784 over land south and east of the Ohio River (Virginia's so-called District of West Augusta: counties of Monongalia, Yohogania, and Ohio)

Cf. F157.W9, Connecticut's old county of Westmoreland

Cf. F247.M7, Monongalia Co., W. Va.

Cf. F247.O3, Ohio Co., W. Va.

157.W8 Wyoming Co.

157.W9 Wyoming Valley

Including Connecticut claims, Susquehanna Company, "Connecticut Gore," Connecticut town and county of Westmoreland

157.Y6 York Co.

For Conewago Creek and Valley, see F157.C75

157.Y7 York Road

157.Y72 Youghiogheny River and Valley (General, and Pennsylvania)

Cf. F187.Y68, Maryland

Cf. F247.Y68, West Virginia

158 **Philadelphia**

158.1 Periodicals. Societies. Collections

158.15 Museums. Exhibitions, exhibits

For Centennial Exposition, 1876, see T825

For Sesquicentennial International Exposition, 1926, see T826.3

158.18 Guidebooks

158.25 Biography (Collective). Genealogy (Collective)

158.27 Historiography

158.29 Study and teaching

158.3 General works. Histories

158.33 Juvenile works

Pamphlets, addresses, essays, etc.

158.35 General

158.36 Anecdotes, legends, pageants, etc.

158.37 Historic monuments. Illustrative material

158.39 Antiquities (Non-Indian)

Pennsylvania

158 **Philadelphia — Continued**

By period

158.4 Early to 1775

158.44 1775-1865

Including merging of the county of Philadelphia into the city; burning of the Orphan Asylum, 1822; riots of 1831, 1838, 1844

Cf. E233, Howe's occupation in 1777

158.5 1865-1950

1951-

158.52 General works

Biography

158.53 Collective

158.54.A-.54.Z Individual, A-Z

GALE NOTE *See note at the head of Table F5 at the end of the text for further instructions on how to subdivide this number*

Sections. Localities. Districts, etc.

158.6 General works

158.61.A-.61.Z Cemeteries

158.61.A1 General works

158.61.M8 Monument Cemetery

158.62.A-.62.Z Churches

158.62.A1 General works

158.62.C5 Christ Church

158.62.F5 First Presbyterian Church

158.625 Hotels, taverns, etc.

158.627 Places of amusement

158.63 Harbor

158.64.A-.64.Z Monuments. Statues

GALE NOTE *The cutter number(s) listed below have been given only as examples by the Library of Congress*

158.64.A1 General works

158.64.G3 Garfield Memorial

158.64.M2 McKinley Statue

158.64.P4 Pennypacker Memorial

158.64.W3 Washington monuments

158.65.A-.65.Z Parks. Squares. Circles

GALE NOTE *The cutter number(s) listed below have been given only as examples by the Library of Congress*

158.65.A1 General works

158.65.F2 Fairmount Park

158.65.I3 Independence National Historical Park

For Independence Hall alone, see F158.8.I3

158.67.A-.67.Z Streets. Bridges. Railroads

GALE NOTE *The cutter number(s) listed below have been given only as examples by the Library of Congress*

158.67.A1 General works

158.67.F17 Fairmount Parkway

158.67.I33 Independence Square

158.67.M34 Market Street

158.68.A-.68.Z Suburbs. Sections of the city. Rivers, etc.

GALE NOTE *The cutter number(s) listed below have been given only as examples by the Library of Congress*

158.68.A1 General works

158.68.E4 Elmwood

158.68.F2 Falls of Schuylkill

Germantown, *see* F159.G3

158.68.L4 League Island

158.68.N8 North Penn Village

158.68.N9 Northern Liberties

	Pennsylvania
158	**Philadelphia**
	Sections. Localities. Districts, etc.
158.68.A-.68.Z	Suburbs. Sections of the city. Rivers, etc. — Continued
158.68.O8	Oxford Township
158.68.P8	Port Royal Farm
158.68.S6	Southwark
158.68.W5	West Philadelphia
158.68.W7	Windmill Island
158.68.W8	Wissahickon Creek
158.69	Wards
	Buildings
158.7	General works. Collective
158.8.A-.8.Z	Individual, A-Z
	GALE NOTE *The cutter number(s) listed below have been given only as examples by the Library of Congress*
158.8.A7	Arsenal, Frankford
158.8.C2	Carpenters' Hall
158.8.C5	City Hall
158.8.C7	Congress Hall
158.8.I3	Independence Hall
	Including Liberty bell
158.8.P4	Pennsylvania Hall
158.8.S8	Strawberry Mansion
158.8.W3	Washington Mansion
	Elements in the population
158.9.A1	General works
158.9.A2-.9.Z	Individual elements
	For a list of racial, ethnic, and religious elements (with cutter numbers), see E184.A+
159.A-.Z	**Other cities, towns, etc., A-Z**
	GALE NOTE *The cutter number(s) listed below have been given only as examples by the Library of Congress*
159.C4	Chambersburg
159.E7	Erie
159.G3	Germantown
159.H3	Harrisburg
	Jim Thorpe, *see* F159.M4
159.J7	Johnstown
159.M4	Mauch Chunk. Jim Thorpe
159.P6	Pittsburgh
	Subarrange by Table F2 at the end of the text
159.R2	Reading
159.S4	Scranton
159.W6	Wilkes-Barre
	Elements in the population
160.A1	General works
160.A2-.Z	Individual elements
	For a list of racial, ethnic, and religious elements (with cutter numbers), see E184.A+
	Delaware
161	**Periodicals. Societies. Collections**
161.5	**Museums. Exhibitions, exhibits**
162	**Gazetteers. Dictionaries. Geographic names**
162.3	**Guidebooks**
163	**Biography (Collective). Genealogy (Collective)**
163.2	**Historiography**
	Historians, *see* E175.5.A+
163.5	**Study and teaching**
164	**General works. Histories**
164.3	**Juvenile works**

Delaware — Continued

Pamphlets, addresses, essays, etc.

164.5 General

164.6 Anecdotes, legends, pageants, etc.

165 **Historic monuments (General). Illustrative material**

166 **Antiquities (Non-Indian)**

By period

167 Early to 1775

Including Swedish settlements on the Delaware River; New Sweden; Dutch conquest, 1655; English conquest, 1664; part of Penn's grant, 1681; the "Lower Counties on the Delaware"

Including biography: Johan Classon Rising, etc.

168 1775-1865

Including biography: Jacob Broom, etc.

Cf. E263.D3, Delaware in the Revolution (General)

Cf. E230+, Military operations and battles in the Revolution

Cf. E500+, Civil War, 1861-1865 (General)

169 1865-1950

Including biography: John Edward Addicks, Edward Woodward Gilpin, etc.

Cf. D570.85.D4+, World War I, 1914-1918

Cf. D769.85.D4+, World War II, 1939-1945

1951-

170 General works

Biography

170.3 Collective

170.4.A-.4.Z Individual, A-Z

GALE NOTE *See note at the head of Table F5 at the end of the text for further instructions on how to subdivide this number*

172.A-.Z **Regions, counties, etc., A-Z**

172.A15 Counties

172.A16 Mountains

172.A17 Rivers

172.A18 Lakes

172.A19 Islands

172.B7 Boundaries

Cf. F157.B7, Pennsylvania boundary; Mason and Dixon's line

Cf. F187.B7, Maryland boundary

172.B78 Brandywine Creek and Valley

Cf. F157.B77, General and Pennsylvania

172.D3 Delaware Bay and region

Including General, and Delaware (State)

Cf. F142.D3, New Jersey

172.D4 Delaware River and Valley, Del.

Cf. F127.D4, New York

Cf.F142.D4, New Jersey

Cf. F157.D4, General, and Pennsylvania

Delmarva Peninsula, *see* F187.E2

172.K3 Kent Co.

172.N35 Nanticoke River and Valley (General and Delaware)

Cf. F187.N35, Maryland

172.N5 New Castle Co.

Including Christina River (Creek)

For Bohemia Manor, see F187.C3

172.S8 Sussex Co.

174.A-.Z **Cities, towns, etc., A-Z**

GALE NOTE *The cutter number(s) listed below have been given only as examples by the Library of Congress*

174.D74 Dover

174.W7 Wilmington

Subarrange by Table F2 at the end of the text

Delaware — Continued

Elements in the population

175.A1 General works

175.A2-.Z Individual elements

For a list of racial, ethnic, and religious elements (with cutter numbers), see E184.A+

Maryland

176 **Periodicals. Societies. Collections**

178 **Museums. Exhibitions, exhibits**

179 **Gazetteers. Dictionaries. Geographic names**

179.3 **Guidebooks**

180 **Biography (Collective). Genealogy (Collective)**

180.2 **Historiography**

Historians, *see* E175.5.A+

180.5 **Study and teaching**

181 **General works. Histories**

181.3 **Juvenile works**

Pamphlets, addresses, essays, etc.

181.5 General

181.6 Anecdotes, legends, pageants, etc.

181.8 **Geography**

182 **Historic monuments (General). Illustrative material**

183 **Antiquities (Non-Indian)**

By period

184 Early to 1775

Including the Calverts, proprietors of Maryland; Kent Island and Claiborne; toleration in Maryland

Including biography: George Calvert, 1st Baron of Baltimore; Cecilius Calvert, 2d Baron of Baltimore; William Claiborne; etc.

Cf. E199, French and Indian Wars, 1755-1763

Cf. F157.B7, Mason and Dixon's line

185 1775-1865

Including biography: Enoch Louis Lowe, John Van Lear McMahon, etc.

Cf. E263.M3, Maryland in the Revolution (General)

Cf. E230+, Military operations and battles in the Revolution

Cf. E359.5.M2, War of 1812 (General)

Cf. E355+, Military operations and battles in the War of 1812

Cf. F189.B1, Baltimore Riot, 1812

Cf. E409.5.M2, War with Mexico, 1845-1848

Cf. E512.1+, Civil War, 1861-1865 (General)

Cf. E470.2+, E471+, Military operations and battles in the Civil War, 1861-1865

Cf. E566.1+, As a Confederate state

186 1865-1950

Including Reconstruction, 1865-1877

Including biography: Aloysius Leo Knott, Charles Edward Phelps

Cf. D570.85.M3+ , World War I, 1914-1918

Cf. D769.85.M3+ , World War II, 1939-1945

1951-

186.2 General works

Biography

186.3 Collective

186.35.A-.35.Z Individual, A-Z

GALE NOTE *See note at the head of Table F5 at the end of the text for further instructions on how to subdivide this number*

186.9 **Western Maryland**

187.A-.Z **Regions, counties, etc., A-Z**

187.A15 Counties

187.A16 Mountains

187.A17 Rivers

187.A18 Lakes

187.A19 Islands

Maryland

187.A-.Z **Regions, counties, etc., A-Z — Continued**

187.A4 Allegany Co.

187.A6 Anne Arundel Co.

Including Severn River and Valley, St. Anne's Parish, St. James' Parish

Assateague Island National Seashore, *see* F187.W7

187.B2 Baltimore Co.

Including Patapsco Neck and River, Hampton National Historic Site

187.B7 Boundaries

Cf. F157.B7, Pennsylvania boundary; Mason and Dixon's line

Cf. F202.B7, District of Columbia boundary

187.C15 Calvert Co.

Including Christ Church Parish, Solomons Island

187.C2 Caroline Co.

187.C25 Carroll Co.

Catoctin Mountain, *see* F187.F8

187.C3 Cecil Co.

Including St. Mary Anne's Parish, Bohemia Manor, Worsell Manor

187.C4 Charles Co.

187.C47 Chesapeake and Ohio Canal area

187.C5 Chesapeake Bay region (General, and Md.)

Including Kent Island, Magothy River and Valley, Smith Island

Cf. F187.E2, Eastern Shore, Md.

Cf. F232.C43, Virginia

Cf. F232.E2, Eastern Shore, Va.

187.C6 Cobb Island

187.D6 Dorchester Co.

Including Blackwater River and Valley, Elliott Island

187.E2 Eastern Shore of Maryland. Delmarva Peninsula

Including Pocomoke River, etc.

Elliott Island, *see* F187.D6

187.F8 Frederick Co.

Including Catoctin Mountain, Prince George's Parish, Sugar Loaf Mountain

187.G2 Garrett Co.

Great Falls of the Potomac, *see* F187.M7

Hampton National Historic Site, *see* F187.B2

187.H2 Harford Co.

Including Deer Creek, St. George's Parish

187.H8 Howard Co.

187.K3 Kent Co.

Including Chester Parish

Kent Island, *see* F187.C5

Magothy River and Valley, *see* F187.C5

Maryland Heights, *see* F187.W3

Mason and Dixon's line, *see* F157.B7

187.M7 Montgomery Co.

Including Great Falls of the Potomac, Prince George's Parish

187.N35 Nanticoke River and Valley

Cf. F172.N35, General and Delaware

187.O27 Octoraro Creek and Valley

Cf. F157.O26, General and Pennsylvania

Patapsco Neck and River, *see* F187.B2

187.P38 Patuxent River and Valley

187.P56 Piscataway Park

Pocomoke River, *see* F187.E2

187.P8 Potomac River and Valley (General, and Md.)

Cf. F202.P8, District of Columbia

Cf. F232.P8, Virginia

Cf. F247.P8, West Virginia

For Great Falls, see F187.M7

Maryland

187.A-.Z **Regions, counties, etc., A-Z — Continued**

187.P9 Prince Georges Co.

Including King George's Parish, Queen Anne's Parish, etc.

187.Q3 Queen Annes Co.

187.S2 St. Marys Co.

Severn River and Valley, *see* F187.A6

Smith Island, *see* F187.C5

Solomons Island, *see* F187.C15

187.S7 Somerset Co.

Sugar Loaf Mountain, *see* F187.F8

187.S8 Susquehanna River and Valley, Md.

Cf. F127.S96, New York

Cf. F157.S8, General, and Pennsylvania

187.T2 Talbot Co.

187.W3 Washington Co.

Including Antietam Creek, Conococheague Creek and Valley, Md., Maryland Heights

Cf. F157.F8, Conococheague Creek and Valley, Pennsylvania

187.W5 Wicomico Co.

187.W7 Worcester Co.

Including Assateague Island National Seashore

187.Y68 Youghiogheny River and Valley

Cf. F157.Y72, General, and Pennsylvania

Cf. F247.Y68, West Virginia

189.A-.Z **Cities, towns, etc., A-Z**

GALE NOTE *The cutter number(s) listed below have been given only as examples by the Library of Congress*

189.A6 Annapolis

Subarrange by Table F2 at the end of the text

189.B1 Baltimore

Subarrange by Table F2 at the end of the text

Elements in the population

190.A1 General works

190.A2-.Z Individual elements

For a list of racial, ethnic, and religious elements (with cutter numbers), see E184.A+

District of Columbia. Washington

191 **Periodicals. Societies. Collections**

191.5 **Museums. Exhibitions, exhibits**

192 **Gazetteers. Dictionaries. Geographic names**

192.3 **Guidebooks**

193 **Biography (Collective). Genealogy (Collective)**

193.2 **Historiography**

Historians, *see* E175.5.A+

193.5 **Study and teaching**

194 **General works. Histories**

194.3 **Juvenile works**

Pamphlets, addresses, essays, etc.

194.5 General

194.6 Anecdotes, legends, pageants, etc.

195 **Historic monuments. Illustrative material**

Including location of national capital, L'Enfant and his plan, retrocession

195.5 **Antiquities (Non-Indian)**

196 **Political and social life**

By period

Including Inauguration ceremonies, 1801-

197 Early to 1815

Cf. E356.W3, Capture by the British, 1814

198 1815-1878

Including biography: William Albert Bradley, Joseph Gales, Walter Lenox, Alexander Robey Shepherd, etc.

District of Columbia. Washington

By period

198 1815-1878 — Continued

Cf. E396, Explosion of frigate Princeton, 1844

Cf. E409.5.D6, War with Mexico, 1845-1848

Cf. E501.1+, Civil War, 1861-1865 (General)

Cf. E470.2+, E471+, Military operations and battles in the Civil War, 1861-1865

Cf. F195, Retrocession of Alexandria County to Virginia, 1846

199 1878-1950

Including Bonus Expeditionary Force, 1932, 1933, etc.

Cf. D570.85.D6, World War I, 1914-1918

Cf. D769.85.D6, World War II, 1939-1945

1951-1980

200 General works

Biography and memoirs

200.2 Collective

200.3.A-.3.Z Individual, A-Z

GALE NOTE *See note at the head of Table F5 at the end of the text for further instructions on how to subdivide this number*

1981-

201 General works

Biography and memoirs

201.2 Collective

201.3.A-.3.Z Individual, A-Z

GALE NOTE *See note at the head of Table F5 at the end of the text for further instructions on how to subdivide this number*

202.A-.Z **Regions, suburbs, etc., A-Z**

202.A5 Anacostia River and Valley

202.B7 Boundaries

Cf. F195, Retrocession of Alexandria County to Virginia, 1846

202.B8 Brightwood

202.B9 Brookland

For West Brookland, see F202.W5

202.C2 Capitol Hill

202.C46 Chinatown

202.C6 Columbia Heights

202.G3 Georgetown

202.L4 Le Droit Park

202.M9 Mount Pleasant

202.N5 Northeast Washington

202.N7 Northwest Washington

202.P8 Potomac River and Valley, D.C

Cf. F187.P8, General, and Maryland

Cf. F203.3, Washington Harbor

Cf. F232.P8, Virginia

Cf. F247.P8, West Virginia

202.S6 Southeast Washington

202.S7 Southwest Washington

202.T4 Temple Heights

202.T43 Tenleytown

Theodore Roosevelt (Analostan) Island, *see* F203.4.T5

202.W5 West Brookland

203 **Localities, etc.**

203.1.A-.1.Z Cemeteries

Cf. RA626+, Management, laying-out, etc., of cemeteries

GALE NOTE *The cutter number(s) listed below have been given only as examples by the Library of Congress*

203.1.A1 General works

Arlington National Cemetery, *see* F234.A7

203.1.C7 Congressional Cemetery

District of Columbia. Washington

203 **Localities, etc.**

203.1.A-.1.Z Cemeteries — Continued

203.1.G5 Glenwood Cemetery

203.1.O12 Oak Hill Cemetery

203.2.A-.2.Z Churches

GALE NOTE *The cutter number(s) listed below have been given only as examples by the Library of Congress*

203.2.A1 General works

203.2.N4 New York Avenue Presbyterian Church

203.2.S14 St. John's Church, Georgetown

203.3 Harbor

203.35 Hotels, taverns, etc.

203.4.A-.4.Z Monuments. Statues. Memorials

GALE NOTE *The cutter number(s) listed below have been given only as examples by the Library of Congress*

203.4.A1 General works

Cf. F204.C2, The Capitol, Statuary Hall

203.4.B7 Braddock's Rock

203.4.C7 Columbus Monument

203.4.E6 Ericsson Monument

203.4.G2 Garfield Statue

203.4.G7 Grant Memorial

203.4.J4 Jefferson Memorial

203.4.L73 Lincoln Memorial

203.4.M5 Meade Monument

203.4.T5 Theodore Roosevelt Island

203.4.W3 Washington Monument

203.5.A-.5.Z Parks. Squares. Circles

GALE NOTE *The cutter number(s) listed below have been given only as examples by the Library of Congress*

203.5.A1 General works

203.5.C2 Capitol Grounds

203.5.L2 Lafayette Park

203.5.M2 The Mall

203.5.P86 Potomac Park

203.5.R6 Rock Creek Park

203.7.A-.7.Z Streets. Bridges. Railroads

GALE NOTE *The cutter number(s) listed below have been given only as examples by the Library of Congress*

203.7.A1 General works

203.7.A6 Arlington Memorial Bridge

203.7.C7 Constitution Avenue

203.7.F7 Fourteenth Street

203.7.L8 Long Bridge

203.7.P4 Pennsylvania Avenue

203.7.S6 Sixteenth Street

203.9 Wards

204.A-.Z **Buildings**

GALE NOTE *The cutter number(s) listed below have been given only as examples by the Library of Congress*

204.A1 General works

204.B5 Blair House

204.C2 Capitol

204.C3 Cathedral of St. Peter and Paul

204.C5 City Hall

204.D43 Department of Commerce Building

204.F6 Ford Theatre

204.H8 House Office Building

204.M5 Memorial Continental Hall

	District of Columbia. Washington
204.A-.Z	**Buildings — Continued**
204.N23	National Theatre
204.O2	Octagon House
204.P47	Petersen House
204.S9	Supreme Court Building
204.U5	Union Railroad Station
204.W5	White House
	Elements in the population
205.A1	General works
205.A2-.Z	Individual elements
	For a list of racial, ethnic, and religious elements (with cutter numbers), see E184.A+
	The South. South Atlantic States
	Region south of Mason and Dixon's line and Ohio River
	Cf. E440.92+, Slavery in the United States
206	**Periodicals. Societies. Collections**
206.5	**Museums. Exhibitions, exhibits**
207	**Gazetteers. Dictionaries. Geographic names**
207.3	**Guidebooks**
207.7	**Dictionaries and encyclopedias of history**
208	**Biography (Collective). Genealogy (Collective)**
208.2	**Historiography**
	Historians, *see* E175.5.A+
208.5	**Study and teaching**
209	**General works. Histories**
209.3	**Juvenile works**
	Pamphlets, addresses, essays, etc.
209.5	General
209.6	Anecdotes, legends, pageants, etc.
209.8	**Geography**
210	**Historic monuments (General). Illustrative material**
	Including life and conditions of Appalachian people (General)
211	**Antiquities (Non-Indian)**
	By period
212	Early to 1775
	Cf. F229, Early grants of Virginia, Raleigh's colonies, etc.
	1775-1865
213	General works
	Including plantation life, etc.
	Cf. E230+, Campaigns of the Revolution
	Cf. E423, Southern Convention, Nashville 1850
	Cf. E440.92+, Slavery
214	Period of the Civil War
	Including description and travel
	Cf. E468+, Civil War, 1861-1865 (General)
	Cf. E482+, Confederate States of America
	1865-1951
215	General works
216	1865-1877. Reconstruction
	Including Northern societies formed to ameliorate conditions in the South, etc.
	Cf. E668 , Histories of reconstruction
216.2	1951-
217.A-.Z	**Regions, A-Z**
217.A15	Counties
217.A16	Mountains
217.A17	Rivers
217.A18	Lakes
217.A19	Islands
217.A3	Allegheny (Alleghany) Mountains
217.A65	Appalachian Mountains, Southern

The South. South Atlantic States

217.A-.Z **Regions, A-Z — Continued**

Atlantic Coast, *see* F106

217.B6 Blue Ridge Mountains

Cf. F232.S48, Shenandoah National Park (Va.)

Cf. F262.B6, North Carolina

217.C45 Chattooga River and Valley

Chesapeake Bay region, *see* F187.C5

Gulf Coast, *see* F296

217.N37 Natchez Trace

Ohio River and Valley, *see* F516+

Old Southwest, Lower Mississippi Valley, *see* F396

Pickwick Landing Reservoir, *see* F217.T3

217.P53 Piedmont Region

Potomac River and Valley, *see* F187.P8

217.T3 Tennessee River and Valley

Including Pickwick Landing Reservoir

Cf. F332.T2, Alabama

Cf. F443.T3, Tennessee

Cf. F457.T3, Kentucky

217.W57 Wiregrass Country

Elements in the population

220.A1A-.A1Z General works

220.A2-.Z Individual elements, A-Z

For list of racial, ethnic and religious elements (with cutter numbers), see E184.A+

Virginia

221 **Periodicals. Societies. Collections**

223 **Museums. Exhibitions, exhibits**

224 **Gazetteers. Dictionaries. Geographic names**

224.3 **Guidebooks**

225 **Biography (Collective). Genealogy (Collective)**

225.2 **Historiography**

Historians, *see* E175.5.A+

225.5 **Study and teaching**

226 **General works. Histories**

226.3 **Juvenile works**

Pamphlets, addresses, essays, etc.

226.5 General

226.6 Anecdotes, legends, pageants, etc.

227 **Historic monuments (General). Illustrative material**

228 **Antiquities (Non-Indian)**

By period

229 Early to 1775

Including Raleigh's explorations and colonies, 1584-1590; Virginia Company of London; Jamestown settlement; Indian massacres; Bacon's Rebellion, 1676; the Parsons' Cause, 1763; etc.

Including biography: William Claiborne, Virginia Dare, Nicolas Martiau, John Smith, Alexander Spotswood, etc.

Cf. E83.759, Cherokee War, 1759-1761

Cf. E83.76, Pontiac's Conspiracy, 1763-1765

Cf. E83.77, Dunmore's War, 1774; Battle of Point Pleasant

Cf. E99.P85, Pocahontas

Cf. E199, French and Indian War, 1755-1763

Cf. F517, Explorations in Ohio Valley

230 1775-1865

Including biography: Archibald Cary, John Floyd, Edmund Pendleton, John Howe Peyton, Edmund Ruffin, etc.

For Kentucky County and District, see F454

Cf. E263.V8, Virginia in the Revolution (General)

Cf. E230+, Military operations and battles in the Revolution

Cf. E234, Clark's conquest of the Northwest

	Virginia
	By period
230	1775-1865 — Continued
	Cf. E309, F483, Cession of territory north of Ohio River
	Cf. E328, Virginia Resolutions, 1798
	Cf. E359.5.V8, War of 1812 (General)
	Cf. E355+, Military operations and battles in the War of 1812
	Cf. E451, John Brown at Harper's Ferry
	Cf. E581.1+, Civil War, 1861-1865 (General)
	Cf. E534.1+, Union history, Civil War, 1861-1865
	Cf. E471+, Military operations and battles in the Civil War, 1861-1865
	Cf. F232.S7, Nat Turner's Insurrection, 1831
	Cf. F241, Separation of West Virginia
	Cf. F454, Final withdrawal of claims to Kentucky
231	1865-1950. Reconstruction
	Including biography: William Mahone, John Edward Massey
	Cf. D570.85.V8+, World War I, 1914-1918
	Cf. D769.85.V8, World War II, 1939-1945
	Cf. F241, Controversies with West Virginia
	1951-
231.2	General works
	Biography
231.3.A2A-.3.A2Z	Collective
231.3.A3-.3.Z	Individual, A-Z
	GALE NOTE *See note at the head of Table F5 at the end of the text for further instructions on how to subdivide this number*
232.A-.Z	**Regions, counties, etc., A-Z**
232.A15	Counties
232.A16	Mountains
232.A17	Rivers
232.A18	Lakes
232.A19	Islands
232.A2	Accomac (Accomack) Co.
	Including Chincoteague Island
	Cf. F232.E2, Eastern Shore of Virginia
232.A3	Albemarle Co.
232.A35	Albemarle Parish
232.A4	Alexandria Co. (To June 6, 1920). Arlington Co. (Since June 6, 1920)
	For retrocession from the District of Columbia, see F195
	Cf. F202.B7, District of Columbia boundary
232.A5	Alleghany Co.
232.A54	Amelia Co.
232.A55	Amherst Co.
232.A6	Appomattox Co.
	Arlington Co., *see* F232.A4
	Arlington National Cemetery, *see* F234.A7
	Assateague Island National Seashore, *see* F187.W7
232.A9	Augusta Co.
	Including Weyer's (Wier's) Cave
232.B24	Back Creek and Valley (General, and Virginia)
	Cf. F247.B14 , West Virginia
232.B3	Bath Co.
232.B4	Bedford Co.
	Blacks Run and Valley, *see* F232.R7
232.B5	Bland Co.
232.B55	Blissland (Blisland) Parish
232.B6	Botetourt Co.
232.B7	Boundaries
	For Mason and Dixon's line, see F157.B7
	Cf. F187.B7, Maryland boundary

Virginia

232.A-.Z **Regions, counties, etc., A-Z**

232.B7 Boundaries — Continued

Cf. F202.B7, District of Columbia boundary

232.B8 Bristol Parish

232.B9 Brunswick Co.

232.B94 Buchanan Co.

232.B96 Buckingham Co.

Cabell Co., *see* F247.C2

232.C15 Campbell Co.

Including Timber Lake

232.C2 Caroline Co.

232.C27 Carroll Co.

232.C3 Charles City Co.

232.C4 Charlotte Co.

232.C43 Chesapeake Bay region, Va.

Including Governor's Land Archaeological District

Cf. F187.C5, General, and Maryland

232.C52 Chesterfield Co.

Chincoteague Island, *see* F232.A2

Clark Mountain, *see* F232.O6

232.C59 Clarke Co.

Including Cunningham Chapel Parish, Frederick Parish

232.C65 Clinch River and Valley (General, and Virginia)

Cf. F443.C57, Tennessee

232.C7 Colonial National Historical Park

232.C8 Craig Co.

232.C9 Culpepper Co.

Cf. F232.S2, St. Mark's Parish

232.C93 Cumberland Co.

232.C94 Cumberland Parish

Dean Mountain, *see* F232.S48

Delmarva Peninsula, *see* F187.E2

232.D2 Dickenson Co.

232.D6 Dinwiddie Co.

232.D7 Dismal Swamp. Lake Drummond

Cf. F262.D7, North Carolina

232.E2 Eastern Shore of Virginia

Cf. F187.E2, Maryland

232.E5 Elizabeth City Co.

232.E6 Elizabeth City Parish

Endless Caverns, *see* F232.S47

232.E7 Essex Co.

Including Rappahannock Co. (1656-1692)

232.F2 Fairfax Co.

232.F3 Fauquier Co.

232.F38 Fincastle Co.

232.F4 Floyd Co.

232.F6 Fluvanna Co.

232.F7 Franklin Co.

232.F75 Frederick Co.

Frederick Parish, *see* F232.C59

232.F76 Fredericksville Parish

232.G38 George Washington Memorial Parkway. Mount Vernon Memorial Highway

232.G4 Giles Co.

Including Mountain Lake

232.G6 Gloucester Co.

Cf. F232.K54, Kingston Parish

Cf. F232.P45, Petsworth Parish

232.G65 Goochland Co.

	Virginia
232.A-.Z	**Regions, counties, etc., A-Z — Continued**
	Governor's Land Archaeological District, *see* F232.C43
232.G7	Grayson Co.
	Great Falls of the Potomac, *see* F187.M7
232.G8	Greene Co.
232.G85	Greensville Co.
	Gwynn Island, *see* F232.M3
232.H17	Halifax Co.
232.H2	Hamilton Parish
232.H23	Hampton Roads
	Cf. F232.J2, James River and Valley
232.H3	Hanover Co.
232.H4	Henrico Co.
232.H5	Henrico Parish
232.H6	Henry Co.
232.H8	Highland Co.
	Holmans Creek, *see* F232.S47
	Hungary Mother Creek and Valley, *see* F232.S6
232.I8	Isle of Wight Co.
232.J13	Jackson River and Valley (General, and Virginia)
	Cf. F247.J22, West Virginia
232.J15	James City Co.
	Cf. F232.B55, Blissland Parish
232.J2	James River and Valley
	Including Mulberry Island, etc.
	Cf. F232.H23, Hampton Roads
	Jones Mountain, *see* F232.S48
	Kentucky County and District, *see* F454
232.K4	King and Queen Co.
232.K45	King George Co.
232.K5	King William Co.
232.K54	Kingston Parish
232.L2	Lancaster Co.
232.L4	Lee Co.
	Lewis Mountain *see* F232.S48
232.L8	Loudoun Co.
	Including Lowes area
232.L85	Louisa Co.
232.L9	Lunenburg Co.
	Luray Caverns, *see* F232.P2
232.M2	Madison Co.
232.M3	Mathews Co.
	Including Gwynn Island, etc.
	Cf. F232.K54, Kingston Parish
232.M4	Mecklenburg Co.
232.M6	Middlesex Co.
	Monongalia Co., *see* F247.M7
232.M7	Montgomery Co.
	Mount Vernon Memorial Highway, *see* F232.G38
	Mulberry Island, *see* F232.J2
232.N2	Nansemond Co.
	Natural Bridge, *see* F232.R68
232.N25	Nelson Co.
	Including Tye River and Valley
232.N3	New Kent Co.
	Including St. Peter's Parish
	Cf. F232.B55, Blissland Parish
	New Market Endless Caverns, *see* F232.S47

Virginia

232.A-.Z Regions, counties, etc., A-Z — Continued

232.N5 New River and Valley, Va.
Cf. F247.N5, General, and West Virginia
Cf. F262.N6, North Carolina

232.N8 Norfolk Co.

232.N85 Northampton Co.
Cf. F232.E2 , Eastern Shore of Virginia

232.N86 Northern Neck

232.N87 Northumberland Co.

232.N9 Nottoway Co.

Ohio Co., *see* F247.O3

232.O6 Orange Co.
Including Clark Mountain

232.O85 Otter, Peaks of

232.O9 Overwharton Parish

232.P2 Page Co.
Including Luray Caverns

232.P25 Pamunkey River and Valley

232.P3 Patrick Co.

232.P45 Petsworth Parish

232.P7 Pittsylvania Co.

232.P8 Potomac River and Valley, Va.
For Great Falls, see F187.M7
Cf. F187.P8, General, and Maryland
Cf. F202.P8, District of Columbia
Cf. F247.P8, West Virginia

232.P816 Powell River and Valley (General, and Virginia)
Cf. F443.P78, Tennessee

232.P82 Powhatan Co.

232.P83 Prince Edward Co.

232.P85 Prince George Co.

232.P86 Prince William Co.
Including Prince William Forest Park

232.P87 Princess Anne Co.
Including Lynnhaven Parish

232.P9 Pulaski Co.

232.R18 Rapidan River and Valley

232.R2 Rappahannock Co.
Cf. F232.E7, Rappahannock Co. (1656-1692)

232.R4 Richmond Co.

232.R6 Roanoke Co.

232.R63 Roanoke River and Valley, Va.
Cf. F262.R5, General, and North Carolina

232.R68 Rockbridge Co.
Including Natural Bridge

232.R7 Rockingham Co.
Including Blacks Run and Valley

232.R9 Russell Co.

232.S15 St. George's Parish

232.S2 St. Mark's Parish

232.S3 Scott Co.

232.S47 Shenandoah Co.
Including Endless Caverns, Holmans Creek

232.S48 Shenandoah National Park
Including Dean Mountain, Jones Mountain, Lewis Mountain

232.S5 Shenandoah River and Valley (Valley of Virginia)
For individual caves, see the county
Cf. F247.S5, West Virginia

Virginia

232.A-.Z **Regions, counties, etc., A-Z — Continued**

232.S6 Smyth Co.

Including Hungary Mother Creek and Valley

232.S7 Southampton Co.

Including Southampton Insurrection, 1831 (Nat Turner's Insurrection, Turner's Negro Insurrection)

232.S8 Spotsylvania Co.

Cf. F232.S15, St. George's Parish

232.S86 Stafford Co.

Cf. F232.O9, Overwharton Parish

232.S9 Surry Co.

Cf. F232.A35, Albemarle Parish

232.S96 Sussex Co.

Cf. F232.A35, Albemarle Parish

232.T15 Tangier Island

232.T2 Tazewell Co.

232.T54 Tidewater Region

Timber Lake, *see* F232.C15

232.T8 Truro Parish

Tye River and Valley, *see* F232.N25

Valley of Virginia, *see* F232.S5

232.W25 Warren Co.

232.W27 Warwick Co.

Including Lake Maury

232.W3 Washington Co.

West Augusta District, *see* F157.W5

232.W4 Westmoreland Co.

232.W8 Wise Co.

Wood Co., *see* F247.W8

232.W9 Wythe Co.

Yohogania Co., *see* F157.W5

232.Y6 York Co.

234.A-.Z **Cities, towns, etc., A-Z**

GALE NOTE *The cutter number(s) listed below have been given only as examples by the Library of Congress*

234.A3 Alexandria

234.A7 Arlington

Including Arlington National Cemetery, Lee Mansion

234.F8 Fredericksburg

234.J3 Jamestown

Monticello, *see* E332.74

Mount Vernon, *see* E312.5

234.N48 New Market

For Endless Caverns, see F232.S47

234.N8 Norfolk

234.R5 Richmond

Subarrange by Table F2 at the end of the text

234.S865 Stratford Hall, Albemarle Co.

234.W7 Williamsburg

234.Y6 Yorktown

Cf. F232.C7, Colonial National Historical Park

Elements in the population

235.A1 General works

235.A2-.Z Individual elements

For a list of racial, ethnic, and religious elements (with cutter numbers), see E184.A+

West Virginia

236 **Periodicals. Societies. Collections**

238 **Museums. Exhibitions, exhibits**

239 **Gazetteers. Dictionaries. Geographic names**

West Virginia — Continued

239.3 **Guidebooks**

240 **Biography (Collective). Genealogy (Collective)**

240.2 **Historiography**

Historians, *see* E175.5.A+

240.5 **Study and teaching**

241 **General works. Histories**

Including by period (Early to 1950) as well as general

For 1951 and later, see F245

Including controversies between Virginia and West Virginia growing out of separation; admission as a state, June 20, 1863; etc.

Including biography: Anne Bailey

Cf. D570.85.W4+ , World War I, 1914-1918

Cf. D769.85.W4+, World War II, 1939-1945

Cf. E536.1+, West Virginia in the Civil War and organization of the state (General)

Cf. E470.3, E471+, Military operations and battles in the Civil War

Cf. E534.1+, Union government of Virginia

Cf. E536.1+, Civil War history of West Virginia

Cf. F582.1+, Confederate history

Cf. F229-230, Virginia (Early to 1865)

241.3 **Juvenile works**

Pamphlets, addresses, essays, etc.

241.5 General

241.6 Anecdotes, legends, pageants, etc.

242 **Historic monuments (General). Illustrative material**

243 **Antiquities (Non-Indian)**

By period

(244) Early to 1950, *see* F229-230 , F241

1951-

245 General works

Biography

245.4 Collective

245.42.A-.42.Z Individual, A-Z

GALE NOTE *See note at the head of Table F5 at the end of the text for further instructions on how to subdivide this number*

247.A-.Z **Regions, counties, etc., A-Z**

247.A15 Counties

247.A16 Mountains

247.A17 Rivers

247.A18 Lakes

247.A19 Islands

Babcock State Park, *see* F247.F2

247.B14 Back Creek and Valley

Cf. F232.B24, General, and Virginia

247.B2 Barbour Co.

247.B5 Berkeley Co.

247.B54 Big Coal River and Valley

247.B55 Birch River and Valley

247.B56 Blennerhassett Island

247.B6 Boone Co.

Including Turtle Creek and Valley

247.B7 Boundaries

Cf. F187.B7, Maryland and old Maryland-Virginia boundary

Cf. F497.B7, Ohio boundary

247.B8 Braxton Co.

247.B9 Brooke Co.

247.C2 Cabell Co.

247.C24 Cacapon River and Valley

247.C3 Calhoun Co.

Campbell's Creek and Valley, *see* F247.K2

West Virginia

247.A-.Z **Regions, counties, etc., A-Z — Continued**

Canaan Valley, *see* F247.T8

Cheat Mountain, *see* F247.R2

247.C5 Clay Co.

247.D6 Doddridge Co.

247.D79 Dry Fork River and region

247.E4 Elk River and Valley

247.F2 Fayette Co.

Including Babcock State Park

247.G5 Gilmer Co.

247.G67 Grant Co.

Great Kanawha River and Valley, *see* F247.K3

247.G7 Greenbrier Co.

247.G73 Greenbrier River Trail

247.H17 Hacker's Creek and Valley

247.H2 Hampshire Co.

247.H24 Hancock Co.

Including Tomlinson Run, Tomlinson Run State Park

247.H28 Hardy Co.

247.H3 Harrison Co.

Indian Creek and Valley (Ritchie County), *see* F247.R6

247.J2 Jackson Co.

247.J22 Jackson River and Valley

Cf. F232.J13 , General, and Virginia

247.J4 Jefferson Co.

247.K2 Kanawha Co.

Including Campbell's Creek and Valley

247.K3 Kanawha River and Valley

247.L6 Lewis Co.

247.L7 Lincoln Co.

247.L8 Logan Co.

247.M2 McDowell Co.

247.M26 Marion Co.

247.M3 Marshall Co.

247.M4 Mason Co.

247.M5 Mercer Co.

247.M55 Mineral Co.

247.M57 Mingo Co.

247.M59 Monongahela National Forest

247.M6 Monongahela River and Valley, W. Va.

Cf. F157.M58, General, and Pennsylvania

247.M7 Monongalia Co.

247.M75 Monroe Co.

247.M8 Morgan Co.

247.N5 New River and Valley (General, and W. Va.)

Cf. F232.N5, Virginia

Cf. F262.N6, North Carolina

247.N6 Nicholas Co.

247.O3 Ohio Co.

247.O4 Ohio River and Valley, W. Va.

Cf. F516+, General

247.P3 Pendleton Co.

247.P5 Pleasants Co.

247.P7 Pocahontas Co.

247.P8 Potomac River and Valley, W. Va.

Cf. F187.P8, General, and Maryland

Cf. F202.P8, District of Columbia

Cf. F232.P8, Virginia

247.P9 Preston Co.

West Virginia

247.A-.Z **Regions, counties, etc., A-Z — Continued**

247.P95 Putnam Co.

247.R15 Raleigh Co.

247.R2 Randolph Co.

Including Cave of Dry Fork of Cheat River, Cheat Mountain

247.R6 Ritchie Co.

Including Indian Creek and Valley

247.R8 Roane Co.

247.S5 Shenandoah River and Valley, W. Va.

Cf. F232.S5, General, and Virginia

247.S9 Summers Co.

247.T3 Taylor Co.

247.T4 Tenmile Creek and Valley

Tomlinson Run, *see* F247.H24

Tomlinson Run State Park, *see* F247.H24

247.T8 Tucker Co.

Including Canaan Valley

Turtle Creek and Valley, *see* F247.B6

247.T9 Tyler Co.

247.U6 Upshur Co.

247.W3 Wayne Co.

247.W37 Webster Co.

247.W5 Wetzel Co.

247.W6 Wirt Co.

247.W8 Wood Co.

247.W9 Wyoming Co.

247.Y68 Youghiogheny River and Valley

Cf. F157.Y72, General, and Pennsylvania

Cf. F187.Y68, Maryland

249.A-.Z **Cities, towns, etc., A-Z**

GALE NOTE *The cutter number(s) listed below have been given only as examples by the Library of Congress*

249.C4 Charleston

249.H2 Harpers Ferry

249.H95 Huntington

249.W5 Wheeling

249.W6 White Sulphur Springs

Elements in the population

250.A1 General works

250.A2-.Z Individual elements

For a list of racial, ethnic, and religious elements (with cutter numbers), see E184.A+

North Carolina

251 **Periodicals. Societies. Collections**

251.5 **Museums. Exhibitions, exhibits**

252 **Gazetteers. Dictionaries. Geographic names**

252.3 **Guidebooks**

253 **Biography (Collective). Genealogy (Collective)**

253.2 **Historiography**

Historians, *see* E175.5.A+

253.5 **Study and teaching**

254 **General works. Histories**

254.3 **Juvenile works**

Pamphlets, addresses, essays, etc.

254.5 General

254.6 Anecdotes, legends, pageants, etc.

254.8 **Geography**

255 **Historic monuments (General). Illustrative material**

256 **Antiquities (Non-Indian)**

North Carolina — Continued

By period

257 Early to 1775

Including grant of Carolina to eight proprietors, 1663; Albemarle and Clarendon settlements; Royal province; Regulator Insurrection, 1766-1771

Including biography: George Burrington, Sir Richard Everard, William Tryon, etc.

Cf. E83.71, Tuscarora War, 1711-1713

Cf. E83.759, Cherokee War, 1759-1761

Cf. E197, Queen Anne's War, 1702-1713

Cf. F229, Raleigh's Roanoke colonies, 1584-1590

Cf. F272, The original grant of Carolina, before the division

Cf. F314, War with Spaniards of Florida, 1740

258 1775-1865

Including biography: Charles Manly, John Motley Morehead, Thomas Ruffin, Benjamin Smith

Cf. E263.N8, North Carolina in the Revolution (General)

Cf. E230+, Military operations and battles in the Revolution

Cf. E215.9, Mecklenburg Resolves, 1775

Cf. E309, North Carolina cessions of 1784 and 1790

Cf. E359.5.N7, War of 1812

Cf. E524.1+, E526.1+, E573.1+, Civil War, 1861-1865 (General)

Cf. E470.6, E471+, Military operations and battles in the Civil War, 1861-1865

259 1865-1950. Reconstruction

Including biography: Charles Brantley Aycock, William Woods Holden, Jonathan Worth

Cf. D570.85.N8+, World War I, 1914-1918

Cf. D769.85.N8+, World War II, 1939-1945

Cf. E726.N8, War of 1898 (Spanish-American War)

1951-

260 General works

Biography

260.4 Collective

260.42.A-.42.Z Individual, A-Z

GALE NOTE *See note at the head of Table F5 at the end of the text for further instructions on how to subdivide this number*

261 **Western North Carolina**

262.A-.Z **Regions, counties, etc., A-Z**

262.A15 Counties

262.A16 Mountains

262.A17 Rivers

262.A18 Lakes

262.A19 Islands

262.A3 Alamance Co.

262.A33 Albemarle region (Northeast coast region)

262.A4 Alexander Co.

262.A45 Alleghany Co.

262.A5 Anson Co.

262.A7 Ashe Co.

Including Pond Mountain

262.A84 Atlantic Coast

262.A9 Avery Co.

Including North Toe River and Valley

Bald Head Island, *see* F262.B9

262.B3 Bald Mountains

Including Big Bald Mountain

Cf. F443.B3, General, and Tennessee

262.B37 Beaufort Co.

262.B38 Bertie Co.

Big Bald Mountain, *see* F262.B3

Big Pine Creek and Valley, *see* F262.M25

262.B4 Black Mountains

Including Mount Mitchell

North Carolina

262.A-.Z **Regions, counties, etc., A-Z — Continued**

262.B45 Bladen Co.

262.B6 Blue Ridge Mountains, N.C.

Including Grandfather Mountain

Cf. F217.B6, General

Bogue Banks, *see* F262.C23

262.B7 Boundaries

Cf. F232.B7, Virginia boundary

Cf. F292.B7, Georgia boundary

262.B89 Broad River and Valley, North Carolina

Cf. F277.B73, General, and South Carolina

262.B9 Brunswick Co.

Including Cape Fear, Smith Island, Bald Head Island

262.B94 Buncombe Co.

262.B96 Burke Co.

262.B97 Bute Co.

262.C12 Cabarrus Co.

262.C15 Caldwell Co.

262.C17 Camden Co.

Cape Fear, *see* F262.B9

262.C2 Cape Fear River and Valley

Cape Hatteras National Seashore, *see* F262.O96

262.C23 Carteret Co.

Including Bogue Banks, Harkers Island, Portsmouth Island

262.C26 Caswell Co.

262.C28 Catawba Co.

262.C3 Catawba River and Valley, N.C.

Cf. F277.C3, South Carolina

Charlotte and Mecklenburg County, *see* F264.C4

262.C4 Chatham Co.

262.C43 Cherokee Co.

262.C44 Chowan Co.

262.C47 Clay Co.

262.C5 Cleveland Co.

262.C6 Columbus Co.

262.C8 Craven Co.

262.C9 Cumberland Co.

262.C95 Currituck Co.

262.D2 Dare Co.

Cf. F262.R4 , Roanoke Island

262.D3 Davidson Co.

262.D4 Davie Co.

262.D7 Dismal Swamp, N.C.

Cf. F232.D7, General, and Virginia

262.D77 Duplin Co.

262.D8 Durham Co.

262.E2 Edgecombe Co.

262.F7 Forsyth Co. Wachovia

Including Tanglewood Park

262.F8 Franklin Co.

262.F85 French Broad River and Valley

Cf. F443.F8, General, and Tennessee

262.G2 Gaston Co.

262.G3 Gates Co.

Goose Creek Island, *see* F262.P2

262.G8 Graham Co.

Grandfather Mountain, *see* F262.B6

262.G85 Granville Co.

Great Smoky Mountains, *see* F443.G7

North Carolina

262.A-.Z Regions, counties, etc., A-Z — Continued

262.G86 Greene Co.

262.G9 Guilford Co.

262.H2 Halifax Co.

Harkers Island, *see* F262.C23

262.H3 Harnett Co.

262.H35 Haywood Co.

Hazel Creek and Valley, *see* F262.S95

262.H47 Henderson Co.

262.H5 Hertford Co.

262.H7 Hoke Co.

262.H9 Hyde Co.

Including Ocracoke Island

262.I7 Iredell Co.

262.J2 Jackson Co.

Including Whiteside Cove

262.J6 Johnston Co.

262.J7 Jones Co.

262.L4 Lee Co.

262.L5 Lenoir Co.

262.L6 Lincoln Co.

262.L64 Little Laurel Creek and Valley

262.M15 McDowell Co.

262.M2 Macon Co.

Including Tellico Creek and Valley

262.M25 Madison Co.

Including Big Pine Creek and Valley, Shelton Laurel Creek and Valley

262.M3 Martin Co.

262.M4 Mecklenburg Co.

Mitchell, Mount, *see* F262.B4

262.M5 Mitchell Co.

262.M6 Montgomery Co.

262.M7 Moore Co.

262.N2 Nash Co.

262.N48 Neuse River and Valley

262.N5 New Hanover Co.

New River and Valley (Onslow Co.), *see* F262.O5

262.N6 New River and Valley (Watauga Co.)

Including Ingles Ferry

Cf. F232.N5, Virginia

Cf. F247.N5, General, and West Virginia

262.N67 Norman, Lake

North Toe River and Valley, *see* F262.A9

262.N7 Northampton Co.

Ocracoke Island, *see* F262.H9

262.O5 Onslow Co.

Including New River and Valley, Topsail Island

262.O7 Orange Co.

262.O96 Outer Banks (General)

Including Cape Hatteras National Seashore

262.P2 Pamlico Co.

Including Goose Creek Island

262.P25 Pasquotank Co.

Pee Dee (Pedee) River and Valley, *see* F262.Y2, F277.P3

262.P35 Peltier Creek and Valley

262.P37 Pender Co.

262.P4 Perquimans Co.

262.P5 Person Co.

262.P6 Pitt Co.

North Carolina

262.A-.Z **Regions, counties, etc., A-Z — Continued**

262.P65 Polk Co.

Pond Mountain (Ashe County), *see* F262.A7

Portsmouth Island, *see* F262.C23

Raleigh's Roanoke Colonies, 1584-1590, *see* F229

262.R2 Randolph Co.

262.R25 Reed Gold Mine State Historic Site

262.R3 Richmond Co.

262.R39 Roan Mountain (General, and N.C.)

Cf. F443.R49, Tennessee

262.R4 Roanoke Island

Including Fort Raleigh National Historic Site

For Raleigh's Roanoke Colonies, 1584-1590, see F229

262.R5 Roanoke River and Valley (General, and N.C.)

Cf. F232.R63, Virginia

262.R6 Robeson Co.

262.R7 Rockingham Co.

262.R8 Rowan Co.

262.R9 Rutherford Co.

262.S3 Sampson Co.

262.S34 Sandhills (General, and N.C.)

Cf. F277.S27, South Carolina

Cf. F292.S25, Georgia

262.S4 Scotland Co.

For Smoky Mountains (The Smokies), see F443.G7

Shelton Laurel Creek and Valley, *see* F262.M25

Smith Island, *see* F262.B9

262.S7 Stanly Co.

262.S8 Stokes Co.

262.S9 Surry Co.

262.S95 Swain Co.

Including Hazel Creek and Valley

Tanglewood Park, *see* F262.F7

Tellico Creek and Valley, *see* F262.M2

Topsail Island, *see* F262.O5

262.T7 Transylvania Co.

Tryon Co. (To 1778), *see* F262.L6 and F262.R9

262.T9 Tyrrell Co.

262.U5 Union Co.

262.V3 Vance Co.

262.W18 Waccamaw River and Valley

Cf. F277.W33 , General, and South Carolina

Wachovia, *see* F262.F7

262.W2 Wake Co.

262.W27 Warren Co.

262.W3 Washington Co.

262.W34 Watauga Co.

For New River and Valley, see F262.N6

262.W4 Wayne Co.

Western North Carolina, *see* F261

Whiteside Cove, *see* F262.J2

262.W6 Wilkes Co.

262.W7 Wilson Co.

262.Y19 Yadkin Co.

262.Y2 Yadkin (Pee Dee) River and Valley

Cf. F277.P3, Pee Dee River of South Carolina

262.Y3 Yancey Co.

North Carolina — Continued

264.A-.Z **Cities, towns, etc., A-Z**

GALE NOTE *The cutter number(s) listed below have been given only as examples by the Library of Congress*

264.A8 Asheville

264.C4 Charlotte

264.R1 Raleigh

264.W8 Winston-Salem

Elements in the population

265.A1 General works

265.A2-.Z Individual elements

For a list of racial, ethnic, and religious elements (with cutter numbers), see E184.A+

South Carolina

266 **Periodicals. Societies. Collections**

266.5 **Museums. Exhibitions, exhibits**

267 **Gazetteers. Dictionaries. Geographic names**

267.3 **Guidebooks**

268 **Biography (Collective). Genealogy (Collective)**

268.2 **Historiography**

Historians, *see* E175.5.A+

268.5 **Study and teaching**

269 **General works. Histories**

269.3 **Juvenile works**

Pamphlets, addresses, essays, etc.

269.5 General

269.6 Anecdotes, legends, pageants, etc.

269.8 **Geography**

270 **Historic monuments (General). Illustrative material**

271 **Antiquities (Non-Indian)**

By period

272 Early to 1775

Including The "Carolana" grant of 1629; province of Carolina (1663-1712); Charleston settlement; Locke's Fundamental constitutions; Spanish attack from Florida in 1680; separation of the two Carolinas

Including biography: Eliza (Lucas) Pinckney, etc.

Cf. E83.759, Cherokee War, 1759-1761

Cf. E197, Queen Anne's War, 1702-1713

Cf. F257, North Carolina settlement

Cf. F289, George settlement, Montgomery's Margravate of Azilia

Cf. F314, Huguenot colony at Port Royal, 1562; St. Augustine Expedition, 1740

273 1775-1865

Including dispute with Massachusetts over the latter's Afro-American citizens, 1845; secession

Including biography: James Henry Hammond, Thomas Lee, James Louis Petigru, Robert Barnwell Rhett

Cf. E263.S7, South Carolina in the Revolution (General)

Cf. E230+, Military operations and battles in the Revolution

Cf. E384.3, Nullification

Cf. E409.5.S7, War with Mexico, 1845-1849

Cf. E577.1+, Civil War, 1861-1865 (General)

Cf. E470.6, E471+, Military operations and battles in the Civil War, 1861-1865

Cf. E529.1+, Union history, Civil War, 1861-1865

Cf. E185.93.S7, Afro-Americans in the Sea Islands, Port Royal mission

Cf. F292.B7, South Carolina's cession of 1787

Cf. HF1754, Tariff of 1828

274 1865-1950. Reconstruction

Including biography: David Henry Chamberlain, Benjamin Franklin Perry, Frederick Adolphus Sawyer, etc.

Cf. D570.85.S6+, World War I, 1914-1918

Cf. D769.85.S6+, World War II, 1939-1945

	South Carolina
	By period — Continued
	1951-
275	General works
	Biography
275.4	Collective
275.42.A-.42.Z	Individual, A-Z
	GALE NOTE *See note at the head of Table F5 at the end of the text for further instructions on how to subdivide this number*
277.A-.Z	**Regions, counties, etc., A-Z**
277.A15	Counties
277.A16	Mountains
277.A17	Rivers
277.A18	Lakes
277.A19	Islands
277.A2	Abbeville Co.
277.A3	Aiken Co.
277.A4	Allendale Co.
277.A5	Anderson Co.
277.A84	Ashley River and Valley
277.A86	Atlantic coast
277.B2	Bamberg Co.
277.B25	Barnwell Co.
277.B3	Beaufort Co. Sea Islands, S.C.
	Including Hilton Head Island, Hunting Island, Kiawah Island, Parris Island, St. Helena Island, Edisto Island
	Cf. E185.93.S7, Afro-Americans in the Sea Islands District
277.B5	Berkeley Co. Craven Co.
	Including Cooper River
277.B7	Boundaries
	Cf. F262.B7, North Carolina boundary
	For South Carolina cession south of Tennessee, see F292.B7
277.B73	Broad River and Valley (General, and South Carolina)
	Cf. F262.B89, North Carolina
	Bullock Creek and Valley, *see* F277.Y6
277.C2	Calhoun Co.
277.C22	Camden District
277.C3	Catawba River and Valley, S.C.
	Cf. F262.C3, North Carolina
277.C4	Charleston Co.
	Including Folly Island, Hampton Plantation State Park, Tea Farm Park, Jehossee Island, Wadmalaw Island, Seabrook Island
	For Sea Islands, S.C., see F277.B3
277.C5	Cherokee Co.
277.C55	Chester Co.
277.C57	Chesterfield Co.
277.C7	Clarendon Co.
277.C8	Colleton Co.
277.C85	Congaree Swamp and Region
	Cooper River, *see* F277.B5
	Craven Co., *see* F277.B5
277.D2	Darlington Co.
277.D5	Dillon Co.
277.D6	Dorchester Co.
277.E2	Edgefield Co.
	Edisto Island, *see* F277.B3
277.F3	Fairfield Co.
277.F5	Florence Co.
	Folly Island, *see* F277.C4

	South Carolina
277.A-.Z	**Regions, counties, etc., A-Z — Continued**
277.G35	Georgetown Co.
	Including Pawleys Island
277.G6	Greenville Co.
277.G7	Greenwood Co.
277.H3	Hampton Co.
	Hampton Plantation State Park, *see* F277.C4
	Hilton Head Island, *see* F277.B3
277.H6	Horry Co.
	Hunting Island, *see* F277.B3
277.J3	Jasper Co.
	Jehossee Island, *see* F277.C4
277.K3	Kershaw Co.
	Kiawah Island, *see* F277.B3
277.K5	Kings Mountain National Military Park
277.L2	Lancaster Co.
277.L3	Laurens Co.
	Including Rosemont Plantation
277.L4	Lee Co.
277.L5	Lexington Co.
277.M15	McCormick Co.
277.M2	Marion Co.
277.M3	Marlboro Co.
277.M87	Murray, Lake, and Region
277.N5	Newberry Co. Newberry District
277.N6	Ninety-Six (District)
277.O3	Oconee Co.
277.O5	Orangeburg Co.
277.O6	Orangeburgh District
	Parris Island, *see* F277.B3
277.P3	Pee Dee region. Pee Dee River and Valley (Great Pedee and Little Pedee Rivers)
	Cf. F262.Y2, North Carolina
277.P35	Pendleton Co. Pendleton District
277.P5	Pickens Co.
277.P95	Prince Frederick Parish
277.P97	Prince William's Parish
277.R49	Richard B. Russell Lake, S.C.
	Cf. F292.R49, General, and Georgia
277.R5	Richland Co.
	St. Helena Island, *see* F277.B3
277.S2	St. Mark's Parish
277.S24	St. Thomas and St. Denis Parish
277.S26	Saluda Co.
277.S27	Sandhills, S.C.
	Cf. F262.S34, General, and North Carolina
	Cf. F292.S25, Georgia
277.S28	Santee River. Santee River system
277.S3	Savannah River and Valley, S.C.
	Including Argyle Island
	Cf. F292.S3, General, and Georgia
	Sea Islands, S.C., *see* F277.B3
	Seabrook Island, *see* F277.C4
277.S7	Spartanburg Co.
277.S77	Sullivans Island
277.S8	Sumter Co.
	Tea Farm Park, *see* F277.C4
277.U5	Union Co.
277.W33	Waccamaw River and Valley (General, and South Carolina)
	Cf. F262.W18, North Carolina

South Carolina

277.A-.Z **Regions, counties, etc., A-Z — Continued**

Wadmalaw Island, *see* F277.C4

277.W7 Williamsburg Co.

277.Y6 York Co.

Including Bullock Creek and Valley

277.Y62 York District

279.A-.Z **Cities, towns, etc., A-Z**

GALE NOTE *The cutter number(s) listed below have been given only as examples by the Library of Congress*

279.C4 Charleston

Subarrange by Table F2 at the end of the text

279.C7 Columbia

279.G79 Greenville

279.S7 Spartanburg

Elements in the population

280.A1 General works

280.A2-.Z Individual elements

For a list of racial, ethnic, and religious elements (with cutter numbers), see E184.A+

Georgia

281 **Periodicals. Societies. Collections**

283 **Museums. Exhibitions, exhibits**

284 **Gazetteers. Dictionaries. Geographic names**

284.3 **Guidebooks**

285 **Biography (Collective). Genealogy (Collective)**

285.2 **Historiography**

Historians, *see* E175.5.A+

285.5 **Study and teaching**

286 **General works. Histories**

286.3 **Juvenile works**

Pamphlets, addresses, essays, etc.

286.5 General

286.6 Anecdotes, legends, pageants, etc.

287 **Historic monuments (General). Illustrative material**

288 **Antiquities (Non-Indian)**

By period

289 Early to 1775

Including Indian affairs; Spanish claims and attacks; Montgomery's Margravate of Azilia; Trustees for establishing the colony of Georgia in America; Royal province

Including biography: James Edward Oglethorpe, etc.

Cf. E197, Queen Anne's War, 1702-1713

Cf. F295.S1, Salzburger immigration

Cf. F314, St. Augustine Expedition, 1740

290 1775-1865

Including cession of western lands to United States, 1802

Including biography: Elijah Clarke, Howell Cobb, Herschel Vespasian Johnson, Charles James McDonald, Thomas Spalding, Linton Stephens, etc.

Cf. E83.813, First Creek War, 1813-1814

Cf. E83.817, First Seminole War, 1817-1818

Cf. E83.836, Second Creek War, 1836

Cf. E99.C5, Cherokee troubles

Cf. E263.G3, Georgia in the Revolution (General)

Cf. E230+, Military operations and battles in the Revolution

Cf. E359.5.G4, War of 1812

Cf. E559.1+, Civil War, 1861-1865 (General)

Cf. E470.6, E471+, Military operations and battles in the Civil War, 1861-1865

Cf. E503.1+, Union history, Civil War, 1861-1865

Cf. F296, F321-350, Western lands ceded to the United States (General)

Cf. F341, Yazoo land companies, Yazoo fraud

	Georgia
	By period — Continued
291	1865-1950. Reconstruction
	Including biography: Rufus Brown Bullock, William Harrell Felton, Charles Jones Jenkins, Eugene Talmadge, etc.
	Cf. D570.85.G4+, World War I, 1914-1918
	Cf. D769.85.G4+, World War II, 1939-1945
	1951-
291.2	General works
	Biography
291.3.A2A-.3.A2Z	Collective
291.3.A3-.3.Z	Individual, A-Z
	GALE NOTE *See note at the head of Table F5 at the end of the text for further instructions on how to subdivide this number*
291.7	**North Georgia**
291.8	**South Georgia**
292.A-.Z	**Regions, counties, etc., A-Z**
292.A15	Counties
292.A16	Mountains
292.A17	Rivers
292.A18	Lakes
292.A19	Islands
292.A6	Appling Co.
	Argyle Island, *see* F292.S3
292.A7	Atkinson Co.
292.A74	Atlantic Coast
292.B13	Bacon Co.
292.B14	Baker Co.
292.B15	Baldwin Co.
292.B2	Banks Co.
292.B27	Barrow Co.
292.B3	Bartow Co.
292.B4	Ben Hill Co.
292.B45	Berrien Co.
292.B5	Bibb Co.
	Billys Island, *see* F292.O5
292.B6	Bleckley Co.
292.B7	Boundaries. South Carolina cession south of Tennessee
	Cf. F277.B7 , South Carolina boundary
	Cf. F317.B7 , Florida boundary
	Cf. F443.B7 , Tennessee boundary
292.B8	Brantley Co.
292.B83	Brooks Co.
292.B85	Bryan Co.
292.B9	Bulloch Co.
292.B95	Burke Co.
292.B97	Butts Co.
292.C15	Calhoun Co.
292.C17	Camden Co.
	Including Kings Bay
	Campbell County, *see* F292.F9
292.C18	Candler Co.
292.C19	Carroll Co.
292.C2	Catoosa Co.
292.C3	Charlton Co.
292.C36	Chatham Co.
	Including Ossabaw Island
292.C39	Chattahoochee Co.
292.C4	Chattahoochee River and Valley (General, and Ga.)
	Cf. F317.J2, Florida

	Georgia
292.A-.Z	**Regions, counties, etc., A-Z**
292.C4	Chattahoochee River and Valley (General, and Ga.) — Continued
	Cf. F332.C4, Alabama
292.C43	Chattooga Co.
292.C47	Cherokee Co.
292.C5	Clarke Co.
292.C53	Clay Co.
292.C54	Clayton Co.
292.C55	Clinch Co.
292.C6	Cobb Co.
292.C63	Coffee Co.
	Colonel's Island, *see* F292.G5
292.C7	Colquitt Co.
292.C73	Columbia Co.
292.C76	Cook Co.
292.C8	Coweta Co.
292.C85	Crawford Co.
292.C93	Crisp Co.
292.C94	Cumberland Island. Cumberland Island National Seashore
292.D15	Dade Co.
292.D2	Dawson Co.
292.D27	Decatur Co.
292.D3	De Kalb Co.
292.D5	Dodge Co.
292.D55	Dooly Co.
292.D6	Dougherty Co.
292.D65	Douglas Co.
292.E2	Early Co.
292.E25	Echols Co.
292.E3	Effingham Co.
292.E4	Elbert Co.
292.E5	Emanuel Co.
292.E9	Evans Co.
292.F2	Fannin Co.
292.F3	Fayette Co.
292.F6	Floyd Co.
292.F67	Forsyth Co.
292.F7	Fort Frederica National Monument
292.F8	Franklin Co.
292.F9	Fulton Co.
	Including Campbell County, Milton County
292.G3	Gilmer Co.
292.G4	Glascock Co.
292.G5	Glynn Co.
	Including Colonel's Island
	For Fort Frederica National Monument, see F292.F7
292.G58	Golden Isles
	Including Jekyl Island, St. Simon's Island
292.G6	Gordon Co.
292.G66	Grady Co.
292.G7	Greene Co.
292.G9	Gwinnett Co.
292.H2	Habersham Co.
292.H25	Hall Co.
292.H3	Hancock Co.
292.H5	Haralson Co.
292.H55	Harris Co.
292.H6	Hart Co.
292.H7	Heard Co.

	Georgia	
292.A-.Z	**Regions, counties, etc., A-Z — Continued**	
292.H73		Henry Co.
292.H8		Houston Co.
292.I67		Irwin Co.
292.J13		Jackson Co.
292.J2		Jasper Co.
292.J25		Jeff Davis Co.
292.J28		Jefferson Co.
		Jekyl Island, *see* F292.G58
292.J4		Jenkins Co.
292.J6		Johnson Co.
292.J7		Jones Co.
		Kings Bay, *see* F292.C17
292.L2		Lamar Co.
		Lanier, Lake, *see* F292.S53
292.L25		Lanier Co.
292.L3		Laurens Co.
292.L4		Lee Co.
292.L6		Liberty Co.
292.L63		Lincoln Co.
		Little Tennessee River and Valley, *see* F443.L64
292.L66		Long Co.
		Lookout Mountain, *see* F443.L8
292.L7		Lowndes Co.
292.L8		Lumpkin Co.
292.M13		McDuffie Co.
292.M15		McIntosh Co.
		Including Sapelo Island
292.M17		Macon Co.
292.M2		Madison Co.
292.M25		Marion Co.
292.M5		Meriwether Co.
292.M6		Miller Co.
		Milton County, *see* F292.F9
292.M65		Mitchell Co.
292.M7		Monroe Co.
292.M73		Montgomery Co.
292.M76		Morgan Co.
292.M8		Murray Co.
292.M9		Muscogee Co.
292.N4		Newton Co.
292.O27		Ocmulgee River
292.O3		Oconee Co.
292.O33		Oconee River and Valley
292.O38		Ogeechee River and Valley
292.O4		Oglethorpe Co.
292.O5		Okefenokee Swamp
		Including Billys Island
		Ossabaw Island, *see* F292.C36
292.P3		Paulding Co.
292.P4		Peach Co.
292.P57		Pickens Co.
292.P61		Pierce Co.
292.P65		Pike Co.
292.P7		Polk Co.
292.P85		Pulaski Co.
292.P9		Putnam Co.
292.Q5		Quitman Co.
292.R3		Rabun Co.

	Georgia
292.A-.Z	**Regions, counties, etc., A-Z — Continued**
292.R35	Randolph Co.
292.R49	Richard B. Russell Lake and region (General, and Georgia) *Cf. F277.R49, South Carolina*
292.R5	Richmond Co.
292.R6	Rockdale Co.
292.S2	St. Marys River and Valley, Ga. *Cf. F317.S3, General, and Florida*
	St. Simon's Island, *see* F292.G58
292.S25	Sandhills, Ga. *Cf. F262.S34, General, and North Carolina* *Cf. F277.S27, South Carolina*
	Sapelo Island, *see* F292.M15
292.S3	Savannah River and Valley (General, and Ga.) *Including Argyle Island* *Cf. F277.S3, South Carolina*
292.S33	Schley Co.
292.S35	Screven Co.
292.S4	Seminole Co.
292.S53	Sidney Lanier, Lake
292.S6	Spalding Co.
292.S7	Stephens Co.
292.S8	Stewart Co.
292.S85	Stone Mountain Memorial
292.S9	Sumter Co.
292.T2	Talbot Co.
292.T23	Taliaferro Co.
292.T27	Tattnall Co.
292.T3	Taylor Co.
292.T35	Telfair Co.
292.T37	Terrell Co.
292.T4	Thomas Co.
292.T5	Tift Co.
292.T6	Toombs Co.
292.T65	Towns Co.
292.T7	Treutlen Co.
292.T75	Troup Co.
292.T8	Turner Co.
292.T9	Twiggs Co.
292.U5	Union Co.
292.U6	Upson Co.
292.W16	Walker Co.
292.W17	Walton Co.
292.W2	Ware Co.
292.W23	Warren Co.
292.W25	Washington Co.
292.W3	Wayne Co.
292.W35	Webster Co.
292.W45	Wheeler Co.
292.W48	White Co.
292.W5	Whitfield Co.
292.W65	Wilcox Co.
292.W7	Wilkes Co.
292.W75	Wilkinson Co.
292.W9	Worth Co.
294.A-.Z	**Cities, towns, etc., A-Z** GALE NOTE *The cutter number(s) listed below have been given only as examples by the Library of Congress*

Georgia

294.A-.Z **Cities, towns, etc., A-Z — Continued**

294.A8 Atlanta

Subarrange by Table F2 at the end of the text

294.A9 Augusta

294.C7 Columbus

294.M2 Macon

294.S2 Savannah

Elements in the population

295.A1 General works

295.A2-.Z Individual elements

For a list of racial, ethnic, and religious elements (with cutter numbers), see E184.A+

295.S1 Salzburgers

296 **Gulf States**

Including Gulf coast after 1803; Gulf of Mexico

For Gulf coast early to 1803, see F372

For Lower Mississippi Valley, see F396

For Mississippi Territory (1798), see F336+

For South Atlantic States, see F206+

For West Florida, see F301

Cf. F332.G9 , Gulf coast of Alabama

Cf. F392.G9 , Gulf coast of Texas; etc.

301 **West Florida**

Cf. F317.W5 , Pensacola District after 1819

Cf. F334.M6, Mobile

Cf. F341, Natchez District

Cf. F377.B7, Louisiana boundary

Cf. F377.F6, Florida parishes of Louisiana, Baton Rouge District since 1812

Florida

306 **Periodicals. Societies. Collections**

308 **Museums. Exhibitions, exhibits**

309 **Gazetteers. Dictionaries. Geographic names**

309.3 **Guidebooks**

310 **Biography (Collective). Genealogy (Collective)**

310.2 **Historiography**

Historians, *see* E175.5.A+

310.5 **Study and teaching**

311 **General works. Histories**

311.3 **Juvenile works**

Pamphlets, addresses, essays, etc.

311.5 General

311.6 Anecdotes, legends, pageants, etc.

311.8 **Geography**

312 **Historic monuments (General). Illustrative material**

313 **Antiquities (Non-Indian)**

By period

314 Early to 1821

Including French Huguenot colonies, 1562-1565; Spanish Colony, 1565-1763, 1783-1821; St. Augustine expeditions, 1740, 1743; East Florida; English Colony, 1763-1783; "Republic of Florida," 1812-1816; MacGregor at Amelia Island, 1817; Treaty of Washington, 1819 (with Spain); Spanish Florida claims (General)

Including biography: Dominique de Gourgues, René Goulaine de Laudonnière, Pedro Menéndez de Avilés, Jean Ribaut (Ribault), etc.

For West Florida, see F301

Cf. E83.813, First Creek War, 1813-1814

Cf. E83.817, First Seminole War, 1817-1818; execution of Arbuthnot and Ambrister

Cf. E359.5.F6, War of 1812

Cf. F319.S2, St. Augustine

Cf. F372, Gulf coast before 1763

Cf. F1410, Spaniards in North America (General)

Florida

By period — Continued

315 1821-1865

Including Andrew Jackson's administration as governor; admission as a state, 1845

Cf. E83.835, Second Seminole War, 1835-1842

Cf. E83.855, Third Seminole War, 1855-1858

Cf. E558.1+, Civil War, 1861-1865 (General)

Cf. E470.7, E471+, Military operations and battles in the Civil War, 1861-1865

Cf. E502.1+, Union history, Civil War, 1861-1865

316 1865-1950

Including Reconstruction; hurricane disasters, 1926, 1927

Cf. D769.85.F5+, World War II, 1939-1945

Cf. E726.F6, War of 1898 (Spanish-American War)

1951-

316.2 General works

Biography

316.22 Collective

316.23.A-.23.Z Individual, A-Z

GALE NOTE *See note at the head of Table F5 at the end of the text for further instructions on how to subdivide this number*

317.A-.Z **Regions, counties, etc., A-Z**

317.A15 Counties

317.A16 Mountains

317.A17 Rivers

317.A18 Lakes

317.A19 Islands

317.A4 Alachua Co.

Including Paynes Prairie

Amelia Island, *see* F317.N3

317.A6 Apalachicola River and Valley

317.A74 Atlantic Coast

317.B2 Baker Co.

317.B3 Bay Co.

317.B54 Big Bend Region

Biscayne Bay, *see* F317.D2

317.B7 Boundaries

Cf. F332.B7, Alabama boundary

317.B75 Bradford Co.

317.B8 Brevard Co.

Including Cape Canaveral, Indian River

317.B85 Broward Co.

317.C3 Calhoun Co.

Cape Canaveral, *see* F317.B8

317.C4 Charlotte Co.

Chattahoochee River and Valley, Fla., *see* F317.J2

317.C5 Citrus Co.

317.C6 Clay Co.

317.C7 Collier Co.

317.C75 Columbia Co.

317.D2 Dade Co.

Including Biscayne Bay, Lake Worth

For Everglades, see F317.E9

317.D4 De Soto Co.

317.D5 Dixie Co.

317.D9 Duval Co.

317.E7 Escambia Co.

For Perdido River and Valley, see F317.P4

317.E9 Everglades

Including Everglades National Park

317.F6 Flagler Co.

	Florida	
317.A-.Z	**Regions, counties, etc., A-Z — Continued**	
	Florida Keys, *see* F317.M7	
317.F63	Florida National Scenic Trail	
	Fort Jefferson National Monument, *see* F317.M7	
317.F7	Franklin Co.	
317.G2	Gadsden Co.	
317.G5	Gilchrist Co.	
317.G6	Glades Co.	
317.G8	Gulf coast of Florida	
		Including Gulf Islands National Seashore (General, and Florida)
		Cf. F347.G9, Gulf Islands National Seashore (Mississippi)
317.G9	Gulf Co.	
	Gulf Islands National Seashore, *see* F317.G8	
317.H2	Hamilton Co.	
317.H3	Hardee Co.	
317.H4	Hendry Co.	
317.H5	Hernando Co.	
317.H54	Highlands Co.	
317.H6	Hillsborough Co.	
317.H7	Holmes Co.	
317.H73	Holmes Creek and Valley (General, and Florida)	
		Cf. F332.H56, Alabama
	Indian River, *see* F317.B8	
317.I5	Indian River Co.	
317.J2	Jackson Co.	
		Including Chattahoochee River and Valley, Fla.
		Cf. F292.C4, General, and Georgia
		Cf. F332.C4, Alabama, etc.
		Cf. F317.A6, Apalachicola River and Valley
317.J4	Jefferson Co.	
317.K57	Kissimmee River and Valley	
317.L15	Lafayette Co.	
317.L2	Lake Co.	
317.L3	Lee Co.	
		Including Pine Island
		For Everglades, see F317.E9
317.L5	Leon Co.	
317.L6	Levy Co.	
317.L7	Liberty Co.	
317.M15	Madison Co.	
317.M2	Manatee Co.	
		Including Manatee River
317.M3	Marion Co.	
		Including Lake Weir
317.M35	Martin Co.	
317.M7	Monroe Co.	
		Including Florida Keys, Fort Jefferson National Monument
		For Everglades, see F317.E9
317.M92	Myakka River State Park	
317.N3	Nassau Co.	
		Including Amelia Island
		Cf. F314, History before 1819
317.O3	Okaloosa Co.	
317.O4	Lake Okeechobee	
317.O43	Okeechobee Co.	
	Okefenokee Swamp, *see* F292.O5	
317.O46	Oklawaha River and Valley	
317.O6	Orange Co.	
317.O7	Osceola Co.	

	Florida
317.A-.Z	**Regions, counties, etc., A-Z — Continued**
317.P2	Palm Beach Co.
317.P3	Pasco Co.
	Paynes Prairie, *see* F317.A4
317.P4	Perdido River and Valley, Fla.
	Cf. F332.P4, General, and Alabama
	Pine Island, *see* F317.L3
317.P6	Pinellas Co.
317.P7	Polk Co.
317.P8	Putnam Co.
317.R43	Red Hills
317.S18	Saint Johns Co.
317.S2	Saint Johns River and Valley
	Including Timucuan Ecological and Historic Preserve
317.S27	Saint Lucie Co.
317.S3	Saint Mary's River and Valley (General, and Fla.)
	Cf. F292.S2, Georgia
317.S37	Sanibel Island
317.S4	Santa Rosa Co.
317.S45	Sarasota Co.
317.S5	Seminole Co.
317.S75	Sumter Co.
317.S78	Suwannee Co.
317.S8	Suwannee River and Valley
317.T3	Taylor Co.
	Timucuan Ecological and Historic Preserve, *see* F317.S2
	Tomoka River, *see* F317.V7
317.U5	Union Co.
317.V7	Volusia Co.
	Including Tomoka River
317.W23	Wakulla Co.
317.W24	Walton Co.
317.W3	Washington Co.
	Including St. Andrews Bay
317.W5	West Florida region
	Including The Pensacola District after 1819
	For the Pensacola district, early to 1819, see F301
319.A-.Z	**Cities, towns, etc., A-Z**
	GALE NOTE *The cutter number(s) listed below have been given only as examples by the Library of Congress*
319.J1	Jacksonville
319.K4	Key West
319.M6	Miami
319.P4	Pensacola
319.S2	St. Augustine
319.S24	St. Petersburg
319.T14	Tallahassee
319.T2	Tampa
	Elements in the population
320.A1	General works
320.A2-.Z	Individual elements
	For a list of racial, ethnic, and religious elements (with cutter numbers), see E184.A+
	Alabama
321	**Periodicals. Societies. Collections**
323	**Museums. Exhibitions, exhibits**
324	**Gazetteers. Dictionaries. Geographic names**
324.3	**Guidebooks**
325	**Biography (Collective). Genealogy (Collective)**

Alabama — Continued

325.2 **Historiography**

Historians, *see* E175.5.A+

325.5 **Study and teaching**

326 **General works. Histories**

Including admission as a state, December 14, 1819

Including by period (Early to 1950)

Including secession; Reconstruction; Ku-Klux Klan

Including biography: John Hollis Bankhead, William Parish Chilton, Thomas Erby Kilby, Thomas Hill Watts, etc.

For West Florida, see F301

Cf. D570.85.A2+, World War I, 1914-1918

Cf. D769.85.A2+, World War II, 1939-1945

Cf. E83.813, First Creek War, 1813-1814

Cf. E83.836, Second Creek War, 1836

Cf. E99.C5, Cherokee Indians

Cf. E551.1+, Civil War, 1861-1865 (General)

Cf. E470.7, E471+, Military operations and battles in the Civil War, 1861-1865

Cf. E495.1+, Union history, Civil War, 1861-1865

Cf. E726.A3, War of 1898 (Spanish-American War)

Cf. F292.B7, South Carolina cession south of Tennessee

Cf. F341, Mississippi Territory

Cf. F372, Early French settlements on the coast (Louisiana)

326.3 **Juvenile works**

Pamphlets, addresses, essays, etc.

326.5 General

326.6 Anecdotes, legends, pageants, etc.

327 **Historic monuments (General). Illustrative material**

328 **Antiquities (Non-Indian)**

By period

(329) Early to 1950, *see* F326

1951-

330 General works

Biography

330.2 Collective

330.3.A-.3.Z Individual, A-Z

GALE NOTE *See note at the head of Table F5 at the end of the text for further instructions on how to subdivide this number*

332.A-.Z **Regions, counties, etc., A-Z**

332.A15 Counties

332.A16 Mountains

332.A17 Rivers

332.A18 Lakes

332.A19 Islands

332.A8 Autauga Co.

332.B2 Baldwin Co.

For Mobile Bay, see F332.M58

For Perdido River and Valley, see F332.P4

332.B3 Barbour Co.

332.B5 Bibb Co.

332.B6 Blount Co.

Including Garfield Colony, Rickwood Caverns State Park

332.B7 Boundaries

Cf. F443.B7, Tennessee boundary

332.B8 Bullock Co.

332.B9 Butler Co.

332.C25 Calhoun Co.

332.C35 Chambers Co.

332.C4 Chattahoochee River and Valley, Ala

Cf. F292.C4, General, and Georgia

Alabama

332.A-.Z **Regions, counties, etc., A-Z**

332.C4 Chattahoochee River and Valley, Ala — Continued

Cf. F317.J2, Florida

332.C44 Cherokee Co.

332.C46 Chilton Co.

332.C48 Choctaw Co.

332.C6 Clarke Co.

332.C62 Clay Co.

332.C63 Cleburne Co.

332.C65 Coffee Co.

332.C68 Colbert Co.

332.C7 Conecuh Co.

332.C74 Coosa Co.

332.C75 Coosa River and Valley

332.C8 Covington Co.

332.C85 Crenshaw Co.

332.C9 Cullman Co.

332.D17 Dale Co.

332.D3 Dallas Co.

Dauphin Island, *see* F332.M6

332.D4 De Kalb Co.

332.E4 Elmore Co.

332.E7 Escambia Co.

332.E8 Etowah Co.

332.F4 Fayette Co.

332.F83 Franklin Co.

332.G4 Geneva Co.

332.G7 Greene Co.

332.G9 Gulf coast of Alabama

For Mobile Bay, see F332.M58

Cf. F296, Gulf coast (General)

332.H3 Hale Co.

332.H4 Henry Co.

332.H56 Holmes Creek and Valley

Cf. F317.H73, General, and Florida

332.H6 Houston (Huston) Co.

332.J2 Jackson Co.

332.J4 Jefferson Co.

Including Rouges Creek and Valley

332.L2 Lamar Co.

332.L3 Lauderdale Co.

332.L4 Lawrence Co.

332.L5 Lee Co.

332.L6 Limestone Co.

332.L7 Lowndes Co.

332.M2 Macon Co.

332.M3 Madison Co.

332.M35 Marengo Co.

332.M37 Marion Co.

332.M4 Marshall Co.

332.M58 Mobile Bay

332.M6 Mobile Co.

Including Dauphin Island

332.M7 Monroe Co.

332.M73 Montgomery Co.

332.M8 Morgan Co.

Muscle Shoals, *see* F332.T2

Oliver Dam, *see* F332.T9

Alabama

332.A-.Z **Regions, counties, etc., A-Z — Continued**

332.P34 Paint Rock River (General, and Alabama)

Cf. F443.P34, Tennessee

332.P37 Pea River and Valley

332.P4 Perdido River and Valley (General, and Ala.)

Cf. F317.P4, Florida

332.P45 Perry Co.

332.P5 Pickens Co.

332.P55 Pike Co.

332.R3 Randolph Co.

Rickwood Caverns State Park, *see* F332.B6

Rouges Creek and Valley, *see* F332.J4

332.R87 Russell Co.

332.S2 St. Clair Co.

332.S5 Shelby Co.

332.S8 Sumter Co.

332.T14 Talladega Co.

332.T15 Tallapoosa Co.

332.T17 Tannehill Historical State Park

332.T2 Tennessee River and Valley, Ala

Including Muscle Shoals (Topography)

Cf. F217.T3, General

332.T6 Tombigbee River and Valley (General, and Ala.)

Cf. F347.T6, Mississippi

332.T9 Tuscaloosa Co.

Including Oliver Dam

332.W3 Walker Co.

332.W4 Washington Co.

332.W48 Wheeler Lake and region

332.W5 Wilcox Co.

332.W54 William B. Bankhead National Forest

332.W6 Winston Co.

334.A-.Z **Cities, towns, etc., A-Z**

GALE NOTE *The cutter number(s) listed below have been given only as examples by the Library of Congress*

334.B6 Birmingham

Subarrange by Table F2 at the end of the text

334.M6 Mobile

334.M7 Montgomery

Subarrange by Table F2 at the end of the text

334.T9 Tuscaloosa

Elements in the population

335.A1 General works

335.A2-.Z Individual elements

For a list of racial, ethnic, and religious elements (with cutter numbers), see E184.A+

Mississippi

336 **Periodicals. Societies. Collections**

338 **Museums. Exhibitions, exhibits, etc.**

339 **Gazetteers. Dictionaries. Geographic names**

339.3 **Guidebooks**

340 **Biography (Collective). Genealogy (Collective)**

340.2 **Historiography**

Historians, *see* E175.5.A+

340.5 **Study and teaching**

341 **General works. Histories**

Including admission as a state, December 10, 1817

Including by period (Early to 1950) as well as general

For 1951 and later, see F345

Including secession; Reconstruction; Yazoo land companies; etc.

	Mississippi
341	**General works. Histories — Continued**
	Including Natchez District of West Florida
	Including biography: Albert Gallatin Brown, Winthrop Sargent, etc.
	For West Florida, Mobile District before 1812, see F301
	Cf. D769.85.M7+, World War II, 1939-1945
	Cf. E83.813, First Creek War, 1813-1814
	Cf. E99.N2, Natchez Indians
	Cf. E568.1+, Civil War (General)
	Cf. E470.7, E471+, Military operations and battles in the Civil War
	Cf. E516.1+, Union history, Civil War, 1861-1865
	Cf. F292.B7, South Carolina cession south of Tennessee
341.3	**Juvenile works**
	Pamphlets, addresses, essays, etc.
341.5	General
341.6	Anecdotes, legends, pageants, etc.
342	**Historic monuments (General). Illustrative material**
343	**Antiquities (Non-Indian)**
	By period
(344)	Early to 1950, *see* F341
	1951-
345	General works
	Biography
345.2	Collective
345.3.A-.3.Z	Individual, A-Z
	Subarrange each by Table F5 at the end of the text
347.A-.Z	**Regions, counties, etc., A-Z**
347.A15	Counties
347.A16	Mountains
347.A17	Rivers
347.A18	Lakes
347.A19	Islands
	Ackia Battleground National Monument, *see* F347.L45
347.A2	Adams Co.
347.A4	Alcorn Co.
347.A5	Amite Co.
347.A7	Attala Co.
347.B4	Benton Co.
347.B6	Bolivar Co.
347.B7	Boundaries
	Cf. F332.B7, Alabama boundary
	Cf. F377.B7, Louisiana boundary
	Cf. F443.B7, Tennessee boundary
347.C2	Calhoun Co.
347.C3	Carroll Co.
347.C4	Chickasaw Co.
347.C45	Choctaw Co.
347.C5	Claiborne Co.
	Including Grand Gulf State Military Park
347.C55	Clarke Co.
347.C6	Clay Co.
347.C7	Coahoma Co.
347.C75	Copiah Co.
347.C8	Covington Co.
347.D4	De Soto Co.
347.F6	Forrest Co.
347.F7	Franklin Co.
347.G4	George Co.
	Grand Gulf State Military Park, *see* F347.C5
347.G65	Greene Co.

	Mississippi
347.A-.Z	**Regions, counties, etc., A-Z — Continued**
347.G7	Grenada Co.
347.G9	Gulf coast of Mississippi *Including Gulf Islands National Seashore* *Cf. F296, Gulf coast (General)* *Cf. F317.G8, Gulf Islands National Seashore (General, and Florida)*
	Gulf Islands National Seashore, *see* F347.G9
347.H2	Hancock Co.
347.H3	Harrison Co. *Including Ship Island*
347.H5	Hinds Co.
347.H6	Holmes Co.
347.H8	Humphreys Co.
347.I7	Issaquena Co.
347.I8	Itawamba Co.
347.J3	Jackson Co.
347.J4	Jasper Co.
347.J48	Jefferson Co.
347.J5	Jefferson Davis Co.
347.J6	Jones Co.
347.K3	Kemper Co.
347.L2	Lafayette Co.
347.L25	Lamar Co.
347.L3	Lauderdale Co.
347.L35	Lawrence Co.
347.L4	Leake Co.
347.L45	Lee Co. *Including Ackia Battleground National Monument*
347.L47	Leflore Co.
347.L6	Lincoln Co.
347.L8	Lowndes Co.
347.M15	Madison Co.
347.M25	Marion Co.
347.M3	Marshall Co.
347.M6	Mississippi River and Valley, Miss. *Cf. F350.5+, General* *Cf. F396, Lower Mississippi Valley*
347.M7	Monroe Co.
347.M75	Montgomery Co.
347.N4	Neshoba Co.
347.N48	Newton Co.
347.N6	Noxubee Co.
347.O4	Oktibbeha Co.
347.P2	Panola Co.
347.P3	Pearl River and Valley (General, and Miss.) *Cf. F377.P3, Louisiana*
347.P33	Pearl River Co.
347.P4	Perry Co.
347.P6	Pike Co.
347.P63	Piney Woods
347.P7	Pontotoc Co.
347.P8	Prentiss Co.
347.Q5	Quitman Co.
347.R3	Rankin Co.
347.S3	Scott Co.
347.S45	Sharkey Co.
347.S5	Simpson Co.
347.S6	Smith Co.
347.S8	Stone Co.

Mississippi

347.A-.Z **Regions, counties, etc., A-Z — Continued**

347.S9 Sunflower Co.

347.T3 Tallahatchie Co.

347.T35 Tate Co.

347.T45 Tippah Co.

347.T5 Tishomingo Co.

347.T6 Tombigbee River and Valley, Miss.

Cf. F332.T6, General, and Alabama

347.T8 Tunica Co.

347.U5 Union Co.

347.W24 Walthall Co.

347.W29 Warren Co.

347.W35 Washington Co.

347.W4 Wayne Co.

347.W45 Webster Co.

347.W65 Wilkinson Co.

347.W7 Winston Co.

347.Y15 Yalobusha Co.

347.Y2 Yazoo Co.

347.Y3 Yazoo River and Valley

349.A-.Z **Cities, towns, etc., A-Z**

GALE NOTE *The cutter number(s) listed below have been given only as examples by the Library of Congress*

349.B5 Biloxi

349.J13 Jackson

349.M5 Meridian

349.N2 Natchez

349.V6 Vicksburg

Elements in the population

350.A1 General works

350.A2-.Z Individual elements

For a list of racial, ethnic, and religious elements (with cutter numbers), see E184.A+

350.3-358.2 **Mississippi River and Valley. Middle West**

350.5 **Biography (Collective). Genealogy (Collective)**

350.8 **Antiquities (Non-Indian)**

351 **General works**

Including the Mississippi Valley under Spain, France, Great Britain, and the United States. History; description, exploration, and travel; manners and customs

Including periodicals, societies, collections, collective biography, etc.

For Louisiana purchase (Diplomatic and political aspects), see E333

Cf. F347.B7, Mississippi-Arkansas boundary

Cf. F366+, Louisiana

Cf. F377.B7, Mississippi-Louisiana boundary

Cf. F396, Lower Mississippi River and Valley

Cf. F516+, Ohio River and Valley

Cf. F547.I2, Illinois River and Valley

Cf. F597, Upper Mississippi River and Valley

Cf. F598, Missouri River and Valley

By period

352 Early to 1803

Including early explorations and discoveries, by Hennepin, La Salle, Marquette

Cf. E125.S7, Soto's explorations (General)

Cf. E234, Clark's Expedition

Cf. E333, Purchase of Louisiana by the United States (Diplomatic and political aspects)

Cf. F372-373, Louisiana (French and Spanish)

Cf. F597, Carver's explorations (Upper Mississippi Valley)

Cf. F1030, New France

Cf. F1030.2, Marquette's explorations (General)

Cf. F1030.3, Joliet's explorations (General)

350.3-358.2 **Mississippi River and Valley. Middle West**
By period
352 Early to 1803 — Continued
Cf. F1030.4, Hennepin's explorations (General)
Cf. F1030.5, La Salle's explorations (General)
Cf. HG6007, Law's Mississippi Scheme
353 1803-1865
Cf. E83.83, Black Hawk War, 1832
Cf. E334, Burr's Conspiracy, 1805-1807
Cf. E471+, Civil War, 1861-1865 (History and campaigns)
Cf. F592, Lewis and Clark Expedition, 1804-1806; Pike's Expedition, 1805-1807
354 1865-1950
Including individual floods, cruises down the river
Cf. TC425.M65, Jetties of the Mississippi
355 1951-
Elements in the population
358 General works
358.2.A-.2.Z Individual elements
For a list of individual racial, ethnic and religious elements (with cutter numbers), see E184.A+
Louisiana
366 **Periodicals. Societies. Collections**
366.5 **Museums. Exhibitions, exhibits**
367 **Gazetteers. Dictionaries. Geographic names**
367.3 **Guidebooks**
367.5 **Directories**
368 **Biography (Collective). Genealogy (Collective)**
368.2 **Historiography**
Historians, *see* E175.5.A+
368.5 **Study and teaching**
369 **General works. Histories**
369.3 **Juvenile works**
Pamphlets, addresses, essays, etc.
369.5 General
369.6 Anecdotes, legends, pageants, etc.
370 **Historic monuments (General). Illustrative material**
371 **Antiquities (Non-Indian)**
By period
372 Early to 1803
Including French Louisiana; Settlement of 1698; Crozat's Grant, 1712-1717; Cession to Spain, 1763
Including biography: Jean Baptiste Le Moyne de Bienville, Pierre Le Moyne d'Iberville, etc.
Cf. E83.739, Chickasaw War, 1739-1740
Cf. F334.M6, Mobile, Ala
Cf. F352, Mississippi Valley
Cf. HG6007, Law's Mississippi scheme, 1717-1720
373 1764-1803
Including Spanish Louisiana; right of navigation of the Mississippi; retrocession to France, 1800-1801
Including biography: Esteban Miró, etc.
For purchase of Louisiana by the United States, see E333
For Spaniards in North America (General), see F1410
374 1803-1865
Including admission as a state, April 30, 1812
Including Province of Louisiana, 1803-1804; Territory of Orleans, 1804-1812; boundary disputes with Spain
Including biography: William Charles Cole Claiborne, Thomas Jefferson Durant, Charles Étienne Arthur Gayarré, Jean Lafitte, Alexander Porter, etc.
Cf. E334, Burr's Conspiracy, 1805-1807
Cf. E355, War of 1812 (Military operations)

Louisiana
By period
374 1803-1865 — Continued
Cf. E565.1+, Civil War (General)
Cf. E470.7, E471+, Military operations and battles in the Civil War
Cf. F301, West Florida
Cf. F314, Spanish Treaty of 1819
Cf. F592, Lewis and Clark Expedition
Cf. F697, The "Indian country"
375 1865-1950. Reconstruction
Including Carpetbag misrule; Committee of Seventy; Ku-Klux Klan
Including biography: Edgar Howard Farrar, Samuel Douglas McEnery, etc.
Cf. D769.85.L6+, World War II, 1939-1945
1951-
376 General works
Biography and memoirs
376.2 Collective
376.3.A-.3.Z Individual, A-Z
GALE NOTE *See note at the head of Table F5 at the end of the text for further instructions on how to subdivide this number*
377.A-.Z **Regions, parishes, etc., A-Z**
377.A15 Counties
377.A16 Mountains
377.A17 Rivers
377.A18 Lakes
377.A19 Islands
377.A2 Acadia Parish
377.A4 Allen Parish
377.A7 Ascension Parish
377.A75 Assumption Parish
377.A78 Atchafalaya River and Swamp
Including Bayou Chene and other bayous in the region
377.A8 Attakapas District
Avery Island, *see* F377.F57
377.A9 Avoyelles Parish
377.B37 Bartholomew Bayou
Class here works limited to the part of the Bartholomew Bayou located in Louisiana
For general works on the Bartholomew Bayou and works limited to the part located in Arkansas, see F417.B27
Bayou Lafourche, *see* F377.L24
Bayou Teche, *see* F377.T4
377.B4 Beauregard Parish
377.B5 Bienville Parish
377.B6 Bossier Parish
377.B7 Boundaries
Cf. F377.F6 , Florida parishes
Caddo Lake, *see* F377.C15
377.C15 Caddo Parish
Including Caddo Lake
Cf. F392.C17 , General, and Texas
377.C2 Calcasieu Parish
377.C23 Caldwell Parish
377.C25 Cameron Parish
Cane River Lake, *see* F377.N4
377.C3 Catahoula Parish
Chalmette National Historical Park, *see* F356.N5
377.C5 Claiborne Parish
377.C7 Concordia Parish
377.D4 Delta region
377.D45 De Soto Parish

	Louisiana
377.A-.Z	**Regions, parishes, etc., A-Z — Continued**
377.E17	East Baton Rouge Parish
377.E2	East Carroll Parish
377.E3	East Feliciana Parish
377.E8	Evangeline Parish
377.F57	Five Islands
	Including Avery Island
377.F6	Florida parishes. Baton Rouge district of West Florida since 1812 (between Pearl and Mississippi rivers)
	For early to 1812, see F301
377.F7	Franklin Parish
	Grand Isle, *see* F377.J4
377.G7	Grant Parish
377.G9	Gulf coast of Louisiana
	Cf. F296, Gulf coast (General)
377.I15	Iberia Parish
377.I2	Iberville Parish
377.J2	Jackson Parish
377.J4	Jefferson Parish
	Including Grand Isle
377.J43	Jefferson Davis Parish
377.L2	Lafayette Parish
377.L24	Lafourche Bayou
377.L25	Lafourche Parish
377.L3	La Salle Parish
377.L5	Lincoln Parish
377.L6	Livingston Parish
377.M2	Madison Parish
377.M6	Mississippi River and Valley, La.
	Cf. F350.5+, General
	Cf. F396, Lower Mississippi Valley
377.M7	Morehouse Parish
	Murphys Lake, *see* F377.N4
377.N4	Natchitoches Parish
	Including Murphys Lake and Cane River Lake
377.O7	Orleans Parish
377.O78	Ouachita Parish
377.O8	Ouachita River and Valley (General, and La.)
	Cf. F417.O83, Arkansas
377.P3	Pearl River and Valley (General, and La.)
	Cf. F347.P3, General, and Mississippi
377.P45	Plaquemines Parish
377.P55	Pointe Coupee Parish
377.P6	Lake Pontchartrain
377.R25	Rapides Parish
	Including Cotile Lake
377.R3	Red River and Valley (General, and La.)
	Cf. F392.R3, Texas
	Cf. F417.R3, Arkansas
	Cf. F702.R3, Oklahoma
	Cf. F802.R36, New Mexico
377.R32	Red River Parish
377.R5	Richland Parish
377.R58	River Road
377.S115	Sabine Parish
377.S116	Sabine River and Valley (General, and La.)
	Cf. F392.S12, Texas
377.S12	St. Bernard Parish
377.S124	St. Charles Parish

Louisiana
377.A-.Z **Regions, parishes, etc., A-Z — Continued**
377.S13 St. Helena Parish
377.S134 St. James Parish
377.S135 St. John the Baptist Parish
377.S14 St. Landry Parish
377.S16 St. Martin Parish
377.S2 St. Mary Parish
377.S3 St. Tammany Parish
377.T3 Tangipahoa Parish
377.T4 Bayou Teche
377.T45 Tensas Parish
377.T5 Terrebonne Parish
377.T6 Toledo Bend Reservoir. Toledo Bend region
377.U5 Union Parish
377.V5 Vermilion Parish
377.V6 Vernon Parish
377.W3 Washington Parish
377.W4 Webster Parish
377.W45 West Baton Rouge Parish
377.W47 West Carroll Parish
377.W5 West Feliciana Parish
377.W6 Winn Parish
379.A-.Z **Cities, towns, etc., A-Z**
GALE NOTE *The cutter number(s) listed below have been given only as examples by the Library of Congress*
379.A15 Cities and towns (Collective and selective)
379.B33 Baton Rouge
379.N5 New Orleans
Subarrange by Table F2 at the end of the text
379.S4 Shreveport
Elements in the population
380.A1 General works
380.A2-.Z Individual elements
For a list of racial, ethnic, and religious elements (with cutter numbers), see E184.A+

Texas
381 **Periodicals. Societies. Collections**
383 **Museums. Exhibitions, exhibits**
384 **Gazetteers. Dictionaries. Geographic names**
384.3 **Guidebooks**
385 **Biography (Collective). Genealogy (Collective)**
385.2 **Historiography**
Historians, *see* E175.5.A+
385.5 **Study and teaching**
386 **General works. Histories**
386.3 **Juvenile works**
Pamphlets, addresses, essays, etc.
386.5 General
386.6 Anecdotes, legends, pageants, etc.
386.8 **Geography**
387 **Historic monuments (General). Illustrative material**
388 **Antiquities (Non-Indian)**
By period
389 Early to 1835
Including Impresarios; Province of Mexico; Coahuila and Texas (Mexican state); Austin's Colony; De Witt's Colony; Las Casas and Sambrano Revolutions, 1811; Fredonian Insurrection, 1826-1827
Including biography: Stephen Fuller Austin, David Gouverneur Burnet, Anson Jones, Thomas Jefferson Rusk, etc.
Cf. E359.5.T47, War of 1812

Texas

By period

389 Early to 1835 — Continued

Cf. F352, La Salle's Colony, 1685-1687

390 1835-1846

Admission as a state, December 29, 1845

Including War of Independence 1835-1836 (Siege of the Alamo, 1836; Battle of San Jacinto, 1836; etc.); Republic of Texas, 1836-1846; Santa Fe Expedition, 1841; Mier Expedition, 1842; annexation to the United States; etc.

Including biography: Samuel Houston, Mirabeau Bonaparte Lamar, Henry Smith, William Alexander Anderson Wallace, etc.

1846-

Including Frontier troubles with Mexico; Session and Reconstruction; frontier and ranch life; Texas Rangers

Including biography: Roy Bean, Charles Goodnight, George Washington Littlefield, William Jesse McDonald, Wilbert Lee O'Daniel, etc.

Cf. D570.85.T4+, World War I, 1914-1918

Cf. D769.85.T4+, World War II, 1939-1945

Cf. E401+, War with Mexico, 1845-1848

Cf. E580.1+, Civil War, 1861-1865 (General)

Cf. E470.9, E471+, Military operations and battles in the Civil War, 1861-1865

Cf. E532.1+, Union history, Civil War, 1861-1865

Cf. F801, Sale of claims to northwest lands, 1850

Cf. F1232, Mexican frontier troubles (General)

391 General works

1951-

391.2 General works

Biography

391.3 Collective

391.4.A-.4.Z Individual, A-Z

GALE NOTE *See note at the head of Table F5 at the end of the text for further instructions on how to subdivide this number*

392.A-.Z **Regions, counties, etc., A-Z**

392.A15 Counties

392.A16 Mountains

392.A17 Rivers

392.A18 Lakes

392.A19 Islands

392.A2 Anderson Co.

392.A25 Andrews Co.

392.A3 Angelina Co.

392.A6 Aransas Co.

392.A65 Archer Co.

Armand Bayou Park and Nature Center, *see* F392.H38

392.A7 Armstrong Co.

392.A8 Atacosa Co.

392.A9 Austin Co.

392.B15 Bailey Co.

392.B17 Balcones Canyonlands National Wildlife Refuge

392.B2 Bandera Co.

392.B23 Bastrop Co.

392.B25 Baylor Co.

392.B3 Bee Co.

392.B34 Bell Co.

Including Tennessee Valley

392.B5 Bexar Co.

392.B53 Big Bend National Park

392.B54 Big Bend region

Big Thicket, *see* F392.H37

392.B55 Blanco Co.

Texas

392.A-.Z **Regions, counties, etc., A-Z — Continued**

392.B57 Bolivar Peninsula

392.B58 Borden Co.

392.B6 Bosque Co.

392.B7 Boundaries

For International boundary, see F786

Cf. F377.B7, Louisiana boundary

392.B74 Bowie Co.

392.B82 Brazoria Co.

392.B84 Brazos Co.

392.B842 Brazos River and Valley

Including South Bend Reservoir

392.B85 Brewster Co.

For Big Bend National Park, see F392.B53

392.B86 Briscoe Co.

392.B88 Brooks Co.

392.B89 Brown Co.

392.B95 Burleson Co.

392.B97 Burnet Co.

392.C17 Caddo Lake (General, and Texas)

Cf. F377.C15, Louisiana

392.C2 Caldwell Co.

392.C22 Calhoun Co.

392.C23 Callahan Co.

392.C25 Cameron Co.

392.C26 Camp Co.

392.C27 Canadian River and Valley, Tex.

Cf. F702.C2, General, and Oklahoma

392.C28 Carson Co.

392.C287 Casa Blanca Land Grant

392.C29 Cass Co.

392.C3 Castro Co.

392.C4 Chambers Co.

392.C44 Cherokee Co.

392.C45 Childress Co.

Choke Canyon Reservoir, *see* F392.F92

392.C5 Clay Co.

392.C517 Coastal Bend

392.C52 Cochino Bayou and Valley

392.C53 Cochran Co.

392.C54 Coke Co.

392.C55 Coleman Co.

392.C56 Collin Co.

392.C57 Collingsworth Co.

392.C58 Colorado Co.

392.C6 Colorado River and Valley

392.C7 Comal Co.

392.C75 Comanche Co.

392.C77 Concho Co.

392.C773 Concho River and Valley

392.C78 Cooke Co.

392.C79 Cooper Lake

392.C8 Coryell Co.

Including Mother Neff State Park

392.C82 Cottle Co.

392.C83 Crane Co.

392.C84 Crockett Co.

392.C85 Crosby Co.

392.C9 Culberson Co.

Texas

392.A-.Z **Regions, counties, etc., A-Z — Continued**

392.D13 Dallam Co.

392.D14 Dallas Co.

392.D25 Dawson Co.

392.D3 Deaf Smith Co.

392.D35 Delta Co.

392.D4 Denton Co.

Including Green Valley

392.D5 De Witt Co.

392.D6 Dickens Co.

392.D65 Dimmit Co.

392.D7 Donley Co.

392.D9 Duval Co.

392.E16 Eastland Co.

Ecleto Creek and Valley, *see* F392.W7

392.E25 Ector Co.

392.E3 Edwards Co.

392.E33 Edwards Plateau

392.E4 Ellis Co.

392.E45 El Paso Co.

392.E64 Enchanted Rock State Natural Area

392.E7 Erath Co.

392.F15 Falls Co.

392.F17 Fannin Co.

392.F2 Fayette Co.

392.F4 Fisher Co.

392.F6 Floyd Co.

392.F65 Foard Co.

392.F7 Fort Bend Co.

Fort Leaton State Park, *see* F392.P7

392.F8 Franklin Co.

392.F85 Freestone Co.

392.F9 Frio Co.

392.F92 Frio River and Valley

Including Choke Canyon Reservoir

392.G2 Gaines Co.

392.G25 Galveston Co.

392.G3 Garza Co.

392.G5 Gillespie Co.

392.G55 Glasscock Co.

392.G6 Goliad Co.

Including Goliad State Park

392.G65 Gonzales Co.

392.G68 Gray Co.

392.G7 Grayson Co.

392.G73 Gregg Co.

392.G75 Grimes Co.

392.G85 Guadalupe Co.

392.G86 Guadalupe Mountains, Texas. Guadalupe Mountains National Park

Cf. F802.G93, General, and New Mexico

392.G9 Gulf coast of Texas

For Padre Island, see F392.P14

Cf. F296, Gulf coast (General)

392.H3 Hale Co.

392.H33 Hall Co.

392.H34 Hamilton Co.

392.H35 Hansford Co.

392.H36 Hardeman Co.

	Texas
392.A-.Z	**Regions, counties, etc., A-Z — Continued**
392.H37	Hardin Co.
	Including Big Thicket
392.H38	Harris Co.
	Including Armand Bayou Park and Nature Center
392.H39	Harrison Co.
392.H4	Hartley Co.
392.H43	Haskell Co.
392.H46	Hays Co.
392.H5	Hemphill Co.
392.H54	Henderson Co.
392.H56	Hidalgo Co.
392.H57	Hill Co.
392.H6	Hockley Co.
392.H65	Hood Co.
392.H67	Hopkins Co.
392.H7	Houston Co.
392.H75	Howard Co.
392.H8	Hudspeth Co.
392.H82	Hueco Mountains (General, and Texas)
	Cf. F802.H84, New Mexico
392.H9	Hunt Co.
392.H95	Hutchinson Co.
	Including Lake Meredith National Recreation Area
392.I6	Irion Co.
392.J22	Jack Co.
392.J24	Jackson Co.
392.J27	Jasper Co.
392.J3	Jeff Davis Co.
392.J33	Jefferson Co.
	Including Sabine Pass Battlefield State Historical Park
392.J48	Jim Hogg Co.
392.J5	Jim Wells Co.
392.J6	Johnson Co.
392.J7	Jones Co.
392.K2	Karnes Co.
392.K25	Kaufman Co.
392.K3	Kendall Co.
392.K32	Kenedy Co.
392.K33	Kent Co.
392.K35	Kerr Co.
392.K4	Kimble Co.
392.K45	King Co.
392.K47	King Ranch
392.K5	Kinney Co.
392.K6	Kleberg Co.
392.K7	Knox Co.
392.L33	La Junta de los Rios
	Lake Meredith National Recreation Area, *see* F392.H95
392.L36	Lamar Co.
392.L37	Lamb Co.
392.L38	Lampasas Co.
392.L4	La Salle Co.
392.L42	Lavaca Co.
392.L45	Lee Co.
392.L46	Leon Co.
392.L5	Liberty Co.
392.L54	Limestone Co.
392.L55	Lipscomb Co.

	Texas	
392.A-.Z	Regions, counties, etc., A-Z — Continued	
392.L58	Live Oak Co.	
392.L6	Llano Co.	
392.L62	Llano Estacado (Staked Plain)	
392.L66	Long Cove	
392.L7	Loving Co.	
392.L8	Lubbock Co.	
392.L87	Lyndon B. Johnson Historical Park	
392.L9	Lynn Co.	
392.M15	McCulloch Co.	
392.M2	McLennan Co.	
392.M23	McMullen Co.	
392.M25	Madison Co.	
392.M3	Marion Co.	
392.M33	Martin Co.	
392.M36	Mason Co.	
392.M4	Matagorda Co.	
	Including Matagorda Bay	
392.M43	Maverick Co.	
392.M44	Medina Co.	
392.M45	Menard Co.	
	Meredith, Lake, National Recreation Area, *see* F392.H95	
392.M5	Midland Co.	
392.M54	Milam Co.	
392.M56	Mills Co.	
392.M6	Mitchell Co.	
392.M67	Montague Co.	
392.M7	Montgomery Co.	
392.M75	Moore Co.	
392.M8	Morris Co.	
	Mother Neff State Park, *see* F392.C8	
392.M85	Motley Co.	
	Mustang Island State Park, *see* F392.N8	
392.N2	Nacogdoches Co.	
392.N24	Nacogdoches District	
392.N3	Navarro Co.	
392.N35	Neches River and Valley	
392.N4	Newton Co.	
392.N6	Nolan Co.	
392.N8	Nueces Co.	
392.N82	Nueces River and Valley	
392.O2	Ochiltree Co.	
392.O4	Oldham Co.	
392.O7	Orange Co.	
392.P14	Padre Island	
392.P16	Palo Duro State Park. Palo Duro Canyon	
392.P165	Palo Pinto Co.	
392.P168	Panhandle	
392.P17	Panola Co.	
392.P2	Parker Co.	
392.P24	Parmer Co.	
392.P28	Pecos Co.	
392.P3	Pecos River and Valley (General, and Tex.)	
	Cf. F802.P3, New Mexico	
392.P55	Polk Co.	
392.P6	Potter Co.	
392.P7	Presidio Co.	
	Including Fort Leaton State Park	
392.R15	Rains Co.	

	Texas
392.A-.Z	**Regions, counties, etc., A-Z — Continued**
392.R2	Randall Co.
392.R22	Ray Roberts Lake
392.R25	Reagan Co.
392.R26	Real Co.
392.R3	Red River and Valley, Tex.
	Cf. F377.R3 , General, and Louisiana
392.R33	Red River Co.
392.R4	Reeves Co.
392.R45	Refugio Co.
392.R48	Richland Creek and Valley
	Including Richland-Chambers Dam and Reservoir
392.R5	Rio Grande (General, and Tex.)
	Including Rio Grande Valley
	For Big Bend National Park, see F392.B53
	Cf. F802.R5, New Mexico
	Cf. F1334, Mexico
392.R6	Roberts Co.
392.R63	Robertson Co.
392.R64	Rocking Chair Ranche
392.R65	Rockwell Co.
392.R75	Runnels Co.
392.R8	Rusk Co.
392.S11	Sabine Co.
	Sabine Pass Battlefield State Historical Park, *see* F392.J33
392.S12	Sabine River and Valley, Tex.
	Cf. F377.S116, General, and Louisiana
392.S19	San Antonio River and Valley
392.S23	San Augustine Co.
392.S234	San Gabriel River and Valley
392.S235	San Jacinto Co.
392.S237	San Patricio Co.
392.S24	San Saba Co.
392.S35	Schleicher Co.
392.S4	Scurry Co.
392.S46	Shackelford Co.
392.S5	Shelby Co.
392.S52	Sherman Co.
392.S55	Smith Co.
392.S65	Somervell Co.
	South Bend Reservoir, *see* F392.B842
	Staked Plain, *see* F392.L62
392.S75	Starr Co.
392.S78	Stephens Co.
392.S8	Sterling Co.
392.S85	Stonewall Co.
392.S9	Sutton Co.
392.S95	Swisher Co.
392.T25	Tarrant Co.
392.T3	Taylor Co.
	Tennessee Valley, *see* F392.B34
392.T4	Terrell Co.
392.T45	Terry Co.
392.T47	Texas Hill Country
392.T5	Throckmorton Co.
392.T55	Titus Co.
	Toledo Bend Reservoir and Toledo Bend region, *see* F377.T6
392.T6	Tom Green Co.
392.T7	Travis Co.

Texas

392.A-.Z **Regions, counties, etc., A-Z — Continued**

392.T8 Trinity Co.

392.T83 Trinity River and Valley

392.T9 Tyler Co.

392.U5 Upshur Co.

392.U6 Upton Co.

392.U9 Uvalde Co.

392.V17 Val Verde Co.

392.V2 Van Zandt Co.

392.V5 Victoria Co.

392.W24 Walker Co.

392.W25 Waller Co.

392.W27 Ward Co.

392.W3 Washington Co.

392.W33 Washita River and Valley (General, and Texas)

Cf. F702.W36, Oklahoma

392.W4 Webb Co.

392.W45 Wharton Co.

392.W47 Wheeler Co.

392.W55 Wichita Co.

392.W6 Wilbarger Co.

392.W64 Willacy Co.

392.W66 Williamson Co.

392.W7 Wilson Co.

Including Ecleto Creek

392.W75 Winkler Co.

392.W8 Wise Co.

392.W9 Wood Co.

392.X2 XIT Ranch

392.Y6 Yoakum Co.

392.Y7 Young Co.

392.Z3 Zapata Co.

392.Z4 Zavala Co.

394.A-.Z **Cities, towns, etc, A-Z**

GALE NOTE *The cutter number(s) listed below have been given only as examples by the Library of Congress*

394.A4 Amarillo

394.A9 Austin

Subarrange by Table F2 at the end of the text

394.B3 Beaumont

394.C78 Corpus Christi

394.D21 Dallas

Subarrange by Table F2 at the end of the text

394.E4 El Paso

394.F7 Fort Worth

394.G2 Galveston

394.H8 Houston

Subarrange by Table F2 at the end of the text

394.S211 San Antonio

Subarrange by Table F2 at the end of the text

394.W12 Waco

Elements in the population

395.A1 General works

395.A2-.Z Individual elements

For a list of racial, ethnic, and religious elements (with cutter numbers), see E184.A+

396 **Old Southwest. Lower Mississippi Valley**

Including biography: John A. Murrell

Cf. E78.S8, Indians of the Old Southwest

Cf. E334, Burr's Conspiracy

396	**Old Southwest. Lower Mississippi Valley — Continued**
	Cf. F296, Gulf coast
	Cf. F350.5+, Mississippi River and Valley
	Cf. F366+, Louisiana
	Cf. F377.R3, Red River, La.
	Cf. F392.B7, Texas boundaries (United States)
	Cf. F417.O9, Ozark Mountain region
	Cf. F786, Mexican boundaries (United States)
	Arkansas
406	**Periodicals. Societies. Collections**
408	**Museums. Exhibitions, exhibits**
409	**Gazetteers. Dictionaries. Geographic names**
409.3	**Guidebooks**
410	**Biography (Collective). Genealogy (Collective)**
410.2	**Historiography**
	Historians, *see* E175.5.A+
410.5	**Study and teaching**
411	**General works. Histories**
	Admission as a state, June 15, 1836
	Including by period (Early to 1950) as well as general
	For 1951 and later, see F415+
	Including Reconstruction
	Including biography: Thomas Chipman McRae, etc.
	Cf. D769.85.A8+, World War II, 1939-1945
	Cf. E553.1+, Civil War, 1861-1865 (General)
	Cf. E470.4+, E471+, Military operations and battles in the Civil War, 1861-1865
	Cf. E496.1+ , Union history, Civil War, 1861-1865
411.3	**Juvenile works**
	Pamphlets, addresses, essays, etc.
411.5	General
411.6	Anecdotes, legends, pageants, etc.
412	**Historic monuments (General). Illustrative material**
413	**Antiquities (Non-Indian)**
	By period
	Early to 1950, *see* F411
	1951-
415	General works
	Biography and memoirs
415.2	Collective
415.3.A-.3.Z	Individual, A-Z
	GALE NOTE *See note at the head of Table F5 at the end of the text for further instructions on how to subdivide this number*
417.A-.Z	**Regions, counties, etc., A-Z**
417.A15	Counties
427.A16	Mountains
417.A17	Rivers
417.A18	Lakes
417.A19	Islands
417.A65	Arkansas Co.
417.A67	Arkansas Delta
417.A7	Arkansas River and Valley (General, and Ark.)
	Cf. F687.A7, Kansas
	Cf. F702.A7, Oklahoma
	Cf. F782.A7, Colorado
417.A8	Ashley Co.
417.B27	Bartholomew Bayou
	Class here general works on the Bartholomew Bayou, and works limited to the part located in Arkansas
	For works limited to the part of the Bartholomew Bayou located in Louisiana, see F377.B37
417.B3	Baxter Co.

	Arkansas
417.A-.Z	**Regions, counties, etc., A-Z — Continued**
417.B4	Benton Co.
	Blue Mountain Lake, *see* F417.L75
417.B6	Boone Co.
417.B7	Boundaries
	Cf. F347.B7, Mississippi boundary
417.B8	Bradley Co.
417.B85	Buffalo River and Valley
417.B86	Bull Shoals Lake and region (General, and Arkansas)
	Cf. F472.B94, Missouri
417.C27	Cadron Creek and Valley
417.C3	Calhoun Co.
	Including Sparta Mine
417.C4	Carroll Co.
417.C45	Chicot Co.
417.C5	Clamorgan land grant (Arkansas and Missouri)
417.C53	Clark Co.
417.C54	Clay Co.
417.C55	Cleburne Co.
417.C56	Cleveland Co.
417.C6	Columbia Co.
417.C7	Conway Co.
	Including Cypress Creek and Valley
417.C8	Craighead Co.
	Crater of Diamonds State Park, *see* F417.P5
417.C87	Crawford Co.
417.C9	Crittenden Co.
417.C95	Cross Co.
	Cypress Creek and Valley, *see* F417.C7
417.D3	Dallas Co.
417.D4	Desha Co.
417.D7	Drew Co.
417.F3	Faulkner Co.
417.F7	Franklin Co.
417.F8	Fulton Co.
417.G3	Garland Co.
417.G7	Grant Co.
417.G8	Greene Co.
417.H4	Hempstead Co.
417.H6	Hot Spring Co.
417.H7	Howard Co.
417.I5	Independence Co.
417.I9	Izard Co.
417.J3	Jackson Co.
417.J4	Jefferson Co.
417.J6	Johnson Co.
417.L2	Lafayette Co.
417.L4	Lawrence Co.
417.L45	Lee Co.
417.L6	Lincoln Co.
417.L64	Little River and Valley, Ark.
	Cf. F702.L55, General and Oklahoma
417.L65	Little River Co.
417.L75	Logan Co.
	Including Blue Mountain Lake
417.L8	Lonoke Co.
417.M3	Madison Co.
417.M35	Marion Co.
417.M5	Miller Co.

Arkansas

417.A-.Z **Regions, counties, etc., A-Z — Continued**

417.M58 Mississippi Co.

417.M6 Mississippi River and Valley, Ark.

Cf. F350.5+, General

Cf. F396, Lower Mississippi Valley

417.M7 Monroe Co.

417.M75 Montgomery Co.

417.N4 Nevada Co.

417.N5 Newton Co.

417.N56 Nimrod Lake and Region

417.O75 Ouachita Co.

417.O77 Ouachita Mountains

Cf. F702.O9, General, and Oklahoma

417.O8 Ouachita National Forest (Arkansas National Forest)

417.O83 Ouachita River and Valley, Ark.

Cf. F377.O8, General, and Louisiana

417.O9 Ozark Mountains (General, and Ark.)

Cf. F472.O9, Missouri

417.P4 Perry Co.

417.P43 Petit Jean Mountain

417.P45 Phillips Co.

417.P5 Pike Co.

Including Crater of Diamonds State Park

417.P65 Poinsett Co.

417.P7 Polk Co.

417.P75 Pope Co.

417.P85 Prairie Co.

417.P98 Pulaski Co.

417.R2 Randolph Co.

417.R3 Red River and Valley, Ark.

Cf. F377.R3, General, and Louisiana

417.S15 St. Francis Co.

417.S2 St. Francis River and Valley (General, and Ark.)

Cf. F472.S25, Missouri

417.S23 Saline Co.

417.S25 Scott Co.

417.S3 Searcy Co.

417.S33 Sebastian Co.

417.S4 Sevier Co.

417.S5 Sharp Co.

Sparta Mine, *see* F417.C3

417.S8 Stone Co.

417.U5 Union Co.

417.V3 Van Buren Co.

417.V55 Village Creek and Valley

417.W3 Washington Co.

417.W4 White Co.

417.W5 White River and Valley (General, and Ark.)

Cf. F472.W5, Missouri

417.W6 Woodruff Co.

417.Y4 Yell Co.

For Blue Mountain Lake, see F417.L75

419.A-.Z **Cities, towns, etc., A-Z**

GALE NOTE *The cutter number(s) listed below have been given only as examples by the Library of Congress*

419.H8 Hot Springs

419.L7 Little Rock

Elements in the population

420.A1 General works

	Arkansas
	Elements in the population — Continued
420.A2-.Z	Individual elements
	For a list of racial, ethnic, and religious elements (with cutter numbers), see E184.A+
	Tennessee
431	**Periodicals. Societies. Collections**
433	**Museums. Exhibitions, exhibits**
434	**Gazetteers. Dictionaries. Geographic names**
434.3	**Guidebooks**
435	**Biography (Collective). Genealogy (Collective)**
435.2	**Historiography**
	Historians, *see* E175.5.A+
435.5	**Study and teaching**
436	**General works. Histories**
	Including the state of Franklin, 1784-1788; admission as a state June 1, 1796
	Including by period (Early to 1950) as well as general
	For 1951 and later, see F440
	Including Pioneer days; Secession and Reconstruction; etc.
	Including biography: David Crockett, Jefferson Dillard Goodpasture, Austin Peay, Archibald Roane, James Robertson, William Tatham, Alfred Alexander Taylor, Robert Love Taylor, etc.
	Cf. D570.85.T2+, World War I, 1914-1918
	Cf. D769.85.T2+, World War II, 1939-1945
	Cf. E83.813, First Creek War, 1813-1814
	Cf. E263.T4, Tennessee in the Revolution, 1775-1783
	Cf. E309, North Carolina cessions of 1784 and 1790
	Cf. E409.5.T4, War with Mexico, 1845-1848
	Cf. E579.1+, Civil War, 1861-1865 (General)
	Cf. E470.4-.5, E471+, Military operations and battles in the Civil War, 1861-1865
	Cf. E531, Union history
	Cf. E726.T4, War of 1898 (Spanish-American War)
436.3	**Juvenile works**
	Pamphlets, addresses, essays, etc.
436.5	General
436.6	Anecdotes, legends, pageants, etc.
437	**Historic monuments (General). Illustrative material**
438	**Antiquities (Non-Indian)**
	By period
	Early to 1950, *see* F436
	1951-
440	General works
	Biography and memoirs
440.2	Collective
440.22.A-.22.Z	Individual, A-Z
	GALE NOTE *See note at the head of Table F5 at the end of the text for further instructions on how to subdivide this number*
442.1	**East Tennessee**
	Including Association of the Territorial Company of Philadelphia, Ocoee District
	Cf. F210, Mountain whites of the South
442.2	**Middle Tennessee. Cumberland Valley**
	Cf. F457.C9, Cumberland Valley, Ky
442.3	**West Tennessee**
	Cf. F443.M6, Mississippi Valley, Tenn.
443.A-.Z	**Regions, counties, etc., A-Z**
443.A15	Counties
443.A16	Mountains
443.A17	Rivers
443.A18	Lakes
443.A19	Islands
443.A5	Anderson Co.

Tennessee

443.A-.Z **Regions, counties, etc., A-Z — Continued**

443.B3 Bald Mountains (General, and Tennessee)
Including Big Bald Mountain
Cf. F262.B3 , North Carolina

443.B33 Bays Mountain

443.B35 Bedford Co.
Including Liberty Gap

443.B4 Benton Co.

Big Bald Mountain, *see* F443.B3

443.B55 Bledsoe Co.

443.B6 Blount Co.

443.B7 Boundaries
Cf. F262.B7, North Carolina boundary
Cf. F457.B7, Kentucky boundary
For South Carolina cession south of Tennessee, see F292.B7

443.B74 Boyd's Creek and Valley

443.B8 Bradley Co.
Including Chatata Creek and Valley

443.C3 Campbell Co.

443.C313 Cannon Co.

443.C316 Carroll Co.

443.C32 Carter Co.
Including Lost Cove

Chatata Creek and Valley, *see* F443.B8

443.C4 Cheatham Co.

443.C45 Chester Co.

443.C47 Chickamauga Lake and region

443.C5 Claiborne Co.

443.C55 Clay Co.

443.C56 Clear Fork River and Valley
Cf. F457.C58, General, and Kentucky

443.C57 Clinch River and Valley

443.C6 Cocke Co.

443.C65 Coffee Co.

443.C7 Crockett Co.

Cumberland Caverns, *see* F443.W2

443.C78 Cumberland Co.

Cumberland River and Valley, *see* F442.2

443.D2 Davidson Co.

443.D25 Decatur Co.

443.D3 De Kalb Co.

443.D5 Dickson Co.

443.D9 Dyer Co.

443.F3 Fayette Co.

443.F34 Fentress Co.

Fort Loudoun Lake, *see* F443.L9

Fort Pillow State Park, *see* F443.L35

443.F7 Franklin Co.

443.F8 French Broad River and Valley (General, and Tennessee)
Cf. F262.F85, North Carolina

443.G35 Gibson Co.

443.G4 Giles Co.

443.G65 Grainger Co.

443.G7 Great Smoky Mountains
Including Great Smoky Mountains National Park

443.G75 Greene Co.

443.G85 Grundy Co.

Hales Bar Dam Region, *see* F443.M32

443.H17 Hamblen Co.

	Tennessee
443.A-.Z	**Regions, counties, etc., A-Z — Continued**
443.H19	Hamilton Co.
443.H24	Hancock Co.
443.H28	Hardeman Co.
443.H3	Hardin Co.
443.H37	Hawkins Co.
443.H4	Haywood Co.
443.H45	Henderson Co.
443.H5	Henry Co.
443.H6	Hickman Co.
443.H7	Holston River and Valley
443.H75	Houston Co.
443.H8	Humphreys Co.
443.J3	Jackson Co.
443.J35	James Co.
443.J5	Jefferson Co.
443.J7	Johnson Co.
443.K6	Knox Co.
443.L25	Lake Co.
443.L35	Lauderdale Co.
	Including Fort Pillow State Park
443.L4	Lawrence Co.
	LeConte, Mount, *see* F443.S45
443.L5	Lewis Co.
	Liberty Gap, *see* F443.B35
443.L6	Lincoln Co.
443.L63	Little River and Valley
443.L64	Little Tennessee River and Valley
443.L8	Lookout Mountain
	Lost Cove (Carter County), *see* F443.C32
443.L9	Loudon Co.
	Including Fort Loudoun Lake
443.M15	McMinn Co.
443.M2	McNairy Co.
443.M23	Macon Co.
443.M25	Madison Co.
443.M32	Marion Co.
	Including Hale's Bar Dam Region
443.M35	Marshall Co.
443.M4	Maury Co.
443.M5	Meigs Co.
443.M6	Mississippi River and Valley, Tenn.
	Cf. F350.5+, General
	Cf. F396, Lower Mississippi Valley
443.M7	Monroe Co.
	Including Fort Loudoun
443.M8	Montgomery Co.
443.M83	Moore Co.
443.M85	Morgan Co.
443.N67	Norris Lake
443.O2	Obion Co.
443.O9	Overton Co.
443.P34	Paint Rock River
	Cf. F332.P34, General, and Alabama
443.P4	Perry Co.
443.P5	Pickett Co.
443.P7	Polk Co.
443.P75	Possum Trot Hollow
443.P78	Powell River and Valley

Tennessee

443.A-.Z **Regions, counties, etc., A-Z — Continued**

443.P9 Putnam Co.

443.R34 Reelfoot Lake and Region

443.R4 Rhea Co.

443.R49 Roan Mountain

Cf. F262.R39, General, and North Carolina

443.R5 Roane Co.

443.R55 Robertson Co.

443.R8 Rutherford Co.

443.S2 Scott Co.

443.S35 Sequatchie Co.

443.S36 Sequatchie River and Valley

443.S45 Sevier Co.

Including Mount LeConte, Sugarlands

443.S5 Shelby Co.

443.S6 Smith Co.

Smoky Mountains (The Smokies), *see* F443.G7

443.S7 Stewart Co.

Sugarlands, *see* F443.S45

443.S8 Sullivan Co.

443.S9 Sumner Co.

443.S97 Sweetwater Valley

443.T3 Tennessee River and Valley, Tenn.

Cf. F217.T3, General

443.T5 Tipton Co.

443.T7 Trousdale Co.

443.U5 Unicoi Co.

443.U6 Union Co.

443.V3 Van Buren Co.

443.W2 Warren Co.

Including Cumberland Caverns, etc.

443.W3 Washington Co.

443.W33 Watts Bar Reservoir and region

443.W4 Wayne Co.

443.W5 Weakley Co.

443.W6 White Co.

443.W7 Williamson Co.

443.W75 Wilson Co.

444.A-.Z **Cities, towns, etc., A-Z**

GALE NOTE *The cutter number(s) listed below have been given only as examples by the Library of Congress*

444.C4 Chattanooga

Subarrange by Table F2 at the end of the text

444.K7 Knoxville

Lookout Mountain, *see* F443.L8

444.M5 Memphis

Subarrange by Table F2 at the end of the text

444.N2 Nashville

Subarrange by Table F2 at the end of the text

444.O3 Oak Ridge

Elements in the population

445.A1 General works

445.A2-.Z Individual elements

For a list of racial, ethnic, and religious elements (with cutter numbers), see E184.A1+

Kentucky

446 **Periodicals. Societies. Collections**

448 **Museums. Exhibitions, exhibits**

449 **Gazetteers. Dictionaries. Geographic names**

449.3 **Guidebooks**

Kentucky — Continued

450 **Biography (Collective). Genealogy (Collective)**

450.2 **Historiography**

Historians, *see* E175.5.A+

450.5 **Study and teaching**

451 **General works. Histories**

451.3 **Juvenile works**

Pamphlets, addresses, essays, etc.

451.5 General

451.6 Anecdotes, legends, pageants, etc.

452 **Historic monuments (General). Illustrative material**

453 **Antiquities (Non-Indian)**

By period

454 Early to 1792

Including Transylvania; County and District of Kentucky; etc.

Including biography: Daniel Boone, James Harrod, Richard Henderson, etc.

Cf. E83.79, Wars with northwestern Indians, 1790-1795

Cf. F517, Early explorations on Ohio River

455 1792-1865

Including admission as a state, June 1, 1792

Including biography: George Michael Bedinger, Joseph Hamilton Daveiss, Harry Innes, Benjamin Sebastian, Isaac Shelby, etc.

Cf. E328, Kentucky and Virginia Resolutions, 1798

Cf. E359.5.K5, War of 1812

Cf. E409.5.K4, War with Mexico, 1845-1848

Cf. E509.1+, Civil War, 1861-1865 (General)

Cf. E470.4+, E471+, Military operations and battles in the Civil War, 1861-1865

Cf. E564.1+, Confederate history, Civil War

Cf. F210, Mountain whites of the South

456 1865-1950

Including biography: William Goebel, etc.

Cf. D570.85.K4+, World War I, 1914-1918

Cf. D769.85.K4+, World War II, 1939-1945

Cf. E726.K37, War of 1898 (Spanish-American War)

1951-

456.2 General works

Biography and memoirs

456.25 Collective

456.26.A-.26.Z Individual, A-Z

GALE NOTE *See note at the head of Table F5 at the end of the text for further instructions on how to subdivide this number*

457.A-.Z **Regions, counties, etc., A-Z**

457.A15 Counties

457.A16 Mountains

457.A17 Rivers

457.A18 Lakes

457.A19 Islands

457.A3 Adair Co.

457.A5 Allen Co.

457.A6 Anderson Co.

457.B16 Ballard Co.

457.B2 Barren Co.

Including Diamond Cave, Great Onyx Cave

457.B23 Bath Co.

457.B4 Bell Co.

Big Bone Lick, *see* F457.B65

457.B5 Big Sandy River and Valley

457.B6 Bluegrass region

457.B65 Boone Co.

Including Big Bone Lick

Kentucky

457.A-.Z **Regions, counties, etc., A-Z — Continued**

457.B7 Boundaries

457.B8 Bourbon Co.

457.B82 Boyd Co.

457.B83 Boyle Co.

457.B84 Bracken Co.

457.B85 Breathitt Co.

457.B9 Breckinridge Co.

457.B92 Bullitt Co.

457.B95 Butler Co.

457.C15 Caldwell Co.

457.C17 Calloway Co.

457.C2 Campbell Co.

457.C25 Carlisle Co.

457.C3 Carroll Co.

457.C35 Carter Co.

457.C37 Casey Co.

457.C55 Christian Co.

457.C56 Clark Co.

457.C57 Clay Co.

457.C58 Clear Fork River and Valley (General, and Kentucky)

Cf. F443.C56, Tennessee

457.C6 Clinton Co.

457.C66 Crittenden Co.

457.C7 Cumberland Co.

457.C77 Cumberland Gap National Historical Park

457.C8 Cumberland Mountains

Cf. F210, Mountain whites of the South

457.C9 Cumberland River and Valley, Ky.

Cf. F442.2, Tennessee

Cypress Creek and Valley, *see* F457.U5

457.D3 Daviess Co.

Diamond Cave, *see* F457.B2

457.E2 Edmonson Co.

For Mammoth Cave, see F457.M2

457.E4 Elliott Co.

457.E7 Estill Co.

457.F2 Fayette Co.

457.F4 Fleming Co.

457.F6 Floyd Co.

457.F8 Franklin Co.

457.F9 Fulton Co.

457.G16 Gallatin Co.

457.G2 Garrard Co.

457.G6 Grant Co.

457.G77 Graves Co.

457.G78 Grayson Co.

Great Onyx Cave, *see* F457.B2

457.G82 Green Co.

457.G85 Green River and Valley

457.G86 Greenup Co.

457.H16 Hancock Co.

457.H2 Hardin Co.

457.H3 Harlan Co.

457.H4 Harrison Co.

457.H43 Hart Co.

457.H5 Henderson Co.

457.H6 Henry Co.

457.H7 Hickman Co.

Kentucky

457.A-.Z **Regions, counties, etc., A-Z — Continued**

457.H8 Hopkins Co.

457.J2 Jackson Co.

457.J23 Jackson Purchase region

457.J4 Jefferson Co.

457.J5 Jessamine Co.

457.J7 Johnson Co.

457.K28 Kenton Co.

457.K29 Kentucky Lake

457.K3 Kentucky River and Valley

457.K5 Knott Co.

457.K6 Knox Co.

457.L2 Larue Co.

457.L25 Laurel Co.

457.L27 Lawrence Co.

457.L45 Lee Co.

457.L47 Leslie Co.

457.L48 Letcher Co.

457.L5 Lewis Co.

457.L6 Lincoln Co.

457.L7 Livingston Co.

457.L8 Logan Co.

457.L9 Lyon Co.

457.M14 McCracken Co.

457.M15 McCreary Co.

457.M16 McLean Co.

457.M17 Madison Co.

457.M18 Magoffin Co.

457.M2 Mammoth Cave

Including Mammoth Cave National Park

457.M3 Marion Co.

457.M34 Marshall Co.

457.M36 Martin Co.

457.M4 Mason Co.

457.M5 Meade Co.

457.M54 Menifee Co.

457.M56 Mercer Co.

457.M57 Metcalfe Co.

457.M6 Mississippi River and Valley, Ky.

Cf. F350.5+, General

457.M7 Monroe Co.

457.M74 Montgomery Co.

457.M8 Morgan Co.

457.M9 Muhlenberg Co.

457.N2 Nelson Co.

457.N5 Nicholas Co.

457.O2 Ohio Co.

457.O3 Ohio River and Valley, Ky.

Cf. F516+, General

457.O4 Oldham Co.

457.O97 Owen Co.

457.O98 Owsley Co.

Payne Hollow, *see* F457.T65

457.P3 Pendleton Co.

457.P4 Perry Co.

457.P6 Pike Co.

457.P7 Powell Co.

457.P8 Pulaski Co.

Kentucky

457.A-.Z **Regions, counties, etc., A-Z — Continued**

457.R4 Red River and Valley

Including Red River Gorge

457.R6 Robertson Co.

457.R65 Rockcastle Co.

457.R7 Rowan Co.

457.R8 Russell Co.

457.S24 Salt Lick Creek and Valley

457.S3 Scott Co.

457.S4 Shelby Co.

457.S5 Simpson Co.

457.S7 Spencer Co.

457.T25 Taylor Co.

457.T3 Tennessee River and Valley, Ky.

Cf. F217.T3, General

For Kentucky Lake, see F457.K29

457.T5 Todd Co.

457.T6 Trigg Co.

457.T65 Trimble Co.

Including Payne Hollow

457.U5 Union Co.

Including Cypress Creek and Valley

457.W2 Warren Co.

457.W3 Washington Co.

457.W4 Wayne Co.

457.W5 Webster Co.

457.W6 Whitley Co.

457.W7 Wolfe Co.

457.W8 Woodford Co.

459.A-.Z **Cities, towns, etc., A-Z**

GALE NOTE *The cutter number(s) listed below have been given only as examples by the Library of Congress*

459.C8 Covington

459.F8 Frankfort

459.L6 Lexington

459.L8 Louisville

Subarrange by Table F2 at the end of the text

Elements in the population

460.A1 General works

460.A2-.Z Individual elements

For a list of racial, ethnic, and religious elements (with cutter numbers), see E184.A+

Missouri

461 **Periodicals. Societies. Collections**

463 **Museums. Exhibitions, exhibits**

464 **Gazetteers. Dictionaries. Geographic names**

464.3 **Guidebooks**

465 **Biography (Collective). Genealogy (Collective)**

465.2 **Historiography**

Historians, *see* E175.5.A+

465.5 **Study and teaching**

466 **General works. Histories**

Admission as a state, August 10, 1821

Including by period (Early to 1950) as well as general

For 1951 and later, see F470

Including The Platt Purchase

Including biography: Frederick Bates, Joseph Wingate Folk, etc.

For local guidebooks, see Class F, e.g. F444.C4, Chattanooga

Cf. D570.85.M8+, World War I, 1914-1918

Cf. D769.85.M8+, World War II, 1939-1945

Missouri

466 **General works. Histories — Continued**

Cf. E373, Missouri Compromise, 1820

Cf. E571.1+, Civil War, 1861-1865 (General)

Cf. E470.4+, E470.9, Military operations and battles in the Civil War, 1861-1865

Cf. E569.1+, Confederate history, Civil War

Cf. E726.M8, War of 1898 (Spanish-American War)

Cf. F685, Kansas troubles, 1854-1859

466.3 **Juvenile works**

Pamphlets, addresses, essays, etc.

466.5 General

466.6 Anecdotes, legends, pageants, etc.

467 **Historic monuments (General). Illustrative material**

468 **Antiquities (Non-Indian)**

By period

(469) Early to 1950, *see* F466

470 1951-

472.A-.Z **Regions, counties, etc., A-Z**

472.A15 Counties

472.A16 Mountains

472.A17 Rivers

472.A18 Lakes

472.A19 Islands

472.A2 Adair Co.

472.A5 Andrew Co.

472.A8 Atchison Co.

472.A9 Audrain Co.

472.B27 Barry Co.

472.B28 Barton Co.

472.B3 Bates Co.

472.B38 Bellevue Valley

472.B4 Benton Co.

Including Harry S. Truman Dam and Reservoir

472.B57 Bollinger Co.

472.B6 Boone Co.

472.B7 Boundaries

472.B9 Buchanan Co.

472.B94 Bull Shoals Lake and region, Mo.

Cf. F417.B86 , General, and Arkansas

472.B96 Butler Co.

472.C2 Caldwell Co.

472.C3 Callaway Co.

472.C32 Camden Co.

472.C33 Cape Girardeau Co.

472.C35 Carroll Co.

472.C36 Carter Co.

472.C37 Cass Co.

472.C4 Cedar Co.

472.C44 Chariton Co.

472.C45 Christian Co.

Clamorgan land grant, *see* F417.C5

472.C47 Clarence Cannon Reservoir

472.C48 Clark Co.

472.C5 Clay Co.

472.C53 Clinton Co.

472.C65 Cole Co.

472.C7 Cooper Co.

472.C8 Crawford Co.

472.C9 Current River and Valley (General, and Mo.)

472.D15 Dade Co.

Missouri

472.A-.Z **Regions, counties, etc., A-Z — Continued**
472.D2 Dallas Co.
472.D25 Daviess Co.
472.D3 De Kalb Co.
472.D35 Dent Co.
472.D4 Des Moines River and Valley, Mo.
Cf. F627.D43, General, and Iowa
472.D6 Douglas Co.
472.D9 Dunklin Co.
472.E4 Eleven Point Wild and Scenic River
472.F6 Franklin Co.
472.G3 Gasconade Co.
472.G4 Gentry Co.
472.G8 Greene Co.
472.G88 Grundy Co.
472.H3 Harrison Co.
Harry S. Truman Dam and Reservoir, *see* F472.B4
472.H6 Henry Co. Rives Co.
472.H65 Hickory Co.
For Harry S. Truman Dam and Reservoir, see F472.B4
472.H7 Holt Co.
472.H8 Howard Co.
472.H9 Howell Co.
472.I7 Iron Co.
472.J2 Jackson Co.
472.J3 Jasper Co.
Including Prosperity Lake and region
472.J4 Jefferson Co.
472.J6 Johnson Co.
472.K6 Knox Co.
472.L15 Laclede Co.
472.L2 Lafayette Co.
472.L4 Lawrence Co.
472.L6 Lewis Co.
472.L7 Lincoln Co.
472.L8 Linn Co.
472.L85 Livingston Co.
472.L88 Loess Hills
Cf. F627.L76 , General and Iowa
Long Branch Lake and region, *see* F472.M2
472.M13 McDonald Co.
Including Jacob's Cavern, etc.
472.M2 Macon Co.
Including Long Branch Lake and region
472.M23 Madison Co.
472.M29 Maries Co.
472.M3 Marion Co.
472.M4 Mercer Co.
472.M45 Miller Co.
Including Bone Cave
472.M55 Mississippi Co.
472.M6 Mississippi River and Valley, Mo.
Cf. F350.5+, General
472.M7 Missouri River and Valley, Mo.
Cf. F598, General
472.M75 Moniteau Co.
472.M76 Monroe Co.
472.M77 Montgomery Co.
472.M8 Morgan Co.

	Missouri
472.A-.Z	**Regions, counties, etc., A-Z — Continued**
472.N4	New Madrid Co.
472.N5	Newton Co.
472.N7	Nodaway Co.
472.O6	Oregon Co.
472.O7	Osage Co.
472.O74	Osage River and Valley
472.O85	Ozark Co.
472.O9	Ozark Mountains, Mo.
	Cf. F417.O9, General, and Arkansas
472.P3	Pemiscot Co.
472.P4	Perry Co.
	Including Tower Rock
472.P5	Pettis Co.
472.P55	Phelps Co.
472.P6	Pike Co.
472.P64	Pine Ford Dam and Reservoir
472.P7	Platte Co.
472.P8	Polk Co.
	Prosperity Lake and region, *see* F472.J3
472.P9	Pulaski Co.
472.P95	Putnam Co.
472.R14	Ralls Co.
472.R15	Randolph Co.
472.R2	Ray Co.
472.R4	Reynolds Co.
472.R6	Ripley Co.
	Rives Co., *see* F472.H6
472.S2	St. Charles Co.
472.S23	St. Clair Co.
472.S25	St. Francis River and Valley, Mo.
	Cf. F417.S2, General, and Arkansas
472.S28	St Francois Co.
472.S3	St. Louis Co.
472.S33	Ste. Genevieve Co.
472.S35	Saline Co.
472.S4	Schuyler Co.
472.S42	Scotland Co.
472.S43	Scott Co.
472.S48	Shannon Co.
472.S5	Shelby Co.
472.S65	Stoddard Co.
472.S7	Stone Co.
472.S8	Sullivan Co.
472.T16	Taney Co.
472.T4	Texas Co.
472.V4	Vernon Co.
472.W17	Warren Co.
472.W2	Washington Co.
472.W3	Wayne Co.
472.W4	Webster Co.
472.W5	White River and Valley, Mo.
	Cf. F417.W5, General, and Arkansas
472.W6	Worth Co.
472.W7	Wright Co.
474.A-.Z	**Cities, towns, etc., A-Z**
	GALE NOTE *The cutter number(s) listed below have been given only as examples by the Library of Congress*
474.J4	Jefferson City

	Missouri
474.A-.Z	**Cities, towns, etc., A-Z — Continued**
474.K2	Kansas City
	Subarrange by Table F2 at the end of the text
474.S18	St. Joseph
474.S2	St. Louis
	Subarrange by Table F2 at the end of the text
474.S7	Springfield
	Elements in the population
475.A1	General works
475.A2-.Z	Individual elements
	For a list of racial, ethnic, and religious elements (with cutter numbers), see E184.A+
476-485	**Old Northwest. Northwest Territory**
	Region between the Ohio and Mississippi Rivers and the Great Lakes
	Cf. F366+, Louisiana
	Cf. F516+, Ohio Valley
	Cf. F597, Upper Mississippi Valley
476	**Periodicals. Societies. Collections**
476.5	**Museums. Exhibitions, exhibits**
477	**Gazetteers. Dictionaries. Geographic names**
477.3	**Guidebooks**
478	**Biography (Collective). Genealogy (Collective)**
478.2	**Historiography**
	Historians, *see* E175.5.A+
478.5	**Study and teaching**
479	**General works. Histories**
	Cf. E78.N76, Indians of the Old Northwest
479.3	**Juvenile works**
	Pamphlets, addresses, essays, etc.
479.5	General
479.6	Anecdotes, legends, pageants, etc.
480	**Historic monuments (General). Illustrative material**
481	**Antiquities (Non-Indian)**
	By period
482	Early to 1763
	Cf. E199, French and Indian War, 1755-1763
	Cf. F517, Ohio Company, 1749
	Cf. F544, Illinois country
	Cf. F572.M16, Mackinac region
	Cf. F574.D4, Detroit, 1701
	Cf. F1030, New France
483	1763-1803
	Including cessions by Virginia and other states, 1781-1786; settlement; Virginia military lands (Chillicothe); the Seven Ranges; Ohio Company, 1786-1795 (Marietta); American and French Scioto companies (Gallipolis); the Miami or Symmes Purchase (Cincinnati)
	Including biography: Manasseh Cutler, Nathaniel Massie, Rufus Putnam, Arthur St. Clair
	Cf. E83.76, Pontiac's Conspiracy, 1763-1765
	Cf. E83.775, Indian wars, 1775-1783
	Cf. E83.79, Indian wars, 1790-1795
	Cf. E83.794, Wayne's Campaign, 1793-1795
	Cf. E263.N84, Old Northwest in the Revolution
	Cf. E234, E237, Clark's campaigns
	Cf. E309, Northwest Ordinance of 1787
	Cf. F230, Virginia
	Cf. F497.W5, Western Reserve of Connecticut
	Cf. F534.V7, Vincennes
	Cf. F1032, Province of Quebec (Canada); Quebec Act
484.3	1803-1865
	Cf. E83.81, Tippecanoe Campaign, 1811
	Cf. E355, War of 1812 (Military operations)

476-485	**Old Northwest. Northwest Territory**
	By period — Continued
484.5	1865-1950
484.6	1951-
	Elements in the population
485.A1	General works
485.A2-.Z	Individual elements
	For a list of racial, ethnic, and religious elements (with cutter numbers), see E184.A+
	Ohio
486	**Periodicals. Societies. Collections**
488	**Museums. Exhibitions, exhibits**
489	**Gazetteers. Dictionaries. Geographic names**
489.3	**Guidebooks**
490	**Biography (Collective). Genealogy (Collective)**
490.2	**Historiography**
	Historians, *see* E175.5.A+
490.5	**Study and teaching**
491	**General works. Histories**
491.3	**Juvenile works**
	Pamphlets, addresses, essays, etc.
491.5	General
491.6	Anecdotes, legends, pageants, etc.
491.8	**Geography**
492	**Historic monuments (General). Illustrative material**
493	**Antiquities (Non-Indian)**
	By period
495	Early to 1865
	Including admission as a state, February 19, 1803
	Including biography: Jacob Burnet, Alfred Kelley, Edward Tiffin, Allen Trimble, Thomas Worthington, etc.
	Cf. E83.81, Tippecanoe Campaign, 1811
	Cf. E359.5.O2, War of 1812 (General)
	Cf. E355+, Military operations, War of 1812
	Cf. E409.5.O3, War with Mexico, 1845-1848
	Cf. E525.1+, Civil War, 1861-1865 (General)
	Cf. E470.4+, Military operations and battles in the Civil War, 1861-1865
	Cf. F483, History before 1803 (Old Northwest)
	Cf. F497.B7, Toledo War, 1836
496	1865-1950
	Including biography: William Allen, Asa Smith Bushnell, George Barnsdale Cox, Donn Piatt, Tom Loftin Johnson, Charles Reemelin, etc.
	Cf. D570.85.O3+, World War I, 1914-1918
	Cf. D769.85.O3+, World War II, 1939-1945
	Cf. E726.O3, War of 1898 (Spanish-American War)
	1951-
496.2	General works
	Biography
496.3	Collective
496.4.A-.4.Z	Individual, A-Z
497.A-.Z	**Regions, counties, etc., A-Z**
497.A15	Counties
497.A16	Mountains
497.A17	Rivers
497.A18	Lakes
497.A19	Islands
497.A2	Adams Co.
497.A4	Allen Co.
497.A7	Ashland Co.
497.A73	Ashtabula Co.
497.A8	Athens Co.

Ohio

497.A-.Z **Regions, counties, etc., A-Z — Continued**

497.A9 Auglaize Co.

Bass Islands, *see* F497.O8

497.B3 Bean Creek and Valley (General, and Ohio)

Cf. F572.B36, Michigan

497.B4 Belmont Co.

Including Raven Rocks

Blennerhassett Island, *see* F247.B56

497.B7 Boundaries

Including Toledo War, 1836 (Ohio-Michigan boundary)

497.B8 Brown Co.

497.B86 Buckeye Lake

497.B9 Butler Co.

497.C2 Carroll Co.

497.C4 Champaign Co.

497.C5 Clark Co.

Including George Rogers Clark Memorial Park

497.C53 Clermont Co.

497.C55 Clinton Co.

497.C6 Columbiana Co.

Including Sandy Beaver Canal

Connecticut Reserve, *see* F497.W5

497.C7 Coshocton Co.

497.C8 Crawford Co.

497.C9 Cuyahoga Co.

497.C95 Cuyahoga River and Valley

Including Tinkers Creek and Valley

497.D2 Darke Co.

497.D25 Defiance Co.

497.D3 Delaware Co.

497.E5 Erie Co.

Including Kelleys Island

For Firelands, see F497.W5

497.E6 Lake Erie region, Ohio

For Bass Islands, see F497.O8

For Kelleys Island, see F497.E5

For Put-in Bay, see F497.O8

For Sandusky Bay, see F497.S23

Cf. F555, General

497.F15 Fairfield Co.

497.F2 Fayette Co.

Firelands, *see* F497.W5

497.F8 Franklin Co.

497.F9 Fulton Co.

497.G15 Gallia Co.

497.G2 Geauga Co.

George Rogers Clark Memorial Park, *see* F497.C5

497.G7 Greene Co.

497.G93 Guernsey Co.

497.H2 Hamilton Co.

Including Duck Creek, Mill Creek

497.H3 Hancock Co.

497.H35 Hanging Rock iron region

497.H4 Hardin Co.

497.H5 Harrison Co.

497.H55 Henry Co.

497.H6 Highland Co.

497.H68 Hocking Co.

497.H7 Hocking River and Valley

Ohio

497.A-.Z **Regions, counties, etc., A-Z — Continued**

497.H74 Holmes Co.

497.H8 Huron Co.

For Firelands, see F497.W5

497.J2 Jackson Co.

497.J4 Jefferson Co.

Including Yellow Creek

Kelleys Island, *see* F497.E5

497.K7 Knox Co.

497.L2 Lake Co.

497.L3 Lawrence Co.

497.L4 Leatherwood Creek and Valley

497.L6 Licking Co.

497.L7 Little Miami River and Valley

Cf. F497.M64, Miami (Great Miami) River and Valley

497.L8 Logan Co.

497.L86 Lorain Co.

497.L9 Lucas Co.

497.M14 Madison Co.

497.M18 Mahoning Co.

497.M2 Mahoning River and Valley (General, and Ohio)

Cf. F157.M3, Pennsylvania

497.M3 Marion Co.

497.M4 Maumee River and Valley (General, and Ohio)

Cf. F532.M62, Indiana

497.M5 Medina Co.

497.M53 Meigs Co.

497.M56 Mercer Co.

497.M6 Miami Co.

497.M64 Miami (Great Miami) River and Valley

Cf. F497.L7 , Little Miami River and Valley

497.M67 Monroe Co.

497.M7 Montgomery Co.

Including Twin Valley

497.M76 Morgan Co.

497.M8 Morrow Co.

497.M9 Muskingum Co.

497.M92 Muskingum River and Valley

497.N6 Noble Co.

497.O3 Ohio River and Valley, Ohio

Cf. F516+, General

497.O8 Ottawa Co.

Including Bass Islands, Put-in Bay

497.P2 Paulding Co.

497.P4 Perry Co.

497.P5 Pickaway Co.

497.P55 Pike Co.

497.P8 Portage Co.

497.P9 Preble Co.

Put-in Bay, *see* F497.O8

497.P96 Putnam Co.

Raven Rocks, *see* F497.B4

497.R5 Richland Co.

497.R7 Rocky River and Valley

497.R8 Ross Co.

497.S2 Sandusky Co.

497.S23 Sandusky River and Valley. Sandusky Bay

Sandy Beaver Canal, *see* F497.C6

497.S3 Scioto Co.

Ohio

497.A-.Z **Regions, counties, etc., A-Z — Continued**

497.S32 Scioto River and Valley

497.S4 Seneca Co.

497.S54 Shelby Co.

497.S7 Stark Co.

497.S9 Summit Co.

Including Portage Path

Tiffin River and Valley, *see* F497.B3

Tinkers Creek and Valley, *see* F497.C95

497.T8 Trumbull Co.

497.T9 Tuscarawas Co.

497.T93 Tuscarawas River and Valley

497.U5 Union Co.

497.V2 Van Wert Co.

497.V5 Vinton Co.

497.W13 Wabash and Erie Canal

Cf. F532.W16, General, and Indiana

497.W2 Warren Co.

497.W3 Washington Co.

For Blennerhassett Island, see F247.B56

497.W4 Wayne Co.

497.W5 Western Reserve (Connecticut Reserve). Firelands

497.W7 Williams Co.

497.W8 Wood Co.

497.W9 Wyandot Co.

499.A-.Z **Cities, towns, etc., A-Z**

GALE NOTE *The cutter number(s) listed below have been given only as examples by the Library of Congress*

499.A3 Akron

499.C2 Canton

499.C4 Chillicothe

499.C5 Cincinnati

Subarrange by Table F2 at the end of the text

499.C6 Cleveland

Subarrange by Table F2 at the end of the text

499.C7 Columbus

Subarrange by Table F2 at the end of the text

499.D2 Dayton

Subarrange by Table F2 at the end of the text

499.M3 Marietta

499.S7 Springfield

499.T6 Toledo

499.Y8 Youngstown

Elements in the population

500.A1 General works

500.A2-.Z Individual elements

For a list of racial, ethnic, and religious elements (with cutter numbers), see E184.A+

Ohio River and Valley

Cf. E78.O4, Indians of the Ohio Valley

Cf. F157.B2, Pennsylvania

Cf. F350.5+, Mississippi River and Valley

Cf. F457.O3, Kentucky

Cf. F497.O3, Ohio

Cf. F532.O4, Indiana

516 **General works**

Including periodicals, societies, collections, biography, etc.

By period

517 Early to 1795

Including Celoron's Expedition, 1749; Ohio Company, 1747-1779

Ohio River and Valley
By period
517 Early to 1795 — Continued
Including biography: Michael Cresap, Simon Girty, Simon Kenton, Lewis Wetzel
Cf. E83.79, Wars with northwestern Indians, 1790-1795
Cf. E199, French and Indian War, 1755-1763
Cf. E234, Clark's Campaign, 1778
Cf. F372, Louisiana before 1803
Cf. F534.V7, Vincennes
Cf. F1030, New France
518 1795-1865
Cf. E470.4+, Civil War, 1861-1865 (General)
519 1865-1950
Including floods, 1884, 1913
520 1951-
Elements in the population
520.5 General works
520.6.A-.6.Z Individual elements, A-Z
For a list of racial, ethnic, and religious elements (with cutter numbers), see E184.A+
Indiana
521 **Periodicals. Societies. Collections**
523 **Museums. Exhibitions, exhibits**
524 **Gazetteers. Dictionaries. Geographic names**
524.3 **Guidebooks**
525 **Biography (Collective). Genealogy (Collective)**
525.2 **Historiography**
Historians, *see* E175.5.A+
525.5 **Study and teaching**
526 **General works. Histories**
Including admission as a state, December 11, 1816
Including biography: James Franklin Doughty Lanier, etc.
For 1951 and later, see F530
Cf. D570.85.I6+, World War I, 1914-1918
Cf. D769.85.I6+, World War II, 1939-1945
Cf. E83.81, Tippecanoe Campaign, 1811
Cf. E355, War of 1812 (Military operations)
Cf. E409.5.I7, War with Mexico, 1845-1848
Cf. E506.1+, Civil War, 1861-1865 (General)
Cf. E470.4+, Military operations in the Civil War, 1861-1865
Cf. E726.I3, War of 1898 (Spanish-American War)
526.3 **Juvenile works**
Pamphlets, addresses, essays, etc.
526.5 General
526.6 Anecdotes, legends, pageants, etc.
527 **Historic monuments (General). Illustrative material**
528 **Antiquities (Non-Indian)**
By period
Early to 1950, *see* F526
1951-
530 General works
Biography and memoirs
530.2 Collective
530.22.A-.22.Z Individual, A-Z
GALE NOTE *See note at the head of Table F5 at the end of the text for further instructions on how to subdivide this number*
532.A-.Z **Regions, counties, etc., A-Z**
532.A15 Counties
532.A16 Mountains
532.A17 Rivers
532.A18 Lakes

Indiana

532.A-.Z **Regions, counties, etc., A-Z — Continued**

532.A19 Islands
532.A2 Adams Co.
532.A4 Allen Co.
For Maumee River, see F532.M62
532.B2 Bartholomew Co.
532.B4 Benton Co.
532.B5 Blackford Co.
532.B6 Boone Co.
532.B7 Boundaries
532.B76 Brown Co.
Calumet region, *see* F532.L2
532.C3 Carroll Co.
532.C4 Cass Co.
532.C5 Clark Co.
532.C6 Clay Co.
Clifty Falls State Park, *see* F532.J5
532.C65 Clinton Co.
532.C8 Crawford Co.
Including Wyandotte Cave
532.D17 Daviess Co.
532.D18 Dearborn Co.
532.D2 Decatur Co.
532.D25 De Kalb Co.
532.D3 Delaware Co.
532.D8 Dubois Co.
Dune region, *see* F532.M67
Dunes State Park, *see* F532.I5
532.E4 Elkhart Co.
532.F2 Fayette Co.
532.F6 Floyd Co.
532.F77 Fountain Co.
532.F8 Franklin Co.
532.F9 Fulton Co.
532.G4 Gibson Co.
532.G7 Grant Co.
532.G75 Greene Co.
532.H2 Hamilton Co.
532.H3 Hancock Co.
532.H4 Harrison Co.
532.H5 Hendricks Co.
532.H6 Henry Co.
532.H75 Hoosier National Forest
532.H8 Howard Co.
532.H9 Huntington Co.
532.I5 Indiana Dunes State Park
532.J14 Jackson Co.
532.J3 Jasper Co.
532.J4 Jay Co.
532.J5 Jefferson Co.
Including Clifty Falls State Park
532.J53 Jennings Co.
532.J6 Johnson Co.
Kankakee-St. Joseph portage, *see* F532.S2
532.K2 Kankakee River and Valley (General, and Ind.)
Cf. F547.K27, Illinois
532.K6 Knox Co.
532.K8 Kosciusko Co.
532.L17 Lagrange Co.

Indiana

532.A-.Z **Regions, counties, etc., A-Z — Continued**
532.L2 Lake Co.
Including Calumet region, Ind.
Cf. F547.C7, Illinois
532.L3 La Porte Co.
532.L4 Lawrence Co.
Including Spring Mill State Park
Lost River and Valley, *see* F532.O63
532.M2 Madison Co.
532.M4 Marion Co.
532.M6 Marshall Co.
532.M613 Martin Co.
532.M62 Maumee River and Valley, Ind.
Cf. F497.M4, General, and Ohio
532.M65 Miami Co.
532.M67 Lake Michigan region, Ind.
Including the dunes of Indiana
For Indiana Dunes State Park, see F532.I5
Cf. F553, General
532.M7 Monroe Co.
532.M75 Montgomery Co.
532.M8 Morgan Co.
532.N5 Newton Co.
Including Beaver Lake
532.N6 Noble Co.
532.O3 Ohio Co.
532.O4 Ohio River and Valley, Ind.
Cf. F516+, General
532.O63 Orange Co.
Including Lost River and Valley
532.O9 Owen Co.
532.P2 Parke Co.
Including Turkey Run State Park
532.P4 Perry Co.
532.P6 Pike Co.
Pokagon State Park, *see* F532.S8
532.P8 Porter Co.
532.P85 Posey Co.
532.P88 Pulaski Co.
532.P9 Putnam Co.
532.R3 Randolph Co.
532.R5 Ripley Co.
532.R95 Rush Co.
532.S2 St. Joseph Co.
Including St. Joseph-Kankakee portage
Cf. F572.S43, St. Joseph River and Valley, Mich.
532.S3 St. Joseph River and Valley (General, and Ind.)
Cf. F572.S43, Michigan
532.S35 Scott Co.
532.S47 Shakamak State Park
532.S5 Shelby Co.
532.S6 Spencer Co.
Including Lincoln Boyhood National Memorial and Nancy Hanks Lincoln Memorial
Spring Mill State Park, *see* F532.L4
532.S7 Starke Co.
532.S8 Steuben Co.
Including Pokagon State Park
532.S9 Sullivan Co.
532.S97 Switzerland Co.

	Indiana
532.A-.Z	**Regions, counties, etc., A-Z — Continued**
532.T6	Tippecanoe Co.
532.T63	Tipton Co.
	Turkey Run State Park, *see* F532.P2
532.U5	Union Co.
532.V2	Vanderburgh Co.
532.V5	Vermillion Co.
532.V7	Vigo Co.
532.W16	Wabash and Erie Canal (General, and Indiana)
	Cf. F497.W13, Ohio
532.W18	Wabash Co.
532.W2	Wabash River and Valley (General, and Ind.)
	Cf. F547.W14, Illinois
532.W3	Warren Co.
532.W4	Warrick Co.
532.W45	Washington Co.
532.W5	Wayne Co.
532.W55	Wells Co.
532.W58	White Co.
532.W59	Whitewater (White Water) River and Valley
532.W6	Whitley Co.
534.A-.Z	**Cities, towns, etc., A-Z**
	GALE NOTE *The cutter number(s) listed below have been given only as examples by the Library of Congress*
534.E9	Evansville
534.F7	Fort Wayne
534.I3	Indianapolis
	Subarrange by Table F2 at the end of the text
534.N5	New Harmony
534.S7	South Bend
534.T3	Terre Haute
534.V7	Vincennes
	Elements in the population
535.A1	General works
535.A2-.Z	Individual elements
	For a list of racial, ethnic, and religious elements (with cutter numbers), see E184.A+
	Illinois
536	**Periodicals. Societies. Collections**
538	**Museums. Exhibitions, exhibits**
539	**Gazetteers. Dictionaries. Geographic names**
539.3	**Guidebooks**
540	**Biography (Collective). Genealogy (Collective)**
540.2	**Historiography**
	Historians, *see* E175.5.A+
540.5	**Study and teaching**
541	**General works. Histories**
541.3	**Juvenile works**
	Pamphlets, addresses, essays, etc.
541.5	General
541.6	Anecdotes, legends, pageants, etc.
541.8	**Geography**
542	**Historic monuments (General). Illustrative material**
543	**Antiquities (Non-Indian)**
	By period
544	Early to 1775. The Illinois country
	Including Illinois under French rule
	Cf. F352, Mississippi River and Valley before 1803
	Cf. F1030, New France, 1603-1763

Illinois

By period — Continued

545 1775-1865

Including admission as a state December 3, 1818

Including biography: John Boyle, Peter Cartwright, Edward Coles, Joseph Duncan, Ninian Edwards, Thomas Ford, Adam Wilson Snyder, Richard Yates, etc.

Cf. E83.83 , Black Hawk War, 1832

Cf. E234, Clark's Campaign, 1778

Cf. E355, War of 1812 (Military operations)

Cf. E409.5.I4, War with Mexico, 1845-1848

Cf. E505.1+, Civil War, 1861-1865 (General)

Cf. E470.4+, Military operations in the Civil War, 1861-1865

Cf. F547.E3, English settlement in Edwards County

Cf. F550.M8, Mormons

546 1865-1950

Including biography: John Peter Altgeld, Edward Fitzsimons Dunne, Frank Orren Lowden, Adlai Ewing Stevenson, John Riley Tanner

Cf. D570.85.I3+, World War I, 1914-1918

Cf. D769.85.I3+, World War II, 1939-1945

Cf. E726.I2, War of 1898 (Spanish-American War)

1951-

546.2 General works

Biography

546.3 Collective

546.4.A-.4.Z Individual, A-Z

GALE NOTE *See note at the head of Table F5 at the end of the text for further instructions on how to subdivide this number*

547.A-.Z **Regions, counties, etc., A-Z**

547.A15 Counties

547.A16 Mountains

547.A17 Rivers

547.A18 Lakes

547.A19 Islands

547.A2 Adams Co.

547.A3 Alexander Co.

Including Horseshoe Lake

547.B6 Bond Co.

547.B65 Boone Co.

547.B7 Boundaries

547.B75 Brown Co.

547.B8 Bureau Co.

547.C13 Cache River and Valley

547.C15 Calhoun Co.

Calumet region, *see* F547.C7

547.C2 Carroll Co.

547.C3 Cass Co.

547.C4 Champaign Co.

547.C45 Chicago River

547.C5 Christian Co.

547.C53 Clark Co.

547.C55 Clay Co.

547.C57 Clinton Co.

547.C6 Coles Co.

547.C7 Cook Co.

Including Calumet region, Ill.

Cf. F532.L2, Indiana

547.C8 Crawford Co.

547.C9 Cumberland Co.

547.D3 De Kalb Co.

547.D4 Des Plaines River and Valley, Ill.

Illinois

547.A-.Z **Regions, counties, etc., A-Z — Continued**

547.D5 De Witt Co.

547.D7 Douglas Co.

547.D9 Du Page Co.

Dunes of Illinois, *see* F547.M56

547.E25 Edgar Co.

547.E3 Edwards Co.

Including English settlement

547.E4 Effingham Co.

547.F35 Fayette Co.

547.F7 Ford Co.

547.F77 Fox River and Valley, Ill.

Cf. F587.F7 , Wisconsin

547.F78 Franklin Co.

547.F8 Fulton Co.

547.G3 Gallatin Co.

547.G7 Greene Co.

547.G8 Grundy Co.

547.H17 Hamilton Co.

547.H2 Hancock Co.

547.H3 Hardin Co.

547.H4 Henderson Co.

547.H52 Henry Co.

Horseshoe Lake, *see* F547.A3

547.I13 Illinois and Michigan Canal National Heritage Corridor

547.I2 Illinois River and Valley

547.I7 Iroquois Co.

547.J2 Jackson Co.

547.J3 Jasper Co.

547.J4 Jefferson Co.

547.J5 Jersey Co.

547.J6 Jo Daviess Co.

547.J8 Johnson Co.

Jubilee College State Park, *see* F547.P4

547.K2 Kane Co.

547.K25 Kankakee Co.

547.K27 Kankakee River and Valley, Ill.

Including Willow Creek and Valley

Cf. F532.K2 , General, and Indiana

547.K4 Kendall Co.

547.K7 Knox Co.

547.L2 Lake Co.

547.L3 La Salle Co.

Including Starved Rock State Park

547.L4 Lawrence Co.

547.L5 Lee Co.

547.L78 Livingston Co.

547.L8 Logan Co.

547.M13 McDonough Co.

547.M14 McHenry Co.

547.M16 McLean Co.

547.M17 Macon Co.

547.M18 Macoupin Co.

547.M2 Madison Co.

547.M3 Marion Co.

547.M34 Marshall Co.

547.M37 Mason Co.

547.M4 Massac Co.

547.M5 Menard Co.

	Illinois
547.A-.Z	**Regions, counties, etc., A-Z — Continued**
547.M55	Mercer Co.
547.M56	Lake Michigan region, Ill.
	Including the dunes of Illinois
	Cf. F553, General
547.M6	Military lands between the Mississippi and Illinois Rivers
	Cf. E359.4, Military bounties (War of 1812)
547.M65	Mississippi River and Valley, Ill.
	Cf. F350.5+ , General
	Cf. F597 , Upper Mississippi Valley
547.M68	Monroe Co.
547.M7	Montgomery Co.
547.M8	Morgan Co.
547.M9	Moultrie Co.
547.O3	Ogle Co.
547.O4	Ohio River and Valley, Ill.
	Cf. F516+, General
547.P4	Peoria Co.
	Including Jubilee College State Park, etc.
547.P45	Perry Co.
	Including White Walnut Creek and Valley
547.P5	Piatt Co.
547.P6	Pike Co.
547.P7	Pope Co.
547.P78	Pulaski Co.
547.P8	Putnam Co.
547.R2	Randolph Co.
547.R5	Richland Co.
547.R6	Rock Island Co.
547.R7	Rock River and Valley (General, and Ill.)
	Cf. F587.R63, Wisconsin
547.S2	St. Clair Co.
547.S24	Saline Co.
547.S3	Sangamon Co.
547.S33	Sangamon River and Valley
547.S4	Schuyler Co.
547.S45	Scott Co.
547.S6	Shelby Co.
547.S65	Spoon River and Valley
547.S7	Stark Co.
	Starved Rock State Park, *see* F547.L3
547.S8	Stephenson Co.
547.S94	Sugar Creek and Valley, Macoupin County and Sangamon County
547.T2	Tazewell Co.
547.U5	Union Co.
547.V2	Vermilion Co.
547.W12	Wabash Co.
547.W14	Wabash River and Valley, Ill.
	Cf. F532.W2, General, and Indiana
547.W2	Warren Co.
547.W23	Washington Co.
547.W25	Wayne Co.
547.W3	White Co.
	White Walnut Creek and Valley, *see* F547.P45
547.W4	Whiteside Co.
547.W5	Will Co.
547.W6	Williamson Co.
	Willow Creek and Valley, *see* F547.K27
547.W7	Winnebago Co.

Illinois

547.A-.Z **Regions, counties, etc., A-Z — Continued**

547.W8 Woodford Co.

Chicago

548.1 Periodicals. Societies. Collections

548.15 Museums. Exhibitions, exhibits

Cf. T500, World's Columbian Exposition, 1893

Cf. T501, Century of Progress International Exposition, 1933-1934

548.18 Guidebooks

548.25 Biography (Collective). Genealogy (Collective)

548.27 Historiography

548.29 Study and teaching

548.3 General works. Histories

548.33 Juvenile works

Pamphlets, addresses, essays, etc.

548.35 General

548.36 Anecdotes, legends, pageants, etc.

548.37 Historic monuments. Illustrative material

548.39 Antiquities (Non-Indian)

By period

Early to 1875

Cf. E356.C53, Fort Dearborn Massacre, 1812

548.4 General works

548.42 1865-1875

Including the great fire of 1871

548.45 1875-1892

Cf. T500, World's Columbian Exposition, 1893

548.5 1892-1950

1951-

548.52 General works

Biography

548.53 Collective

548.54.A-.54.Z Individual, A-Z

GALE NOTE *See note at the head of Table F5 at the end of the text for further instructions on how to subdivide this number*

Sections. Localities. Districts, etc.

548.6 General works

Cemeteries

548.61 General works

548.612.A-.612.Z Individual, A-Z

548.612.G72 Graceland Cemetery

548.62 Churches

548.625 Hotels, taverns, etc.

548.627 Places of amusement

548.63 Harbor

548.64 Monuments. Statues

GALE NOTE *The cutter number(s) listed below have been given only as examples by the Library of Congress*

548.64.A1 General works

548.64.G4 George Washington-Robert Morris-Haym Salomon Monument

548.65 Parks. Squares. Circles

GALE NOTE *The cutter number(s) listed below have been given only as examples by the Library of Congress*

548.65.A1 General works

548.65.D2 Dearborn Park

548.65.L7 Lincoln Park

548.65.S7 South Park

548.67 Streets. Bridges. Railroads

GALE NOTE *The cutter number(s) listed below have been given only as examples by the Library of Congress*

Illinois

Chicago

Sections. Localities. Districts, etc.

548.67 Streets. Bridges. Railroads — Continued

548.67.A1 General works

548.67.M75 Monroe Street

548.68 Suburbs. Sections of the city. Rivers, etc.

GALE NOTE *The cutter number(s) listed below have been given only as examples by the Library of Congress*

548.68.A1 General works

548.68.I7 Irving Park

548.68.N7 North Shore

548.68.R8 Roseland

548.68.S7 South Shore

548.68.W8 Wolf's Point

548.68.W82 Woodlawn

548.69 Wards

Buildings

548.7 General works. Collective

548.8.A-.8.Z Individual, A-Z

GALE NOTE *The cutter number(s) listed below have been given only as examples by the Library of Congress*

548.8.A9 Auditorium Building

548.8.C9 Custom House

548.8.G7 Grand Central Passenger Station

548.8.P17 Palmer House

Elements in the population

548.9.A1 General works

548.9.A2-.9.Z Individual elements

549.A-.Z **Other cities, towns, etc., A-Z**

GALE NOTE *The cutter number(s) listed below have been given only as examples by the Library of Congress*

549.A4 Alton

549.B65 Bloomington

549.C44 Champaign

549.C56 Cicero

549.D3 Decatur

549.E2 East St. Louis

549.E8 Evanston

549.J7 Joliet

549.O13 Oak Park

549.P4 Peoria

549.Q6 Quincy

549.R6 Rock Island

549.R7 Rockford

549.S7 Springfield

Elements in the population

550.A1 General works

550.A2-.Z Individual elements

For a list of racial, ethnic, and religious elements (with cutter numbers), see E184.A+

The Lake region. Great Lakes

The portion of the northern boundary of the United States between the St. Lawrence River and the Lake of the Woods; early French explorations; British posts

Cf. F1030, New France

Cf. GB1627, Physical geography

550.5 **Biography (Collective). Genealogy (Collective)**

551 **General works**

552 **Lake Superior**

Cf. F572.S9, Lake Superior region, Mich.

Cf. F587.A8, Apostle Islands and Chequamegon Bay

The Lake region. Great Lakes
552 **Lake Superior — Continued**
Cf. F587.S9, Lake Superior region, Wis.
Cf. F612.S9, Lake Superior region, Minn.
Cf. F1059.S9, Lake Superior region, Ontario
Cf. F1059.T5, Thunder Bay region, Ontario
553 **Lake Michigan**
Cf. F532.M67, Lake Michigan region, Ind.
Cf. F547.M56, Lake Michigan region, Ill.
Cf. F572.M16, Mackinac Straits and region
Cf. F572.M57, Lake Michigan region, Mich.
Cf. F587.G6, Green Bay
Cf. F587.M57, Lake Michigan region, Wis.
554 **Lake Huron**
Cf. F572.H92, Lake Huron region, Mich.
Cf. F572.S15, Saginaw Bay
Cf. F572.S34, Lake St. Clair
Cf. F1059.G3, Georgian Bay
Cf. F1059.H95, Lake Huron region, Ontario
555 **Lake Erie**
Cf. F127.E65, Lake Erie region, N.Y.
Cf. F127.N6, Niagara region
Cf. F157.E6, Lake Erie region, Pa. (Erie Co.)
Cf. F497.E6, Lake Erie region, Ohio
Cf. F497.W5, Western Reserve
Cf. F1059.E6, Lake Erie region, Ontario
556 **Lake Ontario**
Cf. F127.O72, Lake Ontario region, N.Y.
Cf. F1050, St. Lawrence River
Cf. F1059.O6, Lake Ontario region
Elements in the population
558 General works
558.2.A-.2.Z Individual elements
Michigan
561 **Periodicals. Societies. Collections**
563 **Museums. Exhibitions, exhibits**
564 **Gazetteers. Dictionaries. Geographic names**
564.3 **Guidebooks**
565 **Biography (Collective). Genealogy (Collective)**
565.2 **Historiography**
Historians, *see* E175.5.A+
565.5 **Study and teaching**
566 **General works. Histories**
Including admission as a state, January 26, 1837
Including by period (Early to 1950) as well as general
For 1951 and later, see F570+
Including biography: Aaron Thomas Bliss, Stevens Thomson Mason, Chase Salmon Osborn, William Woodbridge, etc.
Cf. D570.85.M5+, World War I, 1914-1918
Cf. D769.85.M5+, World War II, 1939-1945
Cf. E83.76, Pontiac's War, 1763-1765
Cf. E83.81, Tippecanoe Campaign, 1811
Cf. E237, Clark's campaign against Detroit, 1781
Cf. E355, War of 1812 (Military operations)
Cf. E514.1+, Civil War, 1861-1865 (General)
Cf. E726.M6, War of 1898 (Spanish-American War)
Cf. F497.B7, Toledo War, 1836
566.3 **Juvenile works**
Pamphlets, addresses, essays, etc.
566.5 General

Michigan

Pamphlets, addresses, essays, etc. — Continued

566.6 Anecdotes, legends, pageants, etc.

567 **Historic monuments (General). Illustrative material**

568 **Antiquities (Non-Indian)**

By period

(569) Early to 1950, *see* F566

1951-

570 General works

Biography

570.2 Collective

570.25.A-.25.Z Individual, A-Z

GALE NOTE *See note at the head of Table F5 at the end of the text for further instructions on how to subdivide this number*

572.A-.Z **Regions, counties, etc., A-Z**

572.A15 Counties (Collective and selective)

For Northern Michigan, see F572.N7

For Northern (Upper) Peninsula, see F572.N8

572.A16 Mountains

572.A17 Rivers

572.A18 Lakes

572.A19 Islands

572.A2 Alcona Co.

572.A25 Alger Co.

572.A3 Allegan Co.

572.A4 Alpena Co.

Including Thunder Bay

572.A5 Antrim Co.

572.A7 Arenac Co.

Including Point Lookout

572.B15 Baraga Co.

572.B2 Barry Co.

572.B3 Bay Co.

Including Tobico Marsh

572.B36 Bean Creek and Valley

Cf. F497.B3, General, and Ohio

572.B38 Beaver Island

572.B4 Benzie Co.

Including Crystal Lake, Herring Lake

572.B5 Berrien Co.

Including Paw Paw Lake

572.B7 Boundaries

For Toledo War, 1836 (Michigan-Ohio boundary), see F497.B7

Cf. F497.B7, Ohio boundary

Cf. F532.B7, Indiana boundary

572.B8 Branch Co.

572.B86 Brule River and Valley (General, and Michigan)

Cf. F587.B85, Wisconsin

572.C2 Calhoun Co.

572.C3 Cass Co.

572.C4 Charlevoix Co.

For Beaver Island, see F572.B38

572.C5 Cheboygan Co.

Including Douglas Lake

Cheneaux Islands, *see* F572.L57

572.C54 Chippewa Co.

For Drummond Island, see F572.D88

572.C65 Clare Co.

572.C7 Clinton Co.

572.C9 Crawford Co.

Michigan

572.A-.Z **Regions, counties, etc., A-Z — Continued**

Crystal Lake, *see* F572.B4

572.D4 Delta Co.

572.D46 Detroit River and Valley (General, and Mich.)

Cf. F1059.D46, Ontario

Devils Lake (Lenawee County), *see* F572.L5

572.D5 Dickinson Co.

Douglas Lake, *see* F572.C5

572.D88 Drummond Island

572.E2 Eaton Co.

572.E5 Emmet Co.

Fox Islands, *see* F572.L45

572.G3 Genesee Co.

572.G38 Gladwin Co.

572.G44 Gogebic Co.

572.G45 Grand Island

572.G46 Grand River and Valley

572.G5 Grand Traverse Bay region. The Traverse region

Including Power Island

Cf. F572.L7, Little Traverse Bay region

572.G6 Grand Traverse Co.

572.G8 Gratiot Co.

572.G87 Green Bay region, Mich.

Cf. F587.G6, General, and Wisconsin

572.H6 Hillsdale Co.

572.H8 Houghton Co.

Houghton Lake, *see* F572.R6

572.H9 Huron Co.

Huron Mountains, *see* F572.M33

572.H92 Lake Huron region, Mich.

Cf. F554, General

572.H93 Huron-Manistee National Forests

572.I5 Ingham Co.

572.I6 Ionia Co.

Including Long Lake

572.I63 Iosco Co.

572.I66 Iron Co.

572.I7 Isabella Co.

572.I8 Isle Royale

572.J2 Jackson Co.

572.K2 Kalamazoo Co.

572.K22 Kalamazoo River and Valley

572.K23 Kalkaska Co.

572.K3 Kent Co.

572.K4 Keweenaw Co.

For Isle Royale, see F572.I8

572.K43 Keweenaw Peninsula

572.L2 Lake Co.

572.L3 Lapeer Co.

572.L45 Leelanau Co.

Including Fox Islands

572.L5 Lenawee Co.

Including Devils Lake

572.L57 Les Cheneaux Islands (The Snows)

572.L7 Little Traverse Bay region

Cf. F572.G5 , Grand Traverse Bay region

572.L8 Livingston Co.

Long Lake (Ionia County), *see* F572.I6

Lookout, Point (Arenac Co.), *see* F572.A7

	Michigan
572.A-.Z	**Regions, counties, etc., A-Z — Continued**
572.L9	Luce Co.
572.M14	Mackinac (Mackinaw) Co. Mackinac region. Straits of Mackinac, etc.
	For Les Cheneaux Islands, see F572.L57
572.M16	Mackinac Island. Mackinac Island (City)
572.M2	Macomb Co.
572.M3	Manistee Co.
572.M33	Marquette Co.
	Including Huron Mountains
572.M36	Mason Co.
572.M4	Mecosta Co.
572.M5	Menominee Co.
572.M516	Menominee Range (General, and Michigan)
	Cf. F587.M49, Wisconsin
572.M52	Menominee River and Valley (General, and Mich.)
	Cf. F587.M5, Wisconsin
572.M57	Lake Michigan region, Mich
	Cf. F553, General
	Michilimackinac, *see* F572.M16
572.M6	Midland Co.
572.M65	Missaukee Co.
572.M7	Monroe Co.
572.M8	Montcalm Co.
572.M83	Montmorency Co.
572.M9	Muskegon Co.
572.N5	Newaygo Co.
572.N7	Northern Michigan (Northern part of Lower Peninsula)
572.N8	Northern (Upper) Peninsula
572.O2	Oakland Co.
572.O3	Oceana Co.
572.O4	Ogemaw Co.
572.O6	Ontonagon Co.
572.O62	Ontonagon River and Valley
572.O7	Osceola Co.
572.O73	Oscoda Co.
572.O78	Otsego Co.
572.O8	Ottawa Co.
	Paw Paw Lake, *see* F572.B5
572.P38	Paw Paw River and Valley
572.P46	Pere Marquette River and Valley
572.P5	Pictured Rocks National Lakeshore
572.P53	Pigeon River and Valley. Pigeon River Country State Forest, etc.
	Point Lookout (Arenac Co.), *see* F572.A7
	Power Island, *see* F572.G5
572.P7	Presque Isle Co.
572.R6	Roscommon Co.
	Including Houghton Lake
572.S15	Saginaw Bay region
	Including Fort Saginaw
572.S17	Saginaw Co.
572.S2	Saginaw River and Valley
572.S3	St. Clair Co.
572.S34	Lake St. Clair, Mich.
	Cf. F1059.S3, Ontario
572.S4	St. Joseph Co.
572.S43	St. Joseph River and Valley, Mich.
	Cf. F532.S3, General, and Indiana
572.S5	Sanilac Co.
572.S6	Schoolcraft Co.

	Michigan
572.A-.Z	**Regions, counties, etc., A-Z — Continued**
572.S7	Shiawassee Co.
572.S8	Sleeping Bear Dunes National Lakeshore
	The Snows (Islands), *see* F572.L57
572.S86	South Manitou Island
572.S9	Lake Superior region, Mich.
	Cf. F552, General
572.T58	Thumb District. Thumb Area
	Thunder Bay, *see* F572.A4
	Tiffin River and Valley, *see* F572.B36
	Tobico Marsh, *see* F572.B3
	Traverse region, *see* F572.G5
572.T9	Tuscola Co.
	Upper Peninsula, *see* F572.N8
572.V3	Van Buren Co.
572.W24	Walloon Lake
572.W3	Washtenaw Co.
572.W4	Wayne Co.
572.W5	Wexford Co.
574.A-.Z	**Cities, towns, etc., A-Z**
	GALE NOTE *The cutter number(s) listed below have been given only as examples by the Library of Congress*
574.A6	Ann Arbor
574.B3	Bay City
574.D2	Dearborn
	For Edison Institute (Henry Ford Museum and Greenfield Village), Dearborn, Mich., see E161
574.D4	Detroit
	Subarrange by Table F2 at the end of the text
574.G7	Grand Rapids
574.K1	Kalamazoo
574.L2	Lansing
	Mackinac Island (City), *see* F572.M16
574.M17	Mackinaw
574.M9	Muskegon
574.S15	Saginaw
574.S3	Sault Ste. Marie
	Elements in the population
575.A1	General works
575.A2-.Z	Individual elements
	For a list of racial, ethnic, and religious elements (with cutter numbers), see E184.A+
	Wisconsin
576	**Periodicals. Societies. Collections**
578	**Museums. Exhibitions, exhibits**
579	**Gazetteers. Dictionaries. Geographic names**
579.3	**Guidebooks**
580	**Biography (Collective). Genealogy (Collective)**
580.2	**Historiography**
	Historians, *see* E175.5.A+
580.5	**Study and teaching**
581	**General works. Histories**
581.3	**Juvenile works**
	Pamphlets, addresses, essays, etc.
581.5	General
581.6	Anecdotes, legends, pageants, etc.
581.8	**Geography**
582	**Historic monuments (General). Illustrative material**
583	**Antiquities (Non-Indian)**

Wisconsin — Continued

By period

584 Early to 1848

For biography: Thomas Pendleton Burnett, etc.

585 1836-1848. Wisconsin Territory

586 1848-1950

Admission as a state, May 29, 1848

Including biography: Benjamin Franklin Hopkins, Morgan Lewis Martin, Cadwallader Colden Washburn, etc.

Cf. D570.85.W6+, World War I, 1914-1918

Cf. D769.85.W6+, World War II, 1939-1945

Cf. E537.1+, Civil War, 1861-1865 (General)

Cf. E470.4+, Military operations and battles in the Civil War, 1861-1865

Cf. E726.W6, War of 1898 (Spanish-American War)

1951-

586.2 General works

Biography

586.4 Collective

586.42.A-.42.Z Individual, A-Z

GALE NOTE *See note at the head of Table F5 at the end of the text for further instructions on how to subdivide this number*

587.A-.Z **Regions, counties, etc., A-Z**

587.A15 Counties

587.A16 Mountains

587.A17 Rivers

587.A18 Lakes

587.A19 Islands

587.A2 Adams Co.

Apostle Islands, *see* F587.A8

587.A8 Ashland Co.

Including Apostle Islands, Chequamegon Bay, Madeline Island

587.B25 Barron Co.

587.B3 Bayfield Co.

For Chequamegon Bay, see F587.A8

587.B55 Black River and Valley

Blue Lake, *see* F587.O5

587.B7 Boundaries

Cf. F547.B7, Illinois boundary

Cf. F612.B7, Minnesota boundary

587.B8 Brown Co.

587.B85 Brule River and Valley, Wis.

Cf. F572.B86, General and Michigan

587.B9 Buffalo Co.

587.B95 Burnett Co.

587.C2 Calumet Co.

Chain O' Lakes, *see* F587.W3

Chequamegon Bay, *see* F587.A8

587.C48 Chippewa Co.

587.C5 Chippewa River and Valley

587.C6 Clark Co.

587.C7 Columbia Co.

587.C8 Crawford Co.

Dalles of the Wisconsin, *see* F587.W8

587.D3 Dane Co.

Including Cave of the Mounds, Lake Mendota

Dells of the Wisconsin, *see* F587.W8

587.D6 Dodge Co.

587.D7 Door Co.

Including Rock Island, Washington Island

587.D8 Douglas Co.

	Wisconsin
587.A-.Z	**Regions, counties, etc., A-Z — Continued**
587.D9	Dunn Co.
587.E2	Eau Claire Co.
587.F5	Florence Co.
587.F6	Fond du Lac Co.
587.F65	Forest Co.
587.F7	Fox River and Valley (General, and Waukesha Co., Wisconsin)
	Cf. F547.F77, Illinois
587.F72	Fox River and Valley (Columbia Co.-Brown Co.)
	Lake Geneva, *see* F587.W18
587.G5	Grant Co.
587.G6	Green Bay region (General, and Wis.)
	Cf. F572.G87, Michigan
587.G7	Green Co.
587.G74	Green Lake Co.
587.I6	Iowa Co.
587.I7	Iron Co.
587.J2	Jackson Co.
587.J4	Jefferson Co.
587.J9	Juneau Co.
587.K3	Kenosha Co.
587.K35	Kewaunee Co.
587.K4	Kickapoo River and Valley, Wisc.
587.L14	La Crosse Co.
587.L2	Lafayette Co.
587.L3	Langlade Co.
587.L5	Lincoln Co.
	Madeline Island, *see* F587.A8
587.M2	Manitowoc Co.
587.M3	Marathon Co.
587.M35	Marinette Co.
587.M4	Marquette Co.
587.M49	Menominee Range
	Cf. F572.M516, General, and Michigan
587.M5	Menominee River and Valley, Wis.
	Cf. F572.M52, General, and Michigan
587.M57	Lake Michigan region, Wis.
	Cf. F553, General
587.M6	Milwaukee Co.
587.M63	Mississippi River and Valley, Wis.
	Cf. F350.5, General
	Cf. F597, Upper Mississippi Valley
587.M7	Monroe Co.
587.O2	Oconto Co.
587.O5	Oneida Co.
	Including Blue Lake
587.O93	Outagamie Co.
587.O98	Ozaukee Co.
587.P4	Pepin Co.
587.P6	Pierce Co.
587.P7	Polk Co.
587.P8	Portage Co.
587.P83	Porte des Morts Strait
587.P9	Price Co.
587.R2	Racine Co.
587.R4	Richland Co.
587.R6	Rock Co.
	Rock Island, *see* F587.D7

Wisconsin

587.A-.Z **Regions, counties, etc., A-Z — Continued**

587.R63 Rock River and Valley (Sinnissippi Valley), Wis.

Cf. F547.R7, General, and Illinois

587.R8 Rusk Co.

587.S13 St. Croix Co.

587.S14 St. Croix River and Valley (General, and Wis.)

Cf. F612.S2, Minnesota

587.S2 Sauk Co.

Including Devil's Island, Durward's Glen

587.S3 Sawyer Co.

587.S45 Shawano Co.

587.S5 Sheboygan Co.

587.S9 Lake Superior region, Wis.

Cf. F552, General

587.T3 Taylor Co.

587.T79 Trempealeau Co.

587.V5 Vernon Co.

587.V6 Vilas Co.

587.W18 Walworth Co.

Including Lake Geneva

587.W185 Washburn Co.

587.W19 Washington Co.

Washington Island, *see* F587.D7

587.W2 Waukesha Co.

587.W3 Waupaca Co.

Including Chain O' Lakes

587.W35 Waushara Co.

587.W5 Winnebago Co.

587.W8 Wisconsin River and Valley

Including Dells (Dalles) of the Wisconsin

587.W86 Wolf River. Wolf National Scenic Riverway

587.W9 Wood Co.

589.A-.Z **Cities, towns, etc., A-Z**

GALE NOTE *The cutter number(s) listed below have been given only as examples by the Library of Congress*

589.G7 Green Bay

589.K3 Kenosha

589.L1 La Crosse

589.M1 Madison

Subarrange by Table F2 at the end of the text

589.M6 Milwaukee

Subarrange by Table F2 at the end of the text

589.O8 Oshkosh

589.P8 Prairie du Chien

589.R2 Racine

589.S95 Superior

Elements in the population

590.A1 General works

590.A2-.Z Individual elements

For a list of racial, ethnic, and religious elements (with cutter numbers), see E184.A+

The West. Trans-Mississippi Region. Great Plains

For The "Indian country," 1803-1854, see F697

For Louisiana (Province), see F374

For Middle West, see F350.5+

For Mississippi River and Valley, see F350.5+

For Missouri River and Valley, see F598

For The Northwest (Upper Mississippi Valley), see F597

For Pacific coast, see F851

For Pacific Northwest, see F852

The West. Trans-Mississippi Region. Great Plains — Continued

For Rocky Mountains, see F721

For The Southwest, see F786

Cf. E81+, Indian wars (General)

590.3 **Guidebooks**

590.5 **Biography (Collective). Genealogy (Collective)**

590.6 **Geography**

590.7 **Historic monuments (General). Illustrative material**

591 **General works. Histories**

Cf. E78.W5, Indians of the West

By period

592 Early to 1848

Including United States exploring expeditions: Fremont, Lewis and Clark, Pike

Including biography: James Bridger, Christopher Carson, John Colter, Zebulon Montgomery Pike, Jedediah Strong Smith, William Sherley Williams, etc.

For California, see F864

For the "Indian country," 1821-1854, see F697

For New Mexico (Spanish and Mexican), see F800-801

For Texas, see F390

Cf. E123+, Spanish discoveries

Cf. E401+, War with Mexico, 1845-1848

Cf. E408; F786, Mexican cession of 1848

Cf. F799, Cibola, Quivira

Cf. F868.N5, Donner party

Cf. F880, Oregon question

Lewis and Clark Expedition, 1804-1806

592.3 President Jefferson's message and accompanying documents

Subarrange by date of edition

592.4 Authentic history of the expedition. Lewis and Clark journals

Subarrange by date of edition

592.5 Journals of other members of the expedition. By author

Subarrange by date of edition

592.6 Spurious publications

Subarrange by date of edition

592.7 Other works about the expedition and its members

Subarrange by author or biographee as the case may be

593 1848-1860

Including later United States expeditions; overland journeys to the Pacific

Including biography: Edward Fitzgerald Beale, William Gilpin, etc.

Cf. E83.84, Wars with Pacific coast Indians, 1847-1865

Cf. E83.857, Spirit Lake Massacre, 1857

Cf. E83.858, Mill Creek War, 1857-1865

Cf. F786, Gadsden Purchase, 1853

Cf. F801 , Texas cession of 1850

594 1860-1880

Including biography: Martha Canary ("Calamity Jane"); William Frederick Cody, ("Buffalo Bill"); James Butler Hickok ("Wild Bill Hickok"); Jesse James; Moses Embree Milner ("California Joe"); Cole Younger; etc.

Cf. E83.86, Dakota Indian War, 1862-1863

Cf. E83.863, Indian wars, 1863-1865

Cf. E83.866, Indian wars, 1866-1898

595 1880-1950

Including biography: George Le Roy Parker ("Butch Cassidy")

Cf. E83.866, Indian wars, 1866-1898

595.2 1951-1980

595.3 1981-

596 **Frontier and pioneer life. Ranch life, cowboys, cattle trails, etc.**

Elements in the population

596.2 General works

The West. Trans-Mississippi Region. Great Plains
Elements in the population — Continued
596.3.A-.3.Z Individual elements
For a list of individual elements, see E184.A+
597 **The Northwest**
Including Upper Mississippi Valley; sources of the Mississippi; northern boundary of the United States (from Lake of the Woods to Rocky Mountains), including works on region between Great Lakes and Pacific Ocean, the Oregon Trail, and the Overland Trail
Including biography: Jonathan Carver
For Canadian Northwest, see F1060+
For Pacific Northwest, see F851.72+
Cf. E78.N8 , Indians of the Northwestern States
Cf. F612.I8 , Lake Itasca and park
598 **Missouri River and Valley**
Cf. F472.M7 , Missouri
Cf. F627.M66, Iowa
Cf. F642.M6, North Dakota
Cf. F657.M7, South Dakota
Cf. F672.M6, Nebraska
Cf. F687.M6, Kansas
Cf. F737.M7, Montana
Minnesota
601 **Periodicals. Societies. Collections**
603 **Museums. Exhibitions, exhibits**
604 **Gazetteers. Dictionaries. Geographic names**
604.3 **Guidebooks**
605 **Biography (Collective). Genealogy (Collective)**
605.2 **Historiography**
Historians, *see* E175.5.A+
605.5 **Study and teaching**
606 **General works. Histories**
Including admission as a state, May 11, 1858
For 1951 and later, see F610
Including biography: Willis Arnold Gorman, John Albert Johnson, Floyd Björnsterne Olson, Henry Hastings Sibley, etc.
Cf. D570.85.M6+, World War I, 1914-1918
Cf. D769.85.M6+, World War II, 1939-1945
Cf. E83.86, Dakota Indian War, 1862-1863
Cf. E515.1+, Civil War, 1861-1865 (General)
Cf. E726.M7, War of 1898 (Spanish-American War)
606.3 **Juvenile works**
Pamphlets, addresses, essays, etc.
606.5 General
606.6 Anecdotes, legends, pageants, etc.
607 **Historic monuments (General). Illustrative material**
608 **Antiquities (Non-Indian)**
By period
Early through 1950, *see* F606
1951-
610 General works
Biography
610.2 Collective
610.3.A-.3.Z Individual, A-Z
GALE NOTE *See note at the head of Table F5 at the end of the text for further instructions on how to subdivide this number*
612.A-.Z **Regions, counties, etc., A-Z**
612.A15 Counties
612.A16 Mountains
612.A17 Rivers
612.A18 Lakes

	Minnesota
612.A-.Z	**Regions, counties, etc., A-Z — Continued**
612.A19	Islands
612.A3	Aitkin Co.
612.A6	Anoka Co.
612.B39	Becker Co.
	Including Big Cormorant Lake
612.B43	Beltrami Co.
	Including Star Island
612.B45	Benton Co.
	Big Cormorant Lake, *see* F612.B39
	Big Fork River and Valley, *see* F612.K7
612.B5	Big Stone Co.
612.B6	Blue Earth Co.
612.B7	Boundaries
	For International boundary, see F597
612.B73	Boundary Waters Canoe Area
612.B8	Brown Co.
612.C15	Carlton Co.
612.C2	Carver Co.
612.C25	Cass Co.
612.C4	Chippewa Co.
612.C45	Chisago Co.
612.C6	Clay Co.
612.C63	Clearwater Co.
	For Itasca State Park, see F612.I8
612.C65	Cook Co.
612.C67	Cottonwood Co.
	Crane Island, *see* F612.H5
612.C7	Crow Wing Co.
612.D2	Dakota Co.
612.D6	Dodge Co.
612.D7	Douglas Co.
612.F2	Faribault Co.
612.F25	Father Hennepin State Park
612.F4	Fillmore Co.
	Including Forestville State Park
	Forestville State Park, *see* F612.F4
612.F7	Freeborn Co.
612.G6	Goodhue Co.
	Gooseberry Falls State Park, *see* F612.L3
612.G7	Grant Co.
612.H5	Hennepin Co.
	Including Lake Minnetonka, Crane Island
612.H8	Houston Co.
612.H9	Hubbard Co.
612.I6	Isanti Co.
612.I7	Itasca Co.
612.I8	Itasca Lake. Itasca State Park
612.J2	Jackson Co.
612.K17	Kanabec Co.
612.K2	Kandiyohi Co.
	Including Monogalia Co.
612.K5	Kittson Co.
612.K7	Koochiching Co.
	Including Big Fork River and Valley
612.L2	Lac qui Parle Co.
612.L3	Lake Co.
	Including Gooseberry Falls State Park

Minnesota

612.A-.Z **Regions, counties, etc., A-Z — Continued**

612.L4 Lake of the Woods Co.
Including Northwest Angle
612.L5 Le Sueur Co.
612.L6 Lincoln Co.
612.L9 Lyon Co.
612.M25 McLeod Co.
612.M26 Mahnomen Co.
612.M266 Mankahta Co.
612.M27 Marshall Co.
612.M28 Martin Co.
612.M3 Meeker Co.
612.M36 Mesaba (Mesabi) range
612.M38 Mille Lacs Co.
612.M4 Minnesota River and Valley
612.M5 Mississippi River and Valley, Minn.
Cf. F350.5+, General
Cf. F597, Upper Mississippi Valley
Monogalia Co., *see* F612.K2
612.M88 Morrison Co.
612.M9 Mower Co.
612.M95 Murray Co.
612.N5 Nicollet Co.
612.N7 Nobles Co.
612.N8 Norman Co.
Northwest Angle, *see* F612.L4
612.O5 Olmsted Co.
612.O9 Otter Tail Co.
Including Pelican Lake
Pelican Lake, *see* F612.O9
612.P4 Pennington Co.
612.P42 Pepin, Lake
612.P5 Pine Co.
612.P55 Pipestone Co.
612.P7 Polk Co.
612.P8 Pope Co.
612.R18 Rainy River region
612.R2 Ramsey Co.
612.R25 Red Lake Co.
612.R27 Red River of the North and Valley, Minn.
Cf. F642.R3, North Dakota
Cf. F1064.R3, Manitoba
612.R28 Red River State Recreation Area
612.R3 Redwood Co.
612.R42 Renville Co.
612.R5 Rice Co.
612.R7 Rock Co.
612.R8 Roseau Co.
612.S2 St. Croix River and Valley, Minn.
Cf. F587.S14, General, and Wisconsin
612.S25 St. Louis Co.
Including Side Lake
612.S3 Scott Co.
612.S4 Sherburne Co.
612.S5 Sibley Co.
Side Lake, *see* F612.S25
612.S64 Split Rock Creek and Valley, Minn.
Cf. F657.S73, General and South Dakota
Star Island, *see* F612.B43

Minnesota

612.A-.Z **Regions, counties, etc., A-Z — Continued**

612.S75 Stearns Co.

612.S8 Steele Co.

612.S84 Stevens Co.

612.S86 Straight River and Valley (Steele and Rice Counties)

612.S9 Lake Superior region, Minn.

Cf. F552, General

612.S95 Superior National Forest

612.S98 Swift Co.

612.T6 Todd Co.

612.T7 Traverse Co.

612.V6 Voyageurs National Park

612.W12 Wabasha Co.

612.W14 Wadena Co.

612.W15 Wadsworth Trail

612.W17 Waseca Co.

612.W2 Washington Co.

612.W35 Watonwan Co.

612.W65 Wilkin Co.

612.W7 Winona Co.

Including Rush Creek Valley

612.W9 Wright Co.

612.Y4 Yellow Medicine Co.

614.A-.Z **Cities, towns, etc., A-Z**

GALE NOTE *The cutter number(s) listed below have been given only as examples by the Library of Congress*

614.D8 Duluth

614.F7 Fort Snelling

614.M5 Minneapolis

Subarrange by Table F2 at the end of the text

614.M6 Minneapolis and St. Paul. "The Twin Cities"

614.R6 Rochester

614.S25 St. Cloud

614.S4 St. Paul

614.W7 Winona

Elements in the population

615.A1 General works

615.A2-.Z Individual elements

For a list of racial, ethnic, and religious elements (with cutter numbers), see E184.A+

Iowa

616 **Periodicals. Societies. Collections**

618 **Museums. Exhibitions, exhibits**

619 **Gazetteers. Dictionaries. Geographic names**

619.3 **Guidebooks**

620 **Biography (Collective). Genealogy (Collective)**

620.2 **Historiography**

Historians, *see* E175.5.A+

620.5 **Study and teaching**

621 **General works. Histories**

Including admission as a state, December 28, 1846

Including by period (Early to 1950) as well as general

For 1951 and later, see F625+

Including biography: John Chambers, Augustus Caesar Dodge, Robert Lucas, etc.

Cf. D570.85.I8+, World War I, 1914-1918

Cf. D769.85.I8+, World War II, 1939-1945

Cf. E83.857, Spirit Lake Massacre, 1857

Cf. E409.5.I72, War with Mexico, 1845-1848

Cf. E507.1+, Civil War, 1861-1865 (General)

Cf. E726.I4, War of 1898 (Spanish-American War)

Iowa — Continued

621.3 **Juvenile works**

Pamphlets, addresses, essays, etc.

621.5 General

621.6 Anecdotes, legends, pageants, etc.

622 **Historic monuments (General). Illustrative material**

623 **Antiquities (Non-Indian)**

By period

(624) Early to 1950, *see* F621

1951-

625 General works

Biography

625.4 Collective

625.42.A-.42.Z Individual, A-Z

GALE NOTE *See note at the head of Table F5 at the end of the text for further instructions on how to subdivide this number*

627.A-.Z **Regions, counties, etc., A-Z**

627.A15 Counties

627.A16 Mountains

627.A17 Rivers

627.A18 Lakes

627.A19 Islands

627.A2 Adair Co.

627.A3 Adams Co.

627.A5 Allamakee Co.

627.A6 Appanoose Co.

627.A8 Audubon Co.

627.B4 Benton Co.

627.B5 Big Sioux River and Valley, Iowa

Cf. F657.B5, General, and South Dakota

627.B6 Black Hawk Co.

627.B67 Boone Co.

627.B7 Boundaries

Cf. F472.B7, Missouri boundary

627.B8 Bremer Co.

627.B85 Buchanan Co.

627.B87 Buena Vista Co.

627.B9 Butler Co.

627.C2 Calhoun Co.

627.C25 Carroll Co.

627.C3 Cass Co.

627.C4 Cedar Co.

627.C44 Cerro Gordo Co.

627.C47 Cherokee Co.

627.C5 Chickasaw Co.

627.C53 Clarke Co.

627.C54 Clay Co.

627.C56 Clayton Co.

627.C6 Clinton Co.

627.C8 Crawford Co.

627.D14 Dallas Co.

627.D2 Davis Co.

627.D26 Decatur Co.

627.D3 Delaware Co.

627.D4 Des Moines Co.

627.D43 Des Moines River and Valley (General, and Iowa)

Cf. F472.D4, Missouri

627.D5 Dickinson Co.

Including Okoboji Lake, Spirit Lake

Cf. E83.857, Spirit Lake Massacre, 1857

Iowa

627.A-.Z **Regions, counties, etc., A-Z — Continued**

627.D8 Dubuque Co.

627.E5 Emmet Co.

627.F2 Fayette Co.

627.F5 Floyd Co.

627.F78 Franklin Co.

627.F8 Fremont Co.

Including Waubonsie State Park

Geode State Park, *see* F627.H5

627.G7 Greene Co.

627.G75 Grundy Co.

627.G8 Guthrie Co.

627.H2 Hamilton Co.

627.H25 Hancock Co.

627.H3 Hardin Co.

627.H4 Harrison Co.

627.H5 Henry Co.

Including Geode State Park

627.H7 Howard Co.

627.H8 Humboldt Co.

627.I2 Ida Co.

627.I6 Iowa Co.

627.J2 Jackson Co.

627.J3 Jasper Co.

627.J4 Jefferson Co.

627.J6 Johnson Co.

627.J7 Jones Co.

627.K3 Keokuk Co.

627.K6 Kossuth Co.

627.L4 Lee Co.

627.L7 Linn Co.

627.L76 Loess Hills (General and Iowa)

Cf. F472.L88, Missouri

627.L8 Louisa Co.

627.L85 Lucas Co.

627.L9 Lyon Co.

627.M18 Madison Co.

627.M2 Mahaska Co.

627.M3 Marion Co.

627.M4 Marshall Co.

627.M6 Mills Co.

627.M64 Mississippi River and Valley, Iowa

Cf. F350.5+, General

Cf. F597, Upper Mississippi Valley

627.M66 Missouri River and Valley, Iowa

Cf. F598, General

627.M7 Mitchell Co.

627.M75 Monona Co.

627.M8 Monroe Co.

627.M83 Montgomery Co.

627.M9 Muscatine Co.

627.O2 O'Brien Co.

Okoboji Lakes, *see* F627.D5

627.O8 Osceola Co.

627.P2 Page Co.

627.P3 Palo Alto Co.

627.P5 Plymouth Co.

627.P6 Pocahontas Co.

627.P7 Polk Co.

	Iowa
627.A-.Z	**Regions, counties, etc., A-Z — Continued**
627.P8	Pottawattamie Co.
627.P88	Poweshiek Co.
627.R5	Ringgold Co.
627.S2	Sac Co.
627.S4	Scott Co.
627.S5	Shelby Co.
627.S55	Sioux Co.
	Spirit Lake, *see* F627.D5
627.S8	Story Co.
627.T3	Tama Co.
627.T5	Taylor Co.
627.U5	Union Co.
627.V2	Van Buren Co.
627.W2	Wapello Co.
627.W25	Warren Co.
627.W26	Washington Co.
627.W28	Wayne Co.
627.W3	Webster Co.
627.W65	Winnebago Co.
627.W7	Winneshiek Co.
627.W8	Woodbury Co.
627.W86	Worth Co.
627.W9	Wright Co.
629.A-.Z	**Cities, towns, etc., A-Z**
	GALE NOTE *The cutter number(s) listed below have been given only as examples by the Library of Congress*
629.B9	Burlington
629.C3	Cedar Rapids
629.C8	Council Bluffs
629.D2	Davenport
629.D4	Des Moines
629.D8	Dubuque
629.M9	Muscatine
629.S6	Sioux City
	Elements in the population
630.A1	General works
630.A2-.Z	Individual elements
	For a list of racial, ethnic, and religious elements (with cutter numbers), see E184.A+
	North Dakota
631	**Periodicals. Societies. Collections**
633	**Museums. Exhibitions, exhibits**
634	**Gazetteers. Dictionaries. Geographic names**
634.3	**Guidebooks**
635	**Biography (Collective). Genealogy (Collective)**
635.2	**Historiography**
	Historians, *see* E175.5.A+
635.5	**Study and teaching**
636	**General works. Histories**
	Admission as a state, November 2, 1889
	Including by period (Early to 1950) as well as general
	For early to 1889, see F655
	For 1951 and later, see F640
	Cf. D769.85.N9+, World War II, 1939-1945
636.3	**Juvenile works**
	Pamphlets, addresses, essays, etc.
636.5	General
636.6	Anecdotes, legends, pageants, etc.
637	**Historic monuments (General). Illustrative material**

	North Dakota — Continued
638	**Antiquities (Non-Indian)**
	By period
(639)	Early to 1950, *see* F636 , F655
	1951-
640	General
	Biography
641.A2A-.A2Z	Collective
641.A3-.Z	Individual
	GALE NOTE *See note at the head of Table F5 at the end of the text for further instructions on how to subdivide this number*
642.A-.Z	**Regions, counties, etc., A-Z**
642.A15	Counties
642.A16	Mountains
642.A17	Rivers
642.A18	Lakes
642.A19	Islands
642.A2	Adams Co.
642.B3	Barnes Co.
642.B4	Benson Co.
	For Devils Lake, see F642.D5
642.B5	Billings Co.
642.B6	Bottineau Co.
642.B7	Boundaries
	For International boundary, see F597
642.B75	Bowman Co.
642.B85	Burke Co.
642.B9	Burleigh Co.
642.C34	Cass Co.
642.C4	Cavalier Co.
	Coteau du Missouri, *see* F642.M26
642.D5	Devils Lake
642.D6	Dickey Co.
642.D7	Divide Co.
642.D9	Dunn Co.
	Including Killdeer Mountains, Killdeer Mountain Park
642.E2	Eddy Co.
642.E5	Emmons Co.
642.F6	Foster Co.
642.G6	Golden Valley Co.
642.G7	Grand Forks Co.
642.G75	Grant Co.
642.G8	Griggs Co.
642.H4	Hettinger Co.
642.K5	Kidder Co.
	Kildeer Mountains, *see* F642.D9
642.K54	Knife River and Valley
642.L3	La Moure Co.
642.L5	Little Missouri Badlands
	For Theodore Roosevelt National Memorial Park, see F642.T5
642.L6	Logan Co.
642.M2	McHenry Co.
642.M26	McIntosh Co.
	Including Coteau du Missouri
642.M28	McKenzie Co.
	Including Yellowstone River and Valley
	Cf. F737.Y4 , General, and Montana
642.M29	McLean Co.
642.M5	Mercer Co.

	North Dakota
642.A-.Z	**Regions, counties, etc., A-Z — Continued**
642.M6	Missouri River and Valley, N. Dak.
	Cf. F598, General
642.M7	Morton Co.
642.M8	Mountrail Co.
642.N4	Nelson Co.
642.O4	Oliver Co.
642.P4	Pembina Co.
642.P5	Pierce Co.
642.R17	Ramsey Co.
	For Devils Lake, see F642.D5
642.R2	Ransom Co.
642.R3	Red River of the North and Valley, N. Dak.
	Cf. F612.R27, Minnesota
	Cf. F1064.R3, Manitoba
642.R4	Renville Co.
642.R5	Richland Co.
642.R6	Rolette Co.
642.S2	Sargent Co.
642.S5	Sheridan Co.
642.S55	Sioux Co.
642.S6	Slope Co.
642.S68	Souris River and Valley
	Cf. F1064.S6, Manitoba
	Cf. F1074.S67, General, and Saskatchewan
642.S7	Stark Co.
642.S75	Steele Co.
642.S8	Stutsman Co.
642.T5	Theodore Roosevelt National Memorial Park
642.T6	Towner Co.
642.T7	Traill Co.
642.W3	Walsh Co.
642.W35	Ward Co.
642.W45	Wells Co.
642.W6	Williams Co.
644.A-.Z	**Cities, towns, etc., A-Z**
	GALE NOTE *The cutter number(s) listed below have been given only as examples by the Library of Congress*
644.B6	Bismarck
644.F2	Fargo
644.G8	Grand Forks
	Elements in the population
645.A1	General works
645.A2-.Z	Individual elements
	For a list of racial, ethnic, and religious elements (with cutter numbers), see E184.A+
	South Dakota
	Including works covering both North and South Dakota
646	**Periodicals. Societies. Collections**
648	**Museums. Exhibitions, exhibits**
649	**Gazetteers. Dictionaries. Geographic names**
649.3	**Guidebooks**
650	**Biography (Collective). Genealogy (Collective)**
650.2	**Historiography**
	Historians, *see* E175.5.A+
650.5	**Study and teaching**
651	**General works. Histories**
651.3	**Juvenile works**
	Pamphlets, addresses, essays, etc.
651.5	General

South Dakota

Pamphlets, addresses, essays, etc. — Continued

651.6 Anecdotes, legends, pageants, etc.

651.8 **Geography**

652 **Historic monuments (General). Illustrative material**

653 **Antiquities (Non-Indian)**

By period

655 Early to 1889

Including the Dakota region before 1861, Dakota Territory, 1861-1889

Cf. E83.863, Indian wars, 1863-1865

656 1889-1950

Including admission as a state, November 2, 1889

Including biography: Peter Norbeck

Cf. D570.85.S7+, World War I, 1914-1918

Cf. D769.85.S7+, World War II, 1939-1945

Cf. E83.89, Dakota Indian War, 1890-1891

1951-

656.2 General works

Biography

656.3 Collective

656.4.A-.4.Z Individual, A-Z

GALE NOTE *See note at the head of Table F5 at the end of the text for further instructions on how to subdivide this number*

657.A-.Z **Regions, counties, etc., A-Z**

657.A15 Counties

657.A16 Mountains

657.A17 Rivers

657.A18 Lakes

657.A19 Islands

657.A6 Armstrong Co.

657.A8 Aurora Co.

657.B24 Badlands

657.B3 Beadle Co.

657.B4 Bennett Co.

657.B5 Big Sioux River and Valley (General, and S. Dak.)

Cf. F627.B5, Iowa

657.B6 Black Hills

For Custer State Park, see F657.C92

For Mount Rushmore National Memorial, see F657.R8

For Wind Cave National Park, see F657.W7

657.B65 Bon Homme Co.

657.B7 Boundaries

657.B75 Brookings Co.

657.B76 Brown Co.

657.B77 Brule Co.

657.B8 Buffalo Co.

657.B9 Butte Co.

657.C25 Campbell Co.

657.C4 Charles Mix Co.

657.C55 Clark Co.

657.C6 Clay Co.

657.C8 Codington Co.

657.C83 Corson Co.

657.C9 Custer Co.

For Wind Cave, see F657.W7

657.C92 Custer State Park

657.D25 Davison Co.

657.D3 Day Co.

657.D4 Deuel Co.

657.D45 Dewey Co.

	South Dakota
657.A-.Z	**Regions, counties, etc., A-Z — Continued**
657.D7	Douglas Co.
657.E2	Edmunds Co.
657.F3	Fall River Co.
657.F4	Faulk Co.
	Fort Sisseton State Park, *see* F657.R6
657.G7	Grant Co.
657.G8	Gregory Co.
657.H2	Haakon Co.
657.H3	Hamlin Co.
657.H35	Hand Co.
657.H4	Hanson Co.
657.H45	Harding Co.
657.H8	Hughes Co.
657.H85	Hutchinson Co.
657.H9	Hyde Co.
657.J2	Jackson Co.
657.J4	Jerauld Co.
657.J6	Jones Co.
657.K5	Kingsbury Co.
657.L3	Lake Co.
657.L4	Lawrence Co.
657.L6	Lincoln Co.
657.L9	Lyman Co.
657.M15	McCook Co.
657.M2	McPherson Co.
657.M3	Marshall Co.
657.M4	Meade Co.
	Including Bear Butte
657.M45	Mellette Co.
657.M55	Miner Co.
657.M6	Minnehaha Co.
657.M7	Missouri River and Valley, S. Dak.
	Cf. F598, General
657.M8	Moody Co.
657.P4	Pennington Co.
	For Mount Rushmore National Memorial, see F657.R8
657.P5	Perkins Co.
657.P8	Potter Co.
657.R6	Roberts Co.
	Including Fort Sisseton State Park
657.R8	Mount Rushmore National Memorial
657.S3	Sanborn Co.
657.S5	Shannon Co.
657.S7	Spink Co.
657.S73	Split Rock Creek and Valley (General and South Dakota)
	Cf. F612.S64, Minnesota
657.S8	Stanley Co.
657.S9	Sully Co.
657.T6	Todd Co.
657.T7	Tripp Co.
657.T8	Turner Co.
657.U5	Union Co.
657.W2	Walworth Co.
657.W3	Washabaugh Co.
657.W4	Washington Co.
	In 1944, combined with Shannon County
657.W7	Wind Cave. Wind Cave National Park
657.Y2	Yankton Co.

	South Dakota
657.A-.Z	**Regions, counties, etc., A-Z — Continued**
657.Z5	Ziebach Co.
659.A-.Z	**Cities, towns, etc., A-Z**
	GALE NOTE *The cutter number(s) listed below have been given only as examples by the Library of Congress*
659.A14	Aberdeen
659.P6	Pierre
659.R2	Rapid City
659.S6	Sioux Falls
	Elements in the population
660.A1	General works
660.A2-.Z	Individual elements
	For a list of racial, ethnic, and religious elements (with cutter numbers), see E184.A+
	Nebraska
661	**Periodicals. Societies. Collections**
663	**Museums. Exhibitions, exhibits**
664	**Gazetteers. Dictionaries. Geographic names**
664.3	**Guidebooks**
665	**Biography (Collective). Genealogy (Collective)**
665.2	**Historiography**
	Historians, *see* E175.5.A+
665.5	**Study and teaching**
666	**General works. Histories**
	Including admission as a state, March 1, 1867
	Including by period (Early to 1950) as well as general
	For 1951 and later, see F670
	Including biography: Jules Ami Sandoz, Thomas Clark White
	Cf. D570.85.N19+, World War I, 1914-1918
	Cf. D769.85.N19+, World War II, 1939-1945
	Cf. E433, Kansas-Nebraska Bill, 1854
666.3	**Juvenile works**
	Pamphlets, addresses, essays, etc.
666.5	General
666.6	Anecdotes, legends, pageants, etc.
667	**Historic monuments (General). Illustrative material**
668	**Antiquities (Non-Indian)**
	By period
	Early to 1950, *see* F666
	1951-
670	General works
	Biography
670.3	Collective
670.4	Individual, A-Z
672.A-.Z	**Regions, counties, etc., A-Z**
672.A15	Counties
672.A16	Mountains
672.A17	Rivers
672.A18	Lakes
672.A19	Islands
672.A2	Adams Co.
	Agate Fossil Beds National Monument, *see* F672.S6
672.A6	Antelope Co.
672.A7	Arthur Co.
672.B3	Banner Co.
672.B5	Blaine Co.
672.B6	Boone Co.
672.B7	Boundaries
672.B75	Box Butte Co.
672.B77	Boyd Co.

	Nebraska	
672.A-.Z	**Regions, counties, etc., A-Z — Continued**	
672.B8	Brown Co.	
672.B85	Buffalo Co.	
672.B87	Burt Co.	
672.B9	Butler Co.	
672.C3	Cass Co.	
672.C35	Cedar Co.	
672.C4	Chase Co.	
672.C45	Cherry Co.	
672.C5	Cheyenne Co.	
	Chimney Rock National Historic Site, *see* F672.M7	
672.C6	Clay Co.	
672.C7	Colfax Co.	
672.C8	Cuming Co.	
672.C9	Custer Co.	
672.D2	Dakota Co.	
672.D3	Dawes Co.	
672.D35	Dawson Co.	
672.D4	Deuel Co.	
672.D58	Dixon Co.	
672.D6	Dodge Co.	
672.D7	Douglas Co.	
672.D8	Dundy Co.	
672.F48	Fillmore Co.	
672.F7	Franklin Co.	
672.F8	Frontier Co.	
672.F9	Furnas Co.	
672.G13	Gage Co.	
672.G2	Garden Co.	
672.G3	Garfield Co.	
672.G5	Gosper Co.	
672.G6	Grant Co.	
672.G7	Greeley Co.	
672.H2	Hall Co.	
672.H25	Hamilton Co.	
672.H3	Harlan Co.	
672.H4	Hayes Co.	
672.H5	Hitchcock Co.	
672.H6	Holt Co.	
672.H7	Hooker Co.	
672.H8	Howard Co.	
672.J4	Jefferson Co.	
672.J6	Johnson Co.	
672.K4	Kearney Co.	
672.K45	Keith Co.	
672.K5	Keya Paha Co.	
672.K6	Kimball Co.	
672.K7	Knox Co.	
672.L2	Lancaster Co.	
672.L4	Lincoln Co.	
672.L6	Logan Co.	
672.L7	Loup Co.	
672.L8	Loup River and Valley	
672.M2	McPherson Co.	
672.M3	Madison Co.	
672.M4	Merrick Co.	
672.M6	Missouri River and Valley, Nebr.	
	Cf. F598, General	

	Nebraska
672.A-.Z	**Regions, counties, etc., A-Z — Continued**
672.M7	Morrill Co.
	Including Chimney Rock National Historic Site
672.N3	Nance Co.
672.N4	Nemaha Co.
672.N56	Niobrara River and Valley (General, and Nebraska)
	Cf. F767.N52, Wyoming
672.N8	North Platte River and Valley (General, and Nebr.)
	Cf. F767.N8, Wyoming
672.N9	Nuckolls Co.
672.O8	Otoe Co.
672.P3	Pawnee Co.
672.P4	Perkins Co.
672.P5	Phelps Co.
672.P54	Pierce Co.
672.P58	Platte Co.
672.P6	Platte River and Valley
672.P7	Polk Co.
672.R4	Red Willow Co.
672.R5	Richardson Co.
672.R6	Rock Co.
672.S15	Saline Co.
672.S17	Sandhills
672.S2	Sarpy Co.
672.S24	Saunders Co.
672.S3	Scotts Bluff Co.
672.S5	Seward Co.
672.S53	Sheridan Co.
672.S54	Sherman Co.
672.S6	Sioux Co.
	Including Agate Fossil Beds National Monument
672.S7	South Platte River and Valley (General, and Nebr.)
	Cf. F782.S7, Colorado
672.S8	Stanton Co.
672.T3	Thayer Co.
672.T4	Thomas Co.
672.T5	Thurston Co.
672.V3	Valley Co.
672.W3	Washington Co.
672.W35	Wayne Co.
672.W4	Webster Co.
672.W5	Wheeler Co.
672.Y62	York Co.
674.A-.Z	**Cities, towns, etc., A-Z**
	GALE NOTE *The cutter number(s) listed below have been given only as examples by the Library of Congress*
674.B4	Bellevue
674.G7	Grand Island
674.H3	Hastings
674.L7	Lincoln
674.O5	Omaha
	Subarrange by Table F2 at the end of the text
	Elements in the population
675.A1	General works
675.A2-.Z	Individual elements
	For a list of racial, ethnic, and religious elements (with cutter numbers), see E184.A+
	Kansas
676	**Periodicals. Societies. Collections**
678	**Museums. Exhibitions, exhibits**

Kansas — Continued

679 **Gazetteers. Dictionaries. Geographic names**
679.3 **Guidebooks**
680 **Biography (Collective). Genealogy (Collective)**
680.2 **Historiography**
Historians, *see* E175.5.A+
680.5 **Study and teaching**
681 **General works. Histories**
681.3 **Juvenile works**
Pamphlets, addresses, essays, etc.
681.5 General
681.6 Anecdotes, legends, pageants, etc.
682 **Historic monuments (General). Illustrative material**
683 **Antiquities (Non-Indian)**
By period
685 Early to 1861
Including struggle between proslavery and anti-slavery parties; New England Emigrant Aid Company; armed bands from Missouri; Battle of Osawatomie, 1856; Lecompton Constitution
Including biography: James Henry Lane, Charles Robinson, etc.
Cf. E433, Kansas-Nebraska Bill, 1854
Cf. F799, Quivira
686 1861-1950
Including admission as a state, January 29, 1861
Including biography: Alfred Mossman Landon, etc.
Cf. D570.85.K2+, World War I, 1914-1918
Cf. D769.85.K2+, World War II, 1939-1945
Cf. E508.1+, Civil War, 1861-1865 (General)
Cf. E470.9, Campaigns and battles of the Civil War, 1861-1865
Cf. E474.97, Quantrill's Raid, 1863
Cf. E726.K2, War of 1898 (Spanish-American War)
1951-
686.2 General works
Biography
686.3 Collective
686.4.A-.4.Z Individual, A-Z
GALE NOTE *See note at the head of Table F5 at the end of the text for further instructions on how to subdivide this number*
687.A-.Z **Regions, counties, etc., A-Z**
687.A15 Counties
687.A16 Mountains
687.A17 Rivers
687.A18 Lakes
687.A19 Islands
687.A4 Allen Co.
687.A5 Anderson Co.
687.A7 Arkansas River and Valley, Kans.
Cf. F417.A7, General, and Arkansas
687.A8 Atchison Co.
687.B18 Barber Co.
687.B2 Barton Co.
687.B6 Big Blue River. Blue Valley
687.B7 Boundaries
687.B73 Bourbon Co.
687.B8 Brown Co.
687.B9 Butler Co.
Including El Dorado Lake
Cedar Point Lake, *see* F687.C35
687.C35 Chase Co.
Including Cedar Point Lake
687.C36 Chautauqua Co.

Kansas

687.A-.Z **Regions, counties, etc., A-Z — Continued**

687.C38 Cherokee Co.

687.C5 Cheyenne Co.

687.C52 Cimarron River and Valley

Class here works limited to the part of the Cimarron River and Valley located in Kansas

For works limited to the part of the Cimarron River and Valley located in Colorado, see F782.C57

For works limited to the part of the Cimarron River and Valley located in New Mexico, see F802.C58

For general works on the Cimarron River and Valley, as well as works limited to the part located in Oklahoma, see F702.C53

687.C53 Clark Co.

687.C55 Clay Co.

Clinton Lake, *see* F687.W4

687.C6 Cloud Co.

687.C7 Coffey Co.

687.C75 Comanche Co.

687.C8 Cowley Co.

687.C9 Crawford Co.

Davis Co., *see* F687.G3

687.D4 Decatur Co.

687.D5 Dickinson Co.

687.D6 Doniphan Co.

687.D7 Douglas Co.

687.E2 Edwards Co.

El Dorado Lake, *see* F687.B9

687.E28 Elk Co.

687.E3 Ellis Co.

687.E4 Ellsworth Co.

687.F5 Finney Co.

687.F55 Flint Hills (General, and Kansas)

Cf. F702.F55 , Oklahoma

687.F6 Ford Co.

687.F8 Franklin Co.

687.G3 Geary Co.

Formerly Davis County

687.G72 Gove Co.

687.G74 Graham Co.

687.G75 Grant Co.

687.G78 Gray Co.

687.G8 Greeley Co.

687.G85 Greenwood Co.

687.H3 Hamilton Co.

687.H4 Harper Co.

687.H45 Harvey Co.

687.H5 Haskell Co.

687.H8 Hodgeman Co.

687.J2 Jackson Co.

687.J3 Jefferson Co.

687.J4 Jewell Co.

687.J6 Johnson Co.

687.K3 Kansas River and Valley

687.K4 Kearny Co.

687.K53 Kingman Co.

687.K6 Kiowa Co.

687.L2 Labette Co.

687.L3 Lane Co.

687.L4 Leavenworth Co.

687.L7 Lincoln Co.

	Kansas	
687.A-.Z	**Regions, counties, etc., A-Z — Continued**	
687.L75	Linn Co.	
687.L8	Logan Co.	
687.L9	Lyon Co.	
687.M2	McPherson Co.	
687.M3	Marion Co.	
	For Cedar Point Lake, see F687.C35	
687.M35	Marshall Co.	
687.M48	Meade Co.	
687.M55	Miami Co.	
687.M6	Missouri River and Valley, Kans.	
	Cf. F598, General	
687.M65	Mitchell Co.	
687.M7	Montgomery Co.	
687.M75	Morris Co.	
687.M8	Morton Co.	
687.N3	Nemaha Co.	
687.N4	Neosho Co.	
687.N43	Ness Co.	
687.N8	Norton Co.	
687.O6	Osage Co.	
687.O7	Osborne Co.	
687.O8	Ottawa Co.	
687.P3	Pawnee Co.	
687.P5	Phillips Co.	
687.P8	Pottawatomie Co.	
687.P9	Pratt Co.	
687.R25	Rawlins Co.	
687.R3	Reno Co.	
687.R4	Republic Co.	
687.R45	Rice Co.	
687.R5	Riley Co.	
687.R7	Rooks Co.	
687.R8	Rush Co.	
687.R9	Russell Co.	
687.S16	Saline Co.	
687.S3	Scott Co.	
687.S4	Sedgwick Co.	
687.S45	Seward Co.	
687.S5	Shawnee Co.	
687.S55	Sheridan Co.	
687.S6	Sherman Co.	
687.S8	Smith Co.	
687.S84	Smoky Hill River and Valley (General, and Kansas)	
	Cf. F782.S53, Colorado	
687.S85	Solomon River and Valley	
687.S86	Stafford Co.	
687.S87	Stanton Co.	
687.S88	Stevens Co.	
687.S9	Sumner Co.	
687.T34	Tallgrass Prairie National Preserve	
687.T4	Thomas Co.	
687.T7	Trego Co.	
687.W2	Wabaunsee River and Valley	
687.W4	Wakarusa River and Valley	
	Including Clinton Lake	
687.W43	Wallace Co.	
687.W45	Washington Co.	
687.W6	Wichita Co.	

Kansas

687.A-.Z **Regions, counties, etc., A-Z — Continued**
687.W7 Wilson Co.
687.W73 Wilson Lake
687.W8 Woodson Co.
687.W97 Wyandotte Co.
689.A-.Z **Cities, towns, etc., A-Z**
GALE NOTE *The cutter number(s) listed below have been given only as examples by the Library of Congress*
689.H9 Hutchinson
689.K2 Kansas City
689.L4 Lawrence
689.L5 Leavenworth
689.T6 Topeka
689.W6 Wichita
Elements in the population
690.A1 General works
690.A2-.Z Individual elements
For a list of racial, ethnic, and religious elements (with cutter numbers), see E184.A+

Oklahoma

691 **Periodicals. Societies. Collections**
691.5 **Museums. Exhibitions, exhibits**
692 **Gazetteers. Dictionaries. Geographic names**
692.3 **Guidebooks**
693 **Biography (Collective). Genealogy (Collective)**
693.2 **Historiography**
Historians, *see* E175.5.A+
693.5 **Study and teaching**
694 **General works. Histories**
694.3 **Juvenile works**
Pamphlets, addresses, essays, etc.
694.5 General
694.6 Anecdotes, legends, pageants, etc.
694.8 **Geography**
695 **Historic monuments (General). Illustrative material**
696 **Antiquities (Non-Indian)**
By period
697 Early to 1890
Including the "Indian country," that part of the Louisiana purchase west of Arkansas, Missouri, and the Missouri River, Indian Territory before division in 1890
Including biography: Davis Lewis Payne
1890-1907
698 Indian Territory
699 Oklahoma Territory
700 1907-1950
Including admission as a state, November 16, 1907
Including biography: William Henry Murray
Cf. D570.85.O5+, World War I, 1914-1918
Cf. D769.85.O5+, World War II, 1939-1945
701 1951-
702.A-.Z **Regions, counties, etc., A-Z**
702.A15 Counties
702.A16 Mountains
702.A17 Rivers
702.A18 Lakes
702.A19 Islands
702.A3 Adair Co.
702.A4 Alfalfa Co.
702.A7 Arkansas River and Valley, Okla.
Cf. F417.A7, General, and Arkansas

Oklahoma

702.A-.Z **Regions, counties, etc., A-Z — Continued**

702.A8 Atoka Co.

702.B4 Beaver Co.

702.B45 Beckham Co.

702.B5 Blaine Co.

702.B7 Boundaries

Cf. F392.B7, Texas boundary

Cf. F782.B7, Colorado boundary

702.B8 Bryan Co.

702.C15 Caddo Co.

702.C17 Camp Creek and Valley

702.C18 Canadian Co.

702.C2 Canadian River and Valley (General, and Okla.)

Cf. F392.C27, Texas

Cf. F802.C2, New Mexico

702.C3 Carter Co.

702.C4 Cherokee Co.

702.C42 Cherokee Outlet

Chickasaw National Recreation Area, *see* F702.M84

702.C45 Choctaw Co.

702.C5 Cimarron Co.

702.C53 Cimarron River and Valley

Class here general works on the Cimarron River and Valley, as well as works limited to the part located in Oklahoma

For works limited to the part of the Cimarron River and Valley located in Kansas, see F687.C52

For works limited to the part of the Cimarron River and Valley located in Colorado, see F782.C57

For works limited to the part of the Cimarron River and Valley located in New Mexico, see F802.C58

702.C6 Cleveland Co.

702.C65 Coal Co.

702.C7 Comanche Co.

702.C75 Cotton Co.

702.C8 Craig Co.

702.C85 Creek Co.

702.C9 Custer Co.

702.D4 Delaware Co.

702.D5 Dewey Co.

702.E4 Ellis Co.

702.F55 Flint Hills

Cf. F687.F55, General, and Kansas

702.G25 Garfield Co.

702.G3 Garvin Co.

702.G7 Grady Co.

702.G75 Grant Co.

702.G8 Greer Co.

702.H3 Harmon Co.

702.H35 Harper Co.

702.H4 Haskell Co.

702.H9 Hughes Co.

702.J3 Jackson Co.

702.J4 Jefferson Co.

702.J6 Johnston Co.

702.K23 Kay Co.

702.K4 Kingfisher Co.

702.K5 Kiowa Co.

702.L3 Latimer Co.

702.L4 Le Flore Co.

Oklahoma

702.A-.Z **Regions, counties, etc., A-Z — Continued**

702.L5 Lincoln Co.

Including Robinson Creek and Valley, etc.

702.L55 Little River and Valley (General, and Oklahoma)

Cf. F417.L64, Arkansas

702.L6 Logan Co.

702.L7 Love Co.

702.M2 McClain Co.

702.M3 McCurtain Co.

702.M35 McIntosh Co.

702.M4 Major Co.

702.M5 Marshall Co.

702.M55 Mayes Co.

702.M84 Murray Co.

Including Chickasaw National Recreation Area

For Platt National Park, see F702.P7

702.M9 Muskogee Co.

702.N6 No Man's Land. Oklahoma Panhandle

702.N8 Noble Co.

702.N9 Nowata Co.

702.O5 Okfuskee Co.

702.O55 Oklahoma Co.

Oklahoma Panhandle, *see* F702.N6

702.O6 Okmulgee Co.

702.O7 Osage Co.

Including Salt Creek and Valley

702.O8 Ottawa Co.

702.O9 Ouachita Mountains (General, and Oklahoma)

Cf. F417.O77, Arkansas

Panhandle, *see* F702.N6

702.P35 Pawnee Co.

For Camp Creek and Valley, see F702.C17

702.P4 Payne Co.

For Camp Creek and Valley, see F702.C17

702.P6 Pittsburg Co.

702.P7 Platt National Park

702.P74 Pontotoc Co.

702.P75 Pottawatomie Co.

702.P9 Pushmataha Co.

702.R3 Red River and Valley, Okla.

Cf. F377.R3, General, and Louisiana

Robinson Creek and Valley, *see* F702.L5

702.R6 Roger Mills Co.

702.R7 Rogers Co.

Salt Creek and Valley, *see* F702.O7

702.S35 Seminole Co.

702.S4 Sequoyah Co.

702.S8 Stephens Co.

702.T4 Texas Co.

702.T5 Tillman Co.

702.T8 Tulsa Co.

702.W2 Wagoner Co.

702.W3 Washington Co.

702.W35 Washita Co.

702.W36 Washita River and Valley

Cf. F392.W33, General, and Texas

702.W55 Wichita Mountains and region

702.W7 Woods Co.

702.W8 Woodward Co.

Oklahoma — Continued

704.A-.Z **Cities, towns, etc., A-Z**

GALE NOTE *The cutter number(s) listed below have been given only as examples by the Library of Congress*

704.E6 Enid

704.G9 Guthrie

704.M9 Muskogee

704.N6 Norman

704.O41 Oklahoma City

704.T92 Tulsa

Elements in the population

705.A1 General works

705.A2-.Z Individual elements

For a list of racial, ethnic, and religious elements (with cutter numbers), see E184.A+

Rocky Mountains. Rocky Mountains in the United States

Cf. F782.26, Rocky Mountain region of Colorado, etc.

Cf. F1090, Rocky Mountain region of Canada

721 **General works**

722 **Yellowstone National Park**

Including boundaries

Cf. F737.Y4, Yellowstone River and Valley

Montana

726 **Periodicals. Societies. Collections**

728 **Museums. Exhibitions, exhibits**

729 **Gazetteers. Dictionaries. Geographic names**

729.3 **Guidebooks**

730 **Biography (Collective). Genealogy (Collective)**

730.2 **Historiography**

Historians, *see* E175.5.A+

730.5 **Study and teaching**

731 **General works. Histories**

Including admission as a state, November 2, 1889

Including by period (Early to 1950) as well as general

For 1951 and later, see F735

Including biography: Granville Stuart

Cf. D570.85.M9+, World War I, 1914-1918

Cf. D769.85.M9+, World War II, 1939-1945

Cf. E83.876, Dakota Indian War, 1876

Cf. E83.877, Nez Percé War, 1877

731.3 **Juvenile works**

Pamphlets, addresses, essays, etc.

731.5 General

731.6 Anecdotes, legends, pageants, etc.

731.8 **Geography**

732 **Historic monuments (General). Illustrative material**

733 **Antiquities (Non-Indian)**

By period

(734) Early to 1950, *see* F731

735 1951-

Biography

735.2.A2A-.2.A2Z Collective

735.2.A3-.2.Z Individual, A-Z

GALE NOTE *See note at the head of Table F5 at the end of the text for further instructions on how to subdivide this number*

737.A-.Z **Regions, counties, etc., A-Z**

737.A15 Counties

737.A16 Mountains

737.A17 Rivers

737.A18 Lakes

737.A19 Islands

Montana

737.A-.Z **Regions, counties, etc., A-Z — Continued**

737.A3 Absaroka National Forest
737.B35 Beartooth Mountains (General and Montana)
737.B38 Beaverhead Co.
737.B48 Big Hole River and Valley
737.B49 Big Horn Canyon National Recreation Area
737.B5 Big Horn Co.
737.B53 Big Horn Mountains
Cf. F767.B37, General, and Wyoming
Bird-Truax Trail, *see* F752.B64
737.B6 Bitter Root River and Valley
737.B62 Blackfoot River and Valley
737.B63 Blaine Co.
737.B66 Bob Marshall Wilderness
737.B7 Boundaries
For International boundary, see F597
For Yellowstone National Park boundary, see F722
Cf. F752.B7, Idaho boundary
737.B8 Broadwater Co.
737.C14 Cabinet National Forest
Camas Prairie, *see* F737.M6
737.C25 Carbon Co.
737.C3 Carter Co.
737.C33 Cascade Co.
737.C5 Chouteau Co.
737.C55 Clark Fork and Valley (General, and Montana)
Cf. F752.C57, Idaho
737.C9 Custer Co.
737.D3 Daniels Co.
737.D4 Dawson Co.
737.D5 Deer Lodge Co.
737.F2 Fallon Co.
737.F3 Fergus Co.
737.F58 Flathead Co.
Including Tobacco Plains
737.F6 Flathead Lake and Valley
737.F66 Flying D Ranch
737.G18 Gallatin Co.
737.G2 Gallatin Valley. East and West Gallatin Rivers
737.G3 Garfield Co.
737.G45 Glacier Co.
737.G5 Glacier National Park
Including Lake McDonald, Mount Reynolds
737.G6 Golden Valley Co.
737.G7 Granite Co.
Grant-Kohrs Ranch National Historic Site, *see* F737.P88
737.H55 Hi-Line Region
737.H6 Hill Co.
737.J4 Jefferson Co.
For Lewis and Clark Cavern State Park, see F737.L65
Jocko or Flathead Indian Reservation, *see* E99.S2
737.J8 Judith Basin Co.
737.J83 Judith River and Valley
737.L3 Lake Co.
Including St. Ignatius Mission
For Flathead Lake, see F737.F6
737.L65 Lewis and Clark Cavern State Park
Including Morrison Cave
737.L67 Lewis and Clark Co.

	Montana
737.A-.Z	**Regions, counties, etc., A-Z — Continued**
737.L7	Liberty Co.
737.L8	Lincoln Co.
737.M13	McCone Co.
737.M2	Madison Co.
737.M24	Madison River and Valley, Montana
	Cf. F767.M34 , General, and Wyoming
737.M4	Meagher Co.
737.M48	Milk River and Valley
	Cf. F1079.M54, General and Alberta
737.M5	Mineral Co.
737.M6	Missoula Co.
	Including Camas Prairie
737.M7	Missouri River and Valley, Mont.
	Cf. F598, General
	Morrison Cave, *see* F737.L65
737.M9	Musselshell Co.
737.P23	Park Co.
737.P4	Petroleum Co.
737.P5	Phillips Co.
737.P6	Pondera Co.
737.P8	Powder River Co.
737.P88	Powell Co.
	Including Grant-Kohrs Ranch National Historic Site
737.P9	Prairie Co.
737.P93	Prickly Pear Creek and Valley
737.R3	Ravalli Co.
	Reynolds, Mount, *see* F737.G5
737.R5	Richland Co.
737.R8	Rocky Mountain region, Mont.
	Including Marias Pass
	Cf. F721, General
737.R9	Roosevelt Co.
737.R95	Rosebud Co.
737.R96	Rosebud Creek and Valley
737.S3	Sanders Co.
737.S4	Sheridan Co.
737.S5	Silver Bow Co.
737.S8	Stillwater Co.
737.S84	Sun River and Valley
737.S9	Sweet Grass Co.
	Including West Boulder River and Valley
	Sweet Grass Hills, *see* F737.T6
737.T4	Teton Co.
737.T55	Tongue River and Valley
	Cf. F767.T65, Wyoming
737.T6	Toole Co.
	Including Sweet Grass Hills
737.T7	Treasure Co.
737.V3	Valley Co.
737.W4	Wheatland Co.
737.W5	Wibaux Co.
737.Y3	Yellowstone Co.
	Yellowstone National Park, *see* F722
737.Y4	Yellowstone River and Valley (General, and Montana)
	Including Fort Custer
	Cf. F642.M28, North Dakota
	Cf. F767.Y44, Wyoming

Montana — Continued

739.A-.Z **Cities, towns, etc., A-Z**

GALE NOTE *The cutter number(s) listed below have been given only as examples by the Library of Congress*

739.B5 Billings
739.B8 Butte
739.G7 Great Falls
739.H4 Helena
739.M7 Missoula

Elements in the population

740.A1 General works
740.A2-.Z Individual elements

For a list of racial, ethnic, and religious elements (with cutter numbers), see E184.A+

Idaho

741 **Periodicals. Societies. Collections**
743 **Museums. Exhibitions, exhibits**
744 **Gazetteers. Dictionaries. Geographic names**
744.3 **Guidebooks**
745 **Biography (Collective). Genealogy (Collective)**
745.2 **Historiography**

Historians, *see* E175.5.A+

745.5 **Study and teaching**
746 **General works. Histories**

Including admission as a state, July 3, 1890
Including biography: Frank Steunenberg
Including by period (Early to 1950) as well as general
For 1951 and later, see F750+
Cf. D769.85.I2+, World War II, 1939-1945
Cf. E83.877, Nez Percé War, 1877

746.3 **Juvenile works**

Pamphlets, addresses, essays, etc.

746.5 General
746.6 Anecdotes, legends, pageants, etc.
747 **Historic monuments (General). Illustrative material**
748 **Antiquities (Non-Indian)**

By period

Early to 1950, *see* F746

1951-

750 General works

Biography

750.2 Collective
750.22.A-.22.Z Individual, A-Z

GALE NOTE *See note at the head of Table F5 at the end of the text for further instructions on how to subdivide this number*

752.A-.Z **Regions, counties, etc., A-Z**
752.A15 Counties
752.A16 Mountains
752.A17 Rivers
752.A18 Lakes
752.A19 Islands
752.A3 Ada Co.
752.A4 Adams Co.
752.A55 Albeni Falls Dam and Region
752.A6 Alturas Co. (1864-1895)
752.B2 Bannock Co.
752.B3 Bear Lake Co.
752.B4 Benewah Co.
752.B55 Big Wood River and Valley
752.B6 Bingham Co.
752.B63 Birch Creek Valley

Idaho

752.A-.Z **Regions, counties, etc., A-Z — Continued**

752.B64 Bird-Truax Trail

752.B65 Blaine Co.

Including Sawtooth Mountains and Valley

752.B67 Boise Co.

752.B673 Boise River and Valley

752.B677 Bonner Co.

Including Priest Lake and Region

752.B68 Bonneville Co.

752.B7 Boundaries

For International boundary, see F597, F854, F880

For Yellowstone National Park boundary, see F722

Cf. F897.B7, Washington boundary

752.B73 Boundary Co.

Bruneau River and Valley, *see* F752.O97

752.B9 Butte Co.

752.C17 Camas Co.

752.C2 Canyon Co.

752.C3 Caribou Co.

Including Gem Valley

752.C35 Cassia Co.

Including City of Rocks National Reserve

City of Rocks National Reserve, *see* F752.C35

752.C55 Clark Co.

752.C57 Clark Fork and Valley

Cf. F737.C55, General, and Montana

752.C6 Clearwater Co.

752.C62 Clearwater River and Valley

Coeur d'Alene mining district, *see* F752.S5

752.C65 Coeur d'Alene River and Valley

752.C7 Craters of the Moon National Monument

752.C9 Custer Co.

752.E4 Elmore Co.

752.F68 Frank Church-River of No Return Wilderness

752.F7 Franklin Co.

752.F8 Fremont Co.

752.G4 Gem Co.

Gem Valley, *see* F752.C3

Gilmore Ranch, *see* F752.I2

752.G6 Gooding Co.

Hagerman Fossil Beds National Monument, *see* F752.T8

752.H44 Hells Canyon National Recreation Area

Cf. F882.H44, General and Oregon

752.I2 Idaho Co.

Including Gilmore Ranch, Joseph Plains, Lochea River and Valley

752.I7 Island Park region

752.J4 Jefferson Co.

752.J5 Jerome Co.

752.K8 Kootenai Co.

For Coeur d'Alene mining district, see F752.S5

752.L3 Latah Co.

752.L4 Lemhi Co.

752.L45 Lewis Co.

752.L5 Lincoln Co.

Lochea River and Valley, *see* F752.I2

752.M3 Madison Co.

Mann Creek and Valley, *see* F752.W3

752.M5 Minidoka Co.

752.N57 Nez Perce Co.

Idaho

752.A-.Z **Regions, counties, etc., A-Z — Continued**

752.O5 Oneida Co.

752.O97 Owyhee Co. Owyhee Mountains region

Including Bruneau River and Valley

752.O98 Owyhee River and Valley

Cf. F882.O98, General, and Oregon

752.P23 Pahsimeroi River and Valley

752.P25 Palouse River and Valley (General, and Idaho)

Cf. F897.P24, Washington

752.P3 Payette Co.

752.P33 Payette River and Valley

752.P6 Power Co.

Priest Lake and Region, *see* F752.B677

752.S28 Saint Maries River and Valley

752.S35 Salmon River and Valley

752.S37 Salt Valley

Cf. F767.S37, General, and Wyoming

Sawtooth Mountains and Valley, *see* F752.B65

752.S5 Shoshone Co.

Including Coeur d'Alene mining district

752.S7 Snake River and Valley (General, and Idaho)

Cf. F882.S6, Oregon

Cf. F897.S6, Washington

752.S74 St. Joe River and Valley

752.T4 Teton Co.

752.T5 Teton River and Valley

752.T8 Twin Falls Co.

Including Hagerman Fossil Beds National Monument

752.V3 Valley Co.

752.W27 Wasatch Range

Class here works limited to the part of the Wasatch Range located in Idaho

For general works on the Wasatch Range, as well as works limited to the part located in Utah, see F832.W22

752.W3 Washington Co.

Including Mann Creek and Valley

Yellowstone National Park, *see* F722

754.A-.Z **Cities, towns, etc., A-Z**

GALE NOTE *The cutter number(s) listed below have been given only as examples by the Library of Congress*

754.B65 Boise

754.I2 Idaho Falls

754.L6 Lewiston

754.P7 Pocatello

754.T97 Twin Falls

Elements in the population

755.A1 General works

755.A2-.Z Individual elements

For a list of racial, ethnic, and religious elements (with cutter numbers), see E184.A+

Wyoming

756 **Periodicals. Societies. Collections**

758 **Museums. Exhibitions, exhibits**

759 **Gazetteers. Dictionaries. Geographic names**

759.3 **Guidebooks**

760 **Biography (Collective). Genealogy (Collective)**

760.2 **Historiography**

Historians, *see* E175.5.A+

760.5 **Study and teaching**

761 **General works. Histories**

Including admission as a state, July 10, 1890

	Wyoming
761	**General works. Histories — Continued**
	Including by period (Early to 1950) as well as general
	For 1951 and later, see F765
	Cf. D769.85.W8+, World War II, 1939-1945
	Cf. E83.879, Ute War, 1879
761.3	**Juvenile works**
	Pamphlets, addresses, essays, etc.
761.5	General
761.6	Anecdotes, legends, pageants, etc.
762	**Historic monuments (General). Illustrative material**
763	**Antiquities (Non-Indian)**
	By period
	Early to 1950, *see* F761
	1951-
765	General works
	Biography
765.2	Collective
765.22.A-.22.Z	Individual, A-Z
767.A-.Z	**Regions, counties, etc., A-Z**
767.A15	Counties
767.A16	Mountains
767.A17	Rivers
767.A18	Lakes
767.A19	Islands
767.A3	Albany Co.
767.B23	Beartooth Mountains
	Cf. F737.B35, General, and Montana
	Big Horn Canyon National Recreation Area, *see* F737.B49
767.B35	Big Horn Co.
767.B37	Big Horn Mountains (General, and Wyoming)
	Cf. F737.B53 , Montana
767.B4	Big Horn River and Valley, Wyo.
767.B7	Boundaries
	For Yellowstone National Park boundary, see F722
	Bridger Pass Overland Trail, *see* F767.O94
767.C16	Campbell Co.
767.C2	Carbon Co.
	Casper Mountain, *see* F767.N2
767.C55	Clear Creek and Valley (Big Horn County-Sheridan County)
767.C6	Converse Co.
767.C7	Crook Co.
767.D47	Devils Tower National Monument
	Eden Valley, *see* F767.S9
767.F5	Flaming Gorge National Recreation Area (General, and Wyoming)
	Cf. F832.F52, Utah
767.F8	Fremont Co.
767.F88	Front Range
	Cf. F782.F88, General, and Colorado
	Gibbon Falls, *see* F767.Y44
767.G6	Goshen Co.
	Grand Teton National Park, *see* F767.T3
767.G7	Green River and Valley
	Including Brown's Park
767.H6	Hot Springs Co.
767.I38	Independence Rock
	Jackson Hole, *see* F767.T28
767.J3	Jackson Hole National Monument (1943-1950)
	Included (1950) in Grand Teton National Park, Teton National Forest, and Jackson Hole Wildlife Park

Wyoming

767.A-.Z **Regions, counties, etc., A-Z — Continued**

Jackson Lake, *see* F767.T3

Jenny Lake, *see* F767.T3

767.J8 Johnson Co.

767.L3 Laramie Co.

767.L5 Lincoln Co.

767.M34 Madison River and Valley (General, and Wyoming)

Cf. F737.M24, Montana

767.M42 Medicine Bow Mountains

Cf. F782.M43, General, and Colorado

767.M43 Medicine Bow National Forest

767.N2 Natrona Co.

Including Casper Mountain

For Independence Rock, see F767.I38

767.N5 Niobrara Co.

767.N52 Niobrara River and Valley, Wyoming

Cf. F672.N56, General, and Nebraska

767.N8 North Platte River and Valley, Wyo.

Cf. F672.N8, General, and Nebraska

767.O94 Overland Trail (General, and Wyoming)

Including Bridger Pass Overland Trail

Cf. F597, Overland Trails (Northwest)

Cf. F782.O94, Colorado

767.P3 Park Co.

767.P5 Platte Co.

767.P6 Powder River and Valley, Wyo.

767.S37 Salt Valley (General, and Wyoming)

Cf. F752.S37, Idaho

767.S55 Sheridan Co.

767.S57 Shoshone National Forest

767.S58 Shoshone River and Valley

String Lake, *see* F767.T3

767.S8 Sublette Co.

767.S9 Sweetwater Co.

Including Eden Valley

767.T28 Teton Co.

Including Jackson Hole

Teton Mountains

767.T29 General

767.T3 Grand Teton National Park

Including Jackson Lake, String Lake, Jenny Lake

767.T65 Tongue River and Valley

Cf. F737.T55, General, and Montana

767.U3 Uinta Co.

767.U33 Uinta Mountains

Cf. F832.U39, General, and Utah

767.W3 Washakie Co.

767.W4 Weston Co.

767.W5 Wind River and Valley. Wind River Range

Yellowstone National Park, *see* F722

767.Y44 Yellowstone River and Valley

Including Gibbon Falls

Cf. F737.Y4, General, and Montana

769.A-.Z **Cities, towns, etc., A-Z**

GALE NOTE *The cutter number(s) listed below have been given only as examples by the Library of Congress*

769.C3 Casper

769.C5 Cheyenne

769.L2 Laramie

Wyoming — Continued

Elements in the population

770.A1 General works

770.A2-.Z Individual elements

For a list of racial, ethnic, and religious elements (with cutter numbers), see E184.A+

Colorado

771 **Periodicals. Societies. Collections**

773 **Museums. Exhibitions, exhibits**

774 **Gazetteers. Dictionaries. Geographic names**

774.3 **Guidebooks**

775 **Biography (Collective). Genealogy (Collective)**

775.2 **Historiography**

Historians, *see* E175.5.A+

775.5 **Study and teaching**

776 **General works. Histories**

776.3 **Juvenile works**

Pamphlets, addresses, essays, etc.

776.5 General

776.6 Anecdotes, legends, pageants, etc.

777 **Historic monuments (General). Illustrative material**

778 **Antiquities (Non-Indian)**

By period

780 Early to 1876

Including biography: John Evans, Benjamin Franklin Hall, etc.

Cf. E83.868, Battle of Beecher Island, 1868

Cf. E333, Louisiana Purchase, 1803

Cf. F786, Mexican Cession of 1848

Cf. F801, Purchase of Northwest Texas by United States, 1850

781 1876-1950

Including admission as a state, August 1, 1876

Including biography: Robert Wilbur Steele, Davis Hanson Waite, etc.

Cf. D570.85.C6+, World War I, 1914-1918

Cf. D769.85.C6+, World War II, 1939-1945

Cf. E83.879, Ute Indian War, 1879

781.2 1951-1980

781.3 1981-

782.A-.Z **Regions, counties, etc., A-Z**

782.A15 Counties

782.A16 Mountains

782.A17 Rivers

782.A18 Lakes

782.A19 Islands

782.A2 Adams Co.

782.A4 Alamosa Co.

782.A5 Arapahoe Co.

782.A6 Archuleta Co.

782.A7 Arkansas River and Valley, Colo.

Including Bent's Old Fort National Historic Site

For Royal Gorge, see F782.F8

Cf. F417.A7, General, and Arkansas

782.B2 Baca Co.

782.B33 Battlement National Forest

Beaver Creek and Valley, *see* F782.E15

782.B4 Bent Co.

Bent's Old Fort National Historic Site, *see* F782.A7

782.B45 Big Thompson River and Valley

Including Big Thompson Canyon

782.B5 Black Canyon of the Gunnison National Monument

782.B6 Boulder Co.

For Longs Peak, see F782.L83

Colorado

782.A-.Z **Regions, counties, etc., A-Z — Continued**

782.B7 Boundaries

Bridger Pass Overland Trail, *see* F782.O94

782.C5 Chaffee Co.

Including Chalk Creek

782.C55 Cheyenne Co.

Cheyenne Mountain, *see* F782.E3

782.C57 Cimarron River and Valley

Class here works limited to the part of the Cimarron River and Valley located in Colorado

For works limited to the part of the Cimarron River and Valley located in New Mexico, see F802.C58

For works limited to the part of the Cimarron River and Valley located in Kansas, see F687.C52

For general works on the Cimarron River and Valley, as well as works limited to the part located in Oklahoma, see F702.C53

782.C59 Clear Creek and Valley

782.C6 Clear Creek Co.

782.C66 Cochetopa National Forest

Colorado National Monument, *see* F782.M5

782.C7 Colorado River and Valley, Colo.

Formerly Grand River, Colo.

Cf. F788, General

782.C75 Conejos Co.

782.C8 Costilla Co.

Including Sangre de Cristo Grant (Costilla and Trinchera estates)

782.C9 Crowley Co.

782.C95 Custer Co.

782.D4 Delta Co.

Including Surface Creek and Valley

782.D45 Denver Co.

Dinosaur National Monument, *see* F832.D5

782.D57 Disappointment Creek and Valley

782.D7 Dolores Co.

782.D8 Douglas Co.

782.E15 Eagle Co.

Including Beaver Creek and Valley

782.E25 Elbert Co.

782.E3 El Paso Co.

Including Cave of the Winds, Cheyenne Mountain, Crystal Park, Garden of the Gods

For Pikes Peak, see F782.P63

782.E82 Escalante Canyon

Estes Park region, *see* F782.L2

782.F8 Fremont Co.

Including Royal Gorge (Grand Canyon of the Arkansas)

782.F88 Front Range (General, and Colorado)

Cf. F767.F88, Wyoming

Garden of the Gods, *see* F782.E3

782.G3 Garfield Co.

Including Glenwood Canyon

782.G4 Gilpin Co.

Glenwood Canyon, *see* F782.G3

Grand Canyon of the Arkansas, *see* F782.F8

782.G7 Grand Co.

Including Grand Lake (Lake)

782.G73 Grand Mesa

Grand River and Valley, Colo., *see* F782.C7

782.G78 Great Sand Dunes National Monument

782.G9 Gunnison Co.

782.H5 Hinsdale Co.

Colorado

782.A-.Z **Regions, counties, etc., A-Z — Continued**

782.H6 Holy Cross, Mount of the

782.H8 Huerfano Co.

782.J3 Jackson Co.

Including North Park

782.J4 Jefferson Co.

782.K4 Kiowa Co.

782.K5 Kit Carson Co.

782.L15 Lake Co.

782.L18 La Plata Co.

782.L2 Larimer Co.

Including Estes Park region

782.L3 Las Animas Co.

Including Pinon Canyon

782.L4 Leadville National Forest

Lime Creek and Valley, *see* F782.S18

782.L6 Lincoln Co.

Lodore, Canyon of, *see* F782.M65

782.L8 Logan Co.

782.L83 Longs Peak

Manti La Sal National Forest, *see* F832.M3

Maxwell Land Grant, *see* F802.M38

782.M43 Medicine Bow Mountains (General, and Colorado)

Cf. F767.M42, Wyoming

782.M5 Mesa Co.

Including Colorado National Monument

782.M52 Mesa Verde National Park

Cf. E99.P9, Pueblo Indian antiquities

782.M6 Mineral Co.

782.M65 Moffat Co.

Including Canyon of Lodore

For Dinosaur National Monument, see F832.D5

782.M7 Montezuma Co.

Including Mancos River and Valley, Colo.

782.M8 Montrose Co.

For Uncompahgre Valley, see F782.U5

782.M9 Morgan Co.

North Park, *see* F782.J3

782.O8 Otero Co.

782.O9 Ouray Co.

782.O94 Overland Trail

Including Bridger Pass Overland Trail

Cf. F597, Overland Trails (Northwest)

Cf. F767.O94, Bridger Pass Overland Trail (General, and Wyoming)

782.P3 Park Co.

782.P37 Peak-to-Peak Highway

782.P5 Phillips Co.

782.P52 Piceance Creek and watershed

782.P63 Pikes Peak

Including Pike National Forest

Pinon Canyon, *see* F782.L3

782.P7 Pitkin Co.

782.P8 Prowers Co.

782.P9 Pueblo Co.

782.R36 Red Mountain Mining District

782.R4 Rio Blanco Co.

Including White River and Valley (General, and Colorado)

Cf. F832.U4, White River and Valley, Utah

782.R45 Rio Grande Co.

Colorado

782.A-.Z **Regions, counties, etc., A-Z — Continued**

782.R46 Rio Grande National Forest

782.R52 Roaring Fork Valley

782.R59 Rocky Mountain National Park

For Estes Park region, see F782.L2

For Longs Peak, see F782.L83

782.R6 Rocky Mountain region, Colo.

Including Colorado Trail

For Pikes Peak, see F782.P63

Cf. F721, General

782.R7 Routt Co.

782.R8 Routt National Forest

Royal Gorge, *see* F782.F8

782.S14 Saguache Co.

782.S15 St. Vrain Creek and Valley

782.S17 San Juan Co.

782.S18 San Juan Mountains

Including Lime Creek and Valley

782.S19 San Juan region

782.S2 San Luis Park (Valley)

Cf. F782.C8, Sangre de Cristo Grant

782.S23 San Miguel Co.

Sangre de Cristo Grant, *see* F782.C8

782.S26 Sangre de Cristo Mountains

Cf. F802.S32, General, and New Mexico

782.S4 Sedgwick Co.

782.S53 Smoky Hill River and Valley

Cf. F687.S84, General, and Kansas

782.S6 South Park (Region)

782.S7 South Platte River and Valley, Colo.

Cf. F672.S7, General, and Nebraska

782.S76 Spanish Peaks

782.S95 Summit Co.

Surface Creek and Valley, *see* F782.D4

782.T37 Tarryall Mountains

782.T4 Teller Co.

782.U5 Uncompahgre Valley

Including Uncompahgre National Forest

782.U8 Ute Pass

782.V34 Vallecito Creek and Valley

782.W3 Washington Co.

782.W4 Weld Co.

782.W46 West Elk Loop Scenic and Historic Byway

White River and Valley (General, and Colorado), *see* F782.R4

782.Y8 Yuma Co.

784.A-.Z **Cities, towns, etc., A-Z**

GALE NOTE *The cutter number(s) listed below have been given only as examples by the Library of Congress*

784.A7 Aspen

784.C4 Central City

784.C7 Colorado Springs

784.C8 Cripple Creek

784.D4 Denver

Subarrange by Table F2 at the end of the text

784.G7 Greeley

784.L4 Leadville

784.M3 Manitou

784.P9 Pueblo

Colorado — Continued
Elements in the population
785.A1 General works
785.A2-.Z Individual elements
For a list of racial, ethnic, and religious elements (with cutter numbers), see E184.A+
The New Southwest. Southwestern States
785.3 **Guidebooks**
785.5 **Biography (Collective). Genealogy (Collective)**
786 **1848-1950**
Including the region of the Mexican Cession of 1848, the Texas Purchase of 1850, and the Gadsden Purchase
Including Mexican boundary; Santa Fe Trail; frontier troubles with Mexico; Gadsden Purchase, 1853
Including biography: William H. Bonney (Billy the Kid), etc.
Cf. E78.S7, Indians of the New Southwest
Cf. E401+, War with Mexico, 1845-1848
Cf. E470.9, Civil War, 1861-1865 (Military operations)
Cf. F799+, Southwest before 1848
Cf. F1232, Mexican frontier troubles (General)
787 **1951-**
788 **Colorado River, Canyon, and Valley**
Including Grand Canyon National Park and Lake Mead National Recreation Area
788.5 **Four Corners Region**
789 **Great Basin**
Elements in the population
790.A1 General works
790.A2-.Z Individual elements
For a list of racial, ethnic, and religious elements (with cutter numbers), see E184.A+
New Mexico
791 **Periodicals. Societies. Collections**
793 **Museums. Exhibitions, exhibits**
794 **Gazetteers. Dictionaries. Geographic names**
794.3 **Guidebooks**
795 **Biography (Collective). Genealogy (Collective)**
795.2 **Historiography**
Historians, *see* E175.5.A+
795.5 **Study and teaching**
796 **General works. Histories**
796.3 **Juvenile works**
Pamphlets, addresses, essays, etc.
796.5 General
796.6 Anecdotes, legends, pageants, etc.
797 **Historic monuments (General). Illustrative material**
798 **Antiquities (Non-Indian)**
By period
799 Early to 1822
Including Spanish discoveries and settlements in the Southwest between the Mississippi River and California; seven cities of Cibola; Quivira; Spanish province; Pimería Alta
Including biography: Eusebio Francisco Kino, Diego Dionisio de Peñalosa, etc.
Cf. F1410, Spaniards in North America (General)
800 1822-1848
Including Mexican state, region between Texas and California
Cf. E405.2, Conquest by United States Troops, War with Mexico, 1845-1848
Cf. F389, Texas
Cf. F390, Texan Santa Fe Expedition, 1841
Cf. F786, Santa Fe Trail
Cf. F826, Utah
801 1848-1950
Including admission as a state, January 6, 1912
Including purchase of northwest Texas by United States, 1850

New Mexico
By period
801 1848-1950 — Continued
Including biography: Octaviano Ambrosio Larrazola, Antonio Miguel Otero, etc.
Cf. D769.85.M33+, World War II, 1939-1945
Cf. E83.88, Apache War, 1883-1886
Cf. E423, Compromise of 1850
Cf. E522.1+, Civil War, 1861-1865 (General)
Cf. E470.9, Military operations in the Civil War, 1861-1865
Cf. E571.1+, Confederate history
Cf. F786, Gadsden Purchase, 1853
1951-
801.2 General works
Biography
801.3 Collective
801.4.A-.4.Z Individual, A-Z
802.A-.Z **Regions, counties, etc., A-Z**
802.A15 Counties
802.A16 Mountains
802.A17 Rivers
802.A18 Lakes
802.A19 Islands
Aztec Ruins National Monument, *see* E99.P9
802.B25 Bandelier National Monument
Including Frijoles Canyon
802.B5 Bernalillo Co.
802.B58 Bisti
802.B63 Black Range
802.B7 Boundaries
For International boundary, see F786
Cf. F392.B7, Texas boundary
Cf. F782.B7, Colorado boundary
802.C2 Canadian River and Valley, N. Mex.
Cf. F702.C2, General, and Oklahoma
Capulin Volcano National Monument, *see* F802.U5
802.C28 Carlsbad Caverns
Including Carlsbad Caverns National Park
802.C3 Catron Co.
802.C4 Chaco Canyon
Including Chaco Canyon National Monument
802.C45 Chama Valley
Including Rio Chama
802.C5 Chaves Co.
802.C52 Chihuahuan Desert
802.C54 Cibola Co.
Including El Malpais National Monument, El Malpais National Conservation Area
802.C58 Cimarron River and Valley
Class here works limited to the part of the Cimarron River and Valley located in New Mexico
For works limited to the part of the Cimarron River and Valley located in Colorado, see F782.C57
For works limited to the part of the Cimarron River and Valley located in Kansas, see F687.C52
For general works on the Cimarron River and Valley, as well as works limited to the part located in Oklahoma, see F702.C53
802.C7 Colfax Co.
Including Moreno Creek and Valley
802.C8 Curry Co.
802.D4 De Baca Co.
802.D6 Dona Ana Co.
For Mesilla Valley, see F802.M4

New Mexico

802.A-.Z Regions, counties, etc., A-Z — Continued

802.E2 Eddy Co.

For Carlsbad Caverns, see F802.C28

El Malpais National Conservation Area, *see* F802.C54

El Malpais National Monument, *see* F802.C54

802.E5 El Morro National Monument

802.E8 Española Valley

Frijoles Canyon, *see* F802.B25

Gadsden Purchase, *see* F786

802.G54 Gila River and Valley

Cf. F817.G52, General, and Arizona

802.G62 Gobermador Canyon

802.G7 Grant Co.

Including Mimbres River and Valley

802.G9 Guadalupe Co.

Including Leonard Wood Co. (1903-1904), Santa Rosa Lake and Region

802.G93 Guadalupe Mountains (General, and New Mexico)

Cf. F392.G86, Texas

802.H3 Harding Co.

802.H5 Hidalgo Co.

802.H84 Hueco Mountains

Cf. F392.H82, General, and Texas

Jemez Mountains, *see* F802.S3

Jornada del Muerto Road, *see* F802.J67

802.J67 Jornada del Muerto Wilderness. Jornada del Muerto Road

802.L4 Lea Co.

Leonard Wood Co. (1903-1904), *see* F802.G9

802.L7 Lincoln Co.

802.L84 Los Alamos Co.

802.L9 Luna Co.

802.M2 McKinley Co.

802.M34 Manzano Mountains

802.M38 Maxwell Land Grant

802.M4 Mesilla Valley

For Gadsden Purchase, see F786

Mimbres River and Valley, *see* F802.G7

802.M6 Mora Co.

Moreno Creek and Valley, *see* F802.C7

802.O7 Otero Co.

802.P25 Pajarito Plateau

802.P3 Pecos River and Valley, N. Mex.

Cf. F392.P3, General, and Texas

802.P5 Pine Lawn Valley

802.P83 Puerco River and Valley (General, and New Mexico)

802.Q2 Quay Co.

Red River, *see* F802.T2

802.R36 Red River and Valley

Cf. F377.R3, General, and Louisiana

802.R4 Rio Arriba Co.

Rio Chama, *see* F802.C45

802.R5 Rio Grande and Valley, N. Mex.

Cf. F392.R5, General, and Texas

802.R68 Rocky Mountain region, N. Mex.

Cf. F721, General

802.R7 Roosevelt Co.

802.S13 Salinas National Monument

802.S15 San Andres Mountains

802.S18 San Juan Co.

New Mexico

802.A-.Z **Regions, counties, etc., A-Z — Continued**

San Mateo Mountains, *see* F802.V3

802.S2 San Miguel Co.

802.S28 Sandia Mountains

802.S3 Sandoval Co.

Including Jemez Mountains

For Frijoles Canyon, see F802.B25

For Sangre de Cristo Grant, see F782.C8

802.S32 Sangre de Cristo Mountains (General, and New Mexico)

Cf. F782.S26, Colorado

802.S4 Santa Fe Co.

Santa Rosa Lake and Region, *see* F802.G9

802.S5 Sierra Co.

802.S6 Socorro Co.

802.T2 Taos Co.

Including Red River

Cf. F782.C8 , Sangre de Cristo Grant

802.T47 Tewa Basin

802.T6 Torrance Co.

802.U5 Union Co.

Including Capulin Volcano National Monument

802.V3 Valencia Co.

Including San Mateo Mountains

For Leonard Wood Co. (1903-1904), see F802.G9

802.W44 White Sands Missile Range

802.W45 White Sands National Monument

804.A-.Z **Cities, towns, etc., A-Z**

GALE NOTE *The cutter number(s) listed below have been given only as examples by the Library of Congress*

804.A3 Albuquerque

804.L6 Los Alamos

804.S2 Santa Fe

Subarrange by Table F2 at the end of the text

804.T2 Taos

Elements in the population

805.A1 General works

805.A2-.Z Individual elements

For a list of racial, ethnic, and religious elements (with cutter numbers), see E184.A+

Arizona

806 **Periodicals. Societies. Collections**

808 **Museums. Exhibitions, exhibits**

809 **Gazetteers. Dictionaries. Geographic names**

809.3 **Guidebooks**

810 **Biography (Collective). Genealogy (Collective)**

810.2 **Historiography**

Historians, *see* E175.5.A+

810.5 **Study and teaching**

811 **General works. Histories**

Including admission as a state, February 14, 1912

Including by period (Early to 1950) as well as general

For 1951 and later, see F815

Cf. D769.85.A7+, World War II, 1939-1945

Cf. E83.88, Apache War, 1883-1886

Cf. E470.9, E472.3, E473.4, E474.1, Civil War, 1861-1865

Cf. F786, Mexican Cession of 1848; Gadsden Purchase of 1853

811.3 **Juvenile works**

Pamphlets, addresses, essays

811.5 General

811.6 Anecdotes, legends, pageants, etc.

Arizona — Continued

812	**Historic monuments (General). Illustrative material**
813	**Antiquities (Non-Indian)**
	By period
	Early to 1950, *see* F811
	1951-
815	General works
	Biography
815.2	Collective
815.3.A-.3.Z	Individual, A-Z
	GALE NOTE *See note at the head of Table F5 at the end of the text for further instructions on how to subdivide this number*
817.A-.Z	**Regions, counties, etc., A-Z**
817.A15	Counties
817.A16	Mountains
817.A17	Rivers
817.A18	Lakes
817.A19	Islands
817.A6	Apache Co.
817.A73	Aravaipa Canyon
817.A75	Arizona Strip
817.B5	Big Sandy River and region
	Bonita Creek and Valley, *see* F817.G7
817.B7	Boundaries
	For International boundary, see F786
817.C3	Canyon de Chelly National Monument
817.C35	Casa Grande National Monument
	Chiricahua Mountains, *see* F817.C5
	Chiricahua National Monument, *see* F817.C5
817.C5	Cochise Co.
	Including Chiricahua National Monument, Coronado National Memorial, Sulphur Springs Valley, Chiricahua Mountains
817.C6	Coconino Co.
	Including Sunset Crater Volcano National Monument
817.C7	Colorado River and Valley, Ariz.
	For Grand Canyon, see F788
	Cf. F788, General
	Gadsden Purchase, *see* F786
817.G5	Gila Co.
	Including Pleasant Valley, Tonto National Monument
817.G52	Gila River and Valley (General, and Arizona)
	Cf. F802.G54, New Mexico
	Glen Canyon National Recreation Area, *see* F832.G5
817.G7	Graham Co.
	Including Bonita Creek and Valley
	Grand Canyon National Park, *see* F788
817.G8	Greenlee Co.
	Havasu Canyon, *see* F788
817.L5	Little Colorado River and Valley
817.M3	Maricopa Co.
	Lake Mead National Recreation Area, *see* F788
817.M5	Mohave Co.
	Including Pipe Spring National Monument
	Mohawk Valley, *see* F817.Y9
817.M57	Montezuma Castle National Monument
817.M6	Monument Valley
817.N3	Navajo Co.
817.O7	Organ Pipe Cactus National Monument
817.P2	Painted Desert
817.P4	Petrified Forest National Monument

Arizona

817.A-.Z **Regions, counties, etc., A-Z — Continued**

817.P5 Pima Co.

Including Quijotoa Mountains

For Santa Catalina Mountains, see F817.S28

817.P6 Pinal Co.

Pipe Spring National Monument, *see* F817.M5

Pleasant Valley, *see* F817.G5

Powell, Lake, *see* F832.G5

817.S18 Saguaro National Park

817.S2 Salt River and Valley

817.S25 San Pedro River and Valley (General and Arizona)

Cf. F1346, Mexico

817.S28 Santa Catalina Mountains

817.S3 Santa Cruz Co.

817.S33 Santa Cruz River and Valley

Sulphur Springs Valley, *see* F817.C5

Sunset Crater Volcano National Monument, *see* F817.C6

817.S9 Superstition Mountains

Tonto National Monument, *see* F817.G5

817.T66 Tonto River and Valley

817.T8 Tumacacori National Monument

817.V37 Verde River and Valley

817.W47 Wet Beaver Creek and Valley

817.W8 Wupatki National Monument

817.Y3 Yavapai Co.

817.Y9 Yuma Co.

Including Lechuguilla Desert, Mohawk Valley

819.A-.Z **Cities, towns, etc., A-Z**

GALE NOTE *The cutter number(s) listed below have been given only as examples by the Library of Congress*

819.G5 Globe

819.P57 Phoenix

819.T6 Tombstone

819.T9 Tucson

Subarrange by Table F2 at the end of the text

Elements in the population

820.A1 General works

820.A2-.Z Individual elements

For a list of racial, ethnic, and religious elements (with cutter numbers), see E184.A+

Utah

821 **Periodicals. Societies. Collections**

823 **Museums. Exhibitions, exhibits**

824 **Gazetteers. Dictionaries. Geographic names**

824.3 **Guidebooks**

825 **Biography (Collective). Genealogy (Collective)**

825.2 **Historiography**

Historians, *see* E175.5.A+

825.5 **Study and teaching**

826 **General works. Histories**

Including admission as a state, January 4, 1896

Including by period (Early to 1950) as well as general

For 1951 and later, see F830

Including Mormon settlement; State of Deseret; Mountain Meadows Massacre, 1857; Mormon Rebellion, 1857-1859

Including biography: Jacob Hamblin, John Doyle Lee, etc.

Cf. BX8601-8695, Mormons (Church of Jesus Christ of Latter Day Saints)

Cf. D570.85.U8+, World War I, 1914-1918

Cf. D769.85.U8+, World War II, 1939-1945

Cf. E423, Compromise of 1850

Utah — Continued

826.3 **Juvenile works**

Pamphlets, addresses, essays, etc.

826.5 General

826.6 Anecdotes, legends, pageants, etc.

827 **Historic monuments (General). Illustrative material**

828 **Antiquities (Non-Indian)**

By period

Early to 1950, *see* F826

1951-

830 General works

Biography

830.2 Collective

830.3.A-.Z Individual, A-Z

GALE NOTE *See note at the head of Table F5 at the end of the text for further instructions on how to subdivide this number*

832.A-.Z **Regions, counties, etc., A-Z**

832.A15 Counties

832.A16 Mountains

832.A17 Rivers

832.A18 Lakes

832.A19 Islands

832.A7 Arches National Park

832.B3 Bear River and Valley

832.B35 Beaver Co.

832.B6 Lake Bonneville

832.B7 Boundaries

832.B8 Box Elder Co.

For Bear River and Valley, see F832.B3

Brown's Park, *see* F767.G7

832.B9 Bryce Canyon National Park

832.C3 Cache Co.

Including Cache Valley

832.C35 Cache National Forest

832.C37 Canyonlands National Park

Including Cataract Canyon Wilderness

Capitol Reef National Park, *see* F832.W27

832.C4 Carbon Co.

832.C45 Castle Valley

Cataract Canyon Wilderness, *see* F832.C37

Cedar Breaks National Monument, *see* F832.I6

Cedar Mesa, *see* F832.S4

832.C7 Colorado River and Valley, Utah

Formerly Grand River, Utah

Cf. F788, General

832.D2 Daggett Co.

832.D3 Davis Co.

832.D5 Dinosaur National Monument

For Canyon of Lodore, see F782.M65

832.D8 Duchesne Co.

832.E5 Emery Co.

832.F52 Flaming Gorge National Recreation Area

Cf. F767.F5, General, and Wyoming

832.G3 Garfield Co.

832.G5 Glen Canyon National Recreation Area

Including Lake Powell

832.G65 Grand Co.

Grand River and Valley, Utah, *see* F832.C7

832.G66 Grand Staircase-Escalante National Monument

Utah

832.A-.Z **Regions, counties, etc., A-Z — Continued**

832.G7 Great Salt Lake and region

Including Great Salt Desert

Green River and Valley, *see* F767.G7

Hole in the Rock Trail, *see* F832.S4

832.I6 Iron Co.

Including Cedar Breaks National Monument

832.J8 Juab Co.

832.K3 Kane Co.

Manti Canyon, *see* F832.S42

832.M3 Manti La Sal National Forest

832.M5 Millard Co.

Monument Valley, *see* F817.M6

832.M6 Morgan Co.

832.N55 Nine Mile Canyon

Parley's Canyon, *see* F832.S2

832.P5 Piute Co.

Powell, Lake, *see* F832.G5

832.R3 Rainbow Bridge. Rainbow Bridge National Monument

832.R5 Rich Co.

832.S2 Salt Lake Co.

Including Parley's Canyon

832.S4 San Juan Co.

Including Cedar Mesa, Hole in the Rock Trail

832.S415 San Rafael River and Valley. San Rafael Swell

San Rafael Swell, *see* F832.S415

832.S42 Sanpete Co.

Including Manti Canyon

832.S6 Sevier Co.

832.S9 Summit Co.

832.T6 Tooele Co.

832.U39 Uinta Mountains (General, and Utah)

Cf. F676.U33, Wyoming

832.U4 Uintah Co.

Including Uintah Basin, White River and Valley, Utah

Cf. F782.R4, White River and Valley (General, and Colorado)

Uncompahgre Indian Reservation, *see* E99.U8

832.U8 Utah Co.

Utah National Park, *see* F832.B9

832.W2 Wasatch Co.

832.W22 Wasatch Range

Class here general works on the Wasatch Range, as well as works limited to the part located in Utah

For works limited to the part of the Wasatch Range located in Idaho, see F752.W27

832.W24 Washington Co.

832.W27 Wayne Co.

Including Capitol Reef National Park

832.W3 Weber Co.

Including Ben Lomond

White River and Valley, Utah, *see* F832.U4

832.Z8 Zion National Park

834.A-.Z **Cities, towns, etc., A-Z**

GALE NOTE *The cutter number(s) listed below have been given only as examples by the Library of Congress*

834.L8 Logan

834.O3 Ogden

834.P3 Provo

834.S2 Salt Lake City

Subarrange by Table F2 at the end of the text

Utah — Continued

Elements in the population

835.A1 General works

835.A2-.Z Individual elements

For a list of racial, ethnic, and religious elements (with cutter numbers), see E184.A+

Nevada

836 **Periodicals. Societies. Collections**

838 **Museums. Exhibitions, exhibits**

839 **Gazetteers. Dictionaries. Geographic names**

839.3 **Guidebooks**

840 **Biography (Collective). Genealogy (Collective)**

840.2 **Historiography**

Historians, *see* E175.5.A+

840.5 **Study and teaching**

841 **General works. Histories**

Including admission as a state, October 31, 1864

Including by period (Early to 1950) as well as general

For 1951 and later, see F845+

Including biography: John William Mackay, William Morris Stewart, etc.

Cf. D570.85.N22+, World War I, 1914-1918

Cf. D769.85.N22+, World War II, 1939-1945

841.3 **Juvenile works**

Pamphlets, addresses, essays, etc.

841.5 General

841.6 Anecdotes, legends, pageants, etc.

842 **Historic monuments (General). Illustrative material**

843 **Antiquities (Non-Indian)**

By period

Early to 1950, *see* F841

1951-

845 General works

Biography

845.2 Collective

845.25.A-.25.Z Individual, A-Z

GALE NOTE *See note at the head of Table F5 at the end of the text for further instructions on how to subdivide this number*

847.A-.Z **Regions, counties, etc., A-Z**

847.A15 Counties

847.A16 Mountains

847.A17 Rivers

847.A18 Lakes

847.A19 Islands

847.A42 Amargosa River and Valley (General and Nevada)

847.B53 Black Rock Desert

847.B7 Boundaries

Cf. F868.B7, California boundary

847.C37 Carson River and Valley

847.C4 Churchill Co.

847.C5 Clark Co.

Including Charleston Mountain, Moapa River and Valley, Red Rock Canyon National Conservation Area, Valley of Fire

847.D6 Douglas Co.

847.E4 Elko Co.

Ellsworth Canyon, *see* F847.N9

847.E7 Esmeralda Co.

847.E8 Eureka Co.

847.F6 Fort Churchill Historic State Monument

847.G32 Gabbs Valley

847.G7 Grass Valley

847.G73 Great Basin National Park

	Nevada
847.A-.Z	**Regions, counties, etc., A-Z — Continued**
847.H8	Humboldt Co.
	Including Paradise Valley
847.H85	Humboldt River and Valley
847.L3	Lander Co.
847.L5	Lincoln Co.
847.L9	Lyon Co.
	Lake Mead National Recreation Area, *see* F788
847.M5	Mineral Co.
	Including Walker River and Valley
	Moapa River and Valley, *see* F847.C5
847.N9	Nye Co.
	Including Ellsworth Canyon
847.O6	Ormsby Co.
	Owyhee Mountains region, *see* F752.O97
847.O98	Owyhee River and Valley
	Cf. F882.O98, General, and Oregon
	Paradise Valley, *see* F847.H8
847.P4	Pershing Co.
847.R33	Rainbow Canyon
	Red Rock Canyon National Conservation Area, *see* F847.C5
847.S8	Storey Co.
	Lake Tahoe, *see* F868.T2
	Valley of Fire, *see* F847.C5
	Walker River and Valley, *see* F847.M5
847.W3	Washoe Co.
847.W5	White Pine Co.
849.A-.Z	**Cities, towns, etc., A-Z**
	GALE NOTE *The cutter number(s) listed below have been given only as examples by the Library of Congress*
849.A9	Austin
849.C3	Carson City
	Comstock Lode, *see* F849.V8
849.L35	Las Vegas
849.R4	Reno
849.V8	Virginia City. Comstock Lode
	Elements in the population
850.A1	General works
850.A2-.Z	Individual elements
	For a list of racial, ethnic, and religious elements (with cutter numbers), see E184.A+
	The Pacific States
	Including Pacific coast of North America, works on the coast of America (North and South), Pacific Northwest
	Cf. E78.P2, Indians of the Pacific States
	Cf. E83.84, Wars with the Pacific coast Indians, 1847-1865
850.5	**Biography (Collective). Genealogy (Collective)**
851	**General works**
851.5	**Exploring expeditions to the Pacific coast before 1800**
	For California explorations since 1800, see F864
	For Oregon explorations since 1800, see F880
	For Alaska explorations since 1800, see F907
	For British Columbia explorations since 1800, see F1088
851.7	**Cascade Range**
	Cf. F882.C3, Cascade Range in Oregon
	Cf. F897.C3, Cascade Range in Washington (State)
	The Pacific Northwest
	Including Washington, Oregon, Idaho, Montana, British Columbia
	By period
	Early to 1769, *see* F851.5

The Pacific States
The Pacific Northwest
By period — Continued
1769-1859, *see* F880
852 1859-1950
Cf. E78.N77, Indians of the Pacific Northwest
852.2 1951-1980
852.3 1981-
853 Columbia River and Valley
Cf. F882.C63, Oregon
Cf. F897.C7, Washington
854 Northwest boundary of the United States, 1846-
Including Rocky Mountains to the Pacific
Boundary controversy before 1846, *see* F880
Elements in the population
855 General works
855.2.A-.2.Z Individual elements, A-Z
For a list of racial, ethnic, and religious elements (with cutter numbers), see E184.A+
California
856 **Periodicals. Societies. Collections**
858 **Museums. Exhibitions, exhibits**
859 **Gazetteers. Dictionaries. Geographic names**
859.3 **Guidebooks**
860 **Biography (Collective). Genealogy (Collective)**
860.2 **Historiography**
Historians, *see* E175.5.A+
860.5 **Study and teaching**
861 **General works. Histories**
861.3 **Juvenile works**
861.5 **Pamphlets, addresses, essays, etc.**
861.6 **Anecdotes, legends, pageants, etc.**
861.8 **Geography**
862 **Historic monuments (General). Illustrative material**
Including Spanish mission buildings (General)
863 **Antiquities (Non-Indian)**
By period
864 Early to 1869
Admission as a state, September 9, 1850
Including Spanish explorers after 1769; Spanish California, including Lower and Upper California; Indian missions; American and European intrigues before 1846; Fremont in California, 1846; Bear Flag War, 1846
Including biography: John Bidwell, William Brown Ide, Peter Lassen, Junípero Serra, David Smith Terry, Mariano Guadalupe Vallejo, George Calvert Yount, Agustín Juan Vicente Zamorano, etc.
Cf. E83.84, Wars with Pacific coast Indians, 1847-1865
Cf. E83.858, Mill Creek War, 1857-1865
Cf. E405.2, American military conquest, 1846
Cf. E423, Compromise of 1850
Cf. E497.1+, Civil War, 1861-1865 (General)
Cf. F786, Mexican cession of 1848
Cf. F1089.N8, Nootka Sound Controversy, 1789-1790
Cf. F1246+, Lower California
For explorations before 1769, see F851.5
865 1848-1856
Including gold discoveries; Argonauts; voyages to California by the Cape Horn or Central American isthmus routes; vigilance committees
Including biography: William Tell Coleman, James Wilson Marshall, John Marsh, Joaquin Murrieta, John Augustus Sutter, etc.
Cf. F593, Overland journeys from the East

California

By period — Continued

866 1869-1950

Cf. D570.85.C2+, World War I, 1914-1918

Cf. D769.85.C2+, World War II, 1939-1945

Cf. E83.87, Modoc War, 1872-1873

Cf. E726.C1, War of 1898 (Spanish-American War)

1951-

866.2 General works

Biography

866.3 Collective

866.4.A-.4.Z Individual, A-Z

GALE NOTE *See note at the head of Table F5 at the end of the text for further instructions on how to subdivide this number*

867 **Southern California**

Cf. F864, Early Spanish missions

867.5 **Northern California**

868.A-.Z **Regions, counties, etc., A-Z**

868.A15 Counties

868.A16 Mountains

868.A17 Rivers

868.A18 Lakes

868.A19 Islands

868.A3 Alameda Co.

Including Livermore Valley

Alcatraz Island, *see* F868.S156

Algodones Dunes, *see* F868.I2

868.A35 Alpine Co.

868.A4 Amador Co.

868.A44 American River and Valley

Anacapa Island, *see* F868.V5

Anderson Valley, *see* F868.M5

868.A5 Angeles National Forest

Annadel State Park, *see* F868.S7

Anza-Borrego Desert State Park, *see* F868.S15

Arroyo Grande Creek and Valley, *see* F868.S18

Ashurst Colony, *see* F868.S13

Balboa Island, *see* F868.O6

Barona Valley, *see* F868.S15

Beckworth Trail, *see* F868.S5

Big Creek Lake, *see* F868.S14

868.B5 Big Oak Flat Road

868.B7 Boundaries

868.B8 Butte Co.

868.C14 Calaveras Big Tree National Forest

868.C15 Calaveras Big Trees State Park

868.C16 Calaveras Co.

For Calaveras Big Trees State Park, see F868.C15

California Redwood Park (Santa Cruz Co.), *see* F868.S3

Capay Valley, *see* F868.Y5

Cape Horn, *see* F868.S5

Carquinez Strait, *see* F868.S156

Catalina Island, *see* F868.L8

868.C45 Central Valley

Channel Islands, *see* F868.S232

Chocolate Mountains, *see* F868.I2

Coachella Valley, *see* F868.R6

Colorado Desert, *see* F868.I2

868.C6 Colorado River and Valley, Calif.

Cf. F788, General

California

868.A-.Z **Regions, counties, etc., A-Z — Continued**

868.C7 Colusa Co.

868.C74 Conejo Valley

868.C76 Contra Costa Co.

Including Winter Island, Mount Diablo State Park

Crane Valley Dam and Lake, *see* F868.M2

868.D2 Death Valley

Including Death Valley National Monument, Scotty's Castle

868.D4 Del Norte Co.

Including Smith River National Recreation Area

868.D45 Delta Region

Donner Lake, *see* F868.N5

Eagle Lake, *see* F868.L33

868.E22 East Bay

868.E25 Eel River and Valley

868.E28 El Camino Real

868.E3 El Dorado Co.

Including Wrights Lake

Emerald Bay and region, *see* F868.O6

Emigrant Trail, *see* F868.S5

Empire Mine State Historic Park, *see* F868.N5

868.F24 Farallon Islands (Farallones)

868.F3 Feather River, Canyon, and Valley

Forest of Nisene Marks State Park, *see* F868.S3

868.F8 Fresno Co.

Including Shaver Lake

For San Joaquin Valley, see F868.S173

868.G39 Gazos Creek and Valley

General Grant National Park, *see* F868.K48

868.G5 Glenn Co.

Goat Island, *see* F869.S3

Golden Gate National Recreation Area, *see* F868.S156

Guenoc Valley, *see* F868.L2

Hearst-San Simeon State Historical Monument, *see* F868.S18

Huichica Creek and Valley, *see* F868.N2

868.H8 Humboldt Co.

Including Humboldt Bay, Humboldt Redwoods State Park, Shelter Cove

868.I2 Imperial Co.

Including Chocolate Mountains, Colorado Desert, Imperial Valley, Algodones Dunes

Indian Wells Valley, *see* F868.K3

868.I6 Inyo Co.

Including Manzanar National Historic Site

For Death Valley, see F868.D2

Irvine Park, *see* F868.O6

Jalama Beach Park, *see* F868.S23

John Muir Trail, *see* F868.S5

868.J6 Joshua Tree National Monument

868.K3 Kern Co.

Including Indian Wells Valley, Tejon Ranch

868.K48 Kings Canyon National Park

Including General Grant Grove area (General Grant National Park until 1940)

868.K5 Kings Co.

868.K55 Klamath River and Valley

868.L2 Lake Co.

Including Guenoc Valley

Lake Elsinore and region, *see* F868.R6

868.L33 Lassen Co.

Including Eagle Lake

868.L34 Lassen Peak. Lassen Volcanic National Park

California

868.A-.Z **Regions, counties, etc., A-Z — Continued**

868.L38 Lava Beds National Monument

868.L8 Los Angeles Co.

Including Mount Lowe, Rustic Canyon, San Fernando Valley, San Gabriel Valley, Santa Catalina Island, Santa Clarita Valley, Santa Monica Bay region, Santa Monica Canyon, Los Angeles River

For Channel Islands, see F868.S232

Los Angeles River, *see* F868.L8

868.L83 Los Padres National Forest

Lytle Creek Canyon, *see* F868.S14

868.M2 Madera Co.

Including Crane Valley Dam and Lake

Malakoff Diggins State Historic Park, *see* F868.N5

Manzanar National Historic Site, *see* F868.I6

868.M3 Marin Co.

Including Marin Peninsula, Mount Tamalpais State Park, Muir Woods National Monument

868.M4 Mariposa Co.

Including Fremont Land Grant (Mariposa estate), etc.

868.M5 Mendocino Co.

Including Anderson Valley, Mendocino Headlands State Park, and Round Valley

868.M55 Merced Co.

Mineral King Valley, *see* F868.T8

868.M6 Modoc Co.

Including Surprise Valley

868.M65 Mohave (Mojave) Desert

868.M67 Mono Co.

Including Mono Lake

Mono Lake, *see* F868.M67

Monterey Bay, *see* F868.M7

868.M7 Monterey Co.

Including Point Lobos, Monterey Bay, Pfeiffer Big Sur State Park

Moreno Valley, *see* F868.R6

Mount Diablo State Park, *see* F868.C76

Mount San Jacinto State Park, *see* F868.R6

Muir Trail, *see* F868.S5

Muir Woods National Monument, *see* F868.M3

868.N16 Nacimiento River and Valley

868.N2 Napa Co.

Including Huichica Creek and Valley

868.N5 Nevada Co.

Including Donner Lake, Donner Party Expedition, Empire Mine State Historic Park, Malakoff Diggins State Historic Park

868.N52 New Melones Lake and region

Nobles Trail, *see* F868.S5

Ojai Valley, *see* F868.V5

Old Emigrant Trail, *see* F868.S5

Ontario Colony, *see* F869.O5

868.O6 Orange Co.

Including Balboa Island, Emerald Bay and region, Irvine Park

868.O9 Owens River and Valley

Pajaro River and Valey, *see* F868.S3

868.P33 Pacific Coast

Pfeiffer Big Sur State Park, *see* F868.M7

868.P7 Placer Co.

868.P85 Plumas Co.

868.P9 Point Reyes

868.R32 Rand Mining District

868.R4 Redwood National Park (Humboldt and Del Norte Counties)

Redwood Park (Santa Cruz Co.), *see* F868.S3

California

868.A-.Z **Regions, counties, etc., A-Z — Continued**

868.R6 Riverside Co.

Including Coachella Valley, Lake Elsinore and regions, Moreno Valley, San Jacinto River and Valley, Temecula Creek and Valley, Mount San Jacinto State Park

Roosevelt-Sequoia National Park (Proposed), *see* F868.S4

Round Valley, *see* F868.M5

868.R9 Russian River and Valley

Rustic Canyon, *see* F868.L8

868.S12 Sacramento Co.

868.S13 Sacramento River and Valley

Including Ashurst Colony

868.S132 Saint Helena, Mount

868.S133 Salinas River and Valley

868.S136 San Benito Co.

Including San Juan Valley

868.S14 San Bernardino Co.

Including Lytle Creek Canyon, San Bernardino Valley, Bear Valley, Big Bear Valley, Big Bear Lake

For Ontario Colony, see F869.O5

868.S144 San Bernardino National Forest

868.S15 San Diego Co.

Including Anza-Borrego Desert State Park, Barona Valley, Borrego Valley, Escondido Valley, Palomar Mountain, San Pasqual Valley, San Vicente Valley

For Imperial Valley, see F868.I2

San Fernando Valley, *see* F868.L8

868.S156 San Francisco Bay region

Including Alcatraz Island, Carquinez Strait, Golden Gate National Recreation Area

868.S157 San Francisco Co.

Cf. F869.S3, San Francisco (City)

For Farallon Islands, see F868.F24

San Gabriel Valley, *see* F868.L8

San Jacinto Mountains National Monument, *see* F868.S36

San Jacinto River and Valley, *see* F868.R6

868.S17 San Joaquin Co.

868.S173 San Joaquin River and Valley

Including Tulare Lake and region

San Juan Valley, *see* F868.S136

868.S18 San Luis Obispo Co.

Including Morro Bay, Hearst-San Simeon State Historical Monument, Arroyo Grande Creek and Valley

For Santa Maria River and Valley, see F868.S23

868.S19 San Mateo Co.

San Miguel Island, *see* F868.S23

San Pasqual Valley, *see* F868.S15

868.S2 San Ramon Valley

San Vicente Valley, *see* F868.S15

868.S21 Santa Ana Mountains

868.S22 Santa Ana River and Valley

868.S23 Santa Barbara Co.

Including Jalama Beach Park, San Miguel Island, Santa Barbara Valley, Santa Cruz Island, Santa Maria River and Valley, Santa Rosa Island, Santa Ynez River and Valley, Zaca Lake

Cf. F868.S232, Santa Barbara Islands

868.S232 Santa Barbara (Channel) Islands (General)

For individual islands, see the counties (Santa Barbara, Ventura, and Los Angeles) to which they belong

Santa Catalina Island, *see* F868.L8

868.S25 Santa Clara Co.

Including Santa Clara Valley

For San Juan Valley, see F868.S136

California

868.A-.Z Regions, counties, etc., A-Z — Continued

Santa Clarita Valley, *see* F868.L8

868.S3 Santa Cruz Co.

Including California Redwood Park, Forest of Nisene Marks State Park, Pajaro River and Valley

Santa Cruz Island, *see* F868.S23

868.S33 Santa Cruz Mountains

Including Montara Mountain

868.S34 Santa Margarita River and Valley

Including Rancho Santa Margarita

Santa Maria River and Valley, *see* F868.S23

Santa Monica Canyon, *see* F868.L8

868.S355 Santa Monica Mountains National Recreation Area

868.S36 Santa Rosa and San Jacinto Mountains National Monument

Santa Rosa Island, *see* F868.S23

Santa Ynez River and Valley, *see* F868.S23

868.S37 Searles Valley

Seiad Creek and Valley, *see* F868.S6

868.S4 Sequoia National Park. Sequoia National Forest

Mount Shasta, *see* F868.S6

868.S49 Shasta Co.

Including Whiskeytown-Shasta-Trinity National Recreation Area

For Lassen Peak, see F868.L34

868.S495 Shasta Mountains

Shaver Lake, *see* F868.F8

Shelter Cove, *see* F868.H8

868.S497 Sierra Co.

868.S5 Sierra Nevada Mountains (The Sierras)

Including Beckworth Trail, Cape Horn, John Muir Trail, Old Emigrant Trail, Squaw Valley

For Donner Party Expedition, see F868.N5

For Kings Canyon National Park, see F868.K48

For Lassen Peak, see F868.L34

For Mount Whitney, see F868.W6

For Sequoia National Park, see F868.S4

For Yosemite Valley, see F868.Y6

868.S6 Siskiyou Co.

Including Butte Valley, Mount Shasta, Seiad Creek and Valley, Tule Lake

Smith River National Recreation Area, *see* F868.D4

868.S66 Solano Co.

868.S7 Sonoma Co.

Including Annadel State Park, Arroyo de San Antonio (Estate), Lake Sonoma

Squaw Valley, *see* F868.S5

868.S8 Stanislaus Co.

Surprise Valley, *see* F868.M6

868.S9 Sutter Co.

868.T2 Lake Tahoe

Including Tahoe National Forest

Mount Tamalpais State Park, *see* F868.M3

868.T3 Tehama Co.

Temecula Creek and Valley, *see* F868.R6

868.T58 Trinity Alps

868.T6 Trinity Co.

868.T8 Tulare Co.

For Mt. Whitney, see F868.W6

For Sequoia National Park, see F868.S4

Tulare Lake and region, *see* F868.S173

Tule Lake, *see* F868.S6

868.T9 Tuolumne Co.

For Calaveras Big Trees State Park, see F868.C15

California

868.A-.Z **Regions, counties, etc., A-Z**

868.T9 Tuolumne Co. — Continued

For Calaveras Grove, see F868.C14

868.T92 Tuolumne River and Valley

868.V5 Ventura Co.

Including Anacapa Island, Ojai Valley

Whiskeytown-Shasta-Trinity National Recreation Area, *see* F868.S49

868.W6 Mount Whitney

Winter Island, *see* F868.C76

Wrights Lake, *see* F868.E3

Yerba Buena (Goat) Island, *see* F869.S3

868.Y5 Yolo Co.

Including Capay Valley

868.Y6 Yosemite Valley. Yosemite National Park

Including Half Dome

868.Y8 Yuba Co.

Zaca Lake, *see* F868.S23

869.A-.Z **Cities, towns, etc., A-Z**

GALE NOTE *The cutter number(s) listed below have been given only as examples by the Library of Congress*

869.A15 General

869.B5 Berkeley

869.C27 Carmel

869.G5 Glendale

Including Forest Lawn Memorial Park

869.H74 Hollywood

869.L7 Long Beach

869.L8 Los Angeles

Subarrange by Table F2 at the end of the text

869.O2 Oakland

869.O5 Ontario

Including Ontario Colony

869.P3 Pasadena

869.S12 Sacramento

869.S22 San Diego

869.S3 San Francisco

Subarrange by Table F2 at the end of the text

Including Yerba Buena (Goat) Island

For Farallon Islands, see F868.F24

Cf. F868.S157, San Francisco Co.

Elements in the population

870.A1 General works

870.A2-.Z Individual elements

For a list of racial, ethnic, and religious elements (with cutter numbers), see E184.A+

Oregon

871 **Periodicals. Societies. Collections**

873 **Museums. Exhibitions, exhibits**

874 **Gazetteers. Dictionaries. Geographic names**

874.3 **Guidebooks**

875 **Biography (Collective). Genealogy (Collective)**

875.2 **Historiography**

Historians, *see* E175.5.A+

875.5 **Study and teaching**

876 **General works. Histories**

876.3 **Juvenile works**

Pamphlets, addresses, essays

876.5 General

876.6 Anecdotes, legends, pageants, etc.

877 **Historic monuments (General). Illustrative material**

Oregon — Continued

878 **Antiquities (Non-Indian)**

By period

879 Early to 1792

Cf. F851.5, Exploring expeditions to the Pacific coast before 1800

Cf. F1060.7, Explorations in the Canadian Northwest before 1821

Cf. F1089.N8, Nootka Sound Controversy, 1789-1790

880 1792-1859

Including the Oregon country; "joint occupation" by Great Britain and the United States, 1818-1846; the Oregon question; Northwest boundary to 1846; Oregon Trail

Including biography: Jesse Applegate, Jason Lee, John McLoughlin, Joseph L. Meek, Isaac Ingalls Stevens, Marcus Whitman, etc.

Cf. E83.84, Wars with the Pacific coast Indians, 1847-1865

Cf. F592.3+, Lewis and Clark Expedition

Cf. F854, International boundary since 1846

Cf. F1060+, Hudson Bay Company

Cf. F1086+, British Columbia, the northern part of the Oregon country since 1846

881 1859-1950

Including admission as a state, February 14, 1859

Including biography: Harry Lane, Alfred Benjamin Meacham, etc.

Cf. D570.85.O8+, World War I, 1914-1918

Cf. D769.85.O8+, World War II, 1939-1945

Cf. E83.84, Wars with Pacific coast Indians, 1847-1865

Cf. E83.87, Modoc War, 1872-1873

Cf. E83.877, Nez Percé War, 1877

Cf. E526.1+, Civil War, 1861-1865 (General)

1951-

881.2 General works

Biography

881.3 Collective

881.35.A-.35.Z Individual, A-Z

GALE NOTE *See note at the head of Table F5 at the end of the text for further instructions on how to subdivide this number*

882.A-.Z **Regions, counties, etc., A-Z**

882.A15 Counties

882.A16 Mountains

882.A17 Rivers

882.A18 Lakes

882.A19 Islands

882.A65 Applegate River and Valley

882.B2 Baker Co.

882.B4 Benton Co.

882.B7 Boundaries

Including Sand Island controversy

For International boundary, see F854, F880

Calapooia River and Valley, *see* F882.L7

882.C3 Cascade Range

Including Spencer Butte

882.C5 Clackamas Co.

For Mount Hood, see F882.H85

882.C53 Clatsop Co.

Including Fort Clatsop National Memorial, Fort Stevens State Park

882.C6 Columbia Co.

For Sauvies Island, see F882.S3

882.C63 Columbia River and Valley, Oreg.

Including Columbia River Highway

For Sand Island controversy, see F882.B7

For Sauvies Island, see F882.S3

Cf. F853 , General

	Oregon
882.A-.Z	**Regions, counties, etc., A-Z — Continued**
882.C7	Coos Co.
	Including Coos Bay
	Cow Creek and Valley (Douglas County), *see* F882.D7
882.C8	Crater Lake. Crater Lake National Park
	Including Mount Mazama
882.C83	Crater National Forest
882.C9	Crook Co.
882.C95	Curry Co.
882.D4	Deschutes Co.
	Including Newberry National Volcanic Monument, Paulina Lake
882.D43	Deschutes National Forest
882.D45	Deschutes River and Valley
882.D7	Douglas Co.
	Including Cow Creek and Valley
	Fort Clatsop National Memorial, *see* F882.C53
	Fort Rock Valley, *see* F882.L15
	Fort Stevens State Park, *see* F882.C53
	French Prairie, *see* F882.W6
882.G5	Gilliam Co.
882.G7	Grant Co.
882.H37	Harney Co.
882.H44	Hells Canyon National Recreation Area
	Cf. F752.H44, Idaho
882.H85	Mount Hood
	Including Timberline Lodge
882.H9	Hood River Co.
	Including Hood River and Valley
882.J14	Jackson Co.
882.J4	Jefferson Co.
882.J73	Joaquin Miller Trail
882.J76	John Day River and Valley
882.J8	Josephine Co.
882.K5	Klamath Co.
	For Crater Lake, see F882.C8
882.L15	Lake Co.
	Including Fort Rock Valley
882.L2	Lane Co.
882.L6	Lincoln Co.
882.L7	Linn Co.
	Including Calapooia River and Valley
882.L78	Long Tom River and Valley
882.M2	Malheur Co.
882.M3	Marion Co.
882.M8	Morrow Co.
882.M9	Multnomah Co.
	For Sauvies Island, see F882.S3
	Newberry National Volcanic Monument, *see* F882.D4
882.O16	Ochoco National Forest
	Owyhee Mountains region, *see* F752.O97
882.O98	Owyhee River and Valley (General, and Oregon)
	Cf. F752.O98, Idaho
	Cf. F847.O98, Nevada
882.P34	Pacific Coast
882.P7	Polk Co.
882.R6	Rogue River and Valley
882.S18	Salmon River and Valley
	Sand Island controversy, *see* F882.B7
882.S2	Santiam National Forest

	Oregon
882.A-.Z	**Regions, counties, etc., A-Z — Continued**
882.S3	Sauvies Island
882.S5	Sherman Co.
882.S56	Siskiyou Mountains
882.S58	Siuslaw National Forest
882.S6	Snake River and Valley, Oreg.
	Cf. F752.S7, General, and Idaho
	Spencer Butte, *see* F882.C3
882.T5	Tillamook Co.
882.U4	Umatilla Co.
882.U43	Umpqua Co.
882.U5	Union Co.
882.W2	Wallowa Co.
	Including Wallowa Lake
882.W25	Wallowa National Forest
882.W3	Wasco Co.
	Including Mosier Hills
882.W4	Washington Co.
882.W5	Wheeler Co.
882.W6	Willamette River and Valley
	Including French Prairie
882.Y2	Yamhill Co.
882.Y24	Yaquina River and Valley
884.A-.Z	**Cities, towns, etc., A-Z**
	GALE NOTE *The cutter number(s) listed below have been given only as examples by the Library of Congress*
884.A8	Astoria
884.E9	Eugene
884.K62	Klamath Falls
884.P39	Pendleton
884.P8	Portland
	Subarrange by Table F2 at the end of the text
884.S2	Salem
	Elements in the population
885.A1	General works
885.A2-.Z	Individual elements
	For a list of racial, ethnic, and religious elements (with cutter numbers), see E184.A+
	Washington
886	**Periodicals. Societies. Collections**
888	**Museums. Exhibitions, exhibits**
889	**Gazetteers. Dictionaries. Geographic names**
889.3	**Guidebooks**
890	**Biography (Collective). Genealogy (Collective)**
890.2	**Historiography**
	Historians, *see* E175.5.A+
890.5	**Study and teaching**
890.5.A1-.5.Z8	General works
890.5.Z9A-.5.Z9Z	Catalogs of audiovisual materials
891	**General works. Histories**
	Including admission as a state, November 11, 1889
	Including by period (Early to 1950) as well as general
	For 1951 and later, see F895+
	Cf. D570.85.W3+, World War I, 1914-1918
	Cf. D769.85.W3+, World War II, 1939-1945
	Cf. E83.84, Wars with Pacific coast Indians, 1847-1865
891.3	**Juvenile works**
	Pamphlets, addresses, essays
891.5	General
891.6	Anecdotes, legends, pageants, etc.

Washington — Continued

892 **Historic monuments (General). Illustrative material**
893 **Antiquities (Non-Indian)**
By period
(894) Early to 1950, *see* F891
1951-
895 General works
Biography
895.2 Collective
895.22.A-.22.Z Individual, A-Z
GALE NOTE *See note at the head of Table F5 at the end of the text for further instructions on how to subdivide this number*
897.A-.Z **Regions, counties, etc., A-Z**
897.A15 Counties
897.A16 Mountains
897.A17 Rivers
897.A18 Lakes
897.A19 Islands
Adams, Mount, *see* F897.K6
897.A2 Adams Co.
897.A7 Asotin Co.
Bainbridge Island, *see* F897.K5
Mount Baker, *see* F897.W57
897.B4 Benton Co.
897.B7 Boundaries
For International boundary, see F854, F880
Cf. F882.B7, Oregon boundary and Sand Island controversy
897.C3 Cascade Range
Including North Cascades National Park, Stevens Pass
Chambers Creek, *see* F897.P6
Chehalis Co., *see* F897.G84
897.C4 Chelan Co.
897.C52 Clallam Co.
Including Mount Angeles
For Olympic National Park, see F897.O5
897.C6 Clark Co. (Clarke Co. to 1925)
For Sauvies Island, see F882.S3
Clover Creek, *see* F897.P6
897.C68 Columbia Co.
897.C7 Columbia River and Valley, Wash.
Including Grand Coulee Dam region
For Sand Island controversy, see F882.B7
For Sauvies Island, see F882.S3
Cf. F853, General
897.C8 Columbia National Forest
Colville River and Valley, *see* F897.S9
897.C85 Cowlitz Co.
897.D7 Douglas Co.
Ebey's Landing National Historical Preserve, *see* F897.I7
897.F4 Ferry Co.
897.F8 Franklin Co.
897.G3 Garfield Co.
Ginkgo Petrified Forest State Park, *see* F897.K53
Grand Coulee Dam region, *see* F897.C7
897.G75 Grant Co.
897.G84 Grays Harbor Co. (Chehalis Co., 1854-1915)
Including Grays Harbor
Hartstene Island, *see* F897.M4
897.H63 Hoh River and Valley
Hood Canal, *see* F897.P9

Washington

897.A-.Z **Regions, counties, etc., A-Z — Continued**

897.I7 Island Co.

Including Ebey's Landing National Historical Preserve, Whidbey Island

897.J4 Jefferson Co.

Including Marrowstone Island, Protection Island

897.J9 Juan de Fuca Strait region

Cf. F897.P9, Puget Sound region

Cf. F1089.V3, Vancouver Island

897.K3 Kettle River and Valley

Cf. F1089.K57, General, and British Columbia

897.K4 King Co.

Including Lake Washington, Vashon Island

897.K5 Kitsap Co.

Including Bainbridge Island

897.K53 Kittitas Co.

Including Ginkgo Petrified Forest State Park

897.K6 Klickitat Co.

Including Mount Adams

897.L35 Lake Roosevelt National Recreation Area

Lake Washington, *see* F897.K4

897.L6 Lewis Co.

897.L7 Lincoln Co.

Marrowstone Island, *see* F897.J4

897.M4 Mason Co.

Including Hartstene Island

Naches River and Valley, *see* F897.Y18

Nile Creek and Valley, *see* F897.Y18

North Cascades National Park, *see* F897.C3

897.O4 Okanogan Co.

Including Methow River and Valley

897.O5 Olympic Mountains. Olympic National Park

For Mount Angeles, see F897.C52

897.P2 Pacific Co.

897.P24 Palouse River and Valley, Washington

Cf. F752.P25, General, and Idaho

897.P4 Pend Oreille Co.

897.P6 Pierce Co.

Including Chambers Creek, Clover Creek

For Mount Rainier (Tacoma), see F897.R2

897.P65 Point Roberts

Protection Island, *see* F897.J4

897.P9 Puget Sound region

Including Fort Nisqualli, Hood Canal

Cf. F897.J9, Juan de Fuca Strait region

897.R2 Mount Rainier (Tacoma). Mount Rainier National Park

897.S17 Saint Helens, Mount

897.S2 San Juan Co.

Including San Juan Islands (San Juan, Orcas, Lopez, and Waldron)

Sand Island, *see* F882.B7

Sauvies Island, *see* F882.S3

897.S48 Similkameen River and Valley

Cf. F1089.S48, General, and British Columbia

897.S5 Skagit Co.

897.S52 Skagit River and Valley

897.S53 Skamania Co.

897.S54 Skokomish River and Valley

897.S6 Snake River and Valley, Wash.

Cf. F752.S7, General, and Idaho

	Washington
897.A-.Z	**Regions, counties, etc., A-Z — Continued**
897.S66	Snohomish Co.
	Including Mount Pilchuck, Three Fingers Mountain
897.S67	Snoqualmie River and Valley
897.S7	Spokane Co.
	Including Medical Lake, Spokane River and Valley
897.S9	Stevens Co.
	Including Colville River and Valley
	Stevens Pass, *see* F897.C3
	Mount Tacoma, *see* F897.R2
	Three Fingers Mountain, *see* F897.S66
897.T5	Thurston Co.
	Vancouver Island, *see* F1089.V3
	Vashon Island, *see* F897.K4
897.W15	Wahkiakum Co.
897.W18	Walla Walla Co.
897.W2	Walla Walla River and Valley
897.W44	Wenatchee River and Valley
897.W57	Whatcom Co.
	Including Mount Baker
	Whidbey Island, *see* F897.I7
897.W59	White River and Valley
897.W6	Whitman Co.
897.W65	Whitman National Monument. Whitman Mission National Historic Site
897.Y18	Yakima Co.
	Including Naches River and Valley, Nile Creek and Valley
897.Y2	Yakima River and Valley
899.A-.Z	**Cities, towns, etc., A-Z**
	GALE NOTE *The cutter number(s) listed below have been given only as examples by the Library of Congress*
899.O5	Olympia
899.P8	Port Angeles
899.S4	Seattle
	Subarrange by Table F2 at the end of the text
899.S7	Spokane
899.T2	Tacoma
899.V2	Vancouver
899.Y15	Yakima
	Elements in the population
900.A1	General works
900.A2-.Z	Individual elements
	For a list of racial, ethnic, and religious elements (with cutter numbers), see E184.A+
	Alaska
901	**Periodicals. Societies. Collections**
901.5	**Museums. Exhibitions, exhibits**
902	**Gazetteers. Dictionaries. Geographic names**
902.3	**Guidebooks**
903	**Biography (Collective). Genealogy (Collective)**
903.2	**Historiography**
	Historians, *see* E175.5.A+
903.5	**Study and teaching**
903.5.A1-5.Z8	General works
903.5.Z9	Catalogs of audiovisual materials
904	**General works. Histories**
904.3	**Juvenile works**
	Pamphlets, addresses, essays
904.5	General
904.6	Anecdotes, legends, pageants, etc.
904.8	**Geography**

	Alaska — Continued
905	**Historic monuments (General). Illustrative material**
906	**Antiquities (Non-Indian)**
	By period
907	Early to 1867
	Including exploration; settlement by the Russians; purchase by the United States, 1867 (E669); Rossiĭsko-Amerikanskai͡a kompanii͡a
	Including biography: Aleksandr Andreevich Baranov, etc.
	Cf. F851.5, Early voyages to Northwest
	Cf. G600+, Polar voyages
908	1867-1896
909	1896-1959
910	1959-1981
	Admission as a state, January 3, 1959
	1981-
910.5	General works
	Biography
910.6	Collective
910.7.A-.7.Z	Individual, A-Z
	GALE NOTE *See note at the head of Table F5 at the end of the text for further instructions on how to subdivide this number*
912.A-.Z	**Regions, etc., A-Z**
912.A15	Counties
912.A16	Mountains
912.A17	Rivers
912.A18	Lakes
912.A19	Islands
912.A43	Alaska, Gulf of
	Aleutian Islands, *see* F951
912.A54	Aniakchak National Monument and Preserve
912.B14	Baranof Island
912.B2	Point Barrow
912.B24	Beaufort Sea
	Bering Sea, *see* F951
912.B57	Bird Creek and Valley (Anchorage Borough)
912.B7	Boundaries
912.B74	Bristol Bay
912.B75	Brooks Range
912.C34	Cape Krusenstern National Monument
912.C43	Chandler River and Valley
912.C47	Clark Lake
	Including Clark Lake National Park and Preserve
912.C6	Cook Inlet region
	Including Turnagain Arm
912.C7	Copper River region
912.D58	Deadfish Lake Region
912.D6	Mount Deborah
	Denali National Park and Preserve, *see* F912.M23
912.D65	Denali State Park
912.F2	Mount Fairweather
912.G36	Gates of the Arctic National Park and Preserve
912.G5	Glacier Bay. Glacier Bay National Monument
912.G64	Gold Creek and Valley
912.H37	Hatcher Pass
912.H8	Mount Huntington
912.I44	Iliamna Lake and region
912.I56	Inside Passage
	Cf. F1089.I5, General, and British Columbia
912.K26	Kachemak Bay State Park. Kachemak Bay State Wilderness Park
912.K3	Katmai National Monument

	Alaska
912.A-.Z	**Regions, etc., A-Z — Continued**
912.K4	Kenai Peninsula
	Including Kenai Fjords National Park
912.K56	Klondike Gold Rush National Historical Park
	Klondike River and Valley, *see* F1095.K5
912.K58	Knik Arm
912.K6	Kobuk River and Valley
912.K62	Kodiak Island
912.K66	Kotzebue Sound and region
912.K67	Koyukuk River and Valley
	Krusenstern, Cape, National Monument, *see* F912.C34
912.K85	Kuskokwim River and Valley
	Lake Clark National Park and Preserve, *see* F912.C47
912.L57	Lituya Bay
912.L65	Long Island (Prince of Wales-Outer Ketchikan Census Area)
912.M2	McKinley, Mount (Denali)
912.M23	McKinley, Mount, National Park (Denali National Park and Preserve)
912.M3	Matanuska River and Valley
912.M55	Minook Creek and Valley
	Mount McKinley, *see* F912.M2
912.M9	Muir Glacier
912.N45	Nenana River and Valley
912.N6	Noatak National Preserve
912.N7	Cape Nome region
912.N73	Nome-Taylor Highway
912.N75	Norton Sound and region
912.P9	Pribilof Islands
	Including Alaska Commercial Company, 1868-1940
912.P95	Prince of Wales Island
912.P97	Prince William Sound region
912.R48	Revillagigedo Island
912.S15	Mount St. Elias
912.S2	Saint Lawrence Island
912.S27	Sergief Island
912.S3	Seward Peninsula
912.S38	Shuyak Island State Park
912.S85	Stikine River and Valley
	Cf. F1089.S85, General, and British Columbia
912.S95	Susitna River and Valley
912.T32	Taku River and Valley
	Cf. F1089.T14, General and British Columbia
912.T4	Thomas Bay
912.T64	Tongass National Forest
	Turnagain Arm, *see* F912.C6
912.T85	Twin Lakes region
912.W56	Willow Creek State Recreation Area
912.W64	Wood-Tikchik State Park
912.W72	Wrangell Mountains
912.W74	Wrangell-Saint Elias National Park and Preserve
912.Y2	Yakutat Bay
912.Y9	Yukon River and Valley (General, and Alaska)
	Cf. F1095.Y9, Yukon Territory
914.A-.Z	**Cities, towns, etc., A-Z**
	GALE NOTE *The cutter number(s) listed below have been given only as examples by the Library of Congress*
914.A5	Anchorage
914.F16	Fairbanks
914.J9	Juneau
914.K4	Ketchikan

Alaska

914.A-.Z **Cities, towns, etc., A-Z — Continued**

914.N6 Nome

914.S6 Sitka

914.S7 Skagway

914.W8 Wrangell

Elements in the population

915.A1 General works

915.A2-.Z Individual elements

For a list of racial, ethnic, and religious elements (with cutter numbers), see E184.A+

Klondike River and Valley, see F1095.K5

951 **Bering Sea and Aleutian Islands**

Including discovery and exploration; antiquities

Cf. D769.87.A4, Aleutian Islands in World War II, 1939-1945

Cf. F912.P9, Pribilof Islands

965 **The territories of the United States (General)**

Including since 1912, Alaska, Hawaii, Puerto Rico

970 **Insular possessions of the United States (General)**

Individual possessions are classified according to location: Guam, see DU647; Hawaii, see DU620+; Puerto Rico, *see* F1951+; American Samoa, *see* DU810+; Virgin Islands of the United States, *see* F2136

975 **Central American, West Indian, and other countries protected by and having close political affiliations with the United States (General)**

For Cuba, see F1751+

For Dominican Republic, see F1931+

For Haiti, see F1912+

For Liberia, see DT621+

For Nicaragua, see F1521+

For Republic of Panama, see F1561+

Canada

1001 **Periodicals. Societies. Collections (Serial)**
For Canadian geographical societies, see G4
1003 **Collections (nonserial). Collected works**
1003.5 **Museums. Collections of Canadiana. Exhibitions, exhibits**
1004 **Gazetteers. Geographic names**
1004.7 **Directories**
Biography
1005 Collective
Individual, *see* F1024.6.A+, F1029.92+
1006 **Dictionaries and encyclopedias**
Including chronological tables
1008 **General works**
For New France, see F1030
1008.2 **Juvenile works**
Pamphlets, addresses, essays
1008.3 General
1008.4 Anecdotes, legends, pageants, etc.
Cf. GR113+, Folklore
Cf. Class P, Literature
1009 **Guidebooks. Handbooks**
1010 **Historic monuments (General)**
1011 **Parks of Canada (Collective descriptive works)**
For works on individual parks including theory, management and description, see the subject or local division
For works on theory, management and history, etc., of Canadian parks and public reservations in general, see SB484.C2
1011.3 **Geography**
Description and travel. Views
1012 General works
Early to 1762, *see* F1030
1013 1763-1866
1015 1867-1950
1016 1951-1980
1017 1981-
1019 **Antiquities (Non-Indian)**
For Indians of Canada, see E78.C2 , E92
For individual Indian tribes, see E99.A+
Social life and customs. Civilization. Intellectual life
Including national characteristics
For New France, see F1030
1021 General works
By period
Early to 1945, *see* F1021
1021.2 1945-
Elements in the population, see F1027, F1035.A+
History
For New France, see F1030
1022 Periodicals. Yearbooks
Chronological tables, *see* F1006
Historiography
1024 General works
Biography of historians
1024.5 Collective
1024.6.A-.6.Z Individual, A-Z
GALE NOTE *See note at the head of Table F5 at the end of the text for further instructions on how to subdivide this number*
1025 Study and teaching
1026 General works
Including political history

Canada

History — Continued

1026.4 Comic and satirical works

1026.6 Addresses, essays, lectures, etc.

General special

1027 French Canadians. French Canadian question

If the pertinent number provides for an A-Z arrangement for elements in the population, assign ".F83"

For works on French Canadians in Quebec (Province), see F1052.92+

For works on French Canadians in other provinces, cities, or towns, see the province, city, or town

1027.5 Historical geography

Including general works on boundaries, territorial expansion, geopolitics

1028 Military history

1028.5 Naval history

Diplomatic history. Foreign and general relations

1029 General works

Class general works on the diplomatic history of a period with the period, e.g. F1034.2, Foreign relations after 1945

For works on relations with a specific country regardless of period, see F1029.5.A+

1029.5.A-.5.Z Relations with individual countries, A-Z

1029.9 Other (not A-Z)

By period

Early to 1603, *see* E101+

For Jacques Cartier, see E133.C3

1030 1603-1763. New France

Including history and description. English conquest of 1629; Company of New France, 1629-1663; Royal Province, 1663; Company of the West Indies, 1665-1674; French explorers before 1760

Including biography: François Bigot; Pierre Boucher; Louis de Buade, comte de Frontenac; Pierre Jacques de Taffanel, marquis de La Jonquière; François Xavier de Laval de Montmorency; Pierre du Guast, sieur de Monts; Jean Talon, comte d'Orsainville; Philippe de Rigaud, marquis de Vaudreuil; Jean Baptiste Bissot, sieur de Vincennes; etc.

Cf. E81+, Indian wars

Cf. E195+, Intercolonial wars

Cf. F350.5+, Mississippi River and Valley

Cf. F366+, Louisiana

Cf. F544, The Illinois country

Cf. F1036+, Acadia, Nova Scotia

Cf. F1060+, Hudson's Bay Company and Rupert's Land

Writings of Francis Parkman

1030.P24 Collected works. By date

1030.P245 Partial collections. Selections. By date

1030.P247 Battle for North America

California and Oregon trail, *see* F592

Conspiracy of Pontiac, *see* E83.76

1030.P25 France and England in North America. By date

Selections, *see* F1030.P245

1030.P252-.P268 Individual works

Under each (using successive cutter numbers):

1 English editions

2 Translations

1030.P261-.P262 Pioneers of France

Subarrange by table below F1030.P252-.P268

Jesuits in North America, *see* F1030.7+

LaSalle and the discovery of the Great West, *see* F1030.5

1030.P264-.P265 Old régime in Canada

Subarrange by table below F1030.P252-.P268

Canada

History

By period

1030 1603-1763. New France

Writings of Francis Parkman

1030.P25 France and England in North America. By date

1030.P252-.P268 Individual works — Continued

1030.P267-.P268 Count Frontenac and New France under Louis XIV

Subarrange by table below F1030.P252-.P268

Montcalm and Wolfe, *see* E199

Half century of conflict, *see* E198

1030.1 Champlain, Samuel de

Including Champlain Tercentenary, 1908

For Lake Champlain Tercentenary, 1909, see F127.C6

1030.13 Brulé, Étienne

1030.15 Nicolet, Jean

1030.2 Marquette, Jacques

Cf. F352, Exploration of the Mississippi

1030.3 Joliet, Louis

Cf. F352, Exploration of the Mississippi

1030.4 Hennepin, Louis

Cf. F352, Exploration of the Mississippi

1030.5 La Salle, Robert Cavelier, sieur de

Cf. F352, Exploration of the Mississippi

Jesuits in New France

Including adjacent regions

1030.7.A-.7.Z5 General works

Jesuit relations

1030.7.Z6-.7.Z9 Collective

1030.8 Individual relations and other writings

Including works about individual missionaries

1030.9 1754-1763

Including last years of French rule; the English conquest

Cf. E199, French and Indian War, 1755-1763; Quebec Campaign, 1759

1763-

1031 General works

1031.5 19th century

1032 1763-1867

Including Province of Quebec, 1760; its expansion by Quebec Act of 1774; its division in 1791 and reunion in 1841; Canadian Rebellion, 1837-1838; burning of the "Caroline," 1837; Fenian Raids, 1866-1870; Union of British North American provinces, 1867

Including biography: George Brown, 1818-1880; Joseph Frederick Wallet Des Barres; Lord Dorchester (Guy Carleton); Sir Alexander Tilloch Galt; Sir Frederick Haldimand; Sir Francis Hincks; Sir Louis Hippolyte La Fontaine; Thomas D'Arcy McGee; William Lyon Mackenzie; Louis Joseph Papineau; Lord Sydenham (Charles Edward Poulett Thomson); etc.

Cf. E201+, American Revolution

Cf. E263.C2, E263.N9, British North America

Cf. E231, Quebec Campaign, 1775-1776

Cf. E277+; F1036+ ,F1041+ ,F1056+, American loyalists in Canada

Cf. E359.85, War of 1812

Cf. E355+, Military operations, War of 1812

Cf. E470.95, Confederates in Canada, St. Albans Raid, 1864

1033 1867- . Dominion of Canada

Including annexation question; Fenian invasion of 1870-1871

Including biography: Richard Belford Bennett; Sir George Étienne Cartier; Sir George Eulas Foster; Sir Sam Hughes; William Lyon Mackenzie King; Sir Wilfrid Laurier; Sir John Alexander MacDonald; David Mills; Sir Clifford Sifton; Lord Strathcona and Mount Royal (Donald Alexander Smith); Sir John Sparrow David Thompson; Sir Charles Tupper; etc.

Canada
History
By period
1763-
1033 1867- . Dominion of Canada — Continued
Cf. DT930+, South African War, 1899-1902
Cf. F1060.9, Purchase of Northwest Territories, 1869; Riel Rebellion, 1885
Cf. F1063, Red River Rebellion, 1869-1870
1034 1914-1945
Including New Dominion status, 1926; Statute of Westminster, 1931
Including biography: Pierre Edouard Blondin, Henri Bourassa, etc.
Cf. D501+, World War I, 1914-1918
Cf. D731+, World War II, 1939-1945
Cf. F1123, Newfoundland with Labrador established as a province, 1949
1945-
Cf. DT407.43, Somalia Affair, 1992-1997
1034.2 General works
Biography
1034.3.A2 Collective
1034.3.A3-.3.Z Individual
GALE NOTE *See note at the head of Table F5 at the end of the text for further instructions on how to subdivide this number; the cutter number(s) listed below have been given only as examples by the Library of Congress*
1034.3.D5 Diefenbaker, John George
1034.3.P4 Pearson, Lester B.
1035.A-.Z **Elements in the population**
The cutter numbers are intended to be used as a guide for the best distribution of numbers and not to be used as a fixed standard or to affect numbers already assigned
Including racial and ethnic groups and religious bodies which have significance in the history of Canada
For elements in individual regions, provinces, cities, etc., see the region, province, city, etc.
1035.A1 General works
Including foreign elements (General), minorities, etc.
For race conflicts and problems, see F1027
Acadians, *see* F1027
1035.A5 Americans
1035.A7 Arabs
1035.A74 Armenians
1035.F75 Asians
Asians, South, *see* F1035.S66
1035.A87 Assyrians
1035.A94 Austrians
1035.B3 Basques
1035.B4 Belgians
Blacks, *see* F1035.N3
1035.B7 British
Cf. F1035.E53, Canadians, English-speaking
Cf. F1035.I6, Irish
Cf. F1035.S4, Scotch. Scots
1035.B84 Bulgarians
1035.C27 Cambodians
1035.C3 Catholics
1035.C4 Celts
1035.C48 Chileans
1035.C5 Chinese
1035.C64 Cornish
1035.C7 Croats
1035.C9 Czechs
1035.D3 Danes

Canada

1035.A-.Z **Elements in the population — Continued**

1035.D76 Dukhobors

1035.D8 Dutch

1035.E28 East Europeans

1035.E3 East Indians

1035.E53 English-speaking Canadians

Use only for English speakers in predominantly French-speaking areas, i.e., Quebec

1035.E85 Estonians

1035.E89 Ethiopians

1035.F48 Filipinos

1035.F5 Finns

1035.F8 French

French Canadians (General), *see* F1027

For works on French Canadians in Quebec (Province), see F1053

1035.G3 Germans

1035.G7 Greeks

1035.H34 Haitians

1035.H36 Hawaiians

1035.H54 Hindus

1035.H76 Huguenots

1035.H8 Hungarians

1035.I2 Icelanders

Indians, *see* E78.A+

1035.I55 Indochinese

1035.I58 Iranians

1035.I6 Irish

1035.I8 Italians

1035.J3 Japanese

1035.J5 Jews

1035.K36 Kashubes

1035.K65 Koreans

1035.L27 Latin Americans

1035.L3 Latvians

1035.L43 Lebanese

1035.L5 Lithuanians

1035.M33 Macedonians

1035.M35 Maltese

1035.M45 Mennonites

1035.M67 Mormons

1035.M87 Muslims

1035.N3 Negroes. Blacks

1035.N52 Nigerians

1035.N6 Norwegians

(1035.O6) Orientals, *see* F1035.A75

1035.P34 Pakistanis

1035.P36 Palatines

1035.P6 Poles

1035.P65 Portuguese

1035.R65 Romanians

1035.R79 Russian Germans

1035.R8 Russians

Ruthenians, *see* F1035.U5

1035.S3 Scandinavians

For Danes, see F1035.D3

For Norwegians, see F1035.N6

For Swedes, see F1035.S9

1035.S4 Scotch. Scots

1035.S47 Serbs

1035.S54 Sikhs

Canada

1035.A-.Z **Elements in the population — Continued**

1035.S6 Slavs

1035.S63 Slovaks

1035.S64 Slovenes

1035.S65 Somalis

1035.S66 South Asians

1035.S68 Spaniards

1035.S88 Swabians

1035.S9 Swedes

1035.S94 Swiss

1035.T85 Tunisians

1035.U5 Ukrainians

1035.W44 Welsh

1035.W47 West Indians

1035.W5 White Russians

Regions, provinces, territories

1035.8 Maritime provinces

Including Atlantic coast of Canada

Cf. F106, Atlantic coast of North America

Nova Scotia. Acadia

1036 Periodicals. Societies. Collections

1036.4 Gazetteers. Dictionaries. Geographic names

1036.5 Directories

Biography

1036.8 Collective

Individual, *see* F1038

1037 General works

Including description and travel, social life and customs

1037.4 Juvenile works

Pamphlets, addresses, essays, etc.

1037.5 General

1037.6 Anecdotes, legends, pageants, etc.

Cf. GR113+, Folklore

Cf. Class P, Literature

1037.7 Guidebooks. Handbooks

1037.8 Historic monuments (General). Illustrative material

1037.9 Antiquities (Non-Indian)

For Indians, see E78.A+ , E99.A+

1038 History

Including French beginnings; English conquest; Winslow's Expedition, 1755; removal of Acadians; settlement by New Englanders, 1760-1761

Including biography: Thomas Chandler Haliburton; Sir Brenton Halliburton; Joseph Howe; Charles Amador de Saint-Étienne de la Tour; Sir William Alexander, Earl of Stirling (Cf. PR2369.S5); etc.

Cf. E78.C2, Indians in Canada

Cf. E78.N9, Indians in Nova Scotia

Cf. E83.72, Wars with eastern Indians, 1722-1726

Cf. E184.A2, Acadians in the United States

Cf. E263.N9, American Revolution, 1775-1783

Cf. E277+, American loyalists (General)

Cf. F16+, Maine

Cf. F27.W3, Washington County, including St. Croix Island

Cf. F380, Acadians in Louisiana

Cf. F1030, New France, 1603-1763

1039.A-.Z Regions, counties, etc., A-Z

1039.A2 Annapolis Co.

Including Fort Anne Park

1039.A25 Antigonish Co.

1039.A74 Atlantic Coast

Canada
Regions, provinces, territories
Nova Scotia. Acadia
1039.A-.Z Regions, counties, etc., A-Z — Continued
1039.B7 Boundaries
Including old boundaries of Acadia, etc.
For International boundary since 1783, see E398
Brier Island, *see* F1039.F9
Cabot Trail, *see* F1039.C2
1039.C15 Cape Breton Co.
1039.C2 Cape Breton Island (Île Royale)
Including Cabot Trail
Cf. F1039.C15, Cape Breton Co.
Cf. F1039.I5, Inverness Co.
Cf. F1039.R5, Richmond Co.
Cf. F1039.V5, Victoria Co.
1039.C3 Cape Sable Island
Chezzetcook Inlet, *see* F1039.H3
1039.C5 Chignecto Isthmus
Including Fort Lawrence
1039.C6 Colchester Co.
1039.C8 Cumberland Co.
1039.D5 Digby Co.
1039.F9 Bay of Fundy
Including Brier Island
1039.G8 Guysborough Co.
1039.H3 Halifax Co.
Including Chezzetcook Inlet, McNabs Island, etc.
1039.H4 Hants Co.
Île Royale, *see* F1039.C2
1039.I5 Inverness Co.
1039.J43 Jeddore Harbour
1039.K43 Kejimkujik Lake and region
1039.K44 Kejimkujik National Park
1039.K5 Kings Co.
1039.L9 Lunenburg Co.
McNabs Island, *see* F1039.H3
1039.O35 Oak Island
1039.P6 Pictou Co.
Including Pictou Island
Prince Edward Island, *see* F1046+
1039.Q3 Queens Co.
1039.R5 Richmond Co.
1039.S13 Sable Island
1039.S18 Saint Ann's Bay and region
Gulf of St. Lawrence, *see* F1050
1039.S19 Saint Margaret's Bay and Region
1039.S20 Saint Mary's Bay and region
1039.S27 Saint Paul Island
1039.S5 Shelburne Co.
1039.S55 Shubenacadie River and Valley
Surette's Island, *see* F1039.Y3
1039.T35 Tancook Island. Big Tancook Island
1039.V5 Victoria Co.
1039.Y3 Yarmouth Co.
Including Surette's Island
1039.5.A-.5.Z Cities, towns, etc., A-Z
GALE NOTE *The cutter number(s) listed below have been given only as examples by the Library of Congress*
1039.5.A16 Annapolis Royal

Canada

Regions, provinces, territories

Nova Scotia. Acadia

1039.5.A-.5.Z Cities, towns, etc., A-Z — Continued

1039.5.D3 Dartmouth

1039.5.G5 Glace Bay

1039.5.H17 Halifax

1039.5.L8 Louisburg

Including Fortress of Louisbourg National Historic Park

For Capture of Louisburg, 1745, see E198

For Capture of Louisburg, 1758, see E199

1039.5.S9 Sydney

1039.5.Y3 Yarmouth

Elements in the population

1040.A1 General works

1040.A2-.Z Individual elements

For a list of racial, ethnic, and religious elements, (with cutter numbers), see F1035.A+

New Brunswick

1041 Periodicals. Societies. Collections

1041.4 Gazetteers. Dictionaries. Geographic names

1041.5 Directories

Biography

1041.8 Collective

Individual, *see* F1043-1044.5

1042 General works

Including description and travel, social life and customs

1042.4 Juvenile works

Pamphlets, addresses, essays

1042.5 General

1042.6 Anecdotes, legends, pageants, etc.

Cf. GR113+, Folklore

Cf. Class P, Literature

1042.8 Historic monuments (General). Illustrative material

1042.9 Antiquities (Non-Indian)

For Indians, see E78.A+

1043 History

Entered the Dominion of Canada, 1867

Cf. E263.N9, American Revolution, 1775-1783

Cf. E277+, Loyalists, American Revolution, 1775-1783

Cf. E398, Boundary troubles with the United States

1044.A-.Z Regions, counties, etc., A-Z

1044.A4 Albert Co.

1044.A7 Aroostook River and Valley, N.B.

Cf. F27.A7, General, and Maine

1044.B7 Boundaries

For International boundary since 1783 and Aroostook War, see E398

1044.C2 Campobello Island

1044.C3 Carleton Co.

1044.C4 Chaleur Bay

1044.C5 Charlotte Co.

For Campobello Island, see F1044.C2

For Deer Island, see F1044.D3

For Grand Manan Island, see F1044.G7

Chignecto Isthmus, *see* F1039.C5

1044.D3 Deer Island

1044.F6 Fort Beauséjour National Park

Fundy, Bay of, *see* F1039.F9

1044.F86 Fundy National Park

Gaspé Peninsula, *see* F1054.G2

Canada
Regions, provinces, territories
New Brunswick
1044.A-.Z Regions, counties, etc., A-Z — Continued
1044.G7 Grand Manan Island
1044.K5 Kings Co.
1044.K53 Kingston Peninsula
1044.L35 Lamèque Island
1044.M3 Madawaska Co.
Middle Island, *see* F1044.M5
1044.M5 Miramichi River and Valley
Including Middle Island
1044.M53 Miscou Island
1044.N7 Nepisiguit River and Valley
1044.N83 Northwest Miramichi River and Valley
1044.P3 Passamaquoddy Bay region, N.B
Cf. F27.P3, Maine
1044.S17 St. Croix River and Valley, N.B
Cf. F27.S2 , General, and Maine
1044.S2 St. John River and Valley (General, and New Brunswick)
Cf. F27.S3 , Maine
Gulf of St. Lawrence, *see* F1050
1044.S9 Sugarloaf Provincial Park
1044.T6 Tobique River and Valley
1044.Y65 York County
1044.5.A-.5.Z Cities, towns, etc., A-Z
GALE NOTE *The cutter number(s) listed below have been given only as examples by the Library of Congress*
1044.5.F8 Fredericton
1044.5.M7 Moncton
1044.5.S14 St. John
Elements in the population
1045.A1 General works
1045.A2-.Z Individual elements
For a list of racial, ethnic, and religious elements, (with cutter numbers), see F1035.A+
Prince Edward Island
1046 Periodicals. Societies. Collections
1046.4 Gazetteers. Dictionaries. Geographic names
1046.5 Directories
Biography
1046.8 Collective
Individual, *see* F1048-1049.5
1047 General works
Including description and travel, social life and customs
1047.4 Juvenile works
Pamphlets, addresses, essays
1047.5 General
1047.6 Anecdotes, legends, pageants, etc.
Cf. GR113+, Folklore
Cf. Class P, Literature
1047.7 Guidebooks. Handbooks
1047.8 Historic monuments (General). Illustrative material
1047.9 Antiquities (Non-Indian)
For Indians, see E78.A+, E99.A+
1048 History
Including separating from Nova Scotia, 1769
1049.A-.Z Regions, counties, etc., A-Z
1049.K5 Kings Co.
1049.P7 Prince Co.

Canada
Regions, provinces, territories
Prince Edward Island
1049.A-.Z Regions, counties, etc., A-Z — Continued
1049.Q6 Queens Co.
1049.W47 West River
1049.5.A-.5.Z Cities, towns, etc., A-Z
GALE NOTE *The cutter number(s) listed below have been given only as examples by the Library of Congress*
1049.5.C5 Charlottetown
1049.5.S8 Summerside
Elements in the population
1049.7.A1 General works
1049.7.A2-.7.Z Individual elements
For a list of racial, ethnic, and religious elements (with cutter numbers), see F1035.A+
1050 St. Lawrence Gulf, River, and Valley (General)
Cf. F127.S23, St. Lawrence Valley, N.Y.
Cf. F127.T5, Thousand Islands
Cf. F1054.A6, Anticosti Island
Cf. F1054.O7, Isle of Orleans
Cf. F1054.S26, St. Helen's Island
Cf. F1054.S3, St. Lawrence Valley, Quebec
Cf. F1059.S4, St. Lawrence Valley, Ontario
Cf. F1121+, Newfoundland
Cf. F1170, Saint Pierre and Miquelon
Quebec
1051 Periodicals. Societies. Collections
1051.4 Gazetteers. Dictionaries. Geographic names
1051.5 Directories
Biography
1051.8 Collective
Individual, *see* F1052.96-1054.5.A+
1052 General works
Including description and travel, social life and customs, etc.
1052.4 Juvenile works
Pamphlets, addresses, essays
1052.5 General
1052.6 Anecdotes, legends, pageants, etc.
Cf. GR113+, Folklore
Cf. Class P, Literature
1052.7 Guidebooks. Handbooks
1052.8 Historic monuments (General). Illustrative material
1052.9 Antiquities (Non-Indian)
Indians, *see* E78.A+, E99.A+
History
1052.92 Study and teaching
1052.95 General works
By period
Through 1791, *see* F1030
1053 1791-1960
Including biography: Pierre Stanislas Bedard; RenéEdouard Caron; Earl of Dalhousie (George Ramsay); HonoréMercier; etc.
Cf. E184.F85, French Canadians in the United States
Cf. E231, Quebec Campaign
Cf. E263.C2, American Revolution, 1775-1783
Cf. E277+, F1058, American loyalists
Cf. E355+, Military operations (War of 1812)
Cf. E359.85, Canadian participation (War of 1812)
Cf. F1027, French Canadians (General)

Canada
Regions, provinces, territories
Quebec
History
By period — Continued
1960-
1053.2 General works
Biography
1053.24 Collective
1053.25.A-.25.Z Individual, A-Z
GALE NOTE *See note at the head of Table F5 at the end of the text for further instructions on how to subdivide this number*
1054.A-.Z Regions, counties, seigniories, etc., A-Z
1054.A3 Abitibi Co. Abitibi (region)
1054.A6 Anticosti Island
1054.A67 Argenteuil Co.
1054.A7 Arthabaska Co.
Including Bois-Francs, etc.
1054.B35 Baie Saint-Paul region
1054.B36 Bas-Saint-Láurent
1054.B38 Beauce Co.
1054.B45 Bellechasse Co.
1054.B54 Berthier Co.
1054.B58 Bizard Island
Bois-Francs, *see* F1054.A7
1054.B6 Bonaventure Co.
1054.B63 Bonaventure Island
1054.B7 Boundaries
For International boundary since 1783, see E398
Cf. F42.B7, New Hampshire boundary
Cf. F127.B7, New York boundary
1054.B8 Brome Co.
Including Missisquoi River and Valley, Quebec, etc.
Cf. F57.M7, Vermont
1054.C22 Caplan River and Valley
1054.C4 Cent-Iles
Chaleur Bay, *see* F1044.C4
1054.C44 Chambly Co.
Including Fort Chambly National Historic Park
1054.C445 Charlevoix Region
1054.C45 Chateauguay Co.
1054.C49 Chicoutimi Co.
1054.C7 Compton Co.
1054.C75 Côte de Beaupré (Seigniory)
Côte-du-Sud, *see* F1054.S3
Côte Nord, *see* F1054.S3
1054.C8 Crane Island (Île aux Grues)
1054.D4 Deux Montagnes Co.
1054.D6 Dorchester Co.
1054.D9 Drummond Co.
1054.E13 Eastern Townships
For Bois-Francs, see F1054.A7
1054.G2 Gaspé Peninsula. Gaspé District
Including Île Percée
For Chaleur Bay, see F1044.C4
1054.G26 Gatineau River and Valley
Grosse Île, *see* F1054.S3
Hudson Strait, *see* F1103
1054.H9 Huntington Co.
1054.I3 Île aux Coudres

Canada

Regions, provinces, territories

Quebec

1054.A-.Z Regions, counties, seigniories, etc., A-Z — Continued

1054.I35 Île aux Noix

Including Fort Lennox

1054.I5 Île Verte

James Bay region, *see* F1059.J3

1054.J47 Jesus Island

1054.K2 Kamouraska Co.

1054.L17 Lanaudière

1054.L2 L'Assomption Co.

Laurentian Mountains, *see* F1054.S3

1054.L3 Levis Co.

1054.L57 L'Islet Co.

1054.M18 Magdalen Islands (Îles Madeleine)

1054.M2 Mantawa River and Valley

1054.M35 Massue (Seigniory)

1054.M4 Matane Co.

1054.M42 Matapédia River and Valley

1054.M45 Megantic Co.

For Bois-Francs, see F1054.A7

1054.M5 Lake Memphremagog region, Quebec

Cf. F57.M5, Vermont

1054.M59 Mingan Islands

1054.M6 Missisquoi Co.

1054.M79 Montmagny Co.

1054.M8 Montmorency Co.

1054.M83 Montreal District

1054.N5 New Quebec (Ungava) District

Ungava was created as district of Northwest Territories in 1895; in 1912 was annexed to the province of Quebec as New Quebec

North Shore, *see* F1054.S3

1054.N93 Nunavik

1054.O7 Isle of Orleans

1054.O9 Ottawa River and Valley (General, and Quebec)

Cf. F1059.O91, Ontario

1054.O94 Outaouais region

1054.P36 Parc de la Jacques-Cartier

1054.P365 Parc de Plaisance

1054.P367 Parc des Hautes-Gorges-de-la-Rivière-Malbaie

1054.P37 Parc du Mont-Orford

1054.P54 Piémont des Appalaches

1054.P8 Pontiac Co.

1054.P83 Port Burwell (Island)

1054.P85 Portneuf Co.

1054.Q4 Quebec Co.

1054.Q5 Quebec District

1054.R5 Richelieu River and Valley

1054.R615 Rivière-du-Loup Co. and region

1054.R87 Rupert River and Valley

1054.S13 Saguenay Co.

For New Quebec District, see F1054.N5

1054.S14 Saguenay River and Valley

Cf. F1054.S267, Lake St. John

1054.S254 Saint Francis River and Valley

1054.S26 St. Helen's Island

1054.S264 St. Hyacinthe Co.

1054.S267 Lake St. John

	Canada
	Regions, provinces, territories
	Quebec
1054.A-.Z	Regions, counties, seigniories, etc., A-Z — Continued
1054.S3	St. Lawrence Gulf, River, and Valley, Quebec
	Including Côte-du-Sud, Laurentian Mountains, North Shore, Grosse Île
	Cf. F1050 , General
1054.S33	Saint Maurice River and Valley
1054.S34	Saint-Ours (Seigniory)
1054.S345	Saint Peter, Lake
1054.S48	Shefford Co.
1054.S7	Stanstead Co.
	Lake Tamiscamingue, *see* F1054.T6
	Témiscamingue Co., *see* F1054.T6
1054.T29	Temiscouata Co.
1054.T4	Terrebonne Co.
	Thousand Islands, *see* F127.T5
1054.T5	Three Rivers District
1054.T6	Timiskaming (region). Témiscamingue Co.
	Including Lake Timiskaming
	Trois Rivières Co., *see* F1054.T5
	Two Mountains Co., *see* F1054.D4
	Ungava, *see* F1054.N5
1054.V3	Varennes (Seigniory)
1054.V47	Verchères Co.
1054.Y3	Yamaska Co.
1054.5.A-.5.Z	Cities, towns, etc., A-Z
	GALE NOTE *The cutter number(s) listed below have been given only as examples by the Library of Congress*
1054.5.H8	Hull
1054.5.M8	Montreal
	Subarrange by Table F2 at the end of the text
1054.5.Q3	Quebec
1054.5.S55	Sherbrooke
1054.5.T53	Three Rivers
1054.5.Y2	Yamachiche (Village and parish)
	Elements in the population
1055.A1	General works
1055.A2-.Z	Individual elements
	For a list of racial, ethnic, and religious elements (with cutter numbers), see F1035.A+
	Ontario
1056	Periodicals. Societies. Collections
1056.4	Gazetteers. Dictionaries. Geographic names
1056.5	Directories
	Biography
1056.8	Collective
	Individual, *see* F1058-1059.5.A+
1057	General works
	Including description and travel, social life and customs
1057.4	Juvenile works
	Pamphlets, addresses, essays
1057.5	General
1057.6	Anecdotes, legends, pageants, etc.
	Cf. GR113+, Folklore
	Cf. Class P, Literature
1057.7	Guidebooks. Handbooks
1057.8	Historic monuments (General). Illustrative material
1057.9	Antiquities (Non-Indian)
	For Indians, see E78.O5, E99.A+

Canada
Regions, provinces, territories
Ontario — Continued
1058 History
For early history to 1791, see F1030, F1053
Including United empire loyalists from the United States; political history
Including biography: Richard Cartwright, Sir Oliver Mowat, Sir John Beverley Robinson, John Graves Simcoe, etc.
Cf. E78.C2,E78.O5, Indians
Cf. E277+, American loyalists (General)
Cf. E359.85, War of 1812
Cf. E355+, Military operations, War of 1812
Cf. F1032, Canadian Rebellion, 1837
1059.A-.Z Regions, counties, etc., A-Z
Addington Co., *see* F1059.L5
1059.A3 Algoma District
Cf. F1059.T5, Thunder Bay District
1059.A4 Algonquin Provincial Park
Including Opeongo Lake
1059.A44 Almaguin Highlands
1059.B36 Bathurst District
1059.B53 Blackstone Harbour Provincial Park
1059.B64 Bon Echo Provincial Park
1059.B7 Boundaries
For International boundary, see F550.5
Cf. F1054.B7, Quebec boundary
1059.B82 Brant Co.
1059.B95 Bruce Co.
1059.C3 Carleton Co.
1059.C53 Charleston, Lake and region
1059.C7 Credit River and Valley
1059.D46 Detroit River and Valley
Cf. F572.D46, General, and Mich
Cf. F1059.Y6, Don River and Valley
1059.D88 Dufferin Co.
1059.D9 Dundas Co.
1059.D93 Durham Co.
1059.E4 Elgin Co.
1059.E46 Lake Eloida region, Ont.
1059.E6 Lake Erie region, Ont.
Cf. F555, General
1059.E7 Essex Co.
1059.F3 Fathom Five Provincial Park
1059.F85 French River and Valley
1059.F9 Frontenac Co. Frontenac Provincial Park
1059.G3 Georgian Bay region
1059.G5 Glengarry Co.
1059.G78 Grand River and Valley
1059.G84 Grey Co.
1059.H27 Haliburton Co.
1059.H3 Hastings Co.
1059.H9 Humber River and Valley
1059.H92 Huron Co.
1059.H95 Lake Huron region, Ont.
Cf. F554, General
1059.J3 James Bay region
Joseph, Lake, *see* F1059.M9
1059.K2 Kawartha Lakes
1059.K3 Kent Co.
1059.K5 Killarney Provincial Park

Canada

Regions, provinces, territories

Ontario

1059.A-.Z Regions, counties, etc., A-Z — Continued

1059.K52 Killbear Provincial Park

1059.L2 Lake of the Woods region (General, and Ont.)

Cf. F1064.L2, Manitoba

1059.L23 Lambton Co.

1059.L3 Lanark Co.

1059.L4 Leeds Co.

1059.L5 Lennox and Addington Co.

1059.L8 Long Point

1059.M27 Manitoulin Island

1059.M6 Middlesex Co.

1059.M65 Mississippi River and Valley

1059.M9 Muskoka District. Muskoka Lake region

Including Lake Joseph, Peninsula Lake

Niagara Falls, *see* F127.N8

1059.N5 Niagara Peninsula

Cf. F127.N6, Niagara River region (General, and New York)

Cf. F1059.Q3, Queen Victoria Niagara Falls Park

Cf. F1059.S58, Short Hills Provincial Park

1059.N55 Nipissing District

1059.N6 Norfolk Co.

For Long Point, see F1059.L8

1059.N65 Northumberland Co.

Nym Lake and region, *see* F1059.T5

1059.O5 Ontario Co.

1059.O6 Lake Ontario region, Ont.

Including Toronto Islands, etc.

Cf. F556, General

Opeongo Lake, *see* F1059.A4

1059.O91 Ottawa River and Valley, Ont.

Cf. F1054.O9, General, and Quebec

1059.O98 Oxford Co.

1059.P25 Peel Co.

Peninsula Lake (Muskoka), *see* F1059.M9

1059.P3 Perth Co.

1059.P4 Peterborough Co.

Including Stony Lake

1059.P65 Polar Bear Provincial Park

1059.P75 Prince Edward

1059.Q3 Queen Victoria Niagara Falls Park

Cf. F127.N8, Niagara Falls

1059.Q4 Quetico Provincial Park

1059.Q6 Bay of Quinte

1059.R4 Renfrew Co.

1059.R46 Rideau River and Valley

1059.S3 Lake St. Clair region, Ont.

Cf. F572.S34, Michigan

1059.S33 St. Joseph Island

1059.S4 St. Lawrence River and Valley, Ont.

Cf. F1050, General

1059.S49 Severn River and Valley

Severn-Trent Waterway, *see* F1059.T7

1059.S58 Short Hills Provincial Park

1059.S59 Simcoe, Lake

1059.S6 Simcoe Co.

1059.S63 South Nation River and Valley

1059.S65 Sparrow Lake (Muskoka District and Simcoe County)

Canada

Regions, provinces, territories

Ontario

1059.A-.Z Regions, counties, etc., A-Z — Continued

Stony Lake, *see* F1059.P4

1059.S89 Stormont, Dundas and Glengarry

Cf. F1059.D9, Dundas Co.

Cf. F1059.G5, Glengarry Co.

1059.S9 Lake Superior region, Ont.

Cf. F552, General

1059.T34 Talbot Settlement

1059.T38 Thames River and Valley

1059.T5 Thunder Bay District and region

Including Nym Lake and region

Cf. F1059.A3, Algoma District

1059.T53 Timagani Lake and region

1059.T56 Timiskaming

Toronto Islands, *see* F1059.O6

1059.T7 Trent River and Valley. Trent-Severn Waterway

Trent-Severn Waterway, *see* F1059.T7

1059.W32 Waterloo Co.

1059.W34 Wawa Lake and region

1059.W36 Welland Co.

Including Navy Island

1059.W37 Wellington Co.

1059.W4 Wentworth Co.

1059.W63 Woodland Caribou Provincial Park

1059.Y6 York Co. York Regional Municipality

Including Don River and Valley

1059.5.A-.5.Z Cities, towns, etc., A-Z

GALE NOTE *The cutter number(s) listed below have been given only as examples by the Library of Congress*

1059.5.H2 Hamilton

1059.5.L6 London

1059.5.N5 Niagara

Present name: Niagara-on-the-Lake

1059.5.N55 Niagara Falls

Cf. F127.N8, New York

Cf. F1059.Q3, Queen Victoria Niagara Falls Park

1059.5.O9 Ottawa

1059.5.T68 Toronto

Subarrange by Table F2 at the end of the text

1059.5.W5 Windsor

Elements in the population

1059.7.A1 General works

1059.7.A2-.7.Z Individual elements

For a list of racial, ethnic, and religious elements (with cutter numbers), see F1035.A+

Canadian Northwest. Northwest Territories

Including region to the west and northwest of ancient New France

Including Hudson Bay, Hudson's Bay Company, Rupert's Land, Northwest Company of Canada

For boundaries, see F597, F854, F880, United States; F912.B7, Alaska; F1059.B7, Ontario

Cf. F1060.9, Purchase of Northwest Territories, 1869

Cf. F1090, Canadian Rocky Mountains

Cf. G575+, Polar regions

Cf. G640+, Northwest Passage

1060.A1 Periodicals. Societies. Collections

1060.A2-.Z General works

Including history, description and travel

1060.1 Gazetteers. Dictionaries. Geographic names

Canada

Regions, provinces, territories

Canadian Northwest. Northwest Territories — Continued

1060.15 Museums. Exhibitions, exhibits

1060.2 Directories

Biography

1060.3 Collective

Individual, *see* F1060.7+

1060.35 Juvenile works

Pamphlets, addresses, essays

1060.37 General

1060.38 Anecdotes, legends, pageants, etc.

Cf. GR113+, Folklore

Cf. Class P, Literature

1060.4 Guidebooks. Handbooks

1060.5 Historic monuments (General). Illustrative material

1060.6 Antiquities (Non-Indian)

For Eskimos, see E99.E7

For Indians, see E78.A+ , E99.A+

By period

Including history, explorations, description and travel

1060.7 Early to 1821

Including biography: Médard Chouart, sieur des Groseilliers; Matthew Cocking; Daniel Williams Harmon; Samuel Hearne; Alexander Henry, 1739-1824; Pierre Gautier de Varennes, sieur de La Vérendrye; Sir Alexander Mackenzie; Pierre Esprit Radisson; David Thompson; etc.

Cf. F1030, New France and early French explorations (General)

Cf. F1063, Red River Settlement, 1815-1816

Cf. F1089.N8, Nootka Sound Controversy, 1789-1790

1060.8 1821-1867

Including biography: John McLeod, Sir George Simpson, Thomas Simpson, etc.

Cf. F880, Oregon question and international boundary

Cf. F1086+, British Columbia

Cf. F1089.V3, Vancouver Island

1060.9 1867-1945

Including Purchase from the old Hudson's Bay Company, 1869; Riel Rebellion, 1885; Alaska Highway

Cf. F1061+, Manitoba

Cf. F1070+, Saskatchewan

Cf. F1075+, Alberta

Cf. F1086+, British Columbia

Cf. F1091+, Yukon

Cf. F1096+, Mackenzie

Cf. F1101+, Franklin

Cf. F1106+, Keewatin

1060.92 1945-

1060.94 Frontier and pioneer life. Ranch life, cowboys, cattle trails, etc.

Elements in the population

1060.96 General works

1060.97.A-.97.Z Individual elements, A-Z

For a list of racial, ethnic, and religious elements (with cutter numbers), see F1035.A+

Manitoba

1061 Periodicals. Societies. Collections

1061.4 Gazetteers. Dictionaries. Geographic names

1061.5 Directories

Biography

1061.8 Collective

Individual, *see* F1063-1064.5

Canada
Regions, provinces, territories
Manitoba — Continued
1062 General works
Including description and travel, social life and customs
1062.4 Juvenile works
Pamphlets, addresses, essays
1062.5 General
1062.6 Anecdotes, legends, pageants, etc.
Cf. GR113+, Folklore
Cf. Class P, Literature
1062.7 Guidebooks. Handbooks
1062.8 Historic monuments (General). Illustrative material
1062.9 Antiquities (Non-Indian)
For Indians, see E78.A+, E99.A+
Cf. E73, Mound builders in Manitoba
1063 History
Including admission as a province, 1870
Including Red River Settlement; Red River Rebellion, 1869-1870
Including biography: Thomas Douglas, 5th earl of Selkirk
Cf. F1033, Fenian Raid, 1870-1871
Cf. F1060+, Hudson Bay Company; Rupert's Land
Cf. F1060.9, Riel and his rebellion, 1885
1064.A-.Z Regions, etc., A-Z
1064.B7 Boundaries
For International boundary, see F597
Cf. F1059.B7, Ontario boundary
1064.C58 Churchill River and Valley, Manitoba
Cf. F1074.C58, General, and Saskatchewan
1064.D8 Duck Mountain Provincial Park
1064.G22 Fort Garry (Lower)
1064.H42 Hecla Provincial Park
1064.L2 Lake of the Woods region, Manitoba
Cf. F1059.L2, General, and Ontario
1064.M5 Minnedosa River and Valley
1064.M67 Morris River and Valley
1064.Q34 Qu'Appelle River and Valley (Manitoba)
Cf. F1074.Q34, General, and Saskatchewan
1064.R3 Red River of the North and Red River Valley, Manitoba
Cf. F612.R27, Minnesota
Cf. F642.R3, North Dakota
1064.S6 Souris (Mouse) River and Valley, Manitoba
Cf. F642.S68, North Dakota
Cf. F1074.S67, General, and Saskatchewan
1064.S79 Stuartburn
1064.S9 Swan River and Valley
Cf. F1074.S9, General, and Saskatchewan
1064.W47 Whiteshell Provincial Park
1064.W5 Lake Winnipeg region
1064.5.A-.5.Z Cities, towns, etc., A-Z
GALE NOTE *The cutter number(s) listed below have been given only as examples by the Library of Congress*
1064.5.B73 Brandon
1064.5.S13 Saint Boniface
1064.5.W7 Winnipeg
Elements in the population
1065.A1 General works
1065.A2-.Z Individual elements
For a list of racial, ethnic, and religious elements, (with cutter numbers), see F1035.A+

Canada

Regions, provinces, territories — Continued

1067 Assiniboia

Became part of province of Saskatchewan, September 1, 1905

Saskatchewan

1070 Periodicals. Societies. Collections

1070.4 Gazetteers. Dictionaries. Geographic names

1070.5 Directories

Biography

1070.8 Collective

Individual, *see* F1074.5.A+

1071 General works

Including description and travel, social life and customs

1071.4 Juvenile works

Pamphlets, addresses, essays

1071.5 General

1071.6 Anecdotes, legends, pageants, etc.

Cf. GR113+, Folklore

Cf. Class P, Literature

1071.8 Historic monuments (General). Illustrative material

1071.9 Antiquities (Non-Indian)

For Indians, see E78.A+, E99.A+

1072 History

Province created in 1905

1074.A-.Z Regions, counties, etc., A-Z

Assiniboia, *see* F1067

1074.A75 Athabasca Sand Dunes Provincial Wilderness Park

Battle Valley, *see* F1079.B55

1074.B7 Boundaries

For international boundary, see F597

Cf. F1064.B7, Manitoba boundary

1074.C58 Churchill River and Valley (General, and Saskatchewan)

Cf. F1064.C58, Manitoba

Cypress Hills, *see* F1079.C9

1074.C92 Cypress Hills Provincial Park

1074.G72 Grasslands National Park

1074.G74 Greenwater Lake Provincial Park

1074.L5 Little Pipestone Creek and Valley

1074.L65 Lovering Lake and region

1074.M4 Meadow Lake Provincial Park

1074.M66 Moose Mountain Provincial Park

Motherwell Farmstead National Historic Park, *see* F1074.W28

1074.P7 Prince Albert National Park

1074.Q34 Qu'Appelle River and Valley (General, and Saskatchewan)

Cf. F1064.Q34, Manitoba

Red Deer River and Valley, *see* F1079.R4

1074.R8 Russell Lake region

1074.S3 Saskatchewan River and Valley (General, and Saskatchewan)

1074.S67 Souris (Mouse) River and Valley (General, and Saskatchewan)

Cf. F642.S68, North Dakota

Cf. F1064.S6, Manitoba

1074.S9 Swan River and Valley (General, and Saskatchewan)

Cf. F1064.S9, Manitoba

1074.W28 W.R. Motherwell Farmstead National Historic Park

1074.W65 Wood Mountain (Region)

1074.5.A-.5.Z Cities, towns, etc., A-Z

GALE NOTE *The cutter number(s) listed below have been given only as examples by the Library of Congress*

1074.5.R3 Regina

1074.5.S3 Saskatoon

Canada

Regions, provinces, territories

Saskatchewan — Continued

Elements in the population

1074.7.A1 General works

1074.7.A2-.7.Z Individual elements

For a list of racial, ethnic, and religious elements (with cutter numbers), see F1035.A+

Alberta

1075 Periodicals. Societies. Collections

1075.4 Gazetteers. Dictionaries. Geographic names

1075.5 Directories

Biography

1075.8 Collective

Individual, *see* F1078-1079.5.A+

1076 General works

Including description and travel, social life and customs, etc.

1076.4 Juvenile works

Pamphlets, addresses, essays

1076.5 General

1076.6 Anecdotes, legends, pageants, etc.

Cf. GR113+, Folklore

Cf. Class P, Literature

1076.8 Historic monuments (General). Illustrative material

1076.9 Antiquities (Non-Indian)

For Indians, see E78.A+, E99.A+

History

Class here works on the province formed in 1905

1078 General works

By period

Early to 1970, *see* F1078

1971-

1078.2 General works

Biography

1078.24 Collective

1078.25.A-.25.Z Individual, A-Z

GALE NOTE *See note at the head of Table F5 at the end of the text for further instructions on how to subdivide this number*

1079.A-.Z Regions, counties, etc., A-Z

1079.A8 Athabasca region

1079.B5 Banff National Park

Including Mount Castleguard

1079.B55 Battle Valley

1079.B7 Boundaries

For International boundary, see F597

Cf. F1074.B7, Saskatchewan boundary

1079.B8 Buffalo Hill region

Castleguard, Mount, *see* F1079.B5

1079.C57 Cooking Lake-Blackfoot Grazing, Wildlife, and Provincial Recreation Area

1079.C6 Coyote Flats

1079.C76 Crowsnest Pass. Crowsnest River and Valley (General, and Alberta)

Cf. F1089.C77, British Columbia

1079.C9 Cypress Hills

1079.E24 Eagle Creek and Valley

1079.E5 Elk Island National Park

1079.F67 Forty Mile Coulee and Valley

Including Forty Mile Coulee Reservoir

1079.J27 James River and Valley

1079.J3 Jasper National Park

Including Maligne Lake

Canada

Regions, provinces, territories

Alberta

1079.A-.Z Regions, counties, etc., A-Z — Continued

1079.K34 Kananaskis Country

1079.L47 Lesser Slave Lake

1079.L8 Lake Louise

Maligne Lake and region, *see* F1079.J3

1079.M54 Milk River and Valley (General, and Alberta)

Cf. F737.M48, Montana

1079.P3 Peace River District

Cf. F1089.P3, Peace River and Valley, B.C.

1079.P36 Pembina River and Valley

1079.R4 Red Deer River and Valley

1079.R53 Rife

1079.R66 Rosebud River and Valley

1079.S7 Strathcona

1079.T3 Tail Creek region

1079.T8 Twin Butte region

1079.W3 Waterton Lakes National Park

1079.W6 Wood Buffalo National Park

1079.W74 Writing-on-Stone Provincial Park

Including Writing-on-Stone Northwest Mounted Police Post

1079.Y4 Yellowhead Pass

1079.5.A-.5.Z Cities, towns, etc., A-Z

GALE NOTE *The cutter number(s) listed below have been given only as examples by the Library of Congress*

1079.5.C35 Calgary

1079.5.E3 Edmonton

1079.5.L5 Lethbridge

1079.5.M4 Medicine Hat

Elements in the population

1080.A1 General works

1080.A2-.Z Individual elements

For a list of racial, ethnic, and religious elements (with cutter numbers), see F1035.A+

British Columbia

1086 Periodicals. Societies. Collections

1086.4 Gazetteers. Dictionaries. Geographic names

1086.5 Directories

Biography

1086.8 Collective

Individual, *see* F1088-1089.5.A+

1087 General works

Including description and travel, social life and customs

Cf. F851, Pacific coast of North America

1087.4 Juvenile works

Pamphlets, addresses, essays

1087.5 General

1087.6 Anecdotes, legends, pageants, etc.

Cf. GR113+, Folklore

Cf. Class P, Literature

1087.7 Guidebooks. Handbooks

1087.8 Historic monuments (General). Illustrative material

1087.9 Antiquities (Non-Indian)

For Indians, see E78.A+ , E99.A+

1088 History

Joined the Dominion of Canada in 1871

Including biography: Sir James Douglas, etc.

Cf. E78.B9, Indians in British Columbia

Canada

Regions, provinces, territories

British Columbia

1088 History — Continued

Cf. E78.C2, Indians in Canada

Cf. F851.5 , Exploring expeditions before 1800

Cf. F879-880 , Northwest coast between Alaska and New Spain (California), 1769-1846, including the Oregon question

Cf. F1060+, Hudson's Bay and Northwest companies

1089.A-.Z Regions, etc., A-Z

1089.A4 Alberni region

1089.B43 Bella Coola/Chilcotin Road

1089.B44 Bella Coola River and Valley

1089.B7 Boundaries

For international boundary, see F854, F880

Cf. F912.B7, Alaska boundary

Cf. F1079.B7, Alberta boundary

1089.B74 Bowen Island

1089.B8 Bridge River and Valley

1089.B9 Bulkley River and Valley

1089.C3 Cariboo District

Including Chilako River and Valley, Deka Lake, Mitchell Lake

1089.C35 Cassiar District

Chilako River and Valley, *see* F1089.C3

1089.C42 Chilcotin River and Valley

1089.C45 Chilliwack River and Valley

1089.C47 Christina Lake and region

Clayoquot Sound, *see* F1089.V3

1089.C7 Coast Range

Mount Waddington (Mount George Dawson, Mystery Mountain)

Comox Valley, *see* F1089.V3

1089.C73 Cowichan Lake and region

1089.C75 Creston Valley

1089.C77 Crowsnest Pass. Crowsnest River and Valley, British Columbia

Cf. F1079.C76, General, and Alberta

Deka Lake, *see* F1089.C3

1089.D45 Denman Island

1089.E38 Elk River and Valley

1089.F5 Finlay River and Valley

1089.F54 Fintry Provincial Park

1089.F7 Fraser River and Valley

1089.G3 Garibaldi Provincial Park

1089.G44 Georgia, Strait of, Region

1089.G55 Glacier National Park

1089.G8 Gulf Islands

1089.H6 Hope region

1089.H63 Hornby Island

1089.I5 Inside Passage (General, and B.C.)

Cf. F912.I56, Alaska

1089.J43 Jedediah Island

Juan de Fuca Strait region, *see* F897.J9

1089.K4 Kamloops District

1089.K57 Kettle River and Valley (General, and B.C.)

Cf. F897.K3, Washington

1089.K7 Kootenay (Kootenai) River and Valley, B.C. Kootenay District

1089.L3 Lac La Hache region

1089.L7 Lillooet District

1089.L75 Lonesome Lake and region

1089.M3 Manning Provincial Park

Metchosin District, *see* F1089.V3

Canada

Regions, provinces, territories

British Columbia

1089.A-.Z Regions, etc., A-Z — Continued

Mitchell Lake, *see* F1089.C3

1089.N48 Newcastle Island

1089.N52 Nicola River and Valley

1089.N8 Nootka Sound

Including Nootka Sound controversy, 1789-1790

1089.O5 Okanagan River and Valley, B.C

1089.O55 Omineca River and Valley

1089.P2 Pacific Coast

Pacific Rim National Park, *see* F1089.V3

1089.P3 Peace River and Valley, B.C

Cf. F1079.P3, Peace River District, Alberta

1089.P4 Pemberton Valley

1089.P5 Pitt Lake and region

1089.P77 Princess Louisa Inlet and region

1089.P8 Purcell Range

Quadra Island, *see* F1089.V3

1089.Q3 Queen Charlotte Islands

1089.R62 Robson River and Valley

1089.S2 Saltspring (Salt Spring) Island

San Juan Islands, *see* F897.S2

1089.S4 Selkirk Range

Including Nakimu Caves

1089.S46 Shuswap Lake

1089.S48 Similkameen River and Valley (General, and British Columbia)

Cf. F897.S48, Washington (State)

1089.S5 Skeena River and Valley

1089.S77 Stein River and Valley

1089.S85 Stikine River and Valley (General, and British Columbia)

1089.S88 Stuart Lake and region

1089.S94 Sunshine Coast

1089.T14 Taku River and Valley (General, and British Columbia)

Cf. F912.T32, Alaska

1089.T17 Tatlayoko Lake

1089.T18 Tatshenshini River and Valley

1089.T2 Telkwa River and Valley

1089.T25 Teslin River and Valley

Cf. F1095.T47, General and Yukon

1089.T3 Texada Island

1089.T48 Thompson River and Valley

1089.T85 Tweedsmuir Provincial Park

1089.V3 Vancouver Island

Including Clayoquot Sound, Metchosin District, Pacific Rim National Park, Quadra Island, Comox Valley

For Juan de Fuca Strait region, see F897.J9

1089.W44 Wells Gray Provincial Park

1089.W55 Windermere Lake

1089.Y4 Yale District

Yellowhead Pass, *see* F1079.Y4

1089.5.A-.5.Z Cities, towns, etc., A-Z

GALE NOTE *The cutter number(s) listed below have been given only as examples by the Library of Congress*

1089.5.P7 Prince George

1089.5.V22 Vancouver

1089.5.V6 Victoria

Elements in the population

1089.7.A1 General works

Canada

Regions, provinces, territories

British Columbia

Elements in the population — Continued

1089.7.A2-.7.Z Individual elements

For a list of racial, ethnic, and religious elements (with cutter numbers), see F1035.A+

1090 Rocky Mountains of Canada

Cf. F721, General, and in the United States

Cf. F1011, Canadian national parks (General)

1090.5 Northern regions of Canada (General). Arctic regions

Yukon

District created in 1897; made a territory in 1898

Cf. G770, Arctic regions

1091.A1 Periodicals. Societies. Collections

1091.A2-.Z General works

Including description and travel

For Inuit, see E99.E7

For Indians, see E78.Y8 or individual tribes in E99.A+

1091.4 Juvenile works

1092 Gazetteers. Dictionaries. Geographic names

Biography

1092.8 Collective

Individual, *see* F1093, F1095.A+, F1095.5.A+

1093 History

1095.A-.Z Regions, etc., A-Z

1095.B7 Boundaries

Cf. F912.B7, Alaska boundary

Cf. F1089.B7, British Columbia boundary

1095.F7 Frances Lake

1095.K5 Klondike River and Valley

1095.T47 Teslin River and Valley (General, and Yukon)

Cf. F1089.T25, British Columbia

1095.Y9 Yukon River and Valley

Cf. F912.Y9, Alaska

1095.5.A-.5.Z Cities, towns, etc., A-Z

GALE NOTE *The cutter number(s) listed below have been given only as examples by the Library of Congress*

1095.5.D3 Dawson

1095.5.W5 Whitehorse

Mackenzie

District created in 1895; boundaries redefined in 1918

Cf. G770, Arctic regions

1096.A1 Periodicals. Societies. Collections

1096.A2-.Z General works

Including description and travel

For Eskimos, see E99.E7

For Indians, see E99.A+

1098 History

1100.A-.Z Regions, etc., A-Z

1100.B33 Back River and Valley (General, and Mackenzie)

Cf. F1110.B33, Keewatin

1100.B7 Boundaries

Cf. F1074.B7, Saskatchewan boundary

Cf. F1079.B7, Alberta boundary

Cf. F1089.B7, British Columbia boundary

Cf. F1095.B7, Yukon boundary

Cf. F1110.B7, Keewatin boundary

1100.F7 Franklin Mountains

1100.G7 Great Bear Lake

Canada

Regions, provinces, territories

Mackenzie

1100.A-.Z Regions, etc., A-Z — Continued

1100.G8 Great Slave Lake

1100.K39 Kazan River and Valley (General, and Mackenzie)

Cf. F1110.K39, Keewatin

1100.M3 Mackenzie River and Valley

1100.S6 South Nahanni River and Valley

1100.T54 Thelon River and Valley (General, and Mackenzie)

Cf. F1110.T54, Keewatin

Wood Buffalo National Park, *see* F1079.W6

1100.5.A-.5.Z Cities, towns, etc., A-Z

GALE NOTE *The cutter number(s) listed below have been given only as examples by the Library of Congress*

1100.5.A4 Aklavik

1100.5.F6 Fort Smith

1100.5.N6 Norman Wells

Franklin

District formed in 1895; boundaries redefined in 1897 and 1918; area made a game preserve in 1926

Cf. G770, Arctic regions

1101.A1 Periodicals. Societies. Collections

1101.A2-.Z General works

Including description and travel

For Eskimos, see E99.E7

For Indians, see E78.A+, E99.A+

1103 History

1105.A-.Z Regions, etc., A-Z

GALE NOTE *The cutter number(s) listed below have been given only as examples by the Library of Congress*

1105.A89 Auyuittuq National Park

1105.B3 Baffin Island

Formerly Baffin Land

1105.B7 Boundaries

Cf. F1100.B7, Mackenzie boundary

Cf. F1110.B7, Keewatin boundary

1105.F74 Frobisher Bay

1105.G7 Grinnell Land

1105.K5 King William Island

1105.Q44 Queen Elizabeth Islands

1105.S8 Sverdrup Islands

1105.5.A-.5.Z Cities, towns, etc., A-Z

GALE NOTE *The cutter number(s) listed below have been given only as examples by the Library of Congress*

1105.5.A7 Arctic Bay (Trading post)

1105.5.F6 Fort Ross (Trading post)

1105.7 Hudson Strait

Keewatin

District created in 1876; boundaries redefined in 1912

Cf. G770, Arctic regions

1106.A1 Periodicals. Societies. Collections

1106.A2-.Z General works

Including description and travel, etc.

For Eskimos, see E99.E7

For Indians, see E78.A+, E99.A+

1108 History

1110.A-.Z Regions, etc., A-Z

1110.B33 Back River and Valley

Cf. F1100.B33, General, and Mackenzie

Canada
Regions, provinces, territories
Keewatin
1110.A-.Z Regions, etc., A-Z — Continued
1110.B7 Boundaries
Cf. F1054.B7, Quebec
Cf. F1064.B7, Manitoba
1110.K39 Kazan River and Valley
Cf. F1100.K39, General, and Mackenzie
1110.M5 Melville Peninsula
1110.S6 Southampton Island
1110.T54 Thelon River and Valley
Cf. F1100.T54, General, and Mackenzie
1110.5.A-.5.Z Cities, towns, etc., A-Z
GALE NOTE *The cutter number(s) listed below have been given only as examples by the Library of Congress*
1110.5.B3 Baker Lake (Trading post)
1110.5.C5 Chesterfield Inlet (Trading post)
(1111) Ungava, *see* F1054.N5
Newfoundland
1121 Periodicals. Societies. Collections
1121.4 Gazetteers. Dictionaries. Geographic names
1121.5 Directories
Biography
1121.8 Collective
Individual, *see* F1123-1124.5.A+
1122 General works
Including description and travel, social life and customs
1122.4 Juvenile works
Pamphlets, addresses, essays
1122.5 General
1122.6 Anecdotes, legends, pageants, etc.
Cf. GR113+, Folklore
Cf. Class P, Literature
1122.7 Guidebooks. Handbooks
1122.8 Historic monuments (General). Illustrative material
1122.9 Antiquities (Non-Indian)
For Indians, see E78.A+, E99.A+
1123 History
Province created in 1949, including Labrador
Including Baltimore colony of Avalon, political history
Including biography: Philippe de Pastour, sieur de Costebelle; etc.
1124.A-.Z Regions, counties, etc., A-Z
GALE NOTE *The cutter number(s) listed below have been given only as examples by the Library of Congress*
1124.B7 Boundaries
Cf. F1138.B7, Labrador boundary
1124.F6 Fogo Island
1124.F9 Funk Island
Gulf of St. Lawrence, *see* F1050
Labrador, *see* F1136
1124.5.A-.5.Z Cities, towns, etc., A-Z
GALE NOTE *The cutter number(s) listed below have been given only as examples by the Library of Congress*
1124.5.C6 Corner Brook
1124.5.G3 Gander
1124.5.G7 Grand Falls
1124.5.S14 Saint John's
Elements in the population
1125.A1 General works

Canada

Regions, provinces, territories

Newfoundland

Elements in the population — Continued

1125.A2-.Z Individual elements

For a list of racial, ethnic, and religious elements (with cutter numbers), see F1035.A+

Labrador

1135 Periodicals. Societies. Collections

1135.4 Gazetteers. Dictionaries. Geographic names

1135.5 Directories

Biography

1135.8 Collective

Individual, *see* F1137-1138.A+

1136 General works

Including description and travel, social life and customs

For Indians, see E78.A+, E99.A+

1137 History

Annexed to Newfoundland in 1876

Including biography: Sir William Thomason Grenfell, etc.

1138.A-.Z Regions, etc., A-Z

GALE NOTE *The cutter number(s) listed below have been given only as examples by the Library of Congress*

1138.B7 Boundaries

Cf. F1054.B7, Quebec boundary

1138.G7 Grand Falls

1139 Cities, towns, etc., A-Z

GALE NOTE *The cutter number(s) listed below have been given only as examples by the Library of Congress*

1139.B3 Battle Harbour (Fishing port)

1139.C3 Cartwright (Fishing port)

1139.H6 Hopedale (Fishing port)

1140 The Labrador Peninsula

Cf. F1051+, Quebec

Cf. F1135+, Labrador (Newfoundland)

Nunavut

1141 Periodicals. Societies. Collections

1141.4 Gazetteers. Dictionaries. Geographic names

1141.5 Directories

Biography

1141.8 Collective

Individual, *see* F1143, F1144.A+, F1144.5.A+

1142 General works

Including description and travel, social life and customs

1142.4 Juvenile works

Pamphlets, addresses, essays

1142.5 General works

1142.6 Anecdotes, legends, pageants, etc.

Cf. GR113+, Folklore

Cf. Class P, Literature

1142.8 Historic monuments (General). Illustrative material

1142.9 Antiquities (non-Indian)

For Indians (General), see E78.A+

For Indians (Specific tribes), see E99.A+

For Eskimos, see E99.E7

1143 History

1144.A-.Z Regions, counties, etc., A-Z

1144.E44 Ellesmere Island

1144.5.A-.5.Z Cities, towns, etc., A-Z

Canada

Regions, provinces, territories

Nunavut — Continued

Elements in the population

1145 General works

1145.2.A-.2.Z Individual elements, A-Z

For a list of racial, ethnic, and religious elements (with cutter numbers), see F1035.A+

Other British America

For Bahamas, see F1650+

For Bermudas, see F1630+

For British East and West Florida, 1763-1783, see F301, F314

For British Guiana, see F2361+

For British Honduras, see F1441+

For British West Indies, see F2131

For Falkland Islands, see F3031+

For thirteen North American colonies before 1776, see E186+

Colony in Brazil, 1625-1661, see F2532
Dutch Guiana, see F2401+
Dutch West Indies, see F2141
New Netherlands to 1664, see F122.1
New Sweden (Dutch possession, 1655-1664), see F167

1170 **Saint Pierre and Miquelon**

Including overseas territory of the French union; local autonomy since 1935

Other French America

For Colony in Brazil, 1555-1567, see F2529

For Colony in Florida, 1562-1565, see F314

For French Guiana, see F2441+

For French West Indies, see F2151

For Louisiana, 1698-1803, see F372

For New France and Acadia, 1600-1763, see F1030 , F1038

For General, see salem F1401+
For Saint Pierre and Miquelon, see F1170
For New Spain (Viceroyalty), see F1231

Mexico

1201 **Periodicals. Societies**
For Mexican geographical societies, see G5

1202 **Congresses**

1203 **Collections. Collected works**

Museums. Exhibitions, exhibits

1203.49 General works

1203.5.A-.5.Z Special institutions. By place, A-Z
GALE NOTE *The cutter number(s) listed below have been given only as examples by the Library of Congress*

1203.5.M43 Mexico (City). Galería de Historia - La Lucha del Pueblo Mexicano por su Libertad

1204 **Gazetteers. Dictionaries. Geographic names**

1204.5 **Directories**

Biography

1205 Collective

Individual, *see* F1225.A+

1208 **General works**
Cf. F851, Pacific coast of North America
Cf. F1410, Spaniards in North America

1208.5 **Juvenile works**

Minor works, see F1227

Anecdotes, legends, pageants, etc., *see* F1227.2

1209 **Guidebooks. Handbooks**

1209.5 **Historic monuments (General)**
Cf. F1218.5+, Indian antiquities

1210 **Social life and customs. Civilization. Intellectual life**
Including national characteristics

Elements in the population, other than Indian, see F1392.A+

Indians, *see* F1218.5+

1210.5 **Mexicans in foreign countries (General)**

1210.9 **Geography**

Description and travel. Views

1211 1516-1809
For early discoveries, see E101+

1213 1810-1866

1215 1867-1950
Including Inter-American Highway

1216 1951-1980

1216.5 1981-

Antiquities. Indians

1218.5 Museums. Exhibitions

1218.6 Encyclopedias

1219 General works

1219.1.A-.1.Z Local (Pre-Columbian and Modern), A-Z
Unless otherwise provided for, class individual sites with the state in which they are located
For Mayan sites, see F1435.1.A+
Cf. F799, Cibola, N. Mex.
GALE NOTE *The cutter number(s) listed below have been given only as examples by the Library of Congress*

1219.1.C25 Campeche (State)

1219.1.C3 Casas Grandes

1219.1.C35 Cerro de las Mesas

1219.1.C4 Chametla (Sinaloa)

1219.1.M5 Mexico City

1219.1.M55 Michoacán (State)
Including Apatzingan (District)

Mexico

Antiquities. Indians

1219.1.A-.1.Z Local (Pre-Columbian and Modern), A-Z — Continued

1219.1.M6 Mitla

Officially: San Pablo Villa de Mitla

1219.1.O11 Oaxaca (State)

Including Monte Albán

1219.1.Q5 Quintana Roo

1219.1.S22 San Luis Potosí (State)

1219.1.T13 Tabasco (State)

Including La Venta

1219.1.T24 Tenayuca San Bartolo (Pyramid)

1219.1.T27 Teotihuacán (San Juan Teotihuacán)

1219.1.T43 Ticomán

Including El Arbolillo

1219.1.T7 Tres Zapotes

1219.1.T8 Tula de Allende

Including Tula Site

1219.1.U8 Usumacinta Valley

1219.1.V47 Veracruz (Vera Cruz) (State)

Including Isla de Sacrificios

1219.1.Y8 Yucatan

1219.3.A-.3.Z Special topics (Pre-Columbian and Modern), A-Z

Class here general works on specific topics only

For works on specific topics pertaining to specific peoples, see the people in F1219.7 or F1221

For works on special topics pertaining to specific localities, see the locality in F1219.1.A+

1219.3.A35 Agriculture

1219.3.A42 Alcohol use

1219.3.A5 Anthropometry

1219.3.A6 Architecture

1219.3.A7 Art

1219.3.A85 Astronomy

1219.3.B4 Beadwork

1219.3.B6 Bone carving

1219.3.C2 Calendar. Chronology

1219.3.C4 Census

1219.3.C45 Children

1219.3.C55 Civil rights

Codices, *see* F1219.5+

1219.3.C6 Commerce

1219.3.C65 Cosmogony. Cosmology

1219.3.C75 Costume

1219.3.C8 Craniology

1219.3.C85 Cultural assimilation

Culture, *see* F1219

1219.3.D2 Dances

1219.3.D3 Dentistry

1219.3.D5 Diseases

1219.3.D8 Drama

1219.3.D83 Drug use

1219.3.D9 Dwellings

1219.3.E2 Economic conditions

1219.3.E3 Education

1219.3.E79 Ethnic identity

1219.3.E82 Ethnobotany

1219.3.E83 Ethnozoology

1219.3.F57 Fishing

1219.3.F6 Folklore. Legends

	Mexico
	Antiquities. Indians
1219.3.A-.3.Z	Special topics (Pre-Columbian and Modern), A-Z — Continued
1219.3.F64	Food
1219.3.F85	Funeral customs and rites
1219.3.G3	Games
1219.3.G57	Goldwork
1219.3.G59	Gourds
1219.3.G6	Government relations
1219.3.H56	Historiography
1219.3.I4	Implements
1219.3.I5	Industries
1219.3.I56	Intellectual life
1219.3.I77	Irrigation
1219.3.J48	Jewelry
1219.3.K55	Kings and rulers
1219.3.L34	Land tenure
1219.3.L4	Law
1219.3.M34	Magic
1219.3.M38	Marriage customs and rites
1219.3.M4	Masks
1219.3.M42	Material culture
1219.3.M43	Mathematics
1219.3.M5	Medicine. Surgery
1219.3.M52	Metalwork
1219.3.M54	Migrations
1219.3.M55	Military science
1219.3.M58	Mines and mining. Mineralogy
1219.3.M59	Missions
1219.3.M597	Money
1219.3.M6	Monuments
1219.3.N9	Numeral systems
1219.3.P25	Painting
1219.3.P3	Paper and paper making
1219.3.P46	Petroglyphs. Rock paintings
1219.3.P5	Philosophy
1219.3.P55	Physical characteristics
1219.3.P7	Politics and government
1219.3.P73	Population
1219.3.P8	Pottery
1219.3.P84	Psychology
1219.3.P87	Public opinion
1219.3.P9	Pyramids
1219.3.R38	Religion and mythology
1219.3.R56	Rites and ceremonies
	Rock paintings, *see* F1219.3.P46
1219.3.S38	Sculpture
1219.3.S45	Sexual behavior
1219.3.S5	Slavery
1219.3.S57	Social conditions
1219.3.S6	Social life and customs
1219.3.S64	Societies
1219.3.S7	Statistics
1219.3.T3	Taxation
1219.3.T4	Textile industry and fabrics
1219.3.T73	Transatlantic influences
1219.3.W37	Wars
1219.3.W6	Women
1219.3.W65	Wood carving
1219.3.W94	Writing

Mexico
Antiquities. Indians — Continued
Codices
1219.5 General works
1219.54.A-.54.Z Special. By people, A-Z
GALE NOTE *The cutter number(s) listed below have been given only as examples by the Library of Congress*
1219.54.A98 Aztec
Mayas, *see* F1435.3.W75
1219.54.M59 Mixtec
1219.56.A-.56.Z Individual. By name, A-Z
Under each:
GALE NOTE *".x" represents the cutter number for the name of the codex*
.x Texts. By date
Including translations
.x2 Commentaries
1219.56.A52 Anales de Tecamachalco
1219.56.B53 Biblioteca nazionale centrale di Firenze. Manuscript. Magl. XIII, 3
1219.56.B56 Bibliothèque National de France. Manuscript 210
1219.56.B58 Bibliothèque nationale (France). Manuscript. Mexicain 40
1219.56.B65 Codex Borgianus
1219.56.B67 Códice Boturini
1219.56.B74 British Library. Manuscript. Egerton 2895
1219.56.C38 Codex Azcatitlan
1219.56.C43 Codex Borbonicus
1219.56.C45 Codex Cempoallan
1219.56.C62 Codex Chimalpopocatl
1219.56.C6215 Codex Dresdensis Maya
1219.56.C622 Codex en croix
1219.56.C623 Codex Fejérváry-Mayer
1219.56.C6237-.56.C62372 Codex Ixtlilxochitl
1219.56.C624 Codex Laud
1219.56.C6244 Codex Lopez Ruiz
1219.56.C625 Codex Mendoza
1219.56.C6253 Codex Nuttall
1219.56.C626 Codex Ramírez
1219.56.C627 Codex Telleriano-Remensis
1219.56.C628 Codex Tro-Cortesianus
1219.56.C629 Codex Tulane
1219.56.C633 Codex Vaticanus Lat. 3773
1219.56.C634 Codex Veytia
1219.56.C636 Codex Vindobonensis Mexicanus
1219.56.C64 Codex Xolotl
1219.56.C66 Códice Azoyu 1
1219.56.C68 Códice Baranda
1219.56.C717 Códice Chapultepec
1219.56.C718 Códice Colombino
1219.56.C72 Códice Cospi
1219.56.C725 Codice Cozcatzin
1219.56.C73 Códice Cuauhtinchan
1219.56.C736-.C7362 Códice de Cutzio
1219.56.C74 Códice de Huamantla
1219.56.C743 Códice de Jilotepec
1219.56.C746 Códice de Metepec
1219.56.C7467 Códice de San Antonio Techialoyan
1219.56.C747 Códice de Santa María Asunción
1219.56.C748 Códice de Tlatelolco
1219.56.C7486 Códice de Xicotepec
1219.56.C749 Códice de Yanhuitlan

Mexico

Antiquities. Indians

Codices

1219.56.A-.56.Z Individual. By name, A-Z — Continued

1219.56.C75 Códice Fernández Leal

1219.56.C764 Códice Kingsborough

1219.56.C767 Códice Muro

1219.56.C77 Códice Osuna

1219.56.C78 Códice Sierra

1219.56.C787 Códice Techialoyan de Huixquilucan

1219.56.C788 Códice Techialoyan de San Pedro Tototepec

1219.56.C79 Códice Techialoyan García Granados

1219.56.C82 Códice Xiquipilco-Temoaya

1219.56.G46 Genealogía de Zolín

1219.56.H83 Huexotzinco codex

1219.56.H84 Códice de Huichapan

1219.56.L46-.56.L462 Lienzo de Cuetzpala

1219.56.L48 Lienzo de Parapan

1219.56.L52 Lienzo de Tepetícpac

1219.56.L525 Lienzo de Tiltepec

1219.56.L53 Lienzo de Tlaxcala

1219.56.L536-.56.L5362 Lienzo del pueblo del Señor San Pedro Nexicho

1219.56.L54 Lienzo of Petlacala

1219.56.L55 Lienzo Totomixtlahuaca

1219.56.L57 Lienzos de Acaxochitlán

1219.56.M33 Mapa de Cuauhtinchan núm. 3

1219.56.M36 Mapa de Santiago Guevea

1219.56.M366-.M3662 Mapa Quinatzin

1219.56.M37 Matrícula de tributos

1219.56.O73 Ordenanza del Senor Cuauhtemoc

1219.56.O84 Österreichische Nationalbibliothek. Manuscript. Mexicanus 1

1219.56.P33 Padrones de Tlaxcala del siglo XVI

1219.56.P56 Plano en papel maguey

1219.56.R56 Codex Rios

1219.56.T46 Mapa de Tepechpan

1219.56.T66 Tonalámatl de Aubin

1219.56.T86 Códice Tudela

Pre-Columbian peoples

Class here works on the pre-Columbian period only

For works limited to the post-contact period, as well as comprehensive works on individual peoples existing during both periods, see F1221.A+

For works on local archaeological sites, see F1219.1.A+, except for Mayan sites, see F1435.1.A+

1219.7 General works

Aztecs

Including works on the Nahua peoples (General)

1219.73 General works

Biography

1219.74 Collective

1219.75 Individual, A-Z

GALE NOTE *See note at the head of Table F5 at the end of the text for further instructions on how to subdivide this number; the cutter number(s) listed below have been given only as examples by the Library of Congress*

1219.75.C83 Cuauhtemoc, Emperor of Mexico, 1495-1525

1219.75.M75 Montezuma I, Emperor of Mexico, *ca.* 1398-1468

Montezuma II, *see* F1230

1219.75.N49 Nezahualcóyotl, King of Texcoco, *fl.* 1400-1470

For works on Nezahualcóyotl as a poet, see PM4068

1219.76.A-.76.Z Special topics, A-Z

1219.76.A57 Agriculture

	Mexico
	Antiquities. Indians
	Pre-Columbian peoples
	Aztecs
1219.76.A-.76.Z	Special topics, A-Z — Continued
1219.76.A59	Alcohol use
1219.76.A62	Anthropometry
1219.76.A74	Architecture
1219.76.A78	Art
1219.76.A83	Astrology
1219.76.A84	Astronomy
1219.76.B48	Beverages
1219.76.C35	Calendar. Chronology
1219.76.C37	Cartography
1219.76.C45	Census
1219.76.C53	Chalchihuitl
1219.76.C56	Children
1219.76.C59	City planning
1219.76.C65	Commerce
1219.76.C68	Costume and adornment
	Customs, *see* F1219.76.S64
1219.76.D35	Dance
1219.76.D64	Dolls
1219.76.D76	Drug use
1219.76.E36	Economic conditions
1219.76.E38	Education
1219.76.E47	Employment
1219.76.E83	Ethnobotany
1219.76.E85	Ethnozoology
1219.76.F65	Folklore. Legends
1219.76.F67	Food
1219.76.G35	Games
1219.76.G64	Goldwork
	Government, *see* F1219.76.P75
1219.76.H57	Historiography
1219.76.I53	Industries
1219.76.K53	Kings and rulers
1219.76.K55	Kinship
1219.76.L35	Land tenure
	Legends, *see* F1219.76.F65
1219.76.M35	Magic
1219.76.M37	Material culture
1219.76.M38	Mathematics
1219.76.M43	Medicine
	Mythology, *see* F1219.76.R45
1219.76.N35	Names
1219.76.P35	Painting
1219.76.P37	Paper making
1219.76.P55	Philosophy
1219.76.P75	Politics and government
1219.76.P78	Pottery
1219.76.R45	Religion and mythology
1219.76.R57	Rites and ceremonies
1219.76.S35	Sculpture
1219.76.S53	Slavery
1219.76.S63	Social conditions
1219.76.S64	Social life and customs
1219.76.T39	Taxation
1219.76.U74	Urban residence
1219.76.W37	Wars

Mexico

Antiquities. Indians

Pre-Columbian peoples

Aztecs

1219.76.A-.76.Z Special topics, A-Z — Continued

1219.76.W44 Weights and measures

1219.76.W75 Women

1219.76.W85 Writing

For works limited to the Aztec codices, see F1219.54.A98

1219.8.A-.8.Z Other individual Pre-Columbian peoples or cultures, A-Z

1219.8.A33 Acaxee

1219.8.C52 Chantuto

1219.8.C55 Chichimec

1219.8.H83 Huastec

1219.8.M38 Matlatzinca

Mayas, *see* F1435+

1219.8.M59 Mixtec

Nahua, *see* F1219.73+

1219.8.O56 Olmec

1219.8.O87 Otomi

1219.8.T37 Tarasco

1219.8.T43 Teco

1219.8.T47 Tepanec

1219.8.T49 Tezcucan

1219.8.T52 Tlahuica

1219.8.T53 Tlaxcalan

1219.8.T65 Toltec

1219.8.T68 Totonac

1219.8.Z37 Zapotec

Modern Indian peoples

For works on peoples in both Mexico and the United States, see E99.A+

1220 General works

1221.A-.Z Individual peoples, A-Z

1221.A4 Akwa'ala

1221.A58 Amuzgo

1221.C3 Cahita

1221.C38 Cazcan

Chañabal, *see* F1221.T58

1221.C47 Chatino

1221.C5 Chiapanec

1221.C53 Chichimeca-Jonaz

1221.C56 Chinantec

1221.C567 Chocho

1221.C57 Chol

1221.C58 Chontal

1221.C585 Chuj

1221.C6 Cora

1221.C84 Cuicatec

1221.G79 Guachichile

1221.G82 Guarijío

1221.H8 Huastec

1221.H85 Huave

1221.H9 Huichol

Jacalteca, *see* F1465.2.J3

1221.K35 Kamia

1221.K5 Kiliwa

1221.L2 Lacandon

Mam, *see* F1465.2.M3

1221.M27 Matlatzinca

Mayas, *see* F1435+

Mexico

Antiquities. Indians

Modern Indian peoples

1221.A-.Z Individual peoples, A-Z — Continued

1221.M3 Mayo

1221.M33 Mazahua

1221.M35 Mazatec

1221.M67 Mixe

1221.M7 Mixtec

1221.M74 Motozintlec

1221.N3 Nahua

1221.O6 Opata

1221.O86 Otomi

1221.P3 Pame

1221.P35 Patarabueye

1221.P6 Popoloca

1221.P62 Popoluca (Vera Cruz)

1221.S43 Seri

1221.T25 Tarahumara

1221.T3 Tarasco

1221.T33 Tecuexe

1221.T37 Tepecano

1221.T39 Tepehua

1221.T4 Tepehuan

1221.T5 Tlahuica

1221.T53 Tlapanec

1221.T56 Tlaxcalan

1221.T58 Tojolabal. Chañabal

1221.T6 Totonac

1221.T7 Trique

1221.T8 Tzeltal

1221.T9 Tzotzil

1221.Y3 Yaqui

1221.Y64 Yopi

1221.Z3 Zapotec

1221.Z6 Zoque

History

1223 Chronological tables. Outlines, syllabi, etc. Questions and answers, etc.

Historiography

1224 General works

Biography of historians

1225.A2 Collective

1225.A3-.Z Individual

GALE NOTE *See note at the head of Table F5 at the end of the text for further instructions on how to subdivide this number*

1225.5 Study and teaching

1226 General works

Including political history

Pamphlets, addresses, essays, etc.

1227 General

1227.2 Anecdotes, legends, pageants, etc.

Cf. GR115+, Folklore

Cf. Class P, Literature

General special

1227.5 Military and naval history

Diplomatic history (General). Foreign and general relations

1228 General works

1228.5.A-.5.Z Relations with individual countries, A-Z

1228.9 Other (not A-Z)

Mexico
History — Continued
By period
Pre-Columbian period, *see* F1219.1.A+, F1435.1.A+
1228.98 1492-1519
1519-1824
1229 General works
Including End of Spanish rule, 1824
Cf. E123+, Post-Columbian explorers and explorations (Early to 1607)
Cf. E141+, Early descriptive works on America
1230 1519-1535
Including the Spanish conquest; Cortés and his companions; Bernal Díaz del Castillo; Montezuma II
1231 1535-1810. New Spain (Viceroyalty)
Including period of the viceroys; church and state; expulsion of the Jesuits
Including biography: Luis de Carvajal; José de Iturrigaray y Aróstegui; Guillén Lombardo; Antonio de Mendoza, conde de Tendilla; Juan de Palafox y Mendoza; Melchor de Talamantes Salvador y Baeza; etc.
1810-
1231.5 General works
1232 1810-1849
Including Wars of Independence, 1810-1821; Empire of Iturbide; troubles with France, 1838-1839
Including biography: Lucas Alamán; Ignacio José Allende y Unzaga; Nicolás Bravo; Félix María Calleja, Conde de Calderón; Miguel Hidalgo y Costilla; Augustín de Iturbide; José María Teclo Morelos y Pavón; Antonio López de Santa Anna; etc.
Cf. E401+, War with United States; loss of New Mexico and California
Cf. F390, Revolt and independence of Texas; Texan Mier Expedition, 1842
Cf. F1438, Annexation and secession of Central America
Cf. F1466.4, Annexation and secession of El Salvador
1232.5 1849-1858/1861
Including revolutions; state and church; Constitution of 1857; Raousset-Boulbon and Walker Sonora Expeditions
Including biography: Juan Álvarez; Mariano Arista; Ignacio Comonfort; Gaston Raoux, comte Raousset-Boulbon; etc.
1233 1849/1861-1867
Including European intervention, 1861-1867; French army in Mexico; Empire of Maximilian, 1864-1867
Including biography: Charlotte, consort of Maximilian; Mariana Escobedo; Benito Pablo Juárez; Maximilian, Emperor of Mexico; etc.
For Gadsden Treaty, sale of territory south of the Gila to the United States, see F786
1233.5 1867-1910
Including biography: Porfirio Díaz. etc.
For Apache War, 1883-1886, see E83.88
1234 1910-1946. Mexican Revolution (1910-)
Including frontier troubles with the United States; American occupation of Veracruz, 1914; Pershing's expedition to capture Villa, 1916; Constitution of 1917
Including biography: Plutarco Elías Calles, Manual Ávila Camacho, Lázaro Cárdenas, Venustiano Carranza, Victoriano Huerta, Francisco Indalecio Madero, Álvaro Obregón, Francisco Villa, Emiliano Zapata, etc.
Cf. D501+, World War I, 1914-1918
Cf. D731+, World War II, 1939-1945
Cf. DU950.C5, Clipperton Island dispute
1946-1970
1235 General works
Biography
1235.5.A2 Collective

Mexico
History
By period
1810-
1946-1970
Biography — Continued
1235.5.A3-.5.Z Individual
GALE NOTE *See note at the head of Table F5 at the end of the text for further instructions on how to subdivide this number; the cutter number(s) listed below have been given only as examples by the Library of Congress*
1235.5.E25 Echeverría, Luis, 1922-
1235.5.L6 López Mateos, Adolfo
1235.5.L65 López Portillo, José
1235.5.R8 Ruiz Cortines, Adolfo
1970-
1236 General works
Biography
1236.5 Collective
1236.6.A-.6.Z Individual, A-Z
GALE NOTE *See note at the head of Table F5 at the end of the text for further instructions on how to subdivide this number*
Regions, states, territories, etc.
Including the ecclesiastical subdivisions of New Spain, bishoprics, etc., as well as the provinces of the religious orders which are to be classed with provinces of same name even if they are not identical as to extent
For Indian local history and antiquities, see F1219.1.A+
1240 Islands of Mexico (General)
1241 Aguascalientes
Baja California
Including Baja California (Territory)
Cf. F788, Colorado River
Cf. F864, California before 1869
1246 General works
1246.2 Baja California (State)
1246.3 Baja California Sur
1246.6 Bajío Region
1247 Balsas River
1249 Boundaries
Including Guatemala boundary
Cf. F392.B7, Republic of Texas boundary
Cf. F392.R5, Rio Grande (General, and Texas)
Cf. F786, United States boundary
Cf. F1449.B7, Belize boundary
For Gadsden Purchase, 1853, see F786
For Nootka Sound Controversy with Great Britain, 1789-1790, see F1089.N8
For western boundary of the Louisiana Purchase, see F374
California (Spanish and Mexican province to 1848), *see* F864
1250 California, Gulf of
1251 Campeche
1254 Lake Chapala
1256 Chiapas
Formed one of the Central American states under the Audiencia of Guatemala during colonial period
Cf. DU950.C5, Clipperton Island
Cf. F1437, Central America before 1821
1261 Chihuahua
Province of Nueva Viscaya in colonial period
Including Papigochic River and Valley
Cf. F392.R5, Rio Grande (General, and Texas)
Cf. F786, International boundary

Mexico

Regions, states, territories, etc. — Continued

1262 Chihuahuan Desert

1266 Coahuila

Including Laguna (Region)

Cf. F1234, Frontier troubles

Cf. F392.R5, Rio Grande (General, and Texas)

Cf. F786, International boundary

1271 Colima

1272 Cozumel Island

1276 Durango

1279 Grijalva River

1281 Guanajuato

1286 Guerrero

1291 Hidalgo

Including Ixmiquilpan, Metztitlán, and Pachuca Districts; Mezquital Valley

1294 Huasteca (Region)

1296 Jalisco

Including Nueva Galicia (Audiencia de Guadalajara) covering not only the present states of Jalisco and Zacatecas but the provinces to the north

Laguna Region, *see* F1266

Lower California, *see* F1246+

Mexico (State). Mexico (Archdiocese)

1301 General

Mexico (Federal District and City), *see* F1386

1302 Mexico, Valley of

Including Federal District and parts of states of Mexico, Hidalgo, and Tlaxcala

1306 Michoacán

Including Coalcomán and Jiquilpan Districts

1311 Morelos

1313 Nayarit

In early colonial days the area was part of Nueva Galicia (F1296)

1314 North Mexico

Nueva Galicia, *see* F1296

1316 Nuevo León

In colonial times called "Nuevo Reino de León"

Cf. F391+, F1234, Frontier troubles

Cf. F392.R5, Rio Grande (General, and Texas)

Cf. F786, International boundary

Nuevo Mexico (Spanish and Mexican province to 1848), *see* F799

1321 Oaxaca

Cf. F1359, Isthmus of Tehuantepec

1322 Occidente (State)

Cf. F1341, Sinaloa after 1831

Cf. F1346, Sonora after 1831

1323 Pánuco (Province)

Papigochic River and Valley, *see* F1261

1325 Popocatepetl (Volcano)

Cf. QE523.P8, Geology

1326 Puebla

Including Sierra Norte de Puebla

For Popocatepetl, see F1325

1331 Querétaro

1333 Quintana Roo

Cf. F1272, Cozumel Island

Cf. F1449.B7, Belize boundary

1333.5 Revilla Gigedo Islands

1334 Rio Grande, Mexico

Including Rio Grande Valley

Cf. F392.R5 , General, and Texas

Mexico

Regions, states, territories, etc. — Continued

1335 San Juan de Ulúa Island

1336 San Luis Potosí

1339 Sierra Gorda

1340 Sierra Madre

Including Copper Canyon

1341 Sinaloa

1346 Sonora

Including San Pedro River and Valley, Mexico, and Yaqui River

Cf. F817.S25, San Pedro River and Valley (General and Arizona)

1348 Southeast Mexico

1351 Tabasco

1356 Tamaulipas

Includes Nuevo Santander in colonial times

Cf. F391+, F1234, Frontier troubles

Cf. F392.R5, Rio Grande (General, and Texas)

Cf. F786, International boundary

1359 Isthmus of Tehuantepec

1361 Tepic (Territory)

Texas (Mexican province to 1836), *see* F389

1366 Tlaxcala

1368 Tres Marias Islands

1371 Veracruz (Vera Cruz)

Including cantons: Córdoba, Jalapa (Xalapa), Orizaba, Tuxpan

For Veracruz (Vera Cruz) (City), see F1391.V4

1376 Yucatán Peninsula. Yucatán (State)

Cf. F1449.B7, Belize border

For Indian history and antiquities, see F1219.1.Y8

For local Mayan antiquities, see F1435.1.A+

1381 Zacatecas

In colonial times part of Nueva Galicia (F1296)

Cities, towns, etc.

For Indian local history and antiquities, see F1219.1.A+

1386 Mexico (Federal District and City)

Subarrange by Table F1 at the end of the text

1391.A-.Z Other, A-Z

GALE NOTE *The cutter number(s) listed below have been given only as examples by the Library of Congress*

1391.G9 Guadalajara

1391.G98 Guanajuato

1391.J2 Jalapa (Xalapa)

1391.M5 Mérida

1391.M7 Monterrey

Subarrange by Table F2 at the end of the text

1391.M8 Morelia

1391.O12 Oaxaca

1391.P9 Puebla

1391.Q4 Querétaro

1391.S19 San Luis Potosí

1391.T2 Tampico

1391.T23 Taxco

1391.T3 Tepoztlán

1391.T6 Toluca

1391.V4 Veracruz (Vera Cruz)

Xalapa, *see* F1391.J2

1391.Z2 Zacatecas

1392.A-.Z **Elements in the population, A-Z**

Racial and ethnic groups including religious bodies which have significance in the history of Mexico

	Mexico
1392.A-.Z	**Elements in the population, A-Z — Continued**
	Elements in individual regions, states, cities, etc., are classed with the region, state, city, etc.
1392.A1	General works
	Including foreign elements (General), minorities, race conflicts and problems
1392.A5	Americans
1392.A7	Arabs
1392.B3	Basques
1392.B55	Blacks
1392.C28	Cantabrians
1392.C3	Catalans
1392.C45	Chinese
1392.C8	Cubans
1392.C93	Czechs
1392.E5	English
1392.F8	French
1392.G4	Germans
	Indians, *see* F1218.5+
1392.I82	Italians
1392.J3	Japanese
1392.J4	Jews
1392.K65	Koreans
1392.L4	Lebanese
1392.M6	Mormons
	Negroes, *see* F1392.B55
1392.P6	Poles
1392.S7	Spaniards
1392.V45	Venezuelans
	Latin America (General)
	Cf. F301,F314, Florida before 1819
	Cf. F373, Louisiana, 1764-1803
	Cf. F799+, New Mexico to 1848
	Cf. F864, California to 1848
	Cf. F1201+, Mexico
	Cf. F1421+, Central America
	Cf. F1601+, West Indies
	Cf. F2201+, South America
	Periodicals. Societies. Collections
1401	General
	For geographical societies, see G5
1402	Organization of American States
	Publications on special subjects are to be classed with the subjects in Classes B-Z
	Documents
1402.A1-.A29	Serial
	Nonserial
1402.A3	By the organization as a whole. By date
1402.A4A-.A4Z	By subordinate bodies, departments, etc., A-Z
	For Inter-American Council for Education, Science, and Culture, see F1408.4
1402.A5-.Z	Nonofficial publications
	Including official publications by individual countries of the Organization
	Pan American Union
	Formerly Bureau of the American Republics, and International Bureau of American Republics
	Official publications
1403	By the organization as a whole
1403.3	By subordinate bodies, departments, etc.
1403.5	Nonofficial publications
	Including works about the organization, addresses, essays, etc.
	Congresses
1403.9	General works

Latin America (General)
Congresses — Continued
Pan-American conferences
1404 Early congresses: American Congress, Panama, 1826
International American Conference, 1889-1948
Continued as Inter-American Conference, 1954-
All conferences subarranged like that of the first conference, 1889
Under each:
.A1-.A7 Official publications
.A8-.Z4 Reports of delegations from participating countries
Arranged alphabetically by country
.Z5 Works about the conference
1404.5 General works
1405.3 Inter-American Conference for the Maintenance of Peace, Buenos Aires, 1936
1405.5 Meeting of Consultation of Ministers of Foreign Affairs of American States. By date
1405.9.A-.9.Z Other conferences, congresses, etc., A-Z
GALE NOTE *The cutter number(s) listed below have been given only as examples by the Library of Congress*
1405.9.I5 Inter-American Conference for the Maintenance of Continental Peace and Security, Rio de Janeiro, 1947
1406 **Gazetteers. Dictionaries. Geographic names**
1406.5 **Directories**
Collected works
1406.7 Several authors
1406.8 Individual authors
Including collected papers, addresses, essays, etc.
Biography
1407 Collective
Individual, *see* F1228.96+, F1411+, etc.
1408 **General works**
1408.2 **Juvenile works**
Pamphlets, addresses, essays, etc.
1408.25 General
1408.27 Anecdotes, legends, pageants, etc.
1408.29 **Guidebooks. Handbooks**
Social life and customs. Civilization. Intellectual life
1408.3 General
Including characteristics of the people
For specific periods, see the period
1408.4 Inter-American Council for Education, Science, and Culture
Formerly Inter-American Cultural Council
1408.5 **Historic monuments (General)**
Cf. F1409.5, Antiquities
1408.8 **Historical geography**
1408.9 **Geography**
Description and travel. Views
Early to 1810, *see* E141+
1409 1811-1950
Including Inter-American Highway
Cf. F865, Voyages to the Pacific coast following discovery of gold
1409.2 1951-1980
1409.3 1981-
1409.5 **Antiquities (Non-Indian)**
For Indians of Latin America, see E65
History
1409.6 Chronological tables. Outlines, syllabi, etc. Questions and answers, etc.
Historiography
1409.7 General works
Biography of historians
1409.8.A2 Collective

Latin America (General)

History

Historiography

Biography of historians — Continued

1409.8.A3-.8.Z Individual

GALE NOTE *See note at the head of Table F5 at the end of the text for further instructions on how to subdivide this number*

Study and teaching

1409.9.A-.9.Z8 General works

1409.9.Z9 Audio-visual materials catalogs

1409.95.A-.95.Z By region or country, A-Z

Subarranged by author

1410 General works

Including Spain's government of her American colonies

Including political history

1410.5 Military history

1410.6 Naval history

By period

1411 Early to 1601

Including colonization, treatment of Indians, Las Casas tracts

For biography of Las Casas, see E125.C4

Cf. E141+, Early accounts of America

1412 1601-1830. Wars of independence, 1806-1830

1413 1830-1898

20th century. 1898-

1414 General works

1414.2 1948-

Diplomatic history. Foreign and general relations

1415 General works

Including relations with several countries

1416.A-.Z Relations with individual countries, A-Z

For United States, see F1418

1418 Relations with the United States

Including relations of United States with Latin America

Cf. E18.85, Twentieth century America

Cf. F975, Central American, West Indian, and other countries protected by and having close political affiliations with the United States

Cf. F1403+, Pan American Union, Pan-American Conferences

Cf. JZ1482, Monroe Doctrine

Elements in the population

For interpretation, see F1392.A+

1419.A1 General works

Including foreign elements (General), minorities, race conflicts and problems, etc.

1419.A2-.Z Individual, A-Z

1419.A73 Aragonese

1419.A84 Asians

1419.A87 Asturians

1419.B37 Basques

Blacks, *see* F1419.N4

1419.C26 Canary Islanders

1419.C3 Cantabrians

1419.C94 Czechs

1419.E87 Europeans

1419.G2 Gallegans

1419.G3 Germans

Indians, *see* E65

1419.I8 Italians

1419.J3 Japanese

1419.J4 Jews

1419.M45 Mennonites

Latin America (General)
Elements in the population
1419.A2-.Z Individual, A-Z — Continued
1419.M87 Muslims
1419.N38 Navarrese
1419.N4 Negroes. Blacks
1419.P65 Poles
1419.S5 Slavs
1419.S63 Spaniards
Central America
1421 **Periodicals. Societies. Collections**
For Central American geographical societies, see G5
1422 **Congresses**
Collected works
1423 Several authors
1423.5 Individual authors
Including collected papers, addresses, essays, etc.
1424 **Gazetteers. Dictionaries**
1425 **Directories**
Biography
1426 Collective
Individual, *see* F1435.6.A2+, F1436.92+
1428 **General works**
1428.5 **Juvenile works**
Pamphlets, addresses, essays, etc.
1428.7 General
1428.8 Anecdotes, legends, pageants, etc.
Cf. GR117+, Folklore
Cf. Class P, Literature
1429 **Guidebooks. Handbooks**
1430 **Social life and customs. Civilization. Intellectual life**
Description and travel. Views
1431 Early to 1820
Cf. E101+; F1230, Earliest voyages and explorations
1432 1821-1950
Including voyages to the Pacific coast following discovery of gold
1433 1951-1980
1433.2 1981-
Antiquities. Indians (Ancient and modern)
1434 General works
1434.2.A-.2.Z Topics, A-Z
1434.2.A37 Agriculture
1434.2.A55 Anthropometry
1434.2.A7 Art
1434.2.C58 Civil rights
1434.2.C65 Commerce
1434.2.E38 Education
1434.2.F6 Folklore. Legends
1434.2.G6 Goldwork
1434.2.G68 Government relations
1434.2.H85 Hunting
1434.2.L35 Land tenure
1434.2.M4 Metalwork
1434.2.M6 Missions
1434.2.P76 Politics and government
1434.2.P8 Pottery
1434.2.R3 Religion and mythology
1434.2.S38 Sculpture
1434.2.S62 Social conditions
1434.2.S63 Social life and customs

Central America

Antiquities. Indians (Ancient and modern)

1434.2.A-.2.Z Topics, A-Z — Continued

1434.2.W37 Wars

1434.2.W65 Women

1434.3.A-.3.Z Tribes (other than Mayas), A-Z

For guidance in classification, see note under F2230.2.A+

For Aztecs, see F1219.1.A+

Mayas

Cf. F1445+, British Honduras

Cf. F1465+, Guatemala

1435 General works

1435.A1-.A4 Periodicals. Societies

1435.1.A-.1.Z Local, A-Z

1435.1.A34 Abaj Takalik

1435.1.A35 Acanceh

1435.1.A36 Agua Tibia

1435.1.A38 Alta Verapaz

1435.1.A4 Altar de Sacrificios

1435.1.A57 Altun Ha

1435.1.B35 Balberta

1435.1.B4 Becan

1435.1.B6 Bonampak

1435.1.C32 Cacaxtla

1435.1.C33 Cahal Pech

1435.1.C34 Calakmul

1435.1.C35 Campeche

1435.1.C37 Caracol

1435.1.C38 Cayo

1435.1.C39 Ceren Site

1435.1.C43 Cerros Site

1435.1.C44 Chaguite Site

1435.1.C47 Chan Kom

1435.1.C49 Chiapa de Corso Site

1435.1.C492 Chiapas

1435.1.C494 Chicanná Site

1435.1.C5 Chichén Itzá

1435.1.C54 Chinkultic

1435.1.C56 Cimientos Site

1435.1.C63 Cobá

1435.1.C65 Colha

1435.1.C67 Comalcalco Site

1435.1.C7 Copan

1435.1.C76 Cozumel Island

1435.1.C84 Cuello

1435.1.D67 Dos Pilas

1435.1.D85 Dzibilchaltún

1435.1.D87 Dzibilnocac Site

1435.1.E32 Ecab

1435.1.E37 Edzná Site

1435.1.F45 Felipe Carrillo Puerto

1435.1.H7 Holmul

1435.1.K3 Kaminaljuyu

1435.1.K35 K'axob Site

1435.1.K64 Kohunlich

1435.1.L2 Labná

1435.1.L23 Laguna de On Site

1435.1.L24 Lagunita

1435.1.L64 Loltun Cave

1435.1.L83 Lubaantun

Central America

Antiquities. Indians (Ancient and modern)

Mayas

1435.1.A-.1.Z Local, A-Z — Continued
1435.1.M22 Macanché Island
1435.1.M26 Marco Gonzalez Site
1435.1.M32 Meco Site
1435.1.M64 Mojarra
1435.1.M84 Mul-Chic
1435.1.N35 Naj Tunich
1435.1.N37 Naranjo
1435.1.N55 Nim Li Punit Site
1435.1.N64 Nohmul
1435.1.O94 Oxkintok
1435.1.P2 Palenque
1435.1.P25 Pataxte
1435.1.P38 Paxil
1435.1.P47 Petén
1435.1.P53 Pilar Site
1435.1.P55 Planchon de las Figuras
1435.1.P88 Puuc Region
1435.1.Q78 Quintana Roo
1435.1.Q8 Quirigua
1435.1.R56 Rio Azul Site
1435.1.R67 Rosario Valley
1435.1.S26 San Gervasio Site
1435.1.S29 Sayil
1435.1.S44 Seibal
1435.1.S92 Sumidero
1435.1.T48 Tihosuco
1435.1.T5 Tikal
1435.1.T65 Tonina
1435.1.T67 Topoxté
1435.1.T8 Tulum
1435.1.T96 Tzutzuculi Site
1435.1.U2 Uaxactun
1435.1.U65 Utatlan Site
1435.1.U7 Uxmal
1435.1.W54 Wild Cane Cay Site
1435.1.X26 Xamanhá Site
1435.1.X32 Xcan Cave
1435.1.X35 Xcaret
1435.1.X37 Xculoc Site
1435.1.X7 Xkichmook
1435.1.X73 Xkipché Site
1435.1.X77 Xtacumbilxunaan Cave
1435.1.X82 Xunantunich
1435.1.Y3 Yaxchilán
1435.1.Y89 Yucatán (State)
1435.1.Z3 Zaculeu
1435.3.A-.3.Z Topics, A-Z
1435.3.A37 Agriculture
1435.3.A56 Anthropometry
1435.3.A6 Architecture
1435.3.A7 Art
1435.3.A8 Astrology
1435.3.B37 Basket making
1435.3.C14 Calendar. Chronology. Astronomy
1435.3.C47 Children
1435.3.C49 Chinese influences

Central America

Antiquities. Indians (Ancient and modern)

Mayas

1435.3.A-.3.Z	Topics, A-Z — Continued
1435.3.C57	City planning
1435.3.C58	Civil rights
	Codices, *see* F1435.3.W75
1435.3.C6	Commerce
1435.3.C69	Costume and adornment
1435.3.C75	Crimes against
1435.3.D34	Dances
1435.3.D4	Dentistry
1435.3.D64	Domestic animals
1435.3.D84	Dwellings
1435.3.E27	Economic conditions
1435.3.E37	Education
1435.3.E52	Embroidery
1435.3.E72	Ethnic identity
1475.3.E73	Ethnobiology
1435.3.E74	Ethnobotany
1435.3.E76	Ethnozoology
1435.3.E87	Extraterrestrial influences
1435.3.F57	Fishing
1435.3.F6	Folklore. Legends
1435.3.F7	Food
1435.3.F85	Funeral customs and rites
	Government, *see* F1435.3.P7
1435.3.H85	Hunting
1435.3.I46	Implements
1435.3.I53	Industries
1435.3.J48	Jewelry
1435.3.K55	Kings and rulers
1435.3.K57	Kinship
1435.3.L35	Land tenure
	Legends, *see* F1435.3.F6
1435.3.M3	Masks
1435.3.M32	Material culture
1435.3.M35	Mathematics. Numeration
1435.3.M4	Medicine. Hygiene
1435.3.M49	Middle Eastern influences
1435.3.M53	Missions
1435.3.M6	Mortuary customs
	Mythology, *see* F1435.3.R3
(1435.3.N8)	Numeration, *see* F1435.3.M35
1435.3.O73	Origin
1435.3.P34	Painting
1435.3.P44	Petroglyphs. Rock paintings
1435.3.P5	Philosophy
1435.3.P7	Politics and government
1435.3.P75	Population
1435.3.P8	Pottery
1435.3.R3	Religion and mythology
1435.3.R56	Rites and ceremonies
1435.3.R6	Roads and trails
	Rock painting, *see* F1435.3.P44
1435.3.S24	Salt
1435.3.S32	Science
1435.3.S34	Sculpture
1435.3.S5	Sisal hemp
1435.3.S68	Social conditions

Central America
Antiquities. Indians (Ancient and modern)
Mayas
1435.3.A-.3.Z Topics, A-Z — Continued
1435.3.S7 Social life and customs
1435.3.T48 Textile industry and fabrics
1435.3.T63 Tobacco use
1435.3.W2 Wars
1435.3.W55 Women
1435.3.W6 Wood carving
1435.3.W75 Writing. Codices
History
1435.4 Chronological tables. Outlines, syllabi, etc. Questions and answers, etc.
Historiography
1435.5 General works
Biography of historians
1435.6.A2 Collective
1435.6.A3-.6.Z Individual
GALE NOTE *See note at the head of Table F5 at the end of the text for further instructions on how to subdivide this number*
1435.8 Study and teaching
1436 General works
Including political history
General special
1436.5 Military and naval history
Diplomatic history. Foreign and general relations
1436.7 General works
1436.8.A-.8.Z Relations with individual countries, A-Z
By period
Pre-Columbian period, *see* F1434+
1437 1502-1821
Including Spanish period; Audiencia of Guatemala, 1542-1821
Including biography: Pedro de Alvarado, Pedro Arias de Avila, Juan Vázquez de Coronado, etc.
Cf. E101+, Early explorations and discoveries
Cf. F1232, Mexican wars of independence, 1810-1821
Cf. F1256, Chiapas
Cf. F1441+, F1529.M9, English aggressions on the coast
1438 1821-1950
Including annexation to and separation from Mexico, 1822-1823; Confederación de Centro América, 1823-1838/1842; other attempts at Central American unity; Clayton-Bulwer Treaty of 1850; Filibuster wars, 1855-1860; Zeledon-Wyke Treaty of 1860; Hay-Pauncefote Treaty of 1901
Including biography: Manuel José Arce, José Francisco Barrundia, José Simeón Cañas y Villacorta, Francisco Morazán, Rafael Heliodoro Valle, etc.
Cf. F1526.27, Walker in Nicaragua
1439 1951-1979
Including Organization of Central American States (Charter of Salvador, 1951)
1439.5 1979-
Elements in the population
Including foreign elements (General), minorities, race conflicts and problems, etc.
For interpretation, see F1392.A+
1440.A1 General works
1440.A2-.Z Individual elements, A-Z
1440.A54 Americans
1440.B55 Blacks
1440.G3 Germans
Indians, *see* F1434+
1440.I73 Italians

	Central America
	Elements in the population
1440.A2-.Z	Individual elements, A-Z — Continued
1440.J48	Jews
	Negroes, *see* F1440.B55
1440.P34	Palestinian Arabs
1440.S7	Spaniards
	British Honduras. Belize (Belice)
1441	Periodicals. Societies. Collections
1441.3	Congresses
	Collected works
1441.5	Several authors
1441.6	Individual authors
	Including collected papers, addresses, essays
1441.8	Museums. Exhibitions, exhibits
1442	Gazetteers. Dictionaries. Geographic names
1442.3	Directories
	Biography
1442.7	Collective
	Individual, *see* F1445.7, F1446.92+
1443	General works
1443.2	Juvenile works
	Pamphlets, addresses, essays, etc.
1443.3	General
1443.4	Anecdotes, legends, pageants, etc.
	Cf. GR117+, Folklore
	Cf. Class P, Literature
1443.5	Guidebooks. Handbooks
1443.7	Historic monuments (General)
	For Indian antiquities, see F1445+
1443.8	Social life and customs. Civilization. Intellectual life
	Including national characteristics
	Description and travel. Views
1444	Early to 1950
1444.2	1951-1980
1444.3	1981-
	Antiquities. Indians (Ancient and modern)
	Including Mayas
1445	General works
1445.1.A-.1.Z	Local, A-Z
	For individual Mayan archaeological sites, see F1435.1.A+
1445.2.A-.2.Z	Tribes, A-Z
	Black Carib Indians, *see* F1505.2.C3
	Kekchi, *see* F1465.2.K5
	Mayas, *see* F1445+
1445.3.A-.3.Z	Topics, A-Z
	For topics pertaining to the Mayas only, see F1435.3.A+
	GALE NOTE *The cutter number(s) listed below have been given only as examples by the Library of Congress*
1445.3.P6	Pottery
	History
1445.5	Chronological tables. Outlines, syllabi, etc. Questions and answers, etc.
	Historiography
1445.6	General works
	Biography of historians
1445.7.A2	Collective
1445.7.A3-.7.Z	Individual
	GALE NOTE *See note at the head of Table F5 at the end of the text for further instructions on how to subdivide this number*
1445.8	Study and teaching

Central America

British Honduras. Belize (Belice)

History — Continued

1446 General works

Including political history

General special

1446.3 General

Diplomatic history. Foreign and general relations

1446.4 General works

1446.5.A-.5.Z Relations with individual countries, A-Z

By period

Pre-Columbian period, *see* F1445+

1447 1506-1884

Including self-governing British settlement, 1638-1786; colony with lieutenant governor under governor of Jamaica, 1862-1884; Crown Colony, 1871; separation from Jamaica, 1884

For disputes over claims of Spain, Guatemala, and Mexico, see F1449.B7

1447.5 1884-1945

1448 1945-

For dispute over claim of Guatemala, see F1449.B7G1+

1449.A-.Z Regions, districts, etc., A-Z

1449.A53 Ambergris Cay

1449.B4 Belize

Including Turneffe Island

Boundaries

1449.B7A1-.B7A9 General works

1449.B7G1-.B7G9 Guatemala

1449.B7M1-.B7M9 Mexico

1449.B7S1-.B7S9 Spain

1449.S24 Saint George's Cay

1449.T6 Toledo

Turneffe Island, *see* F1449.B4

1456.A-.Z Cities, towns, etc., A-Z

Cf. F1445.1.A+, Indian local history and antiquities

GALE NOTE *The cutter number(s) listed below have been given only as examples by the Library of Congress*

1456.B4 Belize

Elements in the population

Including foreign elements (General), minorities, race conflicts and problems, etc.

For interpretation, see F1392.A+

1457.A1 General works

1457.A2-.Z Individual elements, A-Z

1457.B4 Belgians

1457.B55 Blacks

Indians, *see* F1445+

1457.M45 Mennonites

Negroes, *see* F1457.B55

Guatemala

For Audiencia or captain-generalcy of Guatemala before 1821, see F1437

1461 Periodicals. Societies. Collections

Collected works

1461.5 Several authors

1461.6 Individual authors

Including collected papers, addresses, essays

1461.8 Museums. Exhibitions, exhibits

1462 Gazetteers. Dictionaries. Geographic names

1462.3 Directories

Biography

1462.7 Collective

Individual, *see* F1465.7.A+, F1466.4+

	Central America
	Guatemala — Continued
1463	General works
1463.2	Juvenile works
	Pamphlets, addresses, essays, etc.
1463.3	General
1463.4	Anecdotes, legends, pageants, etc.
	Cf. GR117+, Folklore
	Cf. Class P, Literature
1463.5	Social life and customs. Civilization. Intellectual life
	Including national characteristics
1463.6	Guidebooks. Handbooks
1463.7	Historic monuments (General)
	For Indian antiquities, see F1465+
	Description and travel. Views
1464	Early to 1950
1464.2	1951-1980
1464.3	1981-
	Antiquities. Indians (Ancient and modern)
1465	General
	Including Mayas
1465.P8	Popul vuh
	Class translations and studies of the contents here
	For original text and linguistic studies, see PM4231.Z6
1465.1.A-.1.Z	Local, A-Z
	For individual Mayan archaeological sites, see F1435.1.A+
	GALE NOTE *The cutter number(s) listed below have been given only as examples by the Library of Congress*
1465.1.A8	Atitlán, Lake
1465.1.C5	Chinautla
1465.2.A-.2.Z	Tribes, A-Z
1465.2.A23	Achi
1465.2.A34	Akatek
	Black Carib, *see* F1505.2.C3
1465.2.C3	Cakchikel
1465.2.C5	Chorti
1465.2.I87	Itza
1465.2.I95	Ixil
1465.2.J3	Jacalteca
1465.2.K36	Kanjobal
1465.2.K5	Kekchi
	Lacandon, *see* F1221.L2
1465.2.M3	Mam
1465.2.M65	Mopan
	Pipil, *see* F1485.2.P5
1465.2.P6	Pokomam
1465.2.Q5	Quichés
(1465.2.R32)	Rabinal Achi, *see* F1465.2.A23
1465.2.T9	Tzutuhil
1465.2.X5	Xinca
1465.3.A-.3.Z	Topics, A-Z
	For topics pertaining to the Mayas only, see F1435.3.A+
1465.3.A37	Agriculture
1465.3.A7	Art
1465.3.C58	Civil rights
1465.3.C77	Commerce
1465.3.C8	Costume and adornment
1465.3.D3	Dances
1465.3.E2	Economic conditions
1465.3.E84	Ethnic identity

Central America
Guatemala
Antiquities. Indians (Ancient and modern)
1465.3.A-.3.Z Topics, A-Z — Continued
1465.3.F6 Folklore. Legends
1465.3.G6 Government relations
1465.3.I5 Industries
1465.3.M36 Masks
1465.3.M4 Medicine
1465.3.M57 Missions
1465.3.P64 Politics and government
1465.3.P68 Pottery
1465.3.R4 Religion and mythology
1465.3.R44 Removal
1465.3.S6 Social conditions
1465.3.S62 Social life and customs
1465.3.T3 Taxation
1465.3.T4 Textiles
1465.3.W37 Wars
History
1465.5 Chronological tables. Outlines, syllabi, etc. Questions and answers, etc.
Historiography
1465.6 General works
Biography of historians
1465.7.A2 Collective
1465.7.A3-.7.Z Individual
GALE NOTE *See note at the head of Table F5 at the end of the text for further instructions on how to subdivide this number*
1465.8 Study and teaching
1466 General works
Including political history
General special
1466.1 Military and naval history
Diplomatic history. Foreign and general relations
Cf. F1469.B7, Boundaries
1466.2 General works
1466.3.A-.3.Z Relations with individual countries, A-Z
1466.35 Other (not A-Z)
By period
Pre-Columbian period, *see* F1465+
1466.4 1523-1838
Including end of Spanish rule, 1821; annexation to and separation from Mexico, 1822-1823; Confederación de Centro América, 1823-1838/1842; earthquake of 1773
1466.45 1838-1945
Including establishment as a republic, April 17, 1839; era of despots; wars with El Salvador; revolutions of 1898, 1906, 1920, 1930, 1944, etc.; epidemic of cholera, 1837; earthquakes of 1902, 1917, 1918
Including biography: Justo Rufino Barrios, Rafael Carrera, Lázaro Chacón, Manuel Estrada Cabrera, Miguel García Granados, Jorge Ubico, etc.
Cf. D731+, World War II, 1939-1945
Cf. F1507.5, Wars with Honduras
1466.5 1945-1985
Including Revolution of 1954
Including biography: Jacobo Arbenz Guzmán, Juan José Arévalo, Carlos Castillo Armas, etc.
1466.7 1985-
1469.A-.Z Regions, departments, etc., A-Z
Alta Vera Paz, *see* F1469.V3
Baja Vera Paz, *see* F1469.V4

	Central America
	Guatemala
1469.A-.Z	Regions, departments, etc., A-Z — Continued
1469.B7	Boundaries
1469.B7A1-.B7A5	General
	British Honduras, *see* F1449.B7
1469.B7A6-.B7Z	Honduras
	Mexico, *see* F1249
	El Salvador, *see* F1489.B7
1469.G9	Guatemala
1469.H8	Huehuetenango
1469.I9	Izabal
	Cf. F1469.S2, Santo Tomas (District)
1469.J8	Jutiapa (Dept.)
1469.M68	Motagua River
1469.P4	Petén
	Including Usumacinta River
1469.Q5	Quezaltenango
1469.S13	Sacatepéquez
1469.S17	San Marcos
1469.S2	Santo Tomas (District)
1469.S64	Sololá
	Including Lake Atitlán
1469.T7	Totonicapán
1469.V3	Vera Paz, Alta
1469.V4	Vera Paz, Baja
	Including former department of Vera Paz
1469.Z3	Zacapa
1476.A-.Z	Cities, towns, etc., A-Z
	Cf. F1465.1.A+, Indian local history and antiquities
	GALE NOTE *The cutter number(s) listed below have been given only as examples by the Library of Congress*
1476.A5	Antigua
1476.G9	Guatemala (City)
1476.P8	Puerto Barrios
1476.Q8	Quezaltenango
	Elements in the population
	For interpretation, see F1392.A+
1477.A1	General works
	Including foreign elements (General), minorities, race conflicts and problems, etc.
1477.A2-.Z	Individual elements
	GALE NOTE *The cutter number(s) listed below have been given only as examples by the Library of Congress*
1477.G3	Germans
	Indians, *see* F1465+
1477.L33	Ladino (Latin American people)
	Salvador (El Salvador)
1481	Periodicals. Societies. Collections
	Collected works
1481.5	Several authors
1481.6	Individual authors
	Including collected papers, addresses, essays, etc.
1481.8	Museums. Exhibitions, exhibits
1482	Gazetteers. Dictionaries. Geographic names
1482.3	Directories
	Biography
1482.7	Collective
	Individual, *see* F1485.7
1483	General works
1483.2	Juvenile works

Central America
Salvador (El Salvador) — Continued

Pamphlets, addresses, essays, etc.
1483.3 General
1483.4 Anecdotes, legends, pageants, etc.
Cf. GR117+, Folklore
Cf. Class P, Literature
1483.5 Guidebooks. Handbooks
1483.7 Historic monuments (General)
For Indian antiquities, see F1485+
1483.8 Social life and customs. Civilization. Intellectual life
Including national characteristics
Description and travel. Views
1484 Early to 1950
1484.2 1951-1980
1484.3 1981-
Antiquities. Indians (Ancient and modern)
1485 General works
1485.1.A-.1.Z Local, A-Z
1485.1.C8 Cuscatlán
1485.2.A-.2.Z Tribes, A-Z
GALE NOTE *The cutter number(s) listed below have been given only as examples by the Library of Congress*
Matagalpa, *see* F1525.2.M3
1485.2.P5 Pipil
1485.3.A-.3.Z Topics, A-Z
For topics pertaining to the Mayas only, see F1435.3.A+
Government, *see* F1485.3.P7
1485.3.N35 Names
1485.3.P7 Politics and government
1485.3.P8 Pottery
1485.3.S6 Social conditions
History
1485.5 Chronological tables. Outlines, syllabi, etc. Questions and answers, etc.
Historiography
1485.6 General works
Biography of historians
1485.7.A2 Collective
1485.7.A3-.7.Z Individual
GALE NOTE *See note at the head of Table F5 at the end of the text for further instructions on how to subdivide this number*
1485.8 Study and teaching
1486 General works
Including political history
General special
1486.1 Military and naval history
Diplomatic history. Foreign and general relations
Cf. F1489.B7, Boundaries
1486.2 General works
1486.3.A-.3.Z Relations with individual countries, A-Z
1486.9 Other (A-Z)
By period
Pre-Columbian period, *see* F1485+
1487 1524-1838
Including end of Spanish rule, 1821; appeal to United States for annexation, 1822; Mexican rule, 1822-1823; Confederación de Centro América, 1823-1838/1842
Including biography: José Matías Delgado, etc.
1487.5 1838-1944. Martínez regime, 1931-1944
Including period of internal struggles and changing constitution; wars with Guatemala; conflicts with Honduras; Revolt of 1944

Central America

Salvador (El Salvador)

History

By period

1487.5 1838-1944. Martínez regime, 1931-1944 — Continued

Including biography: Manuel Enrique Araujo, Maximiliano Hernández Martínez, Alfonso Quiñónez Molina, Pío Romero Bosque, etc.

1488 1944-1979

Including earthquake of May 6, 1951

Including biography: Salvador Castañeda Castro, Oscar Osorio, etc.

1979-1992

1488.3 General works

Biography

1488.4 Collective

1488.42.A-.42.Z Individual, A-Z

GALE NOTE *See note at the head of Table F5 at the end of the text for further instructions on how to subdivide this number*

1992-

1488.5 General works

Biography

1488.52 Collective

1488.53.A-.53.Z Individual, A-Z

GALE NOTE *See note at the head of Table F5 at the end of the text for further instructions on how to subdivide this number*

1489.A-.Z Regions, departments, etc., A-Z

GALE NOTE *The cutter number(s) listed below have been given only as examples by the Library of Congress*

Boundaries

1489.B7A1-.B7A9 General

1489.B7G1-.B7G9 Guatemala

1489.B7H1-.B7H9 Honduras

1489.C8 Cuscatlán

1489.L3 La Unión

1489.M46 Metapán (District)

1489.S2 San Salvador

Unión, *see* F1489.L3

1489.U8 Usulután

1496.A-.Z Cities, towns, etc., A-Z

Cf. F1485.1.A+, Indian local history and antiquities

1496.S2 San Salvador

Including Fire of August 8, 1951

1496.S35 Santa Ana

Elements in the population

Including foreign elements (General), minorities, race conflicts and problems, etc.

For interpretation, see F1392.A+

1497.A1 General works

1497.A2-.Z Individual elements, A-Z

1497.B55 Blacks

Indians, *see* F1485+

Negroes, *see* F1497.B55

Honduras

1501 Periodicals. Societies. Collections

Collected works

1501.5 Several authors

1501.6 Individual authors

Including collected papers, addresses, essays, etc.

1501.8 Museums. Exhibitions, exhibits

1502 Gazetteers. Dictionaries. Geographic names

1502.3 Directories

Central America

Honduras — Continued

Elements in the population

Including foreign elements (General), minorities, race conflicts and problems, etc.

For interpretation, see F1392.A+

1517.A1 General works

1517.A2-.Z Individual elements, A-Z

1517.A73 Arabs

1517.B55 Blacks

Indians, *see* F1505+

Negroes, *see* F1517.B55

Nicaragua

1521 Periodicals. Societies. Collections

Collected works

1521.5 Several authors

1521.6 Individual authors

Including collected papers, addresses, essays, etc.

1521.8 Museums. Exhibitions, exhibits

1522 Gazetteers. Dictionaries. Geographic names

1522.3 Directories

Biography

1522.7 Collective

Individual, *see* F1525.7

1523 General works

1523.2 Juvenile works

Pamphlets, addresses, essays, etc.

1523.3 General

1523.4 Anecdotes, legends, pageants, etc.

Cf. GR117+, Folklore

Cf. Class P, Literature

1523.5 Guidebooks. Handbooks

1523.7 Historic monuments (General)

For Indian antiquities, see F1525+

1523.8 Social life and customs. Civilization. Intellectual life

Including national characteristics

Description and travel. Views

1524 Through 1980

1524.3 1981-

Antiquities. Indians (Ancient and modern)

1525 General works

1525.1.A-.1.Z Local, A-Z

GALE NOTE *The cutter number(s) listed below have been given only as examples by the Library of Congress*

1525.1.Z3 Zapatera Island

1525.2.A-.2.Z Tribes, A-Z

Carib (Black), *see* F1505.2.C3

Chiapanec, *see* F1221.C5

Lenca, *see* F1505.2.L4

1525.2.M3 Matagalpa

Miskito, *see* F1529.M9

1525.2.N5 Nicarao

1525.2.R3 Rama

1525.2.S7 Subtiaba

1525.2.S8 Sumo

(1525.2.T4) Terraba, *see* F1545.2.T4

1525.2.U4 Ulva

1525.3.A-.3.Z Topics, A-Z

1525.3.A7 Art

1525.3.C84 Cultural assimilation

1525.3.E38 Education

	Central America
	Nicaragua
	Antiquities. Indians (Ancient and modern)
1525.3.A-.3.Z	Topics, A-Z — Continued
1525.3.E74	Ethnic identity
1525.3.E76	Ethnobiology
1525.3.G68	Government relations
1525.3.L35	Land tenure
1525.3.M43	Medicine
1525.3.M57	Missions
	Mythology and religion, *see* F1525.3.R44
1525.3.N35	Names
1525.3.P6	Pottery
1525.3.R44	Religion and mythology
1525.3.S38	Sculpture
1525.3.S63	Social conditions
	History
1525.5	Chronological tables. Outlines, syllabi, etc. Questions and answers, etc.
	Historiography
1525.6	General works
	Biography of historians
1525.7.A2	Collective
1525.7.A3-.7.Z	Individual
	GALE NOTE *See note at the head of Table F5 at the end of the text for further instructions on how to subdivide this number*
1525.8	Study and teaching
1526	General works
	Including political history
	General special
1526.1	Military and naval history
	Diplomatic history. Foreign and general relations
	Cf. F1529.B7, Boundaries
1526.2	General works
1526.22.A-.22.Z	Relations with individual countries, A-Z
1526.24	Other (not A-Z)
	By period
	Pre-Columbian period, *see* F1525+
1526.25	1522-1838
	Including end of Spanish rule, 1821; Mexican rule, 1822-1823; Confederación de Centro América, 1823-1838/1842; rivalry between León and Granada; English invasion, 1780-1781
1526.27	1838-1909
	Including foreign intervention, 1848- ; Filibuster War, 1855-1860 (Battle of Rivas, 1856); transfer of Mosquito Territory by Great Britain, 1893; Nicaragua Canal (Cf. TC784)
	Including biography: Pedro Joaquín Chamorro, Roberto Sacasa, William Walker, José Santos Zelaya, etc.
	Cf. F1438, Filibusters in Central America
	Cf. F1529.M9, Mosquito coast and the English protectorate
	Cf. F1536.S2, Bombardment of Greytown, 1854
1526.3	1909-1937
	Including revolts and revolutions of 1909-1910, 1912, 1916, 1926-1929, etc.; United States intervention, 1909-1933; Bryan-Chamorro Treaty, 1916
	Including biography: Emiliano Chamorro, Adolfo Díaz, Juan Bautista Sacasa, Augusto César Sandino, etc.
1527	1937-1979
	Including invasion from El Salvador, 1944; Inter-American Highway
	Including biography: Anastasio Somoza, etc.
	Cf. D731+, World War II, 1939-1945

Central America
Nicaragua
History
By period — Continued
1979-
1528 General works
Biography
1528.2 Collective
1528.22.A-.22.Z Individual, A-Z
GALE NOTE *See note at the head of Table F5 at the end of the text for further instructions on how to subdivide this number*
1529.A-.Z Regions, departments, etc., A-Z
Atlantic Coast, *see* F1529.M9
1529.B7 Boundaries
1529.B7A1-.B7A5 General
1529.B7A6-.B7Z Costa Rica
Honduras, *see* F1509.B7
Saint Andrews Island, *see* F2281.S15
1529.C53 Chontales
1529.J4 Jinotega
1529.M9 Mosquitia (Mosquito Coast). Atlantic Coast, etc.
Including Mosquito Reservation and Miskito Indians
Cf. F1509.M9 , Mosquitia (District) of Honduras
Cf. F1526.27, Transfer of Mosquito Territory by Great Britain, 1893
1529.N5 Lake Nicaragua region
1529.S35 San Juan River and Valley
Cf. F1549.S17, Costa Rica
1529.Z4 Zelaya
Cf. F1529.M9, Mosquitia
1536.A-.Z Cities, towns, etc., A-Z
Cf. F1525.1.A+, Indian local history and antiquities
GALE NOTE *The cutter number(s) listed below have been given only as examples by the Library of Congress*
1536.D5 Diriamba
1536.G72 Granada
Cf. F1526.25, Early history
1536.L4 León
Cf. F1526.25, Early history
1536.M26 Managua
1536.S2 San Juan del Norte. Greytown
Elements in the population
Including foreign elements (General), minorities, race conflicts and problems, etc.
For interpretation, see F1392.A+
1537.A1 General works
1537.A2-.Z Individual elements, A-Z
1537.A5 Americans
1537.B55 Blacks
1537.G47 Germans
Indians, *see* F1525+
Negroes, *see* F1537.B55
Costa Rica
1541 Periodicals. Societies. Collections
Collected works
1541.5 Several authors
1541.6 Individual authors
Including collected papers, addresses, essays, etc.
1541.8 Museums. Exhibitions, exhibits
1542 Gazetteers. Dictionaries. Geographic names
1542.3 Directories

Central America
Costa Rica — Continued
Biography
1542.7 Collective
Individual, *see* F1545.7
1543 General works
1543.2 Juvenile works
Pamphlets, addresses, essays, etc.
1543.3 General
1543.4 Anecdotes, legends, pageants, etc.
Cf. GR117+, Folklore
Cf. Class P, Literature
1543.5 Guidebooks. Handbooks
1543.7 Historic monuments (General)
For Indian antiquities, see F1545+
1543.8 Social life and customs. Civilization. Intellectual life
Including national characteristics
1543.9 Geography
1544 Description and travel. Views
Antiquities. Indians (Ancient and modern)
1545 General works
1545.1.A-.1.Z Local, A-Z
GALE NOTE *The cutter number(s) listed below have been given only as examples by the Library of Congress*
1545.1.V6 Volcán Irazú
1545.15 Museums. Exhibitions
1545.2.A-.2.Z Tribes, A-Z
1545.2.B6 Boruca
1545.2.B7 Bribri
1545.2.C33 Cabecar
1545.2.C48 Chorotega
1545.2.G77 Guatuso
Guaymi, *see* F1565.2.G8
1545.2.G8 Guetar
1545.2.M3 Mangue
1545.2.T4 Terraba
1545.3.A-.3.Z Topics, A-Z
1545.3.A7 Art
1545.3.F6 Folklore. Legends
1545.3.G65 Goldwork
1545.3.J48 Jewelry
1545.3.L34 Land tenure
1545.3.P57 Politics and government
1545.3.P6 Pottery
1545.3.R4 Religion and mythology
1545.3.R44 Reservations
1545.3.S35 Sculpture
1545.3.W2 Warfare
History
1545.5 Chronological tables. Outlines, syllabi, etc. Questions and answers, etc.
Historiography
1545.6 General works
Biography of historians
1545.7.A2 Collective
1545.7.A3-.7.Z Individual
GALE NOTE *See note at the head of Table F5 at the end of the text for further instructions on how to subdivide this number*
1545.8 Study and teaching
1546 General works
Including political history

Central America

Costa Rica

History — Continued

General special

1546.2 Military and naval history

Diplomatic history. Foreign and general relations

For boundary disputes, see F1549.B7

1546.3 General works

1546.4.A-.4.Z Relations with individual countries, A-Z

1546.9 Other (not A-Z)

By period

Pre-Columbian period, *see* F1545+

1547 1502-1838

Including end of Spanish rule, 1821; Mexican rule, 1822-1823; Confederación de Centro América, 1823-1838/1842

1547.5 1838-1948

Including revolutions of 1917, 1919, 1948; Inter-American Highway

Including biography: Tomás Guardia, Rafael Iglesias, Ricardo Jiménez, Juan Rafael Mora, Teodoro Picado Michalski, Bernardo Soto, etc.

1548 1948-1986

Including biography: José Figueres, Otilio Ulate Blanco, etc.

1986-

1548.2 General works

Biography

1548.22 Collective

1548.23.A-.23.Z Individual, A-Z

GALE NOTE *See note at the head of Table F5 at the end of the text for further instructions on how to subdivide this number*

1549.A-.Z Regions, provinces, cantons, etc., A-Z

1549.B7 Boundaries

1549.B7A1-.B7A29 General

Nicaragua, *see* F1529.B7

1549.B7A3-.B7Z Panama

Including ancient Costa Rica-Columbia boundary

1549.C6 Cocos Island

1549.D8 Golfo Dulce (Osa Gulf)

1549.G9 Guanacaste

1549.H5 Heredia

1549.I7 Irazú Volcano

1549.L55 Limón (Province)

1549.N5 Nicoya Peninsula

Osa Gulf, *see* F1549.D8

1549.O83 Osa Peninsula

1549.R5 Rio Grande de Térraba

1549.S15 San José

1549.S17 San Juan River and Valley

Cf. F1529.S35, Nicaragua

1549.T13 Talamanca (District)

Térraba River and Valley, *see* F1549.R5

1556.A-.Z Cities, towns, etc., A-Z

Cf. F1545.1.A+, Indian local history and antiquities

GALE NOTE *The cutter number(s) listed below have been given only as examples by the Library of Congress*

1556.A6 Alajuela

1556.C3 Cartago

Including earthquake of 1910

1556.L5 Limón

1556.S2 San José

Elements in the population

For interpretation, see F1392.A+

	Central America
	Costa Rica
	Elements in the population — Continued
1557.A1	General works
1557.A2-.Z	Individual elements, A-Z
1557.B55	Blacks
1557.C66	Colombians
1557.G3	Germans
	Indians, *see* F1545+
1557.J4	Jews
1557.L42	Lebanese
	Negroes, *see* F1557.B55
1557.N5	Nicaraguans
1557.S7	Spaniards
	Panama
1561	Periodicals. Societies. Collections
	Collected works
1561.5	Several authors
1561.6	Individual authors
	Including collected papers, addresses, essays, etc.
1561.8	Museums. Exhibitions, exhibits
1562	Gazetteers. Dictionaries. Geographic names
1562.3	Directories
	Biography
1562.7	Collective
	Individual, *see* F1565.7
1563	General works
	Cf. F1569.C2, Canal Zone
1563.2	Juvenile works
	Pamphlets, addresses, essays, etc.
1563.3	General
1563.4	Anecdotes, legends, pageants, etc.
	Cf. GR117+, Folklore
	Cf. Class P, Literature
1563.5	Guidebooks. Handbooks
1563.7	Historic monuments (General)
	For Indian antiquities, see F1565+
1563.8	Social life and customs. Civilization. Intellectual life
	Including national characteristics
	Description and travel. Views
1564	Early to 1950
1564.2	1951-1980
1564.3	1981-
	Antiquities. Indians (Ancient and modern)
1565	General works
1565.1.A-.1.Z	Local, A-Z
	GALE NOTE *The cutter number(s) listed below have been given only as examples by the Library of Congress*
1565.1.C6	Coclé
1565.1.D26	Darien
1565.1.V47	Veraguas
1565.2.A-.2.Z	Tribes, A-Z
	Boruca, *see* F1545.2.B6
1565.2.C77	Cueva
1565.2.C8	Cuna
1565.2.D6	Dorask
1565.2.G8	Guaymi
	Terraba, *see* F1545.2.T4
1565.3.A-.3.Z	Topics, A-Z
1565.3.A7	Art

Central America
Panama
Antiquities. Indians (Ancient and modern)
1565.3.A-.3.Z Topics, A-Z — Continued
1565.3.F64 Folklore
1565.3.G68 Government relations
1565.3.I54 Industries
Music, *see* M1685.P2+; ML3572
1565.3.P45 Philosophy
1565.3.T49 Textile industry and fabrics
History
1565.5 Chronological tables. Outlines, syllabi, etc. Questions and answers, etc.
Historiography
1565.6 General works
Biography of historians
1565.7.A2 Collective
1565.7.A3-.7.Z Individual
GALE NOTE *See note at the head of Table F5 at the end of the text for further instructions on how to subdivide this number*
1565.8 Study and teaching
1566 General works
Including political history
For boundary disputes, see F1569.B7
General special
1566.2 Military history
Diplomatic history. Foreign and general relations
Cf. F1569.B7, Boundaries
1566.3 General works
1566.4.A-.4.Z Relations with individual countries, A-Z
1566.44 Other (not A-Z)
By period
Pre-Columbian period, *see* F1565+
1566.45 1501-1903
Including end of Spanish rule, 1821; part of Greater Colombia (Colombian Federation), 1821-1831; under New Granada (later Colombia), 1831-1903; independent in 1841 and 1857; secessionist revolts in 1830, 1831, 1840, 1895, 1898-1903; Massacre of 1856; Panama expeditions, 1741, 1875, 1885
1566.5 1903-1952
Including secession from Colombia, 1903; Hay-Bunau-Varilla Treaty of 1903; Hay-Herrán Treaty of 1903; under protection of the United States, 1903-1936; revolutions of 1931, 1951
Including biography: Manuel Amador Guerrero; Arnulfo Arias Madrid; Pablo Arosemena; Belisario Porras; etc.
1567 1952-
Including biography: José Antonio Remón, etc.
1569.A-.Z Regions, provinces, etc., A-Z
1569.B6 Bocas del Toro
Including Laguna de Chiriqui
1569.B7 Boundaries
1569.B7A1-.B7A5 General
1569.B7A6-.B7A7 Canal Zone
1569.B7A8-.B7Z Colombia
Costa Rica, *see* F1549.B7
Caledonia (Scots' Colony), *see* F2281.D2
1569.C2 Canal Zone. Panama Canal
Including Chagres River
Cf. F1569.B7, Panama boundary
Cf. TC774+, Panama Canal (Construction and maintenance)
Chagres River, *see* F1569.C2

Central America

Panama

1569.A-.Z Regions, provinces, etc., A-Z — Continued

1569.C5 Chiriquí

For Laguna de Chiriqui, see F1569.B6

1569.C6 Coclé

1569.C7 Colón

1569.D3 Darien

Cf. F2281.D2 , Scots' Colony of Darien

Morro Island, *see* F1569.P3

1569.P3 Panama

Including Isla Taboga (Morro Island), Pearl Islands

For Darién Province, see F1569.D3

1569.P35 Panama Bay. Gulf of Panama

Pearl Islands (Islas de las Perlas), *see* F1569.P3

1569.S3 San Blas coast

Scots' Colony of Darien, *see* F2281.D2

Isla Taboga, *see* F1569.P3

1569.V4 Veraguas (Veragua)

1576.A-.Z Cities, towns, etc., A-Z

Cf. F1565.1.A+, Indian local history and antiquities

GALE NOTE *The cutter number(s) listed below have been given only as examples by the Library of Congress*

1576.C7 Colón

1576.P2 Panama

Elements in the population

Including foreign elements (General), minorities, race conflicts and problems, etc.

For interpretation, see F1392.A+

1577.A1 General works

1577.A2-.Z Individual elements, A-Z

1577.B55 Blacks

1577.C48 Chinese

1577.E37 East Indians

Indians, *see* F1565.1.A+

1577.J4 Jews

Negroes, *see* F1577.B55

Caribbean area, see F2155+

West Indies

1601 **Periodicals. Societies. Collections**

Including conferences, congresses, etc.

Collected works

1602 Several authors

1603 Individual authors

Including collected papers, addresses, essays, etc.

1604 **Gazetteers. Dictionaries. Geographic names**

1606 **Directories**

Biography

1607 Collective

Individual, *see* F1620.5.A2+, F1621, F1623

1608 **General works**

1608.3 **Juvenile works**

Pamphlets, addresses, essays, etc.

1608.5 General

1608.7 Anecdotes, legends, pageants, etc.

Cf. GR120+, Folklore

Cf. Class P, Literature

1609 **Guidebooks. Handbooks**

1609.3 **Historic monuments (General)**

For Indian antiquities, see F1619+

West Indies — Continued

1609.5 **Social life and customs. Civilization. Intellectual life**

Including characteristics of the people

Description and travel. Views

1610 Early to 1809

Cf. E141+, Descriptive accounts of America to 1810

1611 1810-1950

1612 1951-1980

1613 1981-

Antiquities. Indians (Ancient and modern)

Works on the aborigines and antiquities of a group of islands or an individual island are classed with the group of islands or the individual island

1619 General works

1619.2.A-.2.Z Tribes, A-Z

GALE NOTE *The cutter number(s) listed below have been given only as examples by the Library of Congress*

Arawak Indians, *see* F2230.2.A7

Carib Indians, *see* F2001

Lucayan Indians, *see* F1655

1619.2.T3 Taino

1619.3.A-.3.Z Topics, A-Z

1619.3.C65 Commerce

1619.3.E83 Ethnic identity. Ethnicity

Ethnicity, *see* F1619.3.E83

1619.3.E85 Ethnobotany

1619.3.F6 Folklore. Legends

1619.3.G68 Government relations

1619.3.I6 Implements (Celts, axes, etc.)

1619.3.P6 Pottery

1619.3.S38 Sculpture

History

1620 Chronological tables. Outlines, syllabi, etc. Questions and answers, etc.

Historiography

1620.3 General works

Biography of historians

1620.5.A2 Collective

1620.5.A3-.5.Z Individual

GALE NOTE *See note at the head of Table F5 at the end of the text for further instructions on how to subdivide this number*

1620.7 Study and teaching

1621 General works

Including general histories and histories of the Spanish West Indies to 1898; naval operations in West Indian waters; Audiencia of Santo Domingo; military and naval history; English West Indian expeditions of 1654-1655, and 1695; George Brydges Rodney and other commanders in the Seven Years' War, 1756-1763; expeditions and campaigns of 1793-1815

Cf. E101+, Early discoveries

Cf. E263.W5, E271+, Naval operations in the American Revolution

Cf. F1411+, Spanish America in general

Cf. F1566.45, Panama Expedition, 1741

Cf. F1781, Capture of Havana, 1762

Cf. F1783, Spanish West Indies in the nineteenth century

Cf. F2041, Ruyter's attack on Barbados, 1655

Cf. F2081, English capture of Martinique, 1809

Cf. F2097, Rodney at St. Eustatius, 1781

Cf. F2161, Buccaneers and pirates in the West Indies

Cf. F2272.5, English West Indian Expedition, 1739-1742

General special

Military and naval history, *see* F1621

Diplomatic history. Foreign and general relations

1621.5 General works

West Indies
History
General special
Diplomatic history. Foreign and general relations — Continued
1622 Relations with the United States
1622.5.A-.5.Z Relations with other countries, A-Z
By period
Early to 1898, *see* F1621
1623 1898-
Cf. F1783, Spanish West Indies, 1810-1898
Elements in the population
Including minorities, race conflicts, problems, etc.
For interpretation, see F1392.A+
1628.8 General works
1629.A-.Z Individual elements, A-Z
1629.B55 Blacks
Cf. HT1071+, Slavery
Indians, *see* F1619+
Negroes, *see* F1629.B55
Bermudas. Somers Islands
1630 Periodicals. Societies. Collections
Collected works
1630.4 Several authors
1630.5 Individual authors
Including collected papers, addresses, essays, etc.
1630.6 Museums. Exhibitions, exhibits
1630.7 Gazetteers. Dictionaries. Geographic names
1630.8 Directories
Biography
1630.9 Collective
Individual, *see* F1635.6, F1636, F1639.A+
1631 General works. Description and travel. Views
1631.2 Juvenile works
Pamphlets, addresses, essays, etc.
1631.3 General
1631.4 Anecdotes, legends, pageants, etc.
Cf. GR120+, Folklore
Cf. Class P, Literature
1632 Guidebooks. Handbooks
1632.5 Historic monuments (General)
1633 Social life and customs. Civilization. Intellectual life
Including characteristics of the people
Description and travel, *see* F1631
1634 Antiquities
History
1635 Chronological tables. Outlines, syllabi, etc. Questions and answers, etc.
Historiography
1635.5 General works
Biography of historians
1635.6.A2 Collective
1635.6.A3-.6.Z Individual
GALE NOTE *See note at the head of Table F5 at the end of the text for further instructions on how to subdivide this number*
1635.7 Study and teaching
1636 General works
Including political history
1637 General special
1639.A-.Z Islands, cities, etc., A-Z
GALE NOTE *The cutter number(s) listed below have been given only as examples by the Library of Congress*

West Indies

Bermudas. Somers Islands

1639.A-.Z Islands, cities, etc., A-Z — Continued

1639.H3 Hamilton

1639.S3 St. George Island

Elements in the population

Including foreign elements (General), minorities, race conflicts and problems, etc.

For interpretation, see F1392.A+

1640.A1 General works

1640.A2-.Z Individual elements, A-Z

1640.B55 Blacks

Negroes, *see* F1640.B55

1640.P67 Portuguese

Bahamas. Bahama Islands. Lucayos

1650 Periodicals. Societies. Collections

Collected works

1650.4 Several authors

1650.5 Individual authors

Including collected papers, addresses, essays, etc.

1650.6 Museums. Exhibitions, exhibits

1650.7 Gazetteers. Dictionaries. Geographic names

1650.8 Directories

Biography

1650.9 Collective

Individual, *see* F1656

1651 General works. Description and travel. Views

1651.2 Juvenile works

Pamphlets, addresses, essays, etc.

1651.3 General

1651.4 Anecdotes, legends, pageants, etc.

Cf. GR120+, Folklore

Cf. Class P, Literature

1652 Guidebooks. Handbooks

1653 Historic monuments (General)

1654 Social life and customs. Civilization. Intellectual life

Including characteristics of the people

Description and travel, *see* F1651

1655 Antiquities. Indians

Including Lucayan Indians (now extinct)

For Taino Indians, see F1619.2.T3

History

1655.3 Chronological tables. Outlines, syllabi, etc. Questions and answers, etc.

Historiography

1655.5 General works

Biography of historians

1655.6.A2 Collective

1655.6.A3-.6.Z Individual

GALE NOTE *See note at the head of Table F5 at the end of the text for further instructions on how to subdivide this number*

1655.7 Study and teaching

1656 General works

Including political history

1657 General special

By period

Early to 1973, *see* F1656

1657.2 1973-

1659.A-.Z Islands, cities, etc., A-Z

GALE NOTE *The cutter number(s) listed below have been given only as examples by the Library of Congress*

1659.C37 Cat Island (Cat Cay)

West Indies

Bahamas. Bahama Islands. Lucayos

1659.A-.Z Islands, cities, etc., A-Z — Continued

1659.N3 Nassau

1659.T9 Turks and Caicos Islands

Elements in the population

Including foreign elements (General), minorities, race conflicts and problems, etc.

For interpretation, see F1392.A+

1660.A1 General works

1660.A2-.Z Individual elements, A-Z

1660.B55 Blacks

Indians, *see* F1655

Negroes, *see* F1660.B55

Greater Antilles

Including Cuba, Haiti, Puerto Rico, Jamaica, and outlying islands. The Windward Passage

1741 General works

Including description and travel, history, antiquities

Cuba

1751 Periodicals. Societies. Collections

Collected works

1752 Several authors

1753 Individual authors

Including collected papers, addresses, essays, etc.

1753.5 Museums. Exhibitions, exhibits

1754 Gazetteers. Dictionaries. Geographic names

1754.5 Directories

1754.7 Guidebooks. Handbooks

Biography

1755 Collective

1758 General works

1758.5 Juvenile works

Pamphlets, addresses, essays, etc.

1759 General

1759.5 Anecdotes, legends, pageants, etc.

Cf. GR120+, Folklore

Cf. Class P, Literature

1759.7 Historic monuments

For Indian antiquities, see F1769

1760 Social life and customs. Civilization. Intellectual life

Including national characteristics

1760.9 Geography

Description and travel. Views

1761 Early to 1810

1763 1811-1897

1765 1898-1951

1765.2 1951-1980

1765.3 1981-

1769 Antiquities. Indians

Including inscriptions, monuments, Ciboney Indians, etc.

For Taino Indians, see F1619.2.T3

History

1772 Chronological tables. Outlines, syllabi, etc. Questions and answers, etc.

Historiography

1773 General works

Biography of historians

1774.A2 Collective

1774.A3-.Z Individual

GALE NOTE *See note at the head of Table F5 at the end of the text for further instructions on how to subdivide this number*

1774.S3 Saco, José Antonio

West Indies

Greater Antilles

Cuba

History — Continued

1775 Study and teaching

1776 General works

Including political history

General special

1776.1 Military and naval history

Diplomatic history. Foreign and general relations

1776.2 General works

1776.3.A-.3.Z Relations with individual countries, A-Z

1778 Other (not A-Z)

By period

Pre-Columbian period, *see* F1769

1492-1810

1779 General

Including Age of buccaneers (16th century); Sir Charles Knowles; Edward Vernon; capture of Spanish silver-fleet in Matanzas Bay, 1628; period of internal development (18th century)

For discovery and exploration, see E101+

1781 1762-1763

Including Siege of Havana; English occupation, 1762-1763

Cf. DA505+,DS674.8, Anglo-Spanish War, 1762-1763

Cf. E199, French and Indian War, 1755-1763

1810-1898

1783 General

Including general works on the Spanish West Indies; question of annexation to the United States; Black Eagle Conspiracy, 1830; Black Conspiracy, 1844

Including biography: Gaspar Betancourt Cisneros; Calixto García; Máximo Gómez y Báez; José Cipriano de la Luz y Caballero; Jose Marti (Cf. PQ7389.M2); Félix Varela y Morales; etc.

Cf. E431, Ostend Manifesto, 1854

Cf. PQ7389.M2, José Martí

1784 Insurrection, 1849-1851. López

Including filibusters and individual biography, e.g. Narciso López

1785 1868-1895

Including Ten Years' War, 1868-1878; Treaty of Zanjon, 1878; the Virginius; the "Little War," 1879-1880

Including biography: Ignacio Agramonte y Loinaz, Francisco Vicente Aguilera, Carlos Manuel de Céspedes y del Castillo

1786 1895-1898

Including Revolution of 1895-1898; question of intervention to February 15, 1898

Including biography: Pedro Estanislao Betancourt y Dávalos, Antonio Maceo, Bartolomé Masó

1787 1898-1933

Including Cuban Republic, 1902- ; Platt Amendment; Revolution of 1906; American occupation, 1906-1909

Including biography: Antonio Sánchez de Bustamente y Sirvén, Tomás Estrada Palma, Juan Gualberto Gómez, Gerardo Machado y Morales, Mario García Menocal, Gonzalo de Quesada, Cosme de la Torriente y Peraza, Alfredo Zayas y Alfonso

1787.5 1933-1959

1959- . Communist regime

Cf. E841+, Cuban missile crisis

1788 General works

1788.2 Addresses, essays, lectures

Biography

1788.22.A2 Collective

	West Indies
	Greater Antilles
	Cuba
	History
	By period
	1959- . Communist regime
	Biography — Continued
1788.22.A3-.22.Z	Individual
	GALE NOTE *See note at the head of Table F5 at the end of the text for further instructions on how to subdivide this number; the cutter number(s) listed below have been given only as examples by the Library of Congress*
1788.22.C3	Castro, Fidel
	Elements in the population
	For interpretation, see F1392.A+
1789.A1	General works
1789.A2-.Z	Individual elements, A-Z
1789.A45	Americans
1789.A7	Asturians
1789.B37	Basques
	Blacks, *see* F1789.N3
1789.C3	Catalans
1789.C53	Chinese
1789.F7	French
1789.G3	Gallegans
	Indians, *see* F1769
1789.J3	Japanese
1789.J4	Jews
1789.K67	Koreans
1789.N3	Negroes. Blacks
1789.S7	Spaniards
	Cf. F1789.A7, Asturians
	Cf. F1789.G3, Gallegans
1789.Y6	Yoruba
	Provinces
	Cf. F1769, Indian history and antiquities
	Camagüey, *see* F1831+
	Havana (Province)
1791	General works
1795	History
1799.A-.Z	Cities, towns, etc., A-Z
	GALE NOTE *The cutter number(s) listed below have been given only as examples by the Library of Congress*
1799.G8	Guanabacoa
1799.H3	Havana (City)
	Subarrange by Table F2 at the end of the text
1799.I8	Isle of Pines
1799.S2	San Antonio de los Baños
	Las Villas, *see* F1821+
	Oriente, *see* F1841+
	Pinar del Rio
1801	General works
1805	History
1809.A-.Z	Cities, towns, etc., A-Z
	GALE NOTE *The cutter number(s) listed below have been given only as examples by the Library of Congress*
1809.M4	Mantua
1809.P5	Pinar del Rio (City)
	Matanzas
1811	General works
1815	History

West Indies
Greater Antilles
Cuba
Provinces
Matanzas — Continued
1819.A-.Z Cities, towns, etc., A-Z
GALE NOTE *The cutter number(s) listed below have been given only as examples by the Library of Congress*
1819.B4 Bellamar Cave
1819.C3 Cárdenas
1819.M4 Matanzas (City)
Las Villas
Formerly Santa Clara
1821 General works
1825 History
1829.A-.Z Cities, towns, etc., A-Z
GALE NOTE *The cutter number(s) listed below have been given only as examples by the Library of Congress*
1829.C5 Cienfuegos
1829.R4 Remedios
1829.S12 Sagua la Grande
1829.S2 Sancti-Spiritus
1829.S3 Santa Clara
1829.T8 Trinidad
Camagüey
Formerly Puerto Principe
1831 General works
1835 History
1839.A-.Z Cities, towns, etc., A-Z
GALE NOTE *The cutter number(s) listed below have been given only as examples by the Library of Congress*
1839.C3 Camagüey (City)
1839.G8 Guáimaro
1839.N9 Nuevitas
Puerto Principe (City), *see* F1839.C3
1839.S23 Santa Cruz del Sur
Oriente
Formerly Santiago de Cuba
1841 General works
1845 History
1849.A-.Z Cities, towns, etc., A-Z
GALE NOTE *The cutter number(s) listed below have been given only as examples by the Library of Congress*
1849.B2 Baracoa
1849.B3 Bayamo
1849.G5 Gibara
1849.H6 Holguín
1849.S3 Santiago de Cuba
1849.T62 Toa River
1849.V5 Victoria de las Tunas
Guantanamo
1850 General works
1850.5 History
1850.9.A-.9.Z Cities, towns, etc., A-Z
Ciego de Avila
1851 General works
1851.5 History
1851.9.A-.9.Z Cities, towns, etc., A-Z
Cienfuegos
1852 General works

West Indies
Greater Antilles
Cuba
Provinces
Cienfuegos — Continued
1852.5 History
1852.9.A-.9.Z Cities, towns, etc., A-Z
Sancti Spíritus
1853 General works
1853.5 History
1853.9.A-.9.Z Cities, towns, etc., A-Z
Holguín Province
1854 General works
1854.5 History
1854.9.A-.9.Z Cities, towns, etc., A-Z
Jamaica
1861 Periodicals. Societies. Collections
Collected works
1862 Several authors
1863 Individual authors
Including collected papers, addresses, essays, etc.
1863.5 Museums. Exhibitions, exhibits
1864 Gazetteers. Dictionaries. Geographic names
1864.5 Directories
Biography
1865 Collective
Individual, *see* F1879.5
1868 General works
1868.2 Juvenile works
Pamphlets, addresses, essays, etc.
1868.3 General
1868.4 Anecdotes, legends, pageants, etc.
Cf. GR120+, Folklore
Cf. Class P, Literature
1869 Guidebooks. Handbooks
1869.5 Historic monuments (General)
For Indian antiquities, see F1875
Description and travel. Views
1870 Early to 1810
1871 1811-1950
1872 1951-1980
1872.2 1981-
1874 Social life and customs. Civilization. Intellectual life
Including characteristics of the people
1874.5 Geography
1875 Antiquities. Indians
History
1878 Chronological tables. Outlines, syllabi, etc. Questions and answers, etc.
Historiography
1879 General works
Biography of historians
1879.5.A2 Collective
1879.5.A3-.5.Z Individual
GALE NOTE *See note at the head of Table F5 at the end of the text for further instructions on how to subdivide this number*
1880 Study and teaching
1881 General works
Including political history
General special
1882 General

West Indies
Greater Antilles
Jamaica
History
General special — Continued
Diplomatic history. Foreign and general relations
1882.2 General works
1882.3.A-.3.Z Relations with individual countries, A-Z
1882.4 Other (not A-Z)
By period
Pre-Columbian period, *see* F1875
1884 1494-1810
Including Spanish rule, 1494-1655; British conquests of 1596, 1643, 1655; Treaty of Madrid, 1670; attempted invasion by France and Spain, 1694, by France alone, 1782, 1806; Maroon War, 1795-1796; Earthquake of 1692
Including biography: Sir Thomas Lynch, etc.
Cf. F2272.5, Admiral Vernon and the English West Indian Expedition of 1739-1742
Cf. F1526.25, British expedition from Jamaica against Nicaragua, 1780-1781
1886 1810-1962
Including Negro insurrection, 1831; Morant Bay Rebellion, 1865-1866; reorganization of Colony, 1844, 1866; earthquake of 1907; hurricanes, 1944, 1951; move toward British West-Indian federation
Including biography: Sir John Peter Grant, Edward John Eyre, etc.
Cf. D501+, World War I, 1914-1918
Cf. D731+, World War II, 1939-1945
Cf. F1447 , British Honduras under governor of Jamaica, 1862-1884
1887 1962-
1891.A-.Z Regions, parishes, etc., A-Z
GALE NOTE *The cutter number(s) listed below have been given only as examples by the Library of Congress*
(1891.C5) Cayman Islands, *see* F2048.5
1891.H2 Hanover Parish
1891.S14 St. James Parish
1891.S2 St. Mary Parish
For Turks and Caicos Islands, see F1659.T9
1895.A-.Z Cities, towns, etc., A-Z
Cf. F1875, Indian local history and antiquities
GALE NOTE *The cutter number(s) listed below have been given only as examples by the Library of Congress*
1895.K5 Kingston
Including earthquake of 1907
1895.M6 Montego Bay
1895.P6 Port Royal
Including earthquake of 1692; hurricanes of 1712, 1714, 1722
1895.S7 Spanish Town
Elements in the population
For interpretation, see F1392.A+
1896.A1 General works
Including race conflicts and problems, etc.
1896.A2-.Z Individual elements, A-Z
Blacks, *see* F1896.N4
1896.C5 Chinese
1896.E2 East Indians
Indians, *see* F1875
1896.I6 Irish
1896.J48 Jews
1896.N4 Negroes. Blacks
Cf. HT1096+, Slavery
Haiti (Island). Hispaniola
1900 Periodicals. Societies. Collections

West Indies

Greater Antilles

Haiti (Island). Hispaniola — Continued

1901 General works

Including description and travel of the whole island

1909 Antiquities. Indians

1911 History (of the island). Spanish Colony, 1492-1795

Spanish Colony of Santo Domingo, 1808-1822, *see* F1938.3

Union of the whole island, 1822-1844, *see* F1924

Haiti (Republic)

1912 Periodicals. Societies. Collections, etc.

Collected works

1912.5 Several authors

1912.6 Individual authors

Including collected papers, addresses, essays, etc.

1912.8 Museums. Exhibitions, exhibits

1913 Gazetteers. Dictionaries. Geographic names

1913.5 Directories

Biography

1914 Collective

Individual, *see* F1920

1915 General works

1915.2 Juvenile works

Pamphlets, addresses, essays, etc.

1915.3 General

1915.4 Anecdotes, legends, pageants, etc.

Cf. GR120+, Folklore

Cf. Class P, Literature

1915.5 Guidebooks. Handbooks

1915.7 Historic monuments (General)

For Indian antiquities, see F1909

1916 Social life and customs. Civilization. Intellectual life

Including national characteristics

1917 Description and travel. Views

Antiquities, Indians, *see* F1909

History

1918 Chronological tables. Outlines, syllabi, etc. Questions and answers, etc.

Historiography

1919 General works

Biography of historians

1920.A2 Collective

1920.A3-.Z Individual

GALE NOTE *See note at the head of Table F5 at the end of the text for further instructions on how to subdivide this number*

1920.5 Study and teaching

1921 General works

Including political history

General special

1921.5 Military and naval history

Diplomatic history. Foreign and general relations

1922 General works

1922.5.A-.5.Z Relations with individual countries, A-Z

1922.9 Other (not A-Z)

By period

Pre-Columbian period, *see* F1909

1923 1492-1803

For period of Spanish control, see F1911

Including French settlement, 1630-1677; Colony of Saint Domingue, 1677-1803; Treaty of Ryswick, 1697; Revolution of 1791-1803; English invasion, 1793-1798; withdrawal of Spain from island, 1795

West Indies

Greater Antilles

Haiti (Island). Hispaniola

Haiti (Republic)

History

By period

1923 1492-1803 — Continued

Including biography: François Dominique Toussaint Louverture, etc.

1924 1804-1843

Including proclamation of independent nation, January 1, 1804; Republic, 1806; separate north and south states, 1806-1820; annexation of Santo Domingo, 1822; Revolution of 1843

Including biography: Jean Pierre Boyer; Henri Christophe (Henri I); Jean Jacques Dessalines; Alexandre Sabès Pétion; etc.

Cf. F1938.3 , Revival of Spanish Colony in the east, 1808-1822

1926 1843-1915

Including loss of Santo Domingo, 1844; period of tumult

Including biography: Fabre Nicolas Geffrard; Pierre Nord Alexis; Louis Étienne Félicité Salomon; Faustino Soulouque (Faustino I, Emperor); etc.

1927 1915-1950

Including United States intervention (Military occupation, 1915-1934; fiscal control ended, 1947); Revolt of 1946

Including biography: Louis Borno, Sudre Dartiguenave, Dumarsais Estimé, Élie Lescot, Sténio Vincent, etc.

1928 1950-1986

Including constitution of 1946 abrogated

Including biography: Paul Eugène Magloire, etc.

1986-

1928.2 General works

Biography

1928.22 Collective

1928.23.A-.23.Z Individual, A-Z

GALE NOTE *See note at the head of Table F5 at the end of the text for further instructions on how to subdivide this number*

1929.A-.Z Regions, departments, cities, etc., A-Z

Cf. F1909, Indian local history and antiquities

GALE NOTE *The cutter number(s) listed below have been given only as examples by the Library of Congress*

1929.B7 Boundaries

Including boundary between Haiti and Dominican Republic

1929.C3 Cap-Haïtien

1929.C8 Cul de Sac

1929.G6 Gonave Island

1929.P8 Port-au-Prince

Elements in the population

Including foreign elements (General), minorities, race conflicts and problems, etc.

For interpretation, see F1392.A+

1930.A1 General works

1930.A2-.Z Individual elements, A-Z

1930.B55 Blacks

1930.F7 French

Indians, *see* F1909

Negroes, *see* F1930.B55

1930.P64 Poles

Dominican Republic. Santo Domingo

1931 Periodicals. Societies. Collections

Collected works

1931.5 Several authors

West Indies
Greater Antilles
Haiti (Island). Hispaniola
Dominican Republic. Santo Domingo
Collected works — Continued
1931.6 Individual authors
Including collected papers, addresses, essays, etc.
1931.7 Museums. Exhibitions, exhibits
1932 Gazetteers. Dictionaries. Geographic names
1932.5 Directories
Biography
1933 Collective
Individual, *see* F1937.6
1934 General works
1934.2 Juvenile works
Pamphlets, addresses, essays, etc.
1934.3 General
1934.4 Anecdotes, legends, pageants, etc.
Cf. GR120+, Folklore
Cf. Class P, Literature
1934.5 Guidebooks. Handbooks
1934.7 Historic monuments (General)
For Indian antiquities, see F1909
1935 Social life and customs. Civilization. Intellectual life
Including national characteristics
1935.5 Geography
Description and travel. Views
1936 Early to 1951
1936.2 1951-1980
1936.3 1981-
Antiquities, Indians, *see* F1909
History
1937 Chronological tables. Outlines, syllabi, etc. Questions and answers, etc.
Historiography
1937.5 General works
Biography of historians
1937.6.A2 Collective
1937.6.A3-.6.Z Individual
GALE NOTE *See note at the head of Table F5 at the end of the text for further instructions on how to subdivide this number*
1937.8 Study and teaching
1938 General works
Including political history
General special
1938.1 Military and naval history
Diplomatic history. Foreign and general relations
1938.2 General works
1938.25.A-.25.Z Relations with individual countries, A-Z
1938.29 Other (not A-Z)
By period
Pre-Columbian period, *see* F1909
1938.3 1492-1844
For Spanish colony, 1492-1795, see F1911
Including period under French or Haitian control, 1795-1808; Spanish colony, 1808-1822; union with Haiti, 1822-1844
1844-1930
1938.4 General
Including establishment of republic, 1844; Spanish regime, 1861-1865; period of revolutions

West Indies
Greater Antilles
Haiti (Island). Hispaniola
Dominican Republic. Santo Domingo
History
By period
1844-1930
1938.4 General — Continued
Including biography: Buenaventura Báez, Juan Pablo Duarte, Ulises Heureaux, Gregorio Luperón, Adolfo Alejandro Nouel y Bobadilla, Francisco del Rosario Sánchez, Pedro Santana, etc.
1938.45 1916-1924
Including period of United States military occupation
1938.5 1930-1961
Including biography: Rafael Leónidas Trujillo Molina, etc.
1961-
1938.55 General works
Biography
1938.57 Collective
1938.58.A-.58.Z Individual, A-Z
GALE NOTE *See note at the head of Table F5 at the end of the text for further instructions on how to subdivide this number*
1939.A-.Z Regions, provinces, cities, etc., A-Z
Cf. F1909, Indian local history and antiquity
GALE NOTE *The cutter number(s) listed below have been given only as examples by the Library of Congress*
1939.A4 Alta Vela (Island). Isla Alto Velo
Boundaries, *see* F1929.B7
Ciudad Trujillo, *see* F1939.S4
1939.C67 Cotuí (Town)
Disitrito Nacional, *see* F1939.S4
1939.I8 Isabela
Ruined town, founded in 1493 by Columbus
La Isabela, *see* F1939.I8
1939.L3 La Vega (City). Concepción de la Vega
1939.M6 Monte Plata (Town)
Monte Tina, *see* F1939.T5
National District, *see* F1939.S4
1939.P9 Puerto Plata (City). San Felipe de Puerto Plata
1939.S15 Salcedo (Province)
1939.S18 Samaná (Town). Santa Bárbara de Samaná
1939.S4 Santo Domingo (National District and City)
Subarrange by Table F2 at the end of the text
Formerly Ciudad Trujillo from 1936 to 1961
1939.T5 Tina (Mountain peak) Monte Tina or Loma Tina
Trujillo (City), *see* F1939.S4
1939.Y38 Yaque del Norte River
Elements in the population
Including foreign elements (General), minorities, race conflicts and problems, etc.
For interpretation, see F1392.A+
1941.A1 General works
1941.A2-.Z Individual elements, A-Z
1941.A73 Arabs
1941.B55 Blacks
1941.C37 Catalans
1941.F5 Flemings
1941.H3 Haitians
Indians, *see* F1909
1941.J3 Japanese
1941.J4 Jews

West Indies
Greater Antilles
Haiti (Island). Hispaniola
Dominican Republic. Santo Domingo
Elements in the population
1941.A2-.Z Individual elements, A-Z — Continued
Negroes, *see* F1941.B55
1941.S7 Spaniards
Puerto Rico. Boriquén
1951 Periodicals. Societies. Collections
Collected works
1952 Several authors
1953 Individual authors
Including collected papers, addresses, essays
1953.5 Museums. Exhibitions, exhibits
1954 Gazetteers. Dictionaries. Geographic names
1954.5 Directories
Biography
1955 Collective
Individual, *see* F1970.6
1958 General works
1958.3 Juvenile works
Pamphlets, addresses, essays, etc.
1958.5 General
1958.7 Anecdotes, legends, pageants, etc.
Cf. GR120+, Folklore
Cf. Class P, Literature
1959 Guidebooks. Handbooks
1959.5 Historic monuments (General)
For Indian antiquities, see F1969
1960 Social life and customs. Civilization. Intellectual life
Including national characteristics
Description and travel. Views
1961 Early to 1897
1965 1898-1950
1965.2 1951-1980
1965.3 1981-
1969 Antiquities. Indians
Including the Borinqueño Indians (now extinct)
History
1970 Chronological tables. Outlines, syllabi, etc. Questions and answers, etc.
Historiography
1970.5 General works
Biography of historians
1970.6.A2 Collective
1970.6.A3-.6.Z Individual
GALE NOTE *See note at the head of Table F5 at the end of the text for further instructions on how to subdivide this number; the cutter number(s) listed below have been given only as examples by the Library of Congress*
1970.6.T3 Tapia y Rivera, Alejandro
1970.8 Study and teaching
1971 General works
Including political history
1972 General special
By period
Pre-Columbian period, *see* F1969
1973 1493-1898
Including period of Spanish rule; attacks by British in 1595, 1598, 1791; attack by Dutch, 1625; revolts against Spain in 1812, 1867; autonomous regime, 1897
Including biography: Eugenio María de Hostos y Bonilla, etc.

West Indies

Greater Antilles

Puerto Rico. Boriquén

History

By period

1973 1493-1898 — Continued

Cf. E717.3, Spanish-American War, 1898

Cf. F1783, Spanish West Indies, 1810-1898

1975 1898-1952

United States possession, 1898; United States Territory (Organized but unincorporated), 1917-1952; hurricanes of 1899, 1928, 1932; etc.

Known as Porto Rico, 1898-1932

Including biography: Jesús T. Piñero, etc.

1952-

1976 General works

Biography

1976.2 Collective

1976.3.A-.3.Z Individual, A-Z

GALE NOTE *See note at the head of Table F5 at the end of the text for further instructions on how to subdivide this number*

1981 Regions, departments, cities, etc., A-Z

Cf. F1969 , Indian local history and antiquities

GALE NOTE *The cutter number(s) listed below have been given only as examples by the Library of Congress*

1981.A26 Aguada

1981.A6 Arecibo (City)

1981.C24 Caguas

1981.C9 Culebra Island

1981.G7 Guayama

1981.M4 Mayagüez (City)

1981.P7 Ponce

1981.R5 Río Piedras

1981.S2 San Juan

Including La Fortaleza (Government house), San Juan National Monument, etc.

1981.U8 Utuado

1981.V5 Vieques Island. Crab Island

Elements in the population

Including foreign elements (General), minorities, race conflicts and problems, etc.

For interpretation, see F1392.A+

1983.A1 General works

1983.A2-.Z Individual elements, A-Z

Blacks, *see* F1983.N4

1983.C83 Cubans

1983.D65 Dominicans

Indians, *see* F1969

1983.N4 Negroes. Blacks

1983.S64 Spaniards

Other islands

1991 Navassa

Lesser Antilles. Caribbees

2001 General works. Cariban Indians

Cf. F2161, The Caribbean Sea with coasts and adjoining islands

Groups of islands, by geographical distribution

For groups by political allegiance, see F2130+

For individual islands, see F2033+

2006 Leeward Islands

Including Anguilla, Antigua, Barbuda, Désirade, Dominica, Guadeloupe, Les Saintes, Marie Galante, Montserrat, Nevis, Redonda, Saba, Saint Bartholomew, Saint Christopher,Saint Croix, Saint Eustatius, Saint John, Saint Martin, Saint Thomas, Virgin Islands

West Indies

Lesser Antilles. Caribbees

Groups of islands, by geographical distribution — Continued

2011 Windward Islands

Including Barbados, Grenada, The Grenadines, Martinique, Saint Lucia, Saint Vincent

2016 Islands along the Venezuela coast

Including Aruba, Bonaire, Curaçao, Tobago, Trinidad

For islands belonging to Venezuela, see F2331.A2

Individual islands (alphabetically)

2033 Anguilla (British)

2035 Antigua and Barbuda

2038 Aruba (Dutch)

2041 Barbados (British)

Including Ruyter's attack on Barbados, 1655

Barbuda, *see* F2035

Basse-Terre Island, *see* F2066

2048 Bonaire. Buen Ayre (Dutch)

2048.5 Cayman Islands (British)

2049 Curaçao (Dutch)

2050 Désirade (French)

2051 Dominica (British)

2056 Grenada (British)

Subarrange by Table F3 at the end of the text

2061 The Grenadines

For Saint Vincent and the Grenadines, see F2106+

2066 Guadeloupe (French)

2070 Les Saintes (French)

2076 Marie Galante (French)

2081 Martinique (French)

Subarrange by Table F3 at the end of the text

2082 Montserrat (British)

2084 Nevis (British). Saint Kitts-Nevis

Redonda, *see* F2035

2088 Saba (Dutch)

2089 Saint Bartholomew. Saint Barthélemy (French)

2091 Saint Christopher. Saint Kitts (British)

For Saint Kitts-Nevis, see F2084

2096 Saint Croix (United States, formerly Danish)

2097 Saint Eustatius (Dutch)

2098 Saint John (United States, formerly Danish)

2100 Saint Lucia (British)

2103 Saint Martin (Dutch and French)

2105 Saint Thomas (United States, formerly Danish)

Saint Vincent. Saint Vincent and the Grenadines

2106 General works

2110.A-.Z Local, A-Z

2116 Tobago

For Trinidad and Tobago, see F2119+

Trinidad. Trinidad and Tobago

2119 General works

By period

2120 Early to 1888

2121 1888-1962

2122 1962-

2123.A-.Z Local, A-Z

2129 Virgin Islands (British)

Class individual islands here

Groups of islands. By political allegiance or national language

2130 English-speaking Caribbean

West Indies

Lesser Antilles. Caribbees

Groups of islands. By political allegiance or national language — Continued

2131 British West Indies (Commonwealth Caribbean)

Including Bahamas, Bermudas, Cayman Islands, Jamaica, the Leeward Islands (Anguilla, Antigua, Barbuda, Dominica, Montserrat, Nevis, Redonda, Saint Christopher), Tobago, Trinidad, the Windward Islands (Barbados, Grenada, The Grenadines, Saint Lucia, Saint Vincent)

For individual groups of islands (geographical distribution) or individual islands, see F1630+, F1650+, F1861+

Cf. E162, E188, English colonies in America before 1775 (General)

Cf. E263.W5, West Indies in the American Revolution, 1775-1783

Cf. F1529.M9, British Protectorate of Mosquito coast

Cf. HT1091+, Slavery

2132 Travel and description, 1951-

2133 History, 1943-

2134 West Indies Federation

Came into effect January 1958. Consists of 10 colonies embracing 13 islands: Antigua, Barbados, Dominica, Grenada, Jamaica, Montserrat, Saint Christopher, Nevis, Anguilla, Saint Lucia, Saint Vincent, Trinidad, and Tobago

2136 Virgin Islands of the United States

Danish West Indies before 1917

For individual islands (Saint Croix), see F2096

For individual islands (Saint John), see F2098

For individual islands (Saint Thomas), see F2105

Cf. E669, Proposed annexation to United States, 1867-1869

Cf. E756, Proposed annexation to United States, 1902

Cf. E768, Purchase by United States, 1917

2141 Netherlands West Indies. Dutch West Indies

Including Aruba, Bonaire, Curaçao, Saba, Saint Eustatius, Saint Martin

For individual islands, see F2038-2103

2151 French West Indies

Leeward Islands (Guadeloupe, Marie Galante, Saint Bartholomew, part of Saint Martin); Martinique (Windward Islands); Les Saintes

For individual islands, see F2066-2103

Saint Domingue (French colony, Haiti), *see* F1923

Spanish West Indies, *see* F1601-1623

Caribbean area. Caribbean Sea

Including the West Indies and coasts of the Caribbean Sea, the Gulf of Mexico, and Spanish Main

2155 Periodicals. Societies. Collections

2155.3 Congresses

Collected works

2156 Several authors

2157 Individual authors

Including collected papers, addresses, essays

2158 Gazetteers. Dictionaries. Geographic names

Biography

2160 Collective

Individual, *see* F2161, F2180.2+

2161 General works

Including pirates and buccaneers

2161.5 Juvenile works

2165 Guidebooks. Handbooks

2169 Social life and customs. Civilization. Intellectual life

Including national characteristics

For specific periods after 1810, see F2181

Description and travel. Views

2171 Early through 1950

2171.2 1951-1980

2171.3 1981-

West Indies
Caribbean area. Caribbean Sea — Continued
2172 Antiquities. Indians
History
2173 Study and teaching
2175 General works
2176 General special
Diplomatic history. Foreign and general relations
2177 General works
2178.A-.Z Relations with individual countries, A-Z
By period
Early through 1810, *see* F2161
1811-
2181 General
2183 1945-
Elements in the population
For interpretation, see F1392.A+
2190 General works
2191.A-.Z Individual elements, A-Z
2191.B55 Blacks
2191.C35 Canary Islanders
2191.C46 Chinese
2191.E27 East Indians
South America
2201 **Periodicals. Societies. Collections**
For South American geographic societies, see G5
2204 **Gazetteers. Dictionaries. Geographic names**
Biography
2205 Collective
Individual, *see* F2230.5, F2232.92+
2208 **General works**
2208.5 **Juvenile works**
Pamphlets, addresses, essays, etc.
2209 General
2209.5 Anecdotes, legends, pageants, etc.
Cf. GR130+, Folklore
Cf. Class P, Literature
2210 **Social life and customs. Civilization. Intellectual life**
Cf. F2239, Elements in the population
2211 **Guidebooks. Handbooks**
2211.5 **Geography**
Regions
2212 Andes Mountains (General). Altiplano (General)
For the Andes or Altiplano in individual countries, see the region of the country, e.g. F2851, Andes in Argentina
2213 Pacific coast
For Galápagos Islands, see F3741.G2
2214 Atlantic coast
2215 Islands of South America (General)
2216 Northern South America
Including Brazil, Colombia, Ecuador, Guiana, Peru and Venezuela
For Amazon River, see F2546
For Spanish Main, see F2161
2217 Southern South America
Including Argentina, Bolivia, Brazil (South), Chile, Paraguay, Peru and Uruguay
Including Gauchos (General)
For Gran Chaco, see F2876
For gauchos in individual countries, see F2621, Brazil; F2682.9, Paraguay; F2722.9, Uruguay; F2926, Argentina
For La Plata region, see F2801+

	South America
	Regions
2217	Southern South America — Continued
	For Falkland Islands, see F3031+
	Description and travel (General). Views
2221	Early to 1810
2223	1811-1950
	Cf. F865, Voyages to the Pacific coast following discovery of gold
2224	1951-1980
2225	1981-
	Antiquities. Indians
2229	General works
2230	Modern Indians (General)
2230.1.A-.1.Z	Topics (Ancient and modern), A-Z
2230.1.A3	Agriculture
2230.1.A4	Anthropometry
2230.1.A5	Architecture
2230.1.A6	Arms and armor
2230.1.A7	Art
2230.1.A85	Astronomy
2230.1.B6	Boats. Canoes
2230.1.B7	Botany (Economics). Ethnobotany
2230.1.C5	Children
2230.1.C75	Commerce
2230.1.C8	Costume and adornment
2230.1.C9	Culture
2230.1.D35	Dance
2230.1.D65	Domestic animals
2230.1.D75	Drinking vessels. Queros
2230.1.D78	Drug use
2230.1.E25	Economic conditions
2230.1.E37	Education
2230.1.E84	Ethnic identity
	Ethnobotany, *see* F2230.1.B7
2230.1.E87	Ethnozoology
2230.1.F2	Feather work
2230.1.F56	Folk literature
2230.1.F6	Folklore. Legends
2230.1.G2	Games
2230.1.G64	Goldwork
2230.1.G68	Government relations
2230.1.H84	Hunting
2230.1.I4	Implements
2230.1.I42	Industries
2230.1.I77	Irrigation
2230.1.K5	Kinship
2230.1.L35	Land tenure
2230.1.M24	Magic
2230.1.M28	Marriage customs and rites
2230.1.M3	Masks
2230.1.M34	Material culture
2230.1.M4	Medicine
2230.1.M43	Metalwork
2230.1.M47	Migrations
2230.1.M5	Missions
	Including biography of missionaries
2230.1.M54	Mixed descent
2230.1.M6	Mortuary customs
	Music, *see* ML3575.A2A+
2230.1.N37	Narcotics

South America

Antiquities. Indians

2230.1.A-.1.Z Topics (Ancient and modern), A-Z — Continued

2230.1.P48 Petroglyphs. Rock paintings

2230.1.P53 Philosophy

2230.1.P65 Politics and government

2230.1.P8 Pottery

Queros, *see* F2230.1.D75

2230.1.R3 Religion and mythology

2230.1.R6 Roads. Trails

Rock paintings, *see* F2230.1.P48

2230.1.S37 Sculpture

2230.1.S44 Semitic influences

2230.1.S54 Shell beads. Shell engraving. Shell jewelry

2230.1.S68 Social conditions

2230.1.S7 Social life and customs

2230.1.T3 Textile industry and fabrics

2230.1.T63 Tobacco use

Trails, *see* F2230.1.R6

2230.1.T7 Treatment of Indians

2230.1.W37 Wars

2230.1.W6 Women

2230.1.W7 Writing

2230.2.A-.2.Z Tribes (Ancient and modern), A-Z

Class here tribes which do not live or are not identified with one particular country

Tribes which live or before extinction have lived in one country or are usually identified with one country, although they may occupy or have occupied areas of one or more adjacent countries, are classed with the individual country

2230.2.A68 Araona Indians

2230.2.A7 Arawak

2230.2.A78 Ashluslay

2230.2.A82 Avachiripá

2230.2.A9 Aymara

2230.2.C3 Caingua

Carib, *see* F2001

2230.2.C5 Chamacoco

(2230.2.C64) Cofán, *see* F3722.1.C67

2230.2.G72 Guarani

2230.2.G75 Guayana

2230.2.G78 Guaycuruan. Guaycuru

2230.2.J58 Jivaran

2230.2.K4 Kechua. Quechua

2230.2.O8 Oyana. Wayana

Quechua, *see* F2230.2.K4

2230.2.T84 Tupi

Wayana, *see* F2230.2.O8

History

2230.3 Chronological tables. Outlines, syllabi, etc. Questions and answers, etc.

Historiography

2230.4 General works

Biography of historians

2230.5.A2 Collective

2230.5.A3-.5.Z Individual

GALE NOTE *See note at the head of Table F5 at the end of the text for further instructions on how to subdivide this number*

2230.6 Study and teaching

2231 General works

General special

2231.5 General

2231.7 Military history

South America
History
General special — Continued
2231.8 Naval history
Diplomatic history. Foreign and general relations
2232 General works
2232.2.A-.2.Z Relations with individual countries, A-Z
By period
Pre-Columbian period, *see* F2229+
2233 1498-1806
Including Colonial period
Cf. E101+, Early discoveries
1806-1830. Wars of independence
2235 General works
2235.3 Bolívar, Simón
Including life and works
2235.36 Guayaquil meeting, 1822
2235.4 San Martín, José de
Including life and correspondence
2235.5.A-.5.Z Other liberators, A-Z
2235.5.R6 Rodríguez, Simón
2235.5.S9 Sucre, Antonio José de
2235.5.U7 Urdaneta, Rafael
1830-
2236 General works
2237 1939-
Cf. D731+, World War II, 1939-1945
Elements in the population
Including foreign elements (General), minorities, race conflicts and problems
For interpretation, see F1392.A+
2239.A1 General works
2239.A2-.Z Individual elements, A-Z
2239.A7 Arabs
2239.B3 Basques
2239.B55 Blacks
2239.B8 British
2239.B9 Bulgarians
2239.C48 Chinese
2239.C76 Croats
2239.D8 Dutch
2239.G3 Germans
2239.G74 Greeks
2239.H85 Hungarians
Indians, *see* F2229+
2239.I8 Italians
2239.J3 Japanese
2239.J5 Jews
2239.K65 Kongo
2239.K67 Koreans
2239.L7 Lithuanians
Negroes, *see* F2239.B55
2239.N6 Norwegians
2239.P6 Poles
2239.P67 Portuguese
2239.S8 Swedes
2239.S9 Swiss
2239.Y83 Yugoslavs
Colombia
2251 Periodicals. Societies. Collections

South America
Colombia — Continued
Collected works
2252 Several authors
2253 Individual authors
Including collected papers, addresses, essays
2253.5 Museums. Exhibitions, exhibits
2254 Gazetteers. Dictionaries. Geographic names
2254.5 Directories
Biography
2255 Collective
Individual, *see* F2270.6, F2272-2279.22
2258 General works
2258.5 Juvenile works
Pamphlets, addresses, essays, etc.
2259 General
2259.3 Anecdotes, legends, pageants, etc.
Cf. GR130+, Folklore
Cf. Class P, Literature
2259.5 Guidebooks. Handbooks
2259.7 Historic monuments (General)
2260 Social life and customs. Civilization. Intellectual life
Including national characteristics
For race conflicts and problems, see F2299
2260.9 Geography
Description and travel. Views
2261 Early to 1809
2263 1810-1950
2264 1951-1980
2264.2 1981-
Antiquities. Indians
2269 General works
2269.1.A-.1.Z Local (Ancient and modern), A-Z
GALE NOTE *The cutter number(s) listed below have been given only as examples by the Library of Congress*
2269.1.A28 Aburrá Valley
2269.1.C95 Cundinamarca
2269.1.P66 Popayán (Province)
2269.1.S24 San Agustin
2269.1.S25 Santa Marta Lagoon region
2269.1.T54 Tierra Adentro
2269.1.V35 Valle del Cauca
2270 Modern Indians (General)
2270.1.A-.1.Z Topics (Ancient and modern), A-Z
2270.1.A47 Agriculture
2270.1.A58 Anthropometry
2270.1.A7 Art
2270.1.C4 Census
2270.1.C58 Civil rights
2270.1.E3 Economic conditions
2270.1.E36 Education
2270.1.E84 Ethnic identity
2270.1.E86 Ethnobotany
2270.1.E88 Ethnozoology
2270.1.F6 Folklore. Legends
2270.1.F85 Funeral customs and rites
2270.1.G57 Goldwork
2270.1.G6 Government relations
Including reservations (General)
2270.1.K55 Kinship

South America

Colombia

Antiquities. Indians

2270.1.A-.1.Z Topics (Ancient and modern), A-Z — Continued

2270.1.L3 Land tenure

Legends, *see* F2270.1.F6

2270.1.M43 Medicine

2270.1.M5 Missions

2270.1.N35 Narcotics. Drugs

2270.1.P4 Petroglyphs. Rock paintings

2270.1.P63 Politics and government

2270.1.P65 Pottery

2270.1.R4 Religion and mythology

Rock paintings, *see* F2270.1.P4

2270.1.S63 Social conditions

2270.1.S64 Social life and customs

2270.1.T38 Taxation

2270.1.T48 Textile industry and fabrics

2270.2.A-.2.Z Tribes and cultures (Ancient and modern), A-Z

2270.2.A3 Achagua

2270.2.A6 Andaqui

2270.2.A63 Anserma

Arawak, *see* F2230.2.A7

2270.2.A67 Arhuaco

Aruac, *see* F2270.2.A67

Baniva, *see* F2520.1.B35

2270.2.B27 Barasana

2270.2.B3 Barbacoa

2270.2.B6 Bora

2270.2.C22 Cabiyari

2270.2.C24 Calima culture

2270.2.C25 Camsa

2270.2.C26 Carapana

2270.2.C27 Carijona

2270.2.C3 Catio

2270.2.C34 Cenu

2270.2.C37 Chamí

2270.2.C4 Chibcha

2270.2.C5 Chimila

2270.2.C6 Choco

2270.2.C63 Churoya

Cobaría, *see* F2270.2.T8

2270.2.C65 Coconuco

2270.2.C67 Colima

2270.2.C68 Coyaima

Cuaiquer, *see* F3722.1.C83

2270.2.C8 Cubeo

Cuna, *see* F1565.2.C8

2270.2.C87 Curripaco

2270.2.D4 Desana

2270.2.E43 Embera

2270.2.E53 Epena Saija

2270.2.G6 Goajiro

Guahibo, *see* F2319.2.G8

2270.2.G8 Guane

2270.2.G83 Guarino

Ijca, *see* F2270.2.A67

2270.2.I53 Ingano

2270.2.K3 Kagaba

Macu, *see* F2520.1.M2

South America

Colombia

Antiquities. Indians

2270.2.A-.2.Z Tribes and cultures (Ancient and modern), A-Z — Continued

2270.2.M33 Macuna

2270.2.M5 Mocoa

2270.2.M6 Moguex

Motilon, *see* F2319.2.M6

2270.2.M75 Muinane

2270.2.M8 Muzo

2270.2.N8 Nukak

2270.2.P3 Paez

Panare, *see* F2319.2.P34

2270.2.P4 Paniquita

2270.2.P44 Pasto

Peban, *see* F3430.1.P4

2270.2.P64 Pijao

2270.2.P8 Puinave

2270.2.Q54 Quillacinga

2270.2.Q8 Quimbaya

Saliva, *see* F2319.2.S3

2270.2.S35 San Agustin culture

2270.2.T3 Tairona

2270.2.T32 Taiwano

2270.2.T34 Tanimuca-Retuama

Timote, *see* F2319.2.T5

Tucano, *see* F2520.1.T9

Tucuna, *see* F2520.1.T925

2270.2.T77 Tukanoan

2270.2.T8 Tunebo

2270.2.W5 Witoto

2270.2.W54 Wiwa

2270.2.Y3 Yakalamarure

2270.2.Y42 Yebamasa

2270.2.Y87 Yucuna

2270.2.Y9 Yuko

Yupa, *see* F2319.2.Y8

History

Including political history

2270.3 Chronological tables. Outlines, syllabi, etc. Questions and answers, etc.

Historiography

2270.4 General works

Biography of historians

2270.5 Collective

2270.6.A-.6.Z Individual, A-Z

GALE NOTE *See note at the head of Table F5 at the end of the text for further instructions on how to subdivide this number*

2270.7 Study and teaching

2271 General works

Including political history

General special

2271.4 Military and naval history

Diplomatic history. Foreign and general relations

2271.5 General works

2271.52.A-.52.Z Relations with individual countries, A-Z

2271.9 Other (not A-Z)

By period

Pre-Columbian period, *see* F2269+

South America
Colombia
History
By period — Continued
1499-1810
2272 General works
Including Viceroyalty and Audiencia of New Granada; conquest of Chibcha Indians, 1536-1538; Siege of Cartagena, 1585, 1697; Insurrection of the Comuneros, 1781
Including biography: Gonzalo Jiménez de Quesada, etc.
Cf. E135.G3, The Welsers, 1529-1556
Cf. F2272.5, Siege of Cartagena 1741
Cf. F2281.D2, Scot's Colony, 1698-1700
2272.5 1739-1742. English West Indian Expedition
Including siege of Cartagena, 1741
Cf. F2272, Siege of Cartagena, 1585 and 1697
Cf. F1621, English West Indian Expedition, 1654-1655, 1695
1810-
2273 General works
Including biography: Francisco de Paula Santander, etc.
2274 1810-1822. War of Independence
Republic of Colombia formed by union of New Granada, Venezuela, and Ecuador, 1819-1822
Including Siege of Cartagena, 1815; Battle of Boyacá, 1819
Including biography: José María Córdoba, José Fernandez Madrid, Antonio Nariño, Antonio Ricaurte y Lozano, etc.
2275 1822-1832
After Venezuela and Ecuador became independent, the name "State of New Granada" was adopted (Law of 1831 and Constitution of 1832)
Including separatist movements, 1829-1830; Battle of Portete de Tarqui, 1829
2276 1832-1886
In modification of Constitution of 1842 and 1843, the name changed to "Republic of New Granada"; under Constitution of 1858, name changed to "Confederation of Granada"; in Pact of 1861 and Constitution of 1863, name changed to "United States of Colombia"
Including biography: Pascual Bravo, Pedro Alcántara Herrán, José Hilario López, Tomás Cipriano de Mosquera, Rafael Núñez, etc.
2276.5 1886-1903
Under the Constitution of 1886, name changed to "Republic of Colombia"
Including Revolution of 1899-1903; Secession of Panama, 1903
Cf. F1566.5, Hay-Herrán Treaty, 1903
Including biography: José Manuel Marroquín, Próspero Pinzón, Manuel Antonio Sanclemente, etc.
2277 1904-1946
Including Conservative rule, 1904-1930; the liberals, 1930-1946; Thomson-Urrutia Treaty, 1914
Including biography: Miguel Antonio Caro, Alfonso López, Enrique Olaya Herrera, Pedro Nel Ospina, Rafael Reyes, Eduardo Santos, etc.
Cf. D501+, World War I, 1914-1918
Cf. D731+, World War II, 1939-1945
Cf. F2281.B7P1+, Leticia Dispute, 1932-1934
2278 1946-1974
Including conservative restoration, 1946; etc.
Including biography: Laureano Gómez, Mariano Ospina Pérez, Gustavo Rojas Pinilla, etc.
1974-
2279 General works
Biography
2279.2 Collective

	South America
	Colombia
	History
	By period
	1810-
	1974-
	Biography — Continued
2279.22.A-.22.Z	Individual, A-Z
	GALE NOTE *See note at the head of Table F5 at the end of the text for further instructions on how to subdivide this number*
2281.A-.Z	Regions, departments, etc., A-Z
	GALE NOTE *The cutter number(s) listed below have been given only as examples by the Library of Congress*
2281.A4	Amazon River and Valley, Colombia
	Cf. F2546, General, and Brazil
2281.A5	Andes Mountains, Colombia
	Cf. F2212, General
2281.A6	Antioquia
2281.A7	Arauca (Dept.)
2281.A79	Atlantic Coast
2281.A8	Atlántico
	Bogotá River, *see* F2281.C9
2281.B6	Bolívar
	Including Barú Island, Rosario Islands, Tierra Bomba Island, San Jorge River, and Sinú River
	Boundaries
2281.B7A1-.B7A9	General
	Brazil, *see* F2554.C7
	Costa Rica (Ancient boundary), *see* F1549.B7
2281.B7E1-.B7E9	Ecuador
	Panama, *see* F1569.B7
2281.B7P1-.B7P9	Peru
	Including Leticia question
	Saint Andrews Island, *see* F2281.S15
2281.B7V1-.B7V9	Venezuela
2281.B8	Boyacá
2281.C25	Caldas
2281.C26	Caquetá
2281.C27	Cartagena (Province)
2281.C3	Cauca
	For Patía River, see F2281.P37
2281.C32	Cauca River and Valley
2281.C4	César
2281.C5	Chocó
2281.C9	Cundinamarca
	Including Bogotá River
	For San Martín (Territory), see F2281.M49
2281.D2	Darien. Scots' Colony (Caledonia)
	For modern Darien, see F1569.D3
2281.G8	Goajira (Territory). La Guajira (Dept.)
	Including Goajira peninsula
2281.H8	Huila
	La Guajira (Dept.), *see* F2281.G8
	Leticia question, *see* F2281.B7P1+
2281.L52	Llanos Orientales
	Cf. F2331.O7, Orinoco River and Valley
2281.M2	Magdalena (Dept.). Santa Marta (Province)
	Including Sierra Nevada de Santa Marta
2281.M23	Magdalena River and Valley
2281.M3	Malpelo Island

South America

Colombia

2281.A-.Z	Regions, departments, etc., A-Z — Continued
2281.M49	Meta (Dept.). San Martín (Territory)
	Including Ariari River
2281.M5	Meta River and Valley
	Morrosquillo, Gulf of, *see* F2281.S82
2281.N3	Nariño
	For Patía River, see F2281.P37
2281.N5	Neiva (Province)
2281.N6	Norte de Santander
2281.P23	Pacific Coast
2281.P3	Pamplona (Province)
2281.P37	Patía River and Valley
2281.P4	Sierra de Perijá
	Cf. F2331.P4, Perijá (District) of Venezuela
2281.P8	Popayán (Province)
2281.P9	Putumayo (Dept.)
	Including Putumayo River and Valley, Colombia, and Sibundoy Valley
	Cf. F3451.P94, General, and Peru
2281.Q55	Quindío (Province)
2281.S15	San Andrés y Providencia (Territory)
	Including Saint Andrews Island, Providence Island
	San Martín (Territory), *see* F2281.M49
	Santa Marta (Province), *see* F2281.M2
	Santa Marta, Sierra Nevada de, *see* P2281.M2
2281.S3	Santander
	Sierra de Perijá, *see* P2281.P4
2281.S82	Sucre (Dept.)
	Including Gulf of Morrosquillo
2281.S86	Sumapaz Region
2281.T6	Tolima
2281.T8	Tunja (Province)
2281.U7	Urabá (Province)
2281.V3	Valle del Cauca
2291.A-.Z	Cities, towns, etc., A-Z
	GALE NOTE *The cutter number(s) listed below have been given only as examples by the Library of Congress*
2291.B3	Barranquilla
2291.B6	Bogotá
	Subarrange by Table F2 at the end of the text
2291.B77	Bucaramanga
2291.B8	Buga
2291.C15	Cali
2291.C3	Cartagena
	For Siege of 1585, see F2272
	For Siege of 1697, see F2272
	For Siege of 1741, see F2272.5
	For Siege of 1815, see F2274
2291.M4	Medellín
2291.P28	Pasto
2291.T8	Tunja
	Elements in the population
	Including foreign elements (General), minorities, race conflicts and problems
	For interpretation, see F1392.A+
2299.A1	General works
2299.A2-.Z	Individual elements
2299.B37	Basques
2299.B55	Blacks
2299.G3	Germans

South America

Colombia

Elements in the population

2299.A2-.Z Individual elements — Continued

Indians, *see* F2269+

2299.J3 Japanese

2299.J5 Jews

2299.L42 Lebanese

Negroes, *see* F2299.B55

Venezuela

2301 Periodicals. Societies. Collections

2301.5 Sources and documents

Collected works

2302 Several authors

2303 Individual authors

Including collected papers, addresses, essays, etc.

2303.5 Museums. Exhibitions, exhibits

2304 Gazetteers. Dictionaries. Geographic names

2304.5 Directories

Biography

2305 Collective

Individual, *see* F2320.6, F2322-2328.52

2308 General works

2308.5 Juvenile works

Pamphlets, addresses, essays, etc.

2309 General

2309.3 Anecdotes, legends, pageants, etc.

Cf. GR130+, Folklore

Cf. Class P, Literature

2309.5 Guidebooks. Handbooks

2309.7 Historic monuments (General)

2310 Social life and customs. Civilization. Intellectual life

Including national characteristics

For race conflicts and problems, see F2349.A+

2310.9 Geography

Description and travel. Views

2311 Early to 1809

2313 1810-1950

2314 1951-1980

2315 1981-

Antiquities. Indians

2318 Museums. Exhibitions

2319 General works

2319.1.A-.1.Z Local (Ancient and modern), A-Z

GALE NOTE *The cutter number(s) listed below have been given only as examples by the Library of Congress*

2319.1.M3 Maracay

2319.1.S8 Sucre (State)

2319.2.A-.2.Z Tribes (Ancient and modern), A-Z

Arawak, *see* F2230.2.A7

Arecuna, *see* F2380.1.A7

2319.2.A73 Arekena

Baniva, *see* F2520.1.B35

Baré, *see* F2520.1.B4

Betoya, *see* F2270.2.T77

2319.2.C28 Caquetio

Carib, *see* F2460.1.C37

Cariban, *see* F2001

Churoya, *see* F2270.2.C63

2319.2.C78 Cuiva

South America

Venezuela

Antiquities. Indians

2319.2.A-.2.Z Tribes (Ancient and modern), A-Z — Continued

2319.2.C8 Cumana

Goajiro, *see* F2270.2.G6

2319.2.G8 Guahibo

2319.2.I7 Irapa

Macu, *see* F2520.1.M2

Macusi, *see* F2380.1.M3

2319.2.M3 Maipure

2319.2.M6 Motilone

2319.2.O8 Otomaco

2319.2.P3 Palenque

2319.2.P34 Panare

2319.2.P37 Paraujano

2319.2.P45 Pemon

2319.2.P5 Piaroa

2319.2.S3 Saliva

2319.2.S52 Sicuane

2319.2.T25 Tamanca

Taurepan, *see* F2380.1.A7

2319.2.T4 Teque

2319.2.T5 Timote

Waica, *see* F2520.1.W3

2319.2.W3 Warao

Yanomamo, *see* F2520.1.Y3

2319.2.Y3 Yaruro

2319.2.Y4 Yecuana

2319.2.Y8 Yupa

2319.3.A-.3.Z Topics (Ancient and modern), A-Z

2319.3.A37 Agriculture

2319.3.A5 Anthropometry

2319.3.A7 Art

2319.3.B37 Baskets

2319.3.C4 Census

2319.3.E26 Economic conditions

2319.3.E46 Employment

(2319.3.F58) Folk literature, *see* F2319.3.F6

2319.3.F6 Folklore. Legends

2319.3.G6 Government relations

2319.3.L35 Land tenure

2319.3.M5 Missions

2319.3.N35 Names

2319.3.P4 Petroglyphs. Rock paintings

2319.3.P6 Pottery

Rock paintings, *see* F2319.3.P4

2319.3.S6 Social conditions

2319.3.S62 Social life and customs

2319.3.T43 Teenagers

History

2319.5 Chronological tables. Outlines, syllabi, etc. Questions and answers, etc.

Historiography

2320 General works

Biography of historians

2320.5 Collective

2320.6.A-.6.Z Individual, A-Z

GALE NOTE *See note at the head of Table F5 at the end of the text for further instructions on how to subdivide this number*

2320.7 Study and teaching

South America

Venezuela

History — Continued

2321 General works

Including political history

General special

2321.1 Military and naval history

Diplomatic history. Foreign and general relations

2321.2 General works

2321.3.A-.3.Z Relations with individual countries, A-Z

2321.9 Other (not A-Z)

By period

Pre-Columbian period, *see* F2318+

2322 1498-1806/1810

Including early settlement; German occupation to 1556; pillage and attacks by English and French, 1595-1798; separation from Viceroyalty of Peru, 1731. In 1777, Captain-Generalcy of Caracas established; in 1786, Audiencia of Caracas created

Including biography: Alonso Andrea de Ledesma

1806/1810-

2322.8 General works

Including biography: José Antonio Páez, etc.

2323 1806-1812

Including Francisco de Miranda's attempts at independence and his biography; Treaty of San Mateo, 1812

2324 1810-1830. War of Independence, 1810-1823

Including earthquake of 1812; Battle of Carabobo, 1821. Province of Republic of Colombia, 1822-1829

Including biography: José Antonio Anzoátegui, José Tomás Boves, Pedro Luis Brión, Pablo Morillo y Morillo, José Félix Ribas, etc.

2325 1830-1935

Including Republic of Venezuela formed in 1830; era of civil wars, 1848-1870; Revolution, 1902-1903; Anglo-German-Italian Blockade, 1902; Dutch Blockade, 1908

Including biography: Cipriano Castro, Joaquín Crespo, Juan Vicente Gómez, Antonio Guzmán Blanco, Santos Michelena, José Tadeo Monagas, Juan Pietri, Arístides Rojas, José María Vargas

2326 1935-1958

Including movement toward democracy, 1935-1948; Revolution of 1945

Including biography: Rómulo Betancourt, Carlos Delgado Chalband, Eleazar López Contreras, Isaías Medina Angarita, Marcos Pérez Jiménez, etc.

Cf. D731+, World War II, 1939-1945

1958-1974

2327 General works

Biography

2327.5 Collective

2327.52.A-.52.Z Individual, A-Z

GALE NOTE *See note at the head of Table F5 at the end of the text for further instructions on how to subdivide this number*

1974-1999

2328 General works

Biography

2328.5 Collective

2328.52.A-.52.Z Individual, A-Z

GALE NOTE *See note at the head of Table F5 at the end of the text for further instructions on how to subdivide this number*

1999-

2329 General works

Biography

2329.2 Collective

South America

Venezuela

History

By period

1806/1810-

1999-

Biography — Continued

2329.22.A-.22.Z Individual, A-Z

GALE NOTE *See note at the head of Table F5 at the end of the text for further instructions on how to subdivide this number*

2331.A-.Z Regions, states, etc., A-Z

2331.A2 Islands along the Venezuela coast (General)

For islands off the coast, belonging to other countries, see F2016

2331.A3 Amazonas (Territory)

2331.A5 Andes Mountains, Venezuela

Cf. F2212, General

2331.A55 Anzoátegui

2331.A65 Apure

2331.A7 Aragua

2331.A9 Aves Islands

2331.A93 Avila Mountain

2331.B3 Barinas (Sur de Occidente, Zamora)

2331.B6 Bolívar

Including Great Savannah

Boundaries

2331.B7 General

Brazil, *see* F2554.V4

2331.B72 British Guiana. Guyana

Colombia, *see* F2281.B7

Guyana, *see* F2331.B72

2331.B75 Bruzual

2331.C3 Carabobo

2331.C5 Chacao (Caracas) Valley

2331.C6 Cojedes

2331.C7 Cubagua Island

2331.D44 Delta Amacuro

2331.F2 Falcón

Including Paraguaná Peninsula

Goajira (Guajira) peninsula, *see* F2281.G8

Great Savannah, *see* F2331.B6

2331.G8 Guárico

2331.G83 Guayana Region

Isla de Patos, *see* F2331.P3

2331.J82 Juan José Mora

Lake Maracaibo Region, *see* F2331.M27

Lake Valencia, *see* F2331.V3

2331.L3 Lara

2331.M27 Maracaibo Lake Region

2331.M3 Margarita (Island)

2331.M5 Mérida

2331.M52 Mérida, Cordillera de (Sierra Nevada de Mérida)

2331.M6 Miranda

2331.M7 Monagas

2331.N8 Nueva Esparta

For Margarita Island, see F2331.M3

2331.O7 Orinoco River and Valley

Cf. F2281.L52, Llanos Orientales

Paraguaná Peninsula, *see* F2331.F2

2331.P3 Isla de Patos

South America

Venezuela

2331.A-.Z Regions, states, etc., A-Z — Continued

2331.P4 Perijá (District)

Cf. F2281.P4, Sierra de Perijá, Colombia

2331.P6 Portuguesa

Roraima, Mount, *see* F2609

2331.S8 Sucre

Sur de Occidente, *see* F2331.B3

2331.T2 Táchira

2331.T7 Trujillo

2331.V3 Lake Valencia

2331.V35 Vargas

2331.Y3 Yaracuy

Zamora, *see* F2331.B3

2331.Z9 Zulia

For Perijá (District), see F2331.P4

2341.A-.Z Cities, towns, etc., A-Z

GALE NOTE *The cutter number(s) listed below have been given only as examples by the Library of Congress*

2341.A2 Collective

2341.B3 Barquisimeto

2341.C2 Caracas

Subarrange by Table F2 at the end of the text

2341.C8 Cumaná

2341.M2 Maracaibó

2341.M25 Maracay

2341.M5 Mérida

2341.S13 San Cristóbal

2341.V25 Valencia

Elements in the population

For interpretation, see F1392.A+

2349.A1 General works

2349.A2-.Z Individual, A-Z

2349.A5 Americans (U.S.)

2349.B3 Basques

2349.B55 Blacks

Cf. HT1151+, Slavery

2349.C35 Canary Islanders

2349.C64 Colombians

2349.C83 Cubans

2349.D8 Dutch

2349.F73 French

2349.G24 Gallegans

2349.G3 Germans

Indians, *see* F2318+

2349.I8 Italians

2349.J48 Jews

2349.L43 Lebanese

2349.P6 Portuguese

2349.S36 Scotch. Scots

Scots, *see* F2349.S36

2349.S7 Spaniards

Guiana

Region between the Amazon and Orinoco although at present usually restricted to British, Dutch, and French Guiana

2351 General works

Cf. E111+, Early voyages

2354 Antiquities. Indians

South America

Guiana — Continued

Guyana. British Guiana

2361 Periodicals. Societies. Collections

Collected works

2362 Several authors

2363 Individual authors

Including collected papers, addresses, essays, etc.

2363.5 Museums. Exhibitions, exhibits

2364 Gazetteers. Dictionaries. Geographic names

2364.5 Directories

Biography

2365 Collective

Individual, *see* F2380.6, F2383-2385

2368 General works

2368.5 Juvenile works

Pamphlets, essays

2369 General

2369.3 Anecdotes, legends, pageants

Cf. GR130, Folklore

Cf. Class P, Literature

2369.5 Guidebooks. Handbooks

2369.7 Historic monuments (General)

2369.8 Social life and customs. Civilization. Intellectual life

Including national characteristics

For race conflicts and problems, see F2391

2369.9 Geography

Description and travel. Views

2370 Early to 1802

2371 1803-1950

2372 1951-1980

2373 1981-

Antiquities. Indians

2379 General works

2380 Modern Indians (General)

Including local (not A-Z)

2380.1.A-.1.Z Tribes (Ancient and modern), A-Z

GALE NOTE *The cutter number(s) listed below have been given only as examples by the Library of Congress*

2380.1.A2 Accawai

Arawak, *see* F2230.2.A7

2380.1.A7 Arecuna

Carib, *see* F2001

2380.1.M3 Macusi

2380.1.P3 Paramona

2380.1.T3 Taruma

Trio, *see* F2420.1.T7

2380.1.W25 Waiwai

2380.1.W3 Wapisiana

2380.2.A-.2.Z Topics (Ancient and modern), A-Z

2380.2.A7 Art

2380.2.F6 Folklore. Legends

2380.2.G3 Games

2380.2.G68 Government relations

2380.2.M44 Medicine

2380.2.M57 Missions

2380.2.S63 Social life and customs

2380.2.S7 String figures

2380.2.W7 Writing

South America

Guiana

Guyana. British Guiana — Continued

History

2380.3 Chronological tables. Outlines, syllabi, etc. Questions and answers, etc.

Historiography

2380.4 General works

Biography of historians

2380.5 Collective

2380.6.A-.6.Z Individual, A-Z

GALE NOTE *See note at the head of Table F5 at the end of the text for further instructions on how to subdivide this number*

2380.7 Study and teaching

2381 General works

Including political history

2382 General special

Diplomatic history. Foreign and general relations

2382.3 General works

2382.4.A-.4.Z Relations with individual countries, A-Z

By period

Pre-Columbian period, *see* F2379+

2383 1580-1803

Including Dutch colonies of Essequibo, Demerara, and Berbice; English conquests; French conquest, 1782

Cf. E129.R2, Raleigh's explorations, 1595-1617

Cf. F2423, English in Dutch Guiana

Cf. F2462, English in French Guiana

2384 1803-1966

Including Great Britain given permanent title by Convention of London, 1814; union of three colonies to form British Guiana, 1831

Including biography: John Smith, 1790-1824; etc.

For boundary disputes with Venezuela, see F2331.B7

For boundary disputes with Brazil, see F2554.B8

Cf. D731+, World War II, 1939-1945

2385 1966-

2387.A-.Z Regions, counties, etc., A-Z

2387.B4 Berbice

2387.B7 Boundaries

2387.B7A1-.B7A5 General

Brazil, *see* F2554.B8

2387.B7A6-.B7Z Surinam. Netherlands or Dutch Guiana

Venezuela, *see* F2331.B72

2387.D4 Demerara

2387.E8 Essequibo

Including Kaieteur Falls

Roraima, Mount, *see* F2609

2389.A-.Z Cities, towns, etc., A-Z

GALE NOTE *The cutter number(s) listed below have been given only as examples by the Library of Congress*

2389.B3 Bartica

2389.G3 Georgetown

2389.N4 New Amsterdam

Formerly Berbice

Elements in the population

For interpretation, see F1392.A+

2391.A1 General works

Including foreign elements (General), minorities, race conflicts and problems

2391.A2-.Z Individual elements

GALE NOTE *The cutter number(s) listed below have been given only as examples by the Library of Congress*

South America
Guiana
Guyana. British Guiana
Elements in the population
2391.A2-.Z Individual elements — Continued
2391.C5 Chinese
2391.E2 East Indians
Indians, *see* F2379+
2391.M37 Maroons
2391.N4 Negroes
Cf. HT1139+, Slavery
Suriname. Netherlands or Dutch Guiana
2401 Periodicals. Societies. Collections
Collected works
2402 Several authors
2403 Individual authors
Including collected papers, addresses, essays
2403.5 Museums. Exhibitions, exhibits
2404 Gazetteers. Dictionaries. Geographic names
2404.5 Directories
Biography
2405 Collective
Individual, *see* F2423-2429
2408 General works
2408.5 Juvenile works
Pamphlets, addresses, essays
2409 General
2409.4 Anecdotes, legends, pageants
Cf. GR130+, Folklore
Cf. Class P, Literature
2409.5 Guidebooks. Handbooks
2409.6 Historic monuments (General)
2409.8 Social life and customs. Civilization. Intellectual life
Including national characteristics
For race conflicts and problems, see F2431
Description and travel. Views
2410 Early to 1813
2411 1814-1950
2412 1951-1980
2413 1981-
Antiquities. Indians
2419 General works
2420 Modern Indians (General)
Including local (not A-Z)
2420.1.A-.1.Z Tribes (Ancient and modern), A-Z
2420.1.A35 Akurio
Arawak, *see* F2230.2.A7
Cariban, *see* F2001
Galibi, *see* F2460.1.C37
2420.1.O8 Oyaricoulet
2420.1.T7 Trio
Warrau, *see* F2319.2.W3
Wayana, *see* F2230.2.O8
2420.2.A-.2.Z Topics (Ancient and modern), A-Z
2420.2.A7 Art
2420.2.P64 Politics and government
History
2420.3 Chronological tables. Outlines, syllabi, etc. Questions and answers, etc.
Historiography
2420.4 General works

South America
Guiana
Suriname. Netherlands or Dutch Guiana
History
Historiography — Continued
Biography of historians
2420.5 Collective
2420.6.A-.6.Z Individual, A-Z
GALE NOTE *See note at the head of Table F5 at the end of the text for further instructions on how to subdivide this number*
2420.7 Study and teaching
2421 General works
Including political history
2422 General special
By period
2423 1604-1814
Including early English settlements; Willoughby and Hyde's Grant, 1663; Dutch West India Company, 1621-1791; etc.
Includes general works on the four Dutch colonies (Essequibo, Demerara, Berbice, and Surinam), 1667-1803
Including biography: Cornelis van Aerssen, heer van Sommelsdijk; Abraham Crijnssen; Jan Jacob Mauricius; etc.
Cf. E129.R2, Raleigh's explorations, 1595-1617
Cf. F2381-2383, Essequibo, Dememrara, and Berbice (Former Dutch colonies)
2424 1814-1950
Including Dutch given permanent title by Treaty of Paris, 1814; member of Dutch American Union, 1828-1845
Cf. D731+, World War II, 1939-1945
2425 1950-1975
As of January 10, 1950, became autonomous within the Dutch Empire
1975-
2425.2 General works
Biography
2425.22 Collective
2425.23.A-.23.Z Individual, A-Z
GALE NOTE *See note at the head of Table F5 at the end of the text for further instructions on how to subdivide this number*
2427.A-.Z Regions, districts, etc., A-Z
2427.B7 Boundaries
2427.B7A1-.B7A5 General
Brazil, *see* F2554.D8
British Guiana, *see* F2387.B7
2427.B7A6-.B7Z French Guiana
2427.M3 Maroni River and Valley, Surinam
Cf. F2467.M3, General, and French Guiana
2429.A-.Z Cities, towns, etc., A-Z
GALE NOTE *The cutter number(s) listed below have been given only as examples by the Library of Congress*
2429.N5 Nieuw Nickerie
2429.P3 Paramaribo
Elements in the population
For interpretation, see F1392.A+
2431.A1 General works
Including foreign elements (General), minorities, race conflicts and problems
2431.A2-.Z Individual elements
2431.B64 Boni
2431.E2 East Indians
Indians, *see* F2419+
2431.J3 Javanese
2431.J4 Jews

South America
Guiana
Suriname. Netherlands or Dutch Guiana
Elements in the population
2431.A2-.Z Individual elements — Continued
2431.N3 Negroes. Blacks
Cf. HT1141+, Slavery
2431.S27 Saramacca
French Guiana
2441 Periodicals. Societies. Collections
Collected works
2442 Several authors
2443 Individual authors
Including collected papers, addresses, essays, etc.
2443.5 Museums. Exhibitions, exhibits
2444 Gazetteers. Dictionaries. Geographic names
2444.5 Directories
Biography
2445 Collective
Individual, *see* F2460.6, F2462-2464
2448 General works
2448.5 Juvenile works
Pamphlets, addresses, essays
2449 General
2449.3 Anecdotes, legends, pageants
Cf. GR130+, Folklore
Cf. Class P, Literature
2449.5 Guidebooks. Handbooks
2449.7 Historic monuments (General)
2449.8 Social life and customs. Civilization. Intellectual life
Including national characteristics
For race conflicts and problems, see F2471
Description and travel. Views
2450 Early to 1813
2451 1814-1950
2452 1951-
Antiquities. Indians
2459 General works
2460 Modern Indians (General)
Including local (not A-Z)
2460.1.A-.1.Z Tribes (Ancient and modern), A-Z
Arawak, *see* F2230.2.A7
2460.1.C37 Carib (Galibi)
Cariban, *see* F2001
2460.1.E5 Emerillon
(2460.1.G3) Galibi, *see* F2460.1.C37
2460.1.O9 Oyampi. Wayampi
2460.1.P3 Palicur
Wayampi, *see* F2460.1.O9
Wayana, *see* F2230.2.O8
2460.2.A-.2.Z Topics (Ancient and modern), A-Z
2460.2.A37 Agriculture
2460.2.E38 Education
2460.2.F64 Folklore. Legends
2460.2.G68 Government relations
Legends, *see* F2460.2.F64
2460.2.P6 Pottery
History
2460.3 Chronological tables. Outlines, syllabi, etc. Questions and answers, etc.

South America
Guiana
French Guiana
History — Continued
Historiography
2460.4 General works
Biography of historians
2460.5 Collective
2460.6.A-.6.Z Individual, A-Z
GALE NOTE *See note at the head of Table F5 at the end of the text for further instructions on how to subdivide this number*
2460.7 Study and teaching
2461 General works
Including political history
By period
Pre-Columbian period, *see* F2459+
2462 1626-1814
Including early English settlements on the Oyapok; first French settlement, 1643; expedition of Kourou, 1763-1765; Portuguese (from Brazil) occupation, 1809-1817
Cf. E129.R2, Raleigh's explorations, 1595-1617
Cf. F2383, French in British Guiana
2463 1814-1946
Including French given permanent title by Treaty of Paris, 1814
For boundary disputes with Brazil, see F2554.F8
For use as a penal colony, see HV8955+
Cf. D731+, World War II, 1939-1945
2464 1947-
As of January 1, 1947, became a department of Metropolitan France
2467.A-.Z Regions, districts, etc., A-Z
2467.B7 Boundaries
Brazil, *see* F2554.F8
Surinam (Dutch Guiana), *see* F2427.B7
2467.I4 Îles du Salut (Devil's Island)
As penal colony, see HV8947.A+
2467.I5 Inine (Territory)
2467.M25 Mana River and Valley
2467.M3 Maroni River and Valley (General, and French Guiana)
Cf. F2427.M3, Surinam
2467.T9 Tumuc-Humac Mountains
2469.A-.Z Cities, towns, etc., A-Z
GALE NOTE *The cutter number(s) listed below have been given only as examples by the Library of Congress*
2469.C3 Cayenne
2469.S3 Saint-Georges (Saint-Georges-de-l'Oyapock)
2469.S5 Saint-Laurent (Saint-Laurent-du-Maroni)
Elements in the population
Including foreign elements (General), minorities, race conflicts and problems
For interpretation, see F1392.A+
2471.A1 General works
2471.A2-.Z Individual elements, A-Z
2471.B55 Blacks
2471.H56 Hmong (Asian people)
Indians, *see* F2459+
Negroes, *see* F2471.B55
Brazil
2501 Periodicals. Societies. Serials
2501.5 Congresses
Collected works (Nonserial)
2502 Several authors

South America
Brazil
Collected works (Nonserial) — Continued
2503 Individual authors
Including collected papers, addresses, essays, etc.
2503.5 Museums. Exhibitions, exhibits
2504 Gazetteers. Dictionaries. Geographic names
2504.5 Directories
Biography
2505 Collective
Individual, *see* F2520.6, F2524-2538.5
2508 General works
2508.5 Juvenile works
Pamphlets, addresses, essays, etc.
2509 General
2509.3 Anecdotes, legends, pageants, etc.
Cf. GR130+, Folklore
Cf. Class P, Literature
2509.5 Guidebooks. Handbooks
2509.7 Historic monuments (General)
2510 Social life and customs. Civilization. Intellectual life
Including national characteristics
For race conflicts and problems, see F2659
2510.5 Brazilians in foreign countries (General)
For Brazilians in a particular country, see the country
2510.9 Geography
Description and travel. Views
2511 Early to 1821
2513 1822-1889
2515 1890-1950
2516 1951-1980
2517 1981-
Antiquities. Indians
2518.5 Museums. Exhibitions
2519 General works
2519.1.A-.1.Z Local (Ancient and modern), A-Z
GALE NOTE *The cutter number(s) listed below have been given only as examples by the Library of Congress*
2519.1.A6 Amazon Valley
2519.1.B3 Bahia (State)
2519.1.G68 Goiás (State). Goyaz (State)
2519.1.L3 Lagoa Santa
2519.1.M37 Maranhão (State)
2519.1.M4 Matto Grosso (State)
2519.1.P2 Pará (State)
2519.1.P3 Paraná (State)
2519.1.P8 Purus River
2519.1.R5 Rio de Janeiro (State)
2519.1.R6 Rio Grande do Sul (State)
2519.1.S2 São Paulo (State)
2519.1.U3 Uaupés Valley
2519.1.X56 Xingu Valley
2519.3.A-.3.Z Topics (Ancient and modern), A-Z
Adornment, *see* F2519.3.C68
2519.3.A42 Alcohol use
2519.3.A5 Anthropometry
2519.3.A7 Art
2519.3.A84 Astronomy
2519.3.B36 Basket making
2519.3.B5 Boats

South America

Brazil

Antiquities. Indians

2519.3.A-.3.Z	Topics (Ancient and modern), A-Z — Continued
2519.3.B6	Bows and arrows
2519.3.C3	Cannibalism
2519.3.C65	Communication
2519.3.C68	Costume and adornment
2519.3.C85	Cultural assimilation
2519.3.D2	Dances
2519.3.D84	Dwellings
2519.3.E2	Education
2519.3.E83	Ethnic identity
2519.3.E85	Ethnobotany
2519.3.F4	Feather work
2519.3.F6	Folklore. Legends
2519.3.F63	Food
2519.3.G3	Games
	Government, *see* F2519.3.P58
2519.3.G6	Government relations
2519.3.H85	Hunting
2519.3.I4	Implements
2519.3.I5	Industries
2519.3.K53	Kings and rulers
2519.3.K55	Kinship
2519.3.L36	Land tenure
2519.3.M37	Mathematics
2519.3.M43	Medicine
2519.3.M5	Missions
2519.3.N35	Names
2519.3.P58	Politics and government
2519.3.P6	Pottery
2519.3.R3	Religion. Mythology
2519.3.S58	Social conditions
2519.3.S6	Social life and customs
2519.3.S94	Suicidal behavior
2519.3.W37	Wars
2519.3.W66	Women
2519.3.W7	Writing
2520	Modern Indians (General)
2520.1.A-.1.Z	Tribes (Ancient and modern), A-Z
2520.1.A4	Akwẽ-Shavante. Xavante
	Amahuaca, *see* F3430.1.A5
2520.1.A6	Apalai
2520.1.A63	Apalakiri
2520.1.A632	Apapocuva
2520.1.A64	Apiacá
2520.1.A65	Apinagé
2520.1.A7	Arara
2520.1.A75	Araua
	Arawak, *see* F2230.2.A7
2520.1.A77	Araweté
	Arecuna, *see* F2380.1.A7
2520.1.A84	Asurini
2520.1.A93	Ava-Canoeiro
2520.1.B3	Bakairi
2520.1.B35	Baniva
2520.1.B4	Baré
	Betoya, *see* F2270.2.T77
	Boro, *see* F2270.2.B6

South America
Brazil
Antiquities. Indians
2520.1.A-.1.Z Tribes (Ancient and modern), A-Z — Continued
2520.1.B75 Bororo
2520.1.B76 Botocudo
2520.1.C3 Cadioeo
Caingua, *see* F2230.2.C3
2520.1.C32 Canella
Canoeiro, *see* F2520.1.R53
2520.1.C35 Caraja
Carib, *see* F2001
2520.1.C37 Caripuna
2520.1.C38 Cashinawa
2520.1.C4 Catoquina
2520.1.C45 Cayapo
Chamacoco, *see* F3320.2.C5
Chapacura, *see* F3320.2.C38
Charrua, *see* F2719.2.C5
Chavante, *see* F2520.1.A4
(2520.1.C6) Chipaya, *see* F3320.2.C388
Chiquito, *see* F3320.2.C3
2520.1.C64 Cinta Larga
2520.1.C67 Craho. Kraho
2520.1.C7 Crichaná
2520.1.C84 Culina
2520.1.D47 Desana
2520.1.F8 Fulnio
2520.1.G37 Gaviões
2520.1.G4 Ge
2520.1.G6 Goyataca
2520.1.G68 Guaharibo
2520.1.G69 Guajá
Guajajara, *see* F2520.1.T4
2520.1.G718 Guana
2520.1.G72 Guanano
Guarani, *see* F2230.2.G72
2520.1.G75 Guató
Guayana, *see* F2230.2.G75
Guayaqui, *see* F2679.2.G9
Guaycuru, *see* F2230.2.G78
2520.1.H48 Heta
2520.1.I6 Ipurucotó
2520.1.I7 Iranxe
2520.1.J8 Juruna. Yuruna
2520.1.K3 Kaingang. Kaingangue
2520.1.K35 Kamaiurá
2520.1.K4 Kariri
Kashinaua, *see* F2520.1.C38
2520.1.K45 Kayabi
Kraho, *see* F2520.1.C67
2520.1.K7 Kreen-Akarore
2520.1.M2 Macu
Macusi, *see* F2380.1.M3
2520.1.M24 Mamaindê
2520.1.M26 Maruba
2520.1.M27 Masacali
2520.1.M3 Maue
Mayoruna, *see* F3430.1.M45
Mbaya, *see* F2679.2.M3

South America

Brazil

Antiquities. Indians

2520.1.A-.1.Z Tribes (Ancient and modern), A-Z — Continued

2520.1.M44 Mehinacu

2520.1.M45 Mekranoti

Mojo, *see* F3320.2.M55

2520.1.M8 Mundurucu

2520.1.M9 Mura

Including Pirahá Indians

2520.1.N3 Nambicuara

Omagua, *see* F3430.1.O5

2520.1.O63 Opaye

Pacaguara, *see* F3320.2.P3

Painguá, *see* F2230.2.C3

2520.1.P32 Pakaa Nova

Palicur, *see* F2460.1.P3

2520.1.P35 Pancararu

Pano, *see* F3430.1.P3

Panoan Indians, *see* F3430.1.P33

2520.1.P38 Parakaña

2520.1.P4 Parintintin

2520.1.P43 Patashó

2520.1.P45 Pauishana

Peban, *see* F3430.1.P4

Pirahá, *see* F2520.1.M9

Piro, *see* F3430.1.P5

2520.1.P68 Potiguara

2520.1.P8 Puri

2520.1.R53 Rikbaktsa. Canoeiro (Mato Grosso)

2520.1.S24 Saluma

2520.1.S3 Sanavirona

Sapuya, *see* F2520.1.K4

2520.1.S47 Sherente

2520.1.S5 Shokleng

2520.1.S86 Surui

2520.1.S89 Suya

2520.1.T2 Tapajo

2520.1.T25 Tapirapé

2520.1.T3 Tapuya

2520.1.T32 Tariana

2520.1.T4 Tenetehara

2520.1.T43 Teremembe

2520.1.T45 Terena. Tereno

2520.1.T5 Timbira

Trio, *see* F2420.1.T7

2520.1.T7 Trumai

2520.1.T9 Tucano

2520.1.T925 Tucuna

Tukanoan, *see* F2270.2.T77

2520.1.T933 Tupari

Tupi, *see* F2230.2.T84

2520.1.T94 Tupinamba

2520.1.T97 Tuxá

2520.1.U3 Uaboi

2520.1.U5 Umotina

2520.1.U7 Urubu Kaapor

2520.1.U74 Uruewawau

2520.1.W3 Waica

2520.1.W34 Waimiri

South America

Brazil

Antiquities. Indians

2520.1.A-.1.Z Tribes (Ancient and modern), A-Z — Continued

Waiwai, *see* F2380.1.W25

Wapisiana, *see* F2380.1.W3

2520.1.W38 Waura

Wayampi, *see* F2460.1.O9

Wayana, *see* F2230.2.O8

2520.1.X33 Xacriaba

Xavante, *see* F2520.1.A4

2520.1.X5 Xikrin

2520.1.Y3 Yanomamo

Yuruna, *see* F2520.1.J8

2520.1.Z65 Zoró

2520.1.Z87 Zuruahá

History

2520.3 Chronological tables. Outlines, syllabi, etc. Questions and answers, etc.

Historiography

2520.4 General works

Biography of historians

2520.5 Collective

2520.6.A-.6.Z Individual, A-Z

GALE NOTE *See note at the head of Table F5 at the end of the text for further instructions on how to subdivide this number; the cutter number(s) listed below have been given only as examples by the Library of Congress*

2520.6.A2 Abreu, João Capistrano de

2520.6.P4 Pereira da Costa, Francisco Augusto

2520.7 Study and teaching

2521 General works

Including political history

General special

2522 Military and naval history

Diplomatic history. Foreign and general relations

2523 General works

2523.5.A-.5.Z Relations with individual countries, A-Z

United States, *see* E183.8.A+

2523.9 Other (not A-Z)

By period

Pre-Columbian period, *see* F2518.5+

1500-1821

2524 General works

2526 1500-1548

Including discovery, exploration, and colonization by Portuguese

Cf. E123, Demarkation line of Alexander VI

1549-1762

2528 General works

Including Bandeiras (General; if limited to a state, class with state); expulsion of Jesuits

Including biography: José de Anchieta; Salvador Correia de Sá e Benavides; Mem de Sá; António Vieira, etc.

Cf. BX4705.V55, Vieira as religious figure

Cf. F2684, Jesuit missions of Paraguay, War of the Seven Reductions (Guarani War), 1754-1756

Cf. F2723, Portuguese settlement at Colonia, Uruguay

2529 French colony at Rio de Janeiro, 1555-1567

Including biography: Nicolas Durand de Villegagnon

2530 Spanish control, 1580-1640

South America
Brazil
History
By period
1500-1821
1549-1762 — Continued
2532 Dutch conquest, 1624-1654
Including capture of Bahia, 1625; battles at Guararapes, 1648 and 1649; capture of Olinda, 1630
Including biography: Henrique Dias, Joao Fernandes Vieira, etc.
2534 1763-1821
Including Portuguese court in Brazil, 1808-1821; revolt in Pernambuco, 1817
Including biography: Joaquim José da Silva Xavier (Tiradentes), etc.
Cf. DP650, João VI, king of Portugal
Cf. F2461, French Guiana
Cf. F2723, Expulsion of Brazilians from Colonia
1822-
2535 General works
2536 Empire, 1822-1889
Including Pedro I, 1822-1831; Regency, 1831-1841; Pedro II, 1841-1889
Including Brazil declared independent of Portugal on September 7, 1822; Empire established on October 12, 1822; Revolution of 1842; separatist movement in Rio Grande do Sul, 1845
Including biography: José Bonifacio de Andrada e Silva (Cf. PQ9697 , as author); Benjamin Constant Botelho Magalhães; Luiz Alves de Lima e Silva, duque de Caxias; Marcilio Dias; Diogo Antonio Feijo; Giuseppe Garibaldi (Cf. DG558.2.G2, as Italian patriot); Irineo Evangelista de Souza, visconde de Maua; Joaquim Nabuco; Joaquim Marques Lisbôa, marques de Tamandare
Cf. F2687, Paraguayan War, 1865-1870
Cf. F2725, War with Argentina over Uruguay, 1825-1828
Cf. F2846.3, War with Argentina, 1849-1852
2537 Republic, 1889-
Including Brazil declared a republic, November 15, 1889
Including special period, 1889-1930; naval revolt of 1893-1894; Conselheiro Insurrection, 1897; military revolution of 1924-1925; etc.
Including biography: Ruy Barbosa; Manuel Ferraz de Campos Salles; Manuel Deodoro da Fonseca; Antonio Vicente Mendes Maciel; Manuel de Oliveira Lima; Floriano Peixoto; José Gomes Pinheiro Machado; José Maria da Silva Paranhos, barão do Rio Branco; etc.
Cf. D501+, World War I, 1914-1918
2538 1930-1954. Period of Vargas
Including Revolution of 1930; Communist Revolution of 1935; Integralist Revolt of 1938
Including biography: Eurico Gaspar Dutra, Getulio Vargas, etc.
Cf. D731+, World War II, 1939-1945
1954-1964
Including administrations of Kubitschek, Quadros, and Goulart
2538.2 General works
Biography
2538.22.A2 Collective
2538.22.A3-.22.Z Individual
GALE NOTE *See note at the head of Table F5 at the end of the text for further instructions on how to subdivide this number; the cutter number(s) listed below have been given only as examples by the Library of Congress*
2538.22.G6 Goulart, João Belchior Marques
2538.22.K8 Kubitschek, Juscelino
1964-1985
2538.25 General works
Biography and memoirs
2538.26 Collective

South America

Brazil

History

By period

1822-

1964-1985

Biography and memoirs — Continued

2538.27.A-.27.Z Individual, A-Z

GALE NOTE *See note at the head of Table F5 at the end of the text for further instructions on how to subdivide this number; the cutter number(s) listed below have been given only as examples by the Library of Congress*

2538.27.F53 Figueiredo, João Baptista de Oliveira, 1918-

2538.27.G44 Geisel, Ernesto

2538.27.P38 Paula, Francisco Julião Arruda de, 1915-

1985-

2538.3 General works

Biography

2538.4 Collective

2538.5.A-.5.Z Individual, A-Z

GALE NOTE *See note at the head of Table F5 at the end of the text for further instructions on how to subdivide this number*

Regions, states, etc.

2539 Islands of Brazil (General)

2540 Acre (Territory)

Cf. F2546, Amazonas boundary

2541 Alagoas

2543 Amapá (Territory)

2546 Amazonas

Including Amazon River and Valley; Içá River; Japurá (Yapurá) River; Javarí (Yavarí) River; Jurua River; Jutaí (Jutahy) River; Purus River; Rio Negro

Cf. F2281.A4, Amazon River and Valley, Colombia

Cf. F3451.A4, Amazonas (Peru)

Cf. F3451.L8, Amazon River and Valley, Peru

2548 Atlantic Coast

2551 Bahia (Baía)

Including Jacuípe River and Valley, and Diamantina Plateau

Cf. F2601, Pernambuco boundary

Cf. F2636, Sergipe boundary

2554 Boundaries

2554.A1-.A8 General

2554.A82 Argentina

For Misiones question, see F2916

2554.B6 Bolivia

Cf. F2540, Acre (Territory)

2554.B8 British Guiana

2554.C7 Colombia

2554.D8 Dutch Guiana. Surinam

2554.F8 French Guiana

2554.P3 Paraguay

2554.P4 Peru

2554.U8 Uruguay

2554.V4 Venezuela

2556 Ceará

2557 Central West Brazil

2558 Counani

Contested territory awarded to Brazil

Distrito Federal, *see* F2646

2561 Espírito Santo

Including colonies of Germans, Poles, Swedes, Tyrolese

South America

Brazil

Regions, states, etc. — Continued

2564 Fernando de Noronha Island (Territory)

2566 Goyaz (Goías, Goiaz)

Including Araguaya River, Tocantins River

2567 Guanabara

Guaporé (Territory), *see* F2624

Guartelá (Region), *see* F2596

2567.3 Ibiapaba

2567.9 Mar Mountains

2568 Marajó (Island)

Including French Colony, 1612-1618

2571 Maranhão

Including Gurupy River, Parnahyba (Parnaíba) River, etc.

2576 Mato Grosso

Including Araguaya River, Garças River, Xingú River

Cf. F2566, Goyaz boundary

Cf. F2684, Jesuit missions of Paraguay

2578 Mato Grosso do Sul

2581 Minas Geraes (Minas Gerais)

Including Jequitinhonha River, Mucury Colony, and Paraibuna River

2582 North Brazil

2583 Northeast Brazil

2585 Pantanal

2586 Pará

Including Rivers: Araguaya, Capim, Gurupy (Gurupi), Tapajos, Tocantins, Parú, Xingú

For Marajó Island, see F2568

Cf. F2546, Amazonas boundary

2591 Parahyba (Paraíba)

2596 Paraná

Including Assunguy Colony, Guartelá (Region), Guayra Falls, Iguazú River and Falls, Paraná River, etc.

Cf. F2909, Argentina

Cf. F2684, Jesuit missions of Paraguay

2601 Pernambuco

Including Itamaracá Island

2606 Piauhy (Piauí)

Including Parnahyba (Parnaíba) River

Cf. F2571, Maranhão boundary

2609 Rio Branco (Territory). Roraima

Including Mount Roraima

2611 Rio de Janeiro (State)

Including Parahyba (Paraíba) do Sul River and Valley, Grande Island Bay

For Rio de Janeiro (Federal District and City), see F2646

2616 Rio Grande do Norte

Cf. F2556, Ceará boundary

2621 Rio Grande do Sul

Including German colonies; Revolution of the Farrapos, 1835-1845; Taquari-Antes River and Valley; gauchos in Brazil

Cf. F2217, Gauchos (General)

Cf. F2684, Jesuit missions; War of the Seven Reductions, 1754-1756

2624 Rondônia (Territory). Rondônia (State)

Including Madeira River

Roraima, *see* F2609

2626 Santa Catharina (Santa Catarina)

Including Santa Catarina Island

Part of Misiones awarded to Brazil

Including German colonies, e.g. Blumenau; Itajahy (Itajaí) River and Valley

South America

Brazil

Regions, states, etc.

2626 Santa Catharina (Santa Catarina) — Continued

Cf. F2596, Paraná boundary

Cf. F2916, Misiones award (General)

Cf. F2916, Misiones Territory of Argentina

2629 São Francisco River and Valley

2631 São Paulo

Including Bandeiras; Revolution of 1932; etc.; Rivers: Aguapehy (Aguapeí), Juquiá, Paraná, Peixe, Piracicaba, Ribeira de Iguape, Tietê

Cf. F2581, Minas Geraes boundary

Cf. F2684, Jesuit missions of Paraguay; War of the Seven Reductions, 1754-1756

2636 Sergipe

2638 Sinos River and Valley

2639 South Brazil

2640 Tocantins State

2641 Vargem Alegre (District)

Cities, towns, etc., A-Z

2646 Rio de Janeiro (City; and Federal District until April 21, 1960)

Subarrange by Table F1 at the end of the text

2647 Brasilia (City; and Federal District, April 21, 1960-)

Subarrange by Table F1 at the end of the text

2651.A-.Z Other, A-Z

GALE NOTE *The cutter number(s) listed below have been given only as examples by the Library of Congress*

Bahia, *see* F2651.S13

2651.B4 Belém

2651.B42 Belo Horizonte

2651.C83 Curitiba

2651.F6 Fortaleza

2651.N5 Niterói (Nictheroy)

2651.O9 Ouro Preto

2651.P15 Palmares

Pará, *see* F2651.B4

Pernambuco, *see* F2651.R4

2651.P8 Porto Alegre

2651.R4 Recife

Subarrange by Table F2 at the end of the text

2651.S13 Salvador

Subarrange by Table F2 at the end of the text

2651.S15 Santos

2651.S2 São Paulo

Subarrange by Table F2 at the end of the text

Elements in the population

For interpretation, see F1392.A+

2659.A1 General works

Including foreign elements (General), minorities, race conflicts and problems

2659.A2-.Z Individual elements, A-Z

2659.A5 Americans

2659.A7 Arabs

2659.A75 Armenians

2659.A84 Asians

2659.A9 Austrians

2659.B4 Belgians

Blacks, *see* F2659.N4

2659.B7 British

2659.C32 Caboclos

2659.D7 Dutch

2659.E8 Estonians

South America
Brazil
Elements in the population
2659.A2-.Z Individual elements, A-Z — Continued
2659.E95 Europeans
2659.F8 French
2659.G3 Germans
2659.H85 Hungarians
Indians, *see* F2518.5+
2659.I8 Italians
2659.J3 Japanese
2659.J5 Jews
Latin Americans, *see* F2659.S65
2659.L38 Latvians
2659.L42 Lebanese
2659.L5 Lithuanians
2659.M69 Mozambicans
2659.N4 Negroes. Blacks
Cf. HT1126+, Slavery
2659.P7 Poles
2659.P8 Portuguese
2659.S45 Slovenes
2659.S63 Spaniards
2659.S65 Spanish Americans (Latin America)
2659.U4 Ukrainians
Paraguay
2661 Periodicals. Societies. Collections
2661.5 Congresses
Collected works
2662 Several authors
2663 Individual authors
Including collected papers, addresses, essays
2663.5 Museums. Exhibitions, exhibits
2664 Gazetteers. Dictionaries. Geographic names
2664.5 Directories
Biography
2665 Collective
Individual, *see* F2679.6, F2683-2689.23
2668 General works
2668.5 Juvenile works
Pamphlets, addresses, essays, etc.
2669 General
2669.3 Anecdotes, legends, pageants, etc.
Cf. GR130+, Folklore
Cf. Class P, Literature
2669.5 Guidebooks. Handbooks
2669.7 Historic monuments (General)
2670 Social life and customs. Civilization. Intellectual life
Including national characteristics
For race conflicts and problems, see F2699
2670.9 Geography
Description and travel. Views
2671 Early to 1810
2675 1810-1950
2676 1951-
Antiquities. Indians
2678 Museums. Exhibitions.
2679 General works
2679.1 Modern Indians (General)

South America

Paraguay

Antiquities. Indians — Continued

2679.15.A-.15.Z Local (Ancient and modern), A-Z

GALE NOTE *The cutter number(s) listed below have been given only as examples by the Library of Congress*

2679.15.C48 Chaco Region

2679.15.M35 Marcelina Kue Site

2679.2.A-.2.Z Tribes (Ancient and modern), A-Z

2679.2.A2 Abipon Indians

Arawak, *see* F2230.2.A7

Caingua, *see* F2230.2.C3

Chamacoco, *see* F2230.2.C5

Chiquito, *see* F3320.2.C39

2679.2.C5 Chiripá Indians

Guarani, *see* F2230.2.G72

2679.2.G9 Guayaki Indians

Guaycuru, *see* F2230.2.G78

2679.2.L4 Lengua

2679.2.M25 Maca

2679.2.M3 Mbaya

2679.2.M34 Mbya

Mocobi, *see* F2823.M6

2679.2.M6 Moro Indians

2679.2.P3 Payagua

Pilaga, *see* F2823.P5

Tereno, *see* F2520.1.T45

Toba, *see* F2823.T7

2679.2.T65 Tomaráxo

2679.3.A-.3.Z Topics (Ancient and modern), A-Z

2679.3.A77 Art

2679.3.C64 Colonization

2679.3.E38 Education

2679.3.F42 Featherwork

2679.3.F64 Folklore. Legends

2679.3.G67 Government relations

Health and hygiene, *see* RA475+

2679.3.I53 Industries

2679.3.L35 Land tenure

Legends, *see* F2679.3.F64

2679.3.M5 Missions

2679.3.P64 Politics and government

2679.3.P66 Population

2679.3.R44 Religion and mythology

2679.3.S65 Social conditions

History

2679.35 Chronological tables. Outlines, syllabi, etc. Questions and answers, etc.

Historiography

2679.4 General works

Biography of historians

2679.5 Collective

2679.6.A-.6.Z Individual, A-Z

GALE NOTE *See note at the head of Table F5 at the end of the text for further instructions on how to subdivide this number*

2679.7 Study and teaching

2681 General works

Including political history

General special

2681.5 Military history

South America
Paraguay
History
General special — Continued
Diplomatic history. Foreign and general relations
2682 General works
2682.5.A-.5.Z Relations with individual countries, A-Z
2682.9 Other (not A-Z)
Cf. F2217, Gauchos (General)
By period
Pre-Columbian period, *see* F2678+
1527-1811
Including before 1620, part of La Plata region; in 1620, Province of Paraguay established under jurisdiction of viceroy at Lima; in 1776, transferred to viceroy at Buenos Aires
Including War of Independence, 1810-1811
2683 General works
2684 Jesuit province. Missions or reductions, 1609-1769
Including Treaty of Madrid, 1750; War of the Seven Reductions (Guarani War), 1754-1756
Cf. F2621, F2723, F2891, F2916, Regions occupied by the missions
1811-1870. Era of three dictators
Including independence from Buenos Aires viceroyalty , 1813; United States Paraguay Expedition, 1858-1859
Including biography: José Gaspar Rodríguez Francia, Carlos Antonio López, Francisco Solano López, etc.
2686 General works
2687 Paraguayan War, 1865-1870
Also called "War of the Triple Alliance"
Including battles at Campo Grande, 1869; Curupaity, 1866; Riachuelo, 1865; Tuyuty, 1866; Yataytу-Corá, 1866
1870-1938
Including biography: Eusebio Ayala, Rafael Franco, Eduardo Schaerer
Cf. D501+, World War I, 1914-1918
2688 General works
2688.5 Chaco War, 1932-1935
Including Chaco Peace Conference at Buenos Aires, 1935-1939; Treaty of Peace, 1938
Cf. F2691.C4 , Chaco Boreal
2689 1938-1989
Including political revolts; Colorados, communists, Franquistas, Tiempistas
Including biography: José Félix Estigarribia, Higinio Morínigo Martínez, etc.
Cf. D731+, World War II, 1939-1945
1989-
2689.2 General works
Biography
2689.22 Collective
2689.23.A-.23.Z Individual, A-Z
GALE NOTE *See note at the head of Table F5 at the end of the text for further instructions on how to subdivide this number*
2691.A-.Z Regions, departments, etc., A-Z
GALE NOTE *The cutter number(s) listed below have been given only as examples by the Library of Congress*
2691.A4 Alto Paraná
Including Colonia Mayntzhusen
Boundaries
2691.B7A1-.B7A5 General
Argentina, *see* F2857.P2

	South America
	Paraguay
2691.A-.Z	Regions, departments, etc., A-Z
	Boundaries — Continued
2691.B7A6-.B7Z	Bolivia
	Chaco Boreal dispute, see F2691.C4
	Brazil, *see* F2554.P3
2691.C4	Chaco Boreal. Paraguayan Chaco. Western Paraguay
	Including territory between the Paraguay and Pilcomayo rivers
	Cf. F2688.5, Chaco War, 1932-1935
	Cf. F2876, El Gran Chaco (General, and Argentina)
	Cf. F3341.C4, Bolivian Chaco
2691.C6	Concepción
2691.P3	Paraguay River and Valley
2695.A-.Z	Cities, towns, etc., A-Z
	GALE NOTE *The cutter number(s) listed below have been given only as examples by the Library of Congress*
2695.A8	Asunción
2695.C7	Concepción
2695.C8	Coronel Oviedo
2695.C9	Curuguaty
2695.E5	Encarnación
	Including Tornado of 1926
2695.H7	Hohenau
2695.T6	Tobatí
2695.V5	Villarrica
	Elements in the population
	Including foreign elements (General), minorities, race conflicts and problems
	For interpretation, see F1392.A+
2699.A1	General works
2699.A2-.Z	Individual elements, A-Z
2699.A72	Arabs
2699.A87	Australians
2699.B67	Brazilians
2699.B7	British
2699.D34	Danes
2699.F7	French
2699.G3	Germans
	Indians, *see* F2678+
2699.I8	Italians
2699.J35	Japanese
2699.J4	Jews
2699.M44	Mennonites
2699.R8	Russians
	Uruguay
2701	Periodicals. Societies. Collections
	Collected works
2702	Several authors
2703	Individual authors
	Including collected papers, addresses, essays
2703.5	Museums. Exhibitions, exhibits, etc.
2704	Gazetteers. Dictionaries. Geographic names
2704.5	Directories
	Biography
2705	Collective
	Individual, *see* F2720.6, F2723-2729.52
2708	General works
2708.5	Juvenile works
	Pamphlets, addresses, essays
2709	General

	South America
	Uruguay
	Pamphlets, addresses, essays — Continued
2709.3	Anecdotes, legends, pageants
	Cf. GR130+, Folklore
	Cf. Class P, Literature
2709.5	Guidebooks. Handbooks
2709.7	Historic monuments (General)
2710	Social life and customs. Civilization. Intellectual life
	Including national characteristics
	For race conflicts and problems, see F2799
	Description and travel. Views
2711	Early to 1810
2713	1811-1950
2714	1951-1980
2715	1981-
	Antiquities. Indians
2719	General works
2719.1.A-.1.Z	Local (Ancient and modern), A-Z
2719.1.C65	Colonia (Dept.)
2719.1.S24	Salto Grand Dept
2719.1.T7	Treinta y Tres (Dept.)
2719.2.A-.2.Z	Tribes (Ancient and modern), A-Z
	Chané, *see* F3320.2.C37
2719.2.C5	Charrua
	Guarani, *see* F2230.2.G72
2719.2.G84	Güenoa
2719.3.A-.3.Z	Topics (Ancient and modern), A-Z
	GALE NOTE *The cutter number(s) listed below have been given only as examples by the Library of Congress*
2719.3.P6	Pottery
2719.3.T6	Tobacco pipes
	History
2720	Chronological tables. Outlines, syllabi, etc. Questions and answers, etc.
	Historiography
2720.3	General works
	Biography of historians
2720.5	Collective
2720.6.A-.6.Z	Individual, A-Z
	GALE NOTE *See note at the head of Table F5 at the end of the text for further instructions on how to subdivide this number*
2720.7	Study and teaching
2721	General works
	Including political history
	General special
2721.5	Military and naval history
	Diplomatic history. Foreign and general relations
2722	General works
2722.5.A-.5.Z	Relations with individual countries, A-Z
2722.9	Other (not A-Z)
	Including gauchos in Uruguay
	Cf. F2217 , Gauchos (General)
	By period
	Pre-Columbian period, *see* F2719+
2723	1516-1811
	Known as the "Banda Oriental." In 1776 placed under the viceroy in Buenos Aires
	Including contests over Colonia; Treaty of San Ildefonso, 1777
	Cf. F2684, Jesuit missions; War of the Seven Reductions, 1754-1756
	Cf. F2845, English invasion of the La Plata, 1806-1807

South America

Uruguay

History

By period — Continued

1811-

2724 General works

2725 1811-1830

In 1821, incorporated in Brazil as Cisplatine Province; declared itself independent, 1825; recognized as independent, 1828

Including wars of independence; Argentine-Brazilian War, 1825-1828 (battles at Sarandi, 1825; Ituzaingó, 1827)

Including biography: José Gervasio Artigas, etc.

2726 1830-1904

Formally constituted as a republic, 1830

Including civil wars between Blancos and Colorados; foreign intervention; Siege of Montevideo, 1843-1851

Including biography: Juan Lindolfo Cuestas, Juan Carlos Gómez, Julio Herrera y Obes; Juan Idiarte Borda, Lorenzo Latorre, Manuel Oribe, José Fructuoso Rivera, Máximo Santos, Aparicio Saravia, etc.

Cf. F2687, Paraguayan War, 1865-1870

Cf. F2846.3, War against Rosas, 1849-1852

2728 1904-1973. Era of Batlle, 1903-1929

Including Revolution of 1904; Battle of Tupambaé, 1904; Revolution of 1910

Including biography: Juan José Amézaga, José Batlle y Ordóñez, Baltasar Brum, Luis Alberto de Herrera, Andrés Martínez Trueba, José Serrato, Gabriel Terra, etc.

Cf. D501+, World War I, 1914-1918

Cf. D731+, World War II, 1939-1945

Cf. D772.G7, Admiral Graf Spee (Battleship)

1973-

2729 General works

Biography

2729.5 Collective

2729.52.A-.52.Z Individual, A-Z

GALE NOTE *See note at the head of Table F5 at the end of the text for further instructions on how to subdivide this number*

2731.A-.Z Regions, departments, etc., A-Z

2731.A7 Artigas

2731.A84 Atlantic Coast

2731.B7 Boundaries (General)

For Argentina, see F2857.U7

For Brazil, see F2554.U8

2731.C22 Canelones

2731.C4 Cerro Largo

2731.C7 Colonia

For Portuguese settlement at Colonia, see F2723

2731.D8 Durazno

2731.F5 Flores

2731.F55 Florida

2731.L3 Lavalleja

2731.M2 Maldonado

Including Punta Ballema

Montevideo, *see* F2781

2731.P3 Paysandú

Polonio, Cape, *see* F2731.R6

2731.R4 Río Negro

2731.R5 Rivera

2731.R6 Rocha

Including Cape Polonio

2731.S2 Salto

South America

Uruguay

2731.A-.Z Regions, departments, etc., A-Z — Continued
2731.S3 San José
2731.S6 Soriano
2731.T3 Tacuarembó
2731.T6 Treinta y Tres
2731.U7 Uruguay River

Cities, towns, etc.
2781 Montevideo
Subarrange by Table F1 at the end of the text
2791.A-.Z Other, A-Z
GALE NOTE *The cutter number(s) listed below have been given only as examples by the Library of Congress*
2791.M3 Maldonado
2791.M55 Mercedes
2791.P34 Paysandú
2791.S2 Salto

Elements in the population
Including foreign elements (General), minorities, race conflicts and problems
For interpretation, see F1392.A+
2799.A1 General works
2799.A2-.Z Individual elements, A-Z
2799.B2 Basques
Blacks, *see* F2799.N3
2799.B7 Brazilians
2799.F7 French
2799.G3 Germans
2799.G74 Greeks
Indians, *see* F2719+
2799.I8 Italians
2799.J36 Japanese
2799.J4 Jews
2799.L4 Lebanese
2799.N3 Negroes. Blacks
2799.S6 Spaniards
2799.S9 Swiss

Argentina. La Plata region

2801 Periodicals. Societies. Collections
2801.5 Congresses
Collected works
2802 Several authors
2803 Individual authors
Including collected papers, addresses, essays
2803.5 Museums. Exhibitions, exhibits, etc.
2804 Gazetteers. Dictionaries. Geographic names
2804.5 Directories
Biography
2805 Collective
Individual, *see* F2829.6, F2841-2849.22
2808 General works
2808.2 Juvenile works
Pamphlets, addresses, essays
2808.3 General
2808.4 Anecdotes, legends, pageants, etc.
Cf. GR130+, Folklore
Cf. Class P, Literature
2808.5 Guidebooks. Handbooks
2809 Historic monuments (General)

South America

Argentina. La Plata region — Continued

2810 Social life and customs. Civilization. Intellectual life

Including national characteristics

For race conflicts and problems, see F3021.A+

2810.9 Geography

Description and travel. Views

2811 Early to 1805

2815 1806-1950

2816 1951-1980

2817 1981-

Antiquities. Indians

2819 Study and teaching

2820 Museums. Exhibitions

2821 General works

2821.1.A-.1.Z Local (Ancient and modern), A-Z

GALE NOTE *The cutter number(s) listed below have been given only as examples by the Library of Congress*

2821.1.A3 Andalgala

2821.1.B8 Buenos Aires (Province)

2821.1.C3 Catamarca (Province)

2821.1.C5 Chubut (Territory)

2821.1.C7 Córdoba (Province)

2821.1.E5 Entre Rios (Province)

2821.1.J9 Jujuy (Province)

2821.1.N4 Neuquén (Province)

2821.1.P22 Paraná Valley

2821.1.P29 Patagonia

2821.1.R58 La Rioja (Province)

2821.1.S15 Salta (Province)

2821.1.S23 Santiago del Estero (Province)

2821.1.T89 Tucumán (Province)

2821.3.A-.3.Z Topics (Ancient and modern), A-Z

2821.3.A3 Agriculture

2821.3.A78 Architecture

2821.3.A8 Art

2821.3.B6 Bolas

2821.3.C4 Census

2821.3.C73 Craniology

2821.3.D4 Dentistry

Including dental mutilation

2821.3.D5 Diseases

2821.3.E84 Ethnic identity

2821.3.F57 First contact with Europeans

2821.3.F6 Folklore. Legends

2821.3.F7 Food

2821.3.G65 Government relations

2821.3.H8 Hunting

2821.3.I5 Implements

2821.3.I6 Industries

2821.3.L35 Land tenure

2821.3.M4 Medicine

2821.3.M5 Missions

2821.3.M6 Mortuary customs

2821.3.N3 Names

2821.3.P6 Petroglyphs. Rock paintings

2821.3.P66 Philosophy

2821.3.P8 Pottery

2821.3.R4 Religion and mythology

Rock paintings, *see* F2821.3.P6

South America

Argentina. La Plata region

Antiquities. Indians

2821.3.A-.3.Z Topics (Ancient and modern), A-Z — Continued

2821.3.S54 Silverwork

2821.3.T6 Tobacco pipes

2821.3.T65 Tombs

2821.3.U7 Urns

Wars, *see* F2822

2822 Modern tribes (General)

Including Indian wars

2823.A-.Z Tribes (Ancient and modern), A-Z

Abipone, *see* F2679.2.A2

Alacaluf, *see* F2986

Araucanian, *see* F3126

Ashluslay, *see* F2230.2.A78

Aymara, *see* F2230.2.A9

Caingua, *see* F2230.2.C3

2823.C2 Calchaqui

2823.C4 Catamarca

Chamacoco, *see* F2230.2.C5

Chané, *see* F3320.2.C37

Charrua, *see* F2719.2.C5

Choroti, *see* F3320.2.C5

2823.C5 Comechingone

2823.D5 Diaguita

Cf. F3070.1.D5, Chile

Fuegian, *see* F2986

Guarani, *see* F2230.2.G72

2823.G8 Guarpe

Kaingangue, *see* F2520.1.K3

Lengua, *see* F2679.2.L4

2823.L8 Lule

2823.M3 Mataco

2823.M6 Mocobi

2823.O34 Ocloya

Ona, *see* F2986

2823.P3 Pampean

Payagua, *see* F2679.2.P3

2823.P5 Pilaga

2823.P8 Puelche

2823.Q4 Querandi

2823.R2 Ranqueles

2823.T7 Toba

2823.T8 Tonocote

Tzoneca, *see* F2936

2823.V5 Vilela

Yahgan, *see* F2986

History

2827 Chronological tables. Outlines, syllabi, etc. Questions and answers, etc.

Historiography

2829 General works

Biography of historians

2829.5 Collective

2829.6.A-.6.Z Individual, A-Z

GALE NOTE *See note at the head of Table F5 at the end of the text for further instructions on how to subdivide this number*

2830 Study and teaching

2831 General works

Including political history

South America

Argentina. La Plata region

History — Continued

General special

2832 Military and naval history

Diplomatic history. Foreign and general relations

2833 General works

Cf. F2857, Boundaries

2833.5.A-.5.Z Relations with individual countries, A-Z

2834 Other (not A-Z)

By period

Pre-Columbian period, *see* F2821+

2841 1516-1810

Including period of discovery, exploration, and settlement. Colonial period. In 1617, Buenos Aires separated from Asunción, became the province of Rio de la Plata under the viceroy of Peru; in 1776, Viceroyalty of La Plata was formed including Argentina, Uruguay, Paraguay, and Bolivia

Including biography: Hernando Arias de Saavedra (Hernandarias); Francisco de Céspedes; Juan de Garay; Domingo Martínez de Irala; Juan de San Martín; Rafael de Sobremonte, marqués de Sobremonte; etc.

Cf. F2683, Paraguay before 1811

Cf. F2684, Jesuit province; War of the Seven Reductions (Guarani War), 1754-1756

Cf. F2723, Brazil's claims to Colonia

Cf. F3301+, Upper Peru and the Audiencia of Charcas

2843 1810-

On May 25, 1810, declared independence from Spain

2845 1806-1817

Including English invasions, 1806-1807; War of Independence, 1810-1817

Including biography: Manuel Belgrano; Guillermo Brown; Martín Miguel Güemes; Santiago Antonio María de Liniers y Bremond, conde de Buenos Aires; Bernardo Monteagudo; Mariano Morena; Juan Martín de Pueyrredón; Cornelio de Saavedra; etc.

1817-1861. Civil wars

Including unitarism versus federalism; secession and return of province of Buenos Aires; battles at Cepeda (1859), Pavón (1861)

Including biography: Manuel Dorrego, Esteban Echeverría, Juan Galo de Lavalle, José María Paz, Juan Facundo Quiroga, Bernardino Rivadavia, Domingo Faustino Sarmiento, Justo José de Urquiza, Dalmacio Vélez Sársfield, etc.

Cf. F2725, War with Brazil over Uruguay, 1825-1828

2846 General works

2846.3 1829-1852. Period of Rosas

Including English and French blockades of Argentine coast, 1838, and of Río de la Plata, 1845-1847; War with Brazil (War against Rosas), 1849-1852; battles at Angaco (1841), Obligado (1845)

Including biography: Juan Manuel José Domingo Ortiz de Rosas

2847 1861-1910

Including League of Córdoba; Civil War, 1880; oligarchy in control, 1890-1910

Including biography: Nicolás Avellaneda, Bartolomé Mitre, Carlos Pellegrini, Julio Argentino Roca, Roque Sáenz Peña, etc.

Cf. F2687, Paraguayan War, 1865-1870

Cf. F2822, Conquista del desierto, 1879-1880

Cf. F2916, Misiones award, 1894

2848 1910-1943

Including radicals in control, 1910-1930; Revolution of 1930; oligarchy in control, 1930-1943

Including biography: Marcelo Torcuato de Alvear, Joaquín Víctor González, Hipólito Irigoyen, Juan Bautista Justo, Lisandro de la Torre, José Félix Uriburu

South America

Argentina. La Plata region

History

By period

2843 1810-

2848 1910-1943 — Continued

Cf. D501+, World War I, 1914-1918

2849 1943-1955

Including the "G.O.U." Coup, 1943; Perón regime, 1943-1955; fascism

Including biography: Juan Domingo Perón, etc.

Cf. D731+, World War II, 1939-1945

1955-2002

2849.2 General works

Biography

2849.22.A2 Collective

2849.22.A3-.22.Z Individual, A-Z

GALE NOTE *See note at the head of Table F5 at the end of the text for further instructions on how to subdivide this number*

2002-

2849.3 General works

Biography

2849.33.A2 Collective

2849.33.A3-.33.Z Individual, A-Z

GALE NOTE *See note at the head of Table F5 at the end of the text for further instructions on how to subdivide this number*

2850-2991 Regions, provinces, etc.

Class an individual department or partido with the province of which it is a part

2850 Territories (General)

2850.4 Aconquija Mountains

2851 Andes Mountains

Including Chilean boundary question

2853 Los Andes (Territory)

Before 1910 was Bolivian territory of Atacama; in 1943, departments were assigned to the provinces of Jujuy, Salta, and Catamarca

2857 Boundaries

2857.A2 General

2857.B6 Bolivia

Cf. F2853, Former Bolivian territory of Atacama

Brazil, *see* F2554.A82, F2916

Chaco Boreal dispute, *see* F2688.5

Chile, *see* F2851, F2853

2857.P2 Paraguay

2857.U7 Uruguay

Buenos Aires (Federal District and City), *see* F3001

2861 Buenos Aires (Province)

Including Avellaneda (Partido); Lechiguanas Islands

For Martin Garcia (Island), see F2909

Cf. F2846, Battles of Cepeda, 1859; Pavón, 1861

Cf. F2886, Córdoba boundary

2871 Catamarca

2876 Chaco. Chaco Austral. El Gran Chaco (General, and Argentina)

Became a province, August 8, 1951

For Bolivian Chaco, see F3341.C4

For Chaco Boreal (Paraguayan Chaco), see F2691.C4

For Chaco Central, see F2901

For Chaco War, 1932-1935, see F2688.5

2881 Chubut (Territory)

For Comodoro Rivadavia, see F2884

2884 Comodoro Rivadavia

Including military zone carved out of Chubut and Santa Cruz Territories in 1946

	South America
	Argentina. La Plata region
2850-2991	Regions, provinces, etc. — Continued
2886	Córdoba
2891	Corrientes
	Including battle of Caá Guazú, 1841
	Cf. F2916, Misiones boundary
	Cuyo, *see* F2911
2896	Entre Rios
	For Lechiguanas Islands, see F2861
	Cf. F2861, Buenos Aires (Province) boundary
2901	Formosa (Territory). Chaco Central
2906	Jujuy
2909	La Plata River and Valley (Rio de La Plata). Paraná River
	Including Iguazú Falls, Martín Garcia (Island)
	Cf. F2596 , Paraná River in Brazil
2911	Mendoza
	Including the ancient Chilean governación of Cuyo
	Including Malargüe (District); Tupungato (Department)
	Cf. F2961, San Juan boundary
2916	Misiones
	Became a province, December 9, 1953
	Including Parque nacional del Iguazú
	Cf. F2554.A82, Brazil-Argentina boundary dispute
	Cf. F2626, Santa Catarina, Brazil (Part of Misiones awarded to Brazil)
	Cf. F2684, Jesuit missions of Paraguay
2921	Neuquén (Territory)
	Including Neuquén River, Parque nacional "Lanín"
2921.5	Northeast Argentina
	Including Chaco, Corrientes, Formosa Misiones, and northern Sante Fe
2922	Northwest Argentina
	Including Calchaqui River
2924	La Pampa
	Became a province, August 8, 1951
2926	Pampas (Region)
	Including region south of Mendoza and San Luis, and west of Buenos Aires, extending to Patagonia (about 40 degrees)
	Cf. F2217, Gauchos (General)
2936	Patagonia
	Including collective works on Patagonia, Falkland Islands, Tierra del Fuego, Strait of Magellan, Cape Horn, etc.; Tzoneca Indians
	Argentine Patagonia is now subdivided into the territories of Chubut, Neuquén, Río Negro, Santa Cruz, and Tierra del Fuego
	Chilean Patagonia covers the Chilean provinces of Chiloé and Magallanes
	Cf. F2986, Tierra del Fuego
	Cf. F3031+, Falkland Islands
	Cf. F3191, Strait of Magellan
2951	Río Negro (Territory)
	Including Nahuel Huapí (Lake), Parque nacional de Nahuel Huapí
2956	La Rioja
2957	Salado River and Valley
	In provinces of Salta, Santiago del Estero, and Santa Fé
2958	Salta
2961	San Juan
2966	San Luis
	Cf. F2886, Córdoba boundary
2971	Santa Cruz (Territory)
	For Comodoro Rivadavia, see F2884
2976	Santa Fé
2981	Santiago del Estero

South America

Argentina. La Plata region

2850-2991 Regions, provinces, etc. — Continued

2986 Tierra del Fuego (Territory and island)

The western part of the island forms part of the Chilean territory of Magallanes

Including Fuegians: The Alacaluf, Ona, and Yahgan

2991 Tucumán (Province)

In colonial times was the gobernación of Tucumán, part of Upper Peru

Cities, towns, etc.

3001 Buenos Aires (Federal District and City)

Subarrange by Table F1 at the end of the text

3011.A-.Z Other, A-Z

GALE NOTE *The cutter number(s) listed below have been given only as examples by the Library of Congress*

3011.A9 Avellaneda

Formerly Barracas al Sud

3011.B3 Bahia Blancha

3011.C7 Córdoba

3011.L4 La Plata

3011.L45 La Rioja

Including earthquake of 1894, etc.

3011.L8 Luján

3011.M29 Mar del Plata

3011.M45 Mendoza

Including earthquake of 1861, etc.

3011.R7 Rosario

3011.S2 Salta

3011.S218 San Juan

Formerly San Juan de la Frontera

Including earthquake of 1944, etc.

San Miguel de Tucumán, *see* F3011.T89

3011.S26 Santa Fé

3011.T89 Tucumán

Elements in the population

Including foreign elements (General), minorities, race conflicts and problems

For interpretation, see F1392.A+

3021.A1 General works

3021.A2-.Z Individual elements, A-Z

3021.A5 Americans

3021.A59 Arabs

3021.A64 Armenians

3021.B2 Basques

3021.B55 Blacks

3021.B65 Bolivians

3021.B86 British

3021.B93 Bulgarians

3021.C3 Catalans

3021.C7 Croats

3021.D2 Danes

3021.D87 Dutch

3021.F56 Finns

3021.F8 French

3021.G2 Gallegans

3021.G3 Germans

3021.H85 Hungarians

Indians, *see* F2821+

3021.I6 Irish

3021.I8 Italians

3021.J36 Japanese

3021.J5 Jews

South America

Argentina. La Plata region

Elements in the population

3021.A2-.Z Individual elements, A-Z — Continued

Negroes, *see* F3021.B55

3021.P6 Poles

3021.P8 Portuguese

3021.R87 Russian Germans

3021.S6 Slovaks

3021.S62 Slovenes

3021.S7 Spaniards

3021.S86 Swedes

3021.S88 Swiss

3021.S95 Syrians

3021.U5 Ukrainians

3021.U7 Uruguayans

3021.Y7 Yugoslavs

3030 **South Atlantic region**

3030.3 Ascension Island

Falkland Islands. Islas Malvinas

Including dependencies: Graham Land (Palmer Peninsula), South Georgia, South Orkneys, South Sheltands, South Sandwich Island

Cf. G890.P3, Palmer Peninsula (Graham Land)

3031 General works

3031.5 Falkland Islands War, 1982

St. Helena, Tristan da Cunha, etc., *see* DT669+

Chile

3051 Periodicals. Societies. Collections

Collected works

3052 Several authors

3053 Individual authors

Including collected papers, addresses, essays

3053.5 Museums. Exhibitions, exhibits, etc.

3054 Gazetteers. Dictionaries. Geographic names

3054.5 Directories

Biography

3055 Collective

Individual, *see* F3076, F3091-3101

3058 General works

3058.5 Juvenile works

Pamphlets, addresses, essays, etc.

3059 General

3059.3 Anecdotes, legends, pageants, etc.

Cf. GR130+, Folklore

Cf. Class P, Literature

3059.5 Guidebooks. Handbooks

3059.8 Historic monuments (General)

3060 Social life and customs. Civilization. Intellectual life

Including national characteristics

For race conflicts and problems, see F3285

3060.9 Geography

Description and travel. Views

3061 Early to 1809

3063 1810-1950

3064 1951-1980

3065 1981-

Antiquities. Indians

3069 General works

South America
Chile
Antiquities. Indians — Continued
3069.1.A-.1.Z Local (Ancient and modern), A-Z
GALE NOTE *The cutter number(s) listed below have been given only as examples by the Library of Congress*
Araucania, *see* F3126
3069.1.A8 Atacama (Province)
3069.1.H8 Huasco (Province)
3069.1.L5 Llaima (Department)
3069.1.L6 Rio Loa region
3069.1.M25 Malloa
3069.1.M6 Molle
3069.1.P5 Pichilemu
3069.1.Q6 Quilpué
3069.3.A-.3.Z Topics (Ancient and modern), A-Z
3069.3.A3 Agriculture
3069.3.A7 Art
3069.3.C66 Commerce
3069.3.E2 Economic conditions
3069.3.E38 Education
3069.3.E46 Employment
3069.3.E84 Ethnobotany
3069.3.F57 Fishing
3069.3.F64 Folklore. Legends
3069.3.G6 Government relations
Legends, *see* F3069.3.F64
3069.3.M4 Metalwork
3069.3.M5 Missions
3069.3.M55 Mixed bloods
3069.3.P76 Population
3069.3.P8 Pottery
3069.3.R44 Religion and mythology
3069.3.T4 Textile industry and fabrics
3069.3.W37 Wars
3070 Modern Indians (General)
3070.1.A-.1.Z Tribes (Ancient and modern), A-Z
Araucanians (Chilote, Huilliche, Mapuche, Pehuenche, and Picunche), *see* F3126
3070.1.A7 Atacameno
3070.1.C5 Chango
3070.1.C6 Chono
3070.1.D5 Diaguita
Cf. F2823.D5, Argentina
Fuegian (Alacaluf, Yahgan), *see* F2986
3072 Ciudad de los Césares
History
3073 Chronological tables. Outlines, syllabi, etc. Questions and answers, etc.
Historiography
3074 General works
Biography of historians
3075 Collective
3076.A-.Z Individual, A-Z
GALE NOTE *See note at the head of Table F5 at the end of the text for further instructions on how to subdivide this number*
3076.B3 Barros Arana, Diego
3077 Study and teaching
3081 General works
Including political history
General special
3082 Military and naval history

South America

Chile

History

General special — Continued

Diplomatic history. Foreign and general relations

3083 General works

3083.5.A-.5.Z Relations with individual countries, A-Z

3083.9 Other (not A-Z)

By period

Pre-Columbian period, *see* F3069+

3091 1535-1810

Including conquest of the Araucanian Indians; history as a Spanish colony

Including biography: Pedro de Valdivia, etc.

1810-

Declared independence from Spain, July 16, 1810

3093 General works

3094 1810-1824. War of Independence

Including battles of Rancagua (1814), Chacabuco (1817), Maipo (1818)

Including biography: José Miguel Carrera, Juan Mackenna, Bernardo O'Higgins, etc.

1824-1920

Including domination of the conservatives, 1830-1861; War with Spain, 1865-1866; bombardment of Valparaiso, 1866; civil wars

Including biography: Manuel Francisco Antonio Julián Montt, Diego José Víctor Portales, Benjamín Vicuña Mackenna, etc.

Cf. D501+, World War I, 1914-1918

Cf. F3447, War with Spain, 1865-1866

3095 General works

War of the Pacific, 1879-1884

3097 General works

3097.3 Territorial questions growing out of the war

Including Tacna-Arica question (Controversial topic until 1929); Treaty of Ancón, 1883; Treaty of Valparaiso, 1884

3098 Revolution of 1891

Including biography: José Manuel Balmaceda, etc.

1921-

Including restoration of presidential power, 1921-1938; Popular Front, 1938-1942; earthquake of 1938

Including biography: Pedro Aguirre Cerda, Arturo Alessandri, Carlos Ibáñez del Campo, etc.

Cf. D731+, World War II, 1939-1945

3099 General works

1970-

3100 General works

Biography

3101.A2 Collective

3101.A3-.Z Individual, A-Z

GALE NOTE *See note at the head of Table F5 at the end of the text for further instructions on how to subdivide this number*

3101.A4 Allende, Salvador

Regions, provinces, etc.

3105 Islands of Chile (General)

3106 Aconcagua

Aisén, *see* F3134

3111 Andes Mountains in Chile

Cf. F2212, South America

Cf. F2851, Argentina

3116 Antofagasta

Formerly Bolivian territory of Atacama

For Taltal (Department), see F3238

South America

Chile

Regions, provinces, etc. — Continued

3126 Arauco

Including ancient and modern Mapuche Indians (Araucanian) and ancient and modern Araucanian Indians in Chile and adjacent areas of Argentina

For Malleco, formerly part of Arauco, see F3196

Arica (Department), *see* F3231

3131 Atacama (Desert and Province)

Including the islands: Gonzalez; Saint Ambrose (San Ambrosio); Saint Felix (San Félix), Huasco River

3134 Aysén (Aisén)

Including Baker River

Baker River, *see* F3134

3136 Bío-Bío

Including Antuco (Volcano)

Boundaries

3139.A1-.A4 General

Argentina, *see* F2851, F2853

3139.A5-.Z Bolivia

Cf. F3097.3, Tacna and Arica question

Cf. F3116, Former Bolivian territory of Atacama

Peru, *see* F3451.B73

Cape Horn, *see* F3186

3141 Cautín

Including Llaima (Department)

3146 Chiloé

A province of Chilean Patagonia

Cf. F2936, Patagonia

Including wreck of the Wager (Ship)

3151 Colchagua

Including Tinguiririca (Volcano)

3156 Concepción

3161 Coquimbo

Including Guayacán Bay

3166 Curicó

Cuyo (Transferred to Viceroyalty of La Plata, 1776), *see* F2911

3169 Easter Island

Including Isla de Pascua, L'ile de Pâques, Rapa Nui, Te Pito te Henua

3170 El Loa

3170.5 Elqui River and Valley

3171 Juan Fernández Islands

Including earthquake of 1835

3174 Laja River and Valley

3176 Linares

Llaima (Department), *see* F3141

3181 Llanquihue

Including Llanquihue Lake, Reloncaví Bay, Rio Cisnes, Rio Puelo

Loa, *see* F3170

3186 Magallanes y Antártica Chilena

Name of Region XII created in 1974 by the union of the former province of Magallanes (western part of the island of Tierra del Fuego, formed as a province of Chilean Patagonia, 1929) and the former Territorio Antártico Chileno (formally claimed by Chile in Nov. 1940)

Including Cape Horn, etc.

For Ultima Esperanza (Department), see F3244

Cf. F2936, Patagonia

Cf. F2986, Tierra del Fuego (Island)

3191 Strait of Magellan

Cf. G286.M2, Life and travels of Fernão de Magalhães (Ferdinand Magellan)

South America

Chile

Regions, provinces, etc.

3191 Strait of Magellan — Continued

Cf. G420.M2, First circumnavigation of the globe by Magellan and crew

3196 Malleco

Including Tolhuaca and Lonquimay Volcanoes

Formerly a part of the Province of Arauco; formed as a separate province, 1887

3201 Maule

3205 North Chile

3206 Ñuble

Including earthquake of 1939

3211 O'Higgins

3214 Pisagua (Department)

3218 Region de los Lagos

3221 Santiago

Cf. F3271, Santiago de Chile (City)

3231 Tacna (Department). Arica (Department)

Between 1883 and 1929, Tacna belonged to Chile; in 1929, became a department of Peru

Before 1883, Arica belonged to Peru

Cf. F3097.3 , Territorial questions arising from war with Peru and Bolivia, 1879-1884

3236 Talca

3238 Taltal (Department)

3241 Tarapacá

Before 1883, belonged to Peru

For departments of Tacna and Arica, see F3231

For Pisagua (Department), see F3214

Cf. F3097.3, Territorial questions arising from war with Peru and Bolivia, 1879-1884

Tierra del Fuego (Chilean part of island), *see* F3186

3244 Ultima Esperanza (Department)

3246 Valdivia

3251 Valparaiso

For Easter Island, see F3169

For Juan Fernández Island, see F3171

Cities, towns, etc.

3271 Santiago de Chile (City)

Subarrange by Table F1 at the end of the text

3281.A-.Z Other, A-Z

3281.A45 Antofagasta

3281.A6 Arica

3281.C46 Chillán

3281.C5 Concepción

3281.I6 Iquique

3281.T17 Talca

3281.T2 Talcahuano

3281.T4 Temuco

3281.V15 Valdivia

3281.V2 Valparaiso

3281.V6 Viña del Mar

Elements in the population

For interpretation, see F1392.A+

3285.A1 General works

Including foreign elements (General), minorities, race conflicts and problems

3285.A2-.Z Individual elements, A-Z

3285.A5 Americans

3285.A7 Arabs

3285.B3 Basques

3285.B53 Blacks

3285.B7 British

3285.C94 Czechs

	South America
	Chile
	Elements in the population
3285.A2-.Z	Individual elements, A-Z — Continued
3285.F8	French
3285.G25	Galicians (Spain)
3285.G3	Germans
	Indians, *see* F3069+
3285.I8	Italians
3285.J4	Jews
3285.P4	Peruvians
3285.S7	Spaniards
3285.S9	Swiss
3285.Y8	Yugoslavs
	Bolivia
3301	Periodicals. Societies. Collections
	Collected works
3302	Several authors
3303	Individual authors
	Including collected papers, addresses, essays
3303.5	Museums. Exhibitions, exhibits
3304	Gazetteers. Dictionaries. Geographic names
3304.5	Directories
	Biography
3305	Collective
	Individual, *see* F3320.6, F3322-3341
3308	General works
3308.5	Juvenile works
	Pamphlets, addresses, essays, etc.
3309	General
3309.4	Anecdotes, legends, pageants, etc.
	Cf. GR130+, Folklore
	Cf. Class P, Literature
3309.5	Guidebooks. Handbooks
3309.7	Historic monuments (General)
3310	Social life and customs. Civilization. Intellectual life
	Including national characteristics
3310.9	Geography
	Description and travel. Views
3311	Early to 1808
3313	1809-1950
3314	1951-1980
3315	1981-
	Antiquities. Indians
3319	General works
3319.1.A-.1.Z	Local (Ancient and modern), A-Z
	GALE NOTE *The cutter number(s) listed below have been given only as examples by the Library of Congress*
3319.1.C4	Chaco (Bolivian)
3319.1.C6	Cochabamba (Department)
3319.1.P6	Potosí
3319.1.S2	Samaypata
3319.1.T55	Tiahuanaco (Tiwanaku, Tiahuanacu)
	Including the Tiwanaku Valley and the Tiwanaku culture
3320	Modern Indians (General)
3320.1.A-.1.Z	Topics (Ancient and modern), A-Z
3320.1.A47	Agriculture
3320.1.A68	Architecture
3320.1.A7	Art
3320.1.C45	Census

	South America
	Bolivia
	Antiquities. Indians
3320.1.A-.1.Z	Topics (Ancient and modern), A-Z — Continued
3320.1.C57	Civil rights
3320.1.C6	Colonization
3320.1.C64	Costume and adornment
3320.1.D35	Dance
3320.1.D83	Dwellings
3320.1.E4	Education
3320.1.E84	Ethnic identity
3320.1.F6	Folklore. Legends
3320.1.F64	Food
3320.1.G35	Games
3320.1.G6	Government relations
3320.1.I45	Implements
3320.1.I54	Industries
3320.1.L35	Land tenure
3320.1.M37	Marriage customs
3320.1.M38	Masks
3320.1.M4	Medicine
3320.1.M43	Metalwork
3320.1.M47	Missions
3320.1.M5	Mixed bloods
3320.1.N37	Narcotics
3320.1.P53	Philosophy
3320.1.P56	Politics and government
3320.1.P6	Pottery
3320.1.P8	Psychology
3320.1.R3	Religion. Mythology
3320.1.S38	Sculpture
3320.1.S62	Social conditions
3320.1.T38	Taxation
3320.1.T48	Textile industry and fabrics
3320.1.W37	Wars
3320.1.W65	Women
3320.2.A-.2.Z	Tribes (Ancient and modern), A-Z
3320.2.A6	Apolista
3320.2.A7	Arauna
	Arawak, *see* F2230.2.A7
	Aymara, *see* F2230.2.A9
3320.2.C3	Callahuaya
3320.2.C33	Canichana
	Caripuna, *see* F2520.1.C37
3320.2.C34	Cavineño
3320.2.C35	Cayubaba
3320.2.C36	Chacobo
	Chamacoco, *see* F2230.2.C5
3320.2.C37	Chané
3320.2.C38	Chapacura
3320.2.C387	Chimane
3320.2.C388	Chipaya
3320.2.C39	Chiquito
3320.2.C4	Chiriguano
3320.2.C5	Choroti
3320.2.C62	Churumata
	Colla, *see* F3430.1.C6
3320.2.G8	Guarayo
	Guaycuru, *see* F2230.2.G78
3320.2.I8	Itene

South America

Bolivia

Antiquities. Indians

3320.2.A-.2.Z Tribes (Ancient and modern), A-Z — Continued

3320.2.J84 Jukumani

Kechua, *see* F2230.2.K4

Lengua, *see* F2679.2.L4

3320.2.M26 Manacica

Mataco, *see* F2823.M3

3320.2.M55 Mojo

3320.2.M57 Mollo culture

3320.2.M6 Moseten

Moxo, *see* F3320.2.M55

3320.2.O3 Ocorona

3320.2.O8 Otuquis

3320.2.P3 Pacaguara

Pano, *see* F3430.1.P3

Panoan Indians, *see* F3430.1.P33

3320.2.P37 Pauserna

Pilaga, *see* F2823.P5

Puquina, *see* F3430.1.P8

Quechua, *see* F2230.2.K4

3320.2.S3 Samucu

3320.2.S5 Siriono

3320.2.T3 Tacana

Toba, *see* F2823.T7

3320.2.T6 Toromona

Tucuna, *see* F2520.1.T925

3320.2.U78 Uru

3320.2.Y78 Yuqui

3320.2.Y8 Yurucari

3320.2.Z3 Zamucoan

History

3320.3 Chronological tables. Outlines, syllabi, etc. Questions and answers

Historiography

3320.4 General works

Biography of historians

3320.5 Collective

3320.6.A-.6.Z Individual, A-Z

GALE NOTE *See note at the head of Table F5 at the end of the text for further instructions on how to subdivide this number*

3320.7 Study and teaching

3321 General works

Including political history

General special

3321.1 Military history

Diplomatic history. Foreign and general relations

3321.2 General works

3321.3.A-.3.Z Relations with individual countries, A-Z

3321.9 Other (not A-Z)

By period

Pre-Columbian period, *see* F3319+

3322 1538-1809. Upper Peru

In colonial times, Bolivia was the southern part of Upper Peru; formed Audiencia of Charcas under viceroy of Peru, 1559-1776 (Cf. F3444, Colonial Peru); under viceroy of Buenos Aires (La Plata), 1776-1810

Cf. F2841, Argentina, 1516-1810

Cf. F2991, Ancient gobernación of Tucumán

Cf. F3444, Insurrection of Tupac Amaru, 1780-1781

3323 1809-1825. Wars of independence

South America
Bolivia
History
By period — Continued
3324 1825-1884
Including independence from Peru declared August 6, 1825. Period of civil wars and conflicts with neighboring countries
For loss of southern Chaco to Argentina, 1878, see F2876
For war with Chile (War of the Pacific), 1879-1884, see F3097
Including biography: Mariano Melgarejo, Andrés Santa-Cruz, etc.
Cf. F3447, Confederación Perú-Boliviana
3325 1884-1938
Including conflicts between the civil and the military; rule of dictators; etc.
Including biography: Mariano Baptista, Ismael Montes, etc.
For loss of Acre District to Brazil (Treaty of Petropolis, 1903), see F2540
For Chaco War, 1932-1935 and Treaty of peace, 1938, see F2688.5
3326 1938-1982
Including biography: Victor Paz Estenssoro, Enrique Peñaranda Castillo, etc.
Cf. D731+, World War II, 1939-1945
3327 1982-
3341.A-.Z Regions, departments, etc., A-Z
3341.A1 Collective
Acre Territory, *see* F2540
3341.A5 Andes Mountains
Cf. F2212, General
Atacama, *see* F2853, Argentine territory of Los Andes; F3116, Chilean province of Antofagasta
3341.A9 Azero (Province)
3341.B4 Beni
3341.B7 Boundaries (General)
For Argentina, see F2857.B6
For Brazil, see F2554.B6
For Chaco Boreal dispute, see F2691.C4
For Chile, see F3139.A1+
For Paraguay, see F2691.B7A+
For Peru, see F3451.B71
3341.C27 Capinota (Province)
3341.C3 Caupolican (Province)
3341.C4 Chaco (Bolivian)
For Chaco War, 1932-1935, see F2688.5
Cf. F2691.C4, Chaco Boreal, Paraguay
Cf. F2876, El Gran Chaco (General, and Argentina)
3341.C5 Chiquitos (Province)
3341.C6 Chuquisaca
For Azero (Province), see F3341.A9
3341.C7 Cochabamba
3341.C75 Cordillera (Province)
3341.I25 Ichilo (Province)
3341.L3 La Paz
For Acre Territory, see F2540
For Caupolican (Province), see F3341.C3
For Lake Titicaca, see F3341.T6
For Nor Yungas (Province), see F3341.N67
3341.L35 Larecaja (Province)
3341.M58 Mizque (Province)
3341.M9 Moxos (Province)
3341.N67 Nor Yungas (Province)
3341.O5 Omasuyos (Province)
3341.O6 Oriente
3341.O7 Oruro
3341.P3 Pando

South America

Bolivia

3341.A-.Z Regions, departments, etc., A-Z — Continued

Piray River and Valley, *see* F3341.S2

3341.P7 Potosí

3341.S2 Santa Cruz

Including Piray River and Valley

Cf. F2691.C4, Chaco Boreal dispute

3341.S9 Sud Chichas

3341.T2 Tarija

Cf. F2691.C4, Chaco Boreal dispute

3341.T3 Territorio Nacional de Colonias

3341.T6 Lake Titicaca region (General, and Bolivia)

Including Titicaca Island

Cf. F3451.P9, Peru

3351.A-.Z Cities, towns, etc., A-Z

GALE NOTE *The cutter number(s) listed below have been given only as examples by the Library of Congress*

3351.C67 Cochabamba

3351.L2 La Paz

Subarrange by Table F2 at the end of the text

3351.O7 Oruro

3351.P85 Potosí

3351.S3 Santa Cruz

3351.S94 Sucre

Formerly known as Charcas, Chuquisaca, and La Plata

Elements in the population

For interpretation, see F1392.A+

3359.A1 General works

Including foreign elements (General), minorities, race conflicts and problems

3359.A2-.Z Individual elements, A-Z

3359.B55 Blacks

3359.B73 Brazilians

3359.G3 Germans

Indians, *see* F3319+

3359.J3 Japanese

3359.J47 Jews

Peru

3401 Periodicals. Societies. Collections

Collected works

3402 Several authors

3403 Individual authors

Including collected papers, addresses, essays

3403.5 Museums. Exhibitions, exhibits

3404 Gazetteers. Dictionaries. Geographic names

3404.5 Directories

Biography

3405 Collective

Individual, *see* F3430.6, F3442-3448.4

3408 General works

3408.5 Juvenile works

Pamphlets, addresses, essays

3409 General

3409.3 Anecdotes, legends, pageants, etc.

Cf. Class P, Literature

3409.5 Guidebooks. Handbooks

3409.7 Historic monuments (General)

3410 Social life and customs. Civilization. Intellectual life

Including national characteristics

For race conflicts and problems, see F3619

	South America
	Peru — Continued
3410.4	Geography
	Description and travel. Views
3410.5	History of travel
3411	Early to 1819
3423	1820-1950
3424	1951-1980
3425	1981-
	Antiquities. Indians
3429	General works
	Including Incas
3429.1.A-1.Z	Local (Ancient and modern), A-Z
	GALE NOTE *The cutter number(s) listed below have been given only as examples by the Library of Congress*
3429.1.A45	Ancachs (Department)
3429.1.A5	Ancón
3429.1.A7	Arequipa (Department)
3429.1.C3	Callejón de Huaylas
3429.1.C47	Chancay Valley
	Including Chancay culture
3429.1.C48	Chavín
	Including Chavín culture
3429.1.C497	Chiribaya Alta. Chiribaya Baja
	Including Chiribaya culture
3429.1.C5	Choqquequirau
3429.1.C8	Cuelap
3429.1.C9	Cuzco
3429.1.E7	Espiritu Pampa
3429.1.H8	Huamachuco
3429.1.H828	Huari
3429.1.L7	Lima (Department)
3429.1.M3	Machu Picchu
3429.1.M35	Maranga
3429.1.N3	Nazca
	Including Nazca culture
3429.1.N5	Nievería
3429.1.P2	Pachacamac
3429.1.P25	Paracas
3429.1.P28	Paramonga
3429.1.P8	Puno (Department)
3429.1.P86	Putumayo Valley
3429.1.R55	Rimac Valley
3429.1.T8	Trujillo (Province)
3429.1.V45	Vicús
	Including Vicús culture
3429.1.V77	Virú Valley
3429.1.V8	Vitcos
3429.3.A-.3.Z	Topics (Ancient and modern), A-Z
3429.3.A37	Aged
3429.3.A4	Agriculture
3429.3.A45	Alcohol use
3429.3.A5	Anthropometry
3429.3.A65	Architecture
3429.3.A7	Art
3429.3.A76	Astronomy
3429.3.A9	Axes
3429.3.B63	Boats
	Burial customs, *see* F3429.3.M7
3429.3.C14	Calendar. Chronology. Astronomy

South America
Peru
Antiquities. Indians

3429.3.A-.3.Z	Topics (Ancient and modern), A-Z — Continued
3429.3.C4	Census
	Ceremonies, *see* F3429.3.R3
3429.3.C56	Civil rights
3429.3.C59	Commerce
3429.3.C594	Communication
3429.3.C6	Consanguinity
3429.3.C74	Cosmology
3429.3.C8	Costume and adornment
3429.3.C85	Craniology
3429.3.D6	Diseases
3429.3.D69	Domestic animals
3429.3.D72	Domestic relations
3429.3.D77	Drinking vessels
3429.3.D79	Drug use
3429.3.E2	Economic conditions
3429.3.E3	Education
3429.3.E35	Egyptian influences
3429.3.E45	Employment
3429.3.E84	Ethnic identity
3429.3.E86	Ethnobotany
3429.3.F55	First contact with Europeans
3429.3.F57	Fishing
3429.3.F6	Folklore. Legends
3429.3.F65	Food
3429.3.F85	Funeral customs and rites
3429.3.G3	Games
3429.3.G4	Genealogy
3429.3.G5	Goldwork
	Government, *see* F3429.3.P65
3429.3.G6	Government relations
3429.3.H5	Historiography
3429.3.I53	Industries
3429.3.I77	Irrigation
3429.3.J8	Judiciary
3429.3.K53	Kings and rulers
3429.3.K55	Kinship
3429.3.L3	Land tenure
3429.3.L45	Law and legislation
	Legends, *see* F3429.3.F6
3429.3.L5	Litters
3429.3.M3	Magic
3429.3.M34	Marriage customs
3429.3.M35	Masks (Sculpture)
3429.3.M36	Mathematics
	For works limited to Quipu, see F3429.3.Q6
3429.3.M4	Medicine
3429.3.M42	Metalwork
3429.3.M6	Missions
3429.3.M63	Mixed bloods
3429.3.M7	Mortuary customs
3429.3.M8	Mummies
3429.3.P34	Painting
3429.3.P47	Petroglyphs. Rock paintings
3429.3.P55	Philosophy
3429.3.P65	Politics and government
3429.3.P68	Population

South America

Peru

Antiquities. Indians

3429.3.A-.3.Z Topics (Ancient and modern), A-Z — Continued

3429.3.P69 Portraits, Indian

3429.3.P7 Postal service

3429.3.P8 Pottery

3429.3.P85 Psychology

3429.3.Q6 Quipu

3429.3.R27 Relations with Blacks

3429.3.R3 Religion. Mythology

3429.3.R58 Rites and ceremonies

3429.3.R6 Roads and trails

Rock paintings, *see* F3429.3.P47

3429.3.S39 Sculpture

3429.3.S45 Sexual behavior

3429.3.S54 Silverwork

3429.3.S59 Social conditions

3429.3.S6 Social life and customs

3429.3.T2 Tattooing

3429.3.T28 Taxation. Tribute

3429.3.T29 Teeth

3429.3.T3 Textile industry and fabrics

3429.3.T7 Trephining

Tribute, *see* F3429.3.T28

3429.3.W2 Warfare

3429.3.W27 Wars

3429.3.W4 Weights and measures

3429.3.W65 Women

3429.3.W7 Writing

3430 Modern Indians (General)

3430.1.A-.1.Z Tribes (Ancient and modern), A-Z

Achuale, *see* F3430.1.A25

3430.1.A25 Achuar. Achuale

3430.1.A35 Aguaruna

3430.1.A5 Amahuaca

3430.1.A54 Amuesha

3430.1.A6 Andoa

3430.1.A7 Arabela

3430.1.A83 Ashaninca

3430.1.A85 Asto

Aymara, *see* F2230.2.A9

Bora, *see* F2270.2.B6

3430.1.C3 Campa

3430.1.C32 Candoshi

3430.1.C34 Capanahua

3430.1.C35 Cashibo

Cashinawa, *see* F2520.1.C38

3430.1.C37 Chachapoya

3430.1.C4 Chanca

Chavín culture, *see* F3429.1.C48

3430.1.C43 Chayahuita

3430.1.C46 Chimu

3430.1.C48 Cholone

3430.1.C5 Chupacho

3430.1.C55 Cocama

3430.1.C6 Colla

Conibo, *see* F3430.1.S5

Culina, *see* F2520.1.C84

3430.1.C8 Cupisnique

South America
Peru
Antiquities. Indians
3430.1.A-.1.Z Tribes (Ancient and modern), A-Z — Continued
3430.1.E78 Ese Ejja
3430.1.H78 Huambisa
3430.1.H8 Huanca
3430.1.H83 Huari
Incas, *see* F3429+
3430.1.I68 Iquito
3430.1.I8 Iscaycinca
3430.1.I85 Itucale
Jivaro, *see* F3722.1.J5
Kechua, *see* F2230.2.K4
3430.1.M3 Machiganga
3430.1.M38 Mashco
3430.1.M4 Mayna
3430.1.M45 Mayoruna
3430.1.M6 Mochica
3430.1.N3 Nasca
3430.1.O25 Ocaina
3430.1.O5 Omagua
3430.1.O74 Orejón
3430.1.P3 Pano
3430.1.P33 Panoan Indians
3430.1.P4 Peban
Pioje, *see* F3722.1.P5
3430.1.P5 Piro
3430.1.P6 Pocra
3430.1.P8 Puquina
3430.1.Q47 Quero
3430.1.S35 Senci
3430.1.S4 Setibo
3430.1.S47 Shapra
3430.1.S48 Sharanahua
3430.1.S5 Shipibo-Conibo. Sipibo
Tacana, *see* F3320.2.T3
3430.1.W35 Wamani
Witoto, *see* F2270.2.W5
3430.1.Y3 Yagua
3430.1.Y34 Yanaconas
3430.1.Y8 Yunca
Zaparo, *see* F3722.1.Z3
History
3430.3 Chronological tables. Outlines, syllabi, etc. Questions and answers, etc.
Historiography
3430.4 General works
Biography of historians
3430.5 Collective
3430.6.A-.6.Z Individual, A-Z
GALE NOTE *See note at the head of Table F5 at the end of the text for further instructions on how to subdivide this number*
3430.7 Study and teaching
3431 General works
Including political history
General special
3432 Military and naval history
Diplomatic history. Foreign and general relations
3433 General works
3434.A-.Z Relations with individual countries, A-Z

South America
Peru
History — Continued
By period
Pre-Columbian period, *see* F3429+
3442 1522-1548
Including Spanish conquest, civil wars, etc.
Including biography: Francisco Pizarro, Gonzalo Pizarro, etc.
For Indians of Peru and the Inca Empire before 1531, see F3429
3444 1548-1820
Including Viceroyalty of Peru, 1542-1824; Insurrection of Tupac Amaru, 1780-1781; sporadic revolts, 1805-1814
Including biography: Vega, Garcilaso de la; Francisco de Toledo; Micaela Villegas; etc.
3446 1820-1829
Including Independence from Spain proclaimed, 1821; battles at Zepita (1823), Colpahuaico (1824), Ayacucho (1824)
Including biography: Juan Antonio Álvarez de Arenales, José de Lamar y Cortazar, William Miller, José Silverio Olaya, etc.
For battle of Portete de Tarqui, see F2275
For loss of Upper Peru, 1825, see F3324
1829-
3446.5 General works
3447 1829-1919
Including civil wars; Battle of Yanacocha, 1835; Confederación Perú-Boliviana, 1835-1839; Spanish question, 1864; War with Spain, 1865-1866; Bombardmentof Callao, 1866; Revolution of 1872; period of reconstruction, 1884-1919
Including biography: Ramón Castilla, Agustín Gamarra, Augusto Bernardino Leguia, Nicolás de Piérola, Leoncio Prado, Mariano Ignacio Prado, Felipe Santiago Salaverry, etc.
For War of the Pacific, 1879-1884, see F3097
Cf. D501+, World War I, 1914-1918
Cf. F3095, War with Spain, 1865-1866
Cf. F3451.P94, Putumayo atrocities
3448 1919-1968
Including rise of liberalism; the Apristas; anti-axis policies
Including biography: Oscar Raimundo Benavides, Víctor Raúl Haya de la Torre, Manuel Artura Odría, Manuel Prado y Ugarteche, etc.
Cf. D731+, World War II, 1939-1945
Cf. F2281.B7P1+, Leticia Dispute, 1932-1934
1968-
3448.2 General works
Biography
3448.3 Collective
3448.4.A-.4.Z Individual, A-Z
GALE NOTE *See note at the head of Table F5 at the end of the text for further instructions on how to subdivide this number; The cutter number(s) listed below have been given only as examples by the Library of Congress*
3448.4.V4 Velasco Alvarado, Juan
3451.A-.Z Regions, departments, etc., A-Z
3451.A4 Amazonas
Amazonas, Bajos, *see* F3451.B3
3451.A43 Anan Yauyo (Province)
3451.A45 Ancachs (Ancash)
Including Callejon de Huaylas
3451.A48 Andahuaylas (Province)
3451.A5 Andes Mountains, Peru
Including Cordillera Blanca
Cf. F2212, General
3451.A54 Andrés Avelino Cáceres

South America

Peru

3451.A-.Z Regions, departments, etc., A-Z — Continued

3451.A6 Apurímac

3451.A7 Arequipa

Including Coropuna, El Misti (Volcano)

Arica (Department), *see* F3231

3451.A87 Ayabaca (Province)

3451.A9 Ayacucho

3451.B3 Bajo Amazonas

Province was named Maynas in 1943

Boundaries

3451.B7 General

3451.B71 Bolivia

Brazil, *see* F2554.P4

3451.B73 Chile

Cf. F3097.3, Tacna and Arica question

Colombia, *see* F2281.B7

3451.B75 Ecuador

Leticia question, *see* F2281.B7P1+

Cáceres Region, *see* F3451.A54

3451.C2 Cajamarca

3451.C23 Calca (Province)

3451.C25 Callao

3451.C28 Canchis

3451.C3 Carabaya (Province)

Cerro Salcantay, *see* F3451.C9

3451.C46 Chancay (Province)

3451.C5 Chincha Valley

3451.C55 Chota (Province)

3451.C6 Chucuito (Province)

3451.C7 Contumazá (Province)

Cordillera Blanca, *see* F3451.A5

3451.C76 Corongo (Province)

3451.C85 Cutervo (Province)

3451.C9 Cuzco (Cusco)

Including Nevado Sarcantay (Cerro Salcantay), Pampaconas River, Urubamba River

Ene River and Valley, *see* F3451.J9

3451.G73 Grau Region

3451.H7 Huamalies (Province)

3451.H75 Huancané (Province)

3451.H76 Huancavelica

3451.H78 Huancayo

3451.H79 Huanta

3451.H8 Huánuco

Including Pozuzo colony

3451.H83 Huaral (Province)

Huaura River and Valley, *see* F3451.L7

Huaylas, Callejon de, *see* F3451.A45

3451.I3 Ica

3451.J33 Jaén (Province)

3451.J9 Junín

Including Ene River and Valley

La Libertad, *see* F3451.L3

3451.L2 Lambayeque

3451.L23 Lampa

3451.L3 Libertad

3451.L7 Lima

Including Huaura River and Valley, Marcahuasi Plateau

Cf. F3601, Lima (City)

South America

Peru

3451.A-.Z Regions, departments, etc., A-Z — Continued

3451.L8 Loreto

Including Amazon River and Valley, Peru, Marañón River, Pichis River, and Ucayali River

3451.M2 Madre de Dios

Including Madre de Dios River

Marcahuasi Plateau, *see* F3451.L7

Maynas (Province), *see* F3451.B3

Misti (Volcano), *see* F3451.A7

3451.M6 La Montaña (region)

3451.M8 Moquegua

Nevado Sarcantay, *see* F3451.C9

3451.N67 Nor Oriental del Marañón

3451.O16 Ocsabamba (Oxapampa) colony

3451.P14 Pachitea (Province)

3451.P19 Pacific coast

3451.P245 Parinacochas (Province)

3451.P247 Pasco

3451.P25 Paucartambo (Province)

3451.P48 Pisco (Province)

3451.P5 Piura

Pozuzo (Posuso) colony, *see* F3451.H8

3451.P9 Puno

Including Peruvian section of Lake Titicaca

Cf. F3341.T6, General, and Bolivia

3451.P94 Putumayo River and Valley

Including rubber atrocities

Cf. F2281.P9, Colombia

Cf. F2546, Brazil, where river is called "Içá"

3451.R6 Rodríguez de Mendoza (Province)

Salcantay, Cerro, *see* F3451.C9

3451.S2 San Marcos (Province)

3451.S24 San Martín

3451.S244 Sandia (Province)

3451.S25 Santa Cruz (District)

Sarcantay, *see* F3451.C9

Tacna (Department), *see* F3231

Tarapacá, *see* F3241

Lake Titicaca region, *see* F3451.P9

3451.T7 Trujillo (Province)

3451.T8 Tumbes

Ucayali River and Valley, *see* F3451.L8

3451.U88 Utcubamba (Province)

White Cordillera, *see* F3451.A5

3451.Y38 Yauyos (Province)

3451.Y47 Yerupaja (El Carnicero, The Butcher)

Cities, towns, etc.

Including individual biography

3601 Lima

Subarrange by Table F1 at the end of the text

Including earthquakes of 1687, 1746, etc.; occupation by Chilean forces, 1881-1883

3611.A-.Z Other, A-Z

GALE NOTE *The cutter number(s) listed below have been given only as examples by the Library of Congress*

3611.A7 Arequipa

3611.C2 Callao

3611.C9 Cusco

3611.H8 Huancavelica

	South America
	Peru
	Cities, towns, etc.
3611.A-.Z	Other, A-Z — Continued
3611.H82	Huancayo
3611.I6	Iquitos
3611.S84	Sullana
3611.T8	Trujillo
	Elements in the population
	Including foreign elements (General), minorities, race conflicts and problems
	For interpretation, see F1392.A+
3619.A1	General works
3619.A2-.Z	Individual elements, A-Z
3619.A5	Americans
3619.B55	Blacks
3619.B7	British
3619.C34	Canary Islanders
3619.C5	Chinese
3619.G3	Germans
	Indians, *see* F3429+
3619.I8	Italians
3619.J3	Japanese
3619.J4	Jews
3619.M47	Mestizos
	Negroes, *see* F3619.B55
3619.P64	Poles
3619.R87	Russians
3619.Y84	Yugoslavs
	Ecuador
3701	Periodicals. Societies. Collections
	Collected works
3702	Several authors
3703	Individual authors
	Including collected papers, addresses, essays
3703.5	Museums. Exhibitions, exhibits
3704	Gazetteers. Dictionaries. Geographic names
3704.5	Directories
	Biography
3705	Collective
	Individual, *see* F3726, F3733-3738.4
3708	General works
3708.5	Juvenile works
	Pamphlets, addresses, essays
3709	General
3709.3	Anecdotes, legends, pageants, etc.
	Cf. Subclasses PN, PQ, etc., Literature
3709.5	Guidebooks. Handbooks
3709.7	Historic monuments (General)
3710	Social life and customs. Civilization. Intellectual life
	Including national characteristics
	For race conflicts and problems, see F3799
3710.9	Geography
	Description and travel. Views
3711	Early to 1808
3714	1809-1950
3715	1951-1980
3716	1981-
	Antiquities. Indians
3721	General works

South America
Ecuador
Antiquities. Indians — Continued
3721.1.A-.1.Z Local (Ancient and modern), A-Z
GALE NOTE *The cutter number(s) listed below have been given only as examples by the Library of Congress*
3721.1.C2 Carchi (Province)
3721.1.G9 Guayas (Province)
3721.1.I3 Imbabura (Province)
3721.1.L36 La Plata Island
3721.1.M2 Manabi
3721.1.T65 Tomebamba
3721.3.A-.3.Z Topics (Ancient and modern), A-Z
3721.3.A35 Agriculture
3721.3.A67 Architecture
3721.3.A7 Art
3721.3.C64 Commerce
3721.3.D35 Dances
Drugs, *see* F3721.3.N35
3721.3.E25 Economic conditions
3721.3.E35 Education
3721.3.E84 Ethnic identity
3721.3.E85 Ethnobotany
3721.3.F65 Folklore. Legends
3721.3.F7 Food
3721.3.G45 Genealogy
3721.3.G68 Government relations
3721.3.I4 Implements
3721.3.M37 Material culture
3721.3.M38 Mathematics
3721.3.M4 Medicine
3721.3.M45 Metalwork
3721.3.M6 Missions
Mythology, *see* F3721.3.R44
3721.3.N35 Narcotics
3721.3.P74 Politics and government
3721.3.P76 Population
3721.3.P8 Pottery
3721.3.R44 Religion. Mythology
3721.3.S24 Salt
3721.3.S65 Social conditions
3721.3.S7 Social life and customs
3721.3.T18 Taxation. Tribute
3721.3.T2 Teeth mutilation and decoration
3721.3.T47 Textile industry and fabrics
Tribute, *see* F3721.3.T18
3721.3.U73 Urban residence
3721.3.W35 Wars
3721.3.W65 Women
3722 Modern Indians (General)
3722.1.A-.1.Z Tribes (Ancient and modern), A-Z
Achuale, *see* F3430.1.A25
Andoa, *see* F3430.1.A6
Arawak, *see* F2230.2.A7
3722.1.C2 Cañari
3722.1.C23 Canelo
3722.1.C25 Cara
3722.1.C3 Cayapa
3722.1.C67 Cofán
3722.1.C7 Colorado

South America
Ecuador
Antiquities. Indians
3722.1.A-.1.Z Tribes (Ancient and modern), A-Z — Continued
3722.1.C83 Cuaiquer
3722.1.E8 Esmeralda
3722.1.G82 Guayacundo
3722.1.H8 Huancavilca
3722.1.H83 Huao
Incas, *see* F3429
3722.1.J5 Jivaro. Shuar
Kechua, *see* F2230.2.K4
3722.1.M3 Manta
3722.1.O8 Otavalo
3722.1.P35 Panzaleo
Pasto, *see* F2270.2.P44
3722.1.P5 Pioje
3722.1.P8 Puruhá
3722.1.Q48 Quijo
3722.1.Q5 Quitu
3722.1.S43 Secoya
Shuar, *see* F3722.1.J5
Tucuna, *see* F2520.1.T925
3722.1.Z3 Zaparo
History
3723 Chronological tables. Outlines, syllabi, etc. Questions and answers, etc.
Historiography
3724 General works
Biography
3725 Collective
3726.A-.Z Individual, A-Z
GALE NOTE *See note at the head of Table F5 at the end of the text for further instructions on how to subdivide this number*
3727 Study and teaching
3731 General works
Including political history
General special
3731.5 Military and naval history
Diplomatic history. Foreign and general relations
3732 General works
3732.5.A-.5.Z Relations with individual countries, A-Z
3732.9 Other (not A-Z)
By period
Pre-Columbian period, *see* F3721+
3733 1526-1809. Colonial period
Including discovery and conquest; civil war among the conquistadores; under viceroyalty of Peru, 1539-1717; under viceroyalty of Nueva Granada, 1717-1723; under viceroyalty of Peru, 1723-1740; under viceroyalty of Nueva Granada, 1740 to independence
Including biography: Sebastián de Belalcázar, Francisco Javier Eugenio, Santa Cruz y Espejo, etc.
3734 1809-1830. Wars of independence
Including revolts against Spain, 1809-1810; Battle of Pichincha, 1822; member of Confederacy known as Republic of Colombia, 1822-1830
Including biography: Abdón Calderón, etc.
1830-
Republic of Ecuador created in 1830 by secession from confederacy
3735 General works
3736 1830-1895. Age of Moreno, 1860-1895
Including civil wars; Concordat of 1862; Theocratic state, 1860-1895; etc.

South America
Ecuador
History
By period
1830-
3736 1830-1895. Age of Moreno, 1860-1895 — Continued
Including biography: Juan José Flores, Gabriel García Moreno, Federico González Suárez, Vicente Rocafuerte, Luis Vargas Torres, etc.
For War with Spain, 1865-1866, see F3447
3737 1895-1944
Including rule of liberals; restriction of church influence; loss of territory to Brazil in 1904, to Peru in 1942; etc.
Including biography: Eloy Alfaro, Carlos Alberto Arroyo del Río, Isidro Ayora, Federico Páez, Leónidas Plaza Gutiérrez, etc.
For Leticia dispute, 1932-1934, see F2281.B7P1+
Cf. D501+, World War I, 1914-1918
Cf. D731+, World War II, 1939-1945
3738 1944-1984
Including revolts and counter revolutions; earthquake of 1949; etc.
Including biography: Galo Plaza Lasso, José María Velasco Ibarra, etc.
1984-
3738.2 General works
Biography
3738.3 Collective
3738.4.A-.4.Z Individual, A-Z
GALE NOTE *See note at the head of Table F5 at the end of the text for further instructions on how to subdivide this number*
3741.A-.Z Regions, provinces, etc., A-Z
3741.A6 Andes Mountains, Ecuador
Cf. F2212, General
Archipiélago de Colón, *see* F3741.G2
3741.A9 Azuay
3741.B5 Bolívar
3741.B7 Boundaries (General)
For Colombia, see F2281.B7
For Leticia question, see F2281.B7P1+
For Peru, see F3451.B75
3741.C25 Cañar
3741.C3 Carchi
Including Rumichaca Grotto
3741.C5 Chimborazo
Colón, Archipiélago de, *see* F3741.G2
3741.C6 Cotopaxi (León)
3741.E4 El Oro
Enchanted Islands, *see* F3741.G2
3741.E6 Esmeraldas
Including Isla de la Tola (Tolita)
3741.G2 Galápagos (Encantadas, Enchanted) Islands. Archipiélago de Colón
3741.G9 Guayas
Cf. F3741.G2, Galápagos Islands
3741.I6 Imbabura
León, *see* F3741.C6
3741.L5 Llanganati (Mountains)
3741.L6 Loja
3741.L7 Los Ríos
3741.M2 Manabí
3741.N3 Napo-Pastaza
Including Oriente (Región oriental)
For Peruvian boundary dispute, see F3451.B75

South America

Ecuador

3741.A-.Z Regions, provinces, etc., A-Z

3741.N3 Napo-Pastaza — Continued

Cf. F3741.S3, Santiago-Zamora

Oriente (Región oriental), *see* F3741.N3

El Oro, *see* F3741.E4

3741.P32 Pacific Coast

3741.P4 Pichincha

Región oriental, *see* F3741.N3

Los Ríos, *see* F3741.L7

3741.S3 Santiago-Zamora

For Oriente (Región oriental), see F3741.N3

Sierra, *see* F3741.A6

3741.S93 Sucumbíos

3741.T7 Tungurahua

Cities, towns, etc.

3781 Quito

Subarrange by Table F1 at the end of the text

3791.A-.Z Other, A-Z

GALE NOTE *The cutter number(s) listed below have been given only as examples by the Library of Congress*

3791.A6 Ambato

3791.C9 Cuenca

3791.G9 Guayaquil

3791.I3 Ibarra

3791.J3 Jipijapa (Canton)

3791.L3 Latecunga

3791.L6 Loja

3791.R6 Riobamba

3791.T8 Tulcán

3791.V7 Vinces

Elements in the population

For interpretation, see F1392.A+

3799.A1 General works

3799.A2-.Z Individual elements, A-Z

3799.B55 Blacks

Indians, *see* F3721+

3799.J4 Jews

Negroes, *see* F3799.B55

3799.S3 Salesians

TABLE E1 FOR INDIVIDUAL BIOGRAPHY

	GALE NOTE *".x" represents the cutter number for the individual*
.xA2	Collected works. By date
.xA25	Selected works. Selections. By date
	Including quotations
.xA3	Autobiography, diaries, etc. By date
.xA4	Letters. By date
.xA5	Speeches, essays, and lectures. By date
.xA6-.xZ	Biography and criticism

TABLE E2 FOR INDIVIDUAL BIOGRAPHY (1 NO.)

.A3	Autobiography, diaries, etc. By date
.A4	Letters. By date
.A6-.Z	Biography and criticism

TABLE E2A FOR INDIVIDUAL BIOGRAPHY (CUTTER NUMBER)

	GALE NOTE *".x" represents the cutter number for the individual*
.xA3	Autobiography, diaries, etc. By date
.xA4	Letters. By date
.xA6-.xZ	Biography and criticism

TABLE E3 FOR COLLECTED WORKS OF AMERICAN STATESMEN

	GALE NOTE *".x" represents the cutter number for the individual*
.x	Collected works. By date
.x2	Selected works. Selections. By date
	Including quotations
	Autobiography, diaries, etc., *see* Table E2 or biography number of individual presidents
	Letters, *see* Table E2 or biography number of individual Presidents
.x4	Essays. By date
.x5	Speeches. By date
.x9A-.x9Z	Special libraries. By author, A-Z

TABLE F1 FOR ONE NUMBER CITIES IN THE AMERICAS

.A2	Periodicals. Societies. Collections
.A3	Museums. Exhibitions, exhibits
.A4	Guidebooks. Gazetteers. Directories
.A5-.Z	General works. Description
.1	Monumental and picturesque
.13	Pamphlets, addresses, essays
.15	Antiquities
.2	Social life and customs. Intellectual life
	History
	Biography
.23.A2	General. Collective
.23.A3-.23.Z	Individual
.25	Historiography. Study and teaching
.3	General works
	Sections. Districts, etc.
.4.A2	General. Collective
.4.A3-.4.Z	Individual
	Cemeteries
.42.A2	General. Collective
.42.A3-.42.Z	Individual
	Monuments. Statues
.5.A2	General. Collective
.5.A3-.5.Z	Individual
	Parks. Squares. Circles
.6.A2	General. Collective
.6.A3-.6.Z	Individual
	Streets
.7.A2	General. Collective
.7.A3-.7.Z	Individual
	Buildings
.8.A2	General. Collective
.8.A3-.8.Z	Individual
	Elements in the population
.9.A2	General. Collective
.9.A3-.9.Z	Individual, A-Z
	For lists of cutter numbers, see E184, United States; F1035, Canada; F1392, Mexico; F1477, Guatemala; etc.

TABLE F2 FOR CUTTER NUMBER CITIES IN THE AMERICAS

	GALE NOTE *".x" represents cutter number for city*
.x	Periodicals. Societies. Collections
.x2	Museums. Exhibitions, exhibits
.x3	Guidebooks. Gazetteers. Directories
.x4	General works. Description
.x43	Monumental and picturesque
.x45	Pamphlets, addresses, essays
.x47	Antiquities
.x5	Social life and customs. Intellectual life
	History
	Biography
.x53A2-.x53A29	General. Collective
.x53A3-.x53Z	Individual
.x55	Historiography. Study and teaching
.x57	General works
	Sections. Districts, etc.
.x6A2	General. Collective
.x6A3-.x6Z	Individual
	Cemeteries
.x62A2	General. Collective
.x62A3-.x62Z	Individual
	Monuments. Statues
.x65A2	General. Collective
.x65A3-.x65Z	Individual
	Parks. Squares. Circles
.x7A2	General. Collective
.x7A3-.x7Z	Individual
	Streets
.x75A2	General. Collective
.x75A3-.x75Z	Individual
	Buildings
.x8A2	General. Collective
.x8A3-.x8Z	Individual
	Elements in the population
.x9A2-.x9A29	General. Collective
.x9A3-.x9Z	Individual, A-Z
	For lists of cutter numbers, see E184, United States; F1035, Canada; F1392, Mexico; F1477, Guatemala; etc.

TABLE F3 FOR COUNTRIES, ISLANDS, REGIONS

.A2	Periodicals. Societies
.A3	Sources and documents. Collections
.A5-.Z	General works
.2	Description and travel. Guidebooks. Gazetteers
.3	Antiquities. Indians
.4	Social life and customs. Civilization
.42	Elements in the population
	History
.5	General works
.6	Biography and memoirs (Collective)
	Political and diplomatic history
.62	General works
.63.A-.63.Z	Relations with individual countries, A-Z
	By period
	Early
.65	General works
	Biography and memoirs
.66	Collective
.67	Individual, A-Z
	Colonial
.7	General works
	Biography and memoirs
.72	Collective
.73.A-.73.Z	Individual, A-Z
	Independent
.8	General works
	Biography and memoirs
.82	Collective
.83.A-.83.Z	Individual, A-Z
.9.A-.9.Z	Local, A-Z

TABLE F4 FOR INDIVIDUAL BIOGRAPHY (ONE NO.)

Use this table to subarrange cutter numbers for individual persons under each class number of the F schedule providing for biography and memoirs. However, in cases where individual biography is classed in numbers designating individual periods, two cutters are assigned, one for the name of the biographee, and one for the author

.A2 Collected works. By date
Including collected or selected works by the individual on general historical or political topics pertaining to the period in which he lived
For his collected or selected works on a special topic, see the topic

.A25 Selected works. By date
Including collected or selected works by the individual on general historical or political topics pertaining to the period in which he lived
For his collected or selected works on a special topic, see the topic

.A3 Autobiography, diaries, etc. By date

.A4 Letters. By date

Speeches, essays, and lectures
Including collected or selected works by the individual on general historical or political topics pertaining to the period in which he lived
For his collected or selected works on a special topic, see the topic
Including interviews

.A49-.A499 Serials. By title

.A5 Monographs. By date

.A6-.Z Biography and criticism

TABLE F5 FOR INDIVIDUAL BIOGRAPHY (CUTTER NO.)

	Use this table to subarrange cutter numbers for individual persons under each class number of the F schedule providing for biography and memoirs, e.g. F1788.22.C3, Castro, Fidel. However, in cases where individual biography is classed in numbers designating individual periods, two cutters are assigned, one for the name of the biographee, and one for the author
	GALE NOTE *".x" represents the cutter number for the individual*
.xA2	Collected works. By date
	Including collected or selected works by the individual on general historical or political topics pertaining to the period in which he lived
	For his collected or selected works on a special topic, see the topic
.xA25	Selected works. By date
	Including collected or selected works by the individual on general historical or political topics pertaining to the period in which he lived
	For his collected or selected works on a special topic, see the topic
.xA3	Autobiography, diaries, etc. By date
.xA4	Letters. By date
	Speeches, essays, and lectures
	Including collected or selected works by the individual on general historical or political topics pertaining to the period in which he lived
	For his collected or selected works on a special topic, see the topic
	Including interviews
.xA49-.xA499	Serials. By title
.xA5	Monographs. By date
.xA6-.xZ	Biography and criticism

INDEX TO CLASSES E-F

D

F

K

S

Z